# Qualified Intermediary

Ross K. McGill · Kirsty V. Pitkin

# Qualified Intermediary

## Practical Compliance in Cross-Border Income Taxation and Anti-Tax Evasion

palgrave
macmillan

Ross K. McGill
TConsult Ltd
Yateley, UK

Kirsty V. Pitkin
TConsult Ltd
Yateley, UK

ISBN 978-3-031-81409-9 ISBN 978-3-031-81410-5 (eBook)
https://doi.org/10.1007/978-3-031-81410-5



This Palgrave Macmillan imprint is published by the registered company Springer Nature Switzerland AG
The registered company address is: Gewerbestrasse 11, 6330 Cham, Switzerland

# Foreword

Ross K. McGill is well known for his prior nine books on the subject of withholding tax, his reputation on the global stage and his work in any number of international committees on taxation. Kirsty Pitkin is becoming increasingly well known and respected for her work in digitisation and tax process transformation having developed the architecture and programming for the first multi-regulatory, digital investor self-declaration tax system and the Tax Compliance Toolkit$^{tm}$.

A number of factors led to the need for this book. The first was the introduction in the US of a new QI Agreement in 2023. The OECD's equivalent to the US QI system the Tax Relief and Compliance Enhancement Implementation Protocol (TRACE IP) gained its first adopter (Finland) in 2021. In parallel, after 35 years of research and discussion, the European Commission finally revealed its plan for harmonisation of withholding tax with the FASTER Directive due to come into force on January 1, 2029.

Where these initiatives focus on the taxation of income, and particularly the trending growth of tax relief at source, other initiatives related to ant-tax evasion have also taken a more prominent role in recent years.

Most people are now aware of the US FATCA framework and are coming to terms with the Common Reporting Standard (CRS) that forms part of the OECD's Automatic Exchange of Information (AEoI). Less well known is the European Union's Directive on Administrative Cooperation (DAC) whose sixth iteration (DAC6) focusses on those who are wilfully trying to evade CRS and which identifies 'Hallmarks' of tax evasion. Where these issues focus on tax evasion by individuals, the OECD has also addressed corporate tax evasion through the Base Erosion and Profit Shifting initiative (BEPS).

The nexus for all these issues are the financial institutions that hold the assets of their investors in safe custody. The problems and compliance challenges that these frameworks cause, such as documentation, due diligence and reporting are compounded by the plethora of other domestic regulation with which these financial institutions must comply.

Ross has written on these subjects individually before and he is particularly well known for his work on US withholding tax and tax reclamation. Kirsty Pitkin, TConsult's co-founder and CEO, has previously been working in the background to create the technological architecture that has transformed their company from a conventional consultancy to a reg-tech firm that is the go-to resource for many. In this book, Ross and Kirsty have collaborated for over a year to bring the industry a single work that brings together the regulations associated with cross-border tax relief at source and anti-tax evasion in their signature no nonsense and pragmatic style.

So, for professionals working in the financial services sector, whether you're in tax, legal, compliance, operations or senior management functions, this book is an absolute must read.

Robert Dombrowski
Chairman and Founder
Viewtrade Holding Corporation
Jersey City, USA

# Acknowledgements

The authors wish to acknowledge the support and contributions given by the following in the construction and development of this book.

Robert Dombrowski, Founder and Chairman, Viewtrade Holdings
Marco Zawar, Affiliate (Hong Kong), TConsult Ltd
Stuart Lipo, Senior Consultant, TConsult Ltd
Stefan Darmanin, Branch Manager, TConsult Ltd
Amanda Hsu, TConsult Taiwan
Alexander Lerch CEO, RAQUEST GmbH
Roman Von der Hoh, Managing Director, RAQUEST GmbH
Yitzhak Zahavy, Chief Compliance Officer, eToro

# Introduction

Most people think of a qualified intermediary as being a financial institution that has signed an agreement with the US government to act as a withholding agent. While this much is true, we cannot avoid the fact that several other jurisdictions have adopted similar models, albeit using slightly different nomenclature, under which non-resident financial institutions can engage with a tax administration either to be a withholding agent in that jurisdiction or to meet certain anti-tax evasion due diligence obligations.

The Japanese have a Qualified Financial Intermediary (QFI) system for Japanese government bonds.

The Irish have an Authorised Withholding Agents (AWA) system based on the US QI model.

The Finnish have adopted the OECD model of using Authorised Intermediaries (AIs) as part of the Tax Relief and Compliance Enhancement framework (TRACE).

The European Union has proposed a Directive called FASTER that uses the concept of Certified Financial Intermediaries (CFIs).

The European Union DAC6 Directive assigns financial institutions the name "intermediary".

The US also has an anti-tax evasion regulation, FATCA, which has many names for intermediaries, the most common being a Reporting Model 1 Foreign Financial Institution (FFI)

In all these cases, the commonality is the appointment, registration or identification of a financial institution outside the home jurisdiction to act as a withholding agent to process tax relief at source, quick refund or standard refunds (as the rules permit) subject to certain compliance obligations, usually including at minimum, due diligence procedural standards and reporting.

All these frameworks are based on two pillars—tax operations and tax compliance. Tax operations are about the day-to-day activities of identifying who your customer is, what jurisdictions they pay tax in, how much tax they should pay on cross-border distributions such as dividends or gross proceeds of equity sales, actually processing these events (corporate actions), keeping good books of record and reporting properly to the authorities.

Compliance, on the other hand, is about the governance of tax operations to make sure that the financial institution, whether they are a QI,QFI, an AI or a CFI, is meeting their obligations under the relevant framework rules. Compliance typically includes registration, the appointment of a responsible officer, obligations for due diligence, withholding, depositing tax and reporting. Compliance also includes enforcement activities including domestic and foreign penalties for material failures or substantial non-compliance.

We wrote this book to address both pillars. Understanding the tax operations and compliance challenges associated with global cross-border withholding tax frameworks, is dependent an understanding of those frameworks. So, in each chapter of this book, we will first describe the relevant framework, whether that be the US QI framework or the Irish QI or Japanese QFI frameworks, then proceed to discuss the compliance challenges raised by those frameworks.

This book will clearly and concisely set out the common principles and legal bases of these frameworks as well as practical information for all concerned parties to minimise risk and maximise efficiency.

Ross has been in the financial services industry since 1996. In 1996, he did not know what a dividend was! So, it's true to say that his learning curve has been almost vertical for most of his career in the industry, which is good, because he likes to learn new things. While he was by no means "fresh out of University" at the time, he still retained enough of that time to know that the best way to acquire knowledge quickly, was to get it from background reading around the subject. That was when he found out that there were no books on withholding tax. After two years he decided that this was definitely the industry for him. His new home. And he decided to right that initial wrong—so he wrote his first book on withholding tax published by Euromoney.

Twenty-one years later, this book, co-authored with Kirsty Pitkin, the CEO of TConsult, will be his eleventh book on the subject of financial services and withholding tax in particular and Kirsty Pitkin's first. Many in that period have prophesied that withholding tax will disappear or that it will be harmonised and automated to the point that it's not worth talking about. So, far, none of this has come to pass and, if anything, the area has become more complex than it ever was, driven mainly by the self-interest of governments taking a short view of the effects of tax on foreign direct investment.

Investors know that they are going to be taxed if they invest in foreign financial instruments. The question is not "if" but "how much?". The author EE Smith observed that criminals are always ahead of the law and the law is always trying to catch up. The same is true of taxation. Irrespective of what tax authorities were asked to do by their governments, foreign investors were always lowest in the long list of priorities, superseded always by taxation of domestic residents. Complex rules surrounding taxation have always attracted those who seek to exploit those rules for their own benefit. Whether that was bricking up windows in England in 1696 to avoid a tax on windows[1], bootlegging to avoid US Prohibition under the 18th Amendment from 1920 to 1933[2], or engaging in tax claims to defraud the Danish government of $1.7Bn[3] between 2012 and 2015. The criminals were always one step ahead of the law simply because the law had to be open, published in advance and visible. Even EE Smith could identify the problem in 1972—"a criminal; can commit a crime and be far away before the crime is even detected"[4]. If the crime occurs across national boundaries, the inefficiencies of governments mean that the criminals have an even greater chance of a clean get away.

We have had the framework for cross-border taxation for several decades now—a system of bilateral tax treaties to provide a framework for the avoidance of double taxation (and double non-taxation) that allows for one or more of three operational models to be adopted—tax relief at source, quick refund and standard refund. The rules, processes and deadlines for each of these three models are set by the home country tax administration.

The problem with a bilateral approach is that each pair of jurisdictions can, and do, adopt different rules in different circumstances. This has led to a lack of standardisation, which in turn has led to a lack of automation

---

[1] Window tax – UK Parliament: https://www.parliament.uk/about/living-heritage/transformingsociety/towncountry/towns/tyne-and-wear-case-study/about-the-group/housing/window-tax/#:~:text=This%20tax%20was%20first%20imposed,exempt%20from%20the%20window%20tax.

[2] Prohibition – Britannica: https://www.britannica.com/event/Prohibition-United-States-history-1920-1933

[3] British financier Sanjay Shah facing charges over $1.7bn fraud extradited to Denmark from UAE. *Sky News*. 6th December 2023: https://news.sky.com/story/british-financier-sanjay-shah-facing-charges-over-1-7bn-fraud-extradited-to-denmark-from-uae-13024051#:~:text=Financier%20Sanjay%20Shah%20was%20convicted,ran%20from%202012%20to%202015.

[4] E.E. Smith, (1972). *Triplanetary.* Panther.

solutions for many years. As EE Smith predicted so well, cross-border withholding tax became a home for wealthy, well-connected criminals to exploit the inefficiencies of the various systems.

As the fiscal problems of the twentieth century came to a head, a focus on anti-tax evasion became more widespread as governments realised they were being ripped off by their own wealthy residents who were choosing to put their wealth somewhere out of the reach of their own tax authority. The US was particularly badly impacted and implemented Title V of the HIRE Act in 2010, now known commonly as FATCA. The OECD quickly followed suit with a simpler system—the Automatic Exchange of Information (AEoI) supported by the Common Reporting Standard (CRS). The EU also began implementing a Directive on Administrative Cooperation (DAC) beginning with DAC1 and up to DAC8. All these initiatives had one thing in common, to get ahead of the criminals by exploiting one fact—they all had to use one or more financial accounts to commit tax evasion. The solution was to force financial institutions to report the accounts of non-residents so that their home governments could figure out whether they were in fact evading tax. But in order to fix that problem, governments had to address the inefficiencies and inequalities of the cross-border tax system at the more general level.

This book has been written because, for the first time in thirty-five years, there is enough of a common approach being adopted by enough jurisdictions to be able to make tax relief at source for most investors a reality in the near future. At the same time, parallel initiatives against tax evasion are coalescing around a single model focused on financial institution due diligence and reporting. It is therefore opportune to focus on these two pillars of international taxation as they will, over time, become the dominant taxation models for international investors.

Finally, the Appendices to this book contain the texts of the most recent regulatory frameworks. While this creates quite lengthy appendices, we feel these are useful to be included in this book to provide a fast, easy-to-use reference for readers rather than having to find these materials on their respective websites.

# Contents

# About the Authors

**Ross K. McGill** 69, born in Newcastle Upon Tyne, England, obtained his Honours degree in Materials Science at the University of Bath in 1978. Married with three children and four grandchildren, he lives in a small town southwest of London. He is the founder and Chairman of TConsult Ltd, a specialist regulatory compliance firm he founded in May 2003, and Chairman of the Association of Qualified andAuthorised Intermediaries (AQAI).

Ross is passionate about tax, standards and automation. Within the industry, in addition to writing ten books, he has held committee positions on the International Capital Markets Services Association (ICMSA), the International Standards Organisation (ISO) Standards Evaluation Group (SEG) and three of its sub-committees on funds management, proxy voting and corporate actions. He provided expert witness testimony to the European Commission (EC) Fiscal Compliance Committee (FISCO) in 2009 and was a full committee member of the European Commission Tax Barriers Business Advisory Group (TBAG) also editing the final report[1] to the Commission in 2013. He founded the non-profit, unincorporated trade Association of Qualified Intermediaries (AQAI[2]) in September 2023 which now has seventy-six QI members in twenty-nine countries.

[1] European Commission, (2016). *Report of the Tax Barriers Business Advisory Group (TBAG).* https://finance.ec.europa.eu/publications/report-tax-barriers-business-advisory-group-tbag_en.

[2] Association of Qualified and Authorised Intermediaries (AQAI): https://aqai.tax.

For his company, Ross managed a transition from consulting to a leading reg-tech firm by establishing the Tax Compliance Toolkit$^{tm}$ (TCT) and the Investor Self-Declaration (ISD), the latter bringing together the regulatory requirements of four of the main pillars of taxation described in this book—the US QI and FATCA regulations and the OECD TRACE IP and Common Reporting Standard (CRS).

**Kirsty V. Pitkin** obtained her Honors degree in Creative Studies in English and Music from Bath Spa University in 2004 and her Master's degree in creative writing and New Media from DeMontfort University in 2008. She lives with her husband, daughter and house rabbit in the World Heritage City of Bath in the southwest of England.

Kirsty co-founded TConsult Ltd with Ross in 2003. In her early years at the company, she focussed on the UK event amplification division of the business, but in 2018 became CEO in charge of all the global operations of the business. In that time, she has guided the company through a phase of digital transformation, developing systems that allow the company to support more clients without compromising on the quality of regulatory opinions that are offered. She has more recently been driving the reg-tech side of the business with the development of the Tax Compliance Toolkit$^{tm}$ and Investor Self-Declaration (ISD) systems.

Kirsty uses her background in communications to help clients understand their obligations and develop effective systems for managing their compliance. She also coordinates work with reg-tech and fintech partners developing compliance software.

Kirsty is passionate about communicating in simple, accessible language that everyone can understand. She specialises in translating complex tax technical documents into a form that allows financial institutions to make more informed compliance decisions.

# Abbreviations

| | |
|---|---|
| ADR | American Depositary Receipt |
| AEoI | Automatic Exchange of Information |
| AI | Authorised Intermediary (Finland)/Artificial Intelligence |
| AIIN | Authorised Intermediary Identification Number |
| AML | Anti Money Laundering |
| AWA | Authorised Withholding Agent |
| BEPS | Base Erosion and Profit Shifting |
| BIAC | Business Industry Advisory Committee |
| CAA | Competent Authority Agreement |
| CAEV | Corporate Action EVent |
| CANO | Corporate Action NOtification |
| CAR | Capital Adequacy Ratio |
| CbCR | Country by Country Reporting |
| CBT | Citizenship-Based Taxation |
| CCG | Consolidated Compliance Group |
| CCP | Common Compliance Program |
| C-DCFFI | Certified Deemed Compliant FFI |
| CFA | Committee on Fiscal Affairs |
| CFC | Controlled Foreign Corporation |
| CFI | Certified Financial Intermediary |
| CiC | Change in Circumstances |
| CIV | Collective Investment Vehicle |
| CLN | Certificate of Loss of Nationality |
| CMU | Capital Markets Union |
| CSD | Central Securities Depository |

| | |
|---|---|
| DCFFI | Deemed Compliant FFI |
| DST | Digital Services Tax |
| EAG | Expanded Affiliate Group |
| EBITDA | Earnings Before Interest, Taxes, Depreciation and Amortisation |
| EC | European Commission |
| ECOFIN | ECOnomic and FInancial affairs COuncil |
| EEA | European Economic Area |
| EFIN | Electronic Filing Identification Number |
| EFTPS | Electronic Federal Tax Payment System |
| EIN | Employer Identification Number |
| EoI | Exchange of Information |
| EPTF | European Post Trade Forum |
| ESMA | European Securities Market Authority |
| eTRC | Electronic Tax Residency Certificate |
| EU | European Union |
| EUID | European Unique IDentifier |
| FASTER | Faster And Simpler Tax Excess Relief |
| FATCA | Foreign Account Tax Compliance Act *(misnomer)* |
| FDAP | Fixed, Determinable, Annual or Periodic Income |
| FDI | Foreign Direct Investment |
| FEIE | Foreign Earned Income Exclusion |
| FFEIN | FFI Employer Identification Number |
| FFI | Foreign Financial Institution |
| FFIA | Foreign Financial Institution Agreement |
| FIP | Foreign Indirect Participant |
| FIRE | Filing Information Returns Electronically |
| FISCO | Fiscal Compliance Experts Group |
| FTC | Foreign Tax Credit |
| FWS | Full Withholding Statement |
| GDR | Global Depositary Receipt |
| GIIN | Global Intermediary Identification Number |
| HCTA | Host Country Tax Authority |
| HIRE | Hiring Incentives to Restore Employment Act (2010) |
| ICG | Informal Consultative Group |
| IDES | International Data Exchange System |
| IDR | International Depositary Receipt |
| IRC | US Internal Revenue Code |
| IRS | Internal Revenue Service (USA) |
| ISIN | International Securities Identification Number |
| ITIN | Individual Taxpayer Identification Number |
| JBESP | Japanese Book-Entry System Participant |
| KYC | Know Your Customer |
| KYT | Know Your Transaction |
| LEI | Legal Entity Identifier |

| | |
|---|---|
| LLM | Large Language Model |
| LoB | Limitation on Benefits |
| MAP | Mutual Agreement Procedure |
| MBT | Main Benefits Test |
| MCAA | Multi Lateral Competent Authority Agreement |
| MDR | Mandatory Disclosure Regulations |
| ML | Machine Learning |
| MLI | Multi-Lateral Instrument |
| MNE | Multi-Ntional Enterprise |
| MoU | Memorandum of Understanding |
| NFFE | Non-Financial Foreign Entity |
| NFT | Non Fungible Tokens |
| NP-FFI | Non-Participating FFI |
| NQI | Nonqualified Intermediary |
| NRA | Non-resident Alien |
| NWFP | Non-Withholding Foreign Partnership |
| NWQI | Non-Withholding Qualified Intermediary |
| OCR | Optical Character Recognition |
| OECD | Organisation for Economic Cooperation and Development |
| OSM | Operational Structure Map |
| OTC | Over the Counter |
| PAI | Private Arrangement Intermediary |
| PE | Permanent Establishment |
| PFFI | Participating FFI |
| PPT | Principal Purpose Test |
| PTIN | Preparer Tax Identification Number |
| QDD | Qualified Derivatives Dealer |
| QFI | Qualified Financial Intermediary (Japan) |
| QFSIT | Qualified Foreign Securities Investment Trust |
| QI | Qualified Intermediary |
| QI-EIN | Qualified Intermediary EIN |
| QSL | Qualified Securities Lender |
| RBT | Residence-Based Taxation |
| R-DCFFI | Registered Deemed Compliant FFI |
| REIT | Real Estate Investment Trust |
| RM[n]-FFI | Reporting Model n FFI (where n = 1A, 1B or 2) |
| SaaS | Software as a Service |
| SSN | Social Security Number |
| SSNA | Social Security Numbering Agency |
| SWIFT | Society for Worldwide Interbank Financial Telecommunications |
| TBAG | Tax Barriers Business Advisory Group |
| TCC | Transmitter Control Code |
| TIN | Tax Identification Number |
| TRACE | Tax Relief and Compliance Enhancement |

| | |
|---|---|
| TRACEIP | TRACE Implementation Protocol |
| USWA | United States Withholding Agent |
| WFP | Withholding Foreign Partnership |
| WFT | Withholding Foreign Trust |
| WQI | Withholding Qualified Intermediary |
| WRPS | Withholding Rate Pool Statement |
| WTCC | Withholding Tax Code of Conduct |

# List of Figures

# List of Tables

# Part I

## Essentials

# 1

# Scope and Purpose

In this chapter, we will bring together, perhaps for the first time, a view of compliance that transcends any one specific jurisdiction.

What is a Qualified Intermediary? For the purposes of this book, and to establish the common thread of the story of cross-border taxation, we are using the term "qualified intermediary" to refer to any financial institution that is subject to an extraterritorial legal or regulatory framework that controls or provides oversight in relation to taxation of cross-border investment income and/or anti-tax evasion principles. This term, and we stress for the purposes of this book specifically, therefore refers to:

(i) Qualified Intermediaries under US tax regulations in US Internal Revenue Code Chapters 3 and 4,
(ii) Authorised Intermediaries under OECD Tax Relief and Compliance Enhancement framework (TRACE),
(iii) Certified Financial Intermediaries under the European Union FASTER Directive,
(iv) Reporting intermediaries under DAC6,
(v) Authorised Withholding Agents (AWAs) and Qualifying Intermediaries under the Irish QI Program
(vi) Qualified Financial Intermediaries (QFIs) under the Japanese Government Bond (JGB) regulations.

Multiple jurisdictions have been and continue to converge their taxation frameworks to eradicate cross-border tax evasion and establish common


R. K. McGill and K. V. Pitkin, *Qualified Intermediary*,
https://doi.org/10.1007/978-3-031-81410-5_1

principles under which non-resident financial institutions can become withholding agents for non-resident investors and establish rules to prevent and detect cross-border tax evasion.

The US began this convergence with its Qualified Intermediary Agreement framework in 2001 with Revenue Procedure 2000–12 (the original QI Agreement). There have been three subsequent 6-year term agreements each building up further benefits for financial institutions and controls on them to ensure effective compliance. The most recent—Revenue Procedure 2022–43—became effective on January 1, 2023, and is complemented by anti-tax evasion principles laid down in Title V of the Hiring Incentives to Restore Employment Act (2010), also known as FATCA.

Ireland followed the US model with its Qualified Intermediary and Authorised Withholding Agent (AWA) program and Japan adopted a Qualified Foreign Intermediary (QFI) system.

In 2013, the OECD published the Tax Relief and Compliance Enhancement Framework (TRACE), comprising an Authorised Intermediary (AI) agreement that complements the OECD anti-tax evasion framework of the Common Reporting Standard (CRS). TRACE was adopted by Finland in 2021.

More recently, in 2023 the European Commission proposed the new Faster and Safer Tax Relief of Excess Withholding Taxes (FASTER) Directive for standardisation and simplification of cross-border withholding tax across twenty-seven Member States. Once agreed upon, the Directive is expected to go into force on January 1, 2030.

All these frameworks have a commonality of purpose and, in many cases, commonality of implementation principles. Differences lie in the practical implementation of these frameworks by financial institutions who may have to adopt different procedures and policies depending on the nature and residency of their clients and the markets in which they choose to invest.

From a tax perspective we know that the European Union has been looking at this for at least 35 years while the US implemented their QI regime 24 years ago. There is no sense therefore in which any of this is "breaking news". The much later frameworks—such as the OECD Automatic Exchange of Information (AEoI) together with its main pillar, the Common Reporting Standard (CRS) and the Tax Relief and Compliance Enhancement (TRACE) implementation protocol—are all based broadly on the US model.

All these models have two things in common. The first is an operational tax framework, that is, what needs to be done on a day-to-day basis to achieve the policy objective of the model. The second is a governance framework designed to establish controls over the operational tax framework. In plain

English, the tax operational framework described *what* must be done, when and how while the governance framework answers the question "*how do you know it's being done properly?*".

So, to describe the scope of this book, we will describe the tax operational components to provide some context, while also spending time on the governance components. Governance, from this perspective, has three elements: (i) control, (ii) oversight and (iii) enforcement. These represent compliance and it is the challenges of these three that will be the main focus of our attention.

The frameworks we've mentioned so far, as well as all the others we will cover in this book, deal with (i) the proper and most efficient investment tax methodologies and (ii) anti-tax evasion.

As Exhibit 1.1 shows, the OECD, EU and US all have a bifurcated model in which the proper taxation of cross-border investment income is handled by a different compliance framework than that of anti-tax evasion. So, in the US, for example, the proper taxation of income paid to non-US recipients is handled mainly through US Internal Revenue Code (IRC) Chapters 1 and 3, collectively referred to as the QI regime. Taxation of US-sourced income paid to US Persons outside the US is handled through IRC Chapters 31 and 61. Anti-tax evasion is handled mainly through IRC Chapter 4 otherwise known as FATCA.

Equally, in the OECD, the proper taxation of cross-border income is handled by the Tax Relief and Compliance Enhancement (TRACE) protocol, while the anti-tax evasion framework is handled by the Common Reporting Standard (CRS) as a supporting element to the Automatic exchange of Information (AEoI). The EU by comparison has been a bit of a mess for some time. While recognising the threat of tax evasion (and doing very little about it), the EU Member States have been unable to come together on a workable model for proper taxation of income as they continue to struggle with the political challenges of the Capital Markets Union (CMU).

However, in contrast to the fanfare of frameworks like FATCA and CRS, the EU has been quietly developing a body of regulation based on the Directive for Administrative Cooperation (DAC) that's designed to standardise and automate what used to be called "fishing expeditions" by tax administrations trying to find potential tax evaders. There have been a number of DACs and in 2024, we are up to DAC8 that deals with the reporting of transfers in crypto-assets, but more of that later.

The scope of this book is therefore inclusive of enough detail about each framework to allow the reader to contextualise the compliance challenges that are described in more detail. The compliance challenges themselves, it must be said, fall mostly on financial institutions such as brokers, prime brokers,

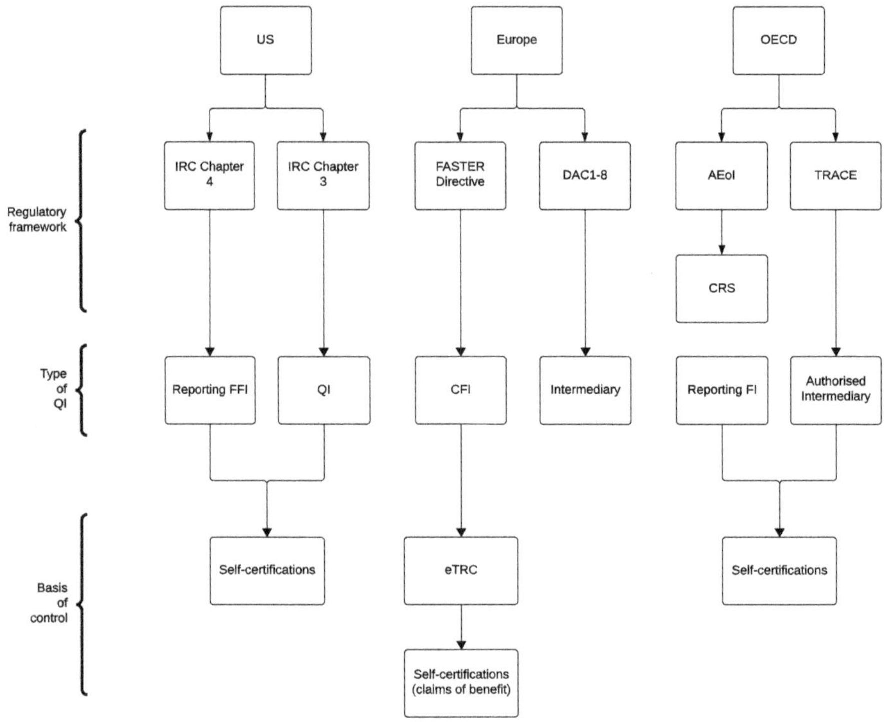


**Exhibit 1.1** Global tax and anti-tax evasion frameworks. *Source* Authors

custodians, central securities depositories, depositaries, with institutional investors coming a close second.

So much for scope. As to purpose, cross-border withholding tax is primarily an issue for tax administrations, investors and financial institutions. For investors, until recently, the main issue has simply been awareness. Institutional investors, such as hedge funds and pension funds and sovereign wealth funds (and every other type of fund in between), have had a slightly higher awareness of these issues than retail investors e.g., individuals running brokerage accounts. The reason is simple: returns. An institutional investor will, as a component of their investment strategy, hold securities "long" i.e., part of their strategy is to deliver returns through increasing share value and through returns delivered from dividends. The sizes and breadth of their holdings will be large enough to make tax optimisation an issue as discussed in more detail in the 2023 second edition of Ross McGill's book *Cross Border Investment Withholding Tax* published by Palgrave Macmillan.[1]

[1] Ross McGill, (2023). *Cross-Border Investment Withholding Tax: A Practical Guide for Investors and Intermediaries.* Palgrave Macmillan. https://link.springer.com/book/10.1007/978-3-031-32785-8.

A retail, investor on the other hand, while having many of the same motivations, is usually dealing with a much smaller portfolio and much smaller amounts of money. The tax component of these portfolios, even at high statutory tax rates, is not material from a numerical viewpoint. As the European Commission Tax Barriers Business Advisory Group found in their 2013 report,[2] most of the cross-border tax that is over-withheld and never reclaimed belongs to small investors who are either unaware of their rights or for whom the effort involved in recovery exceeds the value at risk.

The real compliance question is, therefore, what is mandated by tax administrations for compliance that financial institutions must embed into their business models in order to allow cross-border investing. As one astute person said, “if you think the cost of compliance is high, look at the cost of non-compliance”. Tax administrations are taking an increasingly aggressive approach to non-compliance which can, in some cases, cost millions of dollars before you get to the reputational damage to the firm and to the trust damage for the industry as a whole.

Many firms have come to us, as regulatory compliance specialists, over the years and most want to know how to do the least amount of work possible to tick that compliance box. Compliance departments on the other hand are rightly paranoid about the disproportionate reputational effect that a compliance failure can have on the business, while operational departments really only care about keeping the engine running using the smallest amount of oil.

In our consulting activities in twenty-seven countries, over 20 years, we have consistently observed that operational departments are almost always siloed, narrowly focussed and badly led. They don’t really care about the processes before them or after them, just about their own processes. Their risk management is operationally not business led, but function led. This creates the biggest challenges for compliance because, in most of these tax frameworks, a single person is required to take on responsibility for several compliance objectives across different operational functions.

The purpose of this book is not to provide an easy route to compliance but how to use these frameworks as a tool and guide to motivate the business at a more holistic level to get behind compliance as a proactive activity that can deliver operational and business benefits beyond the day-to-day.

[2] European Commission, (2016). *Report of the Tax Barriers Business Advisory Group (TBAG).* https://finance.ec.europa.eu/publications/report-tax-barriers-business-advisory-group-tbag_en.

# 2

# History and Context

Tax regulation was an invention of the British monarchy in 1799 with the establishment of the Board of Taxes, designed to raise money to help pay for the Napoleonic wars. The subject has been evolving continuously for several hundred years, and for every development in that time there have been those who seek to subvert the government's choices, such as smugglers avoiding excise duty in Cornwall during the seventeenth and eighteenth centuries.[1] It has been an arms race in which the "criminals" (tax evaders) have generally always been one step ahead of the lawmakers. Even when they weren't, the response from those being taxed, such as in the case of the window tax of England's William III in 1696, was rarely benign, leading to unanticipated behaviour, such as bricking up your windows to avoid the tax—from which we get the term "*daylight robbery*"[2]—and occasionally even innovation, such the development of lighter, fluted glass to avoid a tax on glass,[3] which was sold and taxed by weight.

This has led to is an extremely large number of laws and regulation all designed to ensure that tax can be (i) assessed and collected on the one hand, and (ii) not avoided or evaded on the other. In this chapter, we will focus on the more recent history of each of these aspects of tax regulation on the international stage.

[1] Castelow, E., (nd). *Smugglers and Wreckers*. Historic UK. https://www.historic-uk.com/CultureUK/Smugglers-Wreckers/.

[2] Daylight Robbery—Phrase Finder. https://www.phrases.org.uk/meanings/daylight-robbery.html.

[3] Glass tax—Wikipedia: https://en.wikipedia.org/wiki/Glass_tax.


R. K. McGill and K. V. Pitkin, *Qualified Intermediary*,
https://doi.org/10.1007/978-3-031-81410-5_2

## Taxation of Cross-Border Income

The basis of tax relief at source is the existence of bilateral double tax agreements (DTAs) or treaties (DTTs) between pairs of countries. These DTAs, most of which follow the OECD Model Tax Convention on Income and Capital,[4] establish the rights and privileges of recipients of income in one jurisdiction or State when that income was created and distributed from another jurisdiction or State. The current Model Tax Convention is the tenth edition, published in December 2017.

What the DTAs *don't* do is set the actual tax rates involved. Nor do they establish the procedural context in which the DTA is implemented. So, for example, the France-UK DTA may establish that a UK resident individual receiving a dividend from a French corporation may be entitled to be taxed at a treaty rate, as opposed to the French statutory rate, the DTA does not specify what the rate is nor the procedure that the UK resident must follow to ensure that the treaty tax rate is applied. These matters are set by each tax administration.

Historically, the bilateral nature of these DTAs and the administrative approach of each tax authority has meant that, particularly in Europe, a complexity has developed over time that has made tax reclamation, as opposed to tax relief at source, an industry in its own right. Most tax administrations, acting in their own national interests, took the view that they would force domestic corporations to tax cross-border distributions at their domestic statutory rate of tax. This led to a situation in which the DTAs could only be enforced by the recipients of income after statutory rates of tax had been withheld. Tax administrations had to come up with forms and procedures to allow these foreign investors to claim some of the originally taxed distribution back. These procedures and forms were complex, often not in English and had associated deadlines, called statutes of limitation, after which any claim could be rejected.

This complex model was clearly inefficient and harmed the inward investment potential of many countries. It also led to discriminatory practices in which a foreign investor would receive different treatment than a domestic investor of the same type.

Some jurisdictions however established legal frameworks connected to the DTAs that allowed for tax relief at source. However, to retain control, only domestic financial institutions could be withholding agents because the tax

[4] OECD, (2017). Model tax convention on income and on capital: Condensed version 2017. https://www.oecd.org/ctp/treaties/model-tax-convention-on-income-and-on-capital-condensed-version-20745419.htm.

administrations wanted strict liability for underwithholding to lie with an institution over which they had regulatory authority and oversight.

In most of this book, we will be using the example of dividends paid cross-border simply because this accounts for around 80% of all the cross-border investment activity. The world is also split into two types of investors—retail (usually individuals) and institutional, usually legal entities such as funds, although there are a great many different types of institutional investors, such as trusts, partnerships and other collective investment vehicles (CIVs).

The cross-border investment industry operates as a chain of financial institutions, each undertaking different roles, with a corporation at one end of the chain that creates and markets financial instruments (an Issuer) and an investor at the other buying those financial instruments. Corporations and governments are the engine of the investment industry. They create financial instruments and sell these to investors to raise money. For corporations this may be either as equity (shares), debt (bonds) or derivatives (depositary receipts, ETFs, CFDs). Governments typically issue bonds to raise money to fill gaps between tax revenue and government spending or for capital projects. Either way, they sell these financial instruments to investors. The wider the pool of investors the better. So, selling these instruments cross-border via international exchanges increases the amount of money that can be raised. When it comes time to pay investors either as a dividend on their shares, interest on their bonds or dividend equivalents on the underlying securities, these are typically taxed before they are distributed.

In most markets, the financial institution in the chain nearest to the corporation that issued equity or debt instruments acts as a paying agent and withholding agent. Their job is to take the dividend from the corporation and distribute it to the investors. Their other role is to withhold the tax and pay it to the domestic tax authority on behalf of the corporation. When there is only one tax rate, the statutory rate, this is a simple model. Everyone gets taxed at the same rate. However, if the investor is not resident in the same jurisdiction as the corporation, they may be subject to the DTA, under which a lower rate of tax could apply to the proportion of the payment that is allocable to the foreign investor. Multiply this up by many thousands of investors in hundreds of jurisdictions—now you have a payment and tax problem. Exhibit 2.1 provides a basic explanation of this model.

The chain investment model relies on a specific type of account called an omnibus account. So, a financial institution with its own clients will typically operate an omnibus account at another financial institution further up the payment chain. The asses of its clients are co-mingled into this omnibus account so that the financial institution does not have to disclose who its

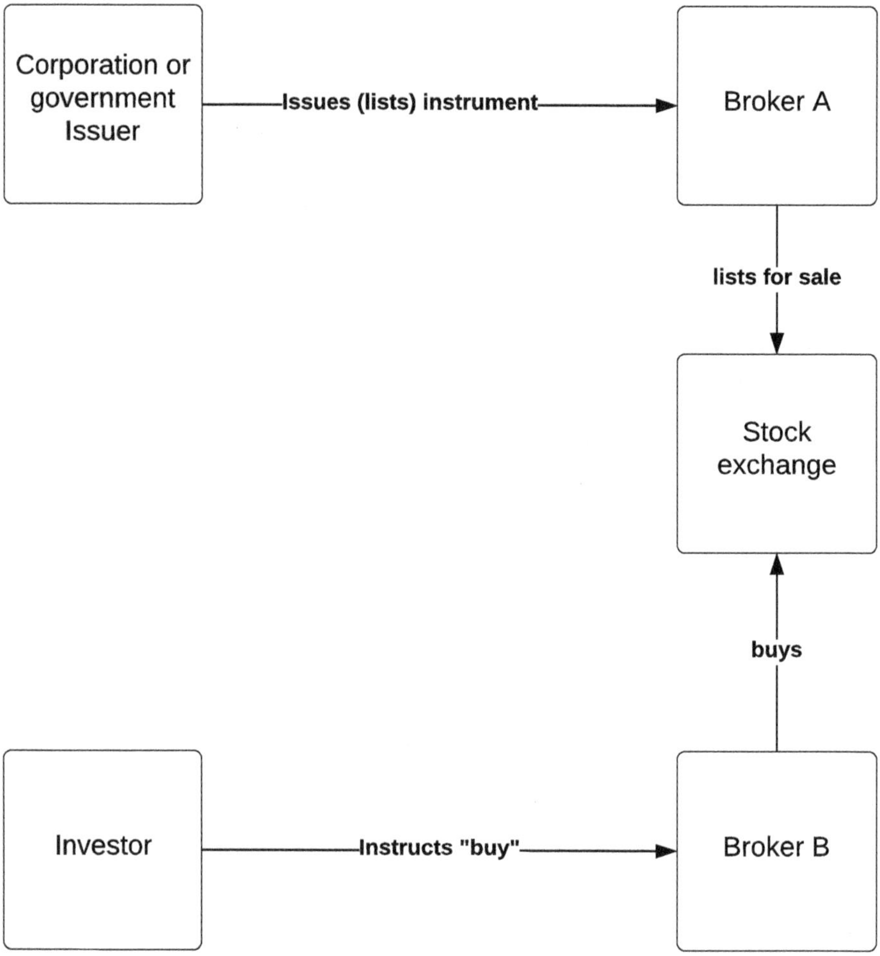


**Exhibit 2.1** Chain of investment model (basic) *Source* Authors

clients are. This is shown in Exhibit 2.2. This continues all the way up until the financial institution that is the paying or withholding agent for the Issuer. At that level, the withholding agent has no knowledge of who the ultimate beneficiary is. Their clients will just be another financial institution with omnibus accounts. While this is fine when only statutory rate tax is applied, it will clearly not work if more than one tax rate must be applied to a distribution.

Because the withholding agent at the top of the chain has strict legal liability for the tax it withholds, a secondary system must apply so that the withholding agent has no *actual* liability. This secondary system is called

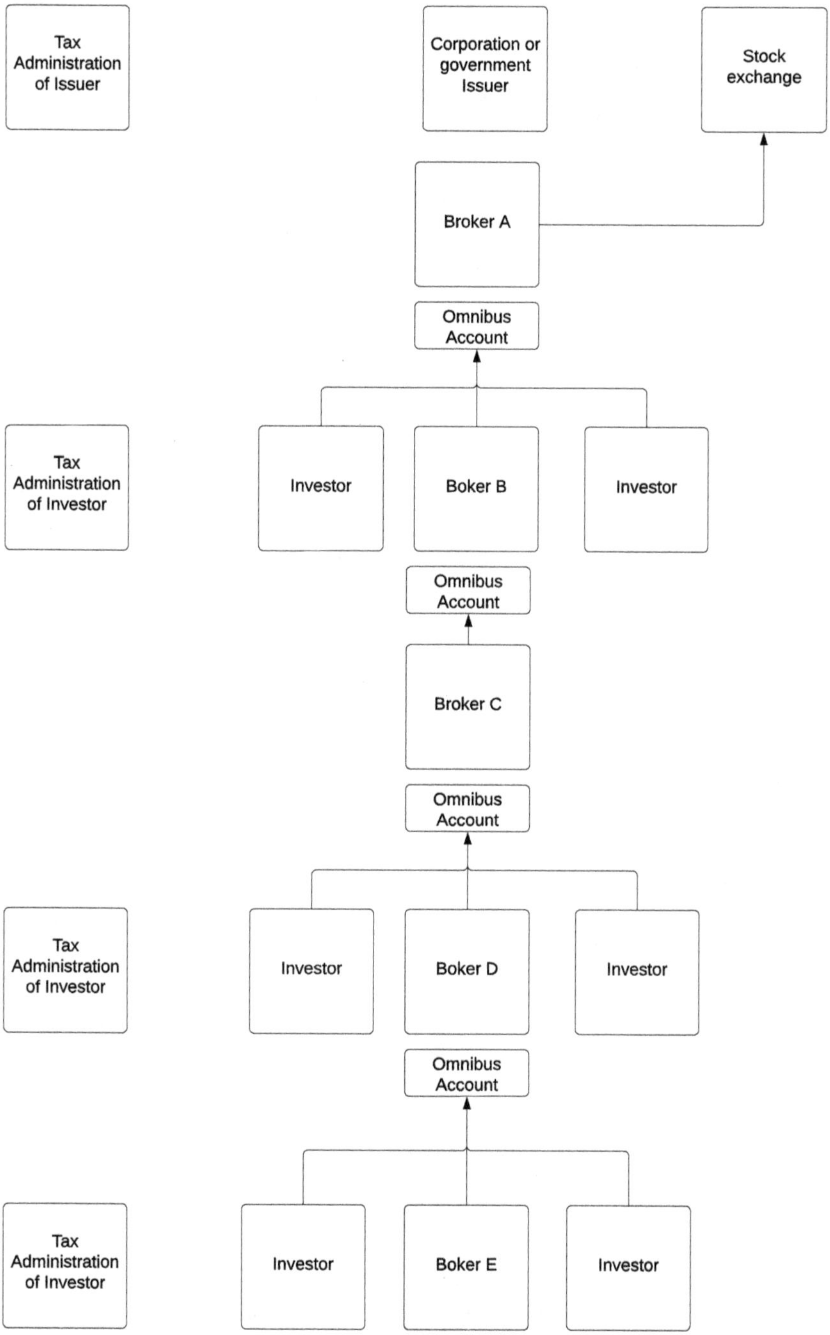


**Exhibit 2.2** The chain of investment using omnibus accounts *Source* Authors

disclosure. In other words, the withholding agent must know who each beneficiary of a payment or part of a payment is, at each level of the payment chain, before they can apply the correct amount of tax. For those parts of the chain, at any level, where disclosure does not occur, no tax relief will be granted, and the statutory rate will be applied.

For example, France operates a tax relief at source system in which the withholding agent at the top of every French payment chain must, by law, be a French bank. If any beneficiary at any point in the payment chain, wants to benefit from tax relief at source under a double tax treaty with France, that beneficiary must provide a form 5000 and a Form 5001, 5002 or 5003 (dependent on the type of income). The Form 5000 is a tax residency certificate that must be stamped by the beneficiary's domestic tax authority first to confirm their residency. These documents are usually provided by the beneficiary to their financial institution who then sends these up the chain of payment together with information about the holdings of the beneficiary, ending with the withholding agent. In the world of the FASTER Directive, as we shall see later, for EU residents, this will be replaced by an electronic tax residency certificate (eTRC).

Once the withholding agent receives all this information, it can compare that to the amounts being distributed (usually by reference to the number of shares in the case of a dividend) and withhold the correct amount of tax which it will send to the tax authorities within a set period of time (often thirty days). Not all financial institutions in markets that allow relief at source have the resources to support complex processes like these.

## Anti-Tax Evasion

The efforts to prevent, detect and deter tax evasion have a much more colourful and complex history. This issue has two parts. The first is the attempt to deter and detect tax evasion conducted by individuals and investing entities such as funds. The second are the attempts by multinational enterprises (MNEs) to evade tax by shifting operating profits to low tax jurisdictions—so-called Base Erosion and Profit Shifting (BEPS). Effectively this means eroding the basis on which tax is assessed in your home jurisdiction (which may also be where most of the economic activity takes place) and shifting the profits to another jurisdiction that taxes those profits at a lower rate than your home jurisdiction.

## Case Study: Apple Inc

In 2014, the European Commission undertook a two-year investigation into tax arrangements between Apple and Ireland, which used a variation of the "double Irish" base erosion and profit shifting (BEPS) tax avoidance tool[5] to shield €110.8 billion of non-US profits from tax in the US over a ten-year period between 2004 and 2014. The European Commission announced its conclusion that Ireland had granted illegal tax benefits to Apple, and ordered Apple to repay €13 billion of back taxes, plus interest.

Somewhat surprisingly, the Irish government chose to appeal this ruling on the grounds that there had been no violation of Irish tax law and national tax policy is explicitly excluded from EU treaties, making the ruling "an intrusion into Irish sovereignty". In July 2020 the European General Court agreed and ruled in favour of Apple. The European Commission has appealed this decision at the European Court of Justice on the grounds that the court did not correctly assess "the substance and consequences of certain methodological errors that, according to the Commission decision, vitiated the tax rulings" (Giovanni Pitruzzella, advocate general to the European Court of Justice). The final judgement is expected in 2024.

Apple has since closed its double Irish tool and restructured into a new Irish BEPS tool called the Capital Allowances for Intangible Assets (CAIA) tool. This required a restatement of Irish GDP, which has been described as "leprechaun economics", and led accusations that Ireland is the world's largest tax haven.

## US

The US began its efforts in the late nineteen nineties culminating in the offset provisions in Title V of the Hiring Incentives to Restore Employment Act (2010) (the HIRE Act), otherwise known as FATCA. The implementing regulation supporting that law is IRC Chapter 4. This was recognised as a major piece of extraterritorial overreach by the US that immediately sparked a push back, particularly from the European Union. The EU at the time had data privacy laws in effect, later to become the General Data Protection Regulation or GDPR. This prevented EU financial institutions from sharing client data outside the border of the EU. FATCA itself, at that time, was focussed on financial institutions and forcing them to divulge US accounts held at

---

[5] *Q&A: What is the double Irish?* Financial Times, October 9, 2014: https://www.ft.com/content/f7a2b958-4fc8-11e4-908e-00144feab7de.

non-US financial institutions. The UBS case was a notable landmark in this process because Switzerland was not an EU member but was in the European Economic Area (EEA). Its well-known approach to client privacy made them a natural target. This push back led to a major change in strategy by the US, which decided that the best way to get around the objections was to engage directly with other tax administrations and sign "intergovernmental agreements" (IGAs). In jurisdictions with an IGA, financial firms would not break data protection laws because they would be reporting US account holders to their local administration, which would then take on the role of reporting to the IRS. This circumvents the issue created by the idiosyncrasy that the US taxes based on citizenship whereas the EU, as with almost everywhere else, taxes based only on residency. So, a US person resident in the EU would be protected under GDPR, yet subject to reporting under FATCA on the grounds of their US citizenship.

The IGAs resulted in a number of jurisdictions transposing FATCA into local law, setting up a legal framework for bilateral information sharing with the US.

## The OECD

The OECD has been involved in taxation for many years. It started with the development of a Model Convention for double tax treaties, which is still used as the basis for most (but not all) tax treaties in force globally. As tax evasion became a bigger issue and tax administrations started to figure out that rich people were hiding assets across borders with the specific intent of evading domestic taxes, the OECD began to formulate approaches to deter and detect it so that its members could adopt a common methodology to combat it. The OECD is not a government and has no power of its own, so its members collaborate towards common goals. But like any collaborative organisation, it is not immune from politics or self-interest. The net result is that it takes longer for these differences to be resolved and incorporated into an agreed model. The OECD's initiatives in tax evasion are focussed on individuals (through AEoI and CRS) and large organisations, multinational enterprises or MNEs (through BEPS). More recently they have been at the forefront of an initiative to establish a common basic rate of corporation tax designed to be a deterrent component of BEPS.

## The European Union

The European Union has been quietly developing and amending a Directive that facilitates the administrative co-operation that one Member State can give another in relation to tax matters, particularly on an automatic basis in the field of taxation. As Directives, these are unanimously agreed upon by all Member States and enacted into local law by each Member State.

DAC1 2011/16/EU sets reporting rules for employment income, capital gains, director's fees and pensions.
DAC2 2014/107/EU sets reporting rules for financial accounts. This has some equivalence to CRS.
DAC3 2015/2376/EU obliges tax administrations to automatically exchange information on advance cross-border rulings and advance pricing agreements. This is also related to BEPS.
DAC4 2016/881/EU establishes rules for country-by-country reporting for multinationals and coordinates with BEPS Action 12.
DAC5 2016/2258/EU combats money laundering by ensuring that authorities have access to beneficial ownership information collected under AML rules.
DAC6 2018/822/EU deals with cross-border arrangements that could have Hallmarks of tax evasion, including the subversion of CRS reporting obligations and tax avoidance.
DAC7 2021/514/EU deals with reporting rules for digital platforms that rent property, transportation, goods or provide personal services.
DAC8 2023/2226/EU deals with the reporting and automatic exchange of information on revenues from transactions in crypto-assets, digital assets and on advance tax rulings for the wealthiest (high-net-worth) individuals.

While the reader may not be as aware of these legal and regulatory structures as they may be of FATCA or CRS, they are nonetheless an important legal framework that applies both in the EU and to any financial institution with any EU clients.

The primary compliance challenge for the DAC system, as an example, is awareness. Most compliance functions focus on FATCA and CRS with a smattering of US QI. Many that we speak to have no awareness of DAC and, to a large extent, have no formalised way to comply. The reason for this is that the framework of DAC is not data based, but pattern based. This highlights a problem for financial institutions. Starting from a basic precept of what a financial institution *is* and what it *does*, there flows an inordinate amount of statute and regulation which was originally designed to make the system more robust and able to properly serve its clients. So, we saw a lot of regulation around consumer rights and payment systems. Then we had the 2008 financial crisis. This woke everyone up to the fact that these financial institutions were operating on shoestring capital and enormous leverage, meaning they had become "*too large to fail*".

As a result, we saw the development of capital adequacy regulation (CAR) and stress testing as governments realised that the financial system was critical to political and economic stability. So, what started out as the original banking system from the twelfth and thirteenth centuries in Renaissance Europe designed to foster trade, has evolved into what we would prefer to describe as a regulatory and enforcement industry that just happens to deal in money as a product.

# 3

# Convergence

This chapter explains the commonalities and differences of the different frameworks and explains how these tax frameworks can be seen to be converging. The practical basis for the frameworks is explained in a comparative way so that the reader can see the overall direction of travel and thus understand and prepare for the likely future events in this space.

All the frameworks discussed in this book have a common set of threads, formed of documentation, due diligence and reporting (Exhibit 3.1).

## Form of Documentation

The US and OECD settled some time ago on the concept of a self-certification of tax residency. The EU on the other hand has recently settled on an electronic tax residency certificate (eTRC) issued by a competent authority.

The European Commission's Tax Barriers Business Advisory Group (TBAG) report of 2013 argued and recommended the use of a self-certification (i) because it would align with other more widespread frameworks and (ii) because it places liability where it belongs—with the investor. However, the European Commission elected not to follow that advice, electing instead to allow Member States to retain control over who could claim double tax treaty benefits through the issuance of eTRCs under the FASTER Directive. That said, even in the FASTER Directive, a claim of benefits is based on an eTRC (or equivalent) plus KYC documentation or, in the case of entities, a separate written claim.


R. K. McGill and K. V. Pitkin, *Qualified Intermediary*,
https://doi.org/10.1007/978-3-031-81410-5_3

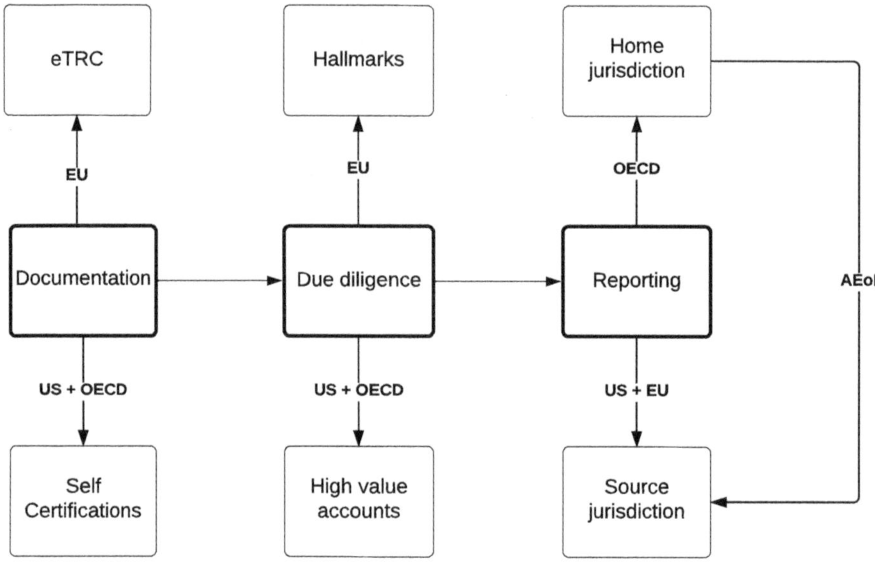


**Exhibit 3.1** Convergence and bifurcation of tax frameworks *Source* Authors

The US and OECD frameworks do allow the flexibility for financial institutions, and their vendor suppliers, to be innovative by allowing the use of electronic signatures and for the forms themselves to be adapted, under certain rules, to the financial institution's onboarding process. As a result, tax documentation has, in recent years, become inextricably linked with KYC and AML because the decision about whether or not to allow an account to be opened now relies just as much on tax certifications as it does on passports for natural persons and incorporation documents for entities. So, there is convergence to the use of self-certifications and convergence to KYC processes too.

## Due Diligence Rules

Once a financial institution has documentation in place, it can do two things. First, it can assess the account holder on an annual basis for anti-tax evasion regulation. Second, it can tax the cross-border income received on behalf of the investor. Both of these fall under the category of due diligence.

In terms of tax operations, the due diligence is centred around an investor's tax residency and any claim of treaty benefits. These can be found in the US W-8 series of self-certifications as well as the OECD's TRACE framework including investor self-declarations (ISDs). Generally, these must be statements by the investor that they beneficially own the income from claimed assets and are claiming a treaty benefit, usually under a penalty of perjury. It's noteworthy for professionals that there is a difference between the beneficial ownership of an asset and beneficial ownership of the income derived from that asset. They are not necessarily always the same. In most cases, we will be talking about beneficial ownership of the income from an asset.

The second category is that of anti-tax evasion and here the rules are much more complex. That said, there is convergence here too. If tax evasion is going to happen, its generally not done in a small way. So, the focus for all parties concerned is really to do with the value of an account (or accounts in aggregate at any one financial institution).

The compliance challenge should be clear to even those most novice in the industry. If you are a financial institution, especially in the European Union, and you have a global client base, you will need to document your clients with up to three different types of tax documentation. You'll need to gather data about *all* accounts then aggregate them to establish the value of those accounts, together with certain information about the account holder. You'll then need to compile reports, know where to send them, when and in what format. You'll also need to continuously monitor these various regulations and laws for any changes each year.

There are other ways of approaching this. Some institutions will first assess the account holders tax residency to see if it could be reportable, then assess the aggregated value of the account to determine if it is above any applicable threshold for reporting.

The convergence of the frameworks does not necessarily mean simplification, as the European Union is finding out with the FASTER Directive. They are essentially transposing one form of complexity with another, at great cost to financial institutions.

The challenge in each phase cannot be understated. Each financial institution will need to assess its pre-existing account holders as well as new clients. In each case, the type of tax identification required, in addition to domestic tax identification numbers (TINs), will vary depending on the markets in which the account holder decides to invest and the jurisdictions in which they hold residency. Much has been written about digitisation and in reality the current regulatory framework could not exist without the facility of digital and electronically signed documents. When reduced to data, many of the tasks involved in tax regulations can be automated. This applies to all except the EU DAC regulation. DAC6 in particular is an update of the DAC 5 designed to catch those who seek to evade the AEoI/CRS framework. It establishes "Hallmarks" which are really descriptions at the highest level of patterns of behaviour and characteristics of products that are at risk of being used for tax evasion. As such it is very difficult to assess these Hallmarks on the basis of data, especially if the arrangements concerned are with and between different financial institutions in different jurisdictions (as any reasonable tax evader would use).

As an example, consider a financial institution with a hundred clients. Each invests in US securities and a range of European securities, including Nokia. These individuals have tax residencies in the UK, France and Germany. For the US securities the financial institution will collect a Form W-8. For the Finnish securities, an investor self-declaration and claim of treaty benefits as laid down in the OECD TRACE Implementation Protocol provided to an Authorised Intermediary (AI). For the other European securities, the financial institution will require the individual to obtain an eTRC from each jurisdiction in which they have residency status and the institution itself will need to be a Certified Financial Intermediary (CFI) to be able to grant treaty benefits based on that eTRC. When it comes to anti-tax evasion, the financial institution will need to obtain an investor self-declaration as laid down by the OECD AEoI/CRS framework. Here the Form W-8 can serve two purposes, so further action is not required in respect of the US market (Exhibit 3.2).

As the reader will see, there are several forms to collect and to validate. This would be challenging in a paper environment with just one customer—who would be rightfully annoyed at the amount of paperwork involved.

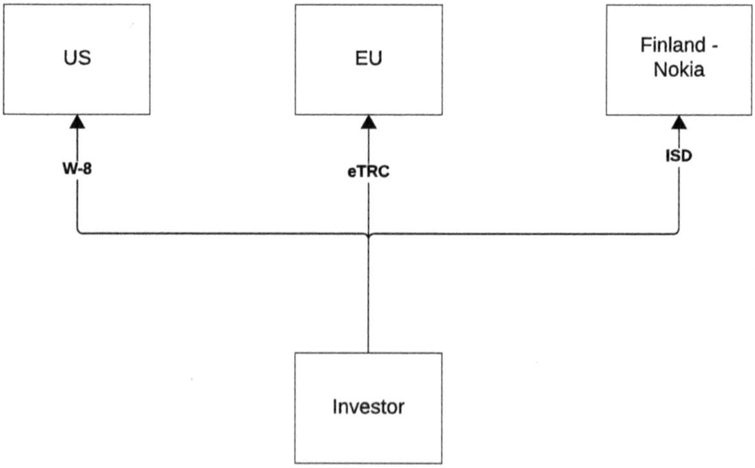


**Exhibit 3.2** Variability in documentation *Source* Authors

In an environment with hundreds, perhaps thousands of customers, digitisation and standardisation become significant factors. There is today, only one firm that has created a single digital self-certification platform[1] that meets the requirements for the US FATCA, the US QI, the OECD TRACE IP and the OECD CRS. The platform, operated by regulatory compliance specialists at TConsult, creates a single, electronically signed, digital Investor Self-Declaration (ISD) that together with an API that allows a data flow to a financial institution that provides the basis for compliance with the documentation obligations of several regulatory frameworks within a KYC environment.[2]

## Reporting Formats

There is some technological convergence in the sphere of reporting. Both FATCA and CRS reporting utilise XML format, and there are sufficient similarities in the schema to allow some jurisdictions to require combined FATCA and CRS reporting. The OCED's TRACE IP also uses XML for reporting.

Currently, the US requires reporting of cross-border income in ASCII format (Forms 1042-S) and on paper (Form 1042), but the IRS is moving towards XML format for Form 1042 reporting in 2026. There is currently no timeline for moving from ASCII to XML format for Form 1042-S reporting.

Convergence in this area will have minimal impact in practice, benefiting only the IT departments within financial institutions that create the final report files.

[1] Tax Compliance Toolkit: https://taxccompliancetoolkit.com.

[2] For example, with Denmark-based KYC provider, Muinmos: https://tconsult-ltd.com/muinmos-and-tconsult-ink-deal-over-digital-investor-tax-self-declarations/.

# 4

# Legal Basis

Some of the frameworks described in this book require a domestic legal basis so that tax administrations have the tools to enforce compliance on their financial institutions. This chapter will explain these legal bases and how they interact with each other. Problems arising from these legal frameworks will also be discussed.

Most, if not all, of the frameworks described in this book have a cross-border extraterritorial component. This presents a legal issue because financial institutions are generally only subject directly to domestic legislation and regulation. Legislation provides the legal basis for compliance. Regulation provides the "how". Tier 1 financial institutions—the largest and most systemically important—are generally multinational enterprises (MNEs) with operations in multiple jurisdictions. While tax frameworks have common components, there are local variations, so these firms need each of their operating locations to keep track of the law and regulation that applies to that operating unit.

## Double Tax Treaties

The foundation of much of the QI world is the concept of a double tax treaty or agreement between pairs of jurisdictions. Most, but not all double tax agreements (DTAs) are based on language created by the OECD's Model Convention on Income and Capital. There have been several versions of


R. K. McGill and K. V. Pitkin, *Qualified Intermediary*,
https://doi.org/10.1007/978-3-031-81410-5_4

this model over the years. The latest was published in 2017.[1] The technical legal basis of these conventions is the agreement between the two governments involved as to the tax treatment of an investor in one jurisdiction compared to the tax treatment of a domestic investor of the other jurisdiction. The DTA conventions establish that each party to the agreement must appoint a Competent Authority (usually their domestic tax administration) to oversee and enforce the DTA and make judgements where there is dispute. This occurs most commonly when the investor is an entity. In most cases, the interpretation of the treaty with regard to individuals is relatively easy. However, many states have some quite strict rules about the treatment of entities since these can, and have been, used for tax evasion and treaty abuse. If there isn't clarity, then it is the job of the Competent Authorities to sort it out.

In some cases, each Competent Authority sticks to its position, at which point the only recourse is to the courts and the issue becomes one of legal jurisdiction. For example, in the European Union if the Competent Authorities can't give a clear judgement, large institutional investors such as pension or sovereign wealth funds will take the matter to the European Court of Justice (ECJ). The most famous of these was the Fokus Bank case in 2004.[2]

As the reader can imagine, these types of claims are rare, very costly and complex. The value of the decision is usually to be measured in billions of euros. It is notable that if an institutional investor or group makes such a claim, usually that they are being treated differently by the other State than their domestic equivalents, the case is almost always won by the plaintiff. This has led to a number of States making rules that clarify these treatments in an effort to avoid litigation.

The challenge for these institutional investors is proving "comparability" or "substantial equivalence". Effectively, the treaties do not go into the micro-detail of the types of investor that may be involved in making tax reclaims. This is effectively left to the equivalent of custom and practice as established by each State.

While this may not be viewed as a compliance issue for the financial institutions involved and more one for the investors themselves, much of the evidence does come from the intermediary in terms of justifying the scale

---

1 OECD, (2017). Model Tax Convention on Income and on Capital: Condensed Version 2017. https://www.oecd.org/ctp/treaties/model-tax-convention-on-income-and-on-capital-condensed-version-20745419.htm.

2 *"Fokus Bank" claims in Spain for non EU resident pension schemes, investment funds and sovereign funds ("third country" claims).* BDO. https://www.bdo.global/en-gb/microsites/tax-newsletters/corporate-tax-news/issue-56-october-2020/spain-fokus-bank"-claims-in-spain-for-non-eu-resident-pension-schemes,-investment-funds-and-sover.

of a claim or claims. In addition, in many cases, it's the intermediary that is filing the claim on behalf of the investor under a power of attorney.

Now, there is an operational issue that is associated with these kinds of claims that should not be overlooked and that is the statute of limitations in the target jurisdiction. There is only a certain amount of time available to claim. If a claim is rejected, as was the case in the Fokus Bank case and others, the market quickly sees the problem and reacts. It is just as possible for a tax administration to abuse *its* obligations by running out the clock on claims. So, the market generally keeps a close eye on these types of claims just in case any of its clients may fall into the same category. In those circumstances, they file what are called protective claims. In other words, until the matter is adjudicated, the tax administration may still be running the statute clock, but the investor, or their agent, may not have clarity about whether the investor is entitled or what evidence may be needed to substantiate the claim. Typically, when these matters are adjudicated, the tax administration can appeal. If not, they will take time to re-write the rules so that there is clarity. This can easily take years. The purpose of a protective claim is to provide notice to a tax administration that an investor has a claim, even though the entitlement is yet to be decided in court.

## FATCA Legal Basis

FATCA is the first truly extraterritorial piece of US legislation that impacted financial institutions of every other market on the planet, irrespective of whether they had any Americans as clients.

The problem started with the US position that Americans were evading US taxes by hiding their assets, and income derived from them, in bank accounts in other countries. This was, and is true, but only to a limited extent and many pundits have argued that FATCA is disproportionate to its purpose. All US citizens, wherever they reside, must disclose assets held outside the US in a Foreign Bank Account Report (FBAR). What the IRS figured out was that all an American had to do to evade US taxes, was to fail to file an FBAR or falsify its contents. Without any other corroborative evidence, the IRS had no way to prove tax evasion. Prior to 2010, the IRS was well known to go on what were called fishing expeditions and this occurred with UBS in 2007 when a whistleblower, Bradley Birkenfield, revealed that UBS had been hiding US clients in numbered Swiss bank accounts. Now, at that time, the IRS knew that there was a problem, but did not have the tools to force

UBS to disclose all its US account holders, only those that Birkenfeld had disclosed (incidentally breaking Swiss bank secrecy laws).

That case led to Switzerland changing its bank secrecy laws and the US fining UBS $780 million as part of a deferred prosecution. By 2010, the IRS had the solution and, after a number of failed attempts, Title V of the Hiring Incentive to Restore Employment Act (2010), now generally known as FATCA, was enacted by Congress.

FATCA has two components, as we will explore in the next chapter. The first was to enshrine a legal obligation on US citizens to file FBARs. The second was to place an obligation on all non-US financial institutions to conduct due diligence on all accounts, identify US accounts and report them back to the IRS. This sounds great, in principle, and would allow the IRS to close the loop on evidence of non-compliance with FBAR obligations by US citizens. There were just two small problems. The first is that there was no legal basis for a non-US financial institution to obey a US statute, unless it was a branch or subsidiary of a US institution. These "foreign" financial institutions just raised their collective hands and said, "you have no jurisdiction over us!".

The second was data protection and, in the EU in particular, the General Data Protection Regulation (GDPR). GDPR comes into play by virtue of the fact that the US taxes based on citizenship, while everywhere else (apart from Eritrea) taxes on the basis of residency. So, if a US citizen resides in an EU Member State, their personal data cannot be sent outside the EU *without the explicit permission of the data subject* under the terms of GDPR.

The IRS solution to this was to create the concept of an Intergovernmental Agreement (IGA). These IGAs forced the partner governments to enact domestic legislation to transpose the requirements of the HIRE Act into local law. The idea was that by using an IGA, the IRS could bypass both arguments. The financial institutions would be compelled by domestic law to transfer data about their account holders to their domestic regulator, not to a foreign government, so GDPR would not be a factor. The IRS went on a binge to establish these IGAs starting in 2014. Most governments did not want to upset the US because of the size of their capital market and its value to their resident investors. They also saw an opportunity to get some reciprocity from the US in the hope that the IRS would apply the same logic in reverse, although to a large extent, this has never happened.

The IGA is an elegant concept that established an international legislative framework. There are several types of IGA, each reflecting the degree to which the pairs of countries already have some sort of information-sharing agreement in place. In broad terms the first two types are Model 1 and

Model 2. In a Model 1 IGA, the most common type of IGA, reporting by financial institutions, is to their domestic tax administration. It is then the tax administration's job to collate all the information from all their financial institutions and send that to the IRS via their International Data Exchange System (IDES). In Model 2 jurisdictions, of which there are only twelve out of the total of 113 (Armenia, Austria, Bermuda, Chile, Iraq, Macao, Moldova, Nicaragua, Paraguay, San Marino, Switzerland and Taiwan), the financial institutions report their US accounts directly to the IRS at IDES. Jurisdictions without an IGA e.g., Russia, must also report directly at IDES. In non-IGA jurisdictions, there continues to be no legislative framework for compliance, other than the pressure provided by financial institutions that want to access the US capital market on behalf of their clients, at almost any cost. In these jurisdictions, the legal framework is replaced with a contractual framework, the FFI Agreement or Revenue Procedure 2017–16 which is similar to the QI Agreement discussed in more detail in this book (Exhibit 4.1).

Equally elegant was the operational concept of keeping track of all these financial institutions using a single tax-identifying number issued by the IRS, the Global Intermediary Identification Number (GIIN).

## US QI Legal Basis

The US QI Agreement has a legal basis in the contractual obligations entered into bilaterally between the IRS and a specific non-US financial institution, which becomes known as a Qualified Intermediary. This Agreement, currently Revenue Procedure 2022–43, is entered into under US law and places each financial institution signatory under a range of obligations as will be discussed in Part II.

Exhibit 4.2 shows the legal basis for the imposition of US tax regulations on non-US financial institutions. The IRS is a subdivision or arm of the US Treasury. It establishes regulations such as IRC Chapters 3 and 4. A nonqualified intermediary will be subject to the US IRC Chapters simply by receiving US-sourced FDAP income on behalf of its clients. A Qualified Intermediary on the other hand will be subject to US tax regulations by receiving US-sourced FDAP income on behalf of its clients AND under the terms of the commercial contract between it and the IRS.

Compliance is a major part of the legal basis for the QI regime. The IRS has been known to issue penalty notices and final demands for up to $900,000 for failure to comply with reporting obligations.

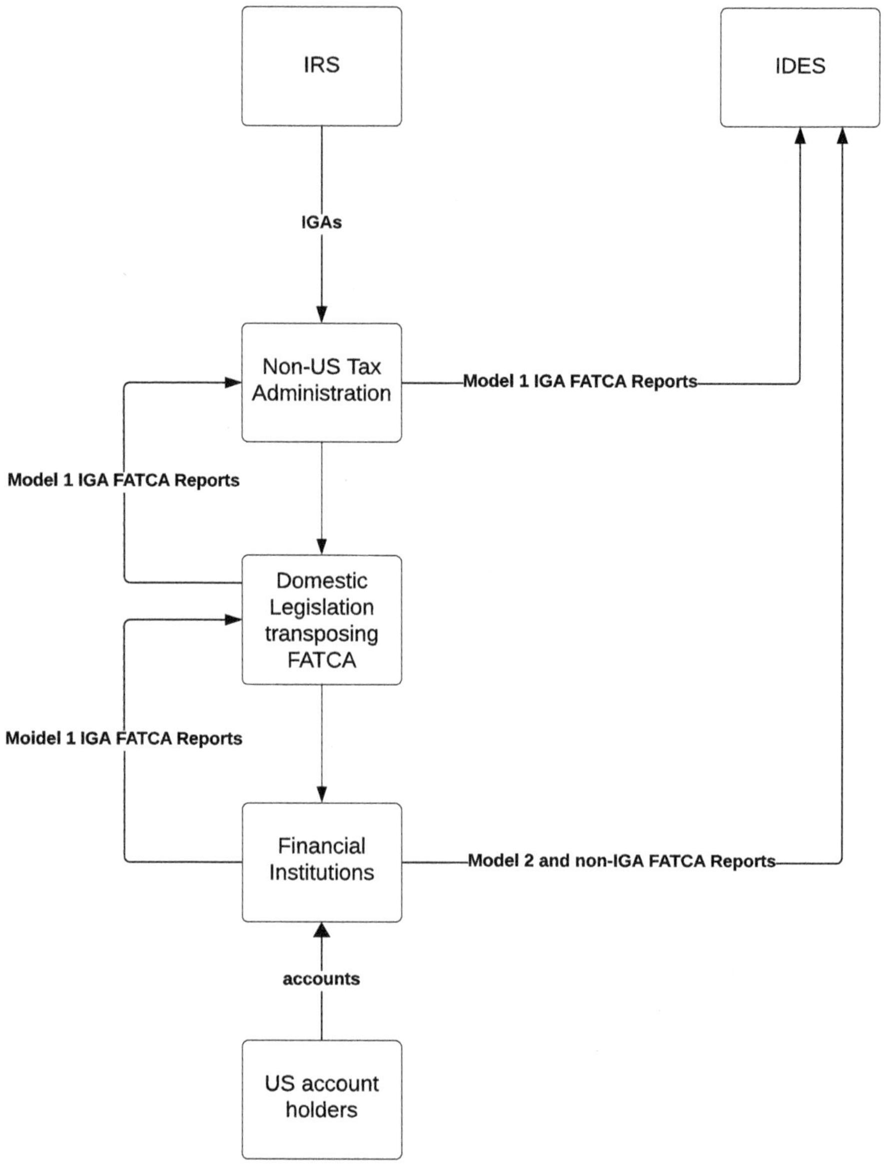


**Exhibit 4.1** Legal basis of FATCA *Source* Authors

What's interesting about the QI regime is that its less to do with QIs and more to do with those financial institutions that are *not* Qis—either by choice or because they are in non-KYC approved jurisdictions and therefore are not eligible to become QIs. There are fifty-two jurisdictions that do not have IRS-approved KYC rules.

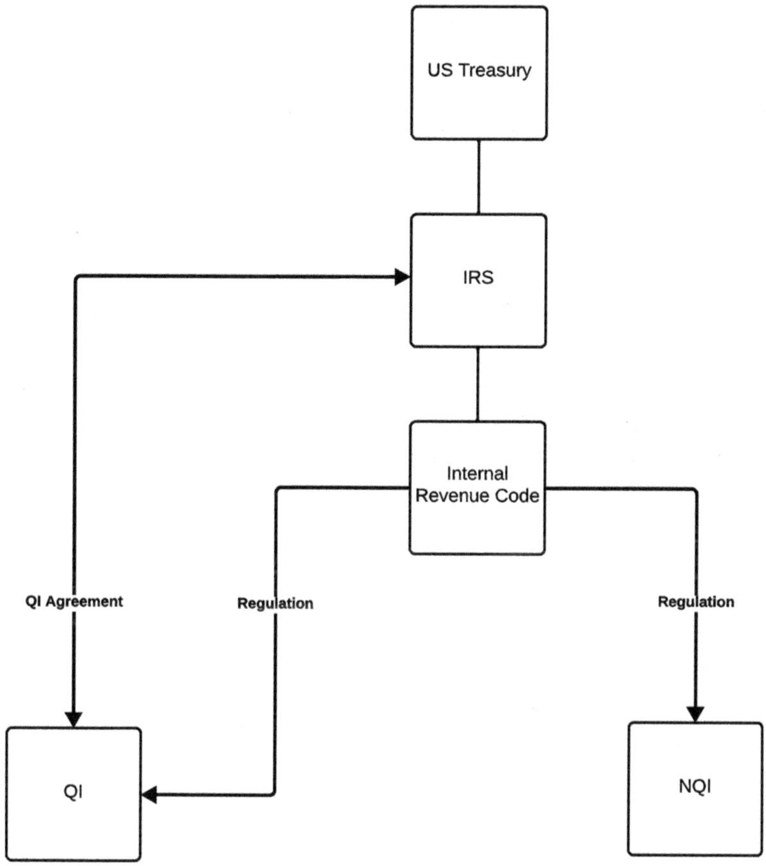


**Exhibit 4.2** Legal Basis of US withholding tax *Sourc* Authors

Almost all non-US financial institutions that receive US-sourced FDAP income on behalf of their clients must file information returns to the IRS on Forms 1042-S. Firms that have signed a QI Agreement with the IRS, around 3,600 worldwide, are permitted to pool their clients for the purpose of withholding taxes and reporting. So, for QIs there is usually no personally identifiable information (PII) being sent to the IRS.

Financial institutions that are not qualified intermediaries are, by default, *non*qualified intermediaries (NQIs). The rule is simple: any client of an NQI receiving US-sourced FDAP income must be disclosed to the IRS on an information return Form 1042-S. This includes name, address, domestic tax ID number, gross US income and US tax withheld.

There are two types of NQI—disclosing and non-disclosing. If an NQI chooses to be non-disclosing, it will be the NQI's obligation to submit the Form 1042-Ss to the IRS electronically (and provide its clients with recipient copies B, C and D). If the NQI chooses to disclose its clients to a QI, then the reporting obligation flows to the QI for those indirect clients that are disclosed. In the latter case, the QI's legal obligation to report the indirect clients of a disclosing NQI cannot be pooled and flows from its contract with the IRS signed under US jurisdiction. Either way, the recipient of the income must be reported to the IRS.

A non-disclosing NQI has no contract with the IRS. Further, it may also have domestic legislation that prevents it from sending client data across national borders. Unlike FATCA where the reporting obligation in most jurisdictions was moved to a domestic tax administration through the use of Intergovernmental Agreements (IGAs), the Form 1042-S information returns are all sent directly to the IRS. So, the question in simple, although the answer may not be: what is the legal basis under which a non-US financial institution can send client data directly to the IRS without breaching domestic data privacy laws?

In the EU, that would be the domestic legislative instruments effected as a result of the FATCA IGAs. The problem is that the same financial institutions are subject to the General Data Protection Regulation or GDPR. It's the GDPR framework that is, ironically, being used to challenge FATCA data transfers of so-called accidental Americans.

The IRS and US Treasury have direct methods to affect the amount of tax that clients of an NQI must suffer. That's typically 30% on dividends. There are many firms, notably in Asia, that see no legal basis to file Form 1042-S returns on the assumption that they've already paid the maximum allowable tax. It is notable that the IRS penalty regime for late Form 1042-S submissions is based on the number of forms filed. But if the firm never files, it is difficult to see how the IRS could impose that penalty. One of the core principles of regulation is the threat of penalties for non-compliance, but the IRS, as far as we know, has not penalised any NQI for non-filing, although this might fall into the category of "intentional disregard". If they have, the other principle is that penalties should be seen to be imposed to deter others from following the same behaviour.

So, it seems that all the mechanics are in place with the exception of a legal basis upon which to impose those mechanics unless the financial institution voluntarily enters into a QI Agreement with the IRS.

## CRS Legal Basis

The Common Reporting Standard (CRS) is a component of the OECD's Automatic Exchange of Information framework (AEoI). It has similarities to the FATCA framework, except that AEoI is a voluntary framework adopted by willing participants rather than a forced extraterritorial framework in which the participants have little or no choice.

As the reader will see from Exhibit 4.3, AEoI has two components. The first are Competent Authority Agreements (CAAs), somewhat analogous to the US IGAs. However, the number possible permutations of jurisdictions desiring to have tax information exchanged leads to a more complex legal structure. There are two types of CAA: bilateral and multilateral. The bilateral CAAs have some similarities to DTAs as they deal only with two parties. The multilateral CAAs (MCAA) can be adopted by one jurisdiction with respect to any other jurisdiction that wants to partner. There are two sub-types of MCAA: one in which there is an existing DTA in effect and one where there is a Tax Information Exchange Agreement (TIEA) already in effect. The TIEAs are the equivalent of what the US was using before FATCA, because they rely on the requesting Competent Authority to ask for information with respect to specific account holders—which pre-supposes that a Competent Authority has sufficient grounds to make the request.

Irrespective of which Competent Authority model a jurisdiction selects, they must transpose this into both primary and secondary legislation to give effect to the due diligence and reporting rules that are set forth in the Common Reporting Standard. It's the CRS that is the compliance obligation of financial institutions, while AEoI is the compliance obligation of the government that is signing up to the framework.

For financial institutions, it is important to understand that, in a perfect world, these rules would be set and be relatively stable over time. This has not proved to be the case. A number of jurisdictions have, on almost an annual basis, changed the deadlines and/or rules applying to the transfer of information. This has led to a compliance burden of monitoring that is heavy for many financial institutions.

The basis of CRS (and by inference AEoI) is the requirement to conduct due diligence on all account holders to determine their residency for tax purposes. Under CRS, this can be accomplished with a self-certification of residency. In the early days, this was achieved in a narrow way. Financial firms would determine the tax residency of their account holders but only maintain such data if any of their declared tax residencies was a partner jurisdiction under AEoI. This is what connects the due diligence to the reporting. So,

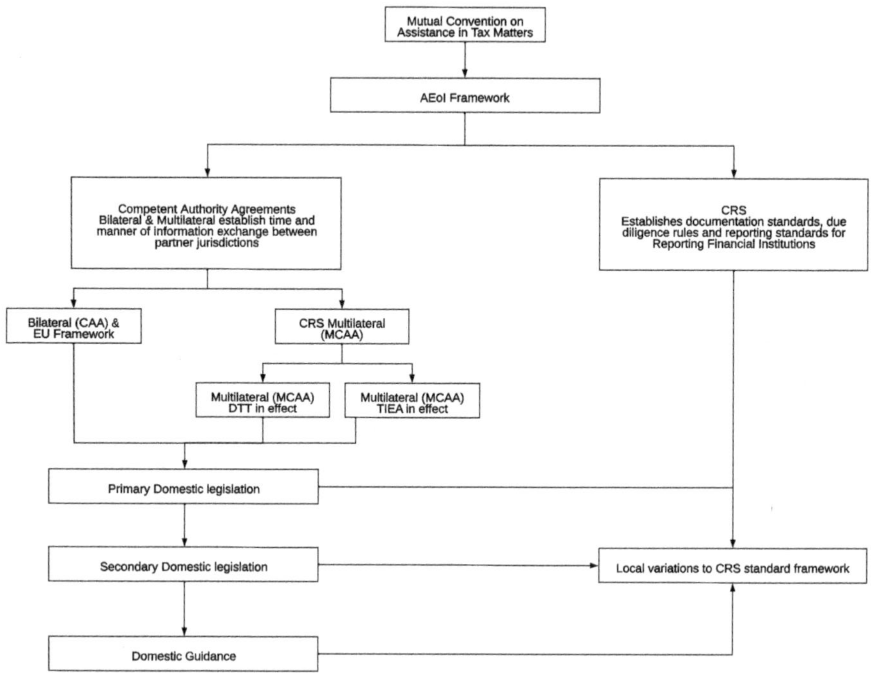


**Exhibit 4.3** Legal basis of AEoI and CRS *Source* Authors

if you have three partner countries, you only need to maintain CRS status for that portion of your client base that are resident in one of those three countries. In more recent times, the OECD has expanded AEoI to allow for a "wider approach". A jurisdiction that adopts the wider approach on a mandatory level will have primary and secondary legislation in place to force their financial institutions to obtain CRS from *all* clients without reference to whether the jurisdiction is a participating CRS partner or not. This has some merits because, as jurisdictions continue to be added to the AEoI family, the wider approach means that financial institutions should already have all the information they need. However, as with all things tax, there are always exceptions. In this case, there are jurisdictions where it is illegal for a financial institution to ask for evidence of tax residency (e.g., Australia). In these instances, the financial institutions must first obtain a waiver of local law to allow their customer to provide their certification.

As we will see later, the OECD's AEoI and CRS framework is also different from the European Union approach. The EU has chosen to go with certifications of tax residency, issued by a Competent Authority, as opposed to the US, which uses the Form W-8 self-certification and the OECD, which uses investor self-declarations (ISDs). This disparity creates an additional compliance burden for financial institutions because they'll need to understand the complexity first, how it applies in their particular circumstances, before they can effectively have a compliance plan.

## FASTER Legal Basis

FASTER is probably the easiest to explain because the legal basis will be an EU Directive. As such, to have effect it must have been unanimously agreed by all 27 Member States and transposed into local law by a set date, in this case, January 1, 2029. By that date, all Member States must have also designed, built and tested an electronic Tax Residency Certification (eTRC) system, as well as a reporting system capable of receiving files from hundreds of financial institutions acting as Certified Financial Intermediaries (CFIs) (Exhibit 4.4).

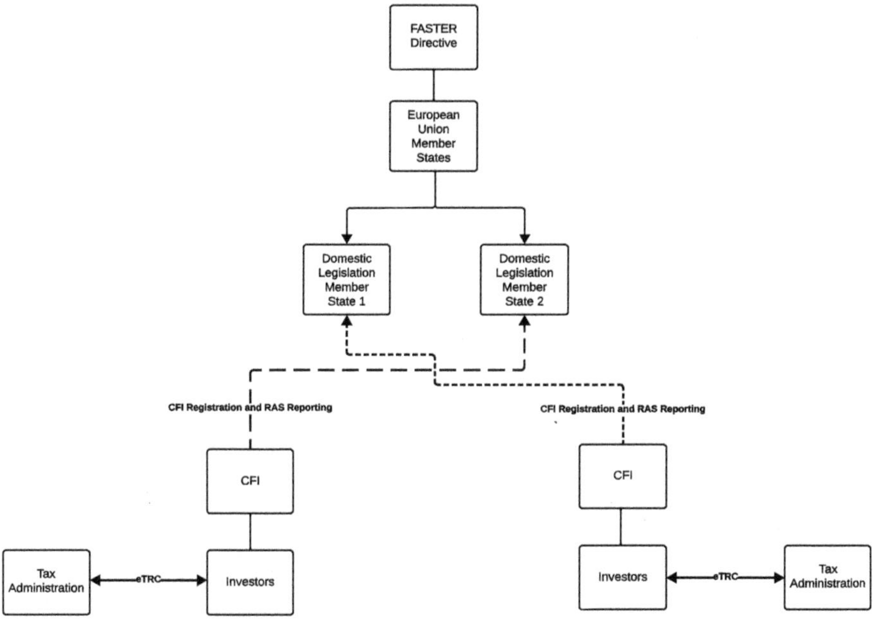


**Exhibit 4.4** FASTER Directive Legal Basis *Source* Authors

## DAC Legal Basis

Again, the Directive on Administrative Co-operation (DAC) has been in force for some years and has been revised and expanded upon several times. While many financial institutions may not be as aware of DAC as they are of FATCA, QI or CRS, it is nonetheless applicable for EU financial institutions or and those outside the EU that have EU residents as customers (Exhibit 4.5).

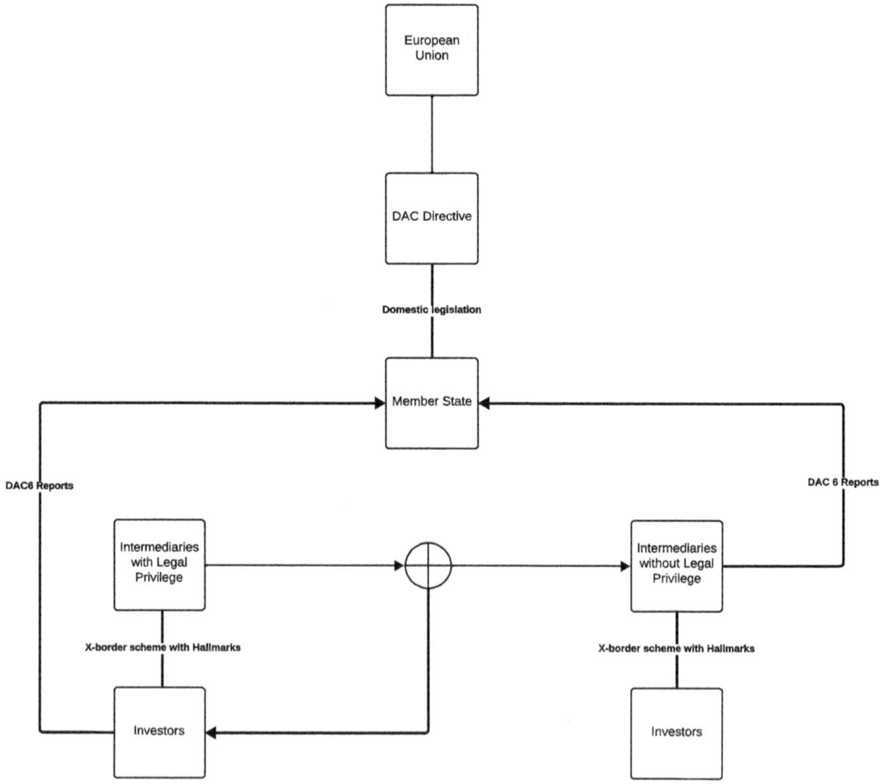


**Exhibit 4.5** DAC6 Legal basis *Source* Authors

# Part II

## United States of America

# 5

# Regulatory Structure

This chapter explains the structure of the US withholding tax space when applied in a cross-border environment, including notably those that choose not to adopt QI status. We will define the actors in the payment chain and their roles, together with an explanation of the options available to financial institutions including, notably, nonqualified intermediary status. Particular attention will be given to summarising the differences between the 2017 QI agreement and the 2023 QI Agreement.

The US securities market represents just under 50% of global capital.[1] It is therefore very difficult to offer investment services to investors without some exposure to the US and a vast number of financial institutions around the world service clients who receive US-sourced FDAP income from their investment portfolio. This is income that is *fixed, determinable, annual,* or *periodic*, including income from dividends and portfolio interest from government or corporate US bonds.

The rules on the taxation of US sourced income paid to a non-US person located outside of the US are set out in Internal Revenue Code (IRC) Chapter 3. However, financial institutions may be affected by Chapters 1, 3, 4, 31 and 61 of the US tax code based on the type of clients they have, or the type of products that they offer. For example, a financial institution with US clients that invest in US securities are affected by Chapter 31 and 61 rules that require backup withholding, currently 24%, on income received by these clients in certain circumstances, while a financial institution that allow their

[1] Visual Capitalist.


R. K. McGill and K. V. Pitkin, *Qualified Intermediary*,
https://doi.org/10.1007/978-3-031-81410-5_5

clients to trade in derivatives with underlying US securities may be affected by Chapter 1, Sect. 871(m).

US-sourced FDAP income can only be issued by a US financial institution, known as a US withholding agent. However, there may be a chain of other financial intermediaries, both within and outside the US, that sit between the US withholding agent and the ultimate beneficial owner. Financial institutions become subject to the US Internal Revenue Code rules as soon as they receive US-sourced FDAP income on behalf of their clients, wherever they are in the world. By default, any income that they handle will be subject to the statutory rate of tax on US-sourced FDAP income (30% for dividends), unless the recipient is entitled to a lower rate or exemption under the terms of a double tax treaty between their country and the US or an exemption.

The US is a combination tax jurisdiction, which means there are several ways that a recipient can claim a reduced rate. They can:

1. Get taxed at the statutory rate of 30%, then make a claim for a tax refund to the IRS in the following 2 years
2. Submit a request for a quick refund
3. Submit documentation to their financial institution prior to a pay date that shows they are entitled to the reduced rate and get tax relief at source.

The IRS prefers the relief at source method, as it allows it to outsource the process of ensuring the client has been taxed at the correct rate, thus relieving the IRS of the work involved in processing a standard refund.

The US was the first jurisdiction to establish a framework to allow the non-US financial institutions in this chain to become withholding agents for the distribution of US-sourced FDAP income. The legal basis for this concept is a simple contract entered into between a financial institution and the US government, in the form of its subsidiary agency the Internal Revenue Service (IRS) known as the QI Agreement (see Exhibit 4.24.2). Financial institutions that choose to enter into this agreement are known as qualified intermediaries, while those who do not are known as nonqualified intermediaries. Nonqualified intermediaries are considered to be potential facilitators of tax evasion[2] as the absence of a contract leaves the IRS with no practical way of enforcing compliance to US tax regulations outside of the US.

The QI Agreement is a 205-page contract established under US contract law. It is published as a Revenue Procedure by the IRS. The first such Revenue

[2] https://obamawhitehouse.archives.gov/realitycheck/the-press-office/leveling-playing-field-curbing-tax-havens-and-removing-tax-incentives-shifting-jobs.

Procedure was Revenue Procedure 2000–12.[3] The QI Agreements are 6-year contracts. Since Revenue Procedure 2000–12, there have been three new versions of the contract—Revenue Procedure 2014–39,[4] Revenue Procedure 2017–15[5] and the latest Revenue Procedure 2022–43.[6] The alert reader will have noticed that there are more than 6 years between each new contract. This is because each QI Agreement contains clauses that allow the agreement to be renewed in its then current form. A new Revenue Procedure only occurs when there is an aggregated substantial difference between it and its predecessor. The latest QI Agreement encompasses new Sections 1446(a) and 1446(f) as well as more detail on dealing with the requirements Chapter 1 Section 871(m), which is currently due to come into effect in January 2027 (see Table 5.1). Between Revenue Procedures, the IRS can unilaterally vary the terms of the QI Agreement by issuing "Notices" or "Announcements", which tell its contractual partners about new rules are and how they should be applied.

The QI Agreement contract provides incentives for financial intermediaries to become qualified intermediaries, including the ability to grant treaty benefits and reduced reporting obligations and flexible operating model choices, which we will discuss in later chapters. Nonqualified intermediaries are not permitted to grant tax relief at source unless they disclose their clients to a qualified intermediary above them in the payment chain.

The QI Agreement is often described as being "signed", but there is no wet signature involved. The IRS will not negotiate any term of the agreement and establishes the agreement's applicability to a specific financial institution by issuing a unique identifying number, known as a QI-EIN.

Structurally, the obligations of a qualified intermediary can be split into two cycles—an operational and a governance cycle, as shown in Exhibit 5.1.

The operational cycle encompasses the tasks of documenting clients, withholding tax at the correct rate, depositing that tax with the US Treasury, and then reporting all that activity to the IRS. Each of these elements builds upon the last. Effective compliance with the terms of the QI Agreement therefore starts with documentation, and everything else flows from there.

The governance cycle relies the appointment of a Responsible Officer, who develops and maintains a compliance program, then arranges a periodic review every 3 years, followed by a certification to the IRS to confirm that effective controls are in place.

---

[3] https://omb.report/icr/201805-1545-001/doc/82748701.

[4] https://www.irs.gov/pub/irs-drop/rp-14-39.pdf.

[5] https://www.irs.gov/pub/irs-drop/rp-17-15.pdf.

[6] https://www.irs.gov/pub/irs-drop/rp-22-43.pdf.

**Table 5.1** Internal Revenue Code Chapters covered in the QI Agreement *Source* Authors

| Chapter | Explanation |
|---|---|
| Chapter 1 | Section 871(m) deals with a financial institution's obligation to determine whether a transaction is a Dividend Equivalent Payment (DEP) or an Equity Linked Instrument (ELI) that represents a US withholdable transaction due to its underlying exposure to US securities |
| Chapter 3 | Section 1441 deals with the due diligence, tax withholding, tax depositing and reporting of US-sourced FDAP income (and dividend equivalent payments) paid to non-US recipients and the application of exemption from withholding on portfolio interest paid to non-US recipients<br>Section 1446(a) deals with taxation and reporting of distributions from publicly traded partnerships (PTPs) with income that is effectively connected to a trade in the US<br>Section 1446(f) deals with gains made on transfers of interests with respect to PTPs with income that is effectively connected to a trade in the US |
| Chapter 4 | Section 1471 deals with anti-tax evasion by US Persons including penalty withholding on US-sourced FDAP income (including DEPs) with respect to recalcitrant account holders and non-participating FFIs. This is an overlap (and addition) to a firm's general exposure to FATCA via domestic law (in the case of an IGA[2] jurisdiction) or an FFI[3] Agreement in the case of a non-IGA jurisdiction<br>Chapter 4 is a negative proof system. All FFIs must document the Chapter 4 status of all customers, irrespective of whether they receive US-sourced income or not, to determine Chapter 4 status and reportability of account holders |
| Chapter 31 | Section 3406 deals with backup withholding and reporting of US (or presumed US) recipients of US-sourced FDAP income |
| Chapter 61 | Sections 6041, 6042, 6045, 6049 and 6050N deal with the identification and reporting of US non-exempt recipients on Forms 1099 |

The details of each of the components of these structural cycles will be discussed in the following chapters.

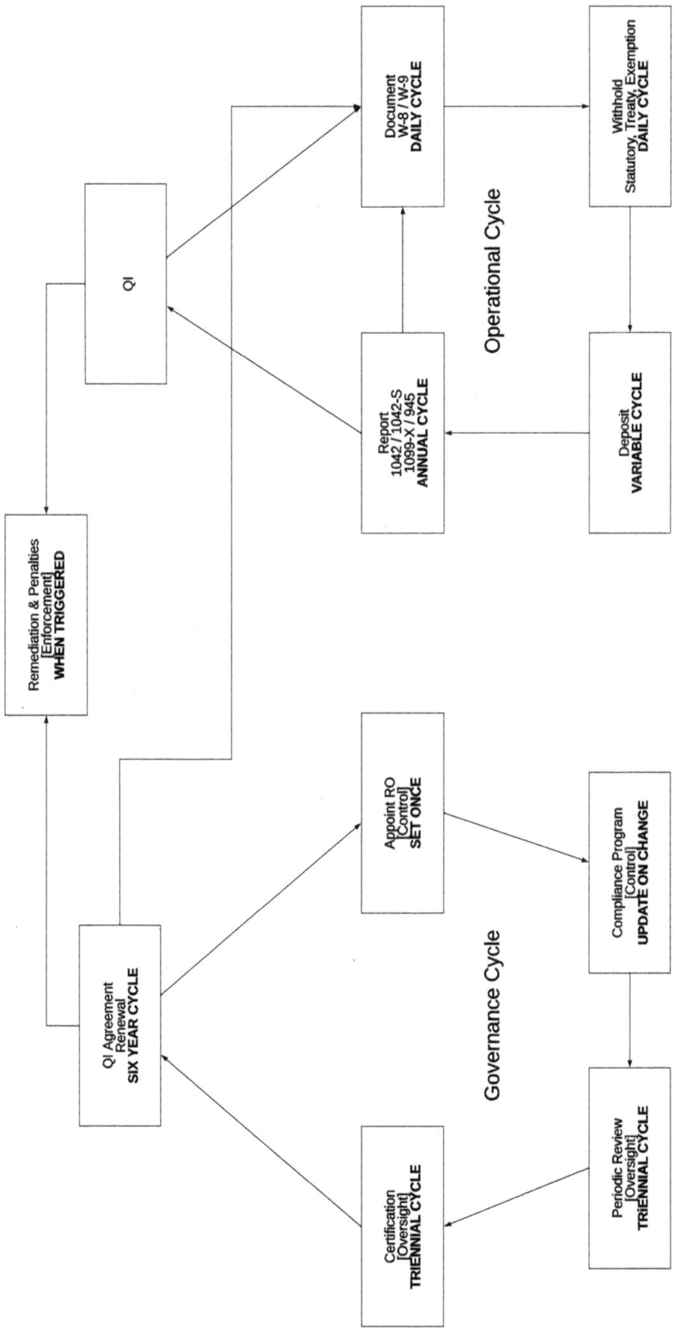


**Exhibit 5.1** QI cyclical compliance approach *Source* Authors

# 6

# Background

In this chapter, we will provide a historical context to the US qualified intermediary program, including a summary of its key components that will be expanded upon in subsequent chapters.

There have been four QI Agreements together with a number of interim revenue procedures and notices containing updates and explanations. From a compliance perspective, the responsible officer should be maintaining a library of these documents and recording which ones remain active at any point in time. It's also important for responsible officers to assess the impact of each revenue procedure and notice on their firm's operating model and practices so that they can keep their compliance program up to date. As you can see from the sheer number of IRS announcements, this is no easy task.

| **Revenue Procedure 2000–12** | **The original and first QI Agreement** |
|---|---|
| Revenue Procedure 2002–55 | Guidance for external auditors |
| Revenue Procedure 2003–09 | TIN matching requirements |
| Revenue Procedure 2003–64 | Partnerships and trusts withholding and reporting |
| Revenue Procedure 2004–21 | WFP and WFT Agreement amendments |
| Revenue Procedure 2005–77 | Withholding on partnerships, trusts and estates |
| Revenue Procedure 2011–42 | Sampling methodologies for auditors |
| Revenue Procedure 2012–24 | NRA deposit and interest regulation |
| Revenue Procedure 2014–10 | First FFI Agreement |
| Revenue Procedure 2014–13 | Updated FFI Agreement |
| Revenue Procedure 2014–38 | Second FFI Agreement |
| **Revenue Procedure 2014–39** | **Second QI Agreement** |
| Revenue Procedure 2014–43 | SSN and TIN requirements |
| Revenue Procedure 2014–47 | Updates to WFP and WFT regulations |
| Revenue Procedure 2014–64 | NRA deposit interest regulations |

(continued)


R. K. McGill and K. V. Pitkin, *Qualified Intermediary*,
https://doi.org/10.1007/978-3-031-81410-5_6

(continued)

| | |
|---|---|
| Revenue Procedure 2015–40 | Competent Authorities |
| Revenue Procedure 2015–40 | Discretionary treaty for LOB |
| Revenue Procedure 2015–43 | Rulings and Determinations letters |
| Revenue Procedure 2015–50 | Updated list of countries for approved AEoI |
| Revenue Procedure 2016–21 | Examination of returns and claims for refunds |
| Revenue Procedure 2016–56 | Bank deposit interest reporting |
| **Revenue Procedure 2017–15** | **Third QI Agreement** |
| Revenue Procedure 2017–16 | Updated FFI Agreement |
| Revenue Procedure 2017–21 | New WFP and WFT Agreements |
| Revenue Procedure 2017–46 | Updates to Rev. Proc. 2014–64 |
| Revenue Procedure 2018–36 | NRA deposit interest regulations |
| Revenue Procedure 2020–20 | Substantial Presence test |
| Revenue procedure 2021–32 | NRA deposit interest reporting |
| **Revenue Procedure 2022–43** | **Fourth and current QI Agreement** |

In more recent times, the IRS has added a Frequently Asked Questions (FAQ) page to its website and a free subscription service by means of which QIs can be kept up to date. While this is useful for specific issues, it is more difficult to understand the broader context of some of these issues. The IRS also has a penchant for giving all the history associated with an issue before summarising its guidance. This can be confusing for many as they try to exclude the wheat from the chaff to get at the core message.

The IRS in 2024 finally released a list of registered QIs.[1] This follows the same logic as GIIN lists[2] that are updated monthly at the IRS website. The latest QI Agreement contains explicit consent for QI's to have their names disclosed. This means that financial institutions receiving a W-8IMY can now check, as part of their form validation procedures, that both the GIIN and the QI-EIN on these certificates are correct for the entity making the certification.

[1] https://www.irs.gov/businesses/corporations/qualified-intermediary-qi-list.

[2] https://apps.irs.gov/app/fatcaFfiList/flu.jsf.

# 7

# FATCA

This chapter explains FATCA as it applies to account holders that receive US sourced income. Diagrams will be used to explain the overlap between FATCA obligations that apply to ALL account holders and obligations that apply to the sub-set of account holders that also receive US-sourced FDAP income.

FATCA is an acronym for the Foreign Account Tax Compliance Act, which refers to a set of measures designed to deter and detect tax evasion by US persons by (i) forcing US taxpayers to disclose their overseas financial accounts to the Internal Revenue Service and (ii) forcing overseas financial institutions to report the accounts of their US clients to the IRS. The IRS then compares the data from the US person and the overseas financial institution to identify taxpayers that have failed to declare overseas income. The rules are described in Chapter 4 of the US Internal Revenue Code, Sections 1471–1474.

Exhibit 7.1 shows the concepts of FATCA. The US operates under what is called the principle of non-duplicative taxation. Under this principle, a financial institution must assess tax penalties in Chapter 4 (FATCA) *before* it assesses taxation in Chapter 3—which is why the chapters on FATCA and QI are ordered the way they are in this book. FATCA comes first, then QI.

FATCA requires an American to file an FBAR—a Foreign Bank Account Report which discloses, as the name implies, any non-US bank accounts that they operate. In addition, an American would also have to report a non-US account in which that person had a financial interest. This ensures that Americans are required to report both types of non-US account—those they have a financial interest in and those that they do not. The question for the US


R. K. McGill and K. V. Pitkin, *Qualified Intermediary*,
https://doi.org/10.1007/978-3-031-81410-5_7

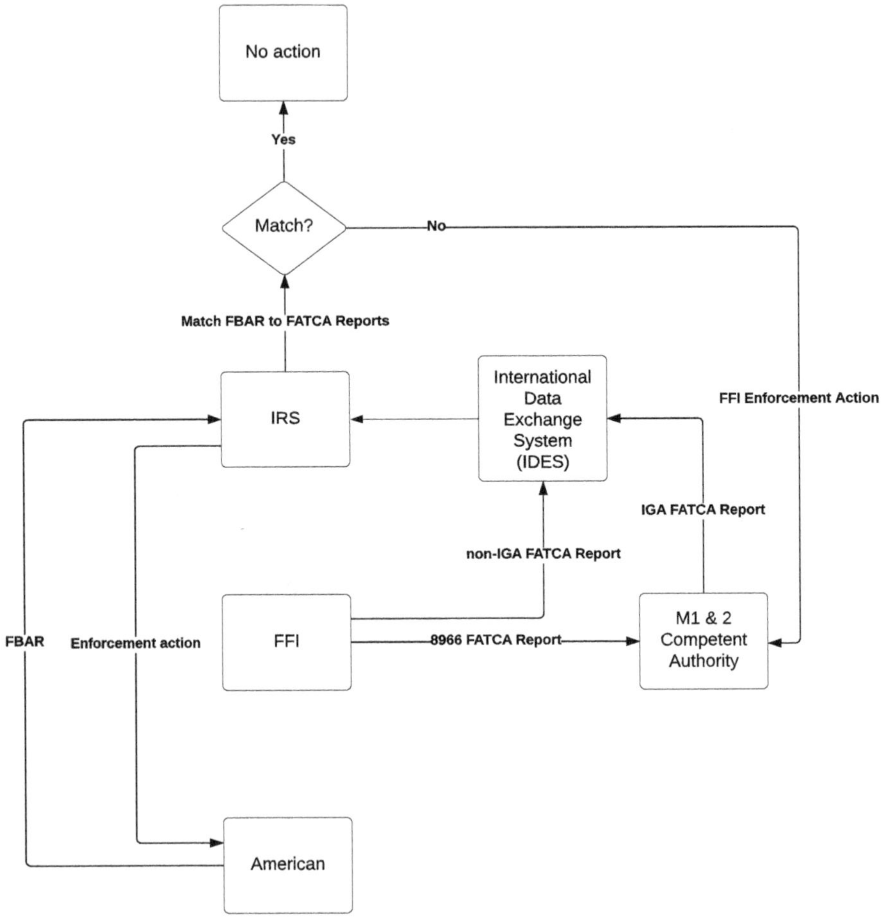


**Exhibit 7.1** FATCA conceptualised *Source* Authors

is—how do they know these Americans are actually disclosing their accounts? The solution, on the right of the diagram, is to force the banks where these accounts are, to report the accounts to the IRS either directly in the case of jurisdictions without an Intergovernmental Agreement, or indirectly in the case of jurisdictions with Model 1 or 2 IGAs. The key in the diagram is the part where the IRS tries to match the bank accounts reported by the financial institutions to the FBARs submitted by the Americans. There are three possibilities:

1. The reports match—no tax evasion

2. The reports exist but do not match—potential tax evasion
3. The reports of one or other party do not exist—likely tax evasion

In the event that there is potential or likely tax evasion, the IRS will take enforcement action to get to the correct answer.

While the QI Agreement is primarily about the taxation of US-sourced FDAP income paid to non-US persons, FATCA is deeply embedded throughout. Qualified intermediaries are required to be FATCA compliant to gain and maintain their QI status. The reason for this is simple: in order to withhold on US-sourced income paid to a non-US person, one must first establish whether the investor *is* a non-US person and not actually a US person who may be evading taxation in the US.

As we will discuss further in Chapter 25, the US is unusual in that it taxes based on both residence *and* citizenship, so there is a much wider range of investors who are subject to US tax. These include:

- US citizens (both US residents and expats living abroad)
- Lawful permanent residents (i.e., Green Card holders)
- Individuals that are considered to be resident because they have been substantially present in the US in the last 3 years
- Corporations that are incorporated in the US, and
- US estates and trusts.

Individuals and entities that meet these criteria are subject to federal taxation in the US on their *worldwide* income. However, the US has probably the largest number of people prepared to avoid or evade taxes if they can. Marginal tax rates for rich Americans can reach as high as 37%, so there is an incentive to put money where it either won't get taxed at all or will be taxed at a relatively low rate under the terms of a double tax treaty.

Tax evasion through offshore accounts has been an issue for a long time, but several legal cases increased the political pressure on the US government to do something about it. In 2009, UBS reached a $780 million settlement[1] with the US government following accusations that it had trained it staff to help US customers avoid detection by US authorities, and engaged in cross-border securities transactions that it knew violated US security laws.[2] UBS

[1] US Department of Justice (2009). https://www.justice.gov/archive/opa/documents/bank-agreement-consent.pdf.

[2] Office of Public Affairs. (2014). Credit Suisse Pleads Guilty to Conspiracy to Aid and Assist U.S. Taxpayers in Filing False Returns https://www.justice.gov/opa/pr/credit-suisse-pleads-guilty-conspiracy-aid-and-assist-us-taxpayers-filing-false-returns.

agreed to provide the identities and account information of its US clients as part of the settlement. In 2014, Credit Suisse pleaded guilty to conspiracy to aid and assist US taxpayers in filing false income tax returns and other documents with the IRS and agreed to pay a fine of US$2.6 billion. As part of the plea agreement Credit Suisse acknowledged that it operated an illegal cross-border banking business for decades and knowingly allowed thousands of US clients to open and maintain undeclared accounts to conceal their offshore assets and income. In 2016, Julius Baer also faced criminal charges requiring payment of $547 million for helping its US clients evade their tax obligations, file false federal tax returns and hide accounts from the IRS between the 1990s until 2009.[3]

FATCA's introduction in 2014 represented a significant effort to tackle the problem by forcing automatic and mandatory reporting by overseas financial institutions about client accounts held by US persons. This was not without controversy. Overseas financial institutions have criticised FATCA as an extraterritorial overreach of US jurisdiction and an unfair burden on their operations. They argue that FATCA compliance is expensive and that it can make it difficult for them to do business with US taxpayers. US taxpayers living abroad have also criticised FATCA, arguing it can make it difficult for them to open or maintain bank accounts and obtain financial investment services. Nevertheless, FATCA has become a model for international efforts to curb tax evasion and improve financial transparency.

As referenced in Chapter 4, FATCA was brought into law as Title V of the HIRE Act (2010). There is actually no such thing as a "Foreign Account Tax Compliance Act" on the US statute books.

There are two components: the first sets an obligation on US citizens with overseas bank accounts to report these accounts each year on an FBAR and on Form 8938,[4] and the second component requires overseas financial institutions to report those accounts to the IRS. Most of the FATCA regulations are set out in Internal Revenue Code Chapter 4, but FATCA also impacts to parts of Chapters 31 and 61, which deal with the identification and reporting of US persons that receive US-sourced FDAP income.

FATCA relies on financial institutions *outside* the US identifying and reporting US Persons. Obviously, financial institutions outside the US are not subject to US laws.

---

[3] Office of Public Affairs. (2016). Criminal Charges Filed Against Bank Julius Baer of Switzerland with Deferred Prosecution Agreement Requiring Payment of $547 Million, as Well as Guilty Pleas of Two Julius Baer Bankers. https://www.justice.gov/opa/pr/criminal-charges-filed-against-bank-julius-baer-switzerland-deferred-prosecution-agreement.

[4] https://www.irs.gov/pub/irs-pdf/f8938.pdf.

FATCA has two mechanisms for solving this problem:

(i) entering into Intergovernmental Agreements (IGAs) with other countries[5] requiring them to put in place domestic laws that compel their financial institutions to identify and report US account holders; and
(ii) offering financial institutions in non-IGA jurisdictions the option to sign a direct contract with the IRS known as the Foreign Financial Institution Agreement (FFIA), which—like the QI Agreement—includes strict terms to reassure the IRS that the financial institution is compliant with FATCA.

The Intergovernmental Agreement route is the preferred option for the IRS, as the existence of an IGA means that a domestic regulator in the financial institution's country will do all the work of policing FATCA compliance for them. IGAs can also help to resolve conflicts between the requirements of FATCA and domestic data protection laws, which might otherwise prevent a financial institution from sharing information about their clients with a foreign government.

Financial institutions in non-IGA jurisdictions that choose *not* to sign an FFI Agreement with the IRS are known as Nonparticipating FFIs (NP-FFI) and are viewed as potential facilitators of tax evasion as there is neither a domestic legal mechanism or a contract in place to provide a legal basis to enforce FATCA.

## Documentation

Under FATCA, financial institutions are required to establish each client's status under Internal Revenue Code Chapter 4. It is a negative proof system, that—in the absence of evidence to the contrary—presumes all individual investors to be Americans intent on evading tax, and all entities to be non-participating foreign financial institutions hiding yet more Americans evading tax.

For individuals, financial institutions can rely on their existing KYC processes to categorise their clients as either, US, foreign (i.e. not a US citizen or resident) or recalcitrant (i.e. there is insufficient information to determine if they are US or not). While KYC *can* provide sufficient information to categorise individual clients for FATCA, there are risks associated with making

[5] A full list of countries with Intergovernmental Agreements with the US can be found on the IRS website: https://home.treasury.gov/policy-issues/tax-policy/foreign-account-tax-compliance-act.

these determinations. As a result, many financial institutions make use of investor self-certifications, which shift the liability associated with the classification from the firm to the investor themselves. Most financial institutions use the Form W-8 and W-9 forms templates for which are issued by the IRS to collect these certifications. We will discuss the challenges associated with these forms in a later chapter. Some institutions choose to develop their own self-certifications, often creating a combined FATCA and CRS form.

Entities are more complex. These can potentially be broadly categorised as US, non-financial foreign entities (NFFEs), foreign financial institutions (FFI) or recalcitrant. However, there are over thirty different Chapter 4 statuses for entities, none of which can be derived purely from KYC. This makes collecting a Form W-8 or W-9 a necessity. Most entities will provide a W-8BENE, but they may provide a Form W-8IMY to show they are acting as an intermediary, or a Form W-8EXP if they are tax exempt (Exhibit 7.2).

It is relatively easy to collect documentation of sufficient quality to determine Chapter 4 status at onboarding. However, this can be harder for pre-existing accounts. FATCA requires financial institutions to carry out due diligence on existing account holders and to submit a Certification of Pre-existing Accounts (COPA) as a one-off exercise. For most institutions, this was completed in 2017, but it is still required for new Participating FFIs and financial institutions in countries that have recently signed an IGA with the US.

The amount of due diligence required depends on whether an account is held by a low or high value account holder. Low value account holders are account holders that have an aggregate account balance of less than US$1 m, while high value account holders have an aggregate account balance of more than US$1 m.

For pre-existing low value account holders, financial institutions must carry out a search of all the electronic records that they hold for the account holder to identify any US indicia. These are specific indicators that the account holder might be a US. person or entity, such as a US place of birth, a current US residence or a US mailing address. The financial institution should also look for evidence of individuals that might have been substantially present in the US over the previous 3 years (see Exhibit 7.4). For pre-existing high value accounts, financial institutions must perform enhanced due diligence checks in addition to the electronic records search, including a relationship manager review to confirm they do not have any knowledge that suggests that the account holder may be US, and reviewing any paper records for evidence of US indicia, as shown in Exhibit 7.3.

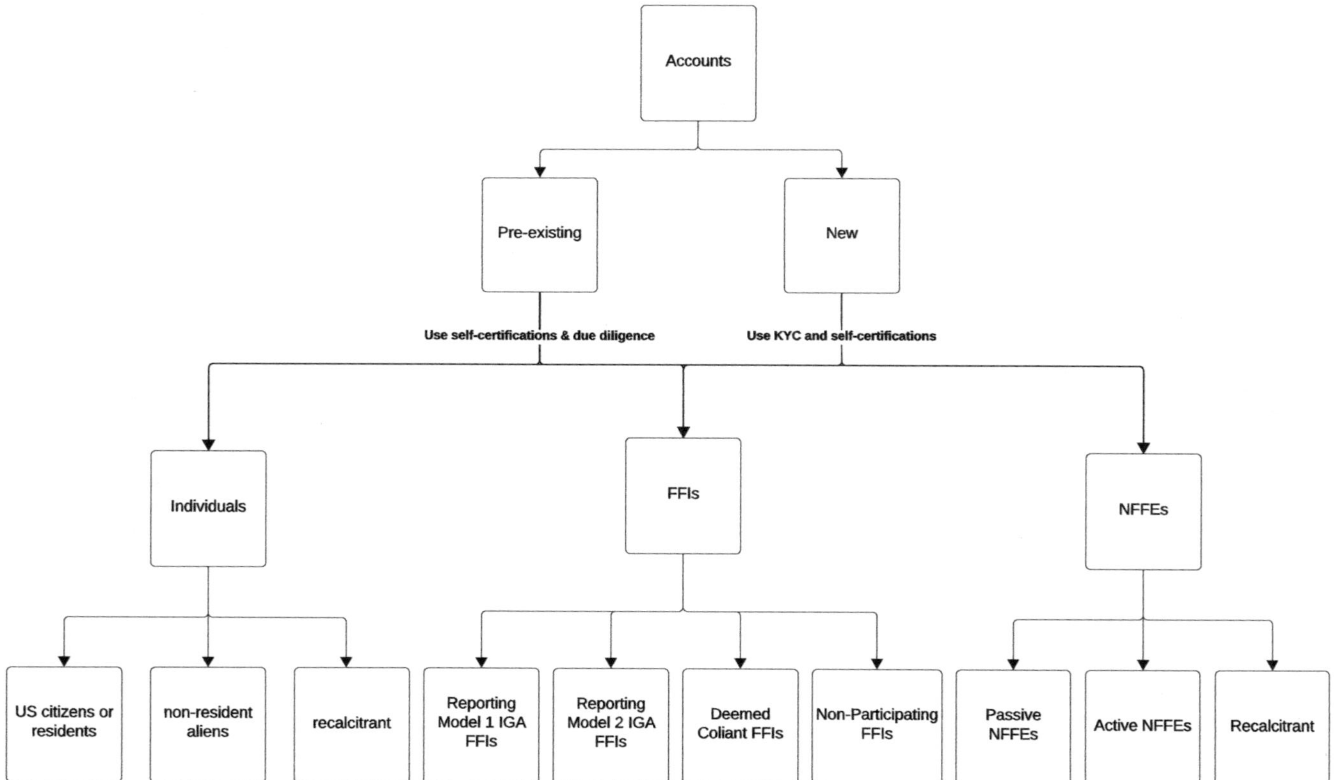


**Exhibit 7.2** Account types and documentation methodologies *Source* Authors

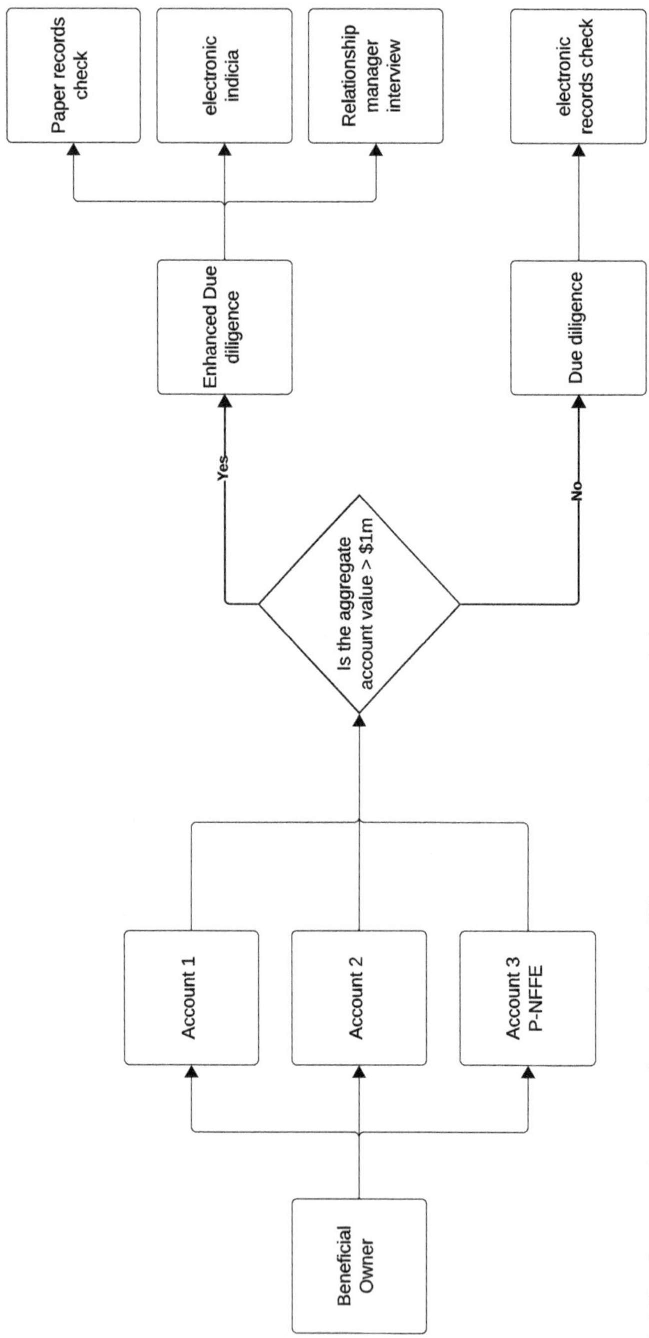


**Exhibit 7.3** Account Aggregation and due diligence rules for pre-existing accounts *Source* Authors

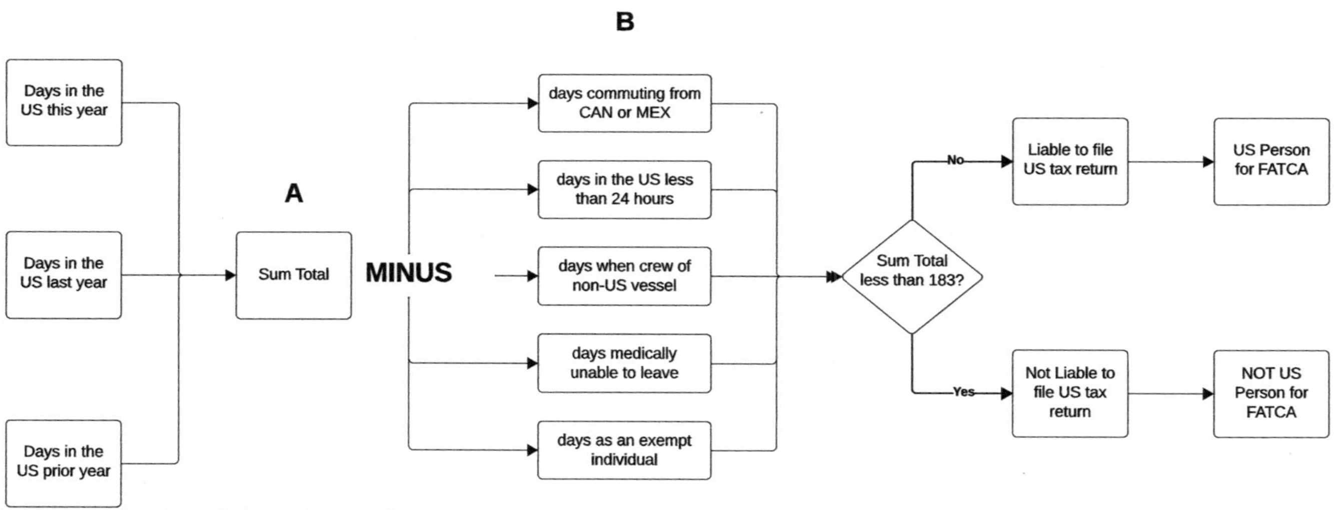


**Exhibit 7.4** Application of the Substantial Prescence Test *Source* Authors

Any US indicia identified during these checks must be cured by collecting additional documentary evidence. Tables 7.1 and 7.2 illustrates how to cure US indicia in individuals and entities, respectively.

If an account holder is not willing or able to provide the additional documentation requested, the account must be treated as a recalcitrant or non-consenting account. A recalcitrant account is any account holder that fails to comply with reasonable requests for information to determine if the account holder is US or not, including known US account holders who fail to provide a valid Form W-9 or US TIN, entities that fail to disclose each substantial US owner, and account holders in non-IGA jurisdictions that fail to provide a waiver of any domestic law that would prevent them from being reported under FATCA. The account holder ceases to be recalcitrant as soon as they provide the necessary documentation.

Recalcitrant account holders are presumed to be US persons that are attempting to evade tax by failing to provide sufficient documentation and are therefore reportable under FATCA. A financial institution failing to provide information must be presumed to be a non-participating FFI (NP-FFI). The IRS expects financial institutions to make reasonable efforts to obtain a FATCA status for any recalcitrant account holders, and to close accounts if this is not forthcoming.

Of course, due diligence is an ongoing process, and client circumstances can change. If the financial institution becomes aware of a change in circumstance that might affect Chapter 4 status of the client, it must make reasonable efforts to obtain new documentation from the client, including a new Form W-8 or W-9, within 90 days. The IRS deems reasonable efforts to include requesting the information more than once during the 90 days and requesting the information via multiple communication channels. If the account holder does not provide the new documentation within 90 days, they become a recalcitrant account holder.

The overlap between FATCA and the terms of the QI Agreement mean that the documentation procedures necessary for compliance with each share many of the same features and challenges, which will be discussed in more detail in Chapter 8.

## Withholding

Under FATCA, any person in whatever capacity having control, receipt, custody, disposal, or payment of any withholdable payment (a withholding agent) making a withholdable payment to a Foreign Financial Institution

**Table 7.1** How to cure US indicia (individuals). *Sourc* Authors

| US Indicia | Cure |
|---|---|
| US place of birth | • Any ID or passport issued by an authorised authority outside of the US **and**<br>• A Certificate of Loss of Nationality in the US<br>Or<br>• Form W-8BEN<br>• A certificate of residency outside of the US **and**<br>• A reasonable written explanation of the renunciation of the US citizenship or why the account holder did not obtained US Citizenship at birth |
| A current US residence address<br>A current US mailing address<br>A current US telephone number | Form W-8BEN *plus*<br>• A certificate of residency<br>• An ID or passport **or**<br>• Any document listed in your jurisdiction's KYC attachment at the IRS website |
| Standing instructions to pay amounts to an account in the US | Form W-8BEN *plus*<br>• A certificate of residency<br>• An ID or passport,<br>• Any document listed in your jurisdiction's KYC attachment at the IRS website, **or**<br>• A written reasonable explanation establishing the account holder's status |
| A current power of attorney or account signatory with an address in the U.S<br>An "in care of" or hold mail address that is the only address you hold for the account holder | Form W-8BEN<br>Or<br>• A certificate of residency<br>• An ID or passport<br>• Any document listed in your jurisdiction's KYC attachment at the IRS website **or**<br>• A written reasonable explanation establishing the account holder's status |

**Table 7.2** How to cure US indicia (entities) *Source* Authors

| US Indicia | Cure |
|---|---|
| US residence address<br>US mailing address<br>Standing instructions to pay amounts to a US account<br>US telephone number only | Form W-8, *plus*:<br>• An organisation document, such as articles of incorporation<br>• A third-party credit report **or**<br>• A government confirmation of tax status |
| US telephone number (in addition to a non-US telephone number)<br>US power of attorney or signatory<br>"In care of" or "hold mai" as the sole address for the entity | • Form W-8<br>• An organisation document, such as articles of incorporation<br>• A third-party credit report **or**<br>• A government confirmation of tax status |

(FFI) must withhold 30% tax of the payment unless the withholding agent is able to treat the FFI as a reporting FFI, participating FFI, deemed-compliant FFI, or exempt beneficial owner. The difference between a participating FFI and a reporting FFI is that a participating FFI is in a non-IGA jurisdiction having signed an FFI Agreement. A reporting FFI will be in a jurisdiction with an IGA and be subject to its domestic law regarding FATCA.

A withholding agent must also withhold 30% on a withholdable payment made to a payee that is a foreign entity other than an FFI (that is, a non-financial foreign entity, or NFFE) that fails to identify its substantial US owners (or certify that it does not have any substantial US owners) unless the payment is excepted from withholding under the regulations to Section 1472.

Finally, a withholding agent must also withhold 30% on a withholdable payment made to a payee that is deemed to be recalcitrant. However, if the financial institution is based in a Model 1 or Model 2 IGA jurisdiction, then withholding on recalcitrant account holders is suspended provided certain conditions are met. Specifically, there is a suspension of withholding, provided the recalcitrant account holder is included in the financial institution's FATCA report. If the account is not reported as recalcitrant in FATCA, then the IRS can issue a group request to the competent authority (usually the financial institution's domestic tax authority) which will trigger a requirement for FATCA withholding, starting six months after the date of the request (Exhibit 7.5).

FATCA withholding ensures that potential tax evaders are taxed at the maximum rate in Chapter 4 and cannot benefit from any reduced rate via a claim of treaty benefits in Chapter 3 under the terms of a double tax treaty. This leverages the existing withholding systems of qualified intermediaries, which we will discuss in more detail in a later chapter.

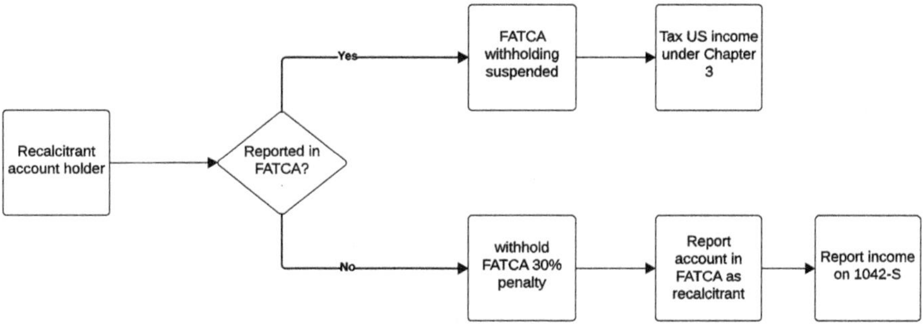


**Exhibit 7.5** Application of the suspension of FATCA withholding on recalcitrant accounts *Source* Authors

## Reporting

Under FATCA, financial institutions are required to report any US Persons, substantial US owners of passive non-financial foreign entities and recalcitrant account holders[6] in their client base each year. Participating FFIs and financial institutions, based in a Model 2 IGA jurisdiction, must file directly to the IRS using the IRS's International Data Exchange Service system, known as IDES[7]. Financial institutions, based in a Model 1 IGA jurisdiction, must file their FATCA reports with their domestic tax authority, who will then combine the data from all financial institutions in that jurisdiction and submit this to the IRS as a single report again, at IDES.

FATCA reports are filed electronically in XML format. The IRS provides an XML schema for use by those filing directly via the IDES system[8], while Model 1 IGA jurisdictions issue their own schemas to accommodate any additional requirements they may have when receiving data domestically. For example, many tax authorities in Model 1 IGA jurisdictions require combined FATCA and CRS reporting, given the similarities between the two frameworks. Some jurisdictions also require an empty or NIL report when the financial institution has no accounts to report.

While this variance complicates the FATCA reporting landscape, it ensures that financial institutions in Model 1 IGA jurisdictions receive guidance in their native language and allows reporting deadlines to be set locally, which can provide operational advantages for financial institutions with various other domestic compliance obligations. As a result, only a small number of

[6] These are known as non-consenting account holders in Model 2 IGA jurisdictions.

[7] IDES: https://www.irs.gov/businesses/corporations/international-data-exchange-service.

[8] FATCA Schema: https://www.irs.gov/businesses/corporations/fatca-xml-schemas-and-business-rules-for-form-8966.

third-party vendors provide global FATCA reporting support, and most focus on specific markets rather than attempting to monitor changes in guidance across all IGA jurisdictions.

A FATCA report will include each reportable account holder's name, address, US TIN, account number, account balance as of 31st December of the previous year (either in US$ or in the currency in which the account is denominated) and payments made to depository, custody or other accounts. If an account is closed during the calendar year, then financial institutions are also required to report the payments and income paid until the date of closure, along with the amount withdrawn when the account was closed.

Financial institutions are permitted to pool reporting of recalcitrant account holders, into the following categories:

- **Passive NFFEs**: Passive NFFEs that failed to provide information about their US substantial owner/controlling persons
- **Recalcitrant account holders that are US Persons**: Account holders that failed to provide a Form W-9 or a valid US TIN
- **Recalcitrant account holders with US Indicia**: Account holders with US indicia that have not been cured during the due diligence process
- **Recalcitrant account holders without US Indicia**: Account holders that failed to respond to the requests for information about their US status
- **Dormant accounts classified as recalcitrant account**: Accounts that have made no transactions in the last 3 years and where the account holder has not communicated with the financial institution for 6 years.

In addition to the FATCA report, financial institutions that applied FATCA withholding must report this income via their Form 1042-S information return and Form 1042 tax return. These will be discussed in more detail in Chapter 11.

## Control and Oversight

The control and oversight measures in FATCA vary depending on the type of jurisdiction. For financial institutions in Model 1 IGA jurisdictions, the terms of the intergovernmental agreement place the responsibility for control and oversight with the host country tax authority, which is then free to define its own measures. In most cases, many of the controls will sit within existing AML and KYC regulations, which underpin the documentation requirements in FATCA. For financial institutions in non-IGA and Model 2 IGA jurisdictions there is a requirement to sign the FFI Agreement, which imposes contractual control and oversight terms similar to those in the QI Agreement, including the appointment of a Responsible Officer, the creation of a written compliance program, conduct of a periodic review and a periodic certification of compliance every 3 years.

All financial institutions must name a Responsible Officer at the FATCA Portal when they register for a Global Intermediary Identification Number (GIIN). This individual is responsible for the creation of the compliance program, and (if required) arranging the conduct of a FATCA periodic review and making the triennial periodic certification to the IRS.

Participating FFIs and Model 2 IGA FFIs must complete a FATCA periodic review and make their periodic certification by 1st July of the year following each certification period. The certification periods are calculated based on the effective date when the institution signed the FFI Agreement. For example, a financial institution that entered an FFI Agreement on 1 January 2021 will have a first certification period that runs until 31 December 2024 and a subsequent certification period of 1 January 2025–31 December 2027. It will have to make a periodic certification on 1 July 2025 and 1 July 2028, respectively.

When a Responsible Officer makes their periodic certification, they will be asked to certify that i) a FATCA compliance program was in place of the date of the certification, ii) that all necessary internal controls are in place, iii) whether there have been any material failures that have not been remediated by the date of the certification, and iv) whether there were any events of default raised by the IRS during the certification period.[9]

A material failure is a failure to comply with your FATCA obligations. This can be due to a deliberate action by one or more employees to circumvent FATCA (e.g., by preventing the accurate reporting of US persons) or failure to implement sufficient internal controls to meet the FATCA requirements. A material failure under FATCA also includes any civil penalty or sanction imposed by a regulator with oversight over the financial institution's compliance with AML due diligence procedures, if that failure is involves failing to identify an account holder under FATCA. If a material failure can be remediated during the certification period, then the Responsible Officer must explain the specific actions taken to remediate the failure, and the measures put in place to prevent the failure from recurring.

[9] The full list of questions your Responsible Office must answer when making their periodic certification is available at the IRS website: https://www.irs.gov/businesses/corporations/fatca-certifications.

An event of default is a more serious failure to comply with FATCA. Examples include failing to reduce the number of recalcitrant account holders over a period of time and failing to establish and maintain a FATCA compliance program. If the IRS finds that a financial institution has committed an event of default, then it will issue a notice of default describing the problem. The financial institution must remediate the event of default in the timeframe provided by the IRS.

For financial institutions that are part of a group, there are options to reduce the costs and administrative burden associated with these control and oversight measures. FATCA includes to concept of an expanded affiliate group, which is a group of financial institutions that agree to establish a consolidated compliance program. A consolidated compliance program is a shared compliance program where all members of the group use the same policies, procedures and systems to meet their obligations. In some cases, they will share the workload too, with one member of the group performing a specific task—such as reporting—for all members. An expanded affiliate group also benefits from only performing one consolidated periodic review on behalf of the whole group.

## Enforcement

In Model 1 and Model 2 IGA jurisdictions, the terms of the intergovernmental agreement are designed to enshrine FATCA obligations into domestic legislation. Penalties and enforcement powers are left to the domestic regulator. There are two types of misconduct that they can penalise: administrative errors and substantial non-compliance.

Generally, domestic regulators will work with a financial institution to resolve administrative errors. However, if the regulator finds that the financial institution is in substantial non-compliance, it can impose sanctions—usually under anti money laundering rules.

The IGAs also contain legal redress by the IRS for "minor administrative failures" and "substantial non-compliance". In the latter case, the IRS has the authority, in conjunction with the domestic tax authority, to impose financial penalties of $10,000 and an additional $50,000 for continued failure to file a FATCA report and also to change the status of the financial institution to non-participating FFI (NP-FFI), which would have the almost immediate effect of applying FATCA withholding at 30% on all of the financial institution's clients' US income as well as effectively disconnecting the NP-FFI from the US securities market by virtue of the fact that, as we have mentioned previously, non-participating FFIs are deemed to be facilitators of tax evasion. Each market will be different. In the UK, the penalties are £300 for each failure to set out a payment accurately in a report subject to a limit of £3,000.

Of course, the enforcement of FATCA also includes penalties for the individuals and entities that fail to disclose their foreign assets to the IRS. These include Form 8938 penalties of up to $10,000 for failure to disclose and an additional $10,000 for each 30 days of non-filing after IRS notice of a failure to disclose, with a potential maximum penalty of $60,000. For those required to submit an FBAR report, wilful failure to disclose will result in a penalty of up to the greater of $100,000 or 50% of account balances. In both cases, criminal penalties may also apply[10]. The IRS does not publish details about how much enforcement action it has taken because of information it has acquired via FATCA reporting from foreign financial institutions, but the deterrence, now there is an effective mechanism by which tax evaders can be identified, is hefty.

## Challenges of FATCA

When FATCA was introduced, many financial institutions opted for strict "No Americans" policies in the mistaken belief that this in some way reduced their obligations. This created significant issues for ordinary American expats, who were not high-net-worth individuals and therefore not really the target of the anti-evasion measures, who suddenly found themselves without access to local banking.

FATCA also caused issues for so-called Accidental Americans. These are individuals who are classed as a US citizens under US tax law, including people who are born in a US territory—even if they leave when at a very young age—and some people born outside the US to parents with US citizenship. Most are unaware that the US government considers them to be citizens and that they are therefore subject to FATCA and FBAR reporting unless they obtain a Certificate of Loss of Nationality to formally renounce their US citizenship, which can be a costly process.

A significant activist community has formed to campaign against FATCA, including launching a class action lawsuit against the US government to recover the cost of renouncing US citizenship ($2,350)[11]. In response,

---

[10] https://www.irs.gov/businesses/comparison-of-form-8938-and-fbar-requirements.

[11] Grunfeld, L. (2024). Cost of renouncing US citizenship. CPAs for expats. https://www.cpasforexpats.com/post/cost-of-renouncing-us-citizenship.

the IRS has launched streamlined filing procedures[12] to support overseas Americans, provided any previous failure to file is not deemed wilful.

The reality is that FATCA does not prevent overseas financial institutions from having US persons as clients, nor does implementing such a policy allow the financial institution to escape the requirements of FATCA, as doing so does not negate the obligation to carry out documentation and due diligence to ascertain the US status of *all* account holders, and to file a FATCA report when required. Realising this and implementing effective procedures to manage the compliance risk could give financial institutions new market opportunities, particularly in jurisdictions with high numbers of US expats.

One of the other challenges of FATCA specifically for qualified intermediaries is the siloed nature of operations within financial institutions. It is not uncommon to see FATCA handled by one department and the QI regime handled by another—both jealously guarding their processes and resources—leading to bifurcation and inefficiency. For example, some institutions use their own internal combined FATCA and CRS self-certifications to collect FATCA status and use Forms W-8 and W-9 for QI purposes. Not only does this force investors to complete duplicate paperwork, but it creates additional validation requirements as the two must be compared to ensure the Chapter 4 status matches. However, in our experience, this cross checking does not happen, resulting in discrepancies that go undetected. Recognising the need for FATCA and QI compliance to be tightly integrated is key to success.

Finally, we have seen a trend in many financial institutions—particularly those with digital onboarding systems—to simply add a check box asking the investor "Are you an American?". Tempting as this may seem to system designers, it is insufficient for proper compliance with FATCA as it does not establish Chapter 4 status (for entities) or leverage the penalty of perjury statement of a Form W-8 to protect the financial institution. In compliance, shortcuts like this are never worth the risk.

[12] IRS streamlined filing compliance procedures: https://www.irs.gov/individuals/international-taxpayers/streamlined-filing-compliance-procedures.

# 8

# Documentation

This chapter and following chapters in this part will focus on the practical aspects of the four pillars of the US QI Agreement that became effective on 1 January 2023. This chapter will deal with documentation of account holders for the purpose of determining Chapter 3 status, Chapter 4 status and any withholding or reporting that flows from such documentation. This chapter will deal with risk and liability and the increasing use of electronically signed digital substitute documentation.

The QI Agreement requires QIs to document their clients to ensure that they meet their FATCA (IRC Chapter 4) obligations and withhold the correct amount of tax. Under the principle of non-duplicative taxation, if there is no FATCA penalty to apply, the QI can move on to decide what rate of tax to apply in Chapter 3. As we touched on in the previous chapter, while it is possible to derive Chapter 4 status with KYC for individuals, most QIs will use either the W-8 and W-9 self-certification forms issued by the IRS, or a digital substitute form because the Chapter 4 status of an entity, partnership, trust or financial institution cannot be derived from KYC data alone. In all cases, a claim of treaty benefits requires either a W-8BEN or W-8BENE (in which the claim of treaty benefits is embedded) or a W-8IMY and a withholding statement allocating portions of a payment to different rates of tax based in turn on the documentation of the underlying client.

Documentation is the foundation of the US tax regulations so it is paramount that they get this right. So, let's define "documentation" first, compared to what the IRS terms "documentary evidence".

"Documentary evidence" refers to material collected under domestic Know Your Customer (KYC) rules. For individuals, this is usually one or more of


R. K. McGill and K. V. Pitkin, *Qualified Intermediary*, https://doi.org/10.1007/978-3-031-81410-5_8

a passport, a national identity card, driver's licence or a utility bill. For entities, this will typically be the corporate founding documents, incorporation certificate, memorandum and articles of association or their equivalent. The problem with documentary evidence is that it has no interest in tax matters. A passport says nothing about your permanent residence (you may have two). Neither does an incorporation certificate (you might have subsidiaries in other jurisdictions or even a holding company). Nor do any of these documents, on their own, provide any rights to a lower rate of taxation on US-sourced income.

The term "documentation" on the other hand means the combination of KYC material *and* a Form W-8 or W-9. These latter two forms add the missing tax pieces to the jigsaw. The W-8 forms each serve two purposes. The first is to establish the tax status of the beneficial owner as a non-US individual, entity, partnership, trust or financial intermediary. The second purpose is to allow the beneficial owner to claim the benefit of a double tax treaty with the US. The effect of this claim is to reduce the effective tax rate on dividends for example, from 30% (the statutory rate) to one of the double tax treaty rates e.g., 10%, 15% or 25%. It is worth noting that KYC alone cannot determine this. There are several financial firms who have been penalised by the IRS for granting treaty benefits solely based on KYC and ignoring the Form W-8. This would be underwithholding. Equally, we've also seen firms penalised for not granting treaty benefits when beneficial owners legitimately claimed it. This would be overwithholding. This latter is often adopted by a financial institution simply because it is easier and cheaper (in the short term) than applying tax relief at different rates. Both underwithholding and overwithholding, when conducted on a systemic regular basis, are Events of Default of the QI Agreement.

So, KYC alone does not allow the QI to provide a tax treaty benefit. If the QI does not have a Form W-8, it can only provide treaty benefits if it has a separate letter from the investor claiming those benefits and agreeing to submit to a penalty of perjury. It is much easier to collect a Form W-8 instead.

There are five types of Form W-8 and one type of W-9:

- Form W-8BEN for individuals
- Form W-8BEN-E for entities and certain types of trust or partnership that are opaque for tax purposes
- Form W-8IMY for financial intermediaries and some types of trust and partnership that are transparent for tax purposes (known as flow-through entities)

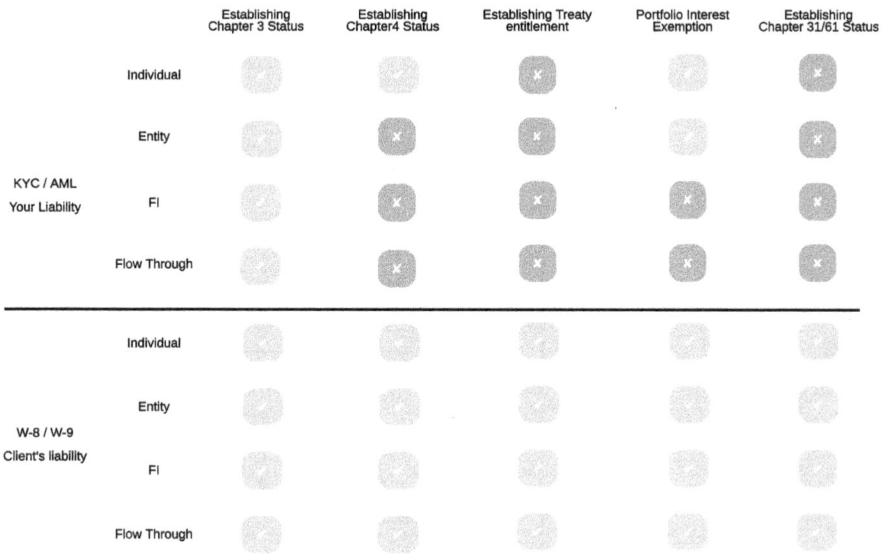


**Exhibit 8.1** Benefits of documentation with W-8 s *Source* Authors

- Form W-8ECI for those with some form of income effectively connected with a US trade or business
- Form W-8EXP for those who are exempt from withholding tax
- Form W-9 is used to document an American, or more precisely, a person that has a tax return obligation to the US.

Exhibit 8.1 shows the obligations that require documentation across the top and the assignment of liability down the left side dependent on the type of account holder. What's important is that a financial institution cannot grant treaty benefits solely using KYC, nor can they establish Chapter 4 status of any entity client. These both require additional documentation in the form of a Form W-8 or W-9. Because of these gaps, most financial institutions use Forms W-8 and W-9 across the board (Exhibit 8.2).

Non-US individuals can claim treaty benefits quite easily. However, for non-US entities it is a bit more difficult because many US tax treaties contain what's known as a limitation on benefits or LOB clause. As the name implies, these are certain conditions under which, even though the entity is resident in a jurisdiction with a tax treaty with the US, the entity does not qualify to claim them. So, to claim those tax treaty benefits, an entity must certify which LOB clause it satisfies to have those benefits granted.

Intermediaries and any type of tax-transparent trust or partnership can only claim treaty benefits if they provide a withholding statement along with

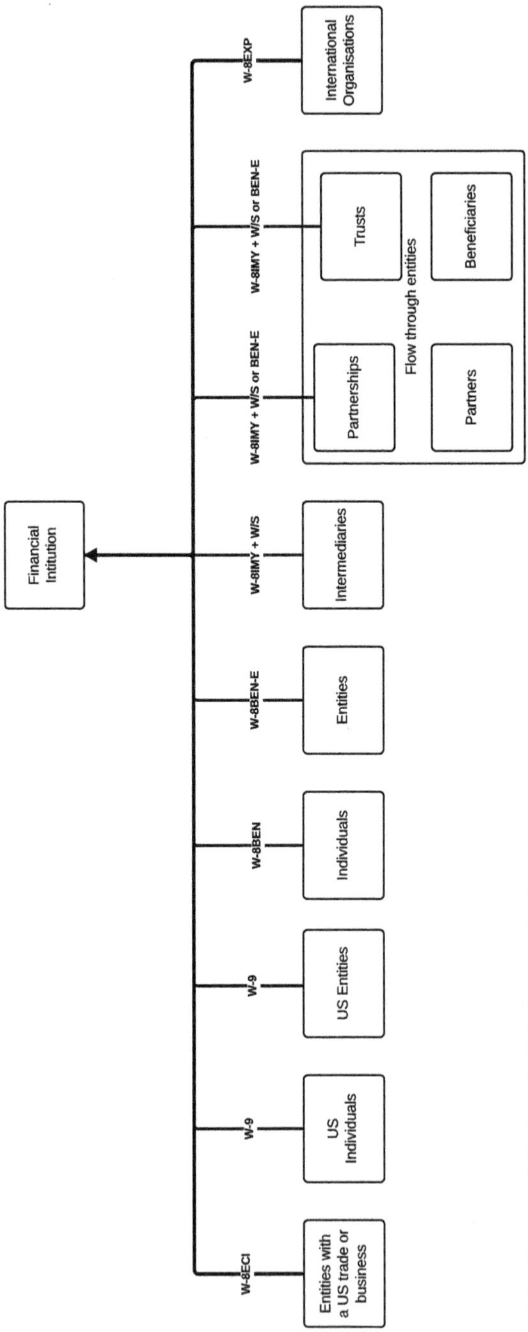


**Exhibit 8.2** Types of W-8 and W-9 *Source* Authors

their W-8IMY, on which they allocate portions of any payment on any given type of income to a particular tax rate. We'll discuss how this is done in the next chapter.

The net result is that the IRS relies on each jurisdiction to have approved KYC rules so that it knows the minimum level of due diligence that a financial institution must apply. Beyond that, to have the tax information necessary to meet FATCA and apply tax treaty benefits, a Form W-8 or W-9 must be in place or some acceptable substitute thereof.

This leads to the next stage: validation. When a financial institution receives a Form W-8 or W-9 it must perform three tasks. These are:

(i) validation on the face
(ii) matching to KYC and
(iii) reason-to-know and actual knowledge check.

Validation-on-the-face involves checking that the relevant form is the correct form (and version) for the client type and that all the information required on the form is present and consistent.

Matching to KYC involves checking that the information on the form matches the KYC data collected by the firm.

Reason-to-know and actual knowledge are tests to make sure that, apart from KYC data and the information on the form, the firm is not aware of any other information that would bring into question any of the information on the form.

All three of these checks take time when performed on paper and must be documented before the form can be treated as valid (Exhibits 8.3, 8.4, 8.5).

*Only* after the financial institution has performed these three tests and documented the results can it show that it has a Chapter 4 tax status (FATCA obligation) and apply any tax treaty benefits (QI obligation).

While most financial firms refuse to onboard Americans in an ill-conceived way to reduce FATCA impacts, there are some who do have American as clients and onboard them by collecting Forms W-9. Some of those Americans are also allowed to trade in US securities and therefore can receive US-sourced FDAP income. Provided the Form W-9 is present and has been validated, the tax rate on US-sourced FDAP income for these clients is 0%. The reason it is 0% is that the American is expected, under FATCA and domestic US law, to disclose the income and pay tax on it domestically. These would be called *US exempt payees (or recipients)*. If the Form W-9 does not contain a validated SSN or EIN, or if the American discloses that the IRS is imposing backup

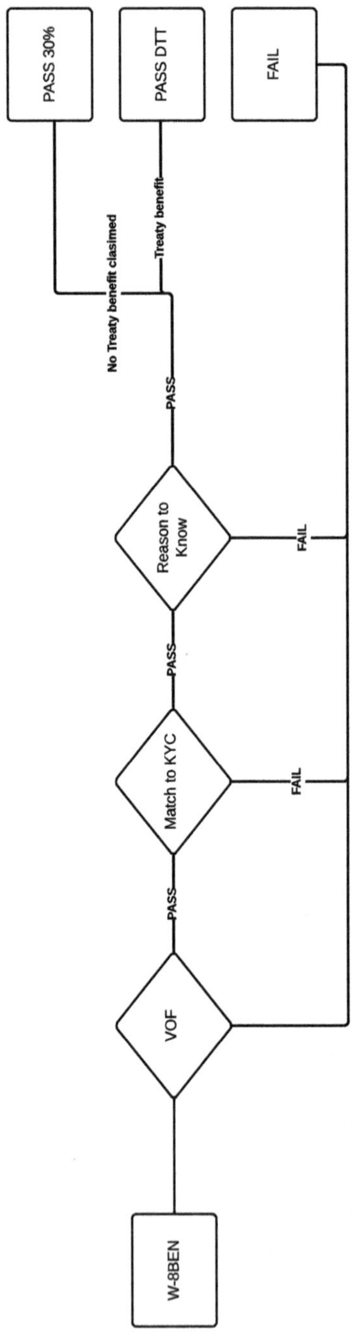


**Exhibit 8.3** Validation of W-8BEN *Source* Authors

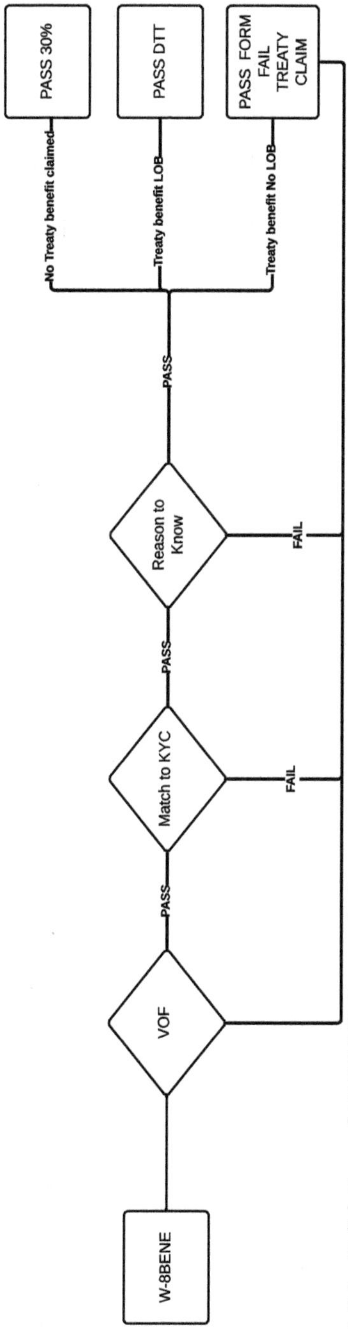


**Exhibit 8.4** Validation of W-8BENE *Source* Authors

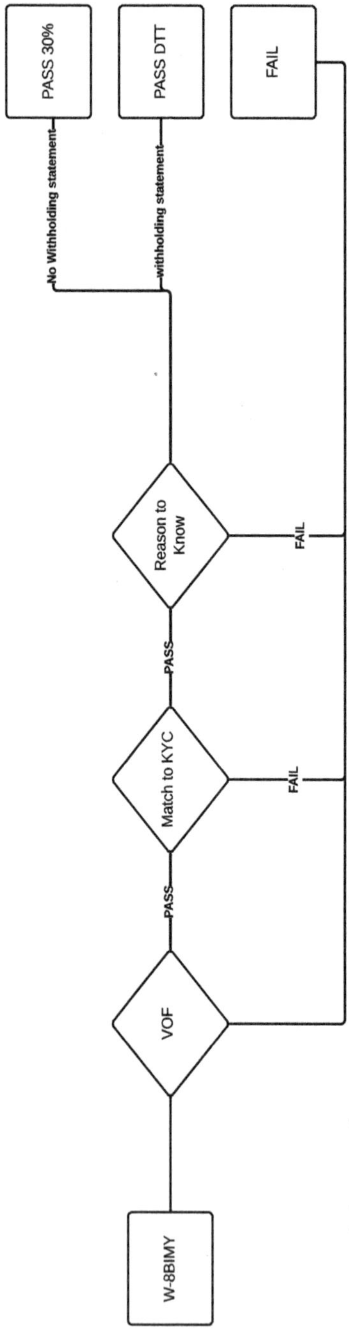


**Exhibit 8.5** Validation of W-8IMY *Source* Authors

withholding, then backup withholding applies and the tax rate is 24% on US-sourced FDAP income. In these cases, the American is called a *US non-exempt recipient*.

All these documentary rules create major challenges for financial institutions—to keep track of the latest forms, to validate those forms and then use the right operating model to withhold tax (or not) on US-sourced FDAP income paid to those clients.

There are two categories of challenges when it comes to documentation. The first is understanding how the rules work. The second is using technology to make compliance easier, cheaper and more robust.

For example, although some firms use online onboarding, there are still a lot of firms, particularly in wealth management, where physical documentation is still used. It can take some time to get tax documentation back, especially if a high-net-worth individual seeks tax advice before filling the forms in. This can lead to a gap between the KYC documentation being received and the tax forms being received. If these clients are allowed to open accounts within that period, technically the financial institution does not have sufficient documentation in place to establish the tax status of that client. This is where the institution needs to understand and apply the "presumption rules". The presumption rules tell the financial institution what to do if it has an account holder for which it has insufficient documentation to establish tax status. The presumption rules for IRC Chapter 4 are different from those in IRC Chapter 3, although in both cases, the QI is allowed a ninety-day grace period before being required to apply them. So the responsible officer needs to know how these work so that they can have policy and procedure in place either to obviate the need to apply the presumption rules (e.g., a policy that prevents an account being opened until all the relevant documentation has been received) or to apply them based on some form of operational trigger.

There are distinct opportunities for technology to play a role the documentation process. In a somewhat prophetic way, the US does allow for substitute forms and also for electronic signatures and sets certain characteristics that an electronic signature must meet in order to be acceptable. The regulations even posit an example of a Form W-8 being embedded into another proprietary form of a financial institution.

This has paved the way for substitute W-8 forms that don't look anything like an IRS W-8. This is important because, in our experience, one of the major hurdles to obtaining a valid form is the awareness and understanding of the beneficial owner when completing the form. The IRS originals are data-dense packed forms, written in what can only be described as "tax technical

American English". For each form there is a set of instructions which, like the form itself, are written in this tax technical language. Both are to a large extent, impenetrable for a non-tax savvy client.

The flow of logic that gets a financial institution from using a paper form in the Form W-8 series to a digital, electronically signed conforming substitute works like this:

### Substitute forms are allowed[1]

You may develop and use your own Form W-8 (a substitute form) for Chapters 3 and 4 purposes if its content is substantially similar to the IRS's official Form W-8 (to the extent required by these instructions), it satisfies certain certification requirements, and it includes a signature under a penalties of perjury statement that is identical to the one stated on the official form.

### Substitute forms can be incorporated into other forms[2]

You may incorporate a substitute Form W-8 into other business forms you customarily use, such as account signature cards, provided the required certifications are clearly set forth.

### Substitute forms must contain at least the same information as a W-8[3]

(2) Same information as paper Form W-8. The electronic transmission must provide the withholding agent or payor with exactly the same information as the paper Form W-8.

### Substitute forms must include the same penalty of perjury language[4]

The perjury statement must contain the language that appears on the paper Form W-8. The electronic system must inform the person whose name is on the Form W-8 that the person must make the declaration contained in the perjury statement and that the declaration is made by signing the Form W-8. The instructions and the language of the perjury statement must immediately follow the person's certifying statements and immediately precede the person's electronic signature.

---

[1] Instructions for the Requestor of Forms W-8BEN, W-8BEN-E, W- 8ECI, W-8EXP, and W-8IMY (06/2022).

[2] Instructions for the Requestor of Forms W-8BEN, W-8BEN-E, W- 8ECI, W-8EXP, and W-8IMY (06/2022).

[3] Section 1.1441–1(e)(4)(iv) (B) (2).

[4] Section 1.1441–1(e)(4)(iv) (B) (3)(i).

## Electronic signatures must be made under penalty of perjury[5]

The electronic transmission must contain an electronic signature by the person whose name is on the Form W-8 and the signature must be under penalties of perjury in the manner described in this paragraph (e)(4)(iv)(B)(3).

## Additional requirements for substitute forms must be met[6]

Additionally, if the substitute form is incorporated into other business forms, the following statement must be presented in the same manner as the penalties of perjury statement and must appear immediately above the single signature line: "The Internal Revenue Service does not require your consent to any provisions of this document other than the certifications required to establish your status as a non-US individual and, if applicable, obtain a reduced rate of withholding".

## Financial institutions must have a standard of confidence in the electronic W-8[7]

(1) In general. The electronic system must ensure that the information received is the information sent, and must document all occasions of user access that result in the submission renewal, or modification of a Form W-8. In addition, the design and operation of the electronic system, including access procedures, must make it reasonably certain that the person accessing the system and furnishing Form W-8 is the person named in the Form.

## The system must be able to produce a hard copy[8]

(4) Requests for electronic Form W-8 data. Upon request by the Internal Revenue Service during an examination, the withholding agent must supply a hard copy of the electronic Form W-8 and a statement that, to the best of the withholding agent's knowledge, the electronic Form W-8 was filed by the person whose name is on the form. The hard copy of the electronic Form W-8 must provide exactly the same information as, but need not be identical to, the paper Form W-8.

---

5 Section 1.1441–1(e)(4)(iv) (B) (3).

6 Instructions for the Requestor of Forms W-8BEN, W-8BEN-E, W-8ECI, W-8EXP, and W-8IMY (06/2022).

7 Section 1.1441-1(e)(4)(iv) (B) (1).

8 Section 1.1441–1(e)(4)(iv) (B) (4).

### Financial institutions can outsource W-8 collection to a third party[9]

You may also rely on an otherwise valid form W-8 received electronically from a third party repository if the form was uploaded or provided to the third party repository and there are processes in place to ensure that the withholding certificate can be reliably associated with a specific request from you and a specific authorization from the person providing the form (or an agent of the person providing the form) for you to receive the withholding certificate.

### Electronic signatures are permitted[10]

Electronic signature. The act of the electronic signature must be effected by the person whose name is on the electronic Form W-8. The signature must also authenticate and verify the submission. For this purpose, the terms authenticate and verify have the same meanings as they do when applied to a written signature on a paper Form W-8. An electronic signature can be in any form that satisfies the foregoing requirements. The electronic signature must be the final entry in the person's Form W-8 submission.

### Electronic signatures must meet certain standards[11]

You may otherwise accept a form W-8 with an electronic signature if the form W-8 reasonably demonstrates that the form has been electronically signed by a person authorised to do so (for example with the time and date stamp and statement that the form has been electronically signed). You may not treat a form W-8 with a typed name in the signature line as validly signed without further information supporting that the signature is an electronic signature.

### Optional field data must be observed[12]

There are a number of specific references to optional fields in the Instructions for Requestors of Forms W-8.

For example:

The substitute form W-8ECI must contain all of the information required in Part I other than line 9. The certifications in Part II of form W-8ECI must be included in a substitute form.

[9] Section 1.1441–1(e)(4)(iv)(E).

[10] Section 1.1441–1(e)(4)(iv) (B) (3)(ii).

[11] Instructions for the Requestor of Forms W-8BEN, W-8BEN-E, W- 8ECI, W-8EXP, and W-8IMY (04/2018).

[12] Instructions for the Requestor of Forms W-8BEN, W-8BEN-E, W- 8ECI, W-8EXP, and W-8IMY (06/2022).

and

> W-8EXP[13] must contain all of the information required in Part I, lines one through 5, line 7 (if a US TIN is required), and line 8. See however [...] earlier, for when you may omit a chapter 4 certification on a substitute form W-8. The substitute form W-8EXP must also contain all of the statements and certifications contained in Parts II and III, as applicable, with respect to the purpose for which the form is provided, but a specific statement or certification needs to be included (in its entirety) only if it is relevant to the type of entity providing the form.

and

> The certifications in Part II of the W-8BEN-E[14] must be included in a substitute form if you are making a withholdable payment to a disregarded entity or a branch that must be reported in Part II. The certifications in Part III must be included only if treaty benefits are claimed, and then only to the extent that the certifications are required.

These mean that if the QI decides to design a substitute W-8 in digital form, it will need to include some programming code to account for different characteristics of each form type. The certification text of each form, for example, is different.

### Certain rules must be met to embed a substitute form into another form[15]

The instructions specify that, for a substitute form incorporated into other business forms:

> [You may not] imply that a person may be subject to 30% withholding or backup withholding unless that person agrees to provisions on the substitute form that are unrelated to the required certifications.

[13] Instructions for the Requestor of Forms W- 8BEN, W-8BEN-E, W-8ECI, W-8EXP, and W-8IMY (06/2022).

[14] Instructions for the Requestor of Forms W-8BEN, W-8BEN-E, W-8ECI, W-8EXP, and W-8IMY (06/2022).

[15] Instructions for the Requestor of Forms W-8BEN, W-8BEN-E, W- 8ECI, W-8EXP, and W-8IMY (06/2022).

### Systems must collect explicit consent for information sharing[16]

> The substitute Form W-8BEN must include a statement that if the person providing the form is a resident in a FATCA partner jurisdiction (that is a Model 1 IGA jurisdiction with reciprocity), certain tax account information may be provided to the jurisdiction of residence.

And finally,

### Systems must not collect unrelated certifications[17]

> [You may not] use a substitute form that requires the payee, by signing, to agree to provisions unrelated to the required certifications.

So, it is clear, albeit represented in a disjointed way in different parts of the regulations and IRS instructions, that, provided a system meets the above requirements, QIs can transition for the use of paper forms to digital forms. We call this, in aggregate, a Statement of Conformity and such a statement would need to be included in a compliance program to replace the manual validation policies and procedures.

The operational opportunity, resilience and cost reduction implications of this are clear. The compliance problem is that many firms, in their zeal to go electronic, made assumptions or just ignored these rules and, for a Form W-8, just used a tick box on an online web-based onboarding system. These approaches are oversimplistic and will not meet the IRS requirements for a conforming digital substitute form.

There is a further beneficial consequence of this digital framework. Other regulations and laws, also described in this book, such as CRS and TRACE, mandate the use of self-certifications. So, by extrapolating the US rules and comparing them to the other rules, you can produce a single digital form with an electronic signature that, at one sitting, collects FATCA status and CRS status to support automated due diligence, as well as QI and TRACE claims of treaty benefits.

So, in concluding this chapter, we would comment that KYC is not a panacea for anti-tax evasion regulations, self-certifications are widely used and digital substitutes with electronic signatures are on the rise which means that compliance is becoming an increasingly digital issue.

---

16 Instructions for the Requestor of Forms W-8BEN, W-8BEN-E, W-8ECI, W-8EXP, and W-8IMY (06/2022).

17 Instructions for the Requestor of Forms W-8BEN, W-8BEN-E, W- 8ECI, W-8EXP, and W-8IMY (06/2022).

Once a firm has followed all these rules, they could drastically reduce paperwork and make due diligence far easier simply by using the electronic data to search for indicia. TConsult's Investor Self-Declaration (ISD) system[18] was built on these principles and the tax logic underpinning the ISD includes questions that relate to US indicia e.g., a substantial presence test. When a financial institution receives an ISD as a substitute Form W-8, they will usually also receive the data associated with the Form W-8 which can then be integrated into internal systems and used to search for indicia (Exhibit 8.6).

Once the financial institution has sufficient documentation, the next stage is to determine withholding, as we will see in the next chapter.

[18] Investor Self Declarations: https://investorselfdeclarations.com/.

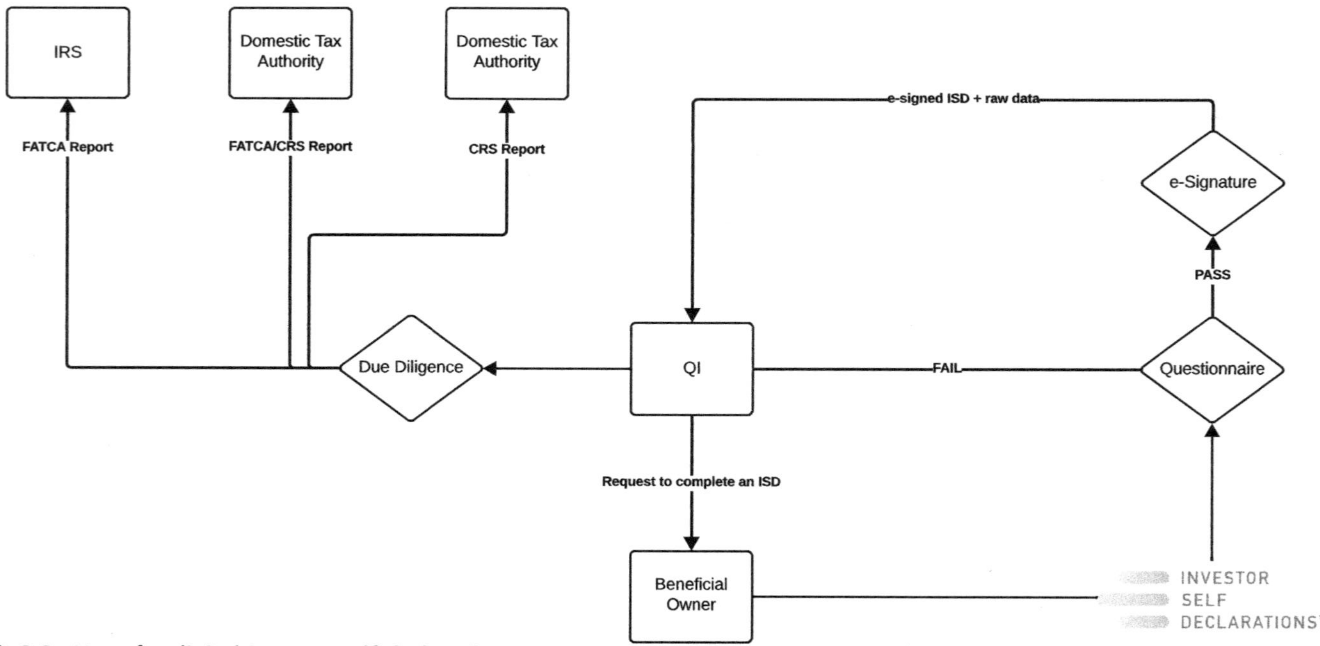


**Exhibit 8.6** Use of a digital investor self-declaration to support due diligence *Source* Authors

# 9

# Withholding

This chapter will explain the trading, safe custody and payment chain in financial institutions together with an explanation of the various operating models that can be used. Particular attention will be given to new Sect. 1446(a) and 1446(f) withholding regulations on the taxation of realised gains on disposal of interests in publicly traded partnerships—which is a new area of the 2023 QI Agreement.

When we say that the US is a relief at source market, this is actually a misnomer. Payments of US-sourced FDAP income are not necessarily taxed at the source by the issuer, but rather at some point along the payment chain before the payment reaches the ultimate beneficial owner.

Each intermediary in the payment chain is a withholding agent from the US perspective. Each has a responsibility to ensure that the correct amount of tax is withheld on payments made to their clients. Which of the intermediaries actually physically withholds and deposits the tax with the US Treasury is essentially a negotiation between the parties in the payment chain. The other intermediaries retain their responsibility to check and, if necessary, correct any mistakes made by others in the payment chain.

The intermediary that physically performs the withholding must have sufficient documentation to apply any treaty rates. If the beneficial owner is their direct client, this is usually not a problem. The complexity arises when the beneficial owner is the client of another intermediary further down the payment chain. That intermediary may be a QI or NQI, and may choose to disclose their clients upstream, or not disclose them. Untangling this


R. K. McGill and K. V. Pitkin, *Qualified Intermediary*,
https://doi.org/10.1007/978-3-031-81410-5_9

complexity and creating a clear map of the payment flow and the corresponding documentation flow is one of the key challenges of the US qualified intermediary regime.

## To Withhold or Not to Withhold?

The QI Agreement allows a QI to choose whether or not it wishes to be the intermediary that physically withholds the tax. This essentially creates two flavours of QI: withholding QIs, and non-withholding Qis (Exhibit 9.1).

A withholding QI provides a Form W-8IMY to the intermediary above them in the payment chain indicating that it wishes to assume primary withholding responsibility. This means that the QI will receive all US-sourced income gross from its upstream counterparty, and then calculate the withholding due to the US Treasury based on the documentation that it holds for each recipient. The operational advantages of this are (i) that the QI only needs one account with its upstream counterparty and (ii) the QI doesn't need

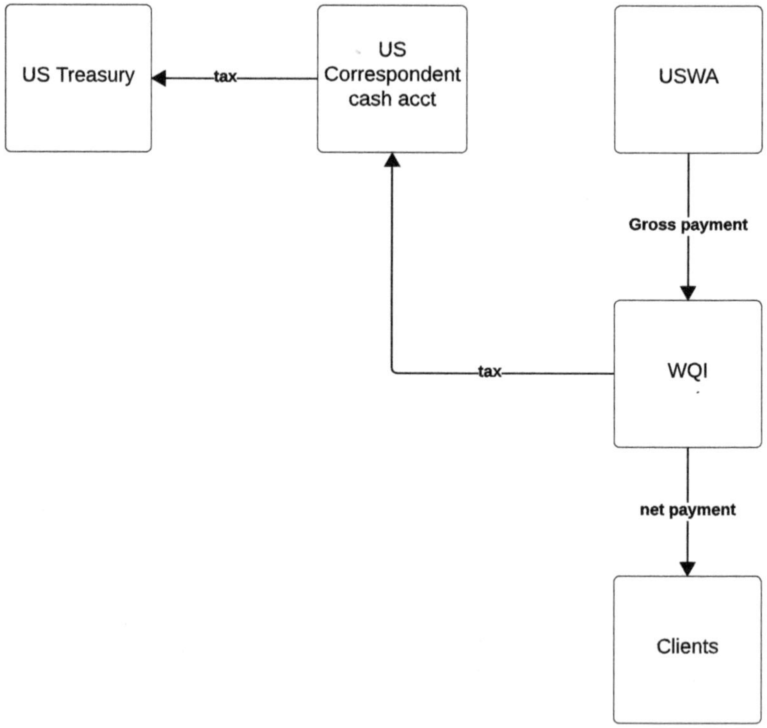


**Exhibit 9.1** Withholding QI operational tax payment model *Source* Authors

to tell its upstream counterparty anything about its clients. It just needs to submit a Form W-8IMY and an annual withholding statements stating that all income paid to its account should be taxed at 0%. However, it will need processes in place to calculate and then deposit the tax within the timeframe specified in the QI Agreement. Procedures will be required for each of these tasks (see Exhibit 9.2).

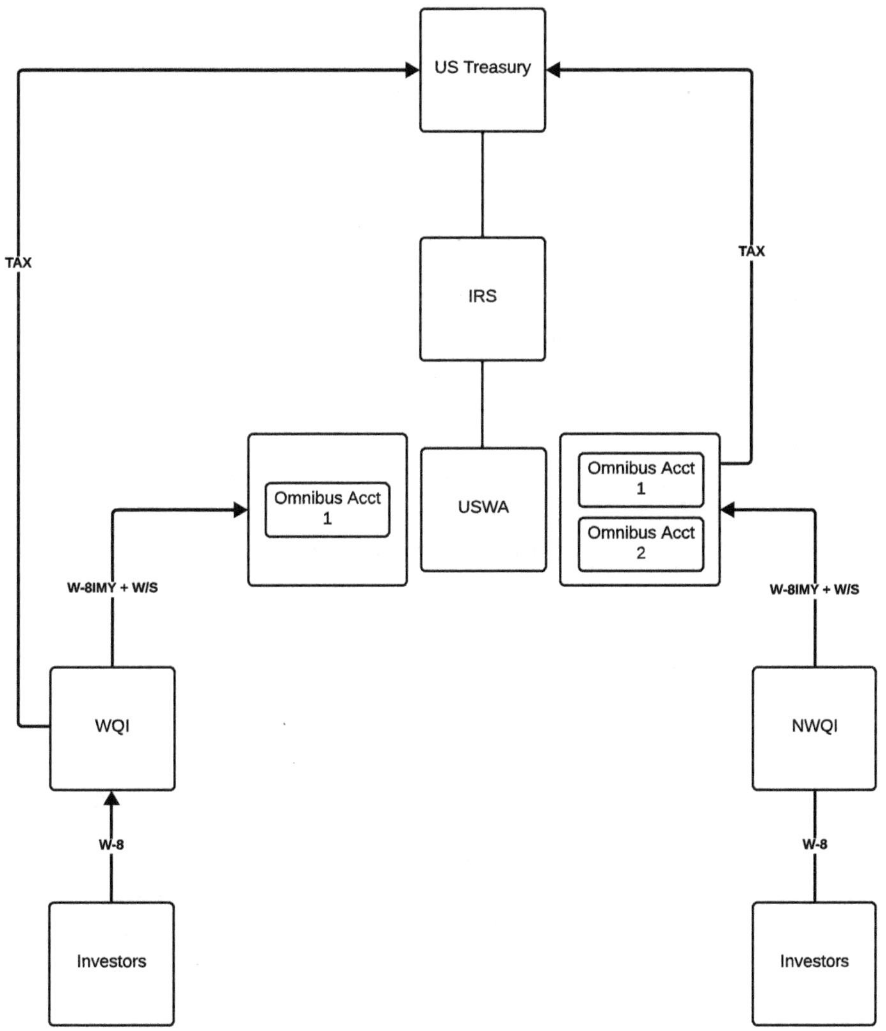


**Exhibit 9.2** Who pays the tax? *Source* Authors

Acting as a withholding QI places a lot of responsibility on the firm to make sure tax is deposited with the US Treasury on time. A lot of qualified intermediaries decide to outsource this task to an upstream financial intermediary in the payment chain by being a non-withholding QI.

A non-withholding QI provides a Form W-8IMY to the intermediary above them in the payment chain indicating that it does **not** wish to assume primary withholding responsibility.

It must then tell the upstream how to tax its clients. There are two ways it can do this:

1. Omnibus rate pool account model
2. Withholding rate pool statement model.

In both models, if the non-withholding QI makes a mistake, and their client gets taxed at a lower rate as a result, the QI will need to withhold the difference and deposit it with the US Treasury itself. While the QI Agreement allows QIs to outsource the activity of withholding, they can't outsource their responsibility to make sure the correct tax is withheld. This means it is essential for the QI to choose the operating model that will work best for them to minimise the risk of mistakes. We strongly advise non-withholding QIs to join the Electronic Federal Tax Payment System (known as EFTPS) just like withholding QIs do. There's no cost associated with this, but it facilitates the non-withholding QI's ability to pay any tax that they withhold to the US Treasury.

## Omnibus Rate Pool Account Model

The omnibus account model is the simplest, and therefore most popular way for a non-withholding QI to operate. The non-withholding QI opens multiple pooled accounts with its upstream counterparty, typically a QI or a US withholding Agent (USWA) and designates a tax rate for each account. The non-withholding QI then places the US assets of all clients that are subject to the same US tax rate in the relevant omnibus account, based on the documentation they hold for the client.

For example, the non-withholding QI might have three omnibus accounts:

- A 30% dividend rate account for clients who should be taxed at the full statutory rate.
- A 15% dividend rate account for clients who are entitled to a 15% treaty rate on dividends.

- A 0% dividend rate account for US clients.

The exact number of omnibus accounts the non-withholding QI will need will vary depending on its client base and the number of applicable tax rates.

The non-withholding QI then instructs the upstream intermediary how to tax each account using a withholding statement. It is effectively fire and forget. While this makes it operationally very simple, this model can require several omnibus accounts, which can be expensive and subject to the commercial policies of the upstream intermediary (Exhibit 9.3).

## Withholding Rate Pool Statement Model

It is also possible to operate as a non-withholding QI with a single upstream account. However, this requires the non-withholding QI to submit instructions to its upstream for each income event, telling the upstream how to tax the account for that specific payment. They use a withholding rate pool statement to provide these instructions.

While this model may be more cost effective in terms of account operating fees, we rarely see this adopted in practice due to the amount of work involved in processing the withholding rate pool statements for both the QI and their upstream counterparty.

In Exhibit 9.4 only one omnibus account is required to hold all US securities. The counterparty sends a message to the QI to inform them of an upcoming corporate actions event (CAEV), typically a SWIFT MT564, and an instruction to provide a withholding statement. On receipt, the QI must calculate which of its clients owns that security, how many shares they own and what tax rate are they entitled to. On record date a second MT564 is sent to the QI confirming the position held by the QI in that security. This crystallises the claimable shares. The QI now sends a withholding rate pool statement instructing the counterparty how many shares to tax at which rate. The counterparty can now apply those rates without knowing who the beneficial owner is, and the net paid to the QI will be at an effectively blended rate i.e., it won't be 30% or a treaty rate, but some other number.

There are one or two firms that operate this model, but it's very time sensitive and labour intensive. If the estimated workload costs less than the cost of operating multiple omnibus rate pool accounts, then it's a viable option.

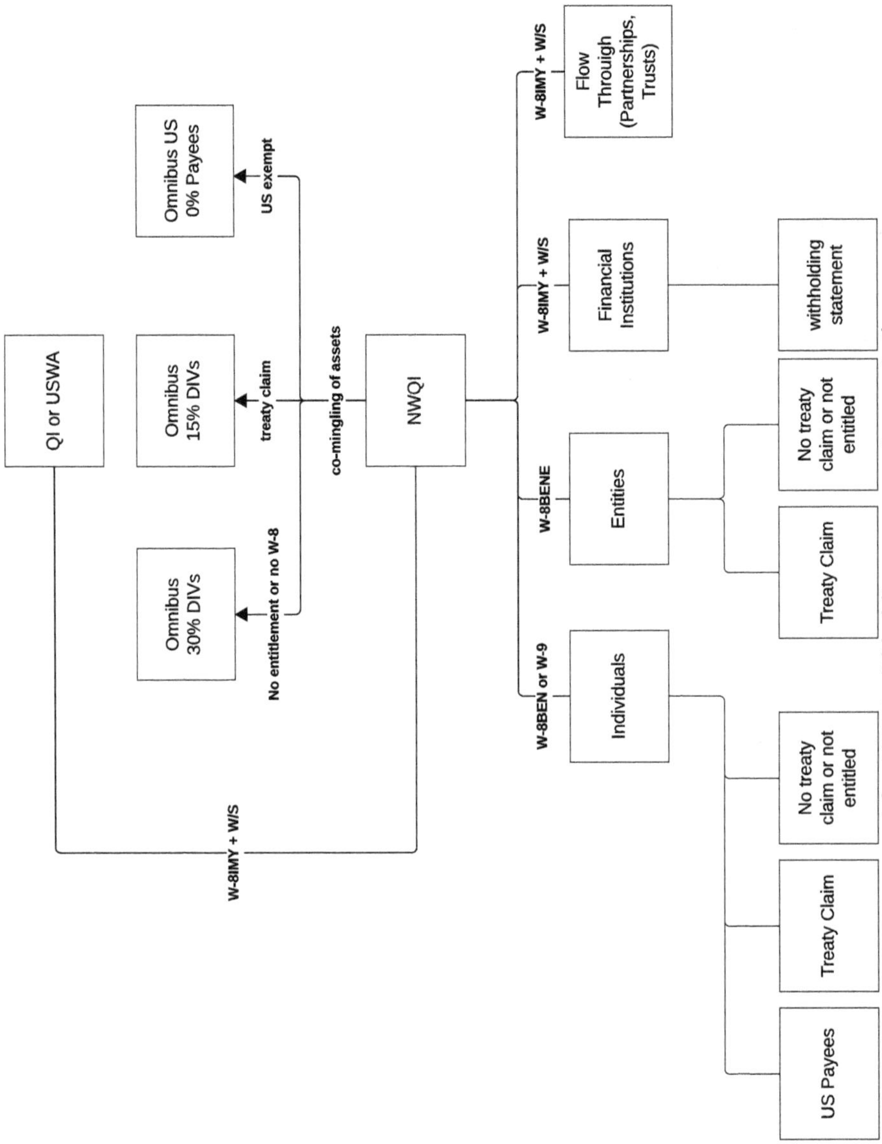


**Exhibit 9.3** Use of omnibus accounts to pool for NWQI withholding purposes *Source* Authors

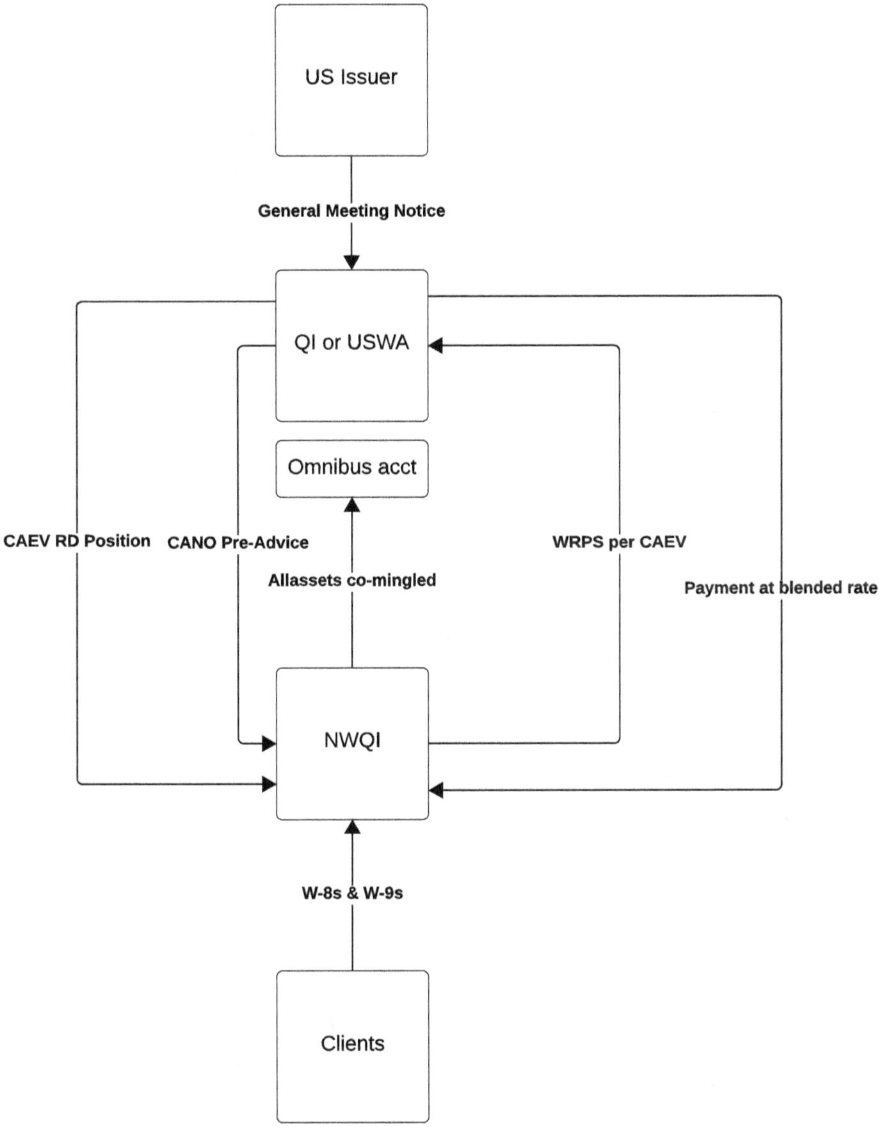


**Exhibit 9.4** Withholding Rate Pool Statement model *Source* Authors

## The Role of Withholding Statements

The key component of both operating models is the withholding statement. A withholding statement is essentially a list of accounts and instructions about how to tax them. The QI Agreement sets out how withholding statements should be used and what information they contain. They are an essential part of the information flow between intermediaries in the payment chain, establishing who is supposed to be applying withholding and at what rate.

A withholding QI will need to give a withholding statement to its upstream counterparty stating that all US-sourced income is paid gross. They will generally have just one omnibus account upstream, so the withholding statement will just list all of the income codes that the account will receive and state that the tax rate should be 0% for each income code. The IRS assigns a two-digit code to each type of income that could be subject to Chapter 3 withholding.

A non-withholding QI may have multiple omnibus accounts, so its withholding statement will include details about each account and how to tax income received under each income code for that account.

The same thing happens downstream. If the QI has another QI as a client, they will provide similar withholding statement telling the upstream QI how to tax *their* accounts. If the client is a nonqualified intermediary, by default they must submit a withholding statement before each pay date. However, the QI Agreement recognises that this may be overly burdensome, so provides the QI with the option to use then "alternative procedure", which allows them to us rate pool omnibus accounts then receive a detailed withholding statement from their NQI clients once a year instead. The QI must grant permission to the NQI in writing allowing them to use the alternative procedure.

The withholding statement is always associated with a specific Form W-8IMY, which is signed under penalty of perjury. This protects the upstream by shifting the liability for applying a reduced rate of withholding onto the intermediary that has submitted the withholding statement.

While the QI Agreement sets out what should be included in a withholding statement and when it is required, it is agnostic on the precise format and means of transmission between intermediaries. Most intermediaries produce their own template for downstream intermediaries to use, which is typically a spreadsheet or PDF.

One of the challenges in standardising withholding statements is that the QI Agreement sets out minimum standards for the information they should contain. QIs can use them to collect additional data that they may find useful or embed them into other business processes.

Another of the challenges relates to the technical systems available to QIs. We often find core banking systems do not store all the information that a QI needs, and there is often an internal resistance to making changes to these systems. As a result, QIs end up supplementing with spreadsheets and manual processes. Withholding statements are one of those aspects of QI compliance that gets relegated to a manually keyed spreadsheet, potentially introducing risk. The introduction of widely adopted standards that automate the transmission of withholding statements would reduce this risk and improve efficiency across the system.

In recent years there have been industry efforts towards standardising withholding statements, including consortiums collaborating to produce standardised spreadsheet templates. At the time of writing, it is unclear what level of industry adoption these templates have.

There are also efforts to submit a business case to the ISO standards committee for an XML standard, although these discussions are currently in the very early phases.[1]

In 2024, the Association of Qualified and Authorised Intermediaries (AQAI) proposed to the International Standards Organisation (ISO) that withholding statements be standardised in an XML format consistent with ISO20022 (Exhibit 9.5).

Because there are several versions of as withholding statement, depending on a financial institution's status and the way it chooses to act with respect to specific accounts that it operates at a counterparty, its necessary to compile a flow chart to help financial institutions make these decisions and, when made, to know what data is required.

As Exhibit 9.6 shows, and as touched on earlier, there are two broad types of withholding statement—pooled and not pooled. Pooled withholding statements are generally used by QIs. A withholding statement is associated with a specific account, unless no account number is specified, in which case, the withholding statement, like the W-8IMY to which it is connected, would apply to all accounts operated by the QI.

Pooled withholding statements can be further subdivided into those that are pooled by a single tax rate for a single income type (rate pools). These are really "fire and forget" because the recipient doesn't care whose assets are in which account. They rely on the sender's obligation to have proper documentation in place and to have placed the assets in the correct pooled account. The other type of pooled statements are those that are blended pools issued for each corporate action event (CAEV). This model is more complex because it requires additional work by both parties. The upstream counterparty that is going to be making the payment, needs to tell the downstream party in advance of an impending corporate action, such as a dividend. This is usually achieved with a SWIFT message MT654 which, in ISO20022, is called a CANO or Corporate Action Notification message. A second CANO

[1] You can follow updates at the Association of Authorised and Qualified Intermediaries (AQAI) website: https://aqai.tax.

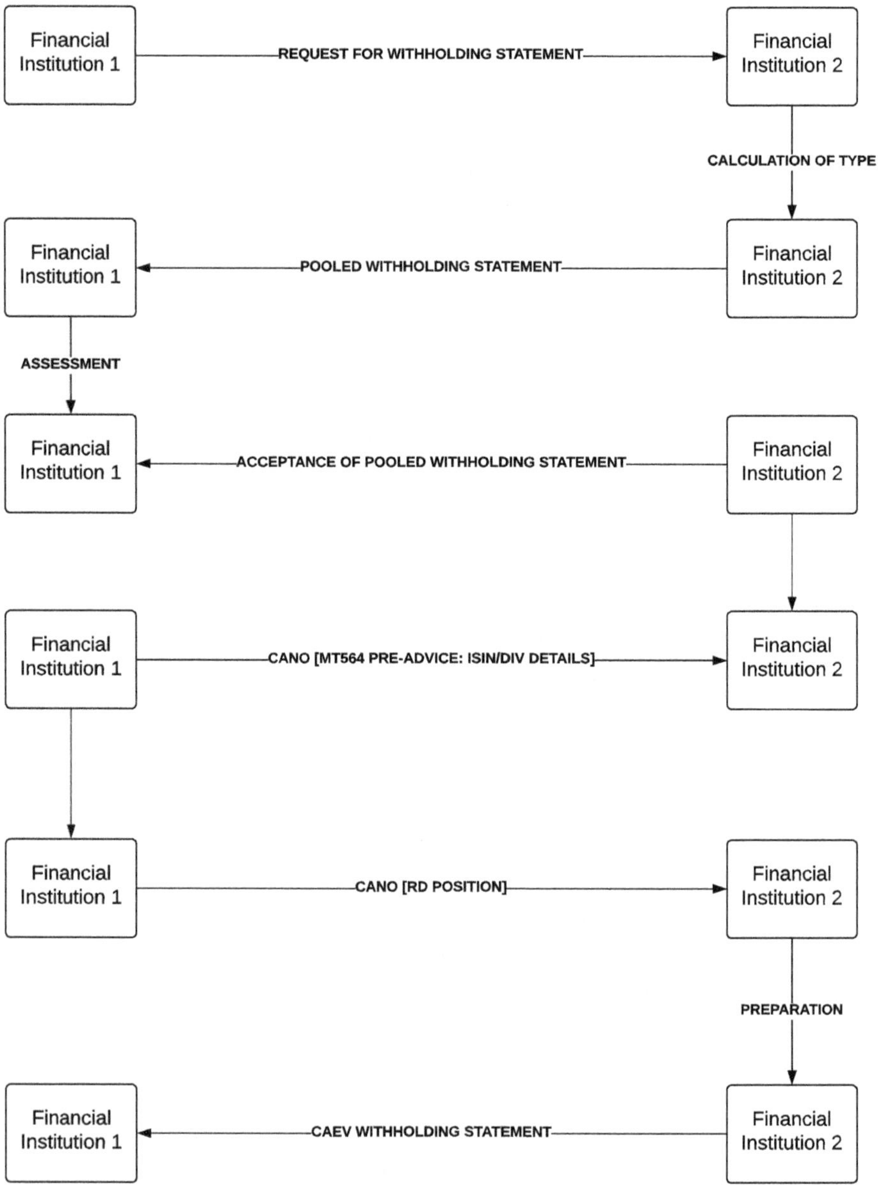


**Exhibit 9.5** Proposed ISO message set for withholding statements *Source* AQAI

is required on the record date to crystallise the number of shares that will be the subject of the payment. The sender of the withholding statement now has to prepare a withholding statement based solely on which clients were holding *that* security on *that* record date. Usually used with a single omnibus account, this means that the payment will be made at an effectively blended

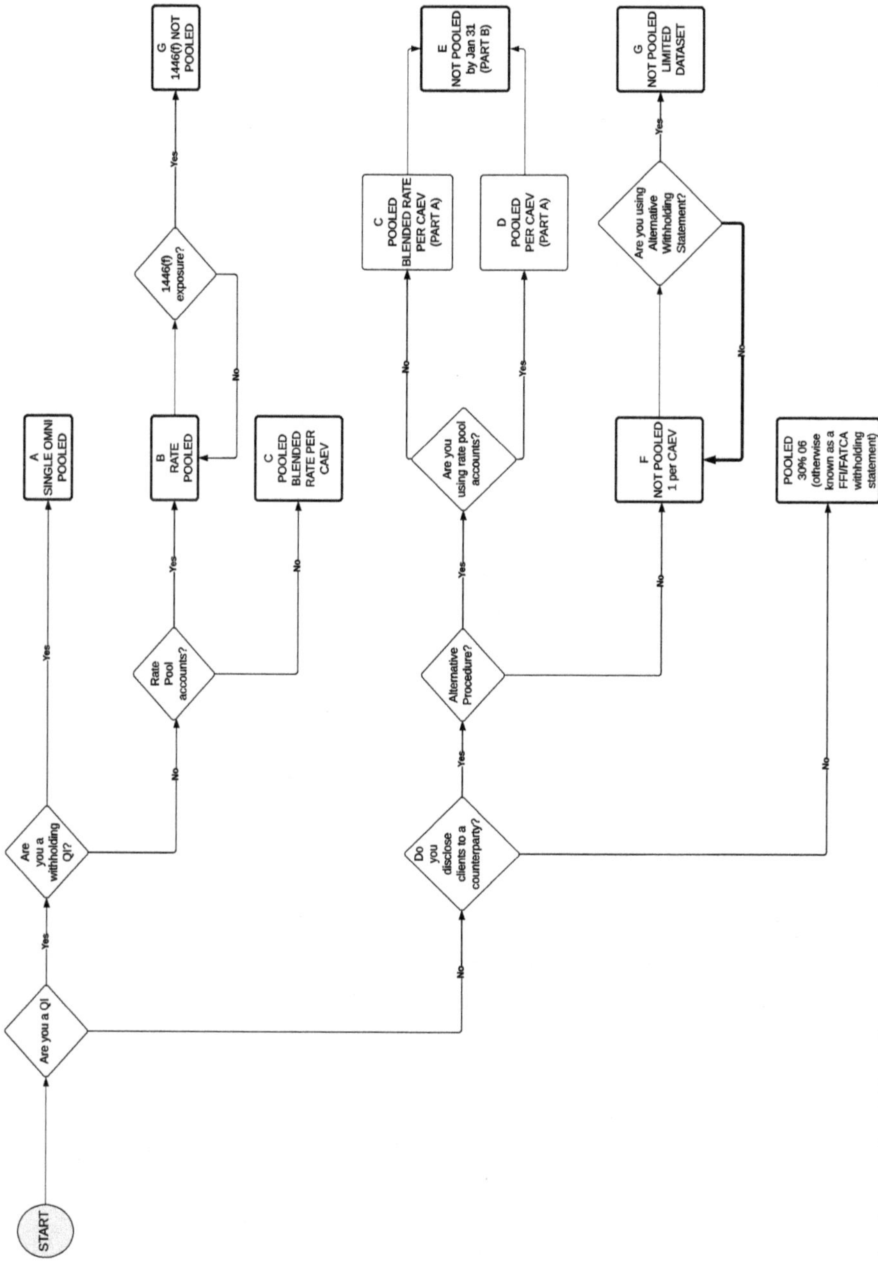


**Exhibit 9.6** Types of withholding statement *Source:* Authors

tax rate. Each party can still report each income type properly because they will both be using the withholding statement to break down the payment into its constituent parts.

Non-Pooled withholding statements per CAEV are the expected standard for NQIs. However, NQIs can use pooled accounts. These can also be subdivided into those that are issued per CAEV and those that are pooled initially but then non-pooled later. The object of these is to allow for simplified processing during the year to avoid a withholding statement for each dividend payment but still meet the obligation of an NQI to disclose its clients (in a non-pooled withholding statement) at an agreed point in the future (January 31st in the case of the US). This is called the Alternative Method.

There is a further subdivision that allows for a more limited data set to be disclosed on the basis that the recipient of the withholding statement has already been provided with underlying documentation (so the recipient can fill in the gaps from the documentation). This is rather confusingly called the Alternative withholding statement.

## Income from Publicly Traded Partnerships (PTPs)

The QI Agreement 2023 introduced new obligations for QIs that allow their customers to trade interests in publicly traded partnerships (PTPs) with income that is effectively connected to a US business or trade.

A publicly traded partnership (PTP) is a type of a limited partnership managed by two or more general partners, including individuals, corporations, or other partnerships. PTPs are capitalised by limited partners who provide capital but have no management role in the partnership. Interests in PTPs are either traded on an established securities market or are readily tradeable on a secondary market.

QIs that allow their account holders to trade interests in PTPs must ensure that the correct amount of tax is withheld when:

- there is a distribution by the PTP—Section 1446(a) typically a dividend.
- there is a gain on the disposition of an interest in a PTP that would be treated as effectively connected with the conduct of a trade or business within the US—Section 1446(f).

Exceptions apply and the rules for calculating the amount of tax to withhold under Sections 1446(a) and (f) are complex, The QI Agreement therefore introduces an extra option: the concept of a disclosing QI. This allows non-withholding QI to disclose its clients to an upstream withholding agent, thus outsourcing the responsibility of calculating the tax rate, in addition to the act of withholding. The QI effectively acts as a disclosing NQI for this income.

Exhibit 9.7 describes the difference between 1446(a) and 1446(f). If a client (BO(1)) purchases an interest in a PTP, the PTP may make distributions such as dividends to its holders. These dividends are taxed at either 37% if the beneficial owner is an individual or 21% if the beneficial owner is an entity.

If the same beneficial owner now decides to sell his interest, 1446(f) applies and a 10% tax on the gross proceeds is payable and reportable by the transferee unless the PTP has issued a Qualified Notice certifying the degree to which an exemption applies to non-US transferees, which will usually be related to the proportion of the PTP's income is effectively connected with a US trade or business.

In practice, most QIs became QIs because they wanted to offer their investors the benefit of reduced rates of withholding *without* disclosing them to another financial intermediary, who may be their competitor. It is not clear how many QIs have opted to become disclosing QIs, but we are seeing significant moves in the marketplace to divest from PTPs in response to these regulations. In the absence of tools to support Section 1446(a) and 1446(f) withholding calculations for small and mid-tier financial institutions, this market is likely to become consolidated by a few big players with the resources to handle this complexity.

## Acting in Different Capacities

The QI Agreement provides QIs with a lot of flexibility when making decisions about whether to withhold themselves or outsource the withholding to another counterparty. A QI can also choose to act in different capacities for different types of payment, different upstream counterparties and for different accounts with the same upstream counterparty.

For example, a QI might assume primary Chapter 3 and 4 withholding responsibility, but not assume primary backup withholding responsibility. This means that the QI will withhold in Chapter 3 and 4, but the upstream withholding agent will be responsible for applying any backup withholding that is due and reporting on forms 1099. Similarly, a QI can choose whether to assume primary withholding responsibility for payments of income related to Publicly Traded Partnerships (PTPs) under Sections 1446(a) and 1446(f)

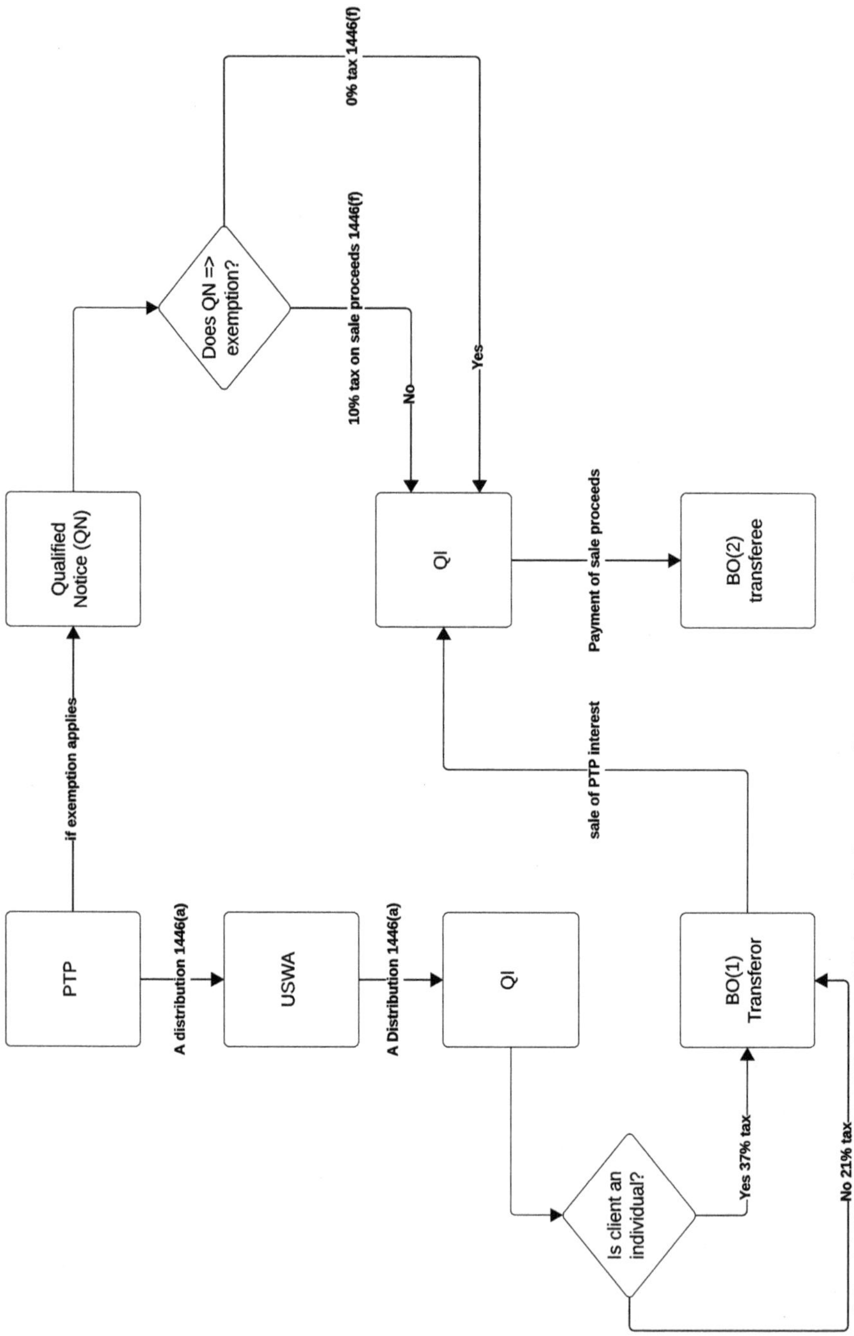


**Exhibit 9.7** 1446(a) and 1446(f) for Publicly traded partnerships *Source* Authors

separate from its decision to assume primary withholding in Chapters 3 and 4.

While most QIs act in one capacity with multiple upstream counterparties, this is also not required. The QI could act as a withholding QI with one counterparty and a non-withholding QI with another. This is communicated via the Form W-8IMY. As a result, the QI may have multiple Forms W-8IMY that it has presented to different intermediaries for different accounts.

Decisions about how to operate are left to the QI and the IRS does not need to be notified. However, the QI may find there are commercial restrictions placed on it by an upstream intermediary that limit its flexibility. For example, some QIs refuse to accept primary backup withholding responsibility, and will reject a Form W-8IMY from a downstream QI that has checked the box indicating that they do not accept this responsibility either. Your choices at that point include looking for an alternative upstream partner to trade with (which could be costly) or to implement policies and procedures that prevent the need for backup withholding in the first place.

As we have seen, the task of withholding the tax on US-sourced FDAP income can take place at various points down the payment chain, and there is a system of communications (Forms W-8IMY accompanied by withholding statements) that allows all the intermediaries in that chain to coordinate who is doing what. In the next chapters, we will explore what QIs need to do with that tax and how it gets reported to the IRS.

Compliance is difficult because so many of the rules are inter-related and interact with each other. Knowledge is the key, but for many smaller QIs, this is simply too expensive. It seems to be a race to the bottom with most firms trying to do as little as possible to get across the compliance threshold.

# 10

# Depositing

To understand depositing of tax, we must consider a few factors. First, the IRS defines all financial institutions in the chain of payment as "withholding agents". All withholding agents have an obligation to withhold and deposit tax to the US Treasury *unless* another withholding agent has already withheld the correct amount of tax.

This means that there are two circumstances in which a non-US financial institution might have to pay money to the US Treasury. The first is if they decide to assume what is called *primary* withholding responsibility. They do this using a Form W-8IMY, which on the October 2021 version of the form would involve checking Line 15a. The exact language is "*I certify that the entity identified in Part 1 of this form assumes primary withholding responsibility for purposes of chapters 3 and 4 for each account identified on a withholding statement attached to this form (or if no withholding statement is attached to this form for all accounts)*".

Remember that the Form W-8IMY, like all the W-8 series of forms, is signed under penalty of perjury. The withholding statement is "associated with" the Form W-8IMY and thus becomes part of the certification and part of the subject to perjury text. This occurs even when the withholding statement is not physically attached to the Form W-8IMY and most financial institutions now include the certification text onto their withholding statement templates, just to be sure.

The second circumstance in which a non-US financial institution might have to make a payment to the US Treasury is if some else makes a mistake or there is an adjustment required. For example, a non-withholding QI would not normally need to withhold tax and pay the Treasury, but if a mistake


R. K. McGill and K. V. Pitkin, *Qualified Intermediary*,
https://doi.org/10.1007/978-3-031-81410-5_10

was made and tax was under-withheld and they have spotted the mistake, it would be their obligation to correct the error, collect the tax and pay the Treasury—because they are by definition, a withholding agent.

However, financial institutions based outside the United States cannot make payments directly to the US Treasury. To make deposits, a QI typically needs to establish a US correspondent banking cash account or make payments via a US affiliate. Operating a US correspondent bank account can be costly, and as a result we tend to see smaller QIs opting to be non-withholding to avoid this requirement. However, this must be accompanied by rigorous procedures to prevent underwithholding to avoid the need for ad hoc deposits to correct underwithholding by an upstream withholding agent. Exhibit 10.1 indicates how, even when an upstream QI that has assumed primary withholding makes a mistake, the lower, non-withholding QI, must correct the error and pay the tax top the Treasury. For this reason, the IRS recommends that all QIs register with the Electronic Federal Tax Payment System (EFTPS).[1] This represents a compliance challenge, not for its own sake, but because it increases the number of systems that non-US financial institutions must interact with. EFTPS sits in the same ecosystem as the FIRE portal (for submission of 1042-S returns) and MeF, the Modernised efile portal (for 1042 tax returns from 2026) and IDES (for submission of FATCA reports from non-IGA and Model 2 IGA jurisdictions). Each of these systems is independent of the others, has its own registration mechanism and its own data formats.

That complexity aside, if tax does have to be deposited, the question is when?

The QI Agreement sets out a formula for calculating how frequently to make payments. If the total amount withheld is very small, QIs can make payments once a year. However, if the amount of tax is very high, the QI will need to apply the formula, which could see you making payments three business days after the end of every quarter-month period.

In practice, many withholding QIs simply assume the worst and make payments three business days after the end of every quarter-month period anyway, rather than applying the formula and risking a mistake.

Non-withholding QIs that are correcting underwithholding must make the payment as soon as possible after discovering underwithholding. Their compliance challenge is that they often don't understand their withholding obligations in these circumstances and so don't have any arrangements or procedures in place to comply.

[1] EFTPS: https://www.eftps.gov/eftps/.

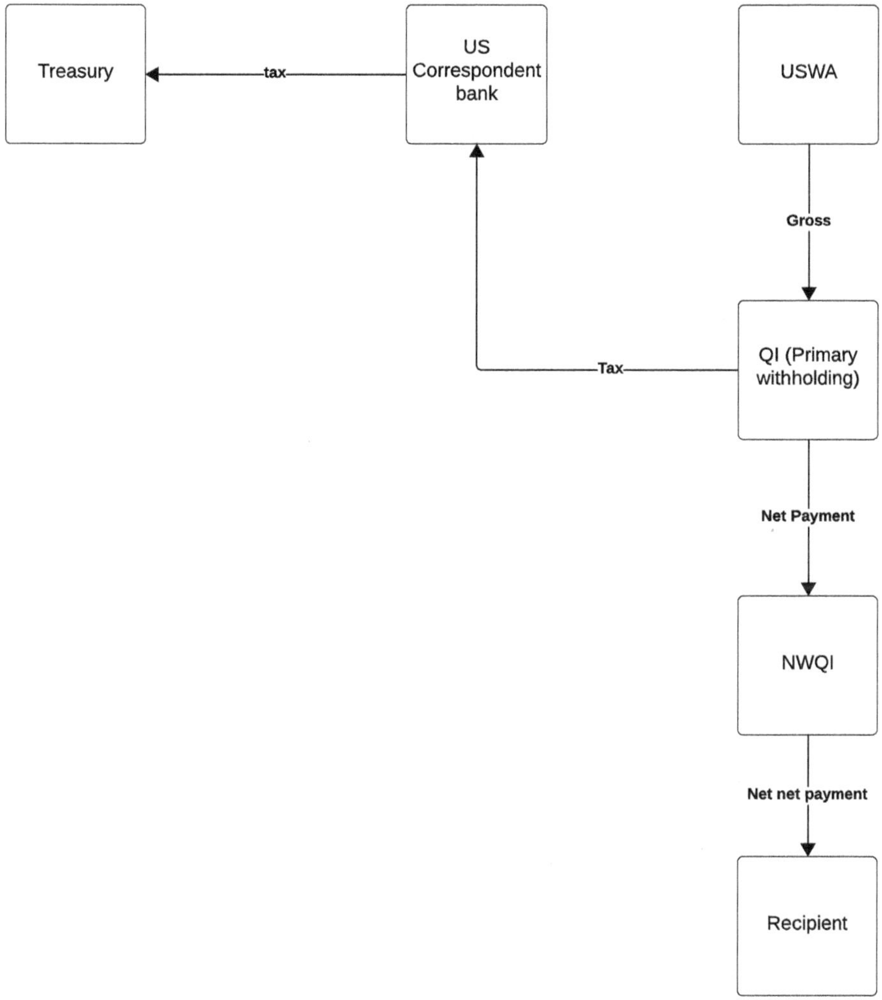


**Exhibit 10.1** Ad hoc payments to US Treasury *Source* Authors

One other complexity associated with depositing tax is concerned with reporting. All financial institutions report tax withheld on Forms 1042-S and Form 1042. The tax that is being withheld is not always deposited at the same time that the tax liability occurs. So, one common error on the Form 1042, the US tax return, is to record the date of payment (i.e., deposited) as if it were the date that the tax liability arose. This is such a common error that the IRS has seen fit to explicitly tell filers, on the form, that the boxes should be completed based on the date that the tax liability arose and not on the date of the payment of the tax to the Treasury. As Exhibit 10.2 shows, a

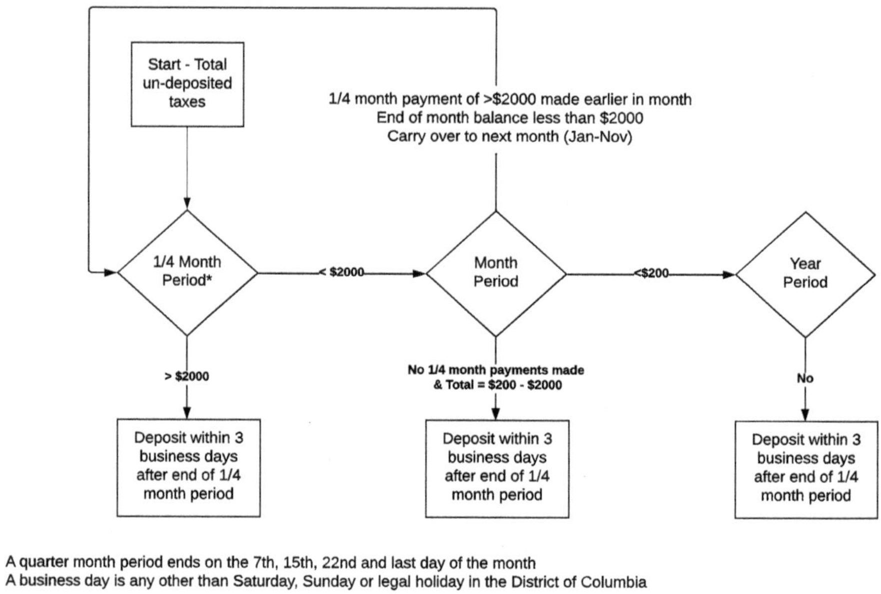


**Exhibit 10.2** How to calculate when to deposit tax *Source* Authors

payment to the US Treasury may take place sometime after the tax liability arose.

# 11

# Reporting

This chapter describes the main reporting obligations of financial institutions that receive US-sourced FDAP income on behalf of their account holders. This includes 1042-S information returns, 1042 tax return and 1099 information returns. This chapter will update the reader on new or updated reporting tools used by the IRS and access requirements.

Reporting payments of US-sourced FDAP income to the US Internal Revenue Service is the final stage in the tax operational cycle. The reporting year runs from January 1st to December 31st.

Qualified intermediaries are potentially subject to up to four types of US tax reporting:

- **Form 1042-S information reporting** of tax withheld on payments of US-sourced income paid to non-US recipients and FATCA withholding penalties applied to non-compliant, or presumed no-non-compliant, investors
- **Form 1042 tax return**, which is the US tax return required from non-US financial institutions that receive US-sourced income
- **Form 1099 reporting**, which involves reporting tax withheld on payments of US-sourced income paid to US recipients, and
- **Form 945 reporting**, which is the tax return required from non-US financial institution that applied backup withholding to US non-exempt recipients.

Strategic choices to restrict US persons from trading US securities, accompanied by strict procedures, can reduce the reporting burden by removing the


R. K. McGill and K. V. Pitkin, *Qualified Intermediary*,
https://doi.org/10.1007/978-3-031-81410-5_11

need for Form 1099 and Form 945 reporting. However, all qualified intermediaries will need to file Form 1042-S information reports and a Form 1042 tax return at a minimum.

## Form 1042-S Information Reporting

Each withholding agent in the chain of payment for US-sourced income must report that US-sourced income to the IRS on a Form 1042-S, regardless of whether they are acting as a qualified or a nonqualified intermediary. It is a cascade reporting system, in which each withholding agent reports electronically directly to the IRS to disclose:

- Details of each investor that received US-sourced income, including their name, address, tax identification number and US tax status
- The type of income received
- The amount of income received
- The upstream withholding agent that it received the income from
- What tax was withheld
- Who withheld the tax (the primary withholding agent)

The withholding agent then issues a copy to each recipient of US-sourced income within 30 days. This is provided in PDF format.

The IRS can use these reports to construct a record of the entire payment chain to identify any discrepancies between what one withholding agent says that it paid to another, and what that other withholding agent says it paid out to its clients.

1042-S reporting is per client, per income type and per withholding agent. For example, imagine Client A holds US securities at a nonqualified intermediary, that it in turn holds with two different upstream withholding agents: Bank B and Bank C. If Client A receives both dividend and interest income from these securities during the tax year, the nonqualified intermediary will be filing four 1042-S reports (Exhibit 11.1):

- One for the dividend income on assets held with Bank B
- One for the interest received on assets held with Bank B
- One for the dividend income on assets held with Bank C
- One for the interest received on assets held with Bank C

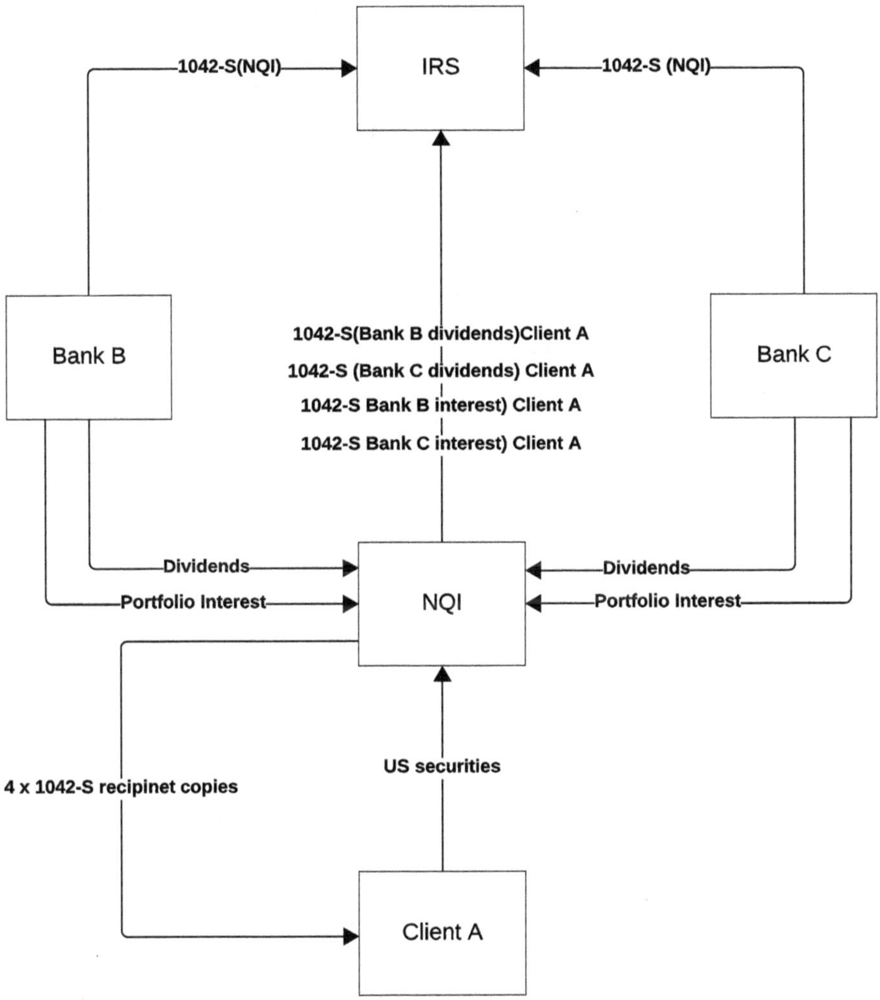


**Exhibit 11.1** Disclosed information returns *Source* Authors

This represents four lines of data in the NQI's 1042-S filing. Bank B and Bank C will each include a single line of data in their 1042-S filing accounting for the income that they paid to the NQI, which the IRS will use in its reconciliations. Any difference in the amount that Bank B or C reported as paid to the NQI and the amount that the NQI paid to its clients will result in a penalty notice to the NQI. It is therefore important for the NQI to check its data against the upstream recipient copies provided by Bank B and C to ensure it matches *before* filing its own 1042-S report with the IRS.

The number of lines of data can get very large, very quickly and the amount of work involved in creating and distributing all those PDF recipient copies also mounts up. This is where the QI Agreement delivers two major operational benefits for qualified intermediaries (Exhibit 11.2):

(i) the ability to pool direct clients for the purpose of reporting, and
(ii) no requirement to provide recipient copies to direct clients, unless a client requests one.

This means that if the QI has 100 clients who all have the same US tax status as Client A, the QI will file **one** 1042-S report per income type, per withholding agent, for the whole group. So, instead of filing 400 lines of 1042-S data and preparing 400 recipient copies, the QI will file just four lines of data representing the whole pool. This is one of the major benefits of QI status in terms of compliance effort (Exhibit 11.3).

There are two caveats. The first is that clients that are financial institutions or flow-through entities such as partnerships and trusts must be reported separately. These cannot be pooled with other clients for the purpose of reporting, as they must receive a recipient copy so that they can reconcile their own reporting with that of their upstream (see Exhibit 11.4). The second is that if the QI accepts disclosing NQIs, each of those disclosed clients must be reported separately and cannot be pooled for the purpose of reporting. Recipient copies will be required for each of these disclosed clients (see Exhibit 11.5).

Exhibit 11.5 shows the difference. Here, BO(1), BO(2) and BO(3) are now customers of a Disclosing NQI (D-NQI). So, the W-8 s that the D-NQI collects are passed on to the QI where they become defined as indirect account holders. The QI can still pool the US assets of these clients for withholding but it must receive a withholding statement from the NQI telling the NQI what rate of tax on which types of income are required. If all the indirect clients are properly documented and specified in a withholding statement, the QI assumes responsibility for including each beneficial owner into its 1042-S return to the IRS and issuing a recipient copy to the beneficial owner. In this case, the QI does not need to issue any 1042-S to the D-NQI because all the income was allocated *past* the NQI to the indirect clients themselves.

Qualified intermediaries often refuse to accept disclosing nonqualified intermediaries as clients because they don't want to take on this extra work. For the NQI, disclosure to a QI is the only way it can obtain treaty benefits for its clients. Without this disclosure, their clients will be automatically taxed at the statutory rate of 30%, as the US views NQIs as potential facilitators of

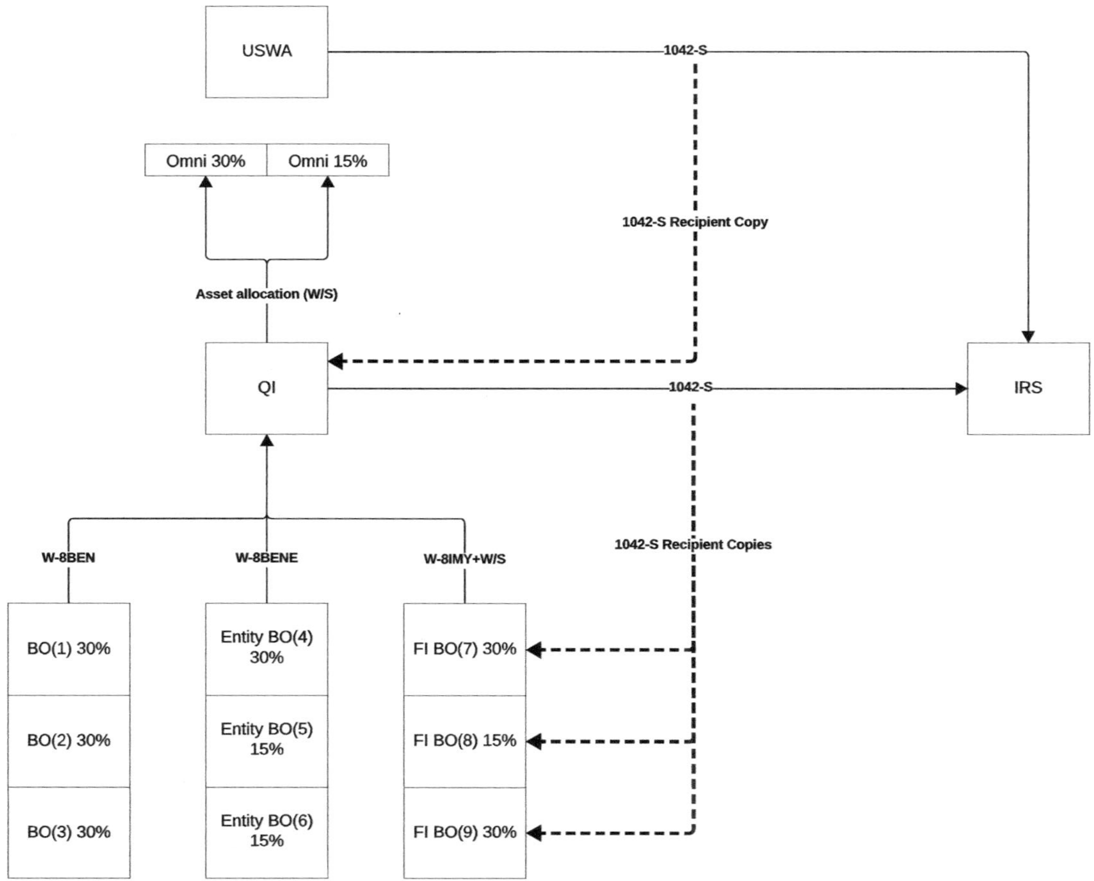


**Exhibit 11.2** Pooled reporting for QIs *Source* Authors

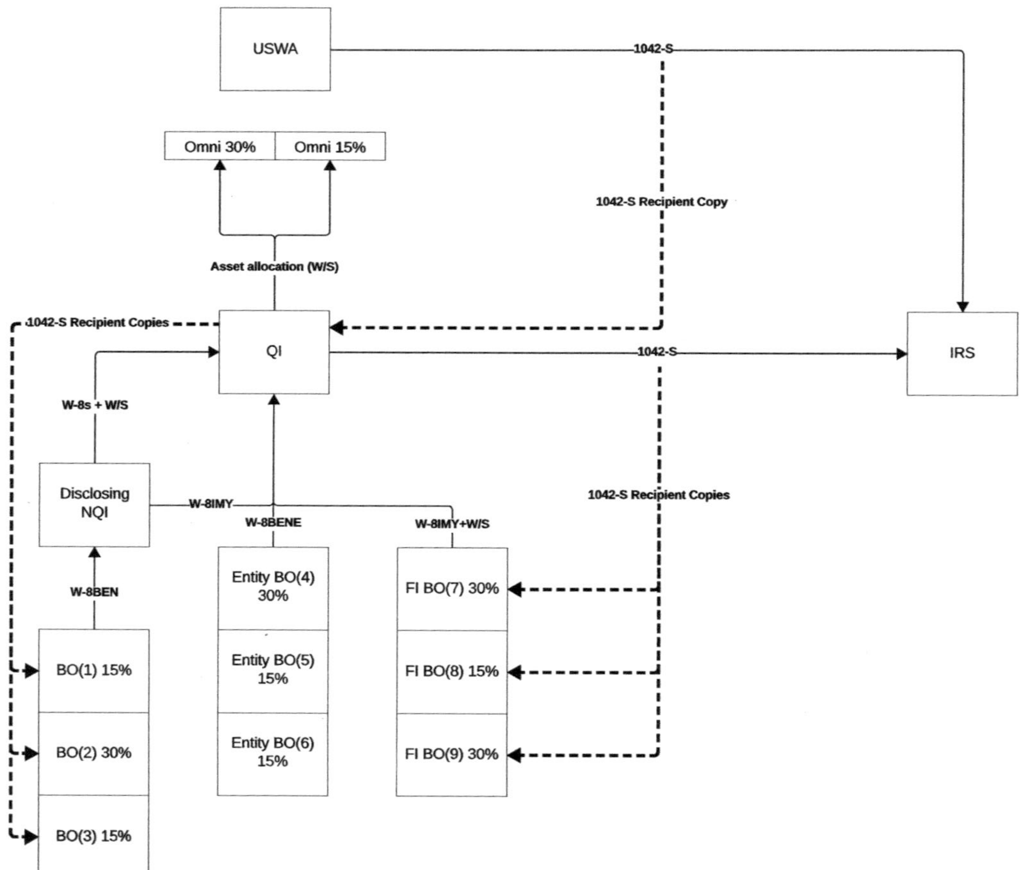


**Exhibit 11.3** Indirect account reporting *Source* Authors

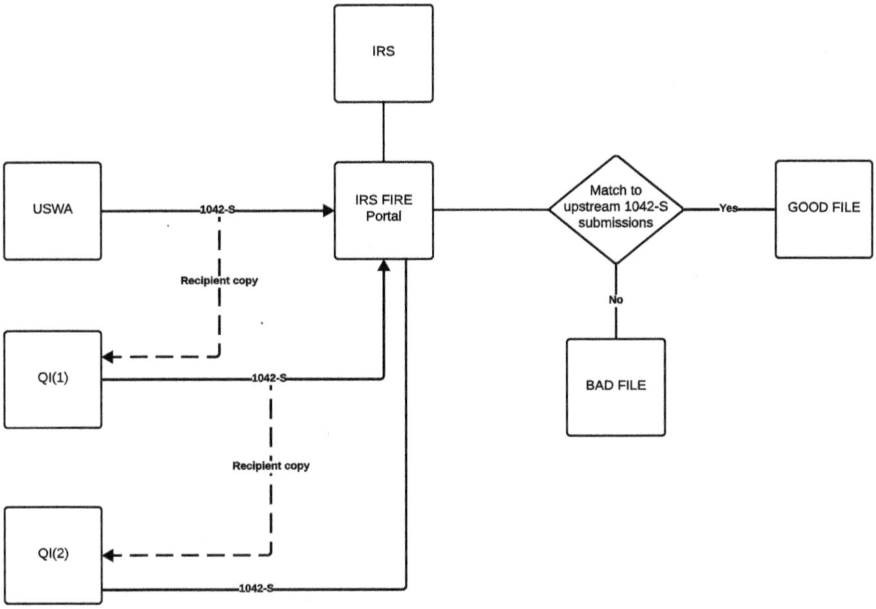


**Exhibit 11.4** Cascade 1042-S information return reporting for QIs *Source* Authors

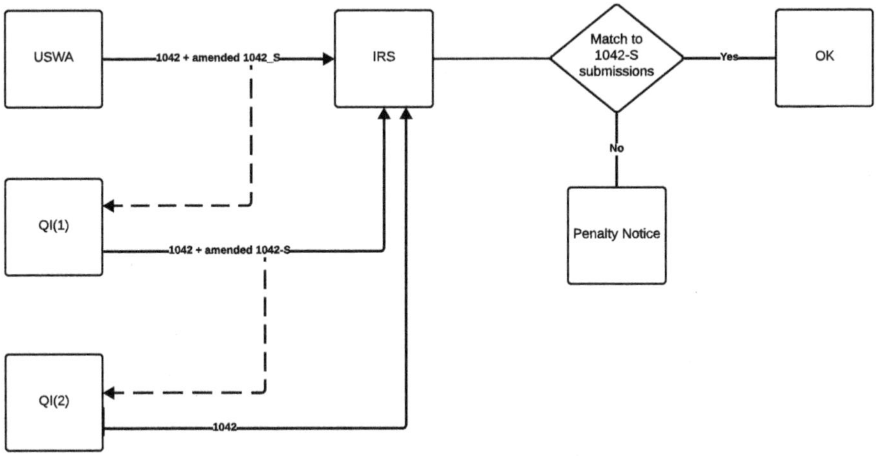


**Exhibit 11.5** 1042 Tax returns *Source* Authors

tax evasion, whereas QIs are trustworthy by virtue of their contract with the IRS.

It is important to note that there is a difference between pooling for the purposes of withholding (discussed in the previous chapter) and pooling for the purposes of reporting. The assets themselves may be pooled in omnibus accounts that are used for the practical administration of withholding, but this does not mean that the income from those assets can be pooled in the reporting.

1042-S reports must be filed electronically in ASCII format. The file is arranged into five sections:

- The **T Record**, which describes the person transmitting the file
- The **W Record**, which describes the withholding agent
- The **Q Records**, which includes the data about who received US-sourced income
- The **C Record**, which provides a reconciliation of all the Q records, and
- The **F Record**, which marks the end of the file.

Full details about how to create the ASCII file are available in Publication 1187, which is updated each year.

Some financial institutions choose to prepare their 1042-S data in an Excel spreadsheet and then get their IT department to convert it into ASCII format. Others use third-party software to create their ASCII file.

All 1042-S reporting to IRS is electronic and conducted at IRS Filing Information Returns Electronically (FIRE) Portal. To file electronically, the QI needs to apply for, and receive, a Transmitter Control Code (TCC), to access this system or use a third-party vendor. With its own TCC to file on their behalf.

There are two major challenges with 1042-S reporting for QIs, even though they benefit from pooled reporting, which simplifies the requirements radically.

The first is caused by the cascade nature of 1042-S reporting. In order to avoid a penalty, the QI's 1042-S filing must match the filing of their upstream withholding agent. To do this, the QI needs the recipient copy issued by that withholding agent showing the amount of income they reported to the IRS as paid to the QI. However, everyone in the payment chain has the same deadline for filing their reports to the IRS: 15th March each year. It is possible to apply for a thirty-day extension, but the reality is that *everyone* in the chain applies for that extension, moving the effective deadline to 14th April. The problem with everyone in the chain sharing a single deadline is that if one withholding agent in the chain leaves it to the last minute to file, all of the downstream intermediaries will not receive their recipient copies in time to perform the necessary checks to ensure that their reporting matches the upstream—leaving them at risk of receiving a penalty notice. While this should not be a problem if the QI has been reconciling its income with statements from its upstream on a regular basis throughout the year, in practice many QIs don't have systems in place to code the data and rely on the 1042-S recipient copy to correctly allocate the income and any exemption codes based on how the upstream has classified the income.

The second challenge is caused by the practice of US issuers re-classifying income after the end of the US tax year. When this happens, the upstream will file an amended 1042-S report to the IRS and send the downstream QI an amended 1042-S recipient copy. This changes a previously issued 1042-S. Amended 1042-S recipient copies are typically issued between April and June each year, usually because of reclassifications of income from US mutual funds or US Real Estate Investment Trusts (known as REITs). They can also be issued if an upstream withholding agent discovers an error that they need to correct.

When a QI receives an amended 1042-S, it must assess the impact of the amendment on any withholding and arrange for additional withholding or refunds, file its own amended 1042-S with the IRS to correct the one it filed earlier, and then issue an amended 1042-S to any of recipients that might need it to adjust their own withholding and reporting. If the QI discovers a mistake in its own reporting after submitting their 1042-S filing in April, it will need to file an amended 1042-S to correct this.

All original and amended 1042-S reports must be filed before the Form 1042 tax return. The deadline for this is 15th March. Again, it is possible to request an extension—this time for six months—thus moving the deadline to the eminently more practical 14th September. *Everyone* requests this extension.

The cascade nature of 1042-S reporting and the practice of amended reporting together create two major crunch points in the year around April and September and extend the time spent on 1042-S reporting over a six-month period. The process is resource intensive, and while solutions exist to outsource the production of the 1042-S report file, the QI must still produce accurate data upon which to base that reporting, which cannot be outsourced.

## Form 1042 Tax Return

Each financial institution in the chain of payment that issues 1042-S information returns must also file a Form 1042 US tax return. This is the summary of the 1042-S reports, together with information about any adjustments you have made to correct any under or over withholding throughout the year.

A QI that also acts as a Qualified Derivatives Dealer (QDD), must complete additional sections, and file Schedule Q with their Form 1042 to reconcile payments withheld under Chapter 1, Sect. 871(m).

The main challenge of the Form 1042 tax return is that it is currently submitted on paper. This might not seem like much of a challenge, but if the QI does not retain proof of postage, it can find itself hit with a late filing penalty if the form is lost in transit.

The IRS is moving towards electronic filing of Form 1042 in XML format via the Modernised e-File (MeF) system. Helpfully, this will mean that QIs need access to two different systems to complete their US tax reporting: the FIRE Portal for Form 1042-S and MeF for Form 1042. The transition to electronic filing was scheduled to come into effect in 2024, but at the time of writing this has been deferred until 2026 to allow the IRS to fix an issue that is emblematic of many of the challenges faced by QIs.

The IRS is—understandably—highly focussed on US taxpayers. Unfortunately, this means that new IT systems are often designed without appropriate consideration for foreign taxpayers, like QIs. The MeF system is one such example. The only way to access MeF is with a US electronic filing identification number (EFIN), which is currently only available to US firms and individuals. This means that unless the QI is part of a group structure that includes a US nexus, it will not be able to access MeF to file its Form 1042 electronically. It will not even be able to download the XML schema to do the necessary preparatory work to create the file, as this is also only accessible to MeF users.

This highlights the need for concerted industry effort to ensure the needs of QIs are considered in these types of modernisation efforts. In 2023, the Association of Qualified and Authorised Intermediaries (AQAI)[1] was established to provide a central trade association to advocate for QIs. At the time of writing, the association has seventy-two members in twenty-eight countries. The association successfully requested a deferral of the introduction of electronic filing for Form 1042 until the IRS has established a mechanism to allow foreign taxpayers to apply for an EFIN to access MeF.

[1] AQAI: https://aqai.tax.

## Form 1099 and Form 945 Reporting

US income paid to a US person or entity must be reported on a Form 1099. There are several different types of Form 1099, depending on the type of income that that the US investor received. For most QIs, the key forms are Form 1099-DIV (used to report dividend income) and Form 1099-INT (used to report interest). Other Form 1099 types are used to report any non-US income that is paid to a US client. The most recent new form 1099 is the 1099-DA to be used for the reporting of digital asset income.

Forms 1099 are filed to the IRS electronically at the FIRE Portal in ASCII format by 31st March each year. The QI must provide a recipient copy of each Form 1099 to the investor by 1st February each year so they can use these to prepare their own domestic US tax return.

The file is arranged into five sections:

- The **T Record**, which describes the person transmitting the file
- The **A Record**, which describes the payer and document type
- The **B Records**, which identify the payee and specific payment amounts
- The **C Record**, which provides a summary of all the B records
- The **K Record**, which is used for State reporting so you can ignore this, and
- The **F Record**, which marks the end of the file.

Full details about how to create a Form 1099 ASCII file are included in Publication 1220, which is updated each year.

Form 945 reporting occurs only if the QI had to apply backup withholding during the calendar year. Backup withholding is required if a US investor has either (i) not provided a valid social security number, or (ii) told you that they are subject to backup withholding on their W-9. The Form 945 report must be filed by 31st January of the following year, or 10th February if the QI deposited the tax on time.

Form 1099 and 945 reporting effectively extend the reporting period from six months (for Forms 1042-S and 1042) to nine months, increasing the cost and resource that QIs need to dedicate to the reporting process. However, there are several ways that a QI can arrange its operations to reduce the impact of Form 1099 and Form 945 reporting.

The first is to implement controls that prevent US persons from trading US securities, thus reducing their Form 1099 reporting and backup withholding obligations entirely. This is a popular strategy, but one that obviously curbs the commercial opportunities that the QI could be exploiting, particularly in markets with large numbers of US expats.

The second is to allow US persons to trade US securities, but implement strict controls to ensure they have a valid social security number that matches the IRS database for every US client and reject Forms W-9 that indicate the client is subject to backup withholding. This reduces the risk that backup withholding and Form 945 reporting will be required but does not remove the QI's Form 1099 reporting obligation.

The third is to disclose its US clients to an upstream withholding agent, thus moving the reporting obligations up to their upstream counterparty. This is done via the Form W-8IMY that the QI uses to document itself to its upstream, where it can indicate that it does not assume primary Form 1099 reporting and backup withholding responsibility. If the QI chooses this option, it must provide a Form W-9 for each US client to its upstream to enable them to carry out Form 1099 reporting and apply any backup withholding that may be required. While the QI Agreement provides the flexibility for the QI to decide whether or not to assume primary Form 1099 reporting and backup withholding responsibility, there may be commercial restrictions imposed by the upstream withholding agent, who may not want to accept the work involved in reporting for the disclosed clients.

# 12

# Control and Oversight

This chapter explains the control and oversight components of the QI Agreement, notably the establishment of certification periods, the requirement to conduct Periodic Reviews and their context in the triennial certification process with the IRS.

In addition to the tax operational aspects of the QI agreement, the contract also has control and oversight provisions. These are contractual obligations to ensure that a QI meets its tax operational obligations.

## Control

The control mechanism is the requirement to appoint a Responsible Officer who is personally responsible for the QI's compliance to the terms of the agreement. This is defined in Section 2.72 and explained in Section 10.02 of the QI Agreement. The primary obligation of the Responsible Officer is to have a written compliance program that transposes the obligations of the QI Agreement into the internal policies and procedures of the firm. This ensures that there is effectively a direct line between the QI Agreement and the practices of the QI at an operational level.

The main obligations of a Responsible Officer are contained in Section 10.02(A)(1)-(7). They include the obligation of the Responsible Officer to (Exhibit 12.1):


R. K. McGill and K. V. Pitkin, *Qualified Intermediary*,
https://doi.org/10.1007/978-3-031-81410-5_12

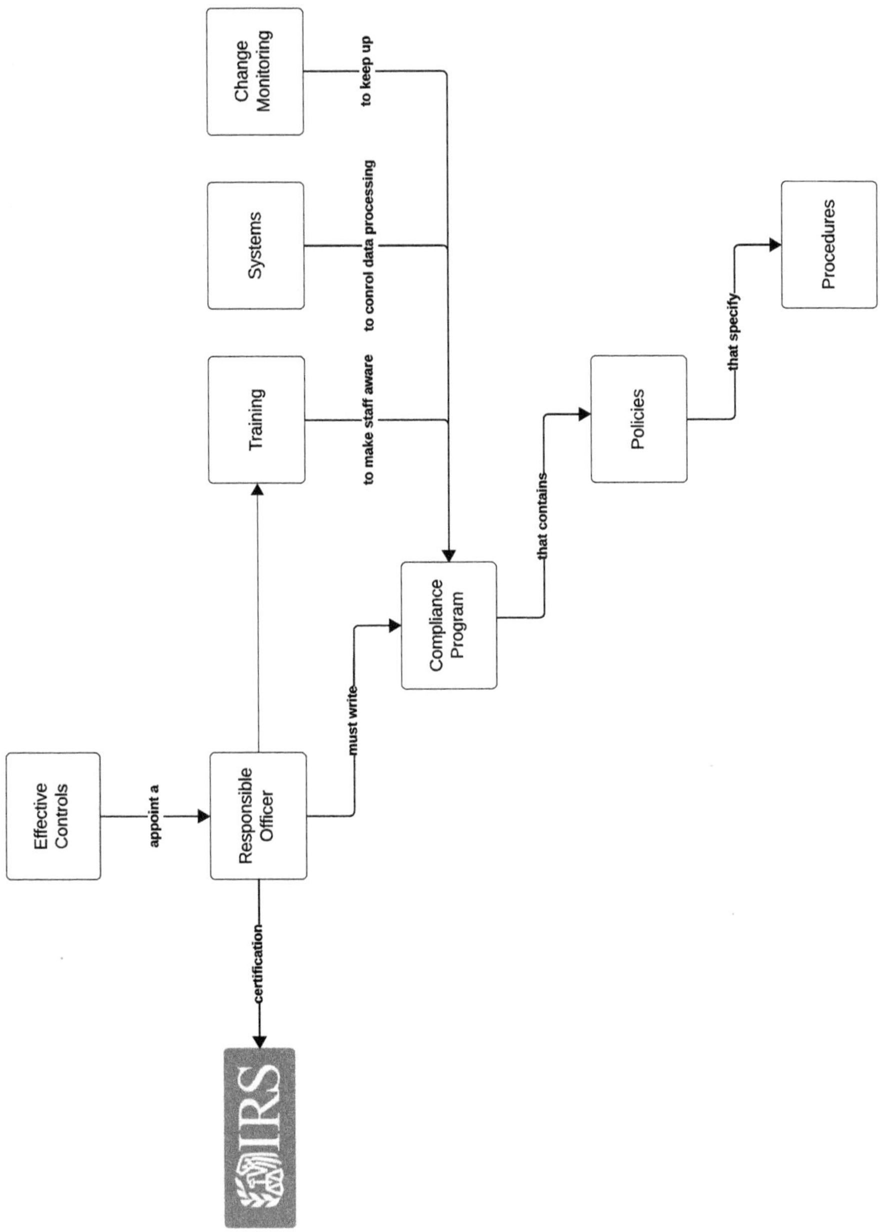


**Exhibit 12.1** Effective control framework for QIs *Source* Authors

1. have a written compliance program document containing policies and procedures by means of which the QI meets its contractual and regulatory obligations[1];
2. provide staff with relevant training concerning the compliance program, particularly with respect to documentation, due diligence, withholding and reporting[2];
3. ensure that systems, typically IT systems, are adequate to meet the withholding and reporting requirements[3];
4. monitor any changes in business practices or circumstances that might affect the compliance of the QI. For example, mergers and acquisitions can affect the exposure of a QI to different parts of the regulations[4];
5. have systems that meet the obligations of a QI that is also a QDD;[5]
6. arrange for the conduct of a Periodic Review with respect to each certification period[6];
7. make a certification of effective controls or a qualified certification every 3 years[7];

In our experience, most, but not all QIs have properly appointed a Responsible Officer. However, it is rare for the Responsible Officer to meet the criteria the IRS stipulates, namely that the Responsible Officer must be of sufficient authority to be able to make changes in the business. Most firms don't prioritise QI compliance and as a result they appoint a lower echelon member of staff to the Responsible Officer position. Without realising it, this puts the QI at greater risk since more senior staff in a variety of departments may make political or operational decisions that do not support compliance to the QI regulations (usually because it would entail additional cost or effort). A cost-cutting or status quo approach within the firm in which change is resisted, even when there is a clear regulatory obligation to change, means the Responsible Officer faces an almost impossible task.

The main challenge for a Responsible Officer is the task of developing a written compliance program. This should clearly state any decisions about how the QI will act and describe the procedures that staff will follow to

[1] Rev. Proc. 2023–43 Sect. 10.02(A)(1).
[2] Rev. Proc. 2023–43 Sect. 10.02(A)(2).
[3] Rev. Proc. 2023–43 Sect. 10.02(A)(3).
[4] Rev. Proc. 2023–43 Sect. 10.02(A)(4).
[5] Rev. Proc. 2023–43 Sect. 10.02(A)(5).
[6] Rev. Proc. 2023–43 Sect. 10.02(A)(6).
[7] Rev. Proc. 2023–43 Sect. 10.02(A)(7).

ensure compliance with the terms of the QI Agreement. This can be a time-consuming process involving representatives any department with a touch point with the QI obligations, such as onboarding, corporate actions, business intelligence, income distributions, tax, legal, reporting and compliance. There may be existing processes that need to be tweaked or significantly revised. There may be entirely new processes that need to be developed, sometimes involving cooperation between departments that don't normally work together. Done well, developing the compliance program is an opportunity to take a holistic look at the firm's operations and ensure that QI compliance is baked in at every level.

Unfortunately, the compliance program is often done badly or not at all. Many QIs fall into the trap of producing a compliance program that simply re-states their obligations and contains only minimal references policy decisions or specific internal procedures that would flow from their obligations. More still fail to keep their compliance program document up to date—it simply gets put in a draw and forgotten about. This is a red flag that shows the Responsible Officer is not actively monitoring changes in the business, assessing their impact on QI compliance, and updating the compliance program accordingly. This usually becomes apparent during a compliance review when we might find significant documentation deficiencies, or during the 1042-S preparation process, when staff might be unable to compile the information that they need to report or to explain any anomalies.

Another significant challenge affects Responsible Officers of QIs are affected by Chapter 1, Sect. 871(m) of the US tax code. Section 871(m) was enacted in 2010 to combat a tax evasion tactic whereby non-US investors would purchase non-US derivative instruments that track US securities, effectively allowing them to derive income from US economic activity, while benefiting from the issuer's lower rate of withholding tax. The regulations require that income from these instruments be taxed as dividend equivalent payments.

The QI Agreement introduced an option for QIs to prevent cascade withholding on dividend equivalent payments by applying to become a qualified derivatives dealer (QDD). A QI can elect to be a QDD if it issues derivative products (typically equity-linked instruments, ETFs, CFDs) that are affected by Sect. 871(m) and it meets certain eligibility criteria, including assuming primary Chapter 3 and 4 withholding responsibility. QDDs benefit from terms in the QI Agreement to help them manage these transactions, including an exemption from withholding on dividend equivalent payments made to QDDs acting as equities dealers.

The rules for QDDs are complex and require the Responsible Officer to have systems in place to identify transactions that are in scope for Sect. 871(m) by performing a series of tests, including (i) determining which party has responsibility for running the following tests and withholding, (ii) determining whether it is a simple or complex contract, (iii) calculating the delta, and (iv) conducting the Substantial Equivalence Test (Exhibit 12.2).

In practice, the requirements are so complex that the industry has successfully lobbied the IRS to delay the full introduction of the rules, originally due in 2017. The introduction of the rules has been delayed five times and is currently due to come into effect on 1st January 2027. Until then, Responsible Officers must demonstrate they meet the Good Faith Efforts standard set out by the IRS in Notice 2016–76.

The Responsible Officer is on the hook for all of this. Personally, they are contractually obliged to enforce effective controls inside the QI, providing the US government with the confidence to allow the QI to grant treaty benefits.

## Oversight

The oversight component of the QI Agreement consists of a Periodic Review and a certification. These allow a QI's Responsible Officer to communicate with the IRS to verify and, as the name implies, certify, that the QI has met all the obligations of the QI Agreement.

### Periodic Review

A periodic review is a mechanical analysis of accounts to determine if the QI properly documented its clients, and correctly withheld, deposited, and reported any US-sourced income in one calendar year of its certification period.

The QI's accounts are grouped into two strata: US accounts that received US-sourced income in the review year and non-US accounts that received US-sourced income in the review year (Exhibit 12.3).

By default, a periodic review will check all accounts in each stratum, but if the number of accounts is prohibitively large (more than sixty accounts per strata), the QI Agreement allows the reviewer to check a sample of accounts instead. The QI Agreement provides a standard sampling methodology (known as the "safe harbor" method) but allows the reviewer to choose their own method—provided that they record their sampling procedure and maintain the ability to reconstruct the sample, upon request.

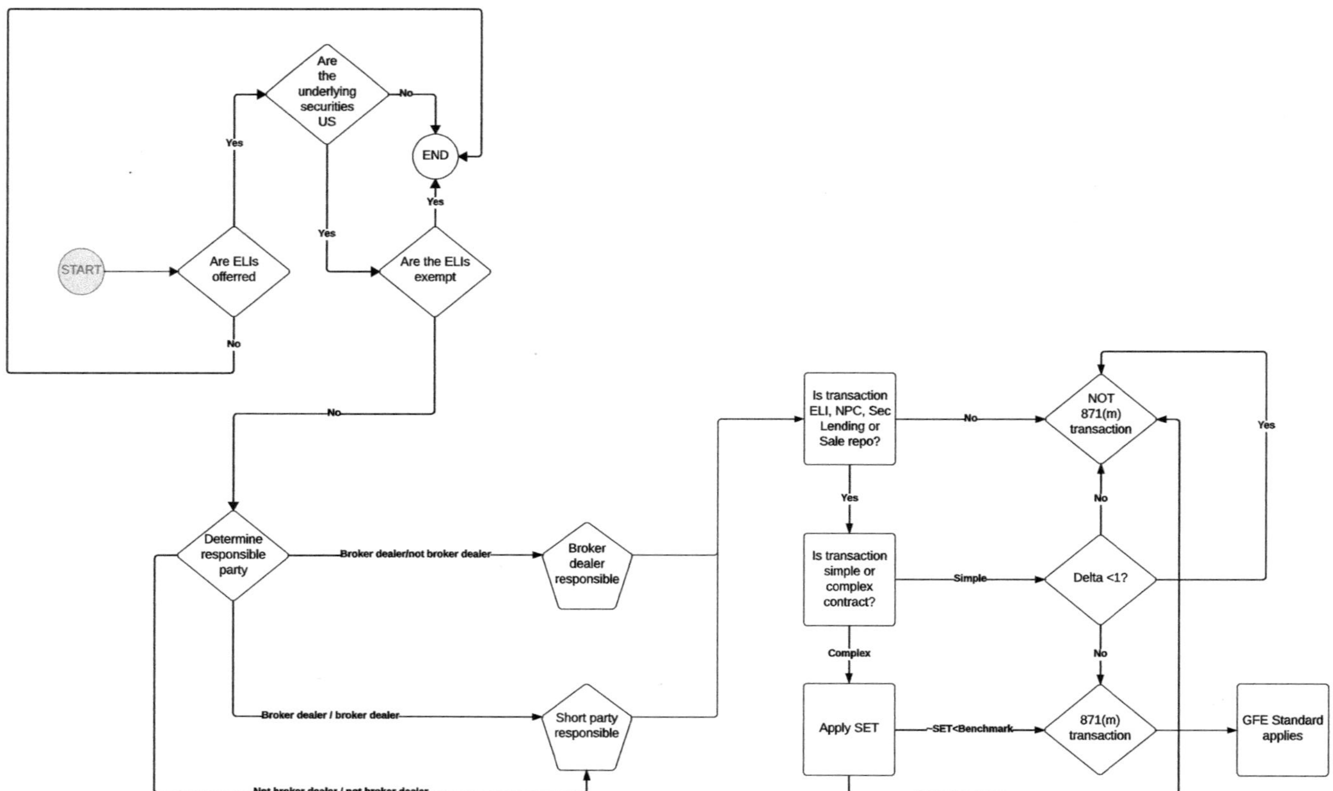


**Exhibit 12.2** Obligations to assess 871(m) applicability *Source* Authors

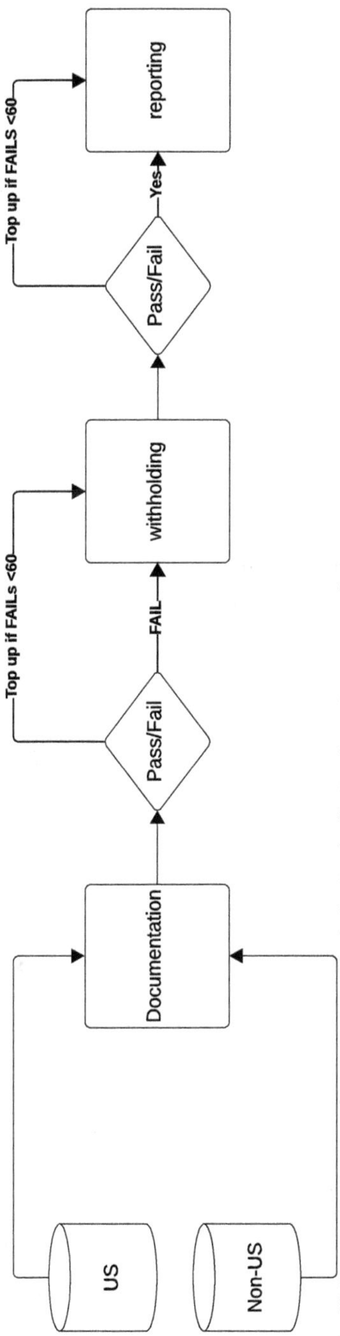


**Exhibit 12.3** Mechanism of account analysis in Periodic Review *Source* Authors

The periodic review differs from an audit in that the QI Agreement sets out a series of specific tests that the reviewer must perform. These are described in in Section 10.05, but broadly these are designed to test:

- The documentation that the QI holds for each account
- The transaction records of each account that received US-sourced FDAP income in the review year
- The 1042-S information reports, and
- The Form 1042 tax return

A periodic review can be a costly and labour-intensive process for a QI, involving gathering and presenting evidence for the reviewer. This must be repeated every 3 years unless the QI qualifies for a waiver, or more frequently if the IRS requests a limited periodic review in response to known deficiencies in the QI's compliance.

A QI can apply for a waiver if it is not a QDD or part of a consolidated compliance program, does not receive reportable amounts of more than $5 million of reportable income in any year of the certification period and has met all its reporting obligations. The IRS can reject a request for a waiver but will grant the QI an extra 6 months to complete its periodic review in such circumstances.

If the QI does not receive a waiver, it must arrange for an independent, competent reviewer to conduct the periodic review with respect to one of the 3 years in their certification period. This can be an external auditor, internal auditor or a third-party consultant.

Achieving independence is a key challenge when selecting a periodic reviewer. The IRS does not provide clear guidance on what it considers to be an acceptable level of independence, so this is left to the judgement of the Responsible Officer. We often find firms engage a consultant to support them with their QI compliance and appoint the same firm (or a different branch or department of the same firm) to conduct their periodic review. To us, this is clearly does not represent independence.

Similarly, the IRS does not define what it deems "competent". Again, the Responsible Officer must make this assessment. It may be tempting to use an internal audit function, but if they lack the specialist knowledge of the QI regime, they may not be considered competent.

Aside from identifying a suitably independent and competent reviewer, the main challenges associated with a periodic review are the cost and the resources required. We frequently see qualified intermediaries fail to allocate sufficient budget and staff time to prepare and support the review. This can be exacerbated if the QI does not have good recordkeeping practices, as staff will struggle to produce the necessary documentation. The QI Agreement does allow the QI to submit additional documentation to cure any failures identified in the reviewer's report, but the findings of the periodic must be reported to the IRS both pre- and post-cure. The periodic review report must also state the dates when curative materials were produced, which can give the IRS a revealing insight into the QI's efficiency. A lack of resource can also result in delays to the delivery of the periodic review report, which can affect the QI's ability to make its certification to the IRS on time.

## Certification

As already discussed, the QI Agreement is a contract that lasts for 6 years. For oversight purposes, it is divided into two certification periods of 3 years each. At the end of each certification period, the Responsible Officer must submit a certification to the IRS including information drawn from the periodic review report.

The deadline for the certification varies depending which year the Responsible Officer selected for its periodic review. If they choose Year 1 or Year 2 of the certification period for the periodic review, then the deadline for certification is 1st July of the year after the certification period has ended. If they choose Year 3 for the periodic review, then the deadline for certification is 31st December of the year after the certification period has ended (Exhibit 12.4).

In reality, almost everyone chooses Year 3 for their periodic review—particularly in their first certification period as a QI, because this is the year where the QI is most likely to have resolved any teething problems encountered in the first 2 years as a QI, giving them the best chance of a good report.

The Responsible Officer must look at the results of the periodic review and any other information they deem relevant and decide what type of certification they will make. This might include training records, policies and procedures, internal reports and compliance reviews.

Based on this evidence, the Responsible Officer has two options:

1. A **Certification of Effective Internal Controls**. This is the ideal certification. The Responsible Officer tells the IRS that the QI has established an effective compliance program and conducted a periodic review that either found no problems or found problems that were identified and corrected before the review, thus demonstrating that the controls worked.

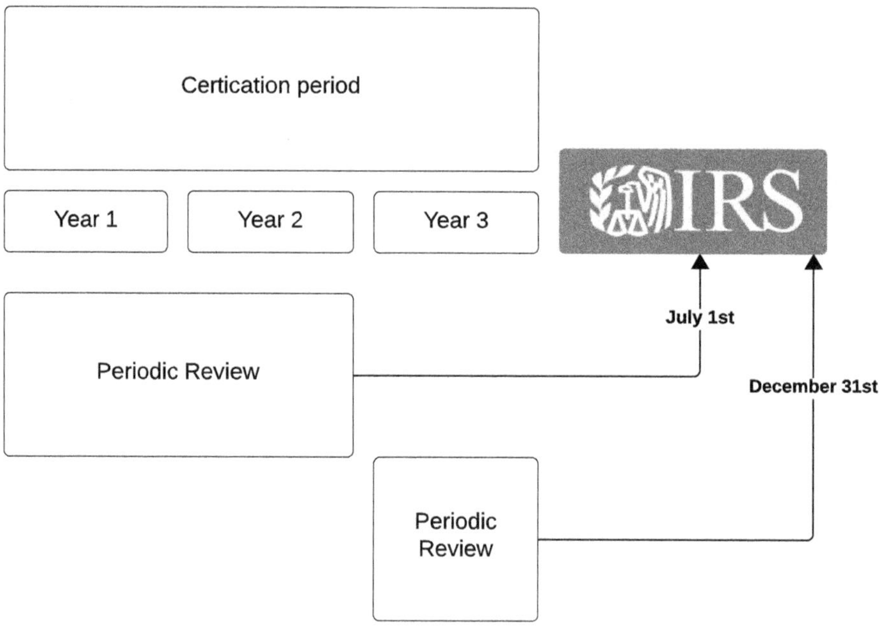


**Exhibit 12.4** Calculating delivery of certification of effective controls *Source* Authors

2. A **Qualified Certification**. This is bad. A QI must make a qualified certification when the Responsible Officer deems that they have not established an effective compliance program, or when the periodic review finds problems that the QI did not identify and correct.

It is important to note that while the periodic review only looks at one year, the certification covers the whole 3-year certification period. This means that if the Responsible Officer is aware of problems that occurred at any point in the certification period, and those issues have not been cured, then they must make a qualified certification, even if the periodic review is perfect.

A qualified certification must be accompanied by a remediation plan and a personal attestation from the responsible officer committing to fix the issues. An effective remediation plan takes time to develop and is difficult to produce at short notice if the periodic review takes place very close to the certification deadline. The IRS will assess the remediation plan and may require extra measures to improve compliance. This can take some time, as the IRS department that manages the QI program is relatively small. The IRS expects the QI to implement its remediation plan straight away, rather than waiting for approval, and then make any further changes at their request later. In our experience, members of the IRS QI team are always keen to stress that they want QIs to succeed and will work with them to help them achieve compliance when they receive a qualified certification.

Both types of certifications must be accompanied by "Factual Information", which is defined in the Annex of the QI Agreement. Much of this Factual Information comes from the periodic review report, so while smaller QIs that qualify for a waiver may save on the time and expense of commissioning a periodic review, they are still required to calculate the figures required for their certification.

The certification is made under penalty of perjury by the Responsible Officer, so they are personally liable for the statements that they make on behalf of the firm to the US government. This brings us full circle: the Responsible Officer is the key control mechanism that the IRS mandates in the QI Agreement, with responsibility for ensuring that the IRS has sufficient information every 3 years to exercise effective oversight over the QI. This allows the IRS to determine if the QI has failed in its contractual obligations and take appropriate enforcement action, which is the subject of our next chapter.

# 13

# Enforcement

This chapter describes the penalties that the IRS can apply for non-compliance, a description of the typical failures found and some case studies describing how such failures can be remediated.

The QI Agreement is enforced through two mechanisms: domestic legislation and contractual obligations.

Clearly US law does not apply to financial institutions outside the US, so the IRS has no way to sanction QIs directly. To combat this, the QI Agreement leverages domestic law to ensure that the documentation requirements necessary for accurate relief at source are met. Financial institutions are only eligible to apply for QI status if they are based in a jurisdiction with KYC rules that have been approved by the IRS.[1] This means that the IRS can rely on domestic KYC regulation that meets its required standard to ensure that the QI will be sanctioned if a breach occurs. Local enforcement for KYC violations varies but will generally result in reputational damage and financial penalties.

Layered on top of the requirements of domestic legislation sit the contractual terms of the QI Agreement, which include financial penalties paid directly to the IRS and the ultimate sanction: loss of QI status. The IRS does not publish details of QIs that have been stripped of this status and instead emphasises its support for struggling QIs to bring them into compliance. While this is usually collaborative, the QI Agreement does provide powers

[1] IRS List of approved KYC rules: https://www.irs.gov/businesses/international-businesses/list-of-approved-kyc-rules.


R. K. McGill and K. V. Pitkin, *Qualified Intermediary*,
https://doi.org/10.1007/978-3-031-81410-5_13

for the IRS to request a replacement Responsible Officer if the one appointed by the firm has not complied with their obligations, and to pre-emptively request remediation or the conduct of a limited periodic review. The IRS can also conduct fact finding via a correspondence review, which can include phone or video interviews with staff if it has concerns.

The QI Agreement sets out the types of failure that will trigger enforcement action. These are grouped into two categories: Material Failures and Events of Default.

Material failures are described in Sect. 10.03(B) of the QI Agreement. A Material Failure is a failure to fulfil the requirements of the QI Agreement, including any failure to comply with FATCA. These include:

- Establishing a tax reserve against future liability (i.e., planning to fail)
- Failure to establish written policies and procedures, or
- Receiving criminal or civil penalties from a regulator or government with respect to KYC or AML violations (Exhibit 13.1).

These failures do not have any limitations. However, other Material Failures *are* limited and are only classed as material if they result from the deliberate actions of an employee of the QI. These include the failure for one or more years to:

- Withhold correctly
- Provide others with proper documentation
- Make deposits in a timely manner or
- Report correctly

Determining whether a failure was the result of a deliberate action of an employee or not can be difficult. We usually find that these types of errors occur due to a lack of appropriate systems and procedures, which result in genuine errors. However, if any of these issues occur on a systemic level, this can represent a deliberate failure on the part of the Responsible Officer for neglecting their duty to establish effective controls. For example, a Responsible Officer may choose to deliberately over withhold by taxing all clients at the statutory rate of 30%, regardless of any treaty claim. This may seem like a risk averse approach to avoid the chance of accidental underwithholding. However, the obligation of the QI is to withhold *correctly*, so systemic over-withholding is still a material failure even if it is to the financial advantage of the US Treasury. Remember, that the purpose of the QI regime is to outsource the administration of relief at source. Systemic over withholding

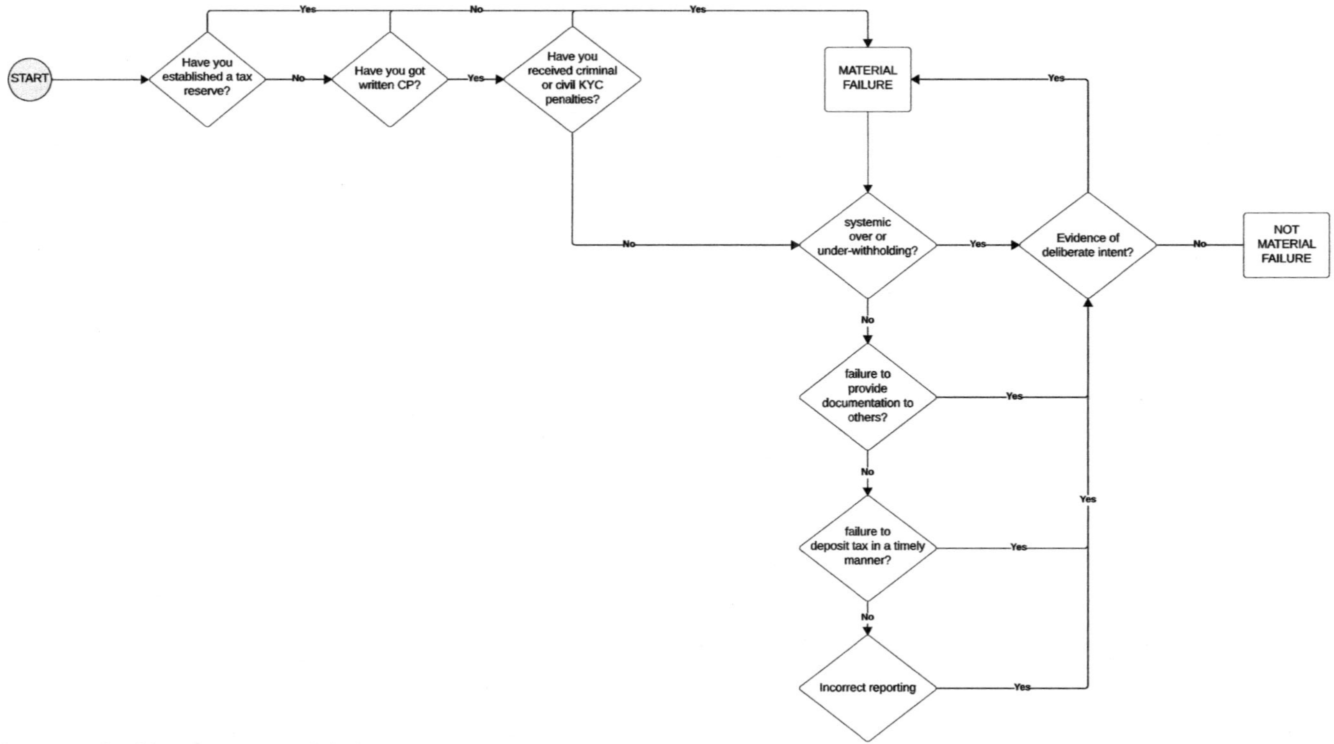


**Exhibit 13.1** Checklist for material failures *Source* Authors

will lead to an increase in the number of tax reclaims made directly to the IRS by investors who should have benefited from a treaty claim administered by the QI, thus resulting in an administrative burden which could lead the IRS to investigate the QI's operations.

Events of Default are described in Sect. 11.06 of the QI Agreement. There are nineteen subsections that define Events of Default, but the relevant ones for most QIs are:

- Failure to implement adequate procedures
- Underwithholding a material amount
- Making excessive reclaims to correct over withholding
- Failure to hold sufficient reliable documentation for a significant number of accounts
- Submitting materially incorrect or fraudulent reports to the IRS
- Failure to meet FATCA requirements
- Failure to perform a Periodic Review
- Failure to cooperate with the IRS
- Failure to inform the IRS of a change to your jurisdiction's KYC rules
- Failure to cure a Material Failure
- Making fraudulent statements or misrepresenting material facts when communicating with the IRS.

The Responsible Officer should disclose Events of Default to the IRS when they happen. The IRS will then trigger a notice and cure procedure, which is described in Sect. 11.07 of the QI Agreement. The IRS will issue a notice for each Event of Default and the QI must respond within 60 days of the date on the notice to propose a cure. If the IRS does not receive a response, it will issue a termination notice. If the IRS is not satisfied by the QI's proposed cure, it may offer a counter proposal, which the QI must implement within 30 days to avoid a termination notice.

The Responsible Officer does not need to notify the IRS if the Event of Default was discovered during a periodic review, provided that the periodic review report describes the cure action.

This system is flawed because it relies on the QI to notify the IRS of an Event of Default. If the QI does not spot a problem or chooses to ignore it, the IRS has no proactive way to detect Events of default, other than through reporting failures or the periodic review process.

## Penalties

The main financial penalties relate to reporting. These penalties are calculated on a per-form basis for each incorrect, late, or missing 1042-S or 1099 report. The penalty amount is capped, unless the IRS deems the QI to be in "intentional disregard".

Given that QIs can pool their reporting for direct clients, they may only have a small number of Forms 1042-S to file, which reduces the risk of large penalties. However, if the QI offers accounts to other financial intermediaries that disclose their clients, these disclosed clients must be reported separately—drastically increasing the financial risk to the QI in the event of a penalty notice.

The penalty for late filing of the Form 1042 tax return is 5% of any unpaid tax per month, up to a maximum of 25%. The penalty for late payment of tax is 1.5% of the unpaid tax, again up to a maximum of 25%. These penalties can be applied on top of each other, so if the QI does not pay the tax on time *and* files its Form 1042 late, then it can end up paying a penalty of 6.5% of any unpaid tax per month. The filing penalties for Forms 1099 and 945 that are used to report income paid to US clients work in a similar way.

These penalties will accrue interest. We have encountered QIs that have received penalty notices of up to $1 million that resulted from late filing penalties that were not paid and therefore built up over time—sometimes accruing interest over a nearly 10-year period. This is a particular risk in jurisdictions where English is not the first language, as the IRS penalty notices may be misunderstood and therefore ignored.

Reporting penalties are not exclusively for qualified intermediaries. Nonqualified intermediaries can also incur reporting penalties. This can be problematic if the NQI later decides to apply for QI status, as the IRS will consider the financial institution's prior compliance as an NQI before approving a QI application. Any outstanding penalty notices must be paid in full before the application can progress.

The IRS only issues financial penalties in relation to the reporting part of the QI operational cycle and relies on domestic regulators to apply appropriate penalties in relation to KYC deficiencies. Withholding and depositing do not have any specific financial penalties, but deficiencies in these areas are usually identified through reporting. The IRS will compare the amounts reported as paid to the QI by an upstream withholding agent with the QI's own reporting and will issue a penalty notice if the amounts do not match. The IRS will also check the reporting against the amount of tax actually deposited and will again issue penalties if there are discrepancies. Thus, the whole cycle of activity is captured with penalties for non-compliance.

If financial penalties don't work, the ultimate sanction that the IRS can impose for non-compliance is to revoke a qualified intermediary's QI status. This can cause reputational damage and result in the QI losing all the competitive advantages that it gained by becoming a QI, such as the ability to offer treaty benefits to their clients without disclosing them to a competitor or the IRS and the ability to use pooled reporting. Historically, the IRS has not published figures on the number of QIs that have been left the QI program—voluntarily or forcibly. However, the 2023 version of the QI Agreement introduced the concept of a register of qualified intermediaries. This was released in October 2024 and enables QIs to verify other financial institutions that represent themselves as QIs. The list will be updated quarterly, giving the sector more insight into the degree of movement in and out of the program. While some QIs will give up their status voluntarily due to internal changes (e.g., acquisitions and mergers, closure of business lines), it should be possible to identify those that have lost their status as a result of enforcement action. This may provide an extra deterrent to QIs that choose not to invest in compliance.

# Part III

## OECD

# 14

# Structure

This chapter provides an overview of the OECD's efforts in the tax space, notably in AEoI/CRS, TRACE and BEPS.

The Organisation for Economic Co-operation and Development (OECD) is a non-governmental body comprising thirty-eight member countries.[1] The OECD works in several areas, including finance and tax.

The aspects of the OECD's work on tax that are of interest to is in this book are structured in a way that broadly mirrors the US approach.

On the cross-border tax front, the OECD introduced its Tax Relief and Compliance Enhancement (TRACE) framework in 2013. This provides member countries with a standardised model to implement their own qualified intermediary-style regime to apply tax relief at source via financial institutions that have been appointed by tax administrations as authorised intermediaries (AIs).

On the anti-tax evasion front, the OECD also has its own version of FATCA: the Automatic Exchange of Information. This enables member countries to exchange information about overseas accounts held by their tax residents. This information is shared using the Common Reporting Standard (CRS), based on data provided by financial institutions in each country.

In addition to these two broad frameworks, the OECD has developed other important initiatives including the Global Minimum Tax (GMT) initiative, which is a part of Pillar 2 of the OECD's Base Erosion and Profit

[1] OECD—Members and partners: https://www.oecd.org/about/members-and-partners/.


R. K. McGill and K. V. Pitkin, *Qualified Intermediary*,
https://doi.org/10.1007/978-3-031-81410-5_14

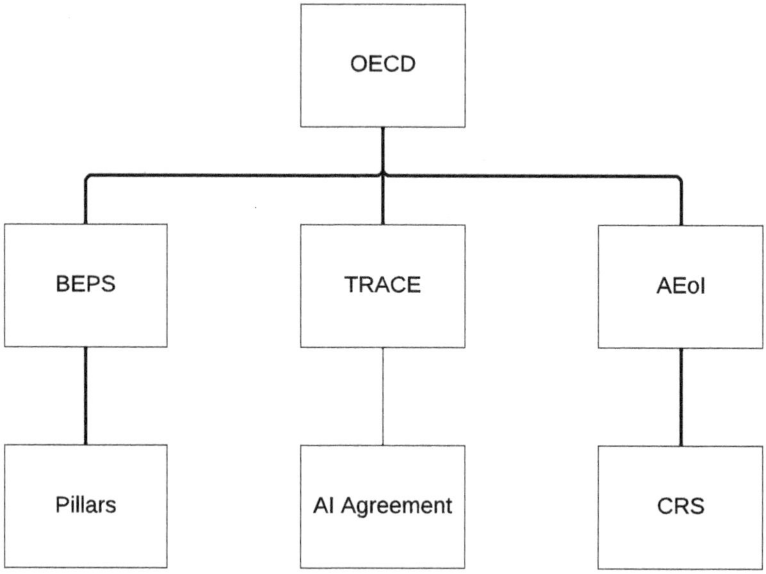


**Exhibit 14.1** OECD tax initiatives *Source* Authors

Shifting (BEPS) framework. BEPS is concerned with addressing corporate tax evasion conducted by MNEs by shifting profits to lower tax jurisdictions. GMT reduces tax rate differentials between jurisdictions to an effective minimum tax rate of 15% tax in each jurisdiction, no matter where it operates, which has potential impacts on the allocation of investment and activity of Multinational Enterprises (MNEs).

Supporting all these frameworks, the OECD has worked on and publishes the Model Tax Convention that many countries use as the basis of their DTAs.

The OECD cannot implement any of these structures directly, but instead develops templates that member countries can choose to adopt into their own domestic law. As such, they can be adapted to meet local requirements. For example, TRACE provides a model for an Authorised Intermediary Agreement (as shown in Exhibit 14.1) that provides similar contractual protections to the US QI Agreement. However, the first country to implement TRACE (Finland) has chosen not to adopt this particular aspect of the framework, as we will discuss in a later chapter. Most countries just make small tweaks to the model frameworks, such as shifting reporting deadlines to accommodate local events or requesting additional data elements. As such, the OECD produces "standards" that operate more as suggestions, allowing member countries to modernise their tax systems in a way that aligns with the rest of the community without reinventing the wheel.

The OECD carries out peer review and monitoring work on these frameworks via the OECD Forum on Harmful Tax Practices[2] to determine if anything implemented in a member country could be harmful to the tax base of other jurisdictions. This provides a mechanism for improving cooperation between OECD members on tax matters and establishing international norms.

[2] OECD – Harmful tax practices: https://www.oecd.org/en/topics/harmful-tax-practices.html.

# 15

# Background

This chapter gives an historical timeline to each of the OECD's initiatives with commentary on each from a global convergence perspective.

The Organisation for Economic Co-operation and Development (OECD) has played a pivotal role in shaping international tax policies and addressing the challenges posed by an increasingly globalised economy. This timeline traces the evolution of OECD tax initiatives, highlighting key milestones and developments that have significantly influenced global tax practices.

## 1961: Establishment of the OECD

The OECD was founded in 1961 as a successor to the Organisation for European Economic Co-operation (OEEC), which was initially created to administer the Marshall Plan[1] after World War II. The OECD's primary aim was to promote economic progress and world trade. It has since adopted a pivotal and central role in the discussion of and development of global tax policy including the Model Tax Convention which is the basis of all but a few double tax treaties (DTTs).

[1] The "Marshall Plan" speech at Harvard University, 5th June 1947. OCED. https://www.oecd.org/en/about/history/the-marshall-plan-speech-at-harvard-university-5-june-1947.html.


R. K. McGill and K. V. Pitkin, *Qualified Intermediary*,
https://doi.org/10.1007/978-3-031-81410-5_15

## 1963: OECD Model Tax Convention

One of the first major tax initiatives by the OECD was the publication of the Model Tax Convention on Income and on Capital in 1963. This convention provided a template for bilateral tax treaties between countries, aiming to eliminate double taxation and prevent tax evasion. The Model Tax Convention has since undergone numerous revisions to address evolving economic realities and tax avoidance strategies.[2]

## 1977: Revision of the Model Tax Convention

The 1977 revision of the Model Tax Convention included significant updates to the original document, reflecting changes in international trade and investment. This version introduced key concepts such as the "permanent establishment" and clarified rules on the taxation of business profits, dividends, interest and royalties.

## 1981: Transfer Pricing Guidelines

In response to growing concerns about multinational enterprises (MNEs) shifting profits to low-tax jurisdictions, the OECD released its first Transfer Pricing Guidelines in 1981. These guidelines provided a framework for pricing transactions between related entities to ensure that profits were appropriately taxed where economic activities occurred.

## 1988: Convention on Mutual Administrative Assistance in Tax Matters

The OECD promotes exchange of information upon request (EOIR) in tax matters, leading to the establishment of the Convention on Mutual Administrative Assistance in Tax Matters.[3]

---

[2] The latest version can be found at https://doi.org/10.1787/9a5b369e-en.

[3] See https://legalinstruments.oecd.org/en/instruments/OECD-LEGAL-0235.

## 1998: Harmful Tax Competition Report

The OECD's 1998 report on "Harmful Tax Competition: An Emerging Global Issue"[4] marked a significant step in addressing the problem of tax havens and harmful tax practices. The report identified harmful tax practices that eroded the tax bases of other countries and set out recommendations for countering these practices. This initiative laid the groundwork for future efforts to combat tax avoidance and evasion.

## 2000: Global Forum on Transparency and Exchange of Information for Tax Purposes

In 2000, the OECD established the Global Forum on Transparency and Exchange of Information for Tax Purposes. This forum brought together OECD and non-OECD countries to promote transparency and the exchange of information between tax authorities. It aimed to curb tax evasion by ensuring that tax authorities had access to the information they needed to enforce tax laws.

## 2002: Model Agreement on Exchange of Information on Tax Matters

To facilitate international cooperation in tax matters, the OECD developed the Model Agreement on Exchange of Information on Tax Matters[5] in 2002. This agreement provided a template for bilateral and multilateral agreements, enabling countries to share information relevant to tax investigations and audits.

## 2008–2009: Global Financial Crisis

The global financial crisis emphasised the need for greater financial transparency and cooperation among tax authorities.

[4] OECD. (1998). *Harmful Tax Competition: An Emerging Global Issue*. https://doi.org/10.1787/9789264162945-en.

[5] OECD, (2002). Model Agreement on Exchange of Information on Tax Matters. https://doi.org/10.1787/97892641110496-8-en.

## 2013: BEPS Action Plan

One of the most significant OECD tax initiatives of the twenty-first century is the Base Erosion and Profit Shifting (BEPS) project, launched in 2013. The BEPS Action Plan outlined fifteen actions to address tax avoidance strategies that exploit gaps and mismatches in tax rules to artificially shift profits to low or no-tax locations. The BEPS project aimed to ensure that profits are taxed where economic activities generating the profits are performed and where value is created.

G20 leaders endorsed the OECD's proposal to develop a global standard for the automatic exchange of financial account information.

## 2014: CRS

The OECD released the Common Reporting Standard (CRS), outlining the information to be exchanged, the financial institutions required to report, and the types of accounts and taxpayers covered. Over one hundred jurisdictions committed to implementing the CRS, agreed to begin exchanging information by 2017 or 2018.

## 2015: Final BEPS Reports

In 2015, the OECD released the final reports for the fifteen BEPS actions. These reports provided detailed recommendations and best practices for governments to implement in their domestic tax laws. Key areas addressed included transfer pricing, hybrid mismatch arrangements, harmful tax practices and treaty abuse. The BEPS project marked a major step forward in international tax cooperation and transparency.

## 2016: Inclusive Framework on BEPS

To broaden participation in the BEPS project, the OECD established the Inclusive Framework on BEPS in 2016. This framework allowed over one hundred countries and jurisdictions to collaborate on implementing BEPS measures and monitoring their effectiveness. The Inclusive Framework ensured that developing countries had a voice in the development of international tax standards.

The first wave of early adopter jurisdictions started collecting data under CRS.

The OECD established the Global Forum on Transparency and Exchange of Information for Tax Purposes to monitor and support CRS implementation.

## 2017: First CRS Exchanges

The first exchanges of information under CRS took place among early adopter jurisdictions. Additional jurisdictions began collecting data for exchange starting in 2018.

## 2018: Interim Report on the Tax Challenges of Digitalisation

The rapid digitalisation of the global economy posed new challenges for international tax policy, particularly concerning the allocation of taxing rights. In 2018, the OECD released an interim report on the tax challenges arising from digitalisation, identifying key issues and potential approaches to address them. This report set the stage for further discussions on how to tax digital businesses fairly and effectively.

The second wave of jurisdictions began exchanging information under CRS. The OECD published the first CRS Implementation Handbook, providing guidance to jurisdictions and financial institutions.

## 2019: Updated CRS Guidelines

The OECD released updated CRS guidelines and a report on the impact of AEoI on tax compliance. Jurisdictions continued to enhance their CRS frameworks, including expanding the scope of reportable information.

## 2020: Pillar One and Pillar Two Blueprints

Building on the work of the BEPS project and the 2018 interim report, the OECD released blueprints for Pillar One and Pillar Two in 2020. Pillar One focussed on reallocating taxing rights to market jurisdictions, ensuring that multinational enterprises paid taxes where they had significant consumer-facing activities. Pillar Two proposed a global minimum tax to address remaining BEPS issues and prevent a "race to the bottom" in corporate tax rates.

## 2021: Historic Agreement on Global Minimum Tax

In July 2021, the OECD announced a historic agreement endorsed by over one hundred and thirty countries to implement a global minimum corporate tax rate of at least 15%. This agreement aimed to ensure that large multinational enterprises paid a minimum level of tax, regardless of where they were headquartered or operated. The global minimum tax represented a significant achievement in the fight against tax avoidance and base erosion.

The OECD explored expanding CRS to cover new financial products and assets, such as cryptocurrencies, to address emerging risks and ensure comprehensive reporting.

## 2022: Implementation Framework for Pillar One and Pillar Two

Throughout 2022, the OECD worked on developing an implementation framework for the Pillar One and Pillar Two agreements. This framework provided detailed guidance for countries on how to incorporate the new rules into their domestic tax systems and ensure consistent application across jurisdictions. The implementation framework aimed to facilitate the smooth transition to the new international tax landscape. Ongoing efforts to enhance and refine the CRS framework, including updates to technical guidance, addressing challenges in implementation and ensuring robust data protection measures.

What this timeline does is remind us that compliance is not a static thing. It evolves over time and so, a challenge for most financial institutions. Will be to monitor changes and, for each change, assess the effect on the institution (Exhibit 15.1).

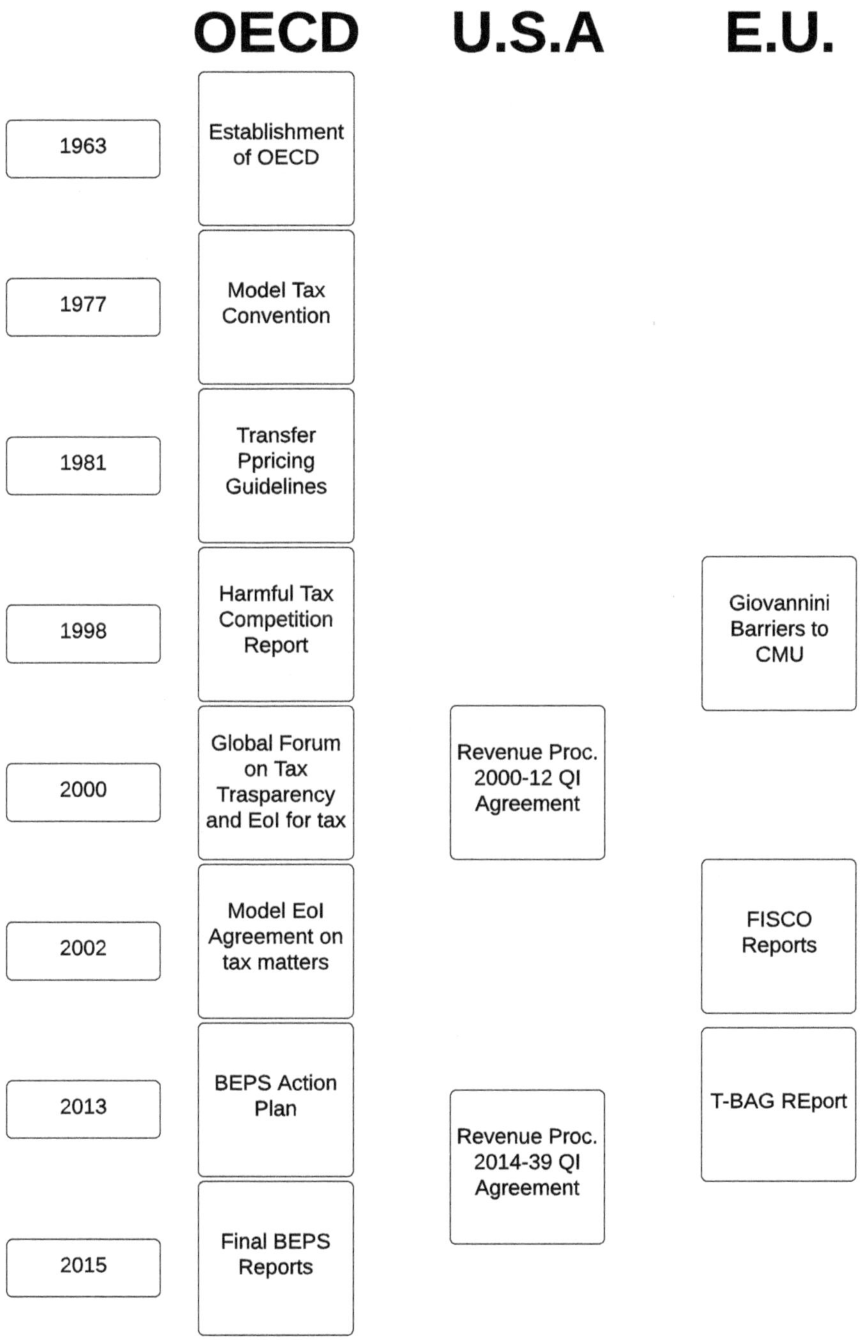


**Exhibit 15.1** History of OECD Progress on tax matters with US and EU for comparison *Source* Authors

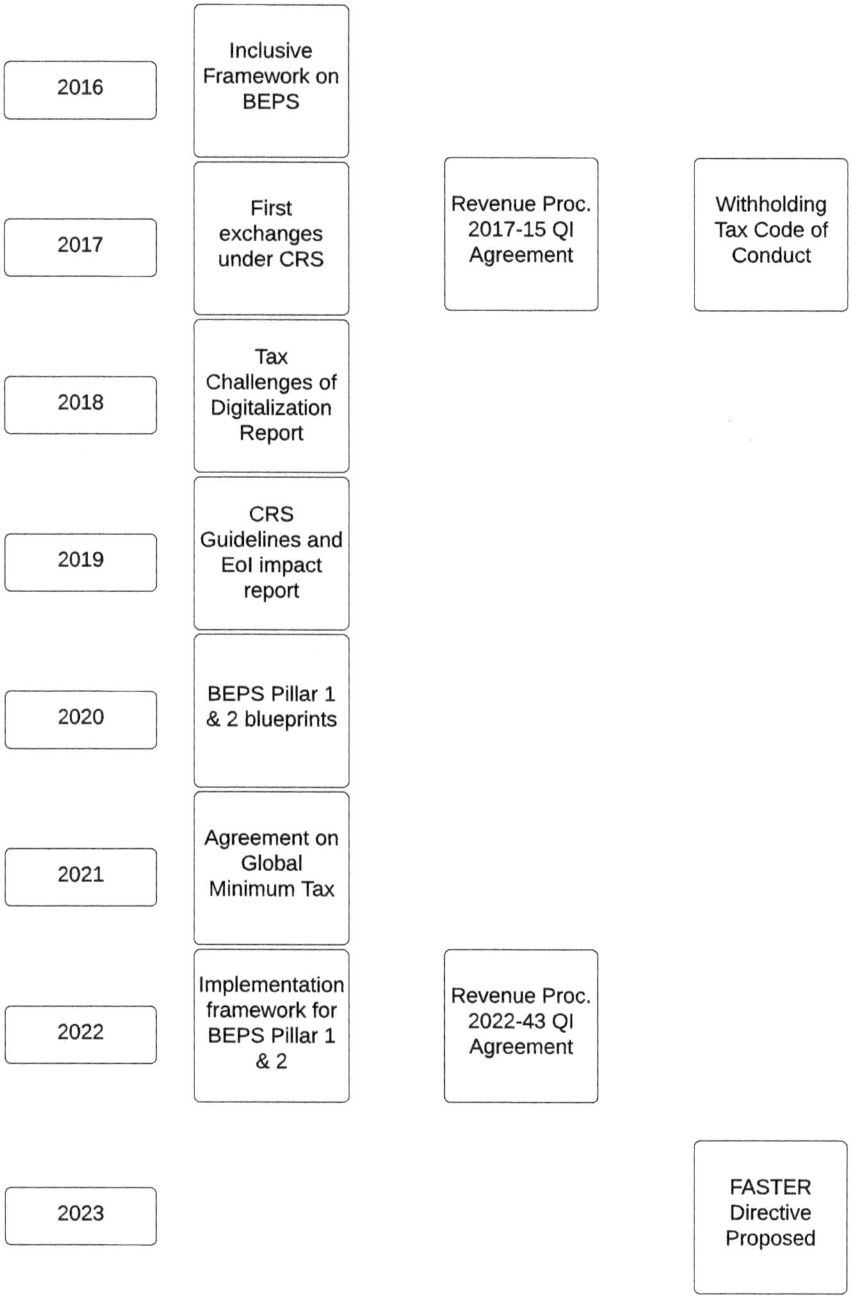


**Exhibit 15.1** (continued)

# 16

# AEoI

This chapter describes the mechanism for automatic exchange of information between tax administrations for the purpose of anti-tax evasion.

In the beginning, there was EoI: the Exchange of Information. The main problem with EoI was that it had to be targeted, and it was reactive. In other words, before a tax administration could request information from another tax administration about a target person that it was concerned about, it would need some evidence to support its request. The problem for EoI was simple, in that the evidence was very difficult, costly and time-consuming to get, often involving sting operations. By the time an EoI request was submitted, the requestor already knew that the target was evading tax and was only asking for enough information to make the final legal argument in court.

What was needed was some way in which administrations could work together to *automatically* share information that might be of interest to other jurisdictions. The common component was tax residency, and that component was most easily obtained by the financial institutions through which any tax evasion would have to take place via financial accounts.

The OECD's answer was a two-pronged approach. The first component was a system in which governments would agree to share certain information with each other based on certain characteristics. This was certainly interesting for many governments in the OECD club.

In Exhibit 16.1, the legal basis for AEoI is an agreement between two jurisdictions to bilaterally share information on an automatic basis, i.e., there is no reactive request required. There is an agreed timetable for events leading to the sharing of information.



R. K. McGill and K. V. Pitkin, *Qualified Intermediary*,
https://doi.org/10.1007/978-3-031-81410-5_16

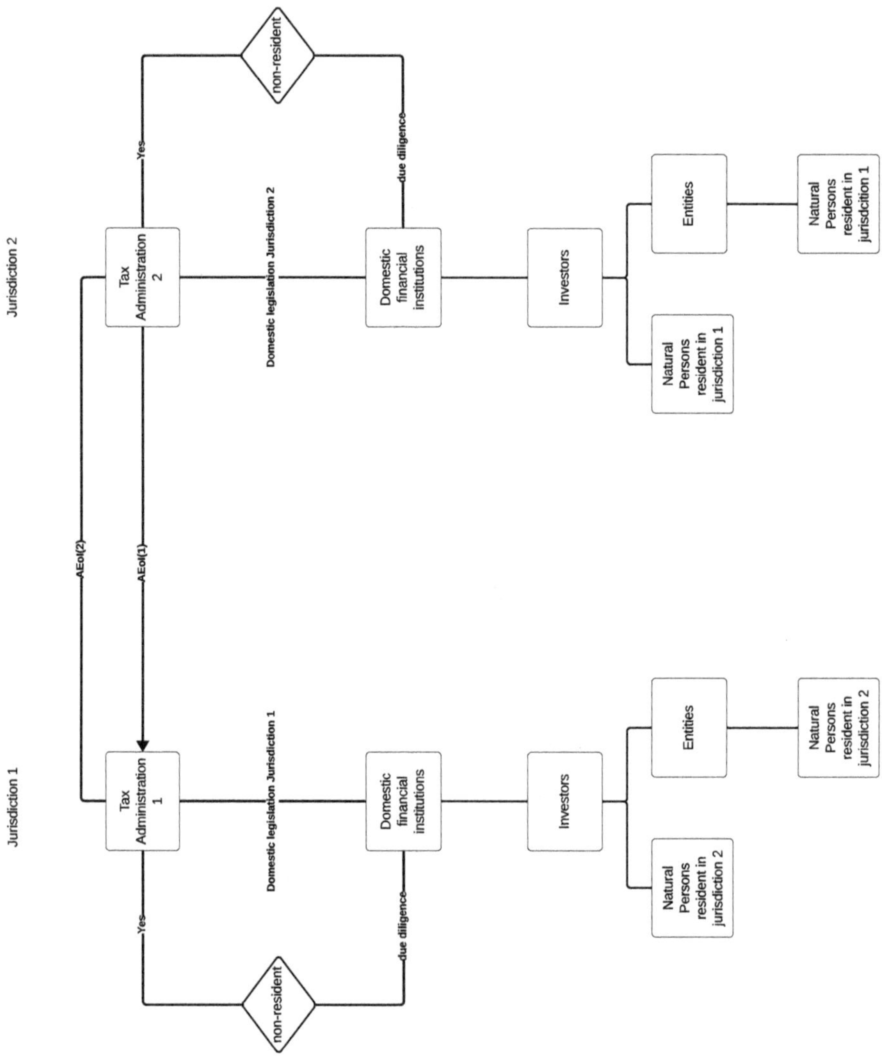


**Exhibit 16.1** AEoI legal basis *Source* Author

To achieve this, each party must have the relevant information. To do this, as the second component, they must each enact domestic legislation forcing their financial institutions to perform sufficient due diligence to identify account holders that are residents of the partner jurisdiction. This would include direct account holders that are natural persons (individuals or joint account holders) as well as the controlling persons of account holders that are entities (bodies corporate).

Provided both parties to the AEoI agreement have set mutually acceptable definitions and processes, and then, each tax administration should receive data from all of their domestic financial institutions, based on their due diligence efforts. This leaves each tax administration, each year, with an enormous number of data files which must be processed to provide a single file per partner jurisdiction.

Exhibit 16.2 shows the complexity involved in the AEoI process from the point of view of Jurisdiction 1. Domestic legislation gives Jurisdiction 1's tax administration the ability to receive multiple files from its financial institutions, each identifying accounts held by residents of Jurisdiction 2. They will have to merge all these files into one file, so they must provide a national standard format for these files so that the financial institutions provide the data in a consistent way. Today, most jurisdictions are using Extended Markup Language (.xml) for this purpose.

Once these files are received, they will go through a validation process to make sure that all the required data is present, e.g., taxpayer identification numbers (TINs), and that the file meets the specified data standard. If the files pass the validation process, then they can go on to the next stage. If they fail, the financial institution concerned will be notified of a "bad file" or "file failure" so that they can correct errors and re-submit.

Now that the files are validated and standardised, they can be merged into a single data file to the data format agreed between the two jurisdictions. This is normally the same format as between the financial institutions and the tax administration, to minimise workload.

The final domestic steps are to compress the data (as these files can be extremely large), then encrypt the data to protect it from cyber-attack and then digitally certificate the file with a private key so that only the correct receiving party can open the file. It can then be deposited at the dedicated AEoI portal of Jurisdiction 2.

This of course also happens in reverse for Jurisdiction 2 and multilaterally if the AEoI agreement is between Jurisdiction1 and multiple other jurisdictions.

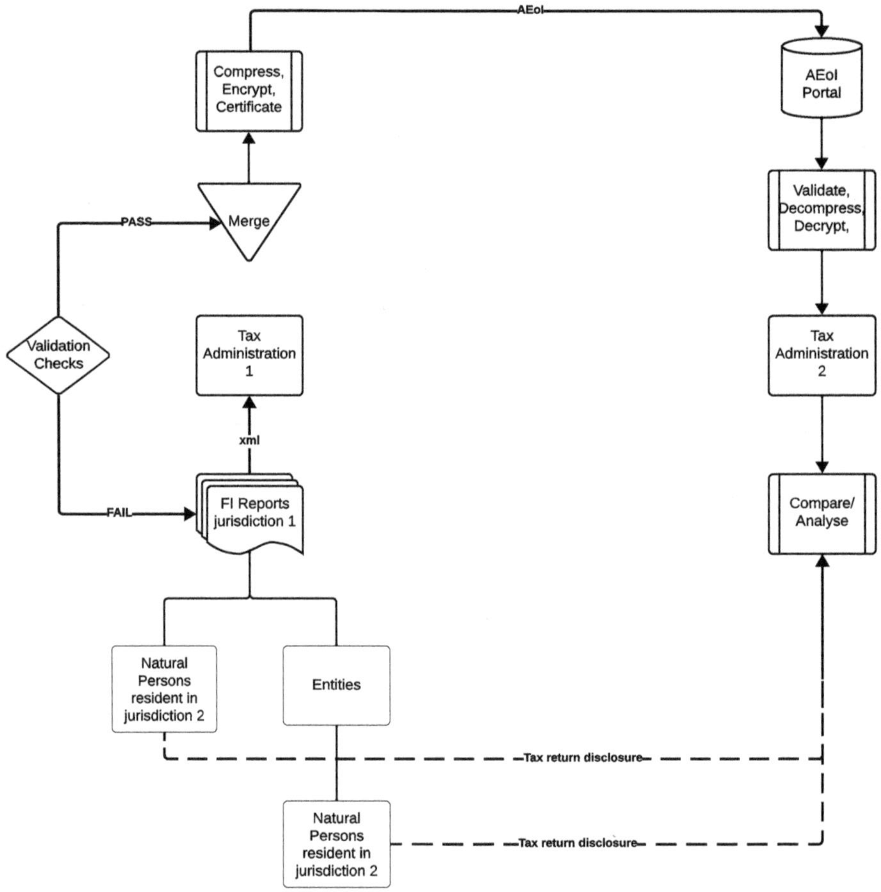


**Exhibit 16.2** Mechanisms of AEoI *Source* Authors

Now, the principle of AEoI is based on one single assumption—that the account holder in Jurisdiction 1 (or their controlling persons) will meet their obligation to file a tax return disclosing their foreign bank account(s) in Jurisdiction 2. So, what are the tax administrations looking for? This has two components. First, they are looking for account holders in the AEoI file that have *not* disclosed the accounts on their domestic tax return. Second, where the account holder *has* disclosed their foreign accounts on their tax return, they are looking for discrepancies or abnormalities between what was reported by the account holder and what was reported by the partner jurisdiction's financial institution(s). If such discrepancies are identified, this can lead to further investigations and request for mutual assistance.

So, being pedantic, AEoI is about the relationship between partner jurisdictions and the reporting obligations each has to the other. It is often confused with CRS, which is the reporting standard designed to make sure that the proper due diligence is performed, and the correct accounts are identified for reporting purposes.

While AEoI is most often used in the context of CRS, AEoI is also a generic term unrelated to the OECD because technically the US FATCA regulations is an example of AEoI, although the US is not a signatory to the AEoI/CRS framework.

The AEoI processes present significant technical challenges for tax administrations as well as additional workload. Where most tax administrations have been paper-based for many years, they are now having to embrace the digital age because there is just no other way that this kind of information sharing would be possible without standards and automation. This is rather like designing a sophisticated rocket, when your experience is based on building paper aeroplanes. Although they don't like to admit it, most jurisdictions have followed the US model where they have the International Data Exchange System (IDES). But it must be said that many jurisdictions have experienced significant technical issues when rolling out IT projects of this scale and have delayed reporting as a result. This does not bode well for the European Union's FASTER Directive, which will require scaling up further and faster and with increased technical agility—words not usually associated with governments or tax administrations! But more on that later.

There is a myth that AEoI is an anti-tax evasion framework. It's not really. It is actually a detection framework designed to provide tax administrations with the raw data they need to detect tax evasion, not prevent it nor even to deter it. It is enabled via the Common Reporting Standard, which is the subject of our next chapter (Exhibit 16.3).

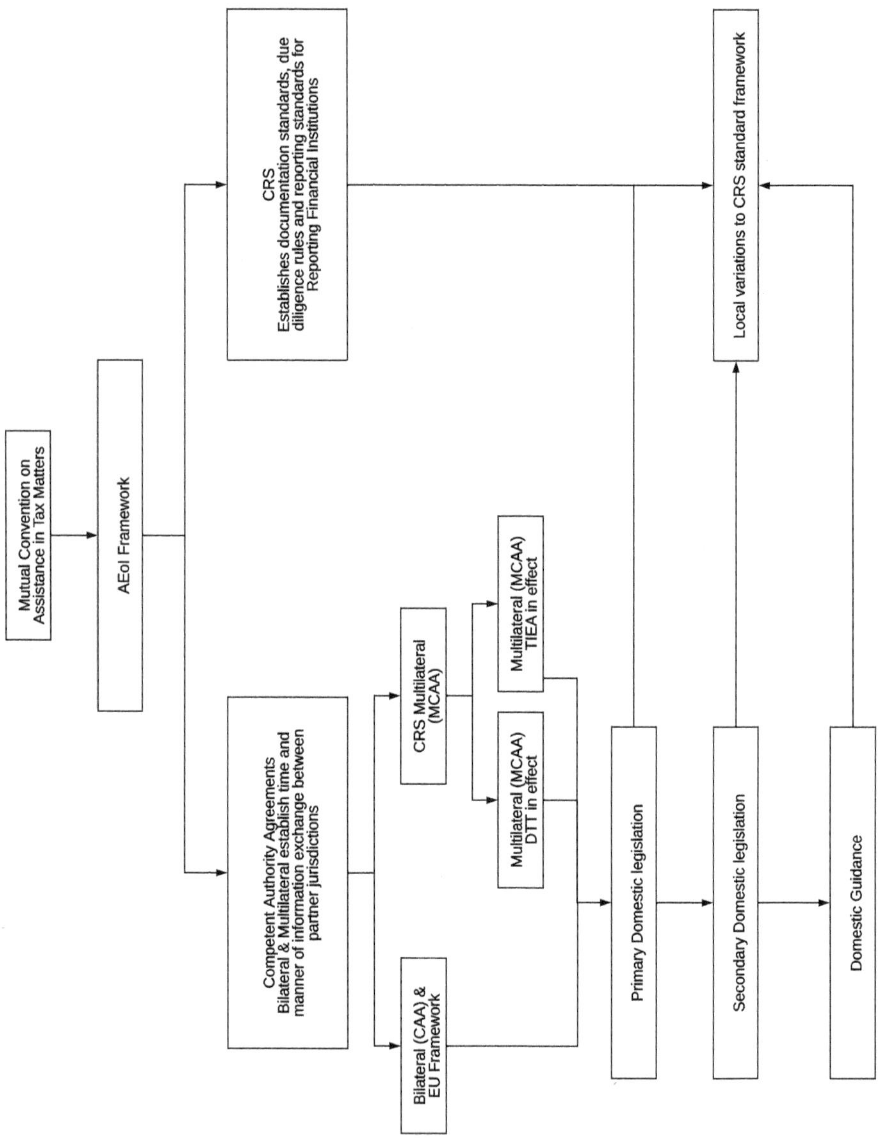


**Exhibit 16.3** AEoI Framework *Source* Authors

# 17

# CRS

This chapter describes the legal basis and rules under which financial institutions subject to CRS must document their account holder's tax residencies and report to their domestic tax administrations obligations under AEoI. This chapter looks at xml schemas to explain data collection and at investor self-declarations as the methodology for collecting data.

Once AEoI was in place to describe the mechanisms for sharing data between governments, it was necessary to make sure that each government was capable of providing that data in a consistent way to their counterparts. This was achieved with the Common Reporting Standard or CRS.

In the same way FATCA contains due diligence rules prior to establishing the reporting rules, CRS also contains the rules that financial firms must follow before creating and submitting their reports.

The big difference between FATCA and CRS is that FATCA is a bilateral relationship between one government (the US) and another (the FATCA partner jurisdiction). CRS, on the other hand, is a multilateral framework between 120 jurisdictions[1] that builds on many of the characteristics of FATCA while also simplifying some of more complex components.

[1] A current list of active exchange agreements is available at https://web-archive.oecd.org/tax/automatic-exchange/international-framework-for-the-crs/exchange-relationships/index.htm.


R. K. McGill and K. V. Pitkin, *Qualified Intermediary*,
https://doi.org/10.1007/978-3-031-81410-5_17

## Due Diligence

CRS has the same basic purpose as FATCA. It is an enabling mechanism to help governments detect and deter potential tax evasion by their residents when holding financial assets across jurisdictional borders. Like FATCA, CRS achieves this on the basis of a self-certification of tax residency.

The OECD publishes template CRS self-certification forms[2] that are similar, but not the same as the US Form W-8 series of self-certifications, the notable difference being that the CRS self-certification does not contain a claim of treaty benefits because it is not concerned with taxation of income, but with the declaration of it. The use of self-certifications is important because it shifts liability for errors or omissions from the financial institution to the investor completing the form. They can be adapted by the individual financial institution and incorporated into proprietary forms. As mentioned previously, we often see firms developing combined FATCA and CRS forms as there is considerable overlap between the data elements on these forms. The key difference is the collection of jurisdiction and TINs for each tax residency, over and above the primary or permanent residence provided on a Form W-8.

As required under FATCA and the QI regime, financial institutions must properly validate these self-certifications against any other KYC or AML evidence they hold, and cannot rely on them as soon as they become aware of a change in client circumstances. CRS is harmonised with the FATCA regime in that it has a 90-day grace period in which to collect new documentation.

CRS is also harmonised with FATCA with regard to its due diligence requirements for pre-existing accounts. These become more onerous for high value account holders, with an aggregate account value of more than $1 m on 31 December, and include a residence test (if permitted under local law) or electronic records test for low value account holders and additional paper record checks and a relationship manager enquiry for high value account holders. So far, so familiar.

In each case, the purpose of the due diligence is to identify and cure any indicia that suggest that the account holder might be resident in a partner jurisdiction—known as a reportable jurisdiction. Examples for individual account holders include:

- Current mailing or residence address (including a PO box) in a reportable jurisdiction

[2] Individual CRS self certification form template: https://www.oecd.org/content/dam/oecd/en/topics/policy-issue-focus/aeoi/crs_individual_self-cert_form.pdf.

- One or more telephone numbers in a reportable jurisdiction (when there is no domestic telephone number)
- Standing instructions to transfer funds to an account in a reportable jurisdiction
- Signing authority granted to a person with an address in a reportable jurisdiction
- "Hold mail" or "in-care-of" address in a reportable jurisdiction (if the financial institution does not hold any other address for the account holder).

Again this list will seem very familiar from our discussions in Chapter 7.

There are subtle differences that can catch out compliance departments as they design systems and procedures. For example, entities that certify as Passive Non-Financial Entities (Passive NFEs) must provide a separate self-certification for each controlling person. It is also possible to determine if an entity is reportable or not based on KYC or publicly available information, including:

- Information published by a government body
- Information in a publicly accessible register maintained by a government body
- Information disclosed on an established securities market
- Any publicly accessible classification based on a standardised industry coding system.

A key challenge for financial institutions is to design documentation and due diligence systems that get maximum benefit from the overlaps with FATCA, while not overlooking the differences between the two frameworks.

## Reporting

Once they have identified reportable account holders, financial institutions are required to report these on an annual basis to their domestic tax authority. This is done using the CRS XML schema according to local guidelines. These guidelines include filing deadlines and data protection measures, which vary by jurisdiction.

The data includes (but is not limited to):

- Name

- Address
- Jurisdiction
- TIN
- Date of birth (individuals only)
- Place of birth (individuals only)
- Controlling person information (entities only)
- Account number
- Account balance
- Information about payments to:
    - o Depository accounts
    - o Custodial accounts
    - o Other financial accounts

Unlike FATCA, CRS is not a negative proof system, so there is no concept of recalcitrant account holders or pooled reporting.

## Control and Oversight

As previously discussed, the nature of AEoI and CRS is such that oversight and subsequent enforcement are baked into domestic law by participating countries, and as such the exact measures and penalties vary. This is only problematic for financial institutions that are part of an international group—and consultants with an international client base, like us.

The OCED has published Model Mandatory Disclosure Rules for CRS Avoidance Arrangements and Offshore Structures,[3] which provide a framework for member countries to enact domestic laws that will compel intermediaries—including tax advisors—to report to their domestic tax authority if they advise on ways to circumvent CRS. As at March 2024, 18 countries have committed to implementing these rules, which are similar to the requirements of DAC6 in the EU (discussed later in Chapter 21).

## Challenges of CRS

The bilateral nature of the CRS and AEoI frameworks means a much greater degree of coordination between partner jurisdictions and some specific challenges for financial institutions. The first of these is language. As we have

[3] OECD (2018), Model Mandatory Disclosure Rules for Addressing CRS Avoidance Arrangements and Opaque Offshore Structures, OECD Publishing, Paris, https://doi.org/10.1787/e3cabd80-en

highlighted many times before, the language of CRS is similar, but not the same as FATCA. In FATCA an NFFE is a non-financial foreign (i.e., non-US) entity. In CRS the equivalent term is an NFE or a non-financial entity. While these two acronyms sound the same, they do have some nuanced differences both in definition and treatment. The CRS status of an entity cannot, therefore, be deduced from US Chapter 4 (FATCA) status, even when the terminology sounds plausibly similar.

The CRS processes for financial institutions are described in Exhibit 17.1. The issues faced by financial institutions are created by:

**The number of clients** that have tax residencies other than those of the financial institution. This will be affected by how "global" the client base is. A financial institution with only domestic resident clients will have minimal exposure to CRS other than perhaps a nil reporting obligation.

**The types of clients** that have multiple tax residencies, notably those that receive more than 50% of their income from passive sources, such as dividends. These are called Passive NFEs or P-NFE. These are a particular target for CRS because they are the most common vehicle that can be used for tax evasion. Most KYC and AML regulation, as well as FATCA and CRS, now

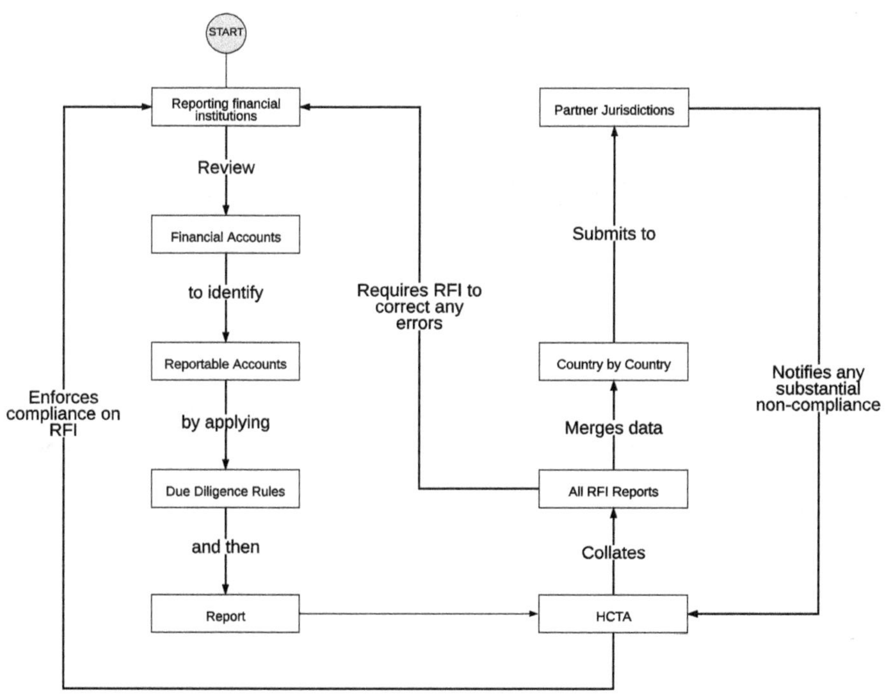


**Exhibit 17.1** CRS Process *Source* Author

require some level of look-through to the controlling persons of such entities to identify any that have more than one tax residency.

Exhibit 17.2 demonstrates that this may not be as easy as it sounds. A Reporting Financial Institution (RFI) may have several different kinds of client. Individuals are the easy part. If an RFI's client is another financial institution, these can have several different sub-types, including nonreporting financial institutions (NR-FI) again, with multiple sub-types. Finally, as described, entities come in two major flavours—passive and active NFEs.

Unlike FATCA, QI or TRACE, there is no direct financial penalty applied via the withholding tax system in CRS. CRS is just a due diligence and reporting system. The penalties, if such are imposed, will be expressed by the financial institution's domestic regulator after relevant investigations and any appeals processes.

**The number of partner jurisdictions** that the host country tax administration (HCTA) has. Because some jurisdictions are smaller than others, they may have challenges to meet their sharing deadlines with a large number of partners. BVI is a good example that has a history of delaying its data sharing to give its financial institutions more time to report.

**Wider approach**. The main obligation of a financial institution is to gather the CRS status of its clients so that they can be properly reported to a partner jurisdiction. If a financial institution has non-resident clients, it only needs to collect CRS status relevant to its country's partner jurisdictions. If it has a non-resident client whose tax residency is not on the partner jurisdiction list, then it does not need to report and, by inference, it does not need to perform due diligence. Indeed, the smarter, more well-informed clients may complain of over-reach in such circumstances. This causes major issues for financial institutions because the partner list can change over time. So, many jurisdictions have adopted the "wider approach". This means that financial institutions can obtain tax residency data for *all* clients, even if their residency is not in the partner list. This protects the financial institution from having to monitor any changes in partner jurisdictions. It also means that there is likely to be more consistency in the xml data definitions making reporting easier.

Unlike FATCA, CRS is not a negative proof system. So, unless the wider approach is in place, the amount of work involved to document non-residents can be limited. However, because FATCA and CRS live in parallel from a compliance perspective, most financial institutions take an inclusive approach and document all new accounts in the same way. With digital online onboarding becoming more prevalent, this is becoming easier,

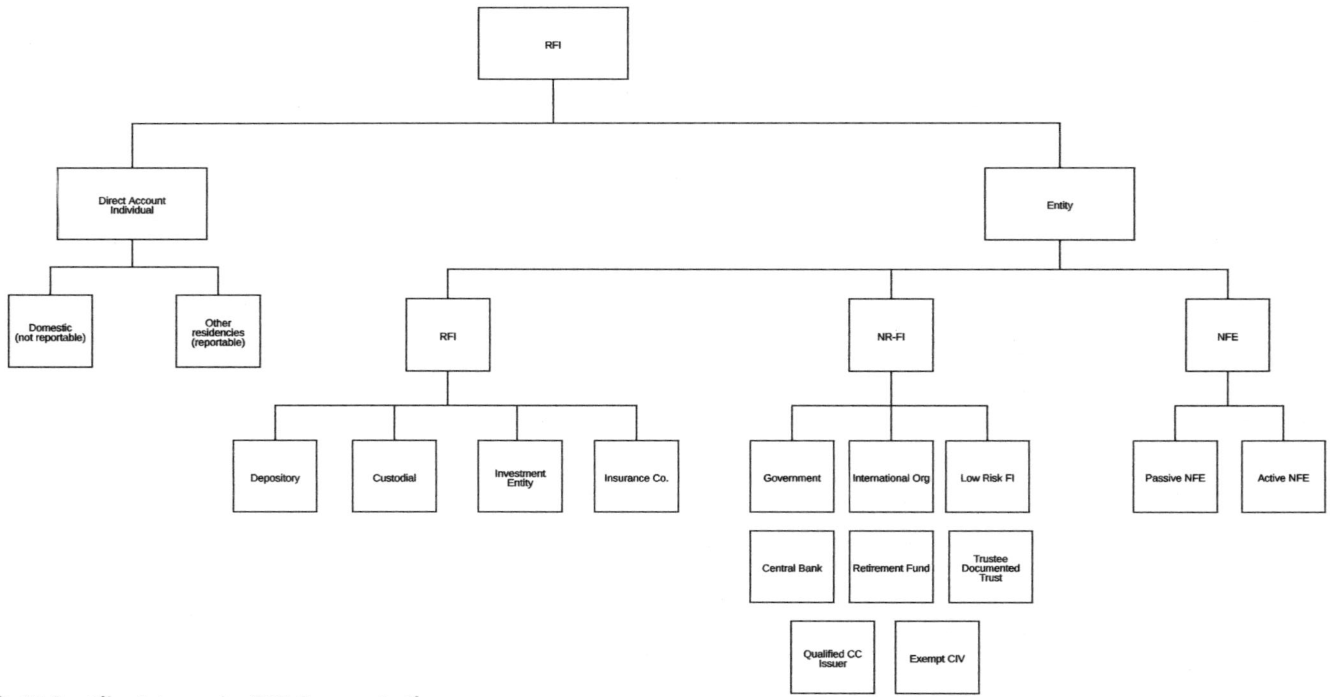


**Exhibit 17.2** Client types in CRS *Source* Authors

although there are rules to follow if an online self-certification is to be held to be valid (Exhibit 17.3).

A host country tax authority (HCTA) has its own problems and challenges in CRS. It must receive xml files from multiple financial institutions in its jurisdiction, to do which it must first have a method to establish such standards, monitor the standard and publish the standard. Today, this is mostly done via an online portal or website. It must also have an agreement in place with each other partner jurisdiction known as a Competent Authority Agreement (CAA), and this can be either bilateral or multilateral (MCAA).

This reminds us that while financial institutions have compliance challenges, technically so do tax administrations who must meet the terms of the agreements between them and partner jurisdictions. From the point of view of CRS, the biggest challenge is ensuring the security and privacy of all the information they are collecting via their financial institutions, packaging it up and sending it to the correct partner competent authority.

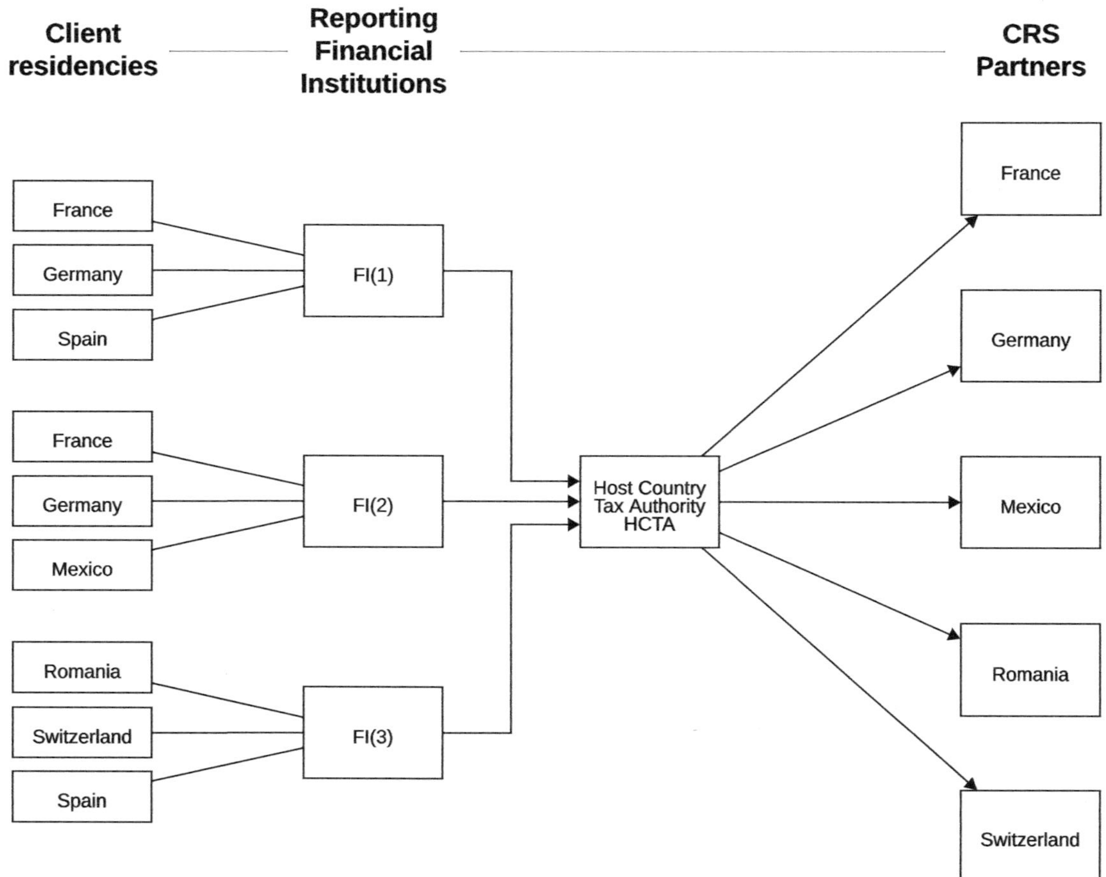


**Exhibit 17.3** Role of the host country tax authority in CRS *Source* Authors

# 18

# TRACE

This chapter deals with the OECD TRACE framework that allows non-resident financial institutions to adopt Authorised Intermediary status in order to offer tax treaty benefits to non-resident investors. We also compare and contrast TRACE to the US Qualified Intermediary Agreement.

Many of the compliance regimes we see are focussed on anti-tax evasion. However, some are concerned with making double tax treaties work more efficiently. The US has its qualified intermediary program. The OECD equivalent is the Tax Relief And Compliance Enhancement protocol, otherwise known as TRACE. TRACE shares similar elements to what was proposed in 2013 the European Commission TBAG Report and the QI program in the United States. In the same way that CRS is an implementation component of AEoI, TRACE has its own set of guidelines for implementing the TRACE system, since any member of the OECD could implement it at any time. These guidelines are known as the Implementation Protocol (IP).[1] So, effectively TRACE IP tells tax administrations how to implement TRACE.

Like the EU's work, the OECD TRACE challenge is creating a framework that is workable and can be adopted most consistently by multiple jurisdictions. The key principles are:

1. An Authorised Intermediary Agreement (AIA)
2. A register of approved Authorised Intermediaries

[1] https://www.oecd.org/ctp/exchange-of-tax-information/TRACE_Implementation_Package_Website.pdf.


R. K. McGill and K. V. Pitkin, *Qualified Intermediary*,
https://doi.org/10.1007/978-3-031-81410-5_18

3. The use of an investor self-declaration (ISD) to establish eligibility and claim of treaty benefits in addition to due diligence procedures,
4. Ability of AIs to implement withholding at reduced rates on a pooled basis
5. Annual reporting according to a.xml schema
6. Control, oversight and enforcement rules embedded into the AIA including an obligation for an independent review.

The only jurisdiction to have implemented TRACE so far is Finland in 2020 (Exhibit 18.1).

As with the QI framework, TRACE has two cycles in operation at the same time—the tax operations cycle that deals with tax relief at source processing and the governance cycle that deals with oversight and enforcement.

The core of TRACE is:

(i) the appointment of non-resident financial institutions to be TRACE withholding agents under an AI Agreement that is substantially similar to the US QI Agreement and
(ii) the use of self-certifications of tax residency and claims of treaty benefits.

The difference between TRACE and the US system is that, under TRACE, *any* OECD member can implement different operational models. Finland, for example, has chosen not to use AI Agreements but instead to use a national register and issue Authorised Intermediary Identification Numbers (AIINs)—similar in concept to the US QIEIN. The list of AIs in Finland, together with their AIINs, is a public register available at the Vero Skatt website.[2]

Implementing Finland's withholding system presented several compliance challenges for financial institutions. While it eliminated tax inefficiencies, financial institutions still have to navigate several complex regulatory, operational, and technical challenges. More importantly, Finland's capital market is quite small, with its most known security being Nokia. While Nokia is an important investment target for several large pension funds, other than this security, the rest of Finland's securities market probably does not commercially warrant the cost of compliance for the benefit gained.

One of the primary compliance challenges with the TRACE system is the need for documentation to confirm the tax residency and eligibility for treaty benefits of non-resident investors. Financial institutions, acting as authorised

[2] Vero Skatt—AI List: https://www.vero.fi/en/businesses-and-corporations/business-operations/financial-sector/nominee-registered-shares/register-of-authorised-intermediaries/public-register-of-authorised-intermediaries/.

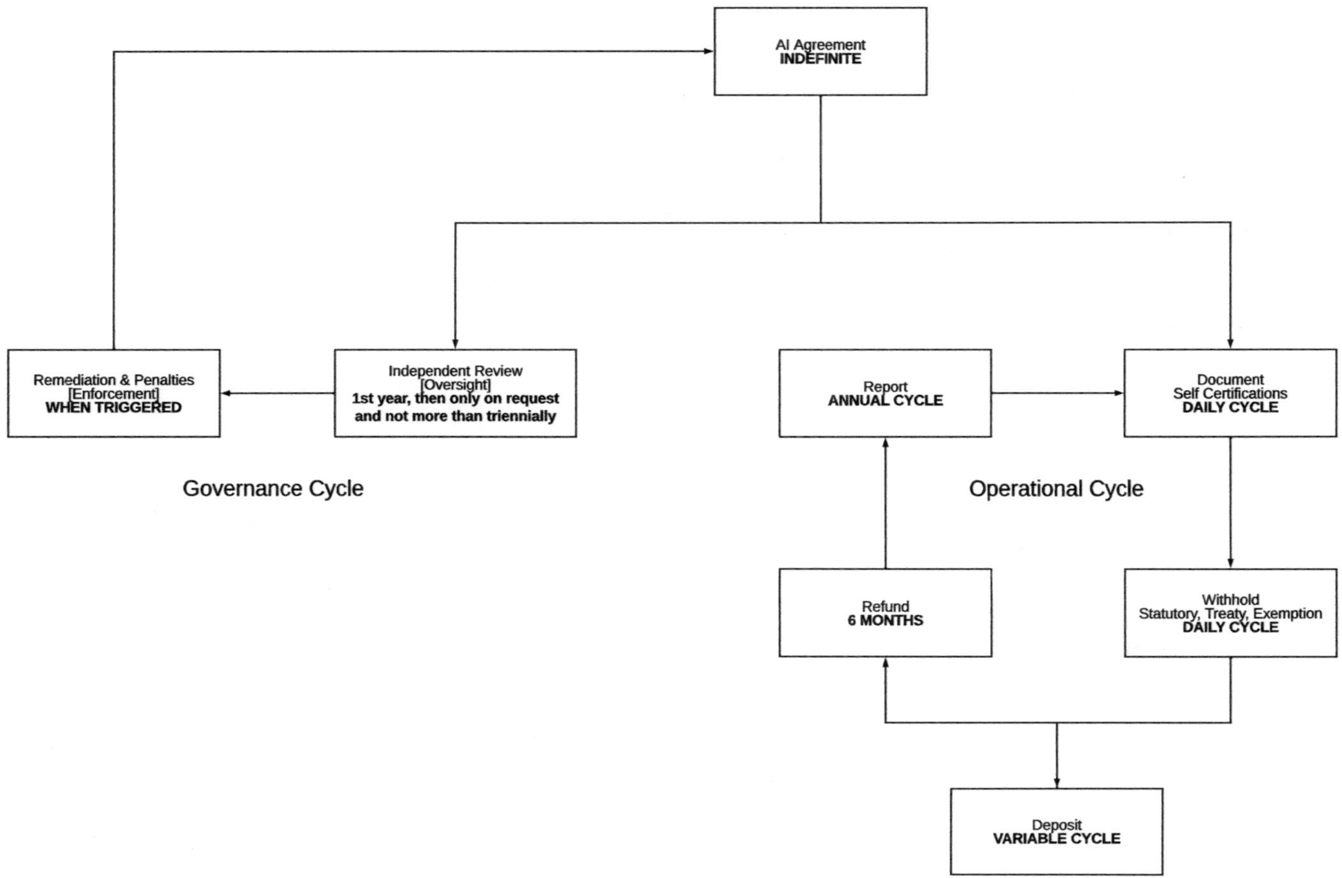


**Exhibit 18.1** TRACE model *Source* Authors

intermediaries (AIs), must ensure they collect, validate and store accurate information to substantiate claims for reduced withholding tax rates. This involves gathering tax residency certificates, investor declarations, and other relevant documents. Some jurisdictions have a form that can be completed by a beneficial owner then stamped by a tax authority. Others require a full certificate issued only by their tax authority and still others permit a self-declaration of tax residency. For those seeking tax relief in a TRACE market, the self-declaration will be sufficient. However, while this makes it easier for the beneficial owner, it imposes more work on the receiving financial institution to properly validate the ISDs, in a similar way to the US, i.e., on the face, to KYC and reason to know.

Financial institutions potentially need to change their current tax processing systems to comply with TRACE's regulatory requirements. This is particularly a problem when the number of adopting jurisdictions is low, as is the case now with just one adopting jurisdiction—Finland. The EU's FASTER Directive causes a problem here simply because it means that Finland, as an EU Member State, either has to revoke its TRACE adoption in order to begin meeting the terms of the Directive or it needs to establish an equivalence between the EU model and the OECD model so that it doesn't have to change much. Finland, unfortunately, sits just above the capital ratio threshold that would otherwise enable it to opt out of FASTER. It is also notable that no other country since 2021 has adopted the TRACE model.

TRACE also introduces new reporting obligations, requiring financial institutions to submit detailed information on beneficiaries and tax treaty claims to the Finnish Tax Administration. In effect, if no treaty claim is made, reporting is not required. Only if a treaty claim is made, will reporting take place and that, unlike the US system, will be at the beneficial owner level, irrespective of where the investor sits in the payment chain. Many institutions will face challenges to ensure that their systems can handle the increased volume of data and documentation.

The main feature of the TRACE system is its reliance on a network of authorised intermediaries (AIs) who process cross-border dividends and apply the appropriate withholding tax relief at source in much the same way as the US QI system. The complexity of coordinating across different chains of intermediaries—such as custodians, sub-custodians, and paying agents—poses a challenge, particularly in ensuring that the correct tax rates are applied to eligible investors at source.

A final challenge lies, as with all the material in this book, in ensuring that staff within financial institutions are adequately trained to manage the complexities of the TRACE system and that written policies and procedures are clear. Employees across various departments, including compliance, legal, IT and operations, need to have a thorough understanding of the new processes, documentation standards and reporting obligations. For multinational financial institutions with large volumes of cross-border transactions, building this internal capacity requires substantial investment in training programs and updating internal guidelines to reflect TRACE's requirements.

While Finland's implementation of TRACE and the model itself aims to modernise and simplify the process of granting tax treaty benefits at source, its implementation, to some extent, contradicts the FASTER Directive, as we will see later. This will cause a problem for any other EU Member States that might be considering implementing TRACE.

To participate in TRACE, financial institutions must address complex documentation requirements, overhaul their operational and technological systems, coordinate across intermediary networks, navigate varying legal regulations and invest in staff training to ensure effective compliance. It is doubtful that the size of Finland's capital market will warrant such investment and it's been noted that several AIs have already withdrawn from the Finnish TRACE system. It remains to be seen if further countries will adopt TRACE, which would help to deliver efficiencies of scale for financial institutions, assuming that those countries do not deviate too far from the core standard.

# 19

# BEPS

**Abstract** This chapter provides an overview, for context, of the OECD Base Erosion and Profit Shifting framework to counteract tax evasion conducted by multinational enterprises (MNEs).

This chapter provides an overview, for context, of the OECD Base Erosion and Profit Shifting framework to counteract tax evasion conducted by multinational enterprises (MNEs).

Base Erosion and Profit Shifting (BEPS) is a reference to tax planning strategies used by multinational enterprises (MNEs) to exploit gaps and mismatches in tax rules to artificially shift profits to low or no-tax jurisdictions where there is little or no economic activity, resulting in little or no overall corporate tax being paid. This phenomenon has significant implications for tax revenues, economic equity, and international tax policy. The Organization for Economic Co-operation and Development (OECD) has spearheaded efforts through a comprehensive set of actions aimed at ensuring that profits are taxed where economic activities generating those profits are performed and where the value is created.

Exhibit 19.1 explains how profit shifting works. An MNE has business entities in more than one location. Its primary source of revenue from its economic activity—let's say, making widgets—takes place in Jurisdiction 1 (e.g., the USA or the UK where profits are taxed at 21% and 19% respectively). An MNE establishes a relationship with its holding company, established in Jurisdiction 2, (e.g., Ireland, where the corporate tax rate 12.5%). The arrangement between the two allows the MNE to transfer any


R. K. McGill and K. V. Pitkin, *Qualified Intermediary*,
https://doi.org/10.1007/978-3-031-81410-5_19

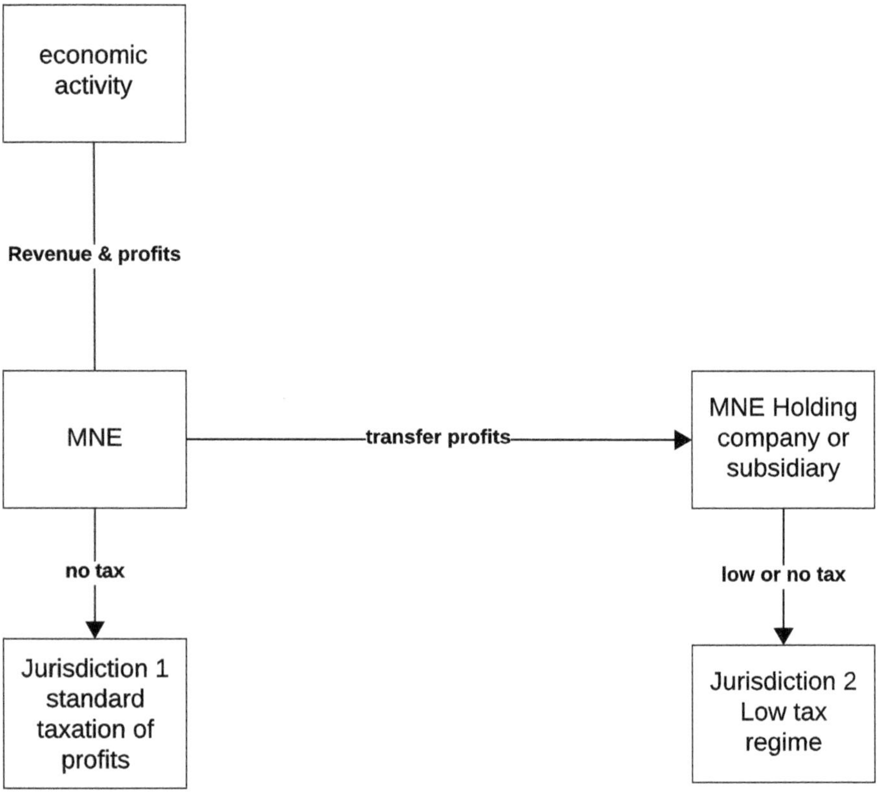


**Exhibit 19.1** How profit shifting works *Source* Authors

profits made in Jurisdiction 1 to Jurisdiction 2. This effectively evades tax in Jurisdiction 1 since there is no profit to tax and taxes those profits in Jurisdiction 2 where the tax rate is much lower than it would otherwise have been. That's a win-win for everyone except Jurisdiction 1 which has lost out on the tax which it could have collected if the profits had been declared in the country where the economic activity took place.

## Historical Context and Evolution of BEPS

BEPS can be traced back to the early days of globalisation when the rise of multinational enterprises began to outpace the development of coherent international tax frameworks. Initially, tax systems were designed with a focus on national economies, with limited consideration for cross-border activities. However, the growth of global trade and investment highlighted significant weaknesses in these systems.

By the mid-twentieth century, the emergence of complex corporate structures, intangible assets, and advanced financial instruments allowed MNEs to manipulate transfer pricing, use tax havens, and engage in aggressive tax planning. The absence of a unified international tax regime meant that countries often competed for investment by offering favourable tax rates, exacerbating the problem.

## Objectives and Actions

In response to growing concerns about BEPS, the OECD, in collaboration with the G20, launched the BEPS Project in 2013. The initiative created a set of international standards to address tax avoidance, improve the coherence of international tax rules, and ensure a more transparent tax environment. The BEPS Action Plan consists of fifteen specific actions grouped into several categories (Exhibit 19.2).

(1) **Digital Economy Challenges (Action 1):** (i) Addresses tax challenges arising from digitalisation and (ii) ensure that digital businesses are taxed where economic activities occur, and value is created. This action focusses on ensuring that countries can tax digital enterprises fairly. Proposed solutions include the introduction of new nexus rules based on significant economic presence and the implementation of measures like digital services taxes (DSTs).

(2) **Hybrid Mismatch Arrangements (Action 2):** Neutralises the effects of hybrid mismatch arrangements that exploit differences in tax treatments across jurisdictions. This action aims to neutralise these mismatches by aligning the tax treatment of instruments and entities in different countries, to prevent double non-taxation or double deductions.

(3) **Controlled Foreign Company (CFC) Rules (Action 3):** Controlled Foreign Company (CFC) rules are designed to prevent companies from shifting profits to subsidiaries in low-tax jurisdictions. This action strengthens these rules by setting out recommendations for effective CFC regimes, including defining CFC income and ensuring it is taxed in the parent company's jurisdiction.

(4) **Interest Deductions (Action 4):** Limits base erosion through the deductibility of interest and other financial payments. This action introduces measures to limit the deductibility of interest payments, such as fixed ratio rules that cap interest deductions based on a

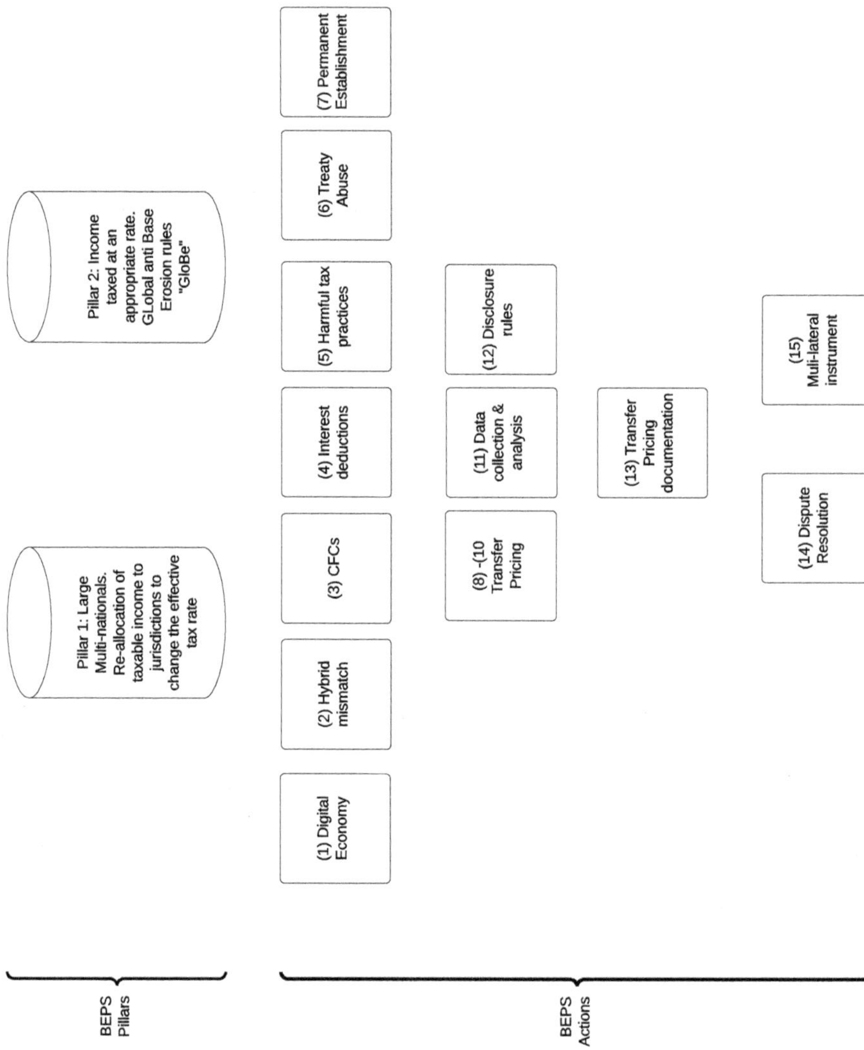


**Exhibit 19.2** A guide to BEPS structures. *Source* Authors

percentage of earnings before interest, taxes, depreciation, and amortisation (EBITDA)

(5) **Harmful Tax Practices (Action 5):** Counters harmful tax practices, with a focus on transparency and substance. This action focusses on identifying and countering harmful tax practices, particularly those that lack substantial economic activity. This includes the establishment of transparency requirements and peer reviews to ensure compliance.

(6) **Treaty Abuse (Action 6):** Prevents treaty abuse to ensure that tax treaties are not used to avoid paying taxes. This action introduces measures to prevent treaty shopping, including the implementation of a Principal Purpose Test (PPT) to deny treaty benefits in cases of abusive arrangements.

(7) **Permanent Establishment (PE) Status (Action 7):** Prevents the artificial avoidance of PE status to ensure taxation where economic activities are performed. This action seeks to prevent the artificial avoidance of PE status by clarifying and expanding the definition of PE to include significant economic presence.

(8) **Transfer Pricing (Actions 8-10):** Assures that transfer pricing outcomes are in line with value creation by aligning transfer pricing rules with economic reality. This includes revising guidelines for the transfer of intangibles, risk and capital allocation, and high-risk transactions to prevent profit shifting.

(9) **Data Collection and Analysis (Action 11):** Establishes methodologies to collect and analyse data on BEPS and its economic impact. This emphasises the need for comprehensive data collection and analysis to assess the scale and economic impact of BEPS. This includes developing methodologies to measure BEPS and its effects on tax revenues.

(10) **Disclosure Rules (Action 12):** Requires taxpayers to disclose aggressive tax planning arrangements. This action requires taxpayers to disclose aggressive tax planning arrangements, enhancing transparency and enabling tax authorities to respond promptly to emerging risks.

(11) **Transfer Pricing Documentation (Action 13):** Develops rules for transfer pricing documentation to enhance transparency. This action introduces a standardised three-tiered approach to transfer pricing documentation: the master file, the local file, and Country-by-Country Reporting (CbCR). This enhances transparency and provides tax authorities with a clearer picture of MNEs' global operations.

(12) **Dispute Resolution (Action 14):** Makes dispute resolution mechanisms more effective to resolve tax treaty-related disputes by improving the Mutual Agreement Procedure (MAP) and ensuring timely resolution of tax treaty-related disputes
(13) facilitates the implementation of BEPS measures through the Multilateral Instrument (MLI), which allows for the amendment of bilateral tax treaties in a coordinated and efficient manner

## Key Measures and Their Impacts

The implementation of the BEPS measures has been a collaborative global effort. Many countries have adopted legislative and administrative changes in line with the BEPS recommendations. The Multilateral Instrument (MLI) has been a key tool in this process, enabling countries to quickly update their bilateral tax treaties to incorporate BEPS measures.

The impact of these measures has been significant. For instance, Country-by-Country Reporting (CbCR) has enhanced transparency, allowing tax authorities to better assess MNEs' global activities and identify profit shifting. Additionally, the limitation of interest deductions and the tightening of transfer pricing rules have curtailed some common BEPS strategies.

However, the digital economy continues to evolve, resulting in ongoing adjustments to tax frameworks. The political and economic interests of different countries can also impede the uniform adoption and enforcement of BEPS measures.

## Challenges

Unlike FATCA and CRS, which are primarily concerned with tax evasion conducted by individuals or entities via the receipt of undisclosed passive income into one or more financial accounts, BEPS is more concerned with large multinational enterprises that are manipulating their accounting methods to gain a tax advantage by moving profits from one jurisdiction to another. While the profits may end up in bank accounts, it would be difficult if not impossible for financial institutions (who may be MNEs themselves) to detect this type of tax evasion.

Despite the progress made through the BEPS Project, there are several challenges associated with its implementation and effectiveness.

The BEPS measures introduce significant complexity to the international tax system, increasing compliance costs for businesses. Smaller enterprises, in particular, may find it challenging to navigate the new rules.

The implementation of BEPS measures varies across countries, leading to potential inconsistencies and gaps that can be exploited by MNEs. Some countries lack the resources or political will to fully implement the recommendations particularly if they have benefitted in the past from increased inbound foreign direct investment (FDI).

While we think BEPS measures have had an overall positive impact, some critics argue that they do not go far enough in addressing the root causes of profit shifting. For example, the reliance on traditional concepts of transfer pricing and Permanent Establishment status may not fully capture the complexities of modern business models.

BEPS requires significant international cooperation, which often conflicts with national interests. Countries may be reluctant to cede tax sovereignty or to adopt measures that could negatively impact their attractiveness as investment destinations.

The taxation of the digital economy remains a contentious issue. While the OECD has proposed solutions, such as the introduction of new nexus rules, achieving global consensus on these measures has been challenging. Some countries have unilaterally implemented digital services taxes, leading to tensions and trade disputes.

BEPS remains a critical issue in the global tax landscape, affecting governments' ability to collect fair tax revenues while maintaining equitable tax systems. The BEPS Project has made significant strides in addressing these challenges through a comprehensive set of actions designed to ensure that profits are taxed where economic activities occur and value is created.

The implementation of BEPS has had a notable impact on international tax policy, enhancing transparency, reducing profit shifting and fostering greater cooperation between and among countries.

# Part IV

## Europe

# 20

# Structure

This chapter provides an overview of the European Union legal and regulatory structure as it applies to cross-border taxation. It provides a brief history of the efforts made by regulators, politicians and business, to understand the nature of the problems, the scope of the problems and proposals for solutions.

The European Union is (currently) a group of twenty-seven independent nation states (Members) who act collectively on several issues of common interest. This includes economic policy. As far as economic policy goes, the EU takes either a voluntary adoption approach or a directive-based approach.

Voluntary adoption means a set of guidelines which Member States can choose to adopt, change or not adopt. It is the least logical approach to taxation issues since each Member State will be resistant to change. This was the case with the Code of Conduct on Withholding Tax[1] that came after the work of the Tax Barriers Business Advisory Group (TBAG). The benefit of a voluntary approach is that you should, in theory, see rapid adoption. The downside is that the adopted approaches may not be consistent with each other.

A Directive is a legislative act that sets out goals that Member States must achieve. It is then up to each Member State to enact domestic legislation and regulation to create the framework for the achievement of the Directive's goal. The legal basis for Directives is Article 288 of the Treaty on the Functioning of the European Union which makes them binding on Member States as to

[1] European Union. (2017). Code of conduct on withholding tax. https://taxation-customs.ec.europa.eu/system/files/2017-12/code_of_conduct_on_witholding_tax.pdf.


R. K. McGill and K. V. Pitkin, *Qualified Intermediary*,
https://doi.org/10.1007/978-3-031-81410-5_20

the result to be achieved. The benefits of a Directive based approach is that Directives must be unanimously voted for at the European Council level. The downside is that, precisely because of the requirement for unanimity, it can take several years to get to a model that is acceptable to all twenty-seven Member States.

Directives fall into one of several categories:

- Free movement and trade
- Social and market regulation (including finance)
- Public regulation
- Other

The financial plan for the European Union centres around the Capital Markets Union project (CMU).

In the 1990s, Alberto Giovanini was tasked by the European Commission to identify the barriers to the efficient operation of capital markets. Table 20.1 summarises the barriers he identified and the current position.

As can be seen, CMU is still not a reality and many aspects are still currently unresolved. Barrier 11 has been a particularly difficult nut to crack given that most Member States take very strong ownership of their individual taxation systems and have been notably reticent to adopt anything that could be described as harmonisation.

The compliance problem for financial institutions represented in European Union Member States or whose clients are resident in once of those Member States is simply a function of the number of laws and regulations and their complexity. These are very difficult to keep track of, let alone understand. Just a few of these regulations are noted below:

SRD II The Shareholder Rights Directive.[2]
MiFID The Markets in Financial Instruments Directive.[3]
DAC Directive on Administrative Cooperation.
EMIR European Markets Infrastructure Regulation.[4]
CSDR Central Securities Depositories Regulation.[5]

[2] https://eur-lex.europa.eu/EN/legal-content/summary/shareholder-rights-directive.html.

[3] https://www.esma.europa.eu/publications-and-data/interactive-single-rulebook/mifid-ii.

[4] https://finance.ec.europa.eu/capital-markets-union-and-financial-markets/financial-markets/post-trade-services/derivatives-emir_en.

[5] https://www.esma.europa.eu/esmas-activities/markets-and-infrastructure/central-securities-depositories.

**Table 20.1** Barriers to the efficient functioning of the EU capital markets. *Source* Alberto Giovanini

| Barrier | European Post Trade Forum (EPTF) Assessment |
|---|---|
| Barrier 1: National differences in information technology and interfaces | Non-standard financial messages persist and cause higher costs and errors |
| Barrier 2: National clearing and settlement restrictions that require the use of multiple systems | Dismantled: direct and indirect access to CSDs now possible |
| Barrier 3: Differences in national rules relating to corporate actions, beneficial ownership and custody | Corporate actions remain fragmented and need market standards to be implemented |
| Barrier 4: Absence of intra-day settlement finality | Dismantled: Now almost the rule in Europe |
| Barrier 5: Practical impediments to remote access to national clearing and settlement systems | Dismantled: No need for multiple CSD memberships any longer |
| Barrier 6: National differences in settlement periods | Dismantled: T + 2 now the rule in Europe |
| Barrier 7: National differences in operating hours/settlement deadlines | Dismantled: T2S brought operating hours into alignment in Europe |
| Barrier 8: National differences in securities issuance practice | Reference data issues with securities and counterparty identifiers still unresolved |
| Barrier 9: National restrictions on the location of securities | Unresolved issues in reference data and identifiers (as with Barrier 8) |
| Barrier 10: National restrictions on the activity of primary dealers and market makers | Primary dealers and market makers must still operate and settle locally |
| **Barrier 11: Domestic withholding tax regulations serving to disadvantage foreign intermediaries** | **FASTER Directive, in progress. Withholding tax reclaim and rebate procedures remain inefficient** |
| Barrier 12: Transaction tax collection integrated into local settlement systems | Transaction tax collection procedures are still not harmonised |
| Barrier 13: The absence of an EU-wide framework for the treatment of interests in securities | Ownership rights in securities held by intermediaries still legally uncertain |
| Barrier 14: National differences in the legal treatment of bilateral netting for financial transactions | Bank risk and CCP default management procedures still legally uncertain |
| Barrier 15: Uneven application of national conflict of law rules | Legal uncertainty over ownership rights in book entry securities and claims persists |

There are many more including several updates related to crypto-currency and crypto-asset regulations and the development of Central Bank Digital Currencies (CBDC).

In a generally siloed financial institution, there is seldom a joining of the dots to create an effective compliance framework in theory or in practice. Most firms just bumble along hoping they won't get caught. When one does, everyone else focusses their attention on just that one issue to make sure they meet a minimum level of compliance. The practical challenges are left to those in each institution that have some level of interest in or knowledge of a particular regulation. They are the ones who "draw the short straw" but they are the go-to people for that organisation at that time. This creates a retention issue because that knowledge represents value and risk reduction. So, these people are sought after and command high salaries.

# 21

# DAC

This chapter provides a context for the European Union Directive on Administrative Cooperation (DAC) and in particular DAC6 as it applies to the CRS.

DAC6 is a European Union Directive 2011/16/EU, amended by Directive 2018/822. It entered into force on June 25, 2018, and was adopted by Member States on December 31, 2019. The acronym stands for the Directive on Administrative Cooperation.

DAC6 is, as the name implies, a European Union Directive including various amendments and updates. The Directive includes:

DAC1 which lays down how Member States will exchange information with each other.
DAC2 which lays own rules for the reporting of financial accounts (similar to FATCA).
DAC3 which lays down rules on the automatic exchange of information related to advance rulings with a cross-border dimension.
DAC4 which describes country by country reporting for groups with a turnover of more than 750 million Euros
DAC5 which provides rules on access to beneficial ownership information
**DAC6 which lays down rules for prevention and detection of potentially aggressive tax planning**
DAC7 which extends DAC6 to cover digital platforms (EU and non-EU)
DAC8 which provides transparency rules for crypto-asset transactions


R. K. McGill and K. V. Pitkin, *Qualified Intermediary*,
https://doi.org/10.1007/978-3-031-81410-5_21

For this chapter, we will focus on DAC6 because of its overlap with the OECD's AEoI and CRS frameworks and its impact on firms that are qualified, authorised or will be certified as financial intermediaries.

One of the problems with CRS is that its relatively easy to circumvent—simply open up your financial account in a country that is not part of CRS. Historically this would have been solved through changes to CRS itself, and this does still happen today. However, it was noted that the jurisdictional issues were only part of the problem. There are instances where tax evasion can take place without a bank account being involved. This posed more problems for CRS, because both CRS and FATCA are focussed on accounts at financial institutions. In the DAC world, the purpose is not to document accounts, but activity patterns. This is done using "Hallmarks", i.e., patterns of activity that trigger a report to a competent authority for further investigation.

Exhibit 21.1 shows the overall framework. The difference between this and FATCA or CRS is that DAC6 defines an intermediary differently than FATCA or CRS.

In DAC6 an intermediary is "*any person* that designs, markets, organises or makes available for implementation or manages the implementation of a reportable cross-border arrangement. It also means any person that, having regard to the relevant facts and circumstances and based on available information and the relevant expertise and understanding required to provide such services, knows or could be reasonably expected to know that they have undertaken to provide, directly or by means of other persons, aid, assistance or advice with respect to designing, marketing, organising, making available for implementation or managing the implementation of a reportable cross-border arrangement. Any person shall have the right to provide evidence that such person did not know and could not reasonably be expected to know that that person was involved in a reportable cross-border arrangement. For this purpose, that person may refer to all relevant facts and circumstances as well as available information and their relevant expertise and understanding".

In order to be an intermediary, a person must meet at least one of the following additional conditions:

1. Be resident for tax purposes in a Member State.
2. Have a permanent establishment in a Member State through which the services with respect to the arrangement are provided.
3. Be incorporated in, or governed by the laws of, a Member State.
4. Be registered with a professional association related to legal, taxation or consultancy services in a Member State.

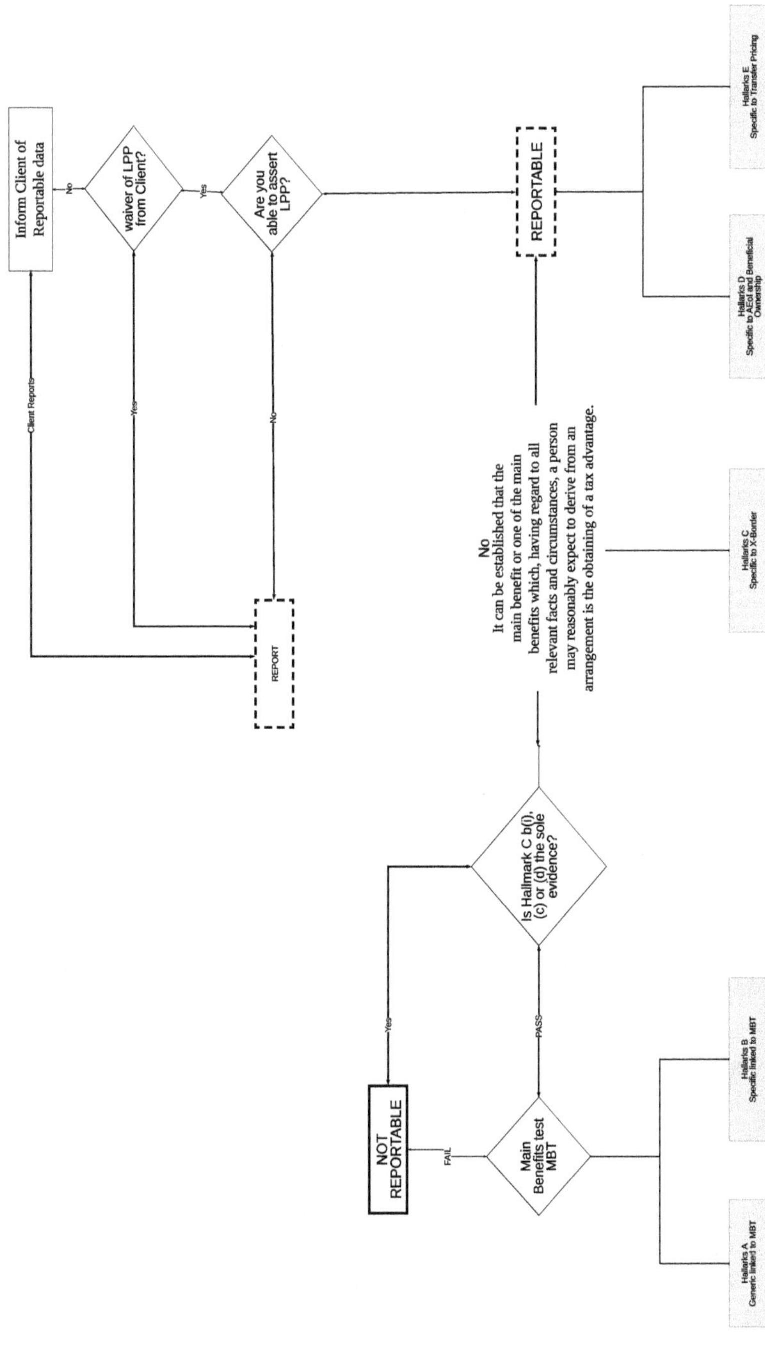


**Exhibit 21.1** DAC6 reporting framework *Source* Authors

The effect of this definitional difference is to bring into play various types of third party such as product designers, developers, market makers, law firms, consultancies and accountancy practices.

Exhibit 21.1 shows the overall framework for reporting that is triggered by the existence of Hallmarks. Exhibits 21.1–21.6 describe Hallmarks A-E that are included in the DAC6 framework.

The other component of note is the Main Benefits Test (MBT) referred to earlier which is only related to Hallmarks A, B and C. The MBT will be satisfied if it can be established that "the main, or one of the main benefits which, having regard to all relevant facts and circumstances, a person may reasonably expect to derive from an arrangement is the obtaining of a tax advantage". In Exhibit 21.1, if the MBT is satisfied, i.e., the main benefit an arrangement is a tax benefit, then the arrangement is still not reportable unless Hallmarks Cb(i), C(c) or C(d) were the sole evidence used to determine whether the MBT test was passed.

There are several compliance challenges associated with DAC6.

The first, as mentioned, is that where an arrangement exists that triggers one of the Hallmarks, there may be several "intermediaries" involved, some of whom may not even know of the existence of the others. This means that where an arrangement is reportable, it may be reported by more than one intermediary dependent on their role in the design, marketing or sale of the arrangement.

The second is that one common feature of such arrangements will be the involvement, directly or indirectly, of legal counsel. Lawyers are included in the definition of an intermediary in DAC6, but are given special rules because of their ability to claim legal professional privilege i.e., they could cite legal professional privilege, (otherwise known as attorney-client privilege) to claim that while they should have reported under DAC6, they could not do so without breaking their legal professional privilege. DAC6 addresses this in a rather blunt fashion. DAC6 states that where legal professional privilege exists, the lawyer concerned must EITHER obtain a waiver of legal professional privilege in order to report the arrangement OR advise their client that the arrangement is reportable. In either case, the naivety of the EU, to expect that anyone who knows that an arrangement will be reportable, is going to report the arrangement or failing that, ask their client to do so, is significant. Bad players are bad players and its unlikely that this aspect of DAC6 will work unless there is clear evidence, potentially from other reporters not restricted by legal professional privilege. If there is, you could argue that the designers have not done a particularly good job.

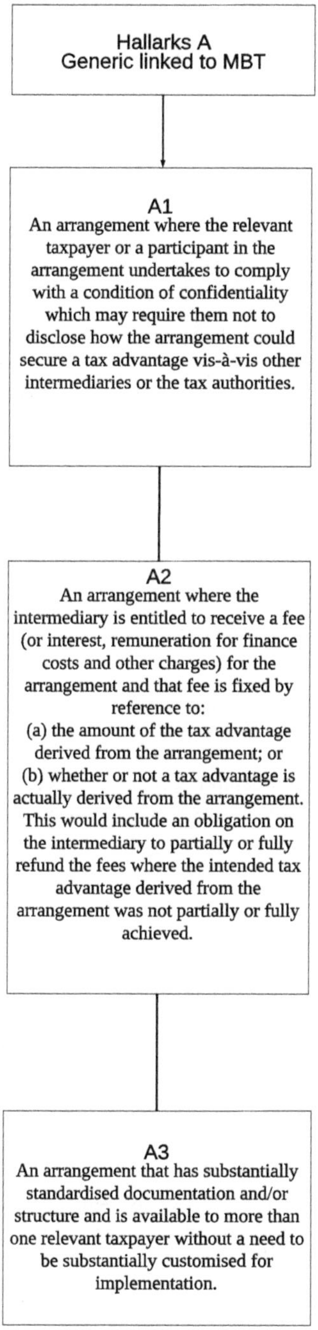


**Exhibit 21.2** DAC6 Hallmarks A1–A3 *Source* Authors

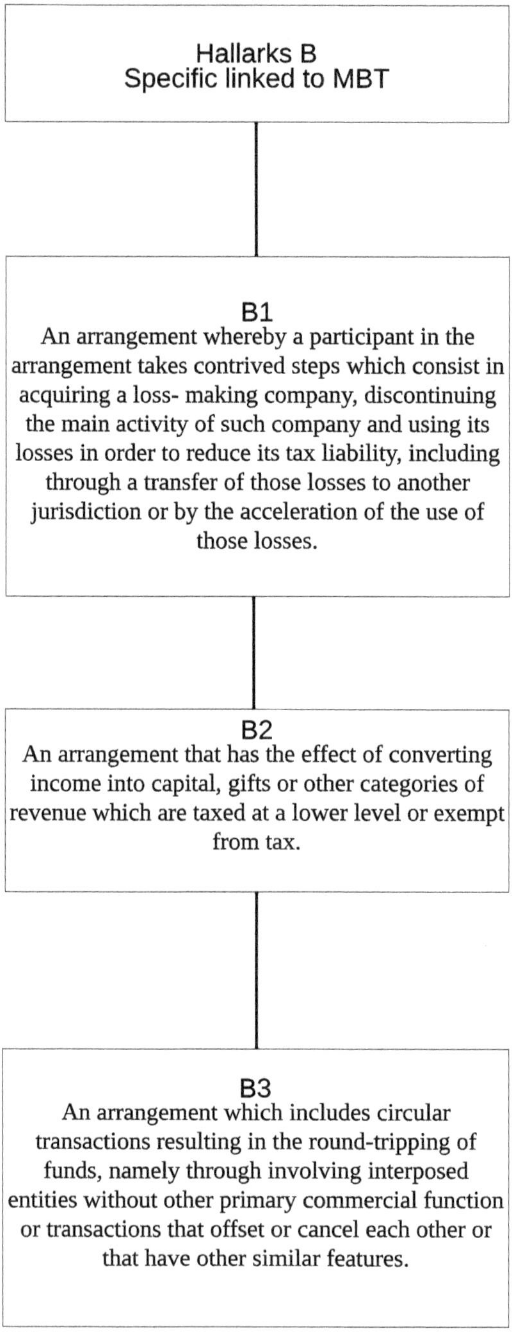


**Exhibit 21.3** DAC6 Hallmarks B1–B3 *Source* Authors

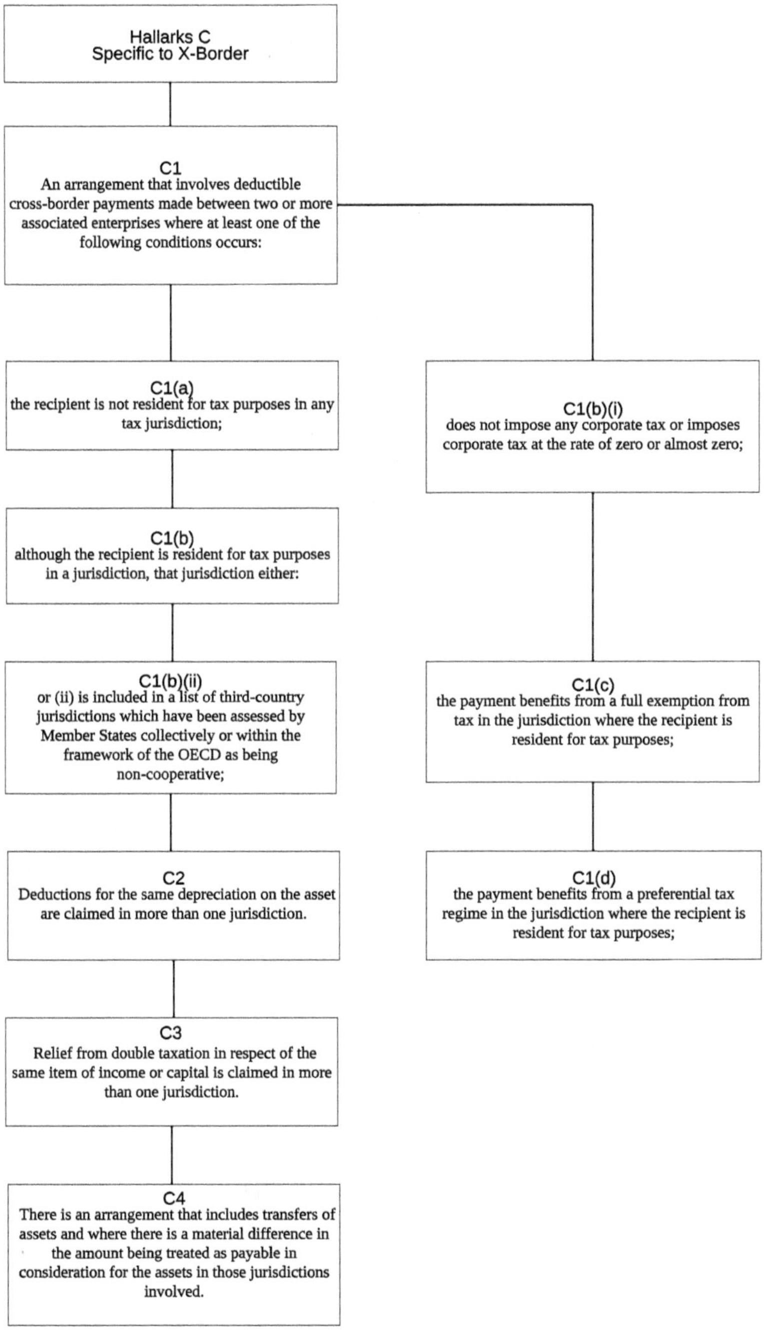


**Exhibit 21.4** DAC6 Hallmarks C1–C4 *Source* Authors

Hallarks D
Specific to AEoI and Beneficial Ownership

D1
An arrangement which may have the effect of undermining the reporting obligation under the laws implementing Union legislation or any equivalent agreements on the automatic exchange of Financial Account information, including agreements with third countries, or which takes advantage of the absence of such legislation or agreements. Such arrangements include at least the following:

(a) the use of an account, product or investment that is not, or purports not to be, a Financial Account, but has features that are substantially similar to those of a Financial Account;

(b) the transfer of Financial Accounts or assets to, or the use of jurisdictions that are not bound by the automatic exchange of Financial Account information with the State of residence of the relevant taxpayer;

(c) the reclassification of income and capital into products or payments that are not subject to the automatic exchange of Financial Account information;

(d) the transfer or conversion of a Financial Institution or a Financial Account or the assets therein into a Financial Institution or a Financial Account or assets not subject to reporting under the automatic exchange of Financial Account information;

(e) the use of legal entities, arrangements or structures that eliminate or purport to eliminate reporting of one or more Account Holders or Controlling Persons under the automatic exchange of Financial Account information;

(f) arrangements that undermine, or exploit weaknesses in, the due diligence procedures used by Financial Institutions to comply with their obligations to report Financial Account information, including the use of jurisdictions with inadequate or weak regimes of enforcement of anti-money-laundering legislation or with weak transparency requirements for legal persons or legal arrangements.

D2
An arrangement involving a non-transparent legal or beneficial ownership chain with the use of persons, legal arrangements or structures:

(a) that do not carry on a substantive economic activity supported by adequate staff, equipment, assets and premises; and

(b) that are incorporated, managed, resident, controlled or established in any jurisdiction other than the jurisdiction of residence of one or more of the beneficial owners of the assets held by such persons, legal arrangements or structures; and

(c) where the beneficial owners of such persons, legal arrangements or structures, as defined in Directive (EU) 2015/849, are made unidentifiable.

**Exhibit 21.5** DAC6 Hallmarks D1–D2 *Source* Authors

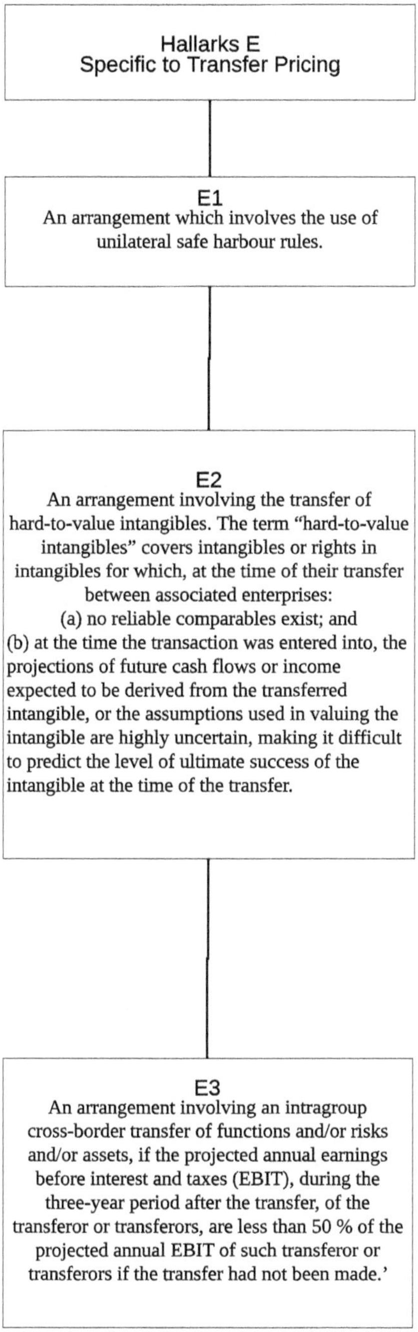


**Exhibit 21.6** DAC6 Hallmarks E1–E3 *Source* Authors

The third feature is that the financial institutions involved in such arrangements may not have enough visibility or information to know whether any of the Hallmarks have been triggered. Worse, their systems are oriented on financial accounts and not on the purpose for which those accounts are used.

The obligation in DAC6 for any intermediary is to have appropriate controls in place to establish monitoring of activity to establish reportability. In both FATCA and AEoI/CRS, the emphasis is on the competent authorities to determine whether tax evasion is occurring and to take relevant action. DAC6 moves that needle towards the intermediary.

So the compliance challenges for financial institutions are mainly around how to establish patterns of client behaviour and characteristics of products that could, on their own or in concert, trigger the Hallmarks and to have systems and processes in place to document such patterns and mechanisms in place to submit reports to the relevant authorities, typically online under the Mandatory Disclosure Regulations (MDR).

# 22

# FASTER Directive

This chapter describes the proposed FASTER directive including a comparison to other frameworks. Attention is given to the methodology for establishing tax residency and new reporting and control mechanisms.

In 2023, the Presidency of the European Union was held by Spain for six months. During their tenure, they proposed a new Directive called the **F**aster **A**nd **S**impler withholding **T**ax **E**xcess **R**elief or FASTER Directive. The FASTER Directive is supposed to simplify and, to some extent, provide the basis for automation of withholding tax between Member States.

The Directive, as proposed, was built on nearly thirty-five years of work starting in 1988 with the proposal for a world-wide tax principle. By 2003, any EU resident financial institution could be a withholding agent in any other EU Member State. The period between 2006 and 2010 was spent by various committees developing the original work of Alberto Giovanini. In 2013, one such committee, the Tax barriers Business Advisory Group (TBAG), has worked out what the withholding tax problem was in the European Union, its scale and the most effective solution. The problem was, of course, a complex set of bilateral treaties with manual paper-based processes with no commonality beyond the principles of the DTAs. The TBAG report was published in 2013.[1] In that report, it was noted that there were two implementation options for the proposed solution, (i) a voluntary approach or (ii) a Directive. Both approaches had their problems. A voluntary approach could get faster adoption, but the adoption may not be homogenous, with

[1] European Commission. (2013). Report of the Tax Barriers Business Advisory Group: https://finance.ec.europa.eu/publications/report-tax-barriers-business-advisory-group-tbag_en.



R. K. McGill and K. V. Pitkin, *Qualified Intermediary*,
https://doi.org/10.1007/978-3-031-81410-5_22

different countries adjusting their models to suit their political situations. The Directive approach would be a better model since it would become enshrined in EU law. However, a Directive requires a unanimous vote in the European Council and often takes five to ten years to get to the text of the Directive (Exhibit 22.1).

In the end, the EU tried the voluntary approach first, with the Withholding Tax Code of Conduct, which no-one formally adopted, but everyone said that their system already met the principles. So, nothing changed. The FASTER Directive is a more formalised approach, although it has some important departures from the TBAG report recommendations.

The proposed FASTER Directive, as it has now been adopted, has twenty-three Articles in four chapters and would be due to come into force on January 1, 2029. However, in the dying days of 2023, following industry commentary, the Spanish proposed that the FASTER Directive be amended—one consequence of which, if adopted, would be a deferral of the implementation date to January 1, 2029. See Appendix 4.

What follows in this chapter is an explanation of the key concepts of the proposed FASTER Directive.

The main reason that FASTER is included in this book is because of one of its principles—the appointment and registration of financial institutions as Certified Financial Intermediaries or CFIs. Unlike the US QI system, the OECD TRACE framework and the TBAG proposal for a contractual agreement with financial institutions, the FASTER Directive is based on the principle of national registers of CFIs. However, the concept of a framework that establishes obligations on financial institutions in return for the ability to offer tax relief at source, is similar enough to allow us to include FASTER as a QI equivalent model.

Let's start with the FASTER proposal issued in February 2024, after its approval by the Economic and Financial Affairs Council (ECOFIN) but before review by the European Securities Market Authority (ESMA).

## Article 1: Subject Matter

Article 1 establishes the basic subject matter, namely the concept that Member States would each establish a national electronic tax residency certification system (eTRC). This poses a challenge because not all Member States are at the same point on these certification systems. Several still use paper

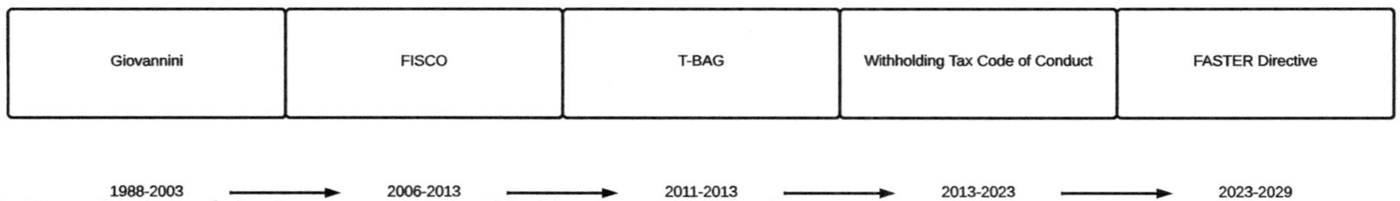


**Exhibit 22.1** Timeline of the EU approach to withholding tax *Source* Authors

certificates and some even require a separate secondary certification or apostille, effectively to certify that the tax residency certificate was issued by a bona fide government department.

## Article 2: Scope

Article 2 lays down how each of the other Chapters will apply to Member States, particularly those that have a tax relief at source model. Not all EU Member States offer all three tax models (tax relief at source, quick refund and standard refund). It is important to understand that the Directive does not go as far as the TBAG recommendations for a tri-model system in each and every Member State.

## Article 3: Definitions

As with all types of tax framework, the devil is in the detail.

Article 3 deals with definitions of terms used in the Directive. This is important because several parts of the proposed Directive reference other Directives that have an impact on how tax administrations can process withholding tax. For example, the definitions article speaks about the European Unique Identifier (EUID) that is contained in Directive 2017/1132.[2] The definitions article also speaks about "large financial institutions" by reference to Article 5(2) of Regulation (EU) 575/2013. However, it is actually Article 142(4) of that regulation that defines a large financial institution as an entity which meets inter alia the condition that its total assets are greater than or equal to a €70 billion threshold.

This seeks to recognise that most, but not all, withholding tax that is optimisable is held by large financial institutions either directly for their own clients or indirectly for other smaller financial institutions through omnibus holding structures. When we come to discuss the purpose of the Directive from a tax administration perspective, one of the key elements is the ability for a tax administration to re-create the payment chain for beneficial owners receiving tax relief at source. The problem this gives us is that if tax relief is technically available, but the investor does not have an account with a CFI, they could be excluded from the process.

---

[2] https://eur-lex.europa.eu/legal-content/EN/TXT/PDF/?uri=CELEX:32017L1132.

## Article 4: Digital Tax Residency Certificates (eTRC)

Article 4 is the first major component of the proposed Directive and is a departure from almost all other tax frameworks, because most other frameworks allow for self-certifications. The proposed Directive establishes that all Member States must provide a digital tax residence certificate to their residents on request. When we say "provide", for most EU tax administrations, this will mean designing, building and testing such a system or making adjustments to existing systems to make sure that they conform to the required standards.

The challenging part of this is not the technology, although tax administrations are not known for their expertise in systems design and development. The challenge is the issuance of these certificates in a way that reduces the risk of cybercrime, prevents fraud and that can be achieved within one day of the request submission.[3]

The information that must be on an eTRC is:

a. the first and last name of the taxpayer, and the date and place of birth or its European Unique Identifier number (EUID), if the taxpayer is an entity
b. tax identification number;
c. address of the taxpayer;
d. date of issuance;
e. the covered period;
f. identification of the tax authority issuing the certificate;
g. any additional information that may be relevant where the certificate is issued to serve purposes other than relief of withholding tax under this Directive or information required to be included in a tax residence certificate under EU law.

The technical implementation also requires that an eTRC will conform if:

a. it has an electronic "seal of conformity"[4]
b. allows for both human and machine-readable format e.g., pdf
c. it is printable
d. it contains an open free text box to allow for conformity to Article 4(2)(g)

[3] Article 4(2).

[4] Regulation (EU) No. 910/2014.

So, while tax administrations will retain control of tax residency certificates, they will have to establish systems for request submission, processing and issuance of these eTRCs to both individuals and entities. If the issuance of an eTRC is expected to take more than one day, the proposed Directive will require the tax administration to communicate with the requestor providing a reason for the delay and expected time of the delay.[5]

The validity period of an eTRC is established as one calendar year from January 1st of the year in which an eTRC is requested or until the holder is no longer a tax resident of the issuing jurisdiction.

While the technical aspects of an eTRC are not particularly onerous, given twenty-seven Member States implementing systems and the likely number of requests, in the first year, these systems will be subject to heavy loads from day one as investors scramble to get their eTRCs in place. Financial institutions will also need to adopt improved systems and automation to handle bifurcated processes. For example, they may be obtaining self-certifications of residency to meet the requirements of the CRS and the US Chapter 3 and Chapter 4 obligations, in addition to the eTRCs for clients that are EU Member State residents who may have entitlements for tax relief from intra-European investment income.

As far as we are concerned, it's regrettable that the EU chose this route because, while it possibly provides a stable system for tax administrations, this will come at a heavy cost for financial institutions that need to understand and handle their clients who are, in turn, unlikely to understand and be frustrated by these different documentation requirements.

It could also be problematic for tax administrations because the eTRC could be considered as a mechanism to facilitate tax treaty abuse. Consider, for example, an investor with two tax residencies who is therefore reportable under CRS based on a self-certification. This investor could obtain two eTRCs, one for each jurisdiction in which they are a tax resident, then pick and choose which eTRC they will use to claim the most optimal tax treaty benefits.

In a digital world, it is also a shame that the EU has not taken the step of allowing the use of non-fungible tokens (NFTs) to represent eTRCs on a blockchain.

[5] Article 4(4).

## Article 5: National Registers of Certified Financial Intermediaries

Article 5 establishes the concept of a "certified financial intermediary" which is why the FASTER Directive deserves its place in this book. The Directive also departs from the TBAG recommendation in that it does not propose a contractual arrangement between a tax administration and a financial institution. Instead it proposes that each tax administration sets up and manages a register of CFIs.

The requirement for a national register has some strings attached, that, again, pose risks and problems for financial institutions. Article 5(1) establishes that if a tax administration operates tax relief at source AND withholds tax on dividends, then they must operate a national register. Article 5(1) and Article 5(2) also note that the requirement for a national register is optional for tax administrations that levy a withholding tax on bonds but do not levy a withholding tax on dividends.

Article 5(3) provides that each Member State must establish a Competent Authority to create and manage the registers.

The registers themselves, if they are used, must include certain information including:

a. name of the certified financial intermediary;
b. date of registration;
c. contact details and any existing website of the certified financial intermediary;
d. the EUID, or, where the certified financial intermediary has no such number, the legal entity identifier (LEI) or any legal entity registration number issued by its country of residence

Its useful to note the different language being used here. The term is financial intermediary and not financial institution. This means that a CFI must be in the chain of payment and acting on behalf of someone else.

Article 5(5) requires that any national register must be publicly available at a dedicated website and updated monthly. This is similar to the requirement in the US for a Global Intermediary Identification Number (GIIN) or the Authorised Intermediary Identification Number (AIIN) used in the OECD TRACE protocol in Finland. This article also addresses one of the key issues identified by the TBAG group, namely the lack of publicly available information on withholding tax matters. One has to pre-suppose that such websites will be available in multiple languages to allow investors in other EU Member States to understand the registers easily.

## Article 6: Development of the European Certified Financial Intermediary Portal

This is a very short Article with only two clauses. The first requires all large financial institutions to register as CFIs with the relevant Competent Authority. The second mandates that Competent Authorities maintain a register and allow the registration of any financial intermediary meeting the requirements of Article 7.

## Article 7 & 8: Requirement to register and Registration Procedure

Article 7(1) requires a Competent Authority to register a financial intermediary as a CFI within three months of the submission of the registration request provided three conditions are met:

1. tax residence in a Member State or third jurisdiction that is not on a non-cooperative jurisdiction list
2. for credit institutions, investment firms and CSDs, an authorisation to provide custodial services under (respectively)
    a. points (12) or (14) of Annex I of Directive 2013/36/EU on access to the activity of credit institutions and the prudential supervision of credit institutions and investment firms
    b. Section B(1) of Annex I of Directive 2014/65/EU on markets in financial instruments (known as MiFID II) or comparable legislation of a third country
    c. Regulation EU 909/2014 on improving securities settlement in the European Union and on central securities depositories (or comparable legislation of a third country of residences
3. A declaration of compliance with the provisions of Council Directive 2014/107/EU41 on the mandatory automatic exchange of information in the field of taxation or the provisions of Directive 2018/843/EU on the prevention of the use of the financial system for the purposes of money laundering or terrorist financing.

This will clearly exclude some financial institutions that have operations in "non cooperative jurisdictions" and will require constant maintenance as many jurisdictions are non-cooperative today but are on track to become cooperative in the future.

As both the Finnish and US authorities have found, establishing these registers is not the problem: it is maintaining the registers. We find that some institutions may fall out of eligibility after registration, or a Competent Authority may hold an enforcement lever over financial institutions (loss of CFI status) for any failures elsewhere in the prudential oversight process.

## Article 9: Removal from the Register

This article stipulates the conditions under which a CFI can be removed from the register. These include:

a. CFI requests removal
b. CFI no longer meets the requirements to be a CFI
c. Repeated and intentional non-compliance with relevant obligations including
    (i) The FASTER Directive
    (ii) Council Directive 2014/107/EU
    (iii) Directive 2018/843/EU
    (iv) comparable legislation of a third country of residence for tax purposes

From a Directive's perspective, this would seem to give financial institutions a reasonable degree of protection without giving a major compliance obligation, other than to stay compliant. The terms *repeated* and *intentional* are undefined and somewhat subjective (two failures three years apart could technically be seen as repeated). However, if the intent is to have an operational model, it would not be reasonable for too many tax administrations to come down too heavily in the early years. Most competent authorities will listen to arguments to defuse compliance issues.

## Article 10: Reporting

FASTER is not, as the TBAG committee hoped, a mandate for tax relief as the preferred model across all Member States. FASTER is actually a reporting model that allows Member States to adopt any of the available models, even if that means no change.

Article 9(1) imposes a requirement on CFIs to report certain data to a competent authority as soon as possible after the record date and within twenty days overall. For trades not settled within twenty days, a further five days are allowed for the CFI to explain why the report has not been submitted.

The format of these reports is mandated in Annex II of the Directive and summarised below.

A. About the submitter

- name, address and TIN of the intermediary
- EUID or LEI of the intermediary
- Email address of the intermediary

B. About the recipient of the dividend or interest

- For all recipients
  - Safekeeping Account number receiving the payment
- For entity recipients
  - Name
  - LEI
  - TIN
  - Address
  - EUID
- For individuals
  - Name
  - TIN
  - Date of birth
  - Address

C. About the payor

- For all recipients
  - Safekeeping Account number where the securities were held by the payor
- For entity recipients
  - Name
  - LEI
  - TIN
  - Address
  - EUID
- For individuals
  - Name

    TIN

Date of birth
Address

D. About the payment

- Issuer name, LEI,TIN or EUID, address
- ISIN
- Security type
- COAF (corporate actions event identifier)
- Ex-date
- Record date
- Pay date
- Settlement date
- Coupon date
- Gross amount of payment
- Net amount of payment
- Tax rate applied
- Amount withheld
- Account number to which payment was made

E. About anti-abuse measures

- Number of shares for shares acquired more than two days before ex date
- Number of shares for shares acquired two days or less from the ex date
- Financial arrangements—Indicate evidence of any financial arrangement involving underlying publicly traded shares that has not been settled, expired or otherwise terminated at the ex-dividend date

We have several comments about reporting. While we could argue that in 2024 and beyond, most financial firms should be able to gather this information from existing systems easily, the reality is that the information required will probably be in different internal systems and require some kind of aggregation and oversight before it can be approved for release to a competent authority.

The twenty-day rule, starting on the record date will create an almost insurmountable problem leading to financial institutions effectively reporting on a daily basis to Competent Authorities. We also have questions about the capabilities of Competent Authorities to handle the vast amounts of data that will be sent in and between at least twenty-seven Member States. We have already seen that the US Internal Revenue Service has been unable to analyse FATCA data received over many years due to under-funding and under-resourcing by Congress. We fully expect that CRS data shared between partner jurisdictions will suffer a similar issue.

It is clear that tax administrations are keen to get as much data as they can about cross-border transactions, particularly those that have a lowered tax rate or exemption associated with them. Its more questionable, given the circumstances, whether those same tax administrations will have the resources or funding to analyse the data and take any effective action. In the case of the FASTER Directive, its may be more about verification than identifying tax abuse.

What is also clear is that the Directive falls short of mandating a fully standardised and automated withholding tax framework. To that extent, the Directive is more akin to the failed Withholding Tax Code Code of Conduct, giving Member States options as to which parts they can adopt and which parts are mandatory.

Now, the original proposed Directive was issued in June 2023. By the end of 2023, the Spanish had proposed a softening of some of the terms of the proposed Directive described in the foregoing. Not least of these was a deferral of transposition into domestic EU law to 2029, two years later than originally planned.

February 28th, 2024, saw a procedural step completed in the progress of the proposed Council Directive on Faster and Safer Relief of Excess Withholding Taxes. In line with the powers of the European Parliament, this was under the consultation procedure—meaning that consultation was obligatory and required, and the proposed Directive cannot acquire force of law unless Parliament has delivered an opinion. It is important to note though that the European Council is not legally obliged to take account of this opinion but in line with the case-law of the European Court of Justice, it must not take a decision without having received it.

The next steps for FASTER were for further discussion within Council and then over to the Economic and Financial Affairs Council (ECOFIN)—which was anticipated for either April or June 2024.

## Article 11: Relief at Source and Quick Refund

This article provides the framework for investors to request tax relief at source or quick refund, where such models are legally permitted and available.

Article 10(1) establishes that the investor (registered owner) has authorised a CFI to act on its behalf and that the CFI has verified and established the investors eligibility for the relief. This is not much of a change to existing models since, in most cases, the financial intermediary is strictly liable for any tax incorrectly withheld. It is therefore logical that, to avoid such risks, the intermediary will take steps to verify any investor's claim.

Article 10(2), however, establishes that a CFI cannot provide tax relief or a quick refund to investors that only held the security paying the dividend for less than two days prior to the ex-date. This is a response to the recent cum-ex and cum-cum scandals that rocked European banks and that were characterised by near ex-date purchases followed by sales shortly after the pay date, leading to duplicate claims by both parties to a given transaction. Article 10(2) also notes that the same restriction applies to transactions that have underlying securities that have not settled, expired or otherwise been terminated.

Finally, Article 10(3) also provides a restriction on tax relief or quick refund below any financial intermediary in a chain of payment that is not a CFI unless that financial intermediary provides a CFI with all the evidence that would be required if they had been a CFI.

## Article 12: Due Diligence

Article 11 establishes the rules for due diligence to make sure that an investor is eligible when a claim is made. In prior years, this has been one of the most controversial areas of withholding tax because each tax administration could, and did, set its own rules for different types of investors. Most of the vendors to the withholding tax reclaim industry maintain a database of at least twenty-seven investor types, each of which has different documentary requirements to establish eligibility in different jurisdictions. In the FASTER Directive landscape, this is simplified.

Article 11(1) requires a CFI to establish that the registered owner is the beneficial owner of the income and has not engaged in a financial arrangement linked to the underlying publicly traded share that has not been settled, expired or otherwise terminated at the ex-dividend date.

Article 11(2) requires a CFI to:

(i) obtain an eTRC or an acceptable equivalent proof of residence if they are in a non-EU jurisdiction
(ii) verify the eTRC or equivalent against AML data and documentation
(iii) verify the correct tax rate and entitlement
(iv) check for any evidence of possible arrangements that are related but are not settled.

Article 11(3) requires Member States to make sure that CFIs have adequate procedures in place to meet the requirements of Article 11(2).

Articles 11(2) and 11(3) here are very similar to the US framework in which due diligence procedures are mandated and financial institutions must have adequate procedures documented to meet the terms of the regulations.

## Article 13: Relief at Source

Article 12 is very simple. It just states that a registered owner, or a CFI on their behalf, can request tax relief by providing the withholding agent with the tax residence information of the registered owner and the applicable tax rate to be applied.

This is a "no change" from current practice in which CFIs will hold assets of investors co-mingled in omnibus accounts in a chain of payment and meet the requirement using withholding statements.

## Article 14: Quick Refund

The quick refund concept relies on the fact that a withholding agent remits then tax it withheld on a regular basis, typically within 30 days of the withholding. On this basis, there is a window of opportunity in which an investor may claim a refund, not from the tax authority (who doesn't have the tax yet), but from the financial institution that withheld it. The mechanism for quick refunds in FASTER will be the same as the process for tax relief at source.

## Compliance Challenges

There is no doubt that the FASTER Directive will pose many challenges, both for financial institutions and for tax administrations. As this book is published in 2024 and the Directive is currently expected to be implemented on January 1st 2029, there are several challenges that could be addressed to make it a more workable solution.

1. The **capital ratio** will lead to smaller Member States being permitted not to implement Chapter III of the Directive – which is counter-productive. The timing of **reporting obligations** in this context could easily be adjusted to allow for smaller jurisdictions below the capital ratio threshold

to report annually while larger Member States, could adopt the twenty-day reporting cycle easily. If the capital ratio was used in this way, rather than a tool to create Member State-level carve-outs, it would lead to less fragmentation without de-grading the amount or quality of data. Everyone would be subject to the Directive with no carve-outs.

2. The **eTRC** concept places the EU as an outlier in this space with the both the OECD (which opted for self-certifications over TRCs in TRACE and CRS) and the US (which uses the W-9 self-certification or the IRS-issued Form 6166).

    a. The Directive's reference to non-EU jurisdiction's participation is based on a level of "equivalence" to be established by a non-EU financial institution. As the rest of the world uses self-certifications, the more logical solution would be to allow electronically signed digital self-certifications to be used as equivalent documents to an eTRC.
    b. The other problem with the eTRC is that it is not a claim of treaty benefits—it is merely a statement of tax residency. The Directive specifically notes that a separate claim of treaty benefits from an entity investor must be part of the process. The US and OECD solved this problem by including a claim of treaty benefits into the self-certification. So, again, if there is some equivalency between self-certifications and eTRCs, this would place non-EU investors and financial institutions at an advantage with only one document required instead of two.
    c. It is also worth observing that the eTRC concept will require a level of IT systems design and implementation that EU Member States are not well known for. An equivalence for **digital self-certifications** in and between Member States would relieve Member States from the burden of building and maintaining such systems and allow financial institutions to leverage their existing systems as a change in scale as opposed to a change in type.
    d. In this area also, no mention is made in the Directive of bulk eTRC applications or the ability for a CFI (or any third party) to request eTRCs on behalf of its clients. In the absence of this kind of operational detail, there will be a massive peak prior to and on January 1st, 2029, as CFIs clamour to get the eTRCs in place quickly enough to allow their clients to benefit from tax relief at source. The tax administrations will get the blame for delays and mistakes, not the CFIs.

3. The use of **thresholds** means that the core principle of being able to reconstruct a payment chain of tax relief by a tax administration won't work, notably because smaller investors will mostly fall beneath the threshold and not be reported at all. Notable given that the basis of FASTER, in context to Giovanini, was to allow small investors easier access to relief at source—which is where most of the lost tax entitlements lie.

Overall, I think the ECOFIN adopted text will not deliver a reduction in fragmentation as hoped for. It will merely change the goalposts and lead to a different kind of fragmentation that will cost yet more money to adapt to. A similar situation will probably occur at the European Securities Market Authority (ESMA) whose role will be to take the implementation phase through the legislative process – which is where many of the detail changes are expected to occur. The ECOFIN text has been superseded by a version issued in December 2024.

As can be seen in the Table 22.1, most of the EU Member States will be eligible for an opt out from parts of the FASTER Directive since they fail to meet the 1.5% market capitalisation threshold.

So, in effect seventeen Member States out of 27 (62.9%) will qualify for an opt-out option from the FASTER Directive based on data as of 31 January 2024. It seems unlikely that many will experience sufficient growth to change that statistic between now and January 2029. This leads us to the uncomfortable conclusion that, given the history of fragmentation and lack of agreement that led us to this place, a Directive that is unanimously agreed to be twenty-seven Member States, seventeen of which must have known that they would be able to opt out is hardly the definition of a homogenous and focussed approach. This is our primary evidence that the FASTER Directive will, likely, be a source of further and continuing fragmentation in the European Union.

**Table 22.1** Proportion of EU Member States with FASTER Opt-out based as at 31/01/2024 *Source* Manfred Artmeier, RAQUEST GmbH

| Rank | Market | Market Cap €Bn | Capital Ratio | Future State |
|---|---|---|---|---|
| 1 | France | 2602.9 | 29.85 | FASTER |
| 2 | Germany | 1791.0 | 20.54 | FASTER |
| 3 | Sweden | 887.4 | 10.18 | FASTER |
| 4 | Netherlands | 760.9 | 8.73 | FASTER |
| 5 | Spain | 643.9 | 7.39 | FASTER |
| 6 | Italy | 574.4 | 6.59 | FASTER |
| 7 | Ireland | 290.6 | 3.33 | FASTER |
| 8 | Denmark | 280.0 | 3.31 | FASTER |
| 9 | Belgium | 207.4 | 2.38 | FASTER |
| 10 | Finland | 169.2 | 1.94 | FASTER |
| 11 | Austria | 130.7 | 1.49 | Opt Out Option |
| 12 | Poland | 74.0 | 0.85 | Opt Out Option |
| 13 | Luxembourg | 62.1 | 0.71 | Opt Out Option |
| 14 | Portugal | 58.5 | 0.67 | Opt Out Option |
| 15 | Greece | 55.0 | 0.63 | Opt Out Option |
| 16 | Czech Rep | 29.6 | 0.34 | Opt Out Option |
| 17 | Romania | 29.0 | 0.33 | Opt Out Option |
| 18 | Croatia | 17.8 | 0.20 | Opt Out Option |
| 19 | Slovenia | 13.5 | 0.15 | Opt Out Option |
| 20 | Hungary | 9.6 | 0.11 | Opt Out Option |
| 21 | Cyprus | 8.6 | 0.10 | Opt Out Option |
| 22 | Malta | 5.4 | 0.06 | Opt Out Option |
| 23 | Bulgaria | 5.3 | 0.06 | Opt Out Option |
| 24 | Lithuania | 4.8 | 0.06 | Opt Out Option |
| 25 | Estonia | 3.7 | 0.04 | Opt Out Option |
| 26 | Slovakia | 3.0 | 0.03 | Opt Out Option |
| 27 | Latvia | 0.6 | 0.01 | Opt Out Option |

# Part V

## Ireland

# 23

# Irish QI Program

This chapter will describe the Irish Qualified Intermediary Agreement, its purpose and key components.

Financial services firms around the world must often act rather like the mythical two-headed dog Janus. Their status and obligations are becoming more and more complex, and these obligations vary depending on which way they are looking on behalf of their investors. The Irish followed the American example with a qualified intermediary system, although much less voluminous in content and depth, it has some significant differences from the American system.

The Irish system is, like the US system, based on a domestic level of withholding which can be mitigated by documentation. There are currently about thirty financial firms signed up as QIs under the Irish system.

There are five significant differences between the US and Irish systems:

- The tax rates are either taxed at the domestic withholding rate or are exempt. There are no bands of withholding or intermediary tax rates
- There is the possibility of a bond or guarantee required by the Irish QI against the risk of its failure to comply, where the US system has a regime of after-the-fact penalties
- The account structure required to operate the Irish QI system is much simpler and more related to pre-existing financial services structures, i.e., exempt and liable.
- Tax information reporting is mandatory in the US scheme but is by notice in the Irish scheme, i.e., the guidance is given in the US regulations for Form 1042 and Form 1099 reporting which must occur each year. The


R. K. McGill and K. V. Pitkin, *Qualified Intermediary*,
https://doi.org/10.1007/978-3-031-81410-5_23

Irish Revenue on the other hand will issue a notice if they want tax information reporting to be performed.
- The existence of a different entity type in the Irish regulations known as a "Special Intermediary" for the purpose of dealing with American Depositary Receipts (ADRs).

The similarities are that both systems:

- establish a matrix of income types and recipient types to whom the tax applies or does not apply
- assume a default domestic level of withholding
- allow documentation to mitigate the withholding level
- require the withholding (exempt or liable) to be established at the time of the distribution
- require documentation to a lower level than previously held by financial firms, i.e., the identification of the real beneficial owner of income
- require increased levels of automation
- require payment in specified time frames

Most of the risks associated with the Irish regime are similar in nature to the US one. So, to that extent we are not going to bore the reader with a replication of comments. Hopefully, having read the US QI description, the reader will be able to infer the risks and issues present in the Irish regime and will find it interesting to see the parallels with the US regulations.

Investors should consider for a moment the difficulties faced by a custodian managing assets in a portfolio including the US, Japan and Ireland where, for example, the custodian is in say France. The custodian may well be an in-country agent for in-bound tax reclaims destined for the French tax authorities, a Qualified Intermediary under the US regulations (because it receives US sourced income for its clients), a Qualified Intermediary under the Irish regulations, because it receives Irish sourced income for its clients and also a Qualified Financial Intermediary with respect to Japanese Government Bond income.

In each case, different documentary requirements apply, different withholding rates and methods of calculating and applying it and, importantly, different requirements for information reporting and oversight compliance.

So, overall, the risk inherent for a custodian is less in the Irish QI regime than in the US, simply because of the simpler structure, although Irish QIs can be required to put up a bond in advance. Also, the costs associated with complying with the Irish regime are likely to be less, as the differences to existing financial services practice are less. However, the absolute value of investments into the US and Ireland are of course quite different which perhaps, to some extent, explains the scale of differences between the two regimes.

The following description of the Irish relief at source regime is provided with grateful thanks to the Irish Revenue Commission for their help and information.

Firstly, and to make life a bit simpler, we must recognise that different terminology exists in each of these sets of regulations, but that the similarities in the words and phrases leave little doubt of the meanings.

An AWA is an authorised withholding agent, i.e., a firm that is authorised to make withholdings of tax on income. This is the same as a straightforward withholding agent described in the US regulations and in the general description of the tax reclaim models. Withholding tax in the context of the Irish regulations is dividend withholding tax, as opposed to the NRA withholding tax in the US regulations which applies to several more types of income. Qualified Intermediaries are the same in principle in the two models, although in the Irish model there is also the concept of a Special Intermediary. The tax authority, which in the US is the IRS, is in Ireland just termed "Revenue".

Dividends paid and other distributions ("relevant distributions") made by Irish-resident companies are generally liable to a dividend withholding tax at the standard rate of income tax for the year of assessment in which the distribution is made.

The Irish resident company making the distribution is required to withhold the tax and pay it over to the Irish Revenue. However, the legislation makes provision for an AWA to act for the company making the distribution. If an AWA is involved, the amount of the distribution can be paid gross by the paying company to the AWA, who then takes over responsibility for applying the withholding tax rules.

The basic principle is that withholding tax must be deducted at the time the distribution is being made unless the company or the AWA has satisfied itself that the recipient is a non-liable person and is entitled to receive the distribution without the deduction of withholding tax. To this extent the Irish rules are the same as the US rules, in terms of the principle applied. The deposit rules are however much simpler. All withholding tax must be paid to Revenue by the 14$^{th}$ of the month following that in which the distribution is made.

Certain recipients of distributions are specifically excluded from the scope of the tax, while certain others are entitled to an exemption. It should be noted that exemption is not automatic and must be established by means of an appropriate declaration of exemption, which must be completed by the applicant and accompanied by the necessary certification. Again, the principle here is the same as the US regulations in that any lower withholding rate (i.e., exemption) that could be applied will only be allowed given the existence of appropriate documentation. The actual documentation, while simple in form, does however have more complexity in structure that the simple W-8BEN forms in the US regulations.

The legislation relating to withholding tax is contained in Chapter 8A of Part 6 and Schedule 2A of the Taxes Consolidation Act, 1997. It was introduced in Sect. 27 of the Finance Act, 1999 and amended by Sections 30 and 59 of the Finance Act, 2000 and Section 43 of the Finance Act, 2001.

So, like the other relief at source regimes, there are types of income that attract different tax treatments and also types of recipient that attract different tax treatments.

Withholding tax at the standard rate of income tax applies to all relevant distributions made by Irish resident-paying companies. For the purposes of the withholding tax legislation, relevant distributions are:

1. **Cash Distributions**
2. **Scrip Dividends:** This is where a shareholder opts to take additional shares instead of a cash dividend in situations where the paying company gives its shareholders the option of taking either cash or additional shares. In such cases the shareholder who elects to take additional shares instead of cash is treated as if they received a distribution of an amount equal to the cash dividend which the shareholder would have received if they had not elected to take the shares. When this happens, the distributing company is required, when issuing the additional shares to each shareholder to issue a reduced number of shares instead of withholding a cash amount from the distribution. The paying company must then pay to the Irish Revenue an amount of withholding tax equal to tax at the standard rate of income tax on the cash amount which the shareholder would have received if they had not elected to take the shares instead of cash.
3. **Distributions in a non-cash form:** This is where a paying company makes a distribution, which consists of something other than cash (but not a scrip dividend). In such cases the paying company which makes the non-cash distribution to the shareholder is liable to pay to the Irish Revenue an amount of withholding tax equal to the tax which would have been payable on the distribution if it had been in cash and taxed at the

standard rate of income tax. Furthermore, since no tax is actually withheld from the non-cash distribution the paying company is empowered to recover from each shareholder (other than shareholders exempted from withholding tax) an amount equal to the tax paid to the Irish Revenue in respect of that shareholder's non-cash distribution.

Distributions not liable to withholding tax include:

1. Distributions made to Ministers of the Government
2. Distributions falling within scope of EU Parent/Subsidiary Directive
3. Stapled Stock arrangements
4. Distributions which are not liable to income tax in the hands of the recipients.
5. Distributions made by an Irish resident company to another Irish resident company of which it is a fifty-one per cent subsidiary.

Persons exempt from withholding tax include:

### Exempt Resident Persons (Excluded Persons)

I won't go into detail on this section because this book deals with cross-border issues, i.e., non-resident aliens. However, it's instructive to realise that such regulations can often have terms which relate to domestic residents too.

### Exempt non-resident persons

Just for clarity, the term "relevant territory" used in the Irish regulations means a Member State of the European Union or a country with which Ireland has a double taxation treaty. Currently, Ireland has double taxation treaties with thirty-nine other countries, including thirteen of the twenty-seven other Member States of the European Union. Ireland does not have a double taxation treaty with Greece but, as a Member State of the European Union, Greece is also treated as a "relevant territory".

The Irish QI system, as we have noted, gives exemption to certain types of recipients on dividend income. As with the US QI system, that exemption must be proved prior to receipt of the payment.

The following is a list of types of non-resident persons exempt from withholding tax:

1. An unincorporated body of persons, such as a charity or superannuation fund, which is resident for the purposes of tax in a relevant territory.
2. Individuals who are neither resident nor ordinarily resident in Ireland but are resident for the purposes of tax, in a relevant territory.
3. Companies resident for the purposes of tax in a relevant territory and which are not controlled by Irish residents.
4. Companies which are not resident in Ireland, which are under the ultimate control of persons who are neither resident nor ordinarily resident in Ireland, but are resident for the purposes of tax in a relevant territory.
5. Companies, the principal class of shares of which (or of a company of which it is at least a seventy-five per cent subsidiary) is substantially and regularly traded on a recognised stock exchange in a relevant territory.
6. Companies which are wholly owned by two or more companies, each of whose principal class of shares is substantially and regularly traded on one or more recognised stock exchanges in a relevant territory.
7. Parent companies in other EU Member States receive distributions from Irish resident unlimited subsidiary companies in which the parent company holds at least 25% of the capital.

Before accepting that non-resident persons are exempt, the paying company or AWA must be satisfied that the person, if not a QI, is the person beneficially entitled to the distribution and has made the appropriate declaration of exemption with supporting certification to the company making the distribution. If the distribution is being paid to an exempt non-resident person through a QI or a chain of QIs, the declaration of exemption and supporting certification must be made to the QI from whom the dividend will be received.

## Irish Resident-Paying Companies

An Irish resident-paying company making relevant distributions is obliged to deduct withholding tax at the standard rate of income tax which applies at the time the distribution is made, unless the company has satisfied itself that:

1. the recipient is a non-liable person and is entitled to receive the distribution without deduction of withholding tax, or
2. the distribution is being made in the first instance to an AWA.

All withholding tax deducted by the paying company must be paid to the Irish Revenue by the 14th of the month following that in which the distribution is made. Payments must be accompanied by a return, which must be in an electronic format approved by the Irish Revenue. In exceptional circumstances, where the Revenue are satisfied that the paying company does not have the facilities to make a return in electronic format, they may authorise the paying company to make the return in writing in a form authorised by the Revenue. Again, there is a clear analogy here with the US regulations and in particular the structure for deposits. The US uses the EFTPS system and the Irish also require an electronic payment method as the default.

The paying company is obliged to retain all declarations and notifications received from shareholders and intermediaries for the longer of 6 years or the period ending 3 years after it ceased to pay distributions to the person who made the declaration or gave the notification to the paying company.

Where company registrars handle distributions on behalf of quoted companies their obligations are similar to those of the paying companies.

An AWA can receive distributions from a paying company without the deduction of withholding tax, regardless of whether the ultimate beneficiary is a liable or an exempt person. However, the AWA then takes over the responsibility of the paying company as far as withholding tax is concerned. It must apply withholding tax, where applicable, when paying on the distributions to its clients, and then pay this withholding tax over to Revenue and make returns to the Revenue, in the same way as paying companies. An AWA must be authorised to act as such by Revenue.

An AWA must give notice of the fact that it is an AWA to each paying company from which it is to receive relevant distributions on behalf of other persons in writing. This allows those companies to make the distributions to the AWA without applying withholding tax. In the absence of such notification, the company must apply withholding tax to the distributions. To this extent, the AWA is essentially acting as a paying agent.

On receiving the distributions, the AWA must operate the withholding tax scheme as if it were the company making the distribution. Thus, the AWA must make the appropriate deduction of withholding tax when it pays on the distributions, or amounts representing the distributions, and must account for that tax to the Irish Revenue by the 14th of the month following that in which the distribution is made by the company.

A substantial portion of investment in Irish companies is made through an intermediary (e.g., a bank or stockbroking firm) or, indeed, through a chain of intermediaries. This is recognised in the withholding tax legislation, which makes provision for exemption at source in such cases provided the intermediary accepts an additional administrative burden. For an intermediary to receive dividends gross on behalf of non-liable clients, the intermediary must have entered into a “Qualifying Intermediary Agreement” with the Irish Revenue. In doing so the intermediary becomes a “Qualifying Intermediary” (QI) under the withholding tax legislation.

To become an Irish QI, an intermediary must:

1. be resident in Ireland,
2. if not resident in Ireland, be resident for tax purposes in a relevant territory,
3. hold (or be wholly owned by a person who holds) a banking license in Ireland or in a relevant territory, or,
4. be a member of the Irish Stock Exchange or a recognised stock exchange in a relevant territory, or,
5. be, in the opinion of the Irish Revenue, a person suitable to be a QI, and
6. enter into a QI agreement with the Irish Revenue and be authorised by the Revenue to act as a QI.

Under the terms of the Irish QI agreement, the intermediary undertakes:

1. to operate the withholding tax scheme (including the making of returns to the Irish Revenue) in a correct and efficient manner,
2. to accept any declaration or notification given to it in connection with the withholding tax scheme and to retain such declarations or notifications for the longer of 6 years, or the period ending 3 years after it has ceased to receive distributions on behalf of the person who made the declaration or gave the notification,
3. to exercise a duty of care and verification in relation to such declarations and notifications,
4. to make available for inspection declarations of exemption and notifications made to the intermediary in connection with the withholding tax scheme,
5. to provide to the Revenue with an auditor’s report on its compliance with the withholding tax scheme after it has been operating the QI agreement for 1 year and to provide further auditor’s reports when requested to do so by the Irish Revenue,
6. to allow for the verification of its compliance with the withholding tax scheme by the Irish Revenue in any manner considered appropriate by the Irish Revenue.

The agreement may also, in certain circumstances, require the provision of a bond or guarantee by the intermediary to protect the Irish Exchequer against fraud or negligence in the operation of the QI agreement and the withholding tax scheme.

The Irish Revenue allows QIs to create and maintain two separate and distinct categories of funds or accounts known respectively as exempt and liable funds or accounts. In advance of a distribution being made, the QI can accept declarations of exemption from non-liable persons and notifications from other QIs and, on receipt of these declarations and notifications, notify the paying company in writing whether the distribution is for the benefit of non-liable or liable persons. The distributions for non-liable persons can then be paid gross by the paying company and will go into the QI's exempt account while the distributions for liable persons will go into the liable account.

In some instances, an intermediary can operate through one or more nominee companies and might want to have these nominee companies covered by the QI authorisation. While this is possible, it can only be allowed where the intermediary advises the Irish Revenue in writing of any nominee companies who wish to operate under the terms of the QI agreement. Such nominee companies must also execute a power of attorney granting the principal full power to enter into a QI agreement with the Irish Revenue on their behalf.

The QI authorisation will expire naturally after 7 years. This doesn't prevent the Irish Revenue and the intermediary from agreeing to renew, or enter into a new, QI agreement, nor does it prevent the Irish Revenue from authorising the intermediary as a QI for a further 7-year period. However, the Irish Revenue reserves the right to revoke a QI authorisation at any time if it is satisfied that the QI has failed to comply with the QI agreement or is otherwise "unsuitable" to be an QI.

Where revocation occurs, the fact that the authorisation has been revoked is published in "Iris Oifigiúil", the official Irish Government gazette. So, there's no hiding place for bad practice and investors have the opportunity to review these publications before selecting a custodian.

A QI, which receives, on behalf of its clients, relevant distributions made by a company resident in Ireland, or amounts representing such distributions paid on to it by another QI, is required to maintain two separate funds or accounts in relation to such distributions and amounts, an "Exempt Fund" and a "Liable Fund". (Exhibit 23.1).

The Exempt Fund or account should include:

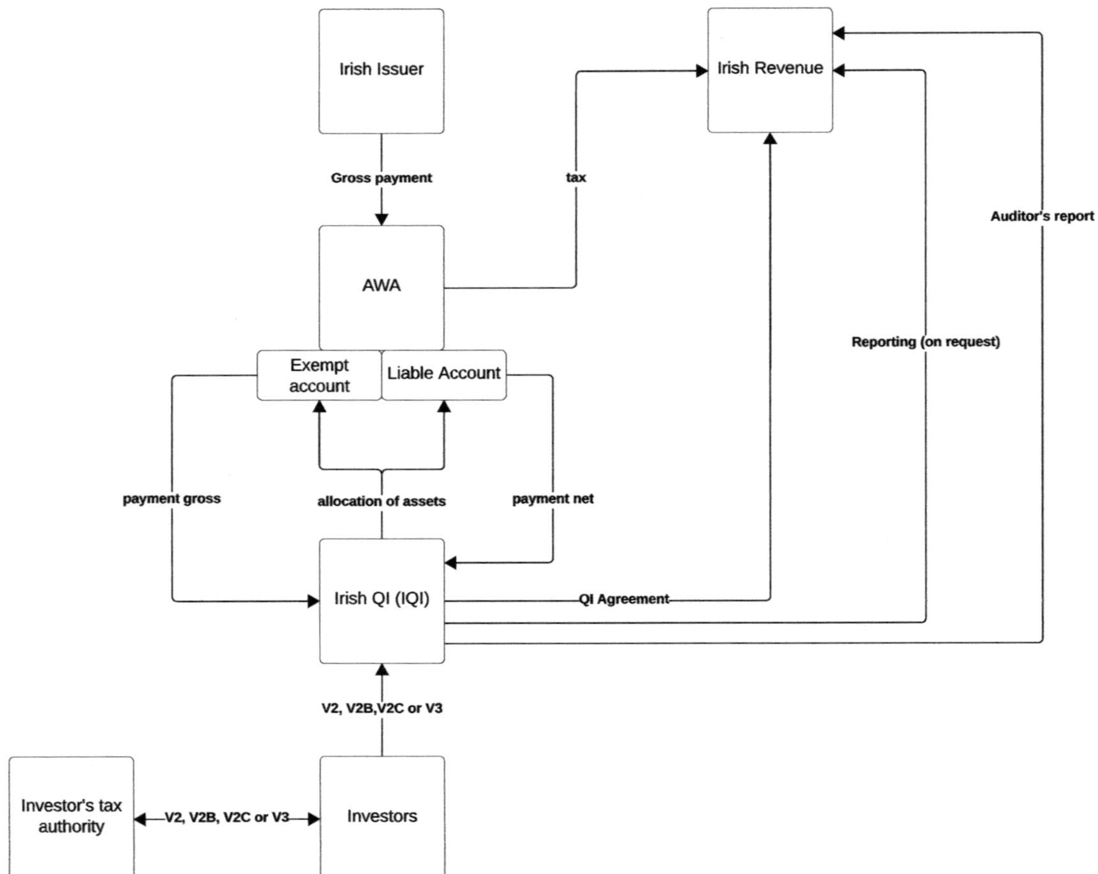


**Exhibit 23.1** Operation of the Irish QI system *Source* Authors

1. excluded persons and qualifying non-resident persons who have made to the QI the appropriate declaration of exemption, and;
2. other QIs who have advised the QI that the distributions, or amounts representing such distributions, to be paid on to them by the QI are to be received by the other QIs on behalf of persons in their Exempt Funds.

The Liable Fund should include the remainder of the QI's clients.

A QI must notify the company making the distributions or, if the distributions are made through a chain of QIs, the QI (if any) immediately above it in the chain, by way of notice in writing, as to whether the distributions to be received by it from the company or the other QI, as the case may be, are to be received for the benefit of persons in its Exempt account or Liable account. The QI must keep its Exempt and Liable Funds up to date and must notify the company, by way of notice in writing, of updates as often as may be necessary. The company must apply withholding tax to a distribution unless it has been notified by the QI that the distribution is to be received by the QI for the benefit of a person in its Exempt Fund.

A QI is obliged to submit a return to Revenue when requested in writing to do so. This return must be made within the time specified, which won't be less than thirty days. When requesting a return, the Revenue may specify that they require only details of a particular class or classes of distributions relating to a specific period, or they may request details of all distributions relating to a specific period. For example, details of all payments over €1,000 might be required or all distributions relating to a particular company or companies. A QI return must be in an electronic format approved by the Irish Revenue.

Each return must contain in relation to the information sought by Revenue:

1. the name and address of each company from which the QI has received distributions on behalf of its clients during the period specified and of each other QI from which it receives amounts representing such distributions on behalf of its clients;
2. the amount of each such distribution;
3. the name and address of the clients to whom the distributions were given by the QI, and
4. whether those clients were liable or non-liable persons.

As mentioned earlier, exemption from withholding tax is not automatic and must be established by means of an appropriate declaration of exemption, which must be completed by the applicant, typically a Form V2.

This declaration must be in a form approved by Revenue and, in the case of qualifying non-resident persons, must, where appropriate be supported by documentary evidence. This equates roughly to the US position on the W-8BEN as the declaration and the application of KYC rules which would provide the supporting documentation.

The supporting documentation is as follows:

1. A declaration made by a non-resident person (not being a company) must be accompanied by a certificate of residence from the tax authority in the country of the person's residence.
2. A declaration by the trustee or trustees of a non-resident discretionary trust must be accompanied by:

    a. a certificate given by the tax authority of the country in which the trust is, by virtue of the law of that territory, resident for the purposes of tax, certifying that the trust is resident in that territory,
    b. a certificate from the trustee or trustees showing the names and addresses of the settlers and beneficiaries of the trust, and
    c. a certificate from the Irish Revenue indicating that they have seen the certification and have noted its contents. In this context it should be noted that the withholding tax legislation defines the term "beneficiary" in a wide manner. The term means any person who, directly or indirectly, is beneficially entitled under the discretionary trust, or may, through the exercise of any power or powers conferred on that person or any other person or persons, reasonably expect to become beneficially entitled under the trust to income or capital or to have any income or capital applied for that person's benefit or to receive any other benefit.

3. A declaration made by a non-resident company which is claiming the exemption on the basis that it is either:

    a. ultimately controlled by persons resident for the purposes of tax in a relevant territory, or
    b. a company, the principal class of shares of which (or of a company of which it is a seventy-five per cent subsidiary) is substantially and regularly traded on a recognised stock exchange in a relevant territory, or

c. a company which is wholly owned by two or more companies, each of whose principal class of shares is substantially and regularly traded on one or more recognised stock exchanges in a relevant territory, must be accompanied by a certificate from the company's auditor certifying that in the opinion of the auditor it meets one of these criteria.

4. A declaration from a company claiming the exemption on the basis that it is resident for the purposes of tax in a relevant territory and is not under the control, directly or indirectly, of a person or persons resident in Ireland must be accompanied by;

   a. a certificate given by the tax authority of the relevant territory in which the company is, by virtue of the law of that territory, resident for the purposes of tax certifying that the company is resident in that territory, and
   b. a certificate signed by the auditor of the company certifying that in the opinion of the auditor the company is not under the control, either directly or indirectly, of a person or persons who is or are resident in the Republic of Ireland.

Exemption declarations for resident (excluded) persons remain valid until such time as:

1. the excluded person notifies the paying company or the QI that they have ceased to be an excluded person, or
2. the paying company or QI becomes aware, for whatever reason, that the person who made the declaration has ceased to be an excluded person.

Exemption declarations for qualifying non-resident persons remain valid for a maximum period of 6 years. This period of validity is determined by the date on which the relevant certificates accompanying the exemption declarations are issued. The legislation confirms that these certificates remain valid for the period from the date of issue until December 31 in the fifth year following the year in which the certificate was issued, thus providing for a maximum period of validity of 6 years where a certificate was issued on 1 January in a particular year. This is analogous to the US form W-8BEN, albeit the validity period is longer. What's also interesting is the more extensive degree to which the declaration by a person is certified accurate by others, such as auditors and local tax authorities. This means that while obtaining the declaration will give the exemption required, obtaining the declaration in correct form for a custodian will be a more costly process. The US Form W-8BEN is a self-certification, whereas the Irish forms are also a sort of self-certification, inasmuch as the person claiming the exemption is the one who ultimately signs the form, but the latter has third parties attesting to its accuracy. The exemption declarations from **excluded** or **qualifying non-resident persons** can only be accepted where the declaration forms have been fully completed and signed and where the recipient of the declaration (paying company, AWA or QI) has no reasonable grounds to believe that the declaration (and any accompanying certificates) is not true or incorrect.

Where a distribution is to be made directly to an exempt shareholder by the company or by the AWA, the shareholder must provide evidence of entitlement to exemption to the company or the AWA. If the distribution is to be made through a QI, the evidence of entitlement to exemption must be given to the QI. That QI will then notify the company of the amount of the distribution to be received on behalf of exempt persons. Where a distribution is to be made to an exempt shareholder through a series of QIs, the evidence of entitlement of the shareholder to an exemption must be given to the QI from whom the shareholder will finally receive payment. In this case that QI will convey to the QI immediately above it, the amount to be received on behalf of exempt persons. That second QI will then convey details (of the amount of the distribution to be received by it which will ultimately be passed on to shareholders who are exempt) to the company. This is a critical issue. As with the US regulations, this requirement is the one that protects the identity of the beneficial owner/recipient from other financial firms in the chain who would otherwise be competitors of the firms below it. This chain approach applies through any number of intermediaries, provided that they are all QIs. If any intermediary in the chain is not a QI, withholding tax will apply. The only exception to this rule is American Depositary Receipts (ADRs), to which special arrangements apply.

ADRs are one of a class of instruments known as Depositary Receipts. Other examples are Global Depositary Receipts (GDRs) and International Depositary Receipts (IDRs). ADRs are US dollar-denominated securities issued by a Depositary bank in the US and representing ownership of non-US shares. A simplified procedure applies to ADRs which establishes a different kind of entity in the chain—the Specified Intermediary. In many respects a Specified Intermediary is like a QI but there are a number of significant differences. Among these are:

1. a Specified Intermediary does not have to be authorised by the Irish Revenue.

2. a Specified Intermediary does not have to enter into an agreement with the Irish Revenue and accordingly doesn't have to provide an auditor's report relating to the intermediary's compliance with an agreement. However a Specified Intermediary does have to enter into an agreement with the QI (or with another Specified Intermediary if it receives distributions through them) under which it undertakes to supply the QI or the other Specified Intermediary, or, if preferred directly to Irish Revenue, returns showing details, such as name and address information and amounts of any distributions, or classes of distributions, which the Revenue has asked for. Such information must be furnished by the Specified Intermediary within twenty-one days of the receipt of a notice requesting such information (Exhibit 23.2)

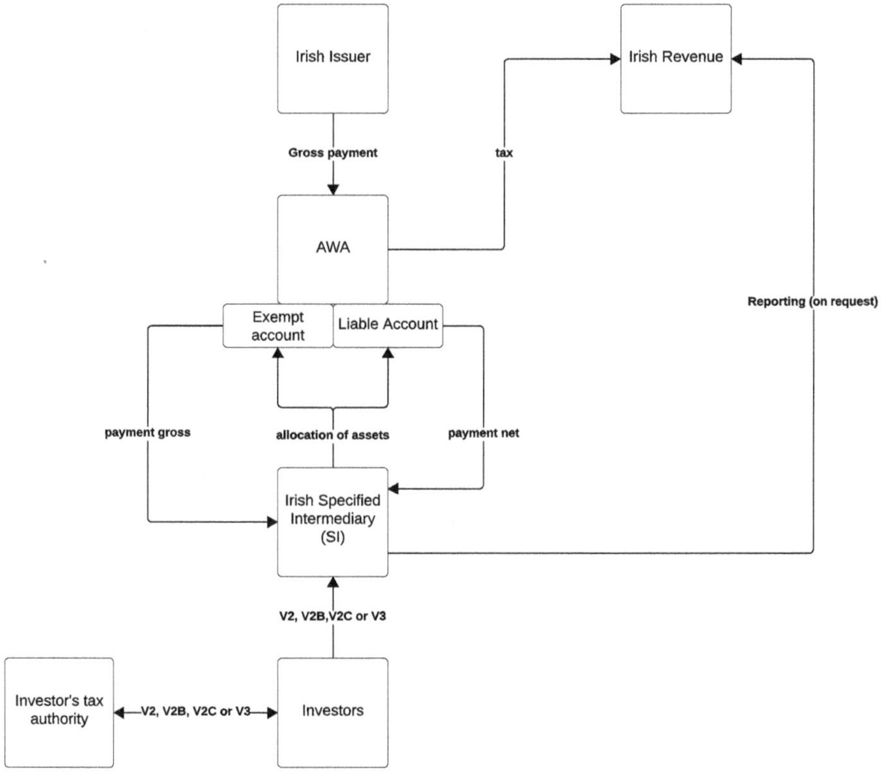


**Exhibit 23.2** Operation of the Irish Specified Intermediary system *Source* Authors

The Irish Revenue does reserve the right to revoke the right of a Specified Intermediary to be treated as a Specified Intermediary for the purposes of the withholding tax scheme if they're satisfied that the Specified Intermediary has failed to comply with its obligations with regard to the withholding tax scheme and particularly the obligation to furnish details such as name and address information and amounts of any distributions, or classes of distributions which Revenue has asked for.

# Part VI

## Japan

# 24

# Japanese QFI Program

This chapter describes the Qualified Financial Intermediary (QFI) program for Japanese Government Bonds (JGBs) including the obligations of the parties.

The QFI system for tax exemptions on interest paid on Japanese government bonds (JGBs) was established in 2001 and launched in 2002. It became fully operational in 2003. There are seven government bonds issued by the Japanese government.[1] They are a 2-year, 5-year, 10-year, 20-year and 30-year yield and 40-year bonds, and the 10-year Japan Climate transition bond.[2]

A QFI is a foreign (non-Japanese) financial institution, such as a global custodian, which has been designated as the account management institution prescribed in the Act on Book-Entry Transfer of Company Bonds, Shares Article 44 (1) (xiii) and has been approved by the Bank of Japan (BOJ) as a foreign indirect participant (FIP) in the JGB Book-Entry System.

The tax exemption scheme for interest on JGBs is only applicable to those firms that hold JGBs in the book-entry transfer account opened with a JGB Book-Entry System Participant in Japan (JBESP) or with the QFI. Therefore, it will not apply to cases where JGBs are held in transfer accounts opened with foreign financial institutions without QFI status.

The Japanese Government promulgated these regulations in order to increase foreign holdings of Japanese government bonds. To that extent the

[1] https://www.bloomberg.com/markets/rates-bonds/government-bonds/japan.

[2] https://www.boj.or.jp/en/statistics/boj/other/mei/release/2024/index.htm.


R. K. McGill and K. V. Pitkin, *Qualified Intermediary*,
https://doi.org/10.1007/978-3-031-81410-5_24

system is far more limited than that which applies from the United States inasmuch as it only applies to a very limited income type. Its intent is also different from the US authorities. Here the espoused intent is to encourage inward investment rather than eradicate abuse of an existing system.

Having said that, it is clear that the Japanese QFI system has many structural similarities, not least in name, to the US system.

Prior to 2001, Japanese regulations granted withholding tax exemption only to the portion of interest arising from JGBs that correspond to the period when JGBs were held by non-resident investors in the Bank of Japan (BOJ) book-entry system. Legislation was introduced in 2001 that would expand this withholding tax exemption to interest on JGBs to include non-resident investors that maintain custody of JGBs through global custodians. This was an important change for the mutual fund industry, since many mutual funds were unable to qualify for the original exemption. The previous law provided that individual non-residents of Japan and foreign corporations were exempt from Japanese withholding tax on interest payments on JGBs, provided certain conditions were met concerning how the securities were held. Some mutual funds were not able to meet those conditions while maintaining custody of JGBs through their global custodians.

The legislation, which became effective for interest payments made on JGBs deposited in the scheme on or after April 1st 2001, allows a non-resident investor, such as a US mutual fund, that uses a qualified foreign intermediary (QFI) or a chain of QFIs to maintain custody of the JGBs to claim the withholding tax exemption. The legislation requires global custodians to obtain QFI status and requires the non-resident investor to submit documentation to the Japanese tax authorities (via the QFI and the local sub-custodian) that would entitle the non-resident investor to claim the withholding tax exemption.

To become a QFI a foreign financial firm must obtain approval from the Bank of Japan as a foreign indirect participant depositing JGBs with a participant or indirect participant (sub-custodian) in the Bank of Japan's book-entry system:

1. The QFI applicant must also obtain approval from the Japanese Tax Authorities
2. QFI applicants must be resident companies of a state which has a tax treaty with Japan and which includes an article on exchange of information with Japan as the partner

3. If a foreign branch of QFI wishes to act in a QFI capacity, the branch office must also be in states with a tax treaty with Japan and which also must have an exchange of information article within the treaty
4. Non-resident investors must submit documentation to identify themselves as well as their ownership period and record of JGBs to the Japanese tax authorities via a QFI and sub-custodian
5. QFI's must keep book records and report information about holdings and records at beneficial owner (investor) level, to sub-custodians
6. QFIs must adhere to procedures and documentation prescribed and published in Cabinet Orders and Ministerial ordinance.

So, from these seven principles, the reader can hopefully see the clear similarities to the US system. Exemption from withholding (i.e., 100% relief) can be gained only by:

- submission of proper documentation
- provision of agreements between foreign intermediaries and tax authorities
- acceptable record keeping
- adherence to rules and
- only within jurisdictions with tax treaties (i.e., acceptable rules).

Exhibit 24.1 shows the effect of the new regulations. The additional functional lines represent each QFI either alone or in a chain, needing to gain the approval of both the BOJ and the Japanese tax authorities. Each line will involve acceptance of the above principles and rules so that foreign investors can gain the benefit of relief from withholding tax on the interest on JGBs.

QFIs are required to submit the Application Form for Withholding Tax Exemption received from non-resident individuals or foreign corporations to the JBESPs under which the QFI concerned has its operation, and QFIs are also required to fulfil the following roles:

(1) QFIs are required to verify with identification documents, the name and address, which are described in the Application Form for Withholding Tax Exemption or the Application Form for Amendment received from non-resident individuals and foreign corporations (in the case where the submitting entities are trustees of Qualified as a Foreign Securities Investment Trusts (QFSITs), the name and address of the trustees, the name of the QFSIT and the fulfilment of the requirements to be a QFSIT are required).

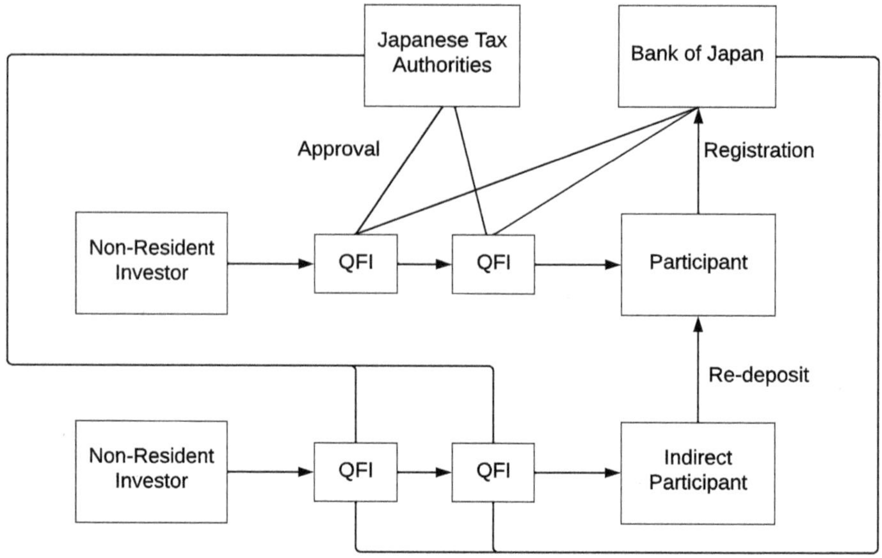


**Exhibit 24.1** Japanese Government Bond QFI system *Source* Authors

(2) When information relating to JGBs has been recorded/described for non-resident individuals or foreign corporations who have submitted the Application Form for Withholding Tax Exemption or an Application Form for Amendment has been submitted or, when an operating partner of partnerships or a trustee of Trusts Taxable on Beneficiaries (excluding FPT) has:

1. submitted the amendment of the following matters in the Notification Form for Amendment:
   a. Name or address of the business office of the partnership or the trust
   b. Name or address, etc. of operating partner of partnerships or trustee of the trust
   c. Proportion of distribution of profits and losses
2. submitted copies of partnership agreement or trust agreement

(3) QFIs must record/describe the following information in the book for each investor (in the case of QFSITs, for each trustee and for each QFSIT or FPT every time, and must keep the book for five years following the year in which the closing date of the book falls:

- Name (in the case of QFSIT/FPT, for each trustee and for each QFSIT/FPT) and address of non-resident individuals or foreign corporations who have submitted the Application Form for Withholding Tax Exemption, and the date of submission
- Issue of the JGBs and redemption amount for each issue
- Date in accordance with the classification mentioned below:
- (When the JGB is acquired) the date when the information relating to the book-entry transfer is described for such acquisition.
- (When the JGB is transferred) the date when the information relating to the book-entry transfer is described for such transfer.
- (When redemption for the JGB is made) the date when the information relating to the book-entry transfer is described for such redemption
- Date of the payment of the interest or profit from redemption (hereinafter referred to as "interests, etc.") for each issue of the JGBs and the amount
- (When Application Form for Amendment is submitted) the date of submission.
- (In the case of the non-resident individual with residence in Japan) any address or location outside Japan
- (In the case of the foreign corporation operating the Japanese branch or plant, etc.) the address of head office or main office outside Japan and
- (When non-resident individuals or foreign corporations who filed Application Form for Withholding Tax Exemption receive the interest payment on the JGBs attributed to partnership property or trust property) (i) Name and address of business office of such partnership or trust, (ii) name and address, etc. of the operating partner or trustee, (iii) proportion of distribution of profits and losses of the non-resident individuals or foreign corporations who filed the Application Form for Withholding Tax Exemption (in the event of amendment of these matters, the date on which the amendment on these matters as well as the amended proportion of distribution of profits and losses would become effective), and (iv) the date of submission of Notification Form for Tax Exemption on Partnership or Trust submitted by the operating partner or trustee, etc.
- Other relevant information

From a compliance perspective, the amount of effort involved in maintaining the books of record for JGBs depends on the size of the market for your financial institution and your clients. Like Finland, Japan is not the largest investment market for non-residents, nor is the JGB portion of it that large either.

There are currently 261 participants in the QFI system, 816 indirect participants and 160 non-Japanese indirect participants.

# Part VII

## Technology & Convergence

# 25

# Residency vs Citizenship

This chapter deals with the major fault line between the US and Eritrea) and the rest of the world. We describe the pitfalls and problems that flow from citizenship-based taxation (CBT) when compared to the residence-based taxation (RBT) used by the rest of the world. We update the reader on efforts to change the US CBT system to a RBT system that would allow the US to revoke its FATCA law and all its inter-governmental agreements (IGAs) and instead, adopt the AEoI/CRS framework.

All but two countries in the world have adopted the principle of taxation based upon the residency of the beneficial owner of the income. This is also sometimes called residency for tax purposes, but generally means that the ultimate owner of the income pays tax on that income in the country of their permanent residence.

The two outliers are the United States, which is already the subject of much discourse in this book, and the African country of Eritrea.

Taxation is a critical component of any nation's fiscal policy, determining how they collect revenues. Among the various approaches to taxation, citizenship-based and residence-based taxation stand out as two distinct models, each with unique implications for taxpayers and governments.


R. K. McGill and K. V. Pitkin, *Qualified Intermediary*,
https://doi.org/10.1007/978-3-031-81410-5_25

## Citizenship-based taxation

Citizen-based taxation requires individuals to pay taxes to their country of citizenship, regardless of where they live or earn their income. The United States is the most prominent example of a country that practices citizenship-based taxation. Under this system, US citizens, including those living abroad, must file annual tax returns and pay taxes on their global income.

The key features of citizen-based taxation are:

1. **Global income taxation**: Citizens are taxed on income earned both domestically and internationally. This includes wages, investment income, and other sources of revenue.
2. **Filing obligations**: Citizens must file tax returns annually, reporting their *worldwide* income to the tax authorities of their home country.
3. **Tax treaties and credits**: To mitigate double taxation, countries with citizen-based taxation systems often enter into tax treaties with other nations. These treaties typically allow for tax credits or deductions to offset taxes paid to foreign governments.[1]

Citizen-based taxation has several significant implications for individuals, particularly those living abroad:

1. **Double taxation risk**: Without adequate tax treaties, individuals may face double taxation on their income – once by the country where they reside and again by their home country.
2. **Complex compliance requirements**: Taxpayers must navigate the tax laws of both their country of citizenship and their country of residence, often leading to complex and burdensome compliance requirements.
3. **Expatriation considerations**: Some individuals may consider renouncing their citizenship to avoid the tax obligations associated with citizen-based taxation. However, this process can be costly and complicated, often involving an exit tax.

[1] McGill, R.K., (2023). *Cross-border investment withholding tax: A practcal guide for investors and intermediaries.* Palgrave Macmillan. https://link.springer.com/book/10.1007/978-3-031-32785-8.

## Residence-based Taxation

Residence-based taxation, on the other hand, taxes individuals based on their residency status rather than their citizenship. Most countries around the world, including Canada, the United Kingdom and Germany, follow this approach. Under this system, individuals are taxed on their global income if they are considered residents of the country for tax purposes.

The key features of residence-based taxation are:

1. **Residency criteria**: Tax residency is usually determined by factors such as the number of days spent in the country, the location of an individual's primary residence, and personal and economic ties.
2. **Global income taxation for residents**: Residents are taxed on their worldwide income, similar to citizen-based taxation, but only while they are considered residents.
3. **Source-based taxation for non-residents**: Non-residents are typically taxed only on income sourced within the country, such as wages earned or investments located there.

Residence-based taxation has distinct implications for individuals, particularly those who move frequently or live abroad:

1. **Flexibility for expats**: Unlike citizen-based taxation, individuals can change their tax residency by moving to another country and meeting its residency requirements, potentially optimising their tax situation.
2. **Simplified compliance**: Taxpayers are generally only subject to the tax laws of their country of residence, simplifying compliance and reducing the risk of double taxation.
3. **Temporary vs. permanent residency**: Some countries differentiate between temporary and permanent residents, with varying tax obligations based on the duration and nature of an individual's stay.

## Comparison

To understand the broader implications of these taxation models, it is essential to compare their impact on various aspects such as complexity, behaviour and mobility.

Citizenship-based taxation leads to higher administrative complexity for both taxpayers and tax authorities. Individuals must keep detailed records of their global income and navigate tax regulations in multiple jurisdictions. Tax authorities must ensure compliance from citizens living abroad, which can be resource intensive as is evidenced by the US QI program and Internal Revenue Code Chapters 3 and 4 discussed earlier in this book.

In contrast, residence-based taxation is administratively simpler. Tax authorities focus on residents within their borders, making enforcement and compliance more straightforward. Taxpayers benefit from dealing with a single set of tax laws related to their country of residence.

Tax policies can significantly influence individual and corporate economic behaviour. Under citizenship-based taxation, individuals are less likely to invest internationally due to the complexities and potential double taxation issues. This can limit international investment opportunities. In the case of the US form example, the introduction of FATCA has led to a quadrupling of the number of US citizens revoking their US citizenship despite its associated costs.

Residence-based taxation, however, can encourage greater international mobility and investment. Individuals can choose to relocate to countries with more favourable tax regimes, potentially boosting global economic integration. However, this system has also led to tax competition among nations, as countries lower their tax rates to attract high-net-worth individuals and businesses.

Citizenship-based taxation acts as a barrier to mobility, as individuals must consider their home country's tax implications when moving abroad. This can be particularly challenging for dual-nationality citizens or those with strong ties to multiple countries.

Residence-based taxation provides greater flexibility for individuals to live and work in different countries without the burden of ongoing tax obligations from their home country. This model supports the growing trend of digital nomadism and the increasing number of expatriates seeking career opportunities worldwide.

Governments must carefully consider the impact of their taxation policies on revenue collection and economic competitiveness. Citizenship-based taxation can provide a stable revenue stream from citizens living abroad, although enforcement and compliance can be challenging and costly.

Residence-based taxation aligns tax revenues more closely with public service provision, as taxes are collected from individuals who reside and benefit from services in the country. However, this system may face challenges from tax avoidance strategies, such as individuals moving to low-tax jurisdictions.

## United States: Citizen-based Taxation in Practice

The United States is the most well-known example of a country with citizen-based taxation. US citizens, including those living abroad, must file annual tax returns and report their worldwide income. The Foreign Earned Income Exclusion (FEIE) and Foreign Tax Credit (FTC) are mechanisms designed to reduce the double taxation burden.

Despite these provisions, many expatriates find the compliance requirements burdensome. The Foreign Account Tax Compliance Act (FATCA) further complicates matters by requiring foreign financial institutions to report accounts held by US citizens, increasing compliance costs and administrative burdens as shown in Exhibit 25.1. For those US citizens that are evading taxes, like any system, FATCA has flaws. One such is that a US person setting up accounts in several countries at several different financial institutions may not hold enough in any one account to trigger enhanced due diligence and thus benefit from reporting exemptions at each financial institution. Under normal circumstances, those accounts would be reported, and the IRS would be the first nexus point to be able to aggregate multiple account balances held at multiple financial institutions. Financial institutions are under no obligation to share data with each other to identify, on a commercial basis, whether they have a common client which when aggregated would be reportable.

The complexity of US tax laws and the potential for double taxation have led some expatriates to renounce their US citizenship, a trend that has raised concerns among policymakers about the impact on global mobility and international relations.

So, citizenship-based and residence-based taxation represent two fundamentally different approaches to taxing individuals in a globalised world. Each system has its advantages and challenges, impacting taxpayers, governments and the broader economy in distinct ways.

Citizen-based taxation ensures that citizens contribute to their home country's revenue regardless of where they live, but it can lead to complex compliance requirements for financial institutions and potential double taxation. Residence-based taxation offers greater flexibility and supports international mobility, but it requires robust residency criteria and enforcement mechanisms to prevent tax evasion.

As the world becomes increasingly interconnected, countries must carefully consider the implications of their tax policies on international mobility, economic behaviour and revenue collection. By striking a balance between fairness, simplicity, and effectiveness, governments can design taxation

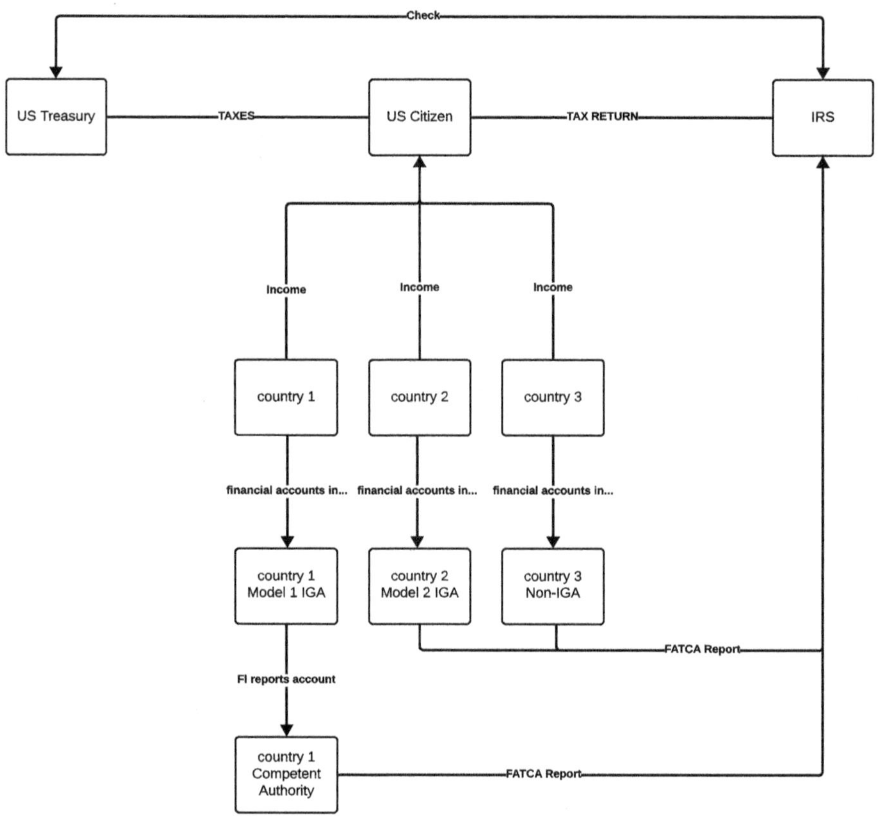


**Exhibit 25.1** Impact of CBT on US citizens *Source* Authors

systems that meet the needs of their citizens and support a dynamic global economy.

Given that primary purpose of FATCA and AEoI/CRS and DAC is the detection and prevention of tax evasion, there are initiatives in play today to put pressure on the US to move from citizenship- to residence-based taxation. A New Zealand-based expatriate filed a request at the IRS Systems Adequacy Management System (SAMS) in 2023 and received a case number which means that the submission is now officially an IRS recommendation for a law change that, if passed, would benefit both the American expatriate community and the American government's efforts to prevent money laundering and tax evasion.

There is also an Association of Accidental Americans dedicated to the change from citizenship- to residence-based taxation for many thousands of Europeans who have fallen foul of the US rules, by not realising that they are technically Americans too.[2] Their website is in French and should not be confused with the American Automobile Association.

[2] Accidental Americans: https://www.americains-accidentels.fr/page/234168-nos-actions.

# 26

# DLT, NFT, Smart Contracts and AI

This chapter describes some of the emergent technologies that could revolutionise the industry. Most notable is the concept of using distributed ledger technology (DLT) to provide standardisation and automation for qualified intermediaries. The conversion of paper documentation into non-fungible tokens (NFTs) will allow for a much greater degree of automation, particularly within smart contracts that can replicate withholding statements and provide straight through processing (STP) of tax events with no human intervention.

One thing is abundantly clear in 2024, technology has found a new home in the tax world. Historically reliant on manual process for everything from onboarding, KYC, through to trading and reporting, the last few years have seen significant changes in the use of technology and the types of technology that can be brought to bear. This chapter will bring new acronyms into the industry and potentially, new and faster ways to comply.

Four technologies are important—Distributed Ledger Technology (DLT) including Blockchain, NFTs and Smart Contracts and Artificial Intelligence (AI).

## DLT

DLT is basically a digital system for recording the transaction of assets in which the transactions and their details are recorded in multiple places at the same time. Unlike traditional databases, distributed ledgers have no central data store or administration functionality.


R. K. McGill and K. V. Pitkin, *Qualified Intermediary*,
https://doi.org/10.1007/978-3-031-81410-5_26

## Blockchain

A blockchain is "a distributed database that maintains a continuously growing list of ordered records, called "blocks". These blocks are linked using cryptography. Each block contains a cryptographic hash of the previous block, a timestamp, and transaction data.

## NFT

Non-Fungible Tokens or NFTs are blockchain-based tokens that each represent a unique asset like a piece of art, digital content, or media. An NFT can be thought of as an irrevocable digital certificate of ownership and authenticity for a given asset, whether digital or physical. In the world of withholding tax, this might be a certificate of residence, an investor self-declaration or even a tax voucher.

## Smart Contracts

Smart contracts are typically used to automate the execution of an agreement so that all participants can be immediately certain of the outcome, without any intermediary's involvement or time loss. They can also automate a workflow, triggering the next action when pre-determined conditions are met.

Smart contracts are programmes that represent automatable components of a contractual obligation. They rely mainly on Boolean logic—e.g., IF x, THEN y.

The combination of DLT, NFTs and smart contracts can, in principle, be used to automate and standardise withholding tax processes.

Consider Exhibit 26.1 in this context. The smart contract is a tax refund contract between the Issuer of financial instruments and tax administrations. The purpose of the smart contract is to encode the terms of a double tax agreement. The smart contract determines the initial state of a distributed ledger as the total number of shares in issue on a record date. This ensures there can be no over-claiming, as the maximum number of claimable shares is set by the Issuer and confirmed on the ledger by the first level of financial institutions in the payment chain. The state of the ledger changes each time a financial institution makes a claim against one of the three blocks. The smart contract also stores information about the three blocks, i.e., opening and closing time frames for submissions and submission requirement such as documentation types.

The blocks in this smart contract represent the three windows of processing—tax relief, quick refund and standard refund. A financial institution can make a claim against each block only to the extent that the previous block window has closed. This effectively integrates the tax processes into one continuous process—something the industry has failed to achieve to date.

The evidence of the investor's eligibility for beneficial rate of tax is a self-certification or an eTRC, both of which would be transmitted as NFTs. In this model, financial institutions would be nodes on the distributed ledger, collecting documentation from their clients to support tax relief processes.

As the reader might imagine, the extent to which existing regulatory processes could cope with a DLT-based tax processing environment is extremely limited. Unfortunately, this DLT-based model has only been proven in the laboratory and has not been seen "*in the wild*".

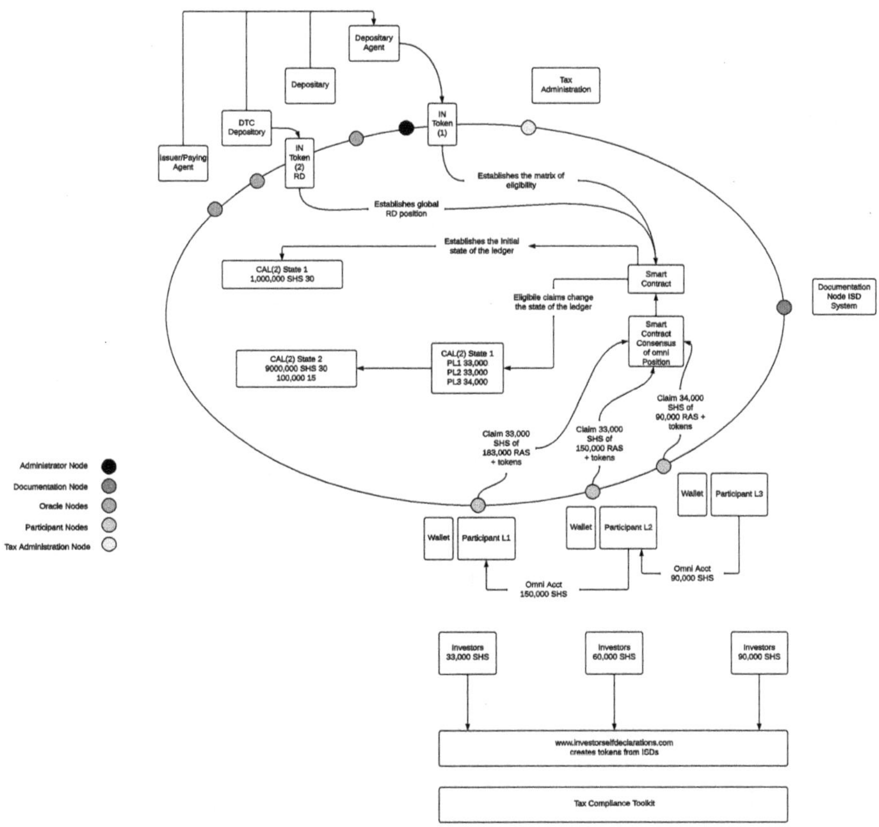


**Exhibit 26.1** DLT, NFT and Smart Contracts in tax processing *Source* Authors

## Artificial Intelligence

One of our greatest criticisms of the financial services industry is its seemingly inexhaustible capacity to be drawn by the new bright shiny thing in front of them and to spend inordinate amounts of money on the off-chance it might be important someday.

DLT was a great example. At the time, it was being hyped as "the next big thing" in financial services off the back of Bitcoin and other digital currencies, which enjoyed rather patchy success. Five years after its launch, even its proponents were publicly acknowledging that DLT was over-hyped, sometimes deliberately, to grab development budgets from financial institutions. And there you have the fintech dilemma: which is in control—the fin or the tech? It seems to me that the tech took charge too much in these firms, hence DLT is now widely regarded as a solution looking for a problem and no-one, in sufficient numbers and throughout the payment and regulatory chain, is really interested enough to allocate the substantial budgets it would need to get anywhere. Enter Artificial Intelligence (AI).

Artificial Intelligence, or AI (not to be confused with the Finnish Authorised Intermediary system), is technology that enables computers and machines to simulate human intelligence and problem-solving capabilities. We found it interesting to note while doing the research for this book, that back in the 1990s the technology to convert cursive writing into typed text, optical character recognition (OCR) was hailed as AI, and from 30,000 feet, it is easy to see why. The act of taking a human scribble and converting it to computer text seemed like magic. Several companies, even today, hail their OCR driven solutions as AI. Thus, we have a difference between the reality and the hype. We all think of AI as being something like Isaac Asimov's robots with their three laws. Many conventions are held each year to discuss the ethics of AI, which predicates the thought that what they are really talking about is artificial consciousness or machine learning, not artificial intelligence.

Machine learning (ML) is a branch of artificial intelligence and computer science that focusses on the using data and algorithms to enable AI to imitate the way that humans learn, gradually improving its accuracy (Exhibit 26.2).

Most AIs today are actually large language models (LLMs) based on machine learning algorithms—not true AI. This just means that a machine is fed a diet of language (the more the better) and it then predicts, using algorithms, what the next term is likely to be. We all see this every day in applications like Google. If you type in a question, however vague, the LLM is trying to figure out what the most likely next words will be. The machine

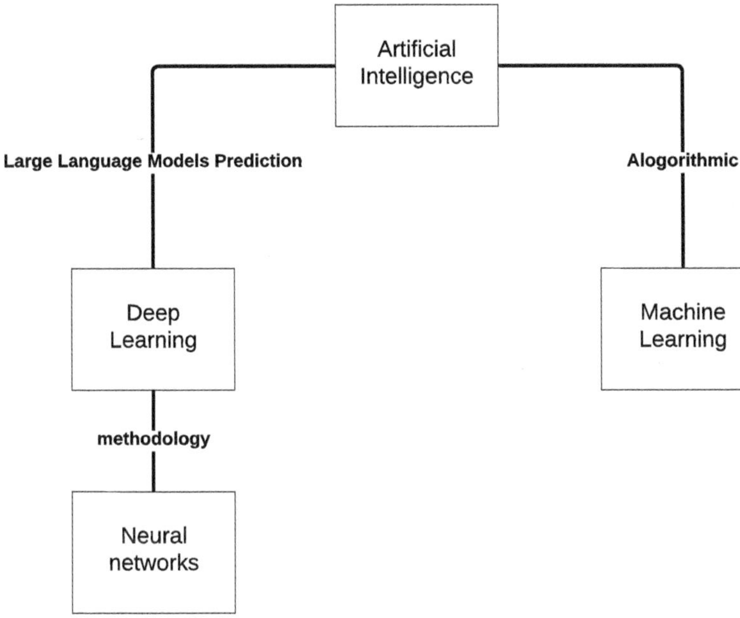


**Exhibit 26.2** AI models *Source* Authors

learning algorithms get better and better the more questions they are asked and the more language they are fed. So, they key is data, lots of it.

A neural network is a method in artificial intelligence that teaches computers to process data in a way that is inspired by the human brain. It is a type of machine learning process, called deep learning, that uses interconnected nodes or neurons in a layered structure that resembles the human brain.

What this allows computers to do is join the dots in a similar way to human's ability to spot patterns. Given that we don't even know how our own brains work, it would be presumptuous to say that an AI is truly intelligent. But enough of the theory. How could what we refer to as AI be of any use in the financial services and particularly the tax world and if so, would there be compliance challenges?

The most obvious candidate would be anti-tax evasion. The current models of FATCA and AEoI means that financial institutions are pumping data into government databases at an alarmingly high rate. Since these institutions do not coordinate with each other, the first point at which systemic tax evasion becomes detectable is at the governmental level. The easiest way to evade tax today would be to hold assets in many financial institutions and in particular where either there are thresholds below which the account won't be reported or in jurisdictions that have not joined the anti-evasion regulatory frameworks.

The following jurisdictions have not joined AEoI or joined the CRS exchange:

- Algeria
- Benin
- Belarus
- Bosnia and Herzegovina
- Botswana
- Burkina Faso
- Vietnam

There are 94 jurisdictions to date that have no FATCA IGA in place. It would therefore not be difficult to map out those jurisdictions that have neither an IGA with the US nor are part of CRS. Those are the jurisdictions that will not be reporting accounts to anyone from a purely regulatory perspective.

If we assume for the moment that there are around 200 financial institutions in each of the 113 FATCA IGA or CRS jurisdictions, that will put the number of reporting institutions at around 22,600. If each of those institutions were reporting say 500 non-resident account holders, the number of account holders to be analysed would be around 11.3 million per year. These are very broad and probably wildly under-stated assumptions, but they do indicate that the likely data set would be in the tens of millions of accounts and more likely hundreds of millions—which would probably make it statistically significant for analysis purposes. We know for example, that there are at least five million[1] Americans alone resident outside the United States and the US has issued over half a. Million GIINs for financial institutions (Exhibit 26.3).

The first step, which would not really need AI, except for the sheer volume of data, would be to cross reference all the primary data to see whether any given account holder had accounts at multiple financial institutions across multiple jurisdictions. Each financial institution only has a small part of the picture, and their data would not, individually, be of statistical significance. Its only when you get to the governmental level that the data becomes meaningful. The key here would be the domestic tax identification number (TIN) of the account holder because this is a required data component in all anti-tax evasion reporting frameworks.

[1] https://www.aaro.org/living-abroad/how-many-americans-live-abroad#:~:text=American%20Citizens%20Abroad%3A%20The%20American,See%20ACA%20Article.

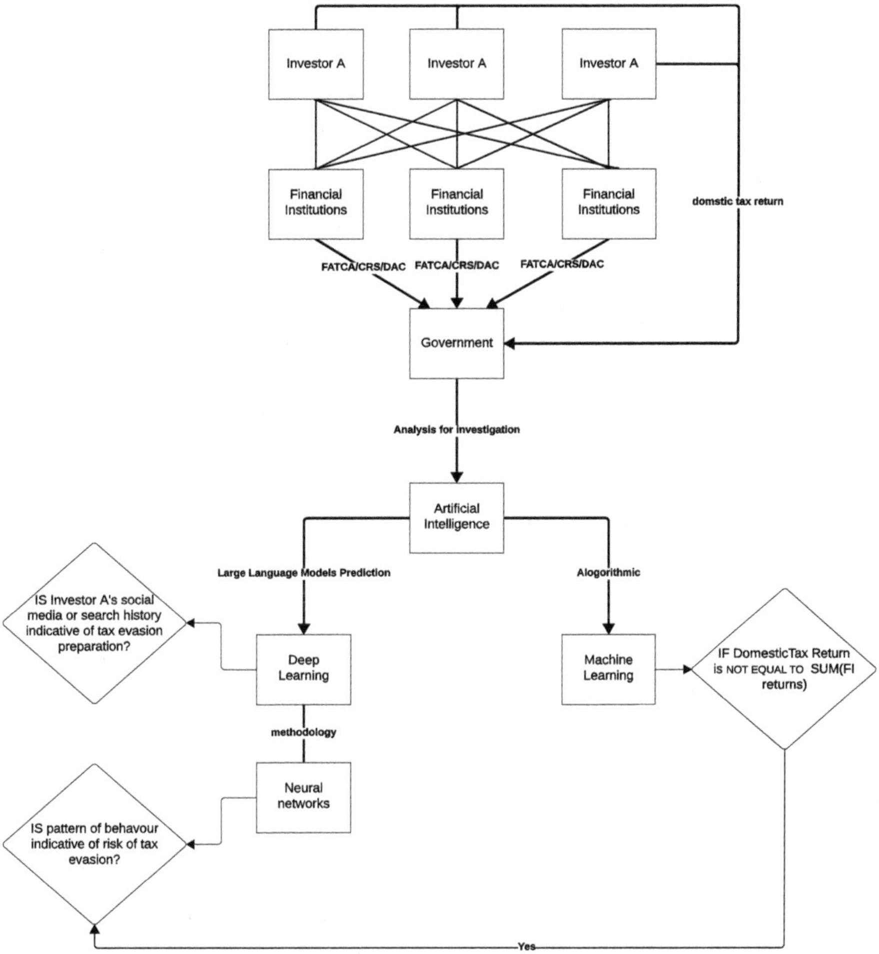


**Exhibit 26.3** Use of AI in anti-tax evasion *Source* Authors

The secondary step would be to cross reference the data against the domestic tax returns of these reported account holders. This is the primary objective of FATCA since Americans must file tax returns irrespective of where they reside. At this point AI does become relevant because the data sets are very large. AI's role would be to look for anomalies or patterns of behaviour that could be indicative of potential tax evasion. A short list of those account holders can then be extracted for investigation. However, for this to work there is one fly in the ointment—data quality.

The framework for reporting does mandate the due diligence required of each financial institution and the format and content of the reportable data. So, if each financial institution's data is of high quality, the governmental data set should also be high quality. The problem is that the assumption is fallacious. Data quality has long been known to be a serious problem for financial institutions. In the tax area, it is particularly bad, with many institutions having real difficulty getting one golden record for their account holders.

So, while the world marvels at the possibilities of AI and Isaac Asimov's robots, we think the impact on financial institutions and their tax compliance for the foreseeable future, will be minimal. What is more likely to be a challenge will be the increasing demands of governments and tax authorities to ask for more and more data, collection of which will be placed at the door of the financial institutions through increased regulation.

The compliance problem for AI is that it's not the end point that's the problem, it's the start point—data quality and the fact that much data is sourced from paper records. As a firm, we provide tax reporting services to financial institution clients every year and every year we spend time analysing data, looking for errors and omissions and helping clients correct their data, just so that they can report correctly. Its unsurprising therefore that our view of data quality in financial services is that it's frighteningly low. And while that data quality is low, analysis of it is effectively meaningless. We are used to specific and well controlled environments, like the weather, where data is huge, precise and error margins low. Tax is not that kind of environment.

The second factor is risk appetite. The regulators have made it clear from their enforcement activity that they want as much information as possible since those volumes are what drive the applicability of AI models. What tends to happen in risk averse financial institutions is that they would rather over-report than under-report. The IRS for example has so-called presumption rules that essentially means that if you're not sure your client isn't an American, you must presume them to be an American. The result is that the IRS has large amounts of reported data which are almost useless to it and, if used in an AI model, would skew any results sufficiently to be almost meaningless for enforcement purposes.

# Part VIII

## Conclusions

# 27

# Challenges, Possibilities, Probabilities and Predictions

In this chapter we bring all the threads of the other chapters together to describe where we think the industry's future lies and what the key hurdles to adoption will be.

This book has had as very wide brief, even though its subject matter is quite narrowly focussed. As we noted at the very beginning, the term "Qualified Intermediary" for our purposes includes any financial institution in any jurisdiction that either acts as a withholding agent in another jurisdiction or is subject to anti-tax evasion regulation or law. From this definition, we drew the parallels to a number of different regulatory and legal frameworks.

The US has had these two frameworks, QI and FATCA, since the year 2000, so they are quite mature from a compliance perspective.

Europe is coming along relatively quickly and has developed the Directive on Administrative Cooperation (DAC) through eight iterations so far, with the most relevant being DAC6 designed to capture CRS evaders. The latest EU initiative, the FASTER Directive, while in theory should be a game changer, we think will, in all likelihood, fall foul of political division and ultimately replace the old form of complexity with another. However, it does mirror the US, with DAC equating to FATCA and FASTER equating to QI.

The OECD has been pivotal because it has pioneered the AEoI, CRS and BEPS initiatives while in parallel launching the TRACE Implementation Protocol, thus establishing the global anti-tax evasion framework as well as the basis for effective taxation for cross-border income at source.

With the addition of double tax treaties, the world now—whether it knows it or not—has an integrated and functioning framework to detect, deter and prosecute those responsible for tax evasion. It also has an established, albeit


R. K. McGill and K. V. Pitkin, *Qualified Intermediary*,
https://doi.org/10.1007/978-3-031-81410-5_27

imperfect, mechanism to allow non-resident financial institutions to be withholding agents in more than one jurisdiction in order to permit tax relief at source on legitimate cross-border investment income (Exhibit 27.1).

So, that's where we are today.

## Practical Compliance Challenges

From a compliance perspective, these regulatory frameworks do have some commonality that drives the number and types of challenges. These are:

1. Siloing
2. Documentation (also ironically known as "papering")
3. Due diligence
4. Reporting
5. Control, oversight and enforcement

Siloing should not be under-estimated because it's connected to awareness and the concept and principle of informed decision-making. In all cases under consideration in this book, more than one function is involved in a series of co-dependent processes. It's not that a department is not aware of the next department to it in the next silo, it's that one department may not be aware of the third or fourth department away from it. The team responsible for onboarding new customers does not know what effect it has on reporting. The income distribution team does not know the effect they have on legal and compliance. None of them individually has the whole picture—and they need it.

The attempt by most regulators to hold one person in a firm responsible for compliance fails in most instances because of the silo effect as shown in Exhibit 27.2. The person that becomes the responsible officer is often the person who draws the short straw but is rarely someone of sufficient authority to meet the obligations that regulators expect. Internal politics, lack of knowledge and authority all contribute to these regulatory frameworks being very weak at the implementational level.

This is not helped by regulators taking either a rules-based approach or a principles-based approach. The European Union's DAC6 for example is a principles-based approach that provides general descriptions of what constitutes a Hallmark of tax evasion, while the US, EU and OECD adopt a rules-based approach that must establish a rule for almost every possible permutation of circumstance to describe a reportable issue.

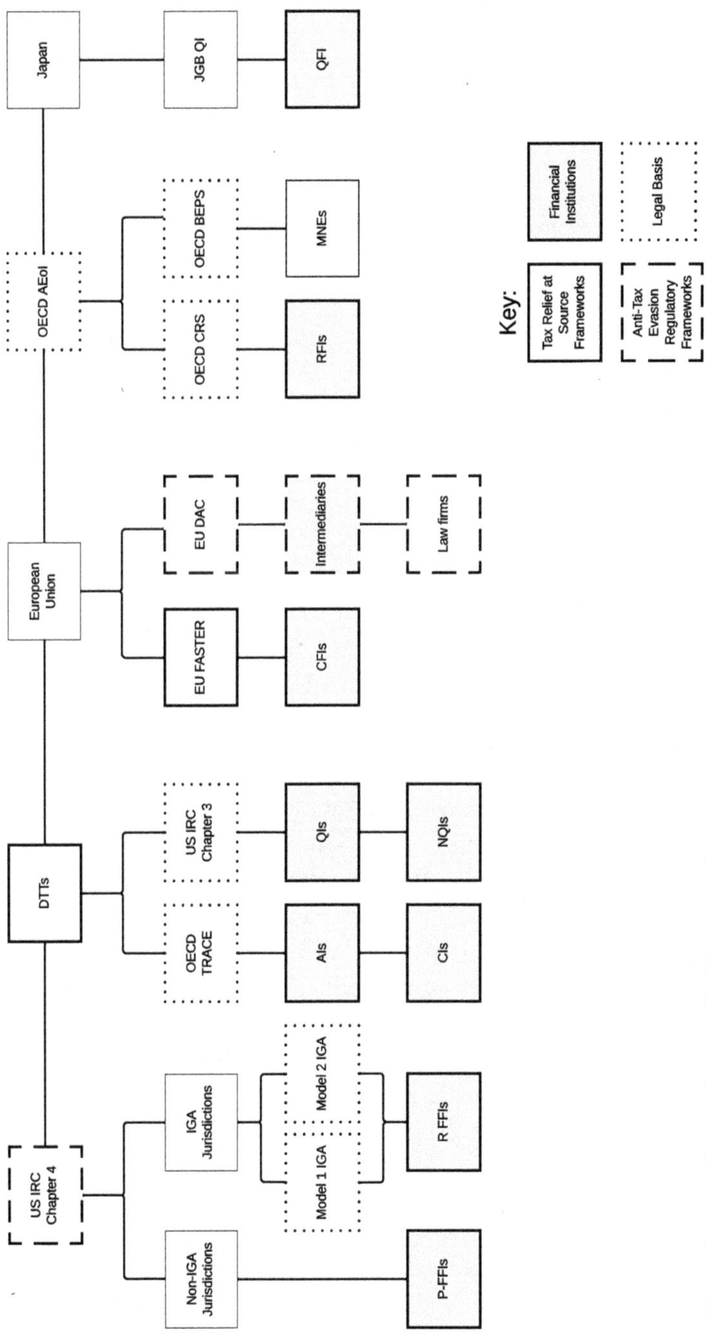


**Exhibit 27.1** Tax evasion and tax relief frameworks *Source* Authors

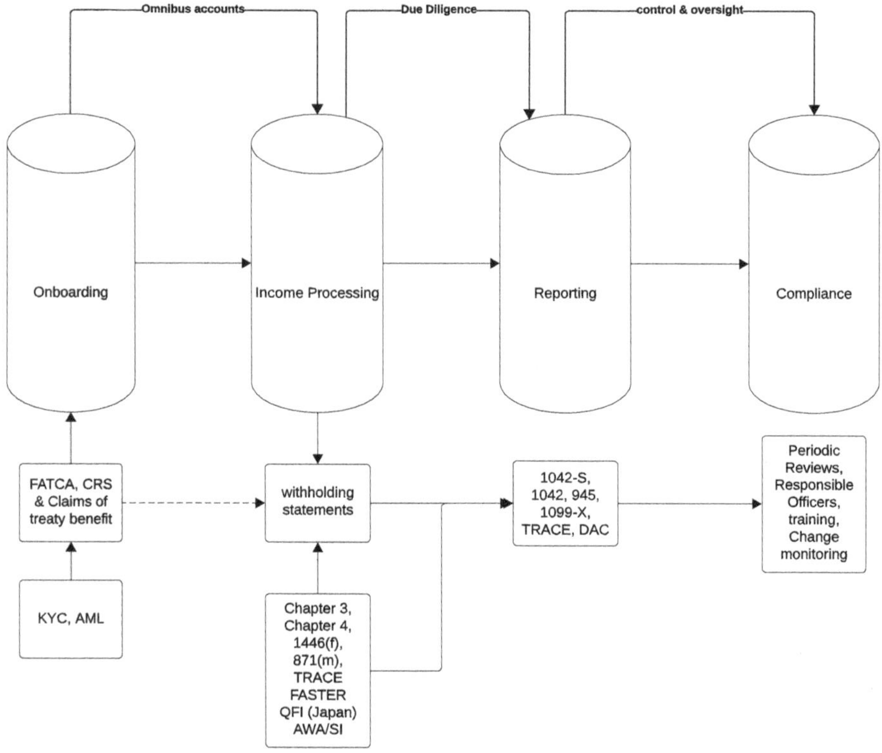


**Exhibit 27.2** The effect of siloing *Source* Authors

The principles-based approach is difficult for financial institutions to implement, because they deal with data. The rules-based approach is equally difficult because, while they have the data, the number of permutations is so large and complex that it's impossible to implement. This, for example, is why the US Chapter 1, Section 871(m) regulations on the taxation of dividend equivalent payments (DEPs) on equity-linked instruments (ELIs) have been such an abject failure and been deferred *five* times by the IRS. It's why the Chapter 3, Section 1446(f) regulations have led to widespread disinvestment in publicly traded partnerships (PTPs). The financial instruments themselves are rather simple to understand. Regulating them is not and the siloing effect simply makes matters worse.

The second challenge is documentation, also known as papering (and for very good and obvious reasons). Recently, it was said that over 60% of corporate actions in financial services still involved paper. That's the same number discussed back in the 1990s, and we can quite believe this. This is a continuing major issue because handling paper creates risk from data re-entry errors or omissions and is highly resource intensive. It is easy for the large financial institutions to rave about the effects of automation and removal of paper, but that's not where the challenge is. The challenge is faced on a daily basis by the very much larger quantity of smaller banks and other tier 2 and tier 3 financial institutions. They are still using paper forms, and the tech sector is ignoring them in its fight to get at the big fish.

One such large institution accepted disclosing nonqualified intermediaries as clients for the US market. This meant that the reporting obligation flowed up to the upstream tier 1 financial institution, in this case a CSD. The US tax rules are that the CSD in this situation had the responsibility not only to report each disclosed beneficial owner's US sourced income, per income type, but also to provide the recipient with copies. They are not allowed to provide those copies to their client, the NQI. However, neither the withholding statements nor the W-8 s included an email address for the recipients. So, to fulfil their contractual obligation to the IRS, they had to physically print out each Form 1042-S on paper, collate them, put them, in envelopes and mail them to the recipients. The NQI could probably have done this electronically, as it would probably have an email address for each client, but it had no obligation to provide that data to its CSD counterparty because that data element is not specified by the IRS.

One bank we know of (and we suspect there are many more in the wealth management space) onboards clients physically at a number of branches and still use paper Forms W-8, validated manually by staff that have a low retention rate (and a low efficiency of validation). This causes increased costs with new staff having to be trained and existing staff having to be re-trained on a regular basis. Paper is increasingly an anathema for financial institutions, yet the industry is unbelievably slow to adapt to new technologies. In fact, the number of new technologies out there far outstrips a bank's ability to adopt them. While we are talking about DLT and AI, most banks are still just moving out of the spreadsheet era into APIs. The financial services industry is by no means homogenous, and it's this lack of homogeneity that creates so much inefficiency.

The third challenge, due diligence, is not the same as documentation. Documentation has its own problems. How to reach out to clients, when to reach out, what documentation to ask for, how to validate it correctly when you get it, how to compare it to KYC and AML. None of these is due diligence. Due diligence is the activity that is mandated to take place before reporting. Consider that you must document all clients as part of the onboarding process. Some of those clients may be retail, low value accounts and some will be high value, often wealth management accounts. Banks don't make money from retail accounts except in very large volumes. One large brokerage we know of has over two million retail accounts, most of which never trade or hold any significant assets.

Regulators are not really interested in low value accounts for tax evasion purposes. They are very interested in low value accounts for taxation of income. As the European Union has found out, most of the tax over-withheld at source is owed to small retail investors and almost none of that is ever recovered by them due to the complexities of the tax refund processes. So, it is not in the interests of many tax authorities to disturb the landscape by making tax relief more accessible, because they get free money from all those investors who never file a claim.

So, due diligence is the process by which accounts that regulators are not really interested in, are excluded from reporting. In general, the 80–20 rule applies, i.e., 80% of a bank's account values are in 20% of its accounts. But how to separate one from the other. From the regulator's perspective this is done with "thresholds". The most common thresholds are $250,000 and $1,000,000 or their local currency equivalent. No-one has yet explained why an account valued at $990,999 is less likely to be used for tax evasion than one valued at $1,000,001, but the due diligence processes generally use this cut-off. The threshold means that a bank needs to undertake additional checks on accounts above the threshold to verify that what it thought was a non-reportable client is still a non-reportable client. So, in the US model, you're looking for a US person hiding their assets in a non-US bank account. Now, your original onboarding may have decided via KYC, AML and a Form W-8 that your clients are not US persons and are therefore not reportable in FATCA. However, when their account value exceeds $1,000,000, you must do additional checks to make sure. That might include interviews with their relationship manager and additional paper checks—all to look for any indicators that they might be an American (so-called US indicia). At the same time, the same regulation allows US persons with depository accounts valued at less than $50,000 to be exempted from reporting—even though they are US persons. Financial institutions like an easy life—just one metric to decide what to do. These types of regulation make it very difficult because they engage multiple metrics with rules, just so you can decide whether the account may be reportable.

The issue for compliance is that you must not only have done the enhanced due diligence, but you must also be able to prove that you did it and show the results when asked. Now in most cases, this enhanced due diligence reveals no additional concerns. So, what was a non-reportable account before, continues to be a non-reportable account after the due diligence. Its worthy of note here that the rules generally means that you have to aggregate accounts beneficially owned by the same person to catch the obvious dodgers who simply think they can open up a number of low value accounts to avoid tripping the threshold. All this to say that additional resources, cost and risk needs to be spent for an activity that, for the most part, does not yield any different result. So, there is a natural resistance to due diligence because it seems like an activity for no purpose. That said, there are technical challenges. How do you aggregate accounts when the data quality of account data is so low. Is Ross McGill the same account holder as Ross K. McGill? And what do you do if you have a passive entity account where Ross McGill is a minority shareholder as well as a direct account of the same person. All these decisions take effort to interpret and implement. The more complex your client base, the more complex due diligence is.

The fourth challenge is reporting.

Reporting is the annual endpoint of the tax operational cycle and you'd think that would be the easy part, right? Not so. You've done your documentation, you've done your due diligence, you've applied all the right tax rates to all the different types of income and now you must report what you did last year. Here's what that looks like in summary. The challenge is keeping track of it, tracking the changes as they occur, planning for changes and having the expertise in place to make it happen (Exhibit 27.3).

You'll be reporting US-sourced FDAP income and tax withheld on Forms 1042-S in an ASCII text file to the FIRE portal, to do which you'll need to register and have a QIEIN or EIN and a transmitter control code (TCC). If you're a non-disclosing NQI (or a QI with indirect account holders), you'll also be printing out recipient copies and mailing them to account holders.

You'll be filing a US tax return, Form 1042, on paper to the IRS, but you'll need to file electronically in 2026, using an XML schema that is currently hidden in the MeF portal which non-US people can't (yet) access and attach upstream Forms 1042-S recipient copies as PDF files within an XML message.

You'll be filing a Form 945 to the IRS is you had US clients that were subject to backup withholding during the year AND you'll be filing Form 1099 electronically to the MeF portal for any that weren't subject to back withholding.

You'll be filing a FATCA report, perhaps even a NIL report to your local tax administration, most commonly using an XML schema or using the IDES portal if you're in a Model 2 IGA or non-IGA jurisdiction.

You'll be filing a CRS report to your local tax administration if you have any non-resident account holders whose country of residence is a partner

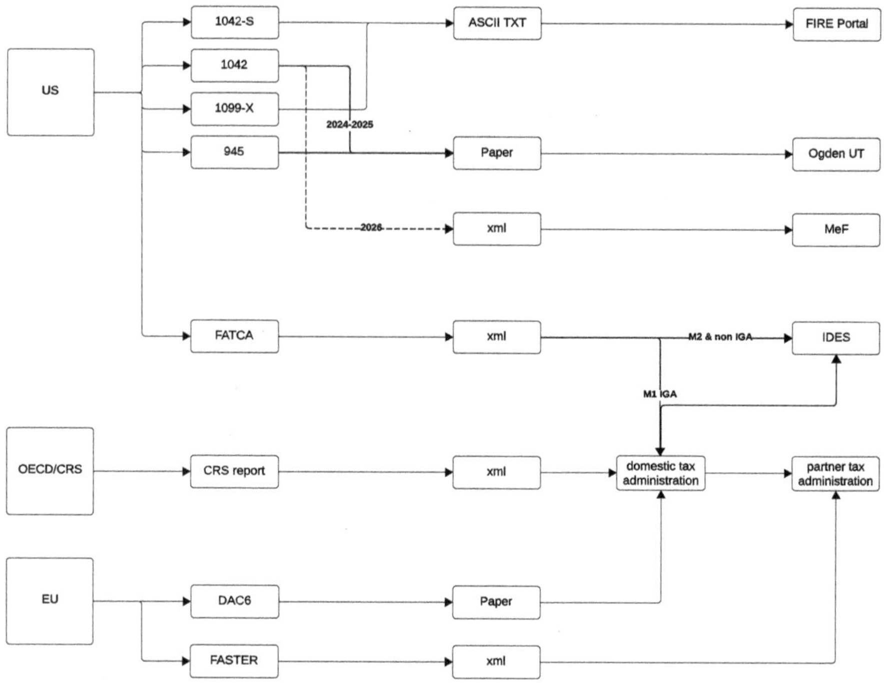


**Exhibit 27.3** Reporting frameworks and formats *Source* Authors

jurisdiction under CRS. Depending on your jurisdiction, you may be lucky and find that is combined with your FATCA report.

You'll be filing a DAC6 report to your local tax administration on paper, if you've figured out how to test for the DAC6 Hallmarks.

So, you'll have multiple systems to deal with, multiple file formats and multiple sets of data to collect, prepare and check. These present formidable challenges for any financial institution with any kind of credible client base. And all that is before you've assessed reporting of those crypto assets you started selling because it's the latest shiny thing your clients want.

## Predictions

Predictions are the fun part of this book. Here, all bets are off and anything can happen if the conditions are right. That said, we are not starting from a clean sheet of paper. We are where we are. We have extensive fragmentation, different views and models of compliance, different drivers for developments and it's certainly not clear what the future may hold. It was less than a 100 years between man's first powered flight by the Wright brothers, to landing a man on the moon. We could perhaps have predicted the moon landing because of the aspirations of the Wright brothers, but not how quickly it would happen or the route we would have to follow to get there.

We asked six of our most trusted partners to give us their insights into the potential developments in the tax industry over the next 10 years–

- Marco Zawar, subject matter expert in Hong Kong,
- Amanda Hsu, TConsult affiliate in Taiwan,
- James St Clair and Kenneth Chan Presidents of Brokerage Services and Technology Services respectively of Viewtrade in New York,
- Yitzhak Zahavy of eToro in Cyprus and
- Roman von der Hoh of RAQUEST GmbH in Germany.

## Marco Zawar

Marco Zawar has the following to say about the future from his perspective in Hong Kong:

The next 10 years will likely see significant evolution in withholding tax compliance, driven by regulatory, technological, and political changes. Three key areas where we can expect transformation are digitisation, the role of artificial intelligence (AI), and the increasing harmonisation of global tax standards.

AI and machine learning are already reshaping industries, and tax compliance is no exception. In the realm of withholding tax, AI could become a powerful tool for both tax authorities and intermediaries. AI algorithms can process vast amounts of data faster than human agents, allowing for near real-time compliance checks and automatic identification of discrepancies or anomalies.

AI could also improve the interpretation of complex tax regulations and treaties, reducing the need for manual intervention and minimising errors. For instance, advanced AI models could predict withholding tax rates and exemptions based on historical data, treaty obligations and the specifics of cross-border transactions. By continuously learning from new data, these systems could adapt to regulatory changes in real time, reducing compliance risk and enhancing the accuracy of reporting.

Tax authorities, particularly in jurisdictions leading the way in tax digitisation like the EU and the US, will likely leverage AI to improve enforcement, using data analytics to detect patterns of tax evasion or avoidance. On the intermediary side, AI could streamline client onboarding, tax determination and withholding processes, ensuring accurate application of treaty benefits and compliance with QI obligations.

### Global Standards and Reporting Harmonisation

The OECD's work on the Common Reporting Standard (CRS) and BEPS has been an essential driver in international tax transparency, and we can expect further progress towards the global harmonisation of tax withholding regimes. As countries continue to embrace automatic exchange of information (AEoI), we may see a move towards more unified withholding tax frameworks, reducing compliance complexity for intermediaries and multinationals operating across borders.

The alignment of reporting standards could be aided by new digital frameworks, potentially led by multinational organisations like the OECD, to streamline withholding tax reporting across jurisdictions. We might even see the emergence of a global withholding tax dashboard—an integrated platform that consolidates information from various jurisdictions, allowing tax authorities and intermediaries to track and verify withholding tax obligations and payments more efficiently.

### Blockchain and Real-Time Withholding

Blockchain technology could play a role in securing and verifying withholding tax transactions. Smart contracts, programmed into blockchain networks, could automatically calculate and remit withholding taxes based on predefined rules, such as treaty rates and domestic regulations. This would reduce administrative burden and enhance transparency for tax authorities. Withholding tax could become real-time, with remittances and reporting occurring instantly, cutting down on delays and potential errors in the current ecosystem.

*Source: Marco Zawar, Hong Kong.*

## Viewtrade

James St Clair and Kenneth Chan of Viewtrade had the following contribution to the debate:

The future of Qualified Intermediaries (QIs) is set for major changes in the coming decade. This transformation will be driven by global regulatory changes, technological advancements, and greater collaboration among tax authorities. Qualified Intermediaries sit at the heart of this evolving landscape, playing a critical role in ensuring accurate tax withholding, reporting, and compliance for multinational transactions.

This chapter outlines the predictions and thoughts on the future of withholding tax and the role of QIs. Industry leaders at ViewTrade share valuable insights into the future of QIs and the impact of technology on the withholding tax environment.

President of Technology Services from ViewTrade, Kenneth Chan, said, "*In the coming decade, we anticipate the emergence of a global withholding tax framework. This will help consolidate tax obligations and standardize withholding requirements, reducing the administrative burden for businesses while improving transparency and compliance. Tax as a Service (TaaS) platforms will become essential for multinational businesses, automating compliance across jurisdictions and integrating with real-time reporting systems. TaaS will dynamically adjust withholding tax rates based on legislative changes, ensuring that businesses remain compliant in an ever-evolving landscape.*

*Furthermore, the integration of Blockchain and AI will allow tax authorities to track transactions in real-time and deliver seamless compliance. Lastly, withholding tax policies will increasingly incentivize companies to meet ESG standards, offering favourable tax rates or credits linked to sustainability targets and further integrating corporate responsibility into the financial landscape*".

**James St Clair**, President of Brokerage Services from ViewTrade, stated,

> In the future, Qualified Intermediaries will experience change driven by blockchain technology and Artificial Intelligence (AI). To begin with, Blockchain will change transaction processing by providing secure information, reducing errors, and ensuring accountability. This shift will improve procedures and increase client trust in the security and precision of their transactions.
> As cross-border transactions increase, QIs must comply with various regulations in different jurisdictions. To stay relevant, QIs need to adopt advanced technology or partner with tech firms that can help.
> AI will provide data analysis and strategic insights for clients' portfolios, allowing QIs to evolve from transaction agents to financial advisors. The future QIs are expected to be adaptable, innovative, and focused on improving client experiences through technology.

In the years ahead, we will see QIs harness the power of emerging technologies like Blockchain, artificial intelligence, and real-time data sharing to ensure compliance and enhance the overall client experience. What was once a manual, complex process will be streamlined and more accurate, giving businesses peace of mind as they navigate the intricate world of cross-border taxation. Ultimately, the future success of QIs will depend on their ability to embrace technology, anticipate challenges, and, most importantly, prioritise the needs of their clients.

The insights industry leaders provide are predictions based on current trends and should not be considered guarantees of future performance or outcomes.

*Source: James St Clair and Kenneth Chan, Viewtrade*

## Yitzhak Zahavy, eToro

Yitzhak Zahavy, Chief Compliance Officer at eToro in Cyprus, has the following comments on the future:

AI is poised to play a transformative role in cross-border income taxation and anti-tax evasion over the next decade, particularly in the realm of withholding taxes. As global financial transactions become increasingly digitised, AI's capacity to automate processes, analyse vast datasets and detect irregularities will be critical in shaping the future of tax compliance.

### Enhanced Data Collection and Reporting

AI will streamline the complex process of data collection and reporting in cross-border taxation. Withholding taxes, which are often applied to payments such as dividends, interest and royalties, vary by jurisdiction and are influenced by international tax treaties. AI-powered systems will help governments and tax authorities automate the collection, analysis, and standardisation of withholding tax data. Global tax regimes like the Common Reporting Standard (CRS) and the Foreign Account Tax Compliance Act (FATCA), which enables the exchange of tax information between jurisdictions, could be enhanced with AI to facilitate real-time data sharing. This will reduce errors, ensure accuracy in tax filings and limit opportunities for evasion by increasing transparency across borders.

### Improved Compliance Monitoring

AI's pattern recognition capabilities will revolutionise compliance monitoring in cross-border taxation. AI can detect irregularities and flag unusual behaviours in financial transactions that may indicate tax evasion or avoidance. For example, it can identify income shifting to low-tax jurisdictions or transactions routed through tax havens. This will improve enforcement by enabling tax authorities to monitor transactions more closely and catch instances of tax evasion earlier. AI will also use predictive analytics to identify high-risk areas for tax evasion, helping governments allocate resources more effectively.

## Automation of Withholding Tax Processes

One of AI's key benefits lies in its ability to automate complex processes. Withholding tax obligations vary across jurisdictions and are governed by international tax treaties, making compliance challenging for multinational corporations. AI can automate the interpretation of tax treaties, ensuring the correct withholding tax rates are applied to cross-border transactions and reducing the risk of double taxation. This will simplify compliance for businesses and improve the accuracy of tax payments. Additionally, AI could be integrated into cross-border payment systems to automatically calculate and deduct withholding taxes in real time, significantly reducing the administrative burden on companies.

## Enhanced Anti-tax Evasion Tools

AI will be an essential tool in the fight against tax evasion. By connecting and analysing data from multiple sources, AI can detect hidden income streams, offshore accounts and shell companies. Furthermore, the integration of AI with blockchain technology could enhance transparency in cross-border transactions, providing a clear audit trail and making it more difficult for individuals and corporations to evade taxes. This will enable tax authorities to track illicit financial flows more effectively and enforce tax laws more efficiently.

## Future Trends in Withholding Tax

Looking ahead, AI will drive a shift towards more automated, data-driven, and harmonised withholding tax regimes. Governments may adopt fully digital tax systems powered by AI, making compliance easier and more transparent for businesses and individuals. AI could also facilitate greater international collaboration between tax authorities, leading to the development of more standardised global or regional withholding tax frameworks. Ultimately, AI may enable real-time calculation and collection of withholding taxes, simplifying the process for taxpayers and ensuring governments collect the appropriate revenues in a timely manner.

In conclusion, AI will play a pivotal role in making cross-border income taxation more efficient, transparent and compliant. As tax authorities and corporations embrace AI-driven technologies, withholding tax processes will become more streamlined, reducing opportunities for tax evasion and ensuring a more equitable global tax system.

*Source: Yitzhak Zahavy, eToro. Cyprus.*

## Amanda Hsu, TConsult

Amanda Hsu, TConsult's affiliate in Taiwan, had the following to say:

Taiwan Financial Supervisory Commission defined "regtech" as the use of information technology to extensively collect financial supervision systems and regulatory requirements from various countries, provide analysis and management tools, and automatically assist financial institutions in complying with regulatory requirements to reduce operational risks.

### Regtech Helps QIs to Conduct Robust Compliance to Their Obligations

The use of technology to comply with regulatory requirements is getting common while the financial institutions are looking at how to implement new technology including AI, machine learning and cryptographic technology to help them develop regtech. So that regtech can help these financial institutions analyse and handle complex situations more quickly and have more consistency and continuity in compliance.

We expect that AI technology and machine learning will make regtech development more intelligent, so that it is closer to practical operations under regulations and can predict potential compliance risks. This not only helps financial institutions, but also relies on the tax experts to train the AI system. Therefore, regtech will play an important role for cross-border taxation and anti-tax evasion in the future.

### Cryptographic Technology Might Change the Way to Exchange the Required Information

Cryptographic technology is a commonly used security protection method at present. It uses technical means to turn important data into garbled codes for encrypted transmission. After reaching the destination, the same or different technical means are used to restore and decrypt it. It can enable financial institutions to share data more safely and efficiently to avoid data leakage.

Under FATCA and CRS regulations, the format of information exchange are XML schema. If the financial institutions use cryptographic technology can help their data protection and make their work more efficient.

Let's imagine that when the financial institutions plan their QI compliance programs, the generative AI might analyse their internal procedures in advance. So that their QI consultants could give advice and train their AI system as well. When the financial institutions do their FATCA or CRS reporting, they use encryption technology to protect their data. We can't wait to see the QI compliance and procedure turning into the regtech world.

*Amanda Hsu, TConsult, Taiwan.*

## RAQUEST GmbH

Roman von der Hoh is the Managing Director of German fintech, RAQUEST GmbH. He had the following to say:

One of the biggest challenges in withholding tax relief services is the growing complexity of global tax regimes. Each jurisdiction may have different rules for applying tax treaties, requiring financial institutions to collect accurate and specific investor documentation to ensure compliance. This variation makes it difficult to standardise relief at source, quick refund, and tax reclaim processes, leading to inefficiencies, delays, and errors.

Compounding the problem is the continuous introduction of new tax reporting regimes and frequent amendments to existing regulations. As tax authorities demand more detailed data and transparency, financial institutions face additional compliance burdens. The constant evolution of these reporting requirements adds strain on operational resources, often pushing withholding tax relief services to a lower priority as institutions focus on meeting stricter regulatory deadlines.

Moreover, in many countries, tax relief services are not yet widely available to investors. As investors become more aware of potential tax savings, financial institutions in these countries will experience increased demand for such services. This will necessitate significant investments in operational capabilities, technical systems, and expertise, as institutions that currently lack infrastructure will need to catch up quickly to meet client expectations.

Despite these challenges, there are promising opportunities for innovation in withholding tax relief services. Technologies such as artificial intelligence (AI) and blockchain offer opportunities to automate processes, reduce errors and improve the transparency of cross-border tax relief. These innovations have the potential to streamline tax relief operations, speeding up the flow of information between institutions and tax authorities.

Additionally, with increasing standardisation and the adoption of more advanced software solutions, even smaller financial institutions will be able to offer tax relief services to their clients. This development lowers the entry barrier, allowing a broader range of institutions to meet growing client demand for these services while reducing operational complexities and costs.

The upcoming European Union FASTER directive, scheduled for 2030, will also create significant opportunities for improving tax relief services within the EU. By introducing standardised formats for documentation and automated digital platforms, FASTER will simplify relief at source and quick refund procedures, reducing the administrative burden on financial institutions and enabling faster, more reliable tax relief for investors.

The probability of widespread adoption of these technological innovations and standardised processes depends largely on regulatory support and industry-wide readiness. The EU's FASTER initiative is likely to improve tax relief services within Europe, but financial institutions operating globally will still face challenges in countries with less harmonised tax systems.

Moreover, financial institutions in countries where tax relief services are not yet offered will need to invest significantly to develop their capabilities. As demand for these services grows, institutions that lag behind in technology or expertise will find themselves under pressure to quickly ramp up their operational capabilities, adding to their costs and complexity.

In parallel, software systems needed to manage evolving tax reporting and relief processes will become more complex and costly. Financial institutions may pass these costs on to investors, increasing fees for tax relief services.

Looking ahead, tax relief services are expected to become more widespread, especially within Europe due to initiatives like the FASTER directive. Relief at source and quick refund applications will likely increase, enabling investors to benefit from reduced withholding tax rates more efficiently. However, globally, financial institutions will continue to face challenges due to the complexity of tax regimes and the need to manage increasingly intricate compliance requirements.

In countries where tax relief services are not yet available, financial institutions will need to make substantial investments in technology and expertise to meet growing client demand. As institutions ramp up these capabilities, operational costs will rise, potentially leading to higher prices for investors.

In conclusion, while the future holds opportunities for greater efficiency and standardisation in withholding tax relief services, financial institutions must navigate a continually evolving regulatory environment. Success will depend on leveraging technology, embracing regulatory changes and managing rising operational costs to deliver effective tax relief services.

*Source: Roman von der Hoh, RAQUEST GmbH.*

## The Authors

We're not sure that the next 10 years are that predictable and there certainly seem to be a lot of possibilities. Everyone seems focussed on AI as taking an important role and we're fine with that. The what is not the issue, it's the how that concerns us.

The convergence of global cross-border taxation to a two-pillar system of tax relief at source and anti-evasion measures, seems to be set for some time and, if the history of the last 35 years is anything to go by we can look forward to a continuing fabric of complex rules-based regulation of financial firms based on a cross-border model involving the appointment, registration or contracting of non-domestic financial firms to act as withholding agents or reporters of financial accounts.

What Marco, Yitzhak and Amanda have highlighted are some of the "how we get there" factors and AI and regtech seem to be the commonly agreed threads—implying a technological solution driven by vendors to the financial firms, but not built by them. This would certainly fit the state of the industry today because only the largest financial firms, global custodians, CSDs and the like, have the budgets to develop these solutions, yet do not seem animated to do so. But we all said that about DLT too 10 years ago, but we still do not have a DLT/blockchain model in live production anywhere in the world.

As authors our view is that AI has similar characteristics to DLT. Its applications in the real world are so numerous and obvious that it seems unlikely to us that AI would be a driver in the backwoods of the corporate actions environment of financial services. It just seems unlikely to us that the immediate benefits would outweigh the costs. What the back-offices of financial institutions do, and regulators support is usually really well-tried and tested technologies that evolve slowly. We mentioned earlier that many financial institutions are only now moving on from paper and spreadsheets. Some of the challenges the industry faces today are born of the very unwillingness to take risks that have created the challenges the industry faces in the first place.

We think the main challenges are:

(1) **Siloing** in the industry that leads to inefficient processes and non-compliance—the left hand doesn't know what the right hand is doing and often doesn't know the right hand exists,
(2) **Attitude**—until the industry starts treating tax as a product and not a task, it will not get the investment it so badly needs. Regtech firms are doing their part because they do treat tax as a service and product. The problem is that their customers see tax as a costly, complex administrative task. It is true that some financial institutions are starting to break tax out of their bundled fee structures, but that's generally because they recognise the increasing costs and they're trying to offset those costs to their customers—that's not the same as treating tax as a product.
(3) **Awareness**—the investors, particularly the institutional investors have some skin in this game, and we continue to be amazed at how little they know about this area. They tend to over-rely on their financial institutions to know what they're doing and assume they're doing it right. In our experience, that's rarely the case.
(4) **Budgets**—the reason that everyone is talking about AI is the same reason that everyone talked about DLT. It is easy to get a CEO to allocate budgets for the new shiny thing that will make their firm look cool and ahead of the curve. As DLT proved, they take too long and rarely deliver the results that the operational folks want in their day-to-day jobs. Until financial firms start budgeting for compliance instead of constraining costs and human resources in a race to the bottom of compliance, all the AI and DLT and other technologies will struggle to get adoption.
(5) **Adoption rates**—even when new technology does come along that is aligned with the problem, as opposed to some theoretical future issue or opportunity, the rate at which the industry adopts these solutions is traditionally very slow. One of the biggest challenges, given a tested solution, is how to engage with the industry in such a way that the industry adopts it quickly and at multiple points in the process simultaneously.

So, we agree, the industry is going to change a lot in the next 10 years. The opportunities we see are tailored to the scale of the regulatory issues and the likely investment (or lack thereof) by financial institutions in compliance related technology. In other words, these opportunities represent changes in scale, not changes in kind (as would be the case with DLT and AI). We don't envy financial institutions today. They have and will continue to be the target of regulators as the nexus from which they can gather the most information. All this in addition to their "day jobs". We see the opportunities as:

(1) **Digitisation**—a continuing drive to replace paper with digital forms. This is likely to increase as technological solutions make it simpler and less costly for financial institutions to use those solutions easily and friction free from their existing processes.
(2) **Integration and consolidation**—tax relief at source, via DTTs, and anti-tax evasion regulations will become ever more integrated with each other.
(3) **Regulation**—rules-based regulation, as opposed to principles-based regulation will flourish because its trackable.
(4) **Compliance automation**—as compliance becomes ever more connected to operational taxes as the source of data for reporting and evasion detection, the obligations of financial institutions will need to be automated too. Regtechs are already working on standardised policies and procedures that are effectively "*pre-compliant*" i.e., if adopted by and implemented in the business, they will automatically generate compliance. This way, firms are buying into the knowledge base of their providers and relying on them to know the regulations and guide them in their compliance.

The possibilities are of course endless, but perhaps these should be tempered by probabilities. So, we are more concerned with those possibilities that stand some reasonable chance of coming to fruition in the next 10 years.

**Centralisation of data**. As more frameworks call for the transfer of large amounts of data, it will become more and more likely that some central trusted authority will take on the role of coordinating these transfers or even of creating a massive data warehouse to which financial institutions contribute and from which governments can extract that data they want (and are authorised to access). There are clear technological and data protection issues at stake, but these don't seem to have stopped key governments from inflicting their rules on everyone else.

**Artificial Intelligence**. While we don't believe we know enough about AI to make intelligent decisions and most AI at the moment is generative (i.e., predicting the next word from a large language model), there is no doubt that AI would be better at pattern matching for tax evasion detection at the tax authority level, where there is sufficient information to make such assessments. Its also possible that AI could predict new forms of tax evasion before they become apparent in the market, providing opportunities for preventative regulation. There remain outstanding ethical concerns about training such a model on the personal data of overseas residents, and the propensity of current models to "hallucinate", which could lead to serious consequences for individuals and entities that could be erroneously identified as tax evaders. There are also environmental concerns about the energy required to run such models that will compete with government net-zero targets and may require tax authorities to be judicious about their use of this technology.

**The EE Smith effect** (criminals are always ahead of the law) will continue to pose problems for regulators and cost for the financial institutions through which these activities flow. That includes the tax evasion we have discussed in this book, whether that be corporate (BEPS) or individual (FATCA/CRS/DAC) as well as abuse of tax relief systems. As the EU progresses towards FASTER, there are already those who are figuring out how to game the system and replicate the treaty abuse scandals of the last decade.

**The rise of rules-based regulation.** At present DAC is the only framework that is principles-based. This is an example of an outlier, a reaction to CRS evasion. Remember that CRS evasion is not tax evasion. The purpose of CRS, as with FATCA, is to allow governments to identify *potential* tax evasion not actual tax evasion. They are simply reporting regimes. But as the criminals get more sophisticated, the regulatory reaction will be to ask more and more of the financial institutions

**Consolidation.** The sheer cost of compliance has and will become such a large budget item that some smaller financial institutions will not be able to commercially meet the rules. We are already seeing this with small tier 3 firms unable to meet the US QI regulations and deliberately using the system of waivers to avoid the checks and balances. That might work for some for a while, but its an unsustainable approach to compliance. The industry is already in a consolidation cycle and we believe this will accelerate as pressure from regulators increases.

**Convergence.** The effect of FATCA and CRS has led to most jurisdictions now adopting one or both models. The EU has, in principle, agreed to a more efficient model, but there are still twelve countries that are blacklisted.

**Tax as a product not a task.** This will become much more prevalent in the next 10 years than it has been in the last thirty-five. As costs of compliance increase, normal market factors will force financial institutions to pass on some or all of these costs to customers. This leads to a need to unbundle custody fees. The more forward looking will make a leap beyond covering costs into the use of tax as a product or service as opposed to its current status as a painfully necessary administrative task. Now, third-party vendors, "Reg-techs" are already at this point because it is their entire business model. We see that these firms will increasingly provide re-saleable services to financial institutions which allows those financial institutions to offset the work (and cost) of compliance and even make a profit by re-selling those services on to their customers (Exhibit 27.4).

So, there you have it. The financial services world in terms of the securities markets appears to be converging on two issues—tax relief and anti-tax evasion. Only a very few countries are not part of some global or bilateral initiatives and eventually, even those blacklisted jurisdictions will join in so as not to be totally excluded from the global capital markets. Technology can certainly help, but neither DLT nor AI are a silver bullet because adoption rates of these technologies by tier 2 and tier 3 institutions will be low and patchy for many decades to come.

We do want to end this book on a high and positive note.

While anti-tax evasion frameworks are generally despised for over-reach, breaches of privacy and reporting complexity and inconsistency, the industry has generally knuckled down and got on with it.

The fragmented nature of the double tax treaties and tax relief efforts are now certainly recognised and initiatives, like FASTER, are being implemented hopefully without replacing one form of complexity with another. Let's hope that it's not another 35 years before we see a more friction-free regulatory and compliance landscape. We are cautiously optimistic.

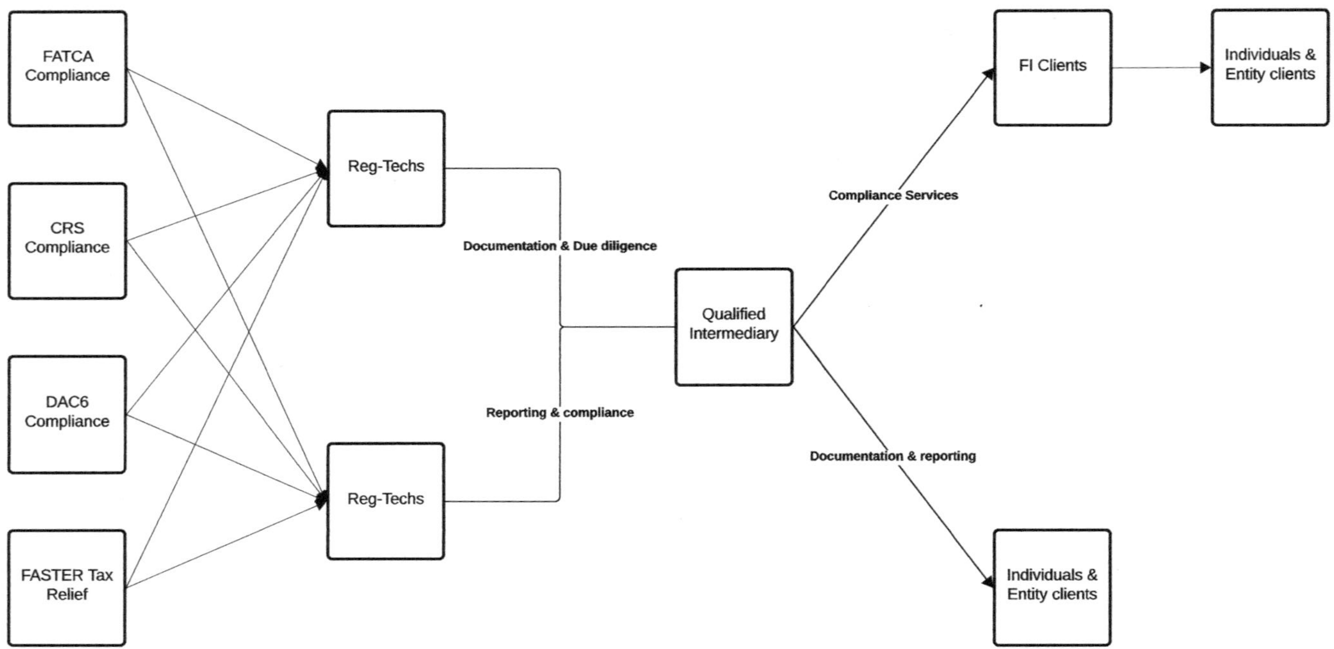


**Exhibit 27.4** Tax as a product not a task *Source* Authors

# Appendix 1: FASTER Directive Approved at ECOFIN 14/05/2024

At the time of writing (Q2 2024) the proposed Directive has already been adjusted ten times prior to submission to ECOFIN. It has now been approved by ECOFIN and can now therefore proceed to the EU Parliament. Various committees are expected to be put in place to manage the detail, but the below text is the final text as approved politically at ECOFIN on May 14, 2024.

## Chapter I
## *General Provisions*

*Article 1*
**Subject Matter**
This Directive lays down rules on the issuance of a digital tax residence certificate by Member States and the procedure to relieve any excess withholding tax that can be withheld by a Member State on dividends from publicly traded shares and, where applicable, interest from publicly traded bonds paid to registered owners who are resident for tax purposes outside that Member State.

*Article 2*
**Scope**

1. Chapters I and IV shall apply to all Member States. Chapter II shall apply to all Member States with regard to all natural persons and entities that are resident for tax purposes in their jurisdiction.
2. Chapter III shall irrevocably apply to all Member States that provide relief of excess withholding tax on dividends paid for publicly traded shares issued by a resident in their jurisdiction if they do not have a comprehensive


R. K. McGill and K. V. Pitkin, *Qualified Intermediary*,
https://doi.org/10.1007/978-3-031-81410-5

relief at source system applicable in such cases or if their market capitalisation ratio is equal to or more than 1.5% for each of the four consecutive years, as set out in the four latest publications by the European Securities and Markets Authority available on the deadline of transposition of this Directive.

3. [deleted]

4. Member States that have a comprehensive relief at source system applicable to the excess withholding tax on dividends paid for publicly traded shares issued by a resident in their jurisdiction may irrevocably apply Chapter III if their market capitalisation ratio is less than 1.5% for at least one of the four consecutive years, as set out in the four latest publications by the European Securities and Markets Authority available on the deadline of transposition of this Directive.

5. Member States shall irrevocably apply Chapter III within five years from the fourth consecutive publication of the data by the European Securities and Markets Authority displaying that their market capitalisation ratio of 1,5% is reached or exceeded during each of the four consecutive years.

6. Member States that provide relief of excess withholding tax on interest paid for publicly traded bonds issued by a resident in their jurisdiction may apply Chapter III.

*Article 3*

**Definitions**

For the purposes of this Directive the following definitions shall apply:

(1) "excess withholding tax" means the difference between the amount of withholding tax levied by a Member State on payments to non-resident owners of dividends or interest from securities by applying the general domestic rate and the lower amount of withholding tax applicable by that Member State on the same dividends or interest in line with a double tax treaty or specific national legislation, as the case may be.

(2) "publicly traded share" means share admitted to trading on a regulated market or traded on a multilateral trading facility as defined under points 21 and 22 of Article 4(1) of Directive

(3) "publicly traded bond" means a bond admitted to trading on a regulated market or traded on a multilateral trading facility or an organised trading facility as defined under points 21, 22 and 23 of Article 4(1) of Directive 2014/65/EU of 15 May 2014 respectively.

(4) "financial intermediary" means a central securities depository as defined in Article 2 (1) of Regulation (EU) 909/2014 of 23 July 2014, a credit institution as defined in point (1) of Article 4(1) of Regulation (EU) No 575/2013 or an investment firm, as defined in point (1) of Article 4(1) in Directive 2014/65/EU, or a branch of those entities, or a third country legal person

that has been authorised to provide services comparable to those provided by a central securities depository, a credit institution or an investment firm, or a branch of those entities, under comparable legislation of a third country of residence, which is part of the securities payment chain between the entity issuing securities and the registered owner receiving payments on such securities.

(4a) "Entity" means a legal person or a legal arrangement, including but not limited to a corporation, partnership, trust, or foundation.

(4b) "Collective investment undertaking" means an undertaking for collective investment in transferable securities (UCITS) as defined in Article 1(2) of Directive 2009/65/EC, an alternative investment fund established in the European Union (EU AIF) or an alternative investment fund managed by an alternative investment fund manager established in the European Union (EU AIFM) as defined in Article 4(1)(k) and Article 4(1)(l), of Directive 2011/61/EU, respectively, or any other collective investment vehicle that, based on the legislation of the source Member State or based on a double tax treaty, is entitled to relief of excess withholding tax or a collective investment vehicle of which the underlying investors are entitled to such relief that can be requested on behalf of them. Where such a collective investment vehicle is established in a third country, and the collective investment itself or its underlying investors are entitled to relief of excess withholding tax, the collective investment vehicle, its manager or its depositary may not be established in a third country listed in Annex I of the EU list as non-cooperative jurisdictions for tax purposes or in Table I of the Annex to Delegated Regulation (EU) 2016/1675.

(4c) "institutions for occupational retirement provision" means an institution as defined in Article 6 (1) of Directive (EU) 2016/2341 of the European Parliament and of the Council

(5) "EUID" means the European Unique Identifier for companies as referred to in Article 16 of Directive (EU) 2017/1132 of the European Parliament and of the Council.

(6) "tax identification number or TIN" means the unique identifier for tax purposes of a registered owner as such in a Member State.

(7) "withholding tax relief procedure" means a procedure whereby a registered owner receiving dividends or interest from securities that can be subject to excess withholding tax is relieved or reimbursed for such excess tax.

(8) "competent authority" means the authority which has been designated by a Member State in accordance with Article 5 and includes any person authorised in accordance with national rules by such authority to act on its behalf for the purposes of this Directive.

(9) "security" means a publicly traded share or a publicly traded bond.

(9a) "depositary receipts" means financial instruments which are negotiable on the capital market of a Member State or a third country and which represent ownership of the securities of an issuer within the European Union while being traded on a trading venue in a Member State or a third country and traded independently of the securities of the issuer.

(10) "large institution" means a large institution as defined in point (146) of Article 4(1) of Regulation (EU) No 575/2013.

(10a) "financial group" means a group as defined in Article 2(12) of Directive (EU) 2002/87/EC of the European Parliament and of the Council

(11) "withholding tax agent" means an entity that has the responsibility under or has been authorised according to the national legislation of the source Member State to deduct the withholding tax from payment of dividends or interest from securities and to transfer such withholding tax to the tax authority of the source Member State.

(12) "record date" means the date set by the issuer of a security, on which the identity of the holder of such security and the rights flowing therefrom shall be determined, based on the settled positions struck in the books of the financial intermediary by book-entry at the close of its business.

(13) "settlement" means the completion of a securities transaction where it is concluded with the aim of discharging the obligation of the parties to that transaction through the transfer of cash or securities or both, as defined in point (7) of Article 2(1) of the Regulation (EU) 909/2014 of 23 July 2014.

(14) "registered owner" means any natural person or entity that is entitled to receive dividend or interest income from securities subject to tax withheld at source in a Member State as the holder of the securities on the record date, without prejudice to the adjustments to transactions pending settlement that could be made in accordance with the law of the source Member State, and that is not a financial intermediary acting for the account of others with respect to that dividend or interest income. Source Member States may consider, in accordance with their national legislation, the holder of depositary receipts as the registered owner, instead of the holder of the underlying securities, as if this holder had directly invested in such securities.

(15) "investment account" means the account or accounts provided by financial intermediaries to registered owners via which their securities are held or registered.

(15a) "cash account" means the account or accounts to which the payments related to the securities held or registered in the investment account are made.

(16) "ex-dividend date" means the date as from which the shares are traded without the rights flowing from the shares, including the right to participate and vote in a general meeting, where relevant.

(16a) "payment date" means the date on which the payment regarding the dividend of a publicly traded share or the interest of a publicly traded bond is due to the registered owner.

(17) "financial arrangement" means, any arrangement or series thereof, or contractual obligation whereby:

i. any part of the ownership of the publicly traded share, on which a dividend is paid, is or could be, either permanently or temporarily transferred to a related or an independent party; or

ii. the dividend is fully or partly compensated, between related or independent parties, in cash or in any other form.

(18) "securities payment chain" means the sequence of financial intermediaries handling the payment of dividends or interest on securities between the securities' issuer and a registered owner to whom dividends or interest from such securities are paid. Brokers that are investment firms authorised under Directive 2014/65/EU, or credit institutions authorised under Directive 2013/36/EU, when providing one or more investment services or performing investment activities, as well as third country legal persons authorised under comparable legislation of a third country of residence when providing investment services or performing investment activities, are considered to be part of the securities payment chain when handling the payment of dividends or interest.

(19) "double tax treaty" means an agreement or convention that provides for the elimination of double taxation of income, and where applicable, capital, in force between two (or more) jurisdictions.

(20) "source Member State" means the Member State of residence of the issuer of the security paying dividend or interest.

(21) "quick refund system" means a system where a payment of dividend or interest is made taking into account the general domestic withholding tax rate followed by a request for refund of the excess withholding tax within the timeframe set in Article 13.

(22) "relief at source system" means a system where the appropriate withholding tax rate, in accordance with the applicable domestic rules or international agreements, such as the relevant double tax treaty, is applied at the moment of payment of dividends or interest.

(22a) "comprehensive relief at source system" means a relief at source system that is applied by a Member State and meets all of the following conditions:

(a) it provides access to relief to any natural person or entity that is entitled to a relief in accordance with the national legislation of the source Member State or a double tax treaty, as applicable;

(aa) if entitled to, it provides relief at the payment date, except in case of failure to report the required information determined by the Member State to apply such relief;

(b) that Member State does not exclude requests for relief other than in circumstances as those set out in Article 10(2);

(c) except in circumstances as those set out in Article 10(2), it neither requires additional information from, nor imposes additional obligations on the natural person or entity entitled to the relief and on the financial intermediary other than the withholding tax agent, other than the information and obligations provided for in Article 11, Article 12, and Article 13a, as applicable;

(d) that Member State has laid down rules on liability for all or part of the loss of withholding tax revenue incurred by that Member State as a result of applying that relief at source system; and

(e) that Member State has laid down rules on effective, proportionate and dissuasive penalties applicable to infringements of national provisions on that relief at source system.

(22b) "market capitalisation" means the total value of the publicly traded shares of the listed companies represented in a Member State as yearly published and provided by the European Securities and Markets Authority.

(22c) "market capitalisation ratio": means the ratio expressed as a percentage of the market capitalisation of a Member State on the 31st of December to the overall market capitalisation of the European Union on the 31st of December, in a given year.

(23) "standard refund system" means a system where a payment of dividends or interest is made taking into account the general domestic withholding tax rate followed by a request for refund of the excess withholding tax outside the procedure set out in Article 13.

## Chapter II
## Digital Tax Residence Certificate

*Article 4*

### Digital Tax Residence Certificate (eTRC)

1. Member States shall provide for an automated process to issue digital tax residence certificates (eTRC) to a natural person or entity deemed resident in their jurisdiction for tax purposes.

2. Member States shall issue the eTRC, based on the information of which the issuing authority has knowledge on the date of issuance, within

14 calendar days from submission of a request, subject to paragraph 4. The eTRC shall comply with the technical requirements of Annex I and shall include the following information:

(a) if the taxpayer is a natural person, the first and last name, the date of birth and the tax identification number or, in its absence, any functional equivalent used for tax purposes;

(b) if the taxpayer is an entity, the name, the tax identification number or, in its absence, any functional equivalent used for tax purposes, and where available, the European Unique Identifier (EUID) or, the legal entity identifier (LEI) or any legal entity registration number which is valid for the entire covered period;

(c) address of the taxpayer;

(d) date of issuance;

(e) the covered period;

(f) identification of the tax authority issuing the certificate;

(fa) one or more double tax treaties pursuant to which the taxpayer requests to be considered resident for tax purposes in the Member State of issuance, where applicable;

(g) any additional information that is necessary for proving the taxpayer's residence for tax purposes insofar as the certificate is not to be used for relief of withholding tax

within the EU.

3. An eTRC shall:

(a) cover a period not exceeding the calendar year or the period of a fiscal year for which it is issued, as applicable in the issuing Member State; and

(b) be valid for certifying the residence of such covered period unless the Member State issuing the eTRC has evidence that the person to which the eTRC refers is not resident for tax purposes in its jurisdiction during all or part of that period and that Member State completely or partially invalidates the eTRC.

4. If more than 14 calendar days are required to verify the tax residency of a specific taxpayer, the Member State shall inform the natural person or entity requesting the certificate of the additional time needed and the reasons for the delay.

5. Member States shall recognise an eTRC issued by another Member State as proof of residence of a taxpayer in that other Member State in accordance with paragraph 3, without prejudice to the possibility for Member States to prove the residence for tax purposes in their jurisdiction.

5a. Member States shall take the appropriate measures to require a natural person or entity deemed resident in their jurisdiction for tax purposes to inform tax authorities issuing the eTRC about any change that could affect the validity or the content of the eTRC.

5b. Member States shall take the necessary measures to require that an eTRC is provided, where a proof of tax residence is required for an natural person or entity deemed resident for tax purposes in a Member State, for the purposes of the application of a relief at source system or a quick refund system in order to obtain relief of excess withholding tax on dividends paid for publicly traded shares, or interests paid for publicly traded bonds, if applicable, issued by a resident in their jurisdiction.

6. The Commission shall adopt implementing acts laying down standard computerised forms, including the linguistic arrangements, and technical protocols, including security standards, for the issuance of an eTRC. Those implementing acts shall be adopted in accordance with the examination procedure referred to in Article 18.

## Chapter III
## Withholding Tax Relief Procedure
## Section 1 Certified Financial Intermediaries

*Article 5*

### National Register of Certified Financial Intermediaries

1. Member States referred to in Article 2, paragraphs 2 and 5, shall establish a national register of certified financial intermediaries.

1a. Member States referred to in Article 2, paragraphs 4 and 6, that opt to apply Chapter III shall establish a national register of certified financial intermediaries.

2. [deleted]

3. Member States establishing a national register according to paragraph 1 and 1a shall designate a competent authority responsible for maintaining and updating that register.

4. The national register shall include the following information on the certified financial intermediaries:

(a) name of the certified financial intermediary;

(b) date of registration;

(c) contact details and any existing website of the certified financial intermediary;

(d) the EUID, or, where the certified financial intermediary has no such number, the legal entity identifier (LEI) or any legal entity registration number issued by its country of residence.

4a. For the purposes of this Article and Articles 9 to 13a, Member States shall permit a certified financial intermediary to assume the obligations and responsibilities set out in Articles 9 to 13a in respect of the position of a financial intermediary that is part of the securities payment chain and is not a certified financial intermediary if both financial intermediaries have agreed on it.

5. The national registers shall be made publicly accessible on a dedicated portal via a website of the Commission (the European Certified Financial Intermediary Portal) and updated at least once a month.

6. Member States shall remain responsible for any decisions regarding registration, rejection, removal and measures imposed on financial intermediaries from their national registers.

7. Any rights and obligations stemming for the decisions referred to in paragraph 6 shall arise from the notification done from the corresponding Member State to the financial intermediary concerned.

8. The Commission shall not be held liable under any circumstances for the content on the European Certified Financial Intermediary Portal or for the failure to exchange information between Member States regarding the registration, the rejection or the removal of a financial intermediary or the measures imposed on certified financial intermediaries.

*Article 5a*

**Development and Operation of the European Certified Financial Intermediary Portal**

1. The Commission shall develop and operate the European Certified Financial Intermediary Portal either by its own means or through a third party.

2. If the Commission decides to develop or operate the European Certified Financial Intermediary Portal through a third party, the choice of the third party and the enforcement by the Commission of the agreement concluded with that third party shall be done in accordance with Regulation (EU, Euratom) No 2018/1046.

3. The European Certified Financial Intermediary Portal shall serve as the electronic access point for financial intermediaries to apply for registration to the registers of the Member States. The portal shall accommodate information exchange between Member States regarding the registration, the rejection, the removal of a financial intermediary or the measures imposed on certified financial intermediaries.

4. Member States shall ensure the information pursuant to Article 6, Article 7 and Article 8 of this Directive is provided to the European Certified Financial Intermediary Portal and the interoperability of their registers within this portal.

5. The Commission shall adopt implementing acts laying down the technical specifications for the operation of the European Certified Financial

Intermediary Portal. Those implementing acts shall be adopted in accordance with the examination procedure referred to in Article 18.

*Article 6*

**Requirement to Register as Certified Financial Intermediary**

1. Member States maintaining a national register in accordance with Article 5 shall require all large institutions that handle payments of dividends and, where relevant, interest on securities issued by a resident in their jurisdiction, and central securities depositories as referred to in Article 3(4) that are the withholding tax agent for the same payments, to register with their national register.

2. Member States maintaining a national register in accordance with Article 5 shall enable, upon request, the registration in that register of any financial intermediary meeting the requirements of Article 7.

*Article 7*

**Registration Procedure**

1. Member States shall ensure that a financial intermediary is registered in their national register of certified financial intermediaries within three months from submission of a request of the financial intermediary that provides evidence of all of the following requirements:

(a) a residence for tax purposes in a Member State or third country jurisdiction not included on Annex I of the EU list of non-cooperative jurisdictions for tax purposes nor on the table I of the Annex to Delegated Regulation (EU) 2016/1675;

(b) if the requesting financial intermediary is a credit institution or an investment firm, an authorisation from the relevant competent authority in the jurisdiction of residence for tax purposes to perform custodial activities; or if the requesting financial intermediary is a central securities depository, an authorisation from the relevant competent authority in the jurisdiction of residence for tax purposes to perform the activities as such. Where the requesting financial intermediary, resident for tax purposes in a third country jurisdiction, has obtained such authorisation under a legislation that is not deemed comparable with Directive 2013/36/EU or Directive

2014/65/EU, as applicable, by a Member State, that Member State may deem this requirement unfulfilled;

(c) a declaration of compliance with the provisions of Directive 2015 / 849 /EU of the European Parliament and of the Council as applicable or with a comparable legislation of a third country jurisdiction not included on Annex I of the EU list of non-cooperative jurisdictions for tax purposes or on the table I of the Annex to Delegated Regulation (EU) 2016/1675. Member States shall permit a certified financial intermediary to act on behalf of another financial intermediary that is part of the same financial group and to assume the obligation set out in Article 6 and the obligations and responsibilities set out in Articles 9 to 13a.

1a. If the financial intermediary submitting the registration request is resident for tax purposes in a third country jurisdiction where the Directive 2010/24/EU or a convention that provides assistance in the collection of taxes does not apply to recover all or part of the loss of withholding tax revenues according to Article 16, Member States may require sufficient and proportionate guarantees to ensure the payment of such loss in relation to the relief requests.

1b. Member States may reject the application for registration if:

(i) the financial intermediaries concerned committed one or more offences or infringements under the national legislation of a Member State or another jurisdiction where such offences or infringements have led to a loss in withholding tax. Such offences or infringements committed by financial intermediaries can only be taken into account by the source Member State to the extent that they were known not more than 10 years prior to the application for the registration; or

(ii) an inquiry is opened by a Member State or another jurisdiction, in relation to the financial intermediary concerned, on potential fraud or tax abuse which may lead to a loss in withholding tax.

2. Financial intermediaries shall notify without undue delay the competent authority of the Member State of any change in the information provided under points (a) to (c).

3. [deleted]

4. Member States shall ensure that the rejected financial intermediary pursuant to paragraph 1b is allowed to re-apply for registration, where Member States have determined that the circumstance that caused it has been remedied.

*Article 8*

**Removal From the National Register**

1. Member States shall remove from their national register any certified financial intermediary that is not a certified financial intermediary on the basis of Article 6(1), where such intermediary:

(a) requests such removal; or

(b) no longer meets the requirements of Article 7.

2. Member States may remove from their national register any certified financial intermediary that is not a certified financial intermediary on the basis of Article 6(1), and:

(a) that has been found to have not complied with its obligations under this Directive or the Directive 2015/849/EU or comparable legislation of a third country of residence for tax purposes; or

(b) that has been found to have committed one or more offences or infringements under the national legislation of a Member State or another jurisdiction where such offences or infringements have led to a loss in withholding tax revenue. Such offences or infringements committed by financial intermediaries can only be taken

into account by the source Member State to the extent that they were known not more than 10 years prior to the removal; or

(c) whereby an inquiry is opened by a Member State or another jurisdiction, in relation to the certified financial intermediary concerned, on potential fraud or tax abuse which may lead to a loss in withholding tax.

2a. Member States may prohibit any certified financial intermediary, on the basis of Article 6(1), to request relief under this Directive:

(a) where such certified financial intermediary has been found to not have complied with its obligations under this Directive or the Directive 2015/849/EU or comparable legislation of a third country of residence for tax purposes; or

(b) where such certified financial intermediary has been found to have committed one or more offences or infringements under the national legislation of a Member State or another jurisdiction where such offences or infringements have led to a loss in withholding tax revenue. Such offences or infringements committed by financial intermediaries can only be taken into account by the source Member State to the extent that they were known not more than 10 years prior to the prohibition to request relief; or

(c) when an inquiry is opened by a Member State or another jurisdiction, in relation to the certified financial intermediary concerned, on potential fraud or tax abuse which may lead to a loss in withholding tax. Where such measure is applied to the certified financial intermediary, upon application thereof, it shall be made part of the information related to that certified financial intermediary in the national register maintained by the Member State that has adopted such measure.

3. [deleted]

4. Member States shall ensure that the financial intermediary that has been removed from the national register pursuant to paragraph 1 or 2, or that has been prohibited to request relief pursuant to paragraph 2a, is re-registered, or allowed to request relief again, where Member States have determined that the circumstance that caused it has been remedied.

## Section 2
## Reporting

*Article 9*
***Obligation to Report***

1. Member States shall take the necessary measures to require certified financial intermediaries in their national register to report to their competent authority the information referred to under heading A to E of Annex II within the second month following the month of the payment date. If a settlement instruction in respect of any part of a transaction is pending, certified financial intermediaries shall indicate the part for which settlement is pending.

1bis. In addition to the information referred to in paragraph 1, Member States may require certified financial intermediaries registered in their national register to report to their competent authority the information referred to under heading F, and where applicable, heading G of Annex II, within the second month following the month of the payment date.

1a. Member States shall take the necessary measures to require that the certified financial intermediary referred to in Article 5(4a) reports to their competent authority the information referred to in paragraph 1 and when applicable paragraph 1bis with respect to a part of the securities payment chain for which the handling financial intermediary is not a certified financial intermediary.

1b. [deleted]

1c. Notwithstanding paragraphs 1, 1bis and 1a, Member States may take the necessary measures to require that only the withholding tax agent or a certified financial intermediary in the relevant security payment chain, appointed by their competent authority or designated under national legislation, reports to the competent authority the information according to those paragraphs. This information is provided by the certified financial intermediaries along the securities payment chain in a sequential order, and in respect of the position of these certified financial intermediaries in the securities payment chain in which they are part of, with an effect that it ultimately reaches the withholding tax agent or the concerned certified financial intermediary.

2. [deleted]

3. Member States referred to in Article 2, paragraph 6, that opt to apply Chapter III and maintain a national register established in accordance with Article 5 shall not require reporting of information under heading E of Annex II.

4. The Commission shall adopt implementing acts laying down standard computerised forms, including the linguistic arrangements, and requirements for the communication channels, for the reporting of information referred to in Annex II. Those implementing acts shall be adopted in accordance with the examination procedure referred to in Article 18.

5. Member States shall require certified financial intermediaries in their national register to keep the documentation supporting the information reported for ten years and to provide access to any other information necessary for the correct application of rules on withholding taxes and shall require certified financial intermediaries to delete or anonymise any personal data included in such documentation as soon as the audit has been completed and at the latest ten years after reporting.

6. [deleted]

## Section 3
## Systems of Relief

*Article 10*

***Request for Relief at Source or Quick Refund***

1. Source Member States shall require a certified financial intermediary, maintaining the investment account of a registered owner receiving dividends distributed or interests paid by a resident in the source Member State, to request relief pursuant to Article 12 or Article 13, as applicable, on behalf of that registered owner if the following conditions are met:

(a) the registered owner has authorised the certified financial intermediary to request relief on its behalf; and

(b) the certified financial intermediary has verified and established the eligibility for the relief in accordance with Article 11 or Article 13a, as applicable.

2. Notwithstanding paragraph 1, Member States may exclude, completely or partially, requests for relief under the systems as provided for under Articles12 and 13 for a request, where any of the following circumstances occur:

(a) the dividend has been paid on a publicly traded share that the registered owner acquired in a transaction carried out within a period of five days before the ex-dividend date;

(b) the dividend payment on the underlying security for which relief is requested is linked to a financial arrangement that has not been settled, expired or otherwise terminated before the ex-dividend date;

(c) at least one of the financial intermediaries in the securities payment chain is not a certified financial intermediary and no certified financial intermediary has assumed the position of that financial intermediary for the purpose of Article 9 according to Article 5(4a).

(d) an exemption of the withholding tax is claimed;

(e) a reduced withholding tax rate not deriving from double tax treaties is claimed;

(f) the dividend payment exceeds a gross amount of at least [100.000 EUR], per registered owner and per payment date. This amount shall be determined by the gross dividend amount per investor holding equity in a collective investment undertaking when this underlying investor is entitled to the relief pursuant to Article 13a(1a)(i) or Article 13a(1a)(ii) as applicable. This point shall not apply when the one entitled to the relief of excess withholding tax is a:

i. statutory pension scheme of a Member State or an institution for occupational retirement provision registered or authorised in a Member State in accordance with Article 9(1) of Directive (EU) 2016/2341; or

ii. collective investment undertaking, that is an undertaking for collective investment in transferable securities (UCITS) as defined in Article 1(2) and established in compliance with Article 1(1) of Directive 2009/65/EC, an

alternative investment fund established in the European Union (EU AIF) or an alternative investment fund managed by an alternative investment fund manager established in the European Union (EU AIFM) as defined in Article 4(1)(k) and Article 4(1)(l), of Directive 2011/61/EU, respectively. Any arrangement whereby the dividend payment is split or any collective investment undertaking other than mentioned in paragraph 2(f)(ii) that has been established with the sole purpose of remaining inferior to this amount leads to the application of this paragraph.

4. Notwithstanding paragraph 1, where a financial intermediary maintaining the investment account of a registered owner is not a certified financial intermediary, Member States shall allow a certified financial intermediary to request relief pursuant to Article 12 or Article 13, as applicable, subject to the provisions of Article 5(4a) and Article 9.

5. The systems of relief pursuant to Article 12 and Article 13, as applicable, shall not reduce the control powers of Member States, according to their national legislation, in relation to the taxable income to which such relief was applied, and do not affect the taxing rights of Member States.

6. Where a Member State has a system for relief at source or quick refund, or a combination thereof, prior to the entry into force of this Directive and where that Member State applies Chapter III pursuant to Article 2, that

Member State shall ensure the compliance of its existing system with the provisions set out in Chapter III for any request of relief covered by this Directive, being dividends arising from publicly traded shares and, only where Member States decide to do so, interest from publicly traded bonds paid to non-residents. Member States may also maintain and apply an existing national relief at source system to cases referred to in paragraph 2(e) in which verifications are performed in order to:

i. ensure equal treatment between domestic and cross-border situations to comply with Chapters 2 and 4 of Title IV of the TFEU; or

ii. apply the reduced withholding tax rates in accordance with Directive 2003/49/EC or

Directive 2011/96/EU.

*Article 11*

***Due Diligence of Registered Owner's Eligibility***

1. Member States shall take the necessary measures to require that the certified financial intermediary requesting relief on behalf of a registered owner under Article 12 and Article 13, as applicable, obtains from such registered owner a declaration that the registered owner:

(a) is the one entitled to the relief of the withholding tax with respect to the dividend or interest in accordance with the national legislation of the source Member State or a double tax treaty, where applicable, including the legal basis and the applicable withholding tax rate; and

(aa) is the beneficial owner, when required by the source Member State, with respect to the dividend or interest in accordance with the national legislation of the source Member State or a double tax treaty, where applicable; and

(b) has engaged or not in a financial arrangement linked to the underlying publicly traded share that has not been settled, expired or otherwise terminated before the ex-dividend date; and

(c) undertakes to inform the certified financial intermediary of any change in their circumstances without undue delay.

2. Member States shall take the necessary measures to require that certified financial intermediaries requesting relief on behalf of a registered owner under Article 12 and Article 13, as applicable, verify, based on the information available to these certified financial intermediaries, the following:

(a) the eTRC of the registered owner or a proof of tax residence in a third country deemed appropriate by the source Member State. For these purposes, a tax residence certificate with equivalent content to that provided for in Article 4(2) and that meets the technical requirements in Annex I, paragraph

1, may be deemed as an appropriate proof of tax residence in a third country by the source Member State;

(aa) notwithstanding point (a) of this paragraph, the documentation deemed appropriate by the source Member State, in cases where a registered owner is an entity for which an eTRC cannot be issued or that cannot obtain a proof of tax residence in a third country because the entity is disregarded for tax purposes and its income (or part thereof) is taxed at the level of the persons who have an interest in that entity, but it is entitled to the relief of the withholding tax with respect to the dividend or interest in accordance with the national legislation of the source Member State or a double tax treaty, where applicable;

(b) the registered owner's declaration and tax residence, against the information that the certified financial intermediary has obtained or has an obligation to obtain, including but not limited to the information collected for other tax purposes or on the basis of anti-money laundering requirements, which the certified financial intermediary is subject to under Directive (EU) 2015/849, or comparable information required in third countries;

(c) the registered owner's entitlement to a specific reduced withholding tax rate in accordance with a double tax treaty between the source Member State and the jurisdictions where the registered owner is resident for tax purposes or specific national legislation of the source Member State;

(d) in case of a dividend payment the possible existence of any financial arrangement that has not been settled, expired or otherwise terminated at the ex-dividend date;

(e) in case of a dividend payment, that the underlying share has been acquired by the registered owner in a transaction carried out earlier or within a period of five days before the ex-dividend date.

2a. Member States may allow a certified financial intermediary to obtain the declaration referred to in paragraph 1 of this Article and to carry out the verifications provided for in paragraph 2, points (a) to (c), of this Article on an annual basis unless the certified financial intermediary knows or has reasons to know that there is a change of circumstances or that the declaration or the information to be verified is incorrect or unreliable.

3. [deleted]

4. In the case provided for in Article 5(4a), Member States shall allow the certified financial intermediary to rely on documentation collected and information verified by the financial intermediary maintaining the investment account of a registered owner according to this Article, without prejudice to the fact that these obligations remain the responsibility of the certified financial intermediary.

5. Member States shall require certified financial intermediaries requesting relief under Article 12 and Article 13, as applicable, keep all supporting documentation and provide access thereto in accordance with Article 9, paragraph 5.

6. The Commission shall adopt implementing acts laying down standard templates of computerised forms for the declaration referred to in this Article, including the linguistic arrangements. Such templates shall encompass the information laid down under letter (a), (b), and (c) of Article 11(1) and enable Member States to request specific additional information. Those implementing acts shall be adopted in accordance with the examination procedure referred to in Article 18.

*Article 12*

***Relief at Source System***

1. Member States may establish a system to allow certified financial intermediaries maintaining a registered owner's investment account to request relief at source on behalf of a registered owner in accordance with Article 10 by providing to the withholding tax agent the following information:

(a) the tax residence of the registered owner or the information contained in the documentation referred to in point (aa) of Article 11, paragraph 2, where applicable; and

(b) the applicable withholding tax rate on the payment in accordance with a double tax treaty or specific national legislation.

*Article 13*

***Quick Refund System***

1. Member States may establish a system to allow certified financial intermediaries maintaining a registered owner's investment account to request a quick refund of the excess withholding tax, on behalf of such registered owner in accordance with Article 10 if the information referred to in paragraph 3 of this Article is provided within the second month following the month of the payment date of the dividend or interest.

2. Without prejudice to paragraph 3a of this Article, Member States shall process a refund request made in accordance with paragraph 1 within 60 calendar days after the end of the period to request the quick refund. Member States shall apply interest in accordance with Article 14 on the amount of such refund for each day of delay after the 60th day.

3. A certified financial intermediary requesting quick refund shall provide the following information to the relevant Member State:

(a1) the identification of the registered owner as referred to in Annex II, heading B;

(a) the identification of the dividend or interest payment as referred to in Annex II, heading D and G, where applicable;

(b) the basis of the applicable withholding tax rate and total amount of excess tax to be refunded;

(c) the tax residence of the registered owner, including the eTRC verification code, where applicable, or the information contained in the documentation referred to in point (aa) of Article 11, paragraph 2, where applicable;

(d) the registered owner's declaration in accordance with Article 11.

3a. Member States may reject a refund request made under this Article in any of the following cases:

(a) the requirements provided for in paragraph 1 or 3 of this Article or in Article 10 or 11 are not met;

(b) the information, necessary to reconstruct the relevant securities payment chain and referred to in Annex II, has not been completely and correctly provided at the end of the period set out in paragraph 1 of this Article;

(c) the Member State, based on risk assessment criteria, initiates any verification procedure or tax audit according to its national legislation with respect to the refund request. Such rejection shall not preclude the application of late payment interest in accordance with paragraph 2 in the event that the refund is finally granted and the circumstances provided for in subparagraphs (a) or (b) do not exist.

3b. The rejection referred to in points (a) and (b) of paragraph 3a of this Article shall be communicated to the requesting certified financial intermediary and shall not preclude the request for a refund under the standard refund system established in the national legislation.

4. The Commission shall adopt implementing acts laying down standard computerised forms, including the linguistic arrangements, and requirements for the communication channels for the submission of requests under this Article. Those implementing acts shall be adopted, in accordance with the examination procedure referred to in Article 18.

*Article 13a*

***Special Provisions for Indirect Investments***

1. Member States shall allow a certified financial intermediary maintaining the investment account of a registered owner receiving dividends or interests, to request relief pursuant to Article 12 and Article 13, as applicable, on behalf of that registered owner, provided that the requirements set out in paragraphs 1a to 1d of this Article have been met.

1a. For the purposes of paragraph 1 of this Article, the registered owner shall be:

(i) a collective investment undertaking, which holds securities for the account of investors entitled to the relief of the withholding tax with respect to the dividends or interest in accordance with the national legislation of the source Member State or a double tax treaty, where applicable; or
(ii) a designated legal person within the fund rules, instruments of incorporation or prospectus of a collective investment undertaking that holds the securities in the investment account that give rise to the dividend or interest, and maintains internal records enabling the individual allocation of these securities to that collective investment undertaking or to the investors in that collective investment undertaking, as applicable, where the collective investment undertaking or the investors in a collective investment undertaking are entitled to the relief of the excess withholding tax with respect to that dividend or interest in accordance with the national legislation of the source Member State or a double tax treaty, where applicable.

1b. For the purposes of paragraph 1 of this Article, the certified financial intermediary requesting the relief shall obtain a declaration from:

(a) each collective investment undertaking entitled to the relief or each investor in the collective investment undertaking entitled to the relief, as applicable, whose securities are held by the registered owner that:

(i) they are entitled to the relief of the withholding tax with respect to the dividend or interest in accordance with the national legislation of the source Member State or a double tax treaty, where applicable, including the legal basis and the applicable withholding tax rate; and

(ia) they are the beneficial owner, when required by the source Member State, with respect to the dividend or interest in accordance with the national legislation of the source Member State or a double tax treaty, where applicable; and

(ii) they have authorised that the relief is requested on their behalf under this Article; and

(iii) if the relief is granted, they waive their right to independently request relief from the source Member State under this Directive or under the systems pursuant to the national legislation of Member States;

(b) the registered owner referred to in point (i) of paragraph 1a of this Article, indicating the applicable withholding tax rates with respect to the dividend or interest paid;

(c) the registered owner referred to in point (ii) of paragraph 1a of this Article, identifying the collective investment undertaking for which the securities giving rise to the dividend or interest are held, in accordance with its internal records, and indicating the applicable withholding tax rates with respect to the dividend or interest paid;

(d) the registered owner with the information referred to in Article 11(1) points (b) and (c).

1c. For the purposes of paragraph 1, the certified financial intermediary requesting the relief at source pursuant to Article 12 shall provide the withholding tax agent with the information referred to in paragraph 1b(b) or 1b(c), as applicable, and with the tax residence or the information contained in the documentation referred to in Article 11(2)(aa) of the collective investment undertaking or the investors in a collective investment undertaking, as applicable, instead of the information referred to in Article 12, and, when the investors in a collective investment undertaking are entitled to the relief, the amount of dividends or interest attributable to each entitled investor pursuant to Article 13a(1a)(i) or Article 13a(1a)(ii) as applicable.

1d. For the purposes of paragraph 1, the certified financial intermediary requesting relief pursuant to Article 13 shall provide the source Member State with the information referred to in paragraph 1b, and with the tax residence of the collective investment undertaking or the investors in a collective investment undertaking, including the eTRC verification code or the information contained in the documentation referred to in Article 11(2)(aa), as applicable, instead of the information referred to in Article 13(3) (c) and (d), and, when the investors in a collective investment undertaking are entitled to the relief, the amount of dividends or interest attributable to each entitled investor in a collective investment undertaking pursuant to Article 13a(1a)(i) or Article 13a(1a)(ii) as applicable.

2. Member States shall take the necessary measures to require that certified financial intermediaries requesting relief under this Article verify, based on the information available to these certified financial intermediaries, the following:

(a) the documentation referred to in Article 11(2) point (a) or (aa) with respect to each collective investment undertaking or each investor in a collective investment undertaking, as applicable, entitled to the relief;

(b) the entitlement of the collective investment undertaking or that of the investors in a collective investment undertaking, as applicable, to a specific exemption or reduced withholding tax rate in accordance with a double tax treaty between the source Member State and the jurisdiction of residence for tax purposes or specific national legislation of the source Member State;

(c) in case of a dividend payment, the possible existence of any financial arrangement that has not been settled, expired or otherwise terminated before the ex-dividend date.

3. [deleted]

4. [deleted]

5. The provisions of paragraphs 1, 2 and 2a of Article 11 shall not apply where the relief is requested pursuant to this Article.

6. The Commission shall adopt implementing acts laying down standard computerised forms, including the linguistic arrangements, and requirements for the communication channels for the submission of requests under paragraph 1d. Those implementing acts shall be adopted in accordance with the examination procedure referred to in Article 18.9925/24 JB/dpn 59

*Article 14*

**Late payment interest**

Pursuant to Article 13(2), Member States shall, where national legislation includes such provisions, apply interest at a rate equal to the interest or equivalent charge applied by the Member State to late payments of withholding tax refunds related to the taxation of dividends or interests, as applicable.

*Article 15*

**Standard refund system**

1. Member States shall ensure that a standard refund system is in place and applicable where requests for relief within the scope of the Directive are excluded from the systems under Article 12 and Article 13, as applicable.

2. Member States shall adopt the necessary measures to require that where Article 12 and Article 13, where applicable, do not apply to dividends due to the conditions set out in this Directive not being met, those entitled to the refund or their authorised representative requesting refund of the excess withholding tax on such dividends provides at least the information required under Annex II, heading E, unless this information has already been provided in accordance with the obligations pursuant to Article 9.

*Article 16*

**Liability**

1. Member States shall take appropriate measures in their national legislation, to ensure that a certified financial intermediary that does not comply, completely or partially, with its obligations under Articles 9, 10, 11, 12, 13 and 13a, can be held liable for all or part of the loss of withholding tax.

2. [deleted]

## Chapter IV
## Penalties and Final Provisions

*Article 17*
**Penalties**
Member States shall lay down the rules on penalties applicable to infringements of national provisions adopted pursuant to this Directive, and shall take all measures necessary to ensure that they are implemented. These penalties shall be effective, proportionate and dissuasive.

*Article 17a*
**Publications by the European Securities and Markets Authority**
1. The European Securities and Markets Authority shall publish, on an annual basis, and within 120 working days of the beginning of each year, starting from 2026 at the latest, the market capitalisation and the market capitalisation ratio of each Member State for at least the preceding year. The European Securities and Markets Authority shall develop draft regulatory technical standards on the methodology for the calculation of market

capitalisation and market capitalisation ratio as defined in Articles 3 (22b) and (22c) respectively. The European Securities and Markets Authority shall submit those draft regulatory technical standards to the Commission by nine months after the entry into force of the Directive.

2. Power is delegated to the Commission to adopt the regulatory technical standards referred to in paragraph 1 in accordance with the procedure laid down in Articles 10 to 14 of Regulation (EU) No 1095/2010.

*Article 18*
**Committee procedure**
1. The Commission shall be assisted by a Committee. That committee shall be a committee within the meaning of Regulation (EU) No 182/2011 of the European Parliament and of the Council.

2. Where reference is made to this paragraph, Article 5 of Regulation (EU) No 182/2011 shall apply.

*Article 19*
**Evaluation**
1. The Commission shall, by 31 December 2032, evaluate the impact on reaching the objectives of the Directive concerning the mechanisms of reporting of article 9 and the case where Member States which meet the conditions of Article 2(4) do not apply Chapter III. The Commission will, within the same timeframe, submit a report to the European Parliament and the Council.

1a. The Commission shall, by 31 December 2034 and every five years thereafter, examine and evaluate the functioning of this Directive, including the potential need to amend specific provisions, and submit a report to the European Parliament and the Council.

2. Member States shall, in accordance with paragraph 3, communicate to the Commission relevant yearly statistical information for the evaluation of the Directive, for the purpose of improving withholding tax relief procedures to reduce double taxation as well as combat tax abuse, in accordance with paragraph 3.

3. The Commission shall, in accordance with the procedure referred to in Article 18(2), determine a list of statistical data which shall be provided by the Member States for the purposes of evaluation of this Directive, as well as the format and the conditions of communication of that information.

4. Information communicated to the Commission pursuant to this Directive shall be kept confidential by the Commission in accordance with the provisions applicable to Union institutions.

5. Information communicated to the Commission by a Member State under paragraph 2, as well as any report or document produced by the Commission using such information, may be transmitted to other Member States. The transmitted information shall be covered by the obligation of official secrecy and enjoy the protection extended to similar information under the national law of the Member State which received it.

*Article 20*

**Personal Data Protection**

1. Member States shall, for the purposes of the correct application of this Directive, restrict the scope of the obligations and rights provided for in Articles 13 to 19 of Regulation (EU) 2016/679 of the European Parliament and of the Council7 to the extent required in order to safeguard the interests referred to in point (e) of Article 23(1) of that Regulation in so far as such obligations or the exercise of such rights may jeopardise the safeguard of those interests.

2. When processing personal data, certified financial intermediaries and the competent authorities of Member States shall be considered as controllers, in the meaning of Article 4, paragraph 7 of Regulation (EU) 2016/679, within the scope of their respective activities under this Directive.

3. Information, including personal data, processed in accordance with this Directive shall be retained for no longer than is necessary to achieve the purposes of this Directive, and in any case in accordance with each data controller's domestic rules on statute of limitations.

*Article 21*

**Notification**

A Member State that establishes and maintains a national register pursuant to Article 5 shall inform

the Commission of any subsequent changes to the rules governing such register. The Commission shall publish in the *Official Journal of the European Union* this information and shall update the information as necessary.

*Article 22*

**Transposition**

1. Member States shall adopt and publish, by 31 December 2028, the laws, regulations and administrative provisions necessary to comply with this Directive. They shall immediately inform the Commission thereof. They shall apply those provisions from 1 January 2030. When Member States adopt those provisions, they shall contain a reference to this Directive or be accompanied by such a reference on the occasion of their official

publication. The methods of making such reference shall be laid down by Member States.

2. Member States shall communicate to the Commission the text of the main provisions of national law which they adopt in the field covered by this Directive.

3. Member States which meet the conditions of Article 2(4) at the time of the transposition of the Directive and do not opt to apply Chapter III, shall notify the Commission by 31 December 2028. They shall communicate to the Commission, without delay, any subsequent change to their national relief at source system concerning the conditions under Article 3 (22a). These Member States shall adopt and publish the laws, regulations and administrative provisions necessary to comply with Chapter III of this Directive as set out in Article 2(4) or within five years from the fourth consecutive publication of the data by the European Securities and Markets Authority, as set out in Article 2(5) displaying that they reach or exceed the market capitalisation ratio threshold as foreseen in Article 2.

*Article 23*

**Entry into force**

This Directive shall enter into force on the twentieth day following that of its publication in the

*Official Journal of the European Union.*

*Article 24*

***Addressees***

This Directive is addressed to the Member States.

# Annex I

## Digital Tax Residence Certificate AS Referred to in Article 4

Technical requirements

1. The digital tax residence certificate shall:

- be issued with an electronic seal in conformity with Regulation (EU) No 910/2014 of the European Parliament and of the Council;
- offer the possibility of both human- and machine-readable format presentations of the digital tax resident certificate with PDF documents or similar other formats which can be used in the automated systems;
- be printable;
- contain an open text box for inclusion of information under Article 4(g).

2. If the legal and technical requirements in the Union are met, Member States may introduce a verification process based on the European Digital Identity Wallet

A Committee shall support the Commission with the implementation of the digital tax residence certificate by Member States. In addition, the Committee may provide technical support regarding any possible changes of the technical basis of the digital tax residence certificate or new technical developments.

# Annex II

## Reporting as Referred to in Articles 9 and 15

Certified financial intermediaries shall provide the following information in the corresponding xml

format:

**A. Information regarding the person that is providing the information**

| Type of Information | Specification |
|---|---|
| Name of the certified financial intermediary or, where applicable, the withholding tax agent | |
| EUID, Legal Entity Identifier (LEI) or alternative | |
| Official address | |
| Other relevant data | Tax identification number assigned by the source Member State, if available, and the tax identification number assigned by the jurisdiction of residence for tax purposes<br>TIN issuing jurisdiction/s<br>E mail address and telephone number |
| Indication if the information is provided pursuant to Article 9.1a | Identification of the financial intermediary that is not a certified financial intermediary<br>(name and EUID, Legal Entity Identifier (LEI) or alternative) |

## B. Information regarding the recipient of the dividend or interest payment

| Type of Information | Specification |
|---|---|
| Identification of the financial intermediary or final investor receiving the dividend or interest payment. When the reporting option of Article 9, §1c is applicable: the withholding tax agent or the designated certified financial intermediary is required to report on the information about the final investor receiving the dividend or interest payment | |
| Natural person | TIN (tax identification number assigned by the source Member State, if available, and the tax identification number assigned by the jurisdiction of residence for tax purposes), TIN issuing jurisdiction/s, date of birth, address |

(continued)

(continued)

| Type of Information | Specification |
|---|---|
| Entity | Name<br>TIN (tax identification number assigned by the source Member State, if available, and the tax identification number assigned by the jurisdiction of residence for tax purposes), TIN issuing jurisdiction/s, address, LEI, where applicable, EUID, where applicable<br>In the absence of an identification number, legal form and date of incorporation<br>Name of country of tax residence |
| In the absence of an identification number, legal form and date of incorporation<br>Information about the tax residence *(to be completed when the person in section A is the certified financial intermediary of the registered owner)* | |
| Investment account number | Number of the safekeeping account where the securities are hold by the financial intermediary/investor receiving the payment |

(continued)

(continued)

| Type of Information | Specification |
|---|---|
| Type of account | The type of account according to Article 38 of Regulation (EU) 909/ 2014 and other accounts:<br>A - Own account (maintained by a participant in the CSD of the securities original register)<br>B- Third party general account (maintained by a participant in the CSD of the securities original register for the account of clients)<br>C- Third party individual account (maintained by a participant in the CSD of the securities original register on behalf of a client)<br>D- Detail register account of a third party general account (securities of a client included in a third party general account maintained by a participant in the CSD of the securities original register)<br>E- Third party global account other than B<br>F- Individual account of a securities holder other than D or C<br>G- Other type of account |

## C. Information regarding the payor of the dividend or interest payment

| Type of Information | Specification |
|---|---|
| Identification of the financial intermediary from whom the reporter receives the dividend or interest payment When the reporting option of Article 9, §1c is applicable: section C contains information about each certified financial intermediary that is part of the security payment chain. This information relates to the sequential payment chain of financial intermediaries | |
| Legal person | Name, LEI, TIN (tax identification number assigned by the source Member State, if available, and the tax identification number assigned by the jurisdiction of residence for tax purposes), TIN issuing jurisdiction/s, address, EUID, where applicable |
| Investment account number | Number of the safekeeping account where the securities were hold by the financial intermediary sending the payment |

(continued)

(continued)

| Type of Information | Specification |
|---|---|
| Type of account | The type of account according to Article 38 of Regulation (EU) 909/2014 and other Accounts:<br>A - Own account (maintained by a participant in the CSD of the securities original register)<br>B- Third-party general account (maintained by a participant in the CSD of the securities original register for the account of clients)<br>C- Third-party individual account (maintained by a participant in the CSD of the securities original register on behalf of a client)<br>D- Detail register account of a third-party general account (securities of a client included in a third-party general account maintained by a participant in the CSD of the securities original register)<br>E- Third-party global account other than B<br>F- Individual account of a securities holder other than D or C<br>G- Other type of account |

## D. Information regarding the dividend or interest payment

| Type of Information | Specification |
|---|---|
| Issuer | Name,<br>TIN or, in its absence, LEI or EUID,<br>official address |
| CSD | Identification of the central securities depository that maintains the original register of the securities |
| ISIN number | Identification of the security |
| Security type | Type of share, underlying of a depository receipt, bond |
| Number of securities that give right to receive the payment | Number of securities settled<br>Number of securities pending settlement |
| Payment type | Cash Shares (indication whether they derive from script dividend and the ISIN number) |

(continued)

(continued)

| Type of Information | Specification |
|---|---|
| COAF (Official Corporate Action Event Identifier) or, if not available, detailed information on the distribution | Identification of the event (dividend/ interest distribution) |
| Relevant dates | Ex-dividend date, record date, payment date |
| Amount of dividend or interest received/to be received and currency | Gross amount,<br>net amount |
| Information about the withholding tax | Withholding Tax rate applied or to be applied, amount withheld, the amount and the rate of a surcharge if applicable<br>The legal basis of the applicable withholding tax rate *(to be completed when the person in section A is the certified financial intermediary of the registered owner)* |
| Cash account IBAN | IBAN of the account to which the payment has been transferred |

Cash account IBAN–IBAN of the account to which the payment has been transferred

**E. Information regarding application of anti-abuse measures to be fulfilled by the certified financial intermediary requesting the relief**

| Type of Information | Specification |
|---|---|
| Information about holding period of underlying publicly traded shares | Two boxes:<br>1) for underlying shares acquired more than five days before the ex-dividend date – number of shares<br>2) for underlying shares acquired within a period of five days before the ex-dividend date – number of shares<br>(First In First Out "FIFO" to be used in case of regular trading positions) |

(continued)

(continued)

| Type of Information | Specification |
|---|---|
| Information about financial arrangement | Indicate evidence of any financial arrangement involving underlying publicly traded shares that has not been settled, expired or otherwise terminated at the ex-dividend date<br>For underlying shares linked to a financial arrangement<br>– number of shares<br>For underlying shares not linked to a financial arrangement<br>– number of shares |

**F. Information regarding transactions that can be requested by the source Member State according to Article 9(1bis)**

| Type of Information | Specification |
|---|---|
| Information about the transactions of the underlying securities from 1 year prior to the record date up to and including 45 days after the record date | Trade dates<br>Contractual or agreed settlement dates<br>Actual settlement dates<br>The respective number of securities that are subject to the trade<br>Transaction type: purchase, sale, loan, transfer, other |

## G. Information regarding depositary receipts that can be requested by the source Member State according to Article 9(1bis)

| Type of Information | Specification |
|---|---|
| When it concerns a dividend payment arising from a depositary receipt | The name, the international securities identification number (ex. ISIN) of the depositary receipts and of the underlying shares<br>The name of the bank in which the ordinary shares are deposited<br>The ratio of the depositary receipts to the ordinary shares<br>The number of depositary receipts held by the registered owner that give right to receive the dividend payment<br>The payment date of the dividend arising from a depositary receipt<br>The total number of issued depositary receipts at the record date<br>The total number of underlying shares for all issued depositary receipts at the record date |

# Appendix 2: The US QI Agreement

This is the text of the IRS Revenue Procedure 2023-43, which is, at the time of writing, the latest QI Agreement. Prior versions of this Revenue Procedure include Rev. proc 2000-12, Rev proc. 2014-39 and Rev. Proc 2017-15.

The preamble to the Agreement has been omitted as this does not contribute further insights to the compliance issues discussed in this book.

THIS AGREEMENT is made under and in pursuance of Sects. 871(m), 1441, 1442, 1443, 1446, 1471, and 1472 and §§1.1441-1(e)(5) and 1.1441-1(e)(6):

**WHEREAS**, QI has submitted an application in accordance with Revenue Procedure 2022-43 to be a qualified intermediary;

**WHEREAS**, QI and the IRS desire to enter into an agreement to establish QI's rights and obligations regarding documentation, withholding, information reporting, tax return filing, deposit, and refund procedures under Sects. 1441, 1442, 1443, 1446, 1461, 1471, 1472, 1474, 3406, 6041, 6042, 6045, 6049, 6050N, 6302, 6402, and 6414, and tax liability under Sects. 871(a) and 881 for a QI that is acting as a qualified

derivatives dealer (QDD), with respect to certain types of payments;

**WHEREAS**, QI represents that there are no legal restrictions that prohibit it from complying with the requirements of this Agreement; and

**WHEREAS**, if QI is a foreign financial institution (FFI), QI represents that, as of the effective date of this Agreement, it has agreed to comply with the requirements of the FFI agreement, in the case of a participating FFI (including a reporting Model 2 FFI); §1.1471-5(f)(1) or the applicable


R. K. McGill and K. V. Pitkin, *Qualified Intermediary*,
https://doi.org/10.1007/978-3-031-81410-5

Model 2 IGA, in the case of a registered deemed- compliant FFI (other than a reporting Model 1 FFI); or the applicable Model 1 IGA, in the

case of a reporting Model 1 FFI or a registered deemed-compliant Model 1 IGA FFI;

**NOW, THEREFORE**, in consideration of the following terms, representations, and conditions, the parties agree as follows:

**Section 1. Purpose and Scope**

**Sec. 1.01. General Obligations.** When the IRS enters into a QI agreement with a foreign person or a foreign branch of a US person, that foreign person (or foreign branch) becomes a QI. QI is a withholding agent under chapters 3 and 4, and a payor under chapter 61 and Sect. 3406, for amounts that it pays to its account holders. QI is also a withholding agent when it receives a PTP distribution for an account holder or it acts as a broker under §1.1446(f)-4 for a payment of an amount realised from the sale of a PTP interest by an account holder.

If QI is an FFI, the requirements that QI has agreed to as a participating FFI, registered deemed-compliant FFI, or registered deemed-compliant Model 1 IGA FFI apply in addition to the requirements under this Agreement. If QI acts as a QI with respect to an account, this Agreement will reference QI's chapter 4 obligations when necessary to facilitate coordination with the QI's obligations under chapters 3, 4, and 61 and Sect. 3406 with respect to such account holders. A participating FFI's (including a reporting Model 2 FFI) obligations are provided in the FFI agreement, a registered deemed- compliant FFI's (other than a reporting Model 1 FFI) obligations are provided in §1.1471-5(f)(1) or the applicable Model 2 IGA, and the obligations of a reporting Model 1 FFI or a registered deemed-compliant Model 1 IGA FFI are provided in the applicable Model 1 IGA. For purposes of chapter 4, QI must comply with its FATCA requirements as a participating FFI, registered deemed-compliant FFI, or registered deemed-compliant Model 1 IGA FFI (as applicable) in order to maintain its required chapter 4 status, as well as the requirements of a withholding agent for any payee that is a

nonparticipating FFI or a NFFE that is not an account holder. If QI is an FFI, QI must also, pursuant to this Agreement, assume primary reporting responsibility for purposes of Sect. 1472, for certain indirect account holders for which it acts as a QI. If QI is an NFFE acting on behalf of persons other than its shareholders, QI must assume primary reporting responsibility for purposes of Sect. 1472 for any person for which it acts as a QI.

If QI acts as a sponsoring entity on behalf of a sponsored FFI (as defined in §1.1471- 1(b)(121)) or sponsored direct reporting NFFE (as defined in

§1.1471-1(b)(123)), it must comply with the due diligence, withholding, reporting, and compliance requirements of a sponsoring entity in addition to its requirements under this Agreement.

For purposes of chapters 3 and 61 and Sect. 3406, QI must act in its capacity as a QI pursuant to this Agreement for those accounts that QI holds with a withholding agent and that QI has identified as accounts for which it acts as a QI. QI is not required to act as a QI for all accounts that it holds with a withholding agent. However, QI must, as part of its QI agreement, materially comply with the requirements of a withholding agent or payor, as applicable to a nonqualified intermediary (NQI) under chapters 3 and 61 and Sect. 3406, for any account for which it does not (or cannot) act as a QI and for any payee that is not an account holder. If QI identifies an account as one for which it will act as a QI, it must act as a QI for all payments made to that account and obtain the documentation required under Sect. 5 of this Agreement for such account. When QI acts as a QI for an account and assumes primary chapter 3 withholding responsibility for payments to the account, QI must also assume primary withholding responsibility for withholdable payments made to such account for chapter 4 purposes.

For amounts subject to withholding on a PTP distribution, QI acts in its capacity as a QI when QI provides a valid withholding certificate described in Sect. 6 of this Agreement indicating that it acts as a nominee for the distribution, provides chapter 3 withholding rate pool information with respect to the distribution under Sect. 6.03 of this Agreement, or acts as a disclosing QI for the distribution. For an amount realised, QI acts in its capacity as a QI when QI provides a valid withholding certificate described in Sect. 6 of this Agreement associated with the amount indicating that QI assumes primary withholding responsibility for the amount under Sect. 1446(f), provides withholding rate pool information with respect to the amount under Sect. 6.03 of this Agreement, or acts as a disclosing QI for the amount.

If QI acts as a QI with respect to payments of substitute interest, as described in Sect. 3.03(A) of this Agreement, it must act as a QI and assume primary withholding responsibility for all such payments of substitute interest.

A QI is permitted to act as a QSL only until December 31, 2024. If QI that is not acting as a QDD acts as a qualified securities lender (QSL) with respect to substitute dividend payments (as defined in §1.861-3(a)(6)), QI is required to act as a QSL and assume primary withholding responsibility for all substitute dividends received and paid by QI when acting as an intermediary or dealer with respect to securities lending and similar transactions. A QI that acts as a QDD may not act as a QSL, except as described in the prior sentence with respect to payments on securities lending or sale-repurchase transactions for which the QI has determined that it is acting as an intermediary. A QI may qualify as a QDD with respect to certain payments on securities lending and sale- repurchase transactions in its qualified derivatives dealer capacity. See below for the requirements, including the eligible entity requirement and which payments are covered. A QI that is not acting as a QSL may still act as a QI for substitute dividend payments received or paid by QI as an intermediary by assuming primary withholding responsibility for all substitute dividends received and paid by QI as an intermediary. QI also may act as a QDD for the transactions covered by the QDD regime.

The home office (as defined in Sect. 2.43 of this Agreement) and each branch of a foreign person that intends to act as a QDD must each separately qualify and be approved for QDD status, as provided in Sect. 1.02 of this Agreement. QDD applicants must follow the naming convention described in Sect. 2.63 of this Agreement on their application and, if approved as a QDD, on any other US tax form, schedule, statement, or other tax material and for any other tax purpose for which the QDD must be identified. A foreign branch of a US financial institution may also apply for QI and QDD status provided it separately qualifies as an eligible entity. If QI acts as a QDD with respect to the home office or branch, the home office or branch, as applicable, must act as a QDD for all payments made as a principal with respect to potential Sect. 871(m) transactions and all payments received as a principal with respect to potential Sect. 871(m) transactions and underlying securities, excluding any payments made or received by the QDD to the extent the payment is treated as effectively connected with the conduct of a trade or business within the United States within the meaning of Sect. 864. A QI may not act as a QDD with respect to any other payments. For purposes of this Agreement, any securities lending or sale-repurchase transaction (as defined in §1.871-15(a)(13)) QI enters into that is a Sect. 871(m) transaction is treated as entered into by QI as a principal unless QI determines that it is acting as an intermediary with respect to that transaction. A QI may not act as a QDD when it receives or makes payments as an intermediary and must act as either a QI or NQI for the payment. A QI acting as a QDD must assume primary chapter 3 and chapter 4 withholding responsibility and primary Form 1099 reporting and backup withholding responsibility under Sect. 3406 for payments made as a QDD with respect to any potential Sect. 871(m) transaction provided the amount paid is an amount subject to chapter 3 or 4 withholding or a reportable payment under chapter 61. A QI acting as a QDD (other than a QDD that is a foreign branch of a US financial institution) also must satisfy its QDD tax liability as determined under Sect. 3.09 of this Agreement. The QDD must report its withholding tax liability under chapters 3 and 4 on Form 1042. In addition, a QDD (other than a QDD that is a foreign branch of a US financial institution or that is a partnership or branch of a partnership) must file a Form 1120-F and report its QDD tax liability on that form, whether or not it would be required to file if it were not a QDD. Similarly, a QDD that is a partnership or a branch of a partnership must file a Form 1065 and report its QDD tax liability on that form, whether or not it would be required to file if it were not a QDD, as well as report on Forms 1042-S with respect to its foreign partners on amounts under Sect. 3.09 of this Agreement as modified for a QDD that is a partnership (or branch of a partnership). A US financial institution with a foreign branch that acts as a QDD must file the appropriate US income tax return (*e.g.*, Form 1120, *US Corporation Income Tax Return*) for the tax year covered by this Agreement to report and pay its tax liability under chapter 1 and would not have a separate QDD tax liability. In each case, the form will be filed by the QI on behalf of its QDD(s).

A dividend or dividend equivalent is treated as received by a QDD acting in its non- equity derivatives dealer capacity if the dividend or dividend equivalent is received by a QDD acting as a proprietary trader. Transactions properly reflected in a QDD's equity. derivatives dealer book are presumed to be held by a dealer in its equity derivatives dealer capacity for purposes of determining the QDD tax liability. In addition, for purposes of determining whether a dealer is acting in its equity derivatives dealer capacity, only the dealer's activities as an equity derivatives dealer are taken into account.

**Sec. 1.02. Parties to the Agreement.** This Agreement applies to:

**(A)** QI; and

**(B)** The Internal Revenue Service.

If QI is an FFI, QI can only act as a QI for an account if the branch of QI that holds the account operates in a KYC jurisdiction identified on the IRS's Approved KYC List. QI may add any jurisdiction in which it operates a branch that is not initially included in its QI application without prior IRS approval if the jurisdiction is identified on the IRS's Approved KYC List and QI updates its information on the Qualified Intermediary Application and Account Management System (QAAMS) with respect to such branch before treating such branch as a QI. Notwithstanding the preceding sentence, a QI may not add a branch that will act as a QDD through QAAMS. Instead, the branch must separately qualify and be approved for QDD status in accordance with the procedures prescribed by the IRS. A branch of a QI that is not subject to the provisions of this Agreement remains subject to the rules of chapters 3, 4, and 61 and Sect. 3406, as provided in Sect. 1.01 of this Agreement.

**Section 2. DEFINITIONS**

For purposes of this Agreement, except as otherwise provided in this Agreement, the terms listed below are defined as follows:

**Sec. 2.01. Account.** "Account" or "financial account" has the meaning given to that term in §1.1471-1(b) with respect to QI's obligations for chapter 4 purposes. For other purposes under this Agreement, "account" or "financial account" means any account for which QI acts as a QI. With respect to a QI acting as a QDD, "account" means any potential Sect. 871(m) transaction or underlying security where QDD receives payments as a principal and any potential Sect. 871(m) transaction where QDD makes payments as a principal. With respect to a QI that assumes primary withholding responsibility for a substitute interest payment as described in Sect. 3.03(A) of this Agreement, an account is treated as held with QI for an account holder described in

Section 2.02 of this Agreement.

**Sec. 2.02. Account Holder.** If QI is an FFI, an "account holder" means any person that is a direct account holder or an indirect account holder of an account that QI has identified to a withholding agent as an account for which it is acting as a QI and also includes any person that receives a US source substitute dividend payment from a QI that is a QSL or is otherwise acting as an intermediary for the payment. "Account holder" also means any person that enters into or holds a potential Sect. 871(m) transaction with a QI acting as a QDD. If QI is an NFFE acting as a QI on behalf of persons other than its shareholders, an "account holder" means any person for whom QI is acting as an intermediary with respect to a reportable payment or withholdable payment. With respect to a QI that assumes primary withholding responsibility for a substitute interest payment, as described in Sect. 3.03(A) of this Agreement, an "account holder" includes any person that receives such a payment from the QI.

**(A) Direct Account Holder.**

A direct account holder is any account holder who has a direct relationship with QI. In the case of an NFFE acting as a QI on behalf of persons other than its shareholders, a direct account holder is any person for whom QI is acting with respect to a reportable payment regardless of whether such person is the beneficial owner. In addition, a direct account holder includes a beneficiary of a trust that holds an account with QI provided the following requirements are satisfied:

(1) the trust is registered with the applicable government as a tax-free plan;
(2) in order to qualify as a tax-free plan, applicable non-US law mandates that where the plan holds assets in a brokerage account, a trust be established for the account holder that is the sole beneficiary under the plan;
(3) the account holder maintains general control over investments in the plan and can withdraw the funds at any time;
(4) QI is required to document the account holder under applicable anti-money laundering/know-your-customer regulations or procedures; and
(5) the trust itself is not eligible for a reduced rate of withholding under an applicable income tax treaty.

**(B) Indirect Account Holder.** An indirect account holder is any account holder who does not have a direct relationship with QI, excluding a beneficiary of a trust described in Sect. 2.02(A) of this Agreement. For example, a person that holds an account with a foreign intermediary that has a direct relationship with QI is an indirect account holder of QI. For chapter 3 and 4 purposes, an indirect account holder also includes a person

holding an interest in a foreign flow-through entity that has a direct relationship with QI. A person is an indirect account holder even if there are multiple tiers of intermediaries or flow-through entities between the person and QI.

**Sec. 2.03. Agreement.** "Agreement" means this Agreement, the Appendices to this Agreement and any amendment to this Agreement in accordance with Sect. 12.02 of this Agreement. QI's application to become a QI, and the know-your-customer rules included in a country attachment on IRS.gov relevant to QI (or a branch of QI) are incorporated into this Agreement by reference.

**Sec. 2.04. Amount Subject to Chapter 3 Withholding.** An "amount subject to chapter 3 withholding" is an amount described in §1.1441-2(a) regardless of whether such amount is withheld upon. Unless indicated otherwise in this Agreement, an amount subject to chapter 3 withholding includes an amount subject to chapter 3 withholding on a PTP distribution. See Sect. 2.91(C) of this Agreement.

**Sec. 2.05. Amount Subject to Chapter 4 Withholding.** An "amount subject to chapter 4 withholding" is a withholdable payment (as defined in §1.1473-1(a)) for which withholding is required under chapter 4 or an amount for which withholding was otherwise applied under chapter 4. Unless indicated otherwise in this Agreement, an amount subject to chapter 4 withholding includes an amount subject to chapter 4 withholding on a PTP distribution. See Sect. 2.91(C) of this Agreement

**Sec. 2.06. Assuming Primary Withholding Responsibility.** "Assuming primary withholding responsibility" refers to when a QI assumes primary chapters 3 and 4 withholding responsibility with respect to payments of US source FDAP income or assumes primary Form 1099 reporting and backup withholding responsibility.

"Assuming primary withholding responsibility" further includes when QI acts as a nominee for a PTP distribution or assumes primary withholding responsibility under Sect. 1446(f) for an amount realised from the sale of a PTP interest. A QI that assumes primary withholding responsibility assumes the primary responsibility for deducting, withholding, and depositing the appropriate amount from a payment. Generally, a QI assuming primary withholding responsibility or assuming primary backup withholding responsibility relieves the person who makes a payment to the QI from the responsibility to withhold. Notwithstanding the preceding sentence, a QI acting as a QDD (that assumes primary withholding responsibility as required by Sect. 3 of this Agreement) remains liable for the tax under Sect. 881 (or in the case of a partnership, its partners remain liable for tax under Sect. 871(a) or 881, as applicable) and remains subject to withholding on all US source FDAP payments with respect to underlying securities; however, a QDD (including a QDD that is a partnership or a branch of a partnership) will not be subject to withholding on amounts described in Sects. 3.03(A)(1) through (3) of this Agreement, and in the case of a QDD that is a partnership or branch of a partnership, its partners will not be subject to withholding on dividends received by the QDD in its equity derivatives dealer capacity in calendar year 2023 or 2024.

**Sec. 2.07. Backup Withholding.** "Backup withholding" means the withholding required under Sect. 3406.

**Sec. 2.08. Beneficial Owner.** A "beneficial owner" has the meaning given to that term in §1.1441-1(c)(6) with respect to an amount subject to chapter 3 withholding.

**Sec. 2.09. Broker Proceeds.** "Broker proceeds" means gross proceeds (as defined in §1.6045-1(d)(5)) from a sale that is reportable under §1.6045-1(c).

**Sec. 2.10.** Chapter 3. Any reference to "chapter 3" means Sects. 1441, 1442, 1443, 1461, 1463, and 1464.

**Sec. 2.11. Chapter 3 Reporting Pool.** A "chapter 3 reporting pool" means a reporting pool described in Sect. 8.03(B) of this Agreement.

**Sec. 2.12. Chapter 4.** Any reference to "chapter 4" means Sects. 1471, 1472, 1473, and 1474.

**Sec. 2.13. Chapter 4 Reporting Pool.** A "chapter 4 reporting pool" means a reporting pool described in Sect. 8.03(A) of this Agreement.

**Sec. 2.14. Chapter 4 Status.** "Chapter 4 status" means the status of a person as a US person, a specified US person, an individual that is a foreign person, a participating FFI, a deemed-compliant FFI, a restricted distributor, an exempt beneficial owner, a nonparticipating FFI, a territory financial institution, an excepted NFFE, or a passive NFFE.

**Sec. 2.15. Chapter 61.** Any reference to "chapter 61" means Sects. 6041, 6042, 6045, 6049, and 6050N.

**Sec. 2.16. Dealer.** A "dealer" has the meaning given to the term dealer in §1.871- 15(a)(2) (*i.e.*, a dealer in securities within the meaning of Sect. 475(c)(1)).

**Sec. 2.17. Deemed-Compliant FFI.** "Deemed-compliant FFI" means an FFI that is treated, pursuant to Sect. 1471(b)(2) and §1.1471-5(f), as meeting the requirements of Sect. 1471(b).

**(A) Certified Deemed-Compliant FFI.** "Certified deemed-compliant FFI" means an FFI described in §1.1471-5(f)(2) and includes a nonreporting IGA FFI but excludes a nonreporting Model 2 FFI that is treated as a registered deemed-compliant FFI.

**(B) Registered Deemed-Compliant FFI.** "Registered deemed-compliant FFI" means an FFI described in §1.1471-5(f)(1) and includes a reporting Model 1 FFI and a nonreporting Model 2 FFI that is treated as registered deemed-compliant FFI. For purposes of this Agreement, a reference to a registered deemed-compliant FFI that is providing a chapter 4 withholding rate pool of US payees includes a registered
deemed-compliant Model 1 IGA FFI.

**(C) Registered Deemed-Compliant Model 1 IGA FFI.** "Registered deemed-compliant Model 1 IGA FFI" means an FFI treated as a deemed-compliant FFI under an applicable Model 1 IGA that is subject to similar due diligence and reporting requirements with respect to US accounts as those applicable to a registered deemed-compliant FFI under §1.1471-5(f)(1), including the requirement to register with the IRS.

**Sec. 2.18. Deposit Interest.** "Deposit interest" means interest described in Sect. 871(i)(2)(A).

**Sec. 2.19. Dividend Equivalent.** A "dividend equivalent" has the meaning given to that term in §1.871-15(c).

**Sec. 2.20. Documentary Evidence.** "Documentary evidence" means any documentation obtained under the appropriate know-your-customer rules, any documentary evidence described in §1.1441-6 sufficient to establish entitlement to a reduced rate of withholding under an income tax treaty, or any documentary evidence

described in §1.6049-5(c) sufficient to establish an account holder's status as a foreign person for purposes of chapter 61. Documentary evidence does not include a Form W- 8 or Form W-9 (or an acceptable substitute Form W-8 or Form W-9).

**Sec. 2.21. Documentation.** "Documentation" means any valid Form W-8, Form W-9 (or an acceptable substitute Form W-8 or Form W-9), or documentary evidence as defined in Sect. 2.20 of this Agreement, including all statements or other information required to be associated with the form or documentary evidence.

**Sec. 2.22. Effective Date.** For a prospective QI that applies to be a QI on or before March 31 of a given calendar year, the effective date of this Agreement will be January 1 of that year. For a prospective QI that applies after March 31 of a given calendar year and that has not received any reportable payments before the date the application is submitted, the effective date of this Agreement will be January 1 of that year. For a prospective QI that applies after March 31 of a given calendar year and that has received a reportable payment in the calendar year before the date the application is submitted, the effective date of this Agreement will be the first of the month in which the QI application is complete and the QI has received its QI-EIN.

**Sec. 2.23. Eligible Entity.** "Eligible entity" for QDD status means a home office or branch that is a QI and that is—

**(A)** An equity derivatives dealer subject to regulatory supervision as a dealer by a governmental authority in the jurisdiction in which it was organised or operates;

**(B)** A bank or bank holding company subject to regulatory supervision as a bank or bank holding company, as applicable, by a governmental authority in the jurisdiction in which it was organised or operates and that, in its equity derivatives dealer capacity, (1) issues potential Sect. 871(m) transactions to customers, and (2) receives dividends with respect to stock or dividend equivalent payments pursuant to potential Sect. 871(m) transactions that hedge potential Sect. 871(m) transactions that it issued;

**(C)** An entity that is wholly-owned (directly or indirectly) by a bank or bank holding company subject to regulatory supervision as a bank or bank holding company, as applicable, by a governmental authority in the jurisdiction in which the bank or bank holding company was organised or operates and that, in its equity derivatives dealer capacity, (1) issues potential Sect. 871(m) transactions to customers, and (2) receives dividends with respect to stock or dividend equivalent payments pursuant to potential Sect. 871(m) transactions that hedge potential Sect. 871(m) transactions that it issued; or

**(D)** A foreign branch of a US financial institution, if the foreign branch would meet the requirements of paragraph (A), (B), or (C), if it were a separate entity.

The home office or any branch that wants to be a QDD must separately meet the requirements of paragraph (A), (B), or (C) as if it were a separate entity.

Eligible entity also includes any other home office or branch that is acceptable to the IRS as provided in §1.1441-1(e)(6)(ii)(D).

**Sec. 2.24. Excepted NFFE.** "Excepted NFFE" means a person described in §1.1471- 1(b)(41).

**Sec. 2.25. Exempt Beneficial Owner.** "Exempt beneficial owner" means a person described in §1.1471-1(b)(42) and includes any person that is treated as an exempt beneficial owner under an applicable Model 1 or Model 2 IGA.

**Sec. 2.26. Exempt Recipient.** For purposes of Form 1099 reporting and backup withholding, an "exempt recipient" means a person described in §1.6049-4(c)(1)(ii) (for interest, dividends, and royalties), a person described in §1.6045-2(b)(2)(i) (for broker proceeds), and a person described in §1.6041-3(q) (for rents, amounts paid on notional principal contracts, and other fixed or determinable income), for which no Form 1099

reporting is required. Exempt recipients are not exempt from reporting or withholding under chapter 3 or 4.

**Sec. 2.27. FATCA Requirements as a Participating FFI, Registered Deemed- Compliant FFI, or Registered Deemed-Compliant Model 1 IGA FFI.** "FATCA requirements as a participating FFI, registered deemed-compliant FFI, or registered deemed-compliant Model 1 IGA FFI" means—

**(A)** For a participating FFI or an FFI that agrees to be treated as a participating FFI, the requirements set forth in the FFI agreement;

**(B)** For a registered deemed-compliant FFI (other than a reporting Model 1 FFI) or an FFI that agrees to be treated as a registered deemed-compliant FFI, the requirements under §1.1471-5(f)(1) or an applicable Model 2 IGA; or

**(C)** For a registered deemed-compliant Model 1 IGA FFI, reporting Model 1 FFI, or an FFI that agrees to be treated as a registered deemed-compliant Model 1 IGA FFI or reporting Model 1 FFI, the requirements under an applicable Model 1 IGA.

**Sec. 2.28. Financial Institution (FI).** "Financial institution" or "FI" is defined in §1.1471- 5(d) and includes a financial institution as defined under an applicable Model 1 or Model 2 IGA.

**Sec. 2.29. Foreign Financial Institution (FFI).** "Foreign Financial Institution" or "FFI" means a foreign entity (as defined in §1.1473-1(e)) that is a financial institution.

**Sec. 2.30. FFI Agreement.** "FFI Agreement" means an agreement described in §1.1471-4(a) and provided in Rev. Proc. 2017-16, 2017-3 I.R.B. 501 (and any superseding revenue procedure).

**Sec. 2.31. Flow-Through Entity.** A flow-through entity is a foreign partnership described in §301.7701-2 or 3 (other than a withholding foreign partnership), a foreign trust (other than a withholding foreign trust) that is described in Sect. 651(a), or a foreign trust if all or a portion of such trust is treated as owned by the grantor or other person under Sects. 671 through 679. For an item of income for which a treaty benefit is claimed, an entity is also a flow-through entity to the extent it is treated as fiscally transparent under Sect. 894 and the regulations thereunder. For an amount realised or amount subject to withholding under Sect. 1446(a) on a PTP distribution, a flow-through entity includes a US grantor trust.

**Sec. 2.32. Foreign Person.** A "foreign person" is any person that is not a "United States person" and includes a "nonresident alien individual", a "foreign corporation", a "foreign partnership", a "foreign trust", and a "foreign estate", as those terms are defined in Sect. 7701. For purposes of chapters 3 and 4, the term foreign person also means, with respect to a payment by a withholding agent, a foreign branch (including a foreign

disregarded entity) of a US person that provides a valid Form W-8IMY on which it represents that it is a QI. A foreign branch of a US person that is a QI is, however, a US payor for purposes of chapter 61 and Sect. 3406.

**Sec. 2.33. Foreign TIN.** A "foreign TIN" is a taxpayer identification number issued by a foreign person's country of residence.

**Sec. 2.34. Form W-8.** "Form W-8" means IRS Form W-8BEN, *Certificate of Foreign Status of Beneficial Owner for United States Tax Withholding (Individuals)*; IRS Form W-8BEN-E, *Certificate of Status of Beneficial Owner for United States Tax Withholding and Reporting (Entities)*; IRS Form W-8ECI, *Certificate of Foreign Person's Claim That Income is Effectively Connected With the Conduct of a Trade or Business in the United States*; IRS Form W-8EXP, *Certificate of Foreign Government or Other Foreign Organization for United States Tax Withholding and Reporting*; and IRS Form W-8IMY, *Certificate of Foreign Intermediary, Foreign Flow-Through Entity, or Certain US Branches for*

*United States Tax Withholding and Reporting*, as appropriate. It also includes any acceptable substitute Form W-8.

**Sec. 2.35. Form W-9.** "Form W-9" means IRS Form W-9, *Request for Taxpayer Identification Number and Certification*, or any acceptable substitute Form W-9.

**Sec. 2.36. Form 945.** "Form 945" means IRS Form 945, *Annual Return of Withheld Federal Income Tax*.

**Sec. 2.37. Form 1042.** "Form 1042" means IRS Form 1042, *Annual Withholding Tax Return for US Source Income of Foreign Persons*.

**Sec. 2.38. Form 1042-S.** "Form 1042-S" means IRS Form 1042-S, *Foreign Person's US Source Income Subject to Withholding*.

**Sec. 2.39. Form 1099.** "Form 1099" means IRS Form 1099-B, *Proceeds From Broker and Barter Exchange Transactions*; IRS Form 1099-DIV, *Dividends and Distributions*; IRS Form 1099-INT, *Interest Income*; IRS Form 1099-MISC, *Miscellaneous Income*; IRS Form 1099-OID, *Original Issue Discount*; and any other form in the IRS Form 1099 series appropriate to the type of payment required to be reported.

**Sec. 2.40. Form 8966.** "Form 8966" means IRS Form 8966, *FATCA Report*.

**Sec. 2.41. Form 1099 Reporting.** "Form 1099 reporting" means the reporting required on Form 1099.

**Sec. 2.42. Global Intermediary Identification Number (GIIN).** "Global intermediary identification number" or "GIIN" means the identification number that is assigned to a participating FFI, registered deemed-compliant FFI, direct reporting NFFE, or sponsoring entity of a direct reporting NFFE. The term also includes the identification number assigned to a reporting Model 1 FFI or registered deemed-compliant Model 1 IGA FFI that is a QI for the purpose of identifying itself to withholding agents.

**Sec. 2.43. Home Office.** "Home office" means a foreign person, excluding any branches of the foreign person, that applies for QDD status.

**Sec. 2.44. Intermediary.** An "intermediary" means any person that acts on behalf of another person such as a custodian, broker, nominee, or other agent.

**Sec. 2.45. Know-Your-Customer Rules.** "Know-your-customer rules" refers to the applicable laws, regulations, rules, and administrative practices and procedures governing the requirements of QI to obtain documentation confirming the identity of QI's account holders.

**Sec. 2.46. Marketable Securities.** For purposes of this Agreement, the term "marketable securities" means those securities described in §1.1441-6 for which a US TIN (or foreign TIN) is not required to obtain treaty benefits with respect to an amount subject to chapter 3 withholding.

**Sec. 2.47. Net Delta Exposure.** Net delta exposure to an underlying security is the amount (measured in number of shares) by which (A) the aggregate number of shares in an underlying security that the QDD has exposure to as a result of positions in the underlying security (including as a result of owning the underlying security) with values that move in the same direction as the underlying security (the "long positions") exceeds (B) the aggregate number of shares of in an underlying security that the QDD has exposure to as a result of positions in the underlying security with values that move in the opposite direction from the underlying security (the "short positions"). The net delta exposure calculation only includes long positions and short positions that the QDD holds in its equity derivatives dealer business. Any long positions or short positions that are treated as effectively connected with the QDD's conduct of a trade or business in the United States for US federal income tax purposes are excluded from the net delta exposure computation. The net delta exposure to an underlying security is determined at the end of the day on the date provided in §1.871-15(j)(2) for the applicable dividend. For purposes of this calculation, net delta must be determined in a commercially reasonable manner. If a QDD calculates net delta for non-tax business purposes, the net delta ordinary will be the delta used for this purpose, subject to the modifications required by this definition. Each QDD must determine its net delta exposure separately only taking into account transactions that exist and are attributable to that QDD for US federal income tax purposes.

**Sec. 2.48. Non-Consenting US Account.** For purposes of a reporting Model 2 FFI, "non-consenting US account" has the meaning that such term has under an applicable Model 2 IGA.

**Sec. 2.49. Non-Exempt Recipient.** A "non-exempt recipient" means a person that is not an exempt recipient under the definition in Sect. 2.26 of this Agreement.

**Sec. 2.50. Non-Financial Foreign Entity (NFFE).** A "non-financial foreign entity" or "NFFE" means a foreign entity that is not a financial institution (including an entity that is incorporated or organised under the laws of any US territory and that is not a financial institution). The term also means a foreign entity treated as an NFFE pursuant to a Model 1 or Model 2 IGA.

**Sec. 2.51. Nonparticipating FFI.** A "nonparticipating FFI" means an FFI other than a participating FFI, a deemed-compliant FFI, or an exempt beneficial owner.

**Sec. 2.52. Nonqualified Intermediary (NQI).** A "nonqualified intermediary" or "NQI" is any intermediary that is not a qualified intermediary. An

NQI includes any intermediary that is a foreign person unless such person enters an agreement to be a QI and acts in such capacity. An NQI also includes an intermediary that is a territory FI unless such institution agrees to be treated as a US person.

**Sec. 2.53. Non-US Payor.** A "non-US payor" means a payor other than a US payor as defined in this Sect. 2.81 of this Agreement.

**Sec. 2.54. Non-withholding Foreign Partnership.** A "nonwithholding foreign partnership" means a foreign partnership other than a withholding foreign partnership as defined in §1.1441–5(c)(2)(i).

**Sec. 2.55. Non-withholding Foreign Trust.** A "nonwithholding foreign trust" means a foreign trust (as defined in Sect. 7701(a)(31)(B)) that is a foreign simple trust or a foreign grantor trust and that is not a withholding foreign trust.

**Sec. 2.56. Overwithholding.** The term "overwithholding" means any amount actually withheld (determined before application of the adjustment procedures described in Sect. 9 of this Agreement) from an item of income or other payment that is in excess of:

**(A)** The amount required to be withheld under chapter 4 with respect to such item of income or other payment, if applicable;

**(B)** In the case of an amount subject to chapter 3 withholding, the actual tax liability of the beneficial owner of the income or payment to which the withheld amount is attributable, regardless of whether such overwithholding was in error or appeared correct when it occurred; and,

**(C)** In the case of the withholding required under Sect. 1446(a) or (f), the excess of the amount withheld over the amount required to be withheld under §1.1446-4 or §1.1446(f)-4, respectively. For purposes of Sect. 3406, the term "overwithholding" means the excess of the amount actually withheld under Sect. 3406 over the amount required to be withheld.

**Sec. 2.57. Participating FFI.** A "participating FFI" means an FFI described in §1.1471- 1(b)(91). The term participating FFI also includes a QI branch of a US financial institution unless such branch is a reporting Model 1 FFI.

**Sec. 2.58. Payee.** For chapter 4 purposes, a "payee" means a person described in §1.1471-3(a). For purposes of chapter 61, a "payee" means the person to whom a payment is made. For purposes of chapter 3, a "payee" means a person described in §1.1441-1(c)(12).

**Sec. 2.59. Payment.** A "payment" is considered made to a person if that person realises income, whether or not such income results from an actual transfer of cash or other property. See §1.1441-2(e). For example, a payment includes crediting an amount to an account. For any payment of a dividend equivalent, a "payment" has the meaning provided in §1.871-15(i).

**Sec. 2.60. Payor.** A "payor" is defined in §31.3406(a)-2 and §1.6049-4(a)(2) and generally means any person required to make an information return under chapter 61. The term includes any person that makes a payment, directly or indirectly, to QI and to whom QI provides information, pursuant to this Agreement, so that such person can report a payment on Form 1099 and, if appropriate, backup withhold. See also Sects. 2.81 and 2.53 of this Agreement for the definition of US payor and non-US payor.

**Sec. 2.61. Potential Sect. 871(m) Transaction.** A "potential Sect. 871(m) transaction" is any securities lending or sale-repurchase transaction, notional principal contract (NPC), or equity linked instrument (ELI) that references one or more underlying securities. For purposes of this definition, securities lending or sale-repurchase transaction, NPC, ELI, reference, and underlying security have the meaning given to the terms in §§1.871-15(a)(13), (7), (4), (11), and (15), respectively.

**Sec. 2.62. Private Arrangement Intermediary (PAI).** A "private arrangement intermediary" or "PAI" is an intermediary described in Sect. 4 of this Agreement.

**Sec. 2.63. Qualified Derivatives Dealer (QDD).** A "qualified derivatives dealer" or "QDD" is an eligible entity that agrees to meet the requirements of §1.1441-1(e)(6)(i) and of this Agreement with respect to payments on potential Sect. 871(m) transactions and underlying securities that it receives or makes as a principal. In order to act as a QDD, the home office or branch, as applicable, must qualify and be approved for QDD status and must represent itself as a QDD on its Form W-8IMY and separately identify the home office or branch as the recipient on a withholding statement (if necessary). Each home office or branch that obtains QDD status is treated as a separate QDD and must use the name specified on its application for QDD status when representing its status as a QDD. For the QDD's application, a home office must use the name of the legal entity applying for QDD status, and a branch of the legal entity must add the following to the Home Office Name: QDD-BRANCH-(Branch QDD COUNTRY, and branch identifier, if necessary), for example: ABC Bank-QDD-BRANCH-SINGAPORE (Disregarded Entity Name)). Each QDD of a QI must have a different name.

**Sec. 2.64. QDD Tax Liability**. A "QDD tax liability" is the amount described in Sect. 3.09 of this Agreement.

**Sec. 2.65. Qualified Intermediary (QI).** A "qualified intermediary" or "QI" is a person (or branch) described in §1.1441-1(e)(5)(ii) that has in effect an agreement with the IRS to be treated as a QI and acts as a QI.

**Sec. 2.66. QI-EIN.** A "QI-EIN" means the employer identification number assigned by the IRS to a QI. QI's QI-EIN is only to be used when QI is acting as a QI. For example, QI must give a withholding agent its EIN (other than its QI-EIN), if any, if it is receiving income as a beneficial owner (excluding when it receives income as a principal when acting as either a QDD or QSL, or when a QI assumes primary withholding responsibility for a substitute interest payment under this Agreement). QI must also use its non-QI EIN, if any, when acting as an NQI. Each signatory to this Agreement must have its own QI-EIN.

**Sec. 2.67. Qualified Securities Lender (QSL).** A "qualified securities lender" or "QSL" is a person described as a qualified securities lender in Notice 2010-46, 2010-24 I.R.B. 757. A QI that acts as a QSL with respect to a substitute dividend payment (as defined in §1.861-3(a)(6)) is required to act as a QSL for all US source substitute dividends received by the QI when acting as an intermediary or dealer with respect to securities lending and similar transactions, except as otherwise provided in Sect. 1.01 of this Agreement. A QI is only permitted to act as a QSL until December 31, 2024.

**Sec. 2.68. Reportable Amount.** A "reportable amount" means US source FDAP income that is an amount subject to chapter 3 withholding, US source deposit interest, and US source interest or original issue discount paid on the redemption of short-term obligations. The term does not include payments on deposits with banks and other financial institutions that remain on deposit for two weeks or less. It also does not include amounts of original issue discount arising from a sale and repurchase transaction completed within a period of two weeks or less, or amounts described in §1.6049-5(b)(7), (10), or (11) (relating to certain foreign targeted registered obligations and certain obligations issued in bearer form).

**Sec. 2.69. Reportable Payment.** For purposes of this Agreement, a "reportable payment" means an amount described in Sect. 2.69(A) of this Agreement, in the case of a US payor, and an amount described in Sect. 2.69(B) of this Agreement, in the case of a non-US payor.

**(A) US Payor.** If QI is a US payor, a "reportable payment" means, unless an exception to reporting applies under chapter 61,

**(1)** Any reportable amount;

**(2)** Any broker proceeds from a sale reportable under §1.6045-1(c); and

**(3)** Any foreign source interest, dividends, rents, royalties, or other fixed and determinable income.

**(B) Non-US Payor.** If QI is a non-US payor, a "reportable payment" means, unless an exception to reporting applies under chapter 61,

**(1)** Any reportable amount;

**(2)** Any broker proceeds from a sale effected at an office inside the United States, as defined in §1.6045-1(g)(3)(iii); and

**(3)** Any foreign source interest, dividends, rents, royalties, or other fixed and determinable income if such income is not paid outside the United States as described under Sect. 5.13(C)(1) of this Agreement.

**Sec. 2.70. Reporting Model 1 FFI.** A "reporting Model 1 FFI" means an FFI with respect to which a foreign government or agency thereof agrees to obtain and exchange information pursuant to a Model 1 IGA, other than an FFI that is treated as a nonreporting Model 1 FFI (including a registered deemed-compliant Model 1 IGA FFI) or a nonparticipating FFI under an applicable Model 1 IGA.

**Sec. 2.71. Reporting Pool.** A "reporting pool" is defined in Sect. 8 of this Agreement.

**Sec. 2.72. Responsible Officer.** A "responsible officer" of a QI means an officer of the QI with sufficient authority to fulfil the duties of a responsible officer as described in Sect. 10 of this Agreement, including the requirements to periodically certify and to respond to requests by the IRS for additional information to review the QI's compliance.

**Sec. 2.73. Section 871(m) Amount.** For each dividend on each underlying security, the "Sect. 871(m) amount" is (A) the QDD's net delta exposure to the underlying security for the applicable dividend multiplied by (B) the applicable dividend amount per share. These amounts are treated as dividend equivalent amounts under Sect. 871(m).

**Sec. 2.74. Section 871(m) Transaction.** A "Sect. 871(m) transaction" is any securities lending or sale-repurchase transaction, specified NPC, or specified ELI described in §1.871-15(a)(13), (d), and (e), respectively.

**Sec. 2.75. Short-Term Obligation.** A "short-term obligation" is any obligation described in Sect. 871(g)(1)(B)(i).

**Sec. 2.76. Substitute Interest.** "Substitute interest" means a substitute interest payment described in §1.861-2(a)(7).

**Sec. 2.77. Underlying Security.** For purposes of a QI acting as a QDD or any determination relating to Sect. 871(m), "underlying security" has the meaning provided in §1.871-15(a)(15).

**Sec. 2.78. Underwithholding.** "Underwithholding" means the excess of the amount required to be withheld under chapter 3 or 4 or Sect. 3406 over the amount actually withheld.

**Sec. 2.79. Undocumented Account Holder.** An "undocumented account holder" is an account holder for whom QI does not hold valid documentation.

**Sec. 2.80. US Account.** A "US account" is any financial account maintained by an FFI that is held by one or more specified US persons or US-owned foreign entities that such FFI reports or elects to report under the FFI Agreement or §1.1471-5(f), as applicable.

**Sec. 2.81. US Payor.** The term "US payor" has the same meaning as in §1.6049-5(c)(5).

**Sec. 2.82. US Person.** A "US person" (or "United States person") is a person described in Sect. 7701(a)(30), the US government (including an agency or instrumentality thereof), a State of the United States (including an agency or instrumentality thereof), or the District of Columbia (including an agency or instrumentality thereof). An individual will not be treated as a US person for purposes of this section for a taxable year or any portion of a taxable year that the individual is a dual resident taxpayer (within the meaning of §301.7701(b)-7(a)(1)) who is treated as a nonresident alien pursuant to §301.7701(b)-7 for purposes of computing his or her US tax liability. The term "US person" or "United States person" also means a foreign insurance company that has made an election under Sect. 953(d), provided that either the foreign insurance company is not a specified insurance company (as described in §1.1471-5(e)(1)(iv)), or the foreign insurance company is a specified insurance company and is licensed to do business in any State of the United States.

**Sec. 2.83. US Reportable Account.** A "US reportable account" means a financial account maintained by a reporting Model 1 FFI or registered deemed-compliant Model 1 IGA FFI that such FFI reports or elects to report under the applicable domestic law for compliance with and implementation of FATCA.

**Sec. 2.84. US Source FDAP.** "US source FDAP" means amounts from sources within the United States that constitute fixed or determinable annual or periodical income, as defined in §1.1441-2(b)(1).

**Sec. 2.85. US TIN.** A "US TIN" means a US taxpayer identification number assigned under Sect. 6109.

**Sec. 2.86. Withholding Agent.** A "withholding agent" has the same meaning as set forth in §1.1441-7(a) for purposes of chapter 3 and as set forth in §1.1473-1(d) for purposes of chapter 4 and includes a payor (as defined in Sect. 2.60 of this Agreement), a broker (as defined in Sect. 2.91(D) of this Agreement), or a nominee (as defined in Sect. 2.91(G) of this Agreement with respect to §1.1446-4).

**Sec. 2.87. Withholding Foreign Partnership (WP).** A "withholding foreign partnership" or "WP" means a partnership, described in §1.1441-5(c)(2), that has entered into a withholding agreement with the IRS to be treated as a withholding foreign partnership.

**Sec. 2.88. Withholding Foreign Trust (WT).** A "withholding foreign trust" or "WT" means a trust, described in §1.1441-5(e)(5)(v), that has entered into a withholding agreement with the IRS to be treated as a withholding foreign trust.

**Sec. 2.89. Withholdable Payment.** A "withholdable payment" means an amount described in §1.1473-1(a).

**Sec. 2.90. Withholding Rate Pool.** A "withholding rate pool" is defined in Sect. 6.03 of this Agreement and includes a chapter 3 withholding rate pool and a chapter 4 withholding rate pool.

**Sec. 2.91. Terms Applicable to Sect. 1446(a) and (f) Requirements.** The following terms apply in connection with QI's requirements with respect to QI's account holders holding PTP interests for purposes of Sect. 1446(a) and (f):

**(A) Amount Realised**. For purposes of Sect. 1446(f), an "amount realized" on a sale of a PTP interest is the amount of gross proceeds (as defined in §1.6045-1(d)(5)) paid or credited to the partner or broker that is the transferor of the interest. The "amount realized" on a PTP distribution is the amount of the distribution reduced by the portion of the distribution that is attributable to the cumulative net income of the partnership (as determined under §1.1446(f)-4(c)(2)(iii)).

**(B) Amount Subject to Reporting under Sect. 1446(f).** An "amount subject to reporting under Sect. 1446(f)" is the amount realised on the transfer of a PTP interest paid to a foreign partner (including a partner presumed to be foreign) unless an exception to withholding applies under §1.1446(f)-4(b)(2) through (4). See §1.1461-1(c)(2)(i)(Q).

**(C) Amount Subject to Withholding on a PTP Distribution.** An "amount subject to withholding on a PTP distribution" is the amount of the distribution subject to withholding under chapter 3 or 4 and/or under Sect. 1446(a) or (f).

**(D) Broker.** The term "broker" has the meaning described in §1.1446(f)-1(b)(1), when referenced in connection with the transfer of a PTP interest.

**(E) Disclosing QI.** For purposes of Sect. 1446(a) or (f), a "disclosing QI" is a QI that does not assume the primary withholding obligation under Sect. 1446(a) or (f) for a payment and that provides with its withholding statement the specific payee documentation referenced in §1.1446(f)-4(a)(7)(iii) (for an amount realised) or §1.1446- 4(e)(4) (for withholding on a PTP distribution under Sect. 1446(a)) instead of the chapter 3 withholding rate pool information otherwise permitted to be included on the withholding statement and, for an amount realised, a chapter 4 withholding rate pool of US payees when permitted for chapter 4 purposes in lieu of specific payee documentation (that is, Forms W-9) for those payees. A QI that acts as a disclosing QI for a payment must act as a disclosing QI for the entire payment of an amount realised from the sale of a PTP interest or a PTP distribution (regardless of the number of account holders that are partners receiving the payment). For purposes of the preceding sentence, a QI will be treated as having acted as a disclosing QI with respect to an account holder that is a foreign person regardless of whether the Form W-8 that QI provides with its withholding statement for the foreign person includes a US TIN. See, however, Sect. 5.01(A) of this Agreement for a QI's requirement to request US TINs from its account holders for purposes of Sects. 1446(a) and (f).

**(F) Modified Amount Realised.** In the case of an amount realised paid to a transferor of a PTP interest that is a foreign partnership, the "modified amount realized" is the amount determined under §1.1446(f)-4(c)(2)(ii), as modified by Sect. 4.06 or 5 of this Agreement with respect to the partner information required for determining the amount.

**(G) Nominee.** Except as otherwise provided in this Agreement, the term "nominee" means a person that, under §1.1446-4(b)(3), holds an interest in a PTP on behalf of a foreign person and that is either a US person or QI that assumes primary withholding responsibility for a PTP distribution or a US branch of a foreign person (or territory financial institution) that agrees to be treated as a US person with respect to the distribution.

**(H) Partner.** When referenced in connection with Sect. 1446(a) and (f), a "partner" is a person holding a PTP interest, including a partnership or trust but excluding a grantor trust and including the trust's grantors or owners to the extent of their respective interests in the trust, and excluding an intermediary. When referenced in connection with §1.6031(c)-1 T, a partner is a person to whom a partnership is required to issue a statement under Sect. 6031(b). See Sect. 8.07 of this Agreement.

**(I) PTP Interest.** A "PTP interest" is an interest in a publicly traded partnership if the interest is publicly traded on an established securities market or is readily tradable on a secondary market (or the substantial equivalent thereof).

**(J) PTP Distribution.** A "PTP distribution" is a distribution made by a publicly traded partnership.

**(K) Publicly Traded Partnership (PTP).** The term "publicly traded partnership" (PTP) has the same meaning as in Sect. 7704 and §§1.7704-1 through 1.7704-4 but does not include a publicly traded partnership treated as a corporation under that section.

**(L) Qualified Notice.** A "qualified notice" is a notice issued by a PTP for a PTP distribution as described in §1.1446-4(b)(4).

**(M) Transfer.** A "transfer" is a sale, exchange, or other disposition of a PTP interest and includes a distribution from a partnership to a partner, as well as a transfer treated as a sale or exchange under Sect. 707(a)(2)(B). With respect to a PTP distribution, however, see Sects. 2.91(A) and 3.01(C)(2) of this Agreement for the extent of an amount realised on the distribution for purposes of QI's requirement to withhold under Section 1446(f).

**(N) Transferor.** A "transferor" is any person, foreign or domestic, that transfers a PTP interest. In the case of a trust, to the extent all or a portion of the income of the trust is treated as owned by the grantor or another person under Sects. 671 through 679, the term transferor means the grantor or other person.

**Sec. 2.92. Other Terms.** Any term not defined in this section has the same meaning that it has under the Code, including the income tax regulations under the Code, any applicable income tax treaty, or any applicable Model 1 or Model 2 IGA with respect to a QI's FATCA requirements as a participating FFI, registered deemed-compliant FFI, or registered deemed-compliant Model 1 IGA FFI. Except as expressly provided in this Agreement, any term relating to a QDD or Sect. 871(m) has the same meaning given to the term in §1.871-15.

## Section 3. Withholding Responsibility and QDD Tax Liability

### Sec. 3.01. Chapters 3 and 4 Withholding Responsibilities and Withholding with respect to PTP Interests.

**(A) Chapter 4 Withholding.**

QI is a withholding agent for purposes of chapter 4 and subject to the withholding and reporting provisions applicable to withholding agents under Sects. 1471 and 1472 with respect to its accounts. QI is required to withhold 30 per cent of any withholdable payment made after June 30, 2014, to an account holder that is an FFI unless either QI can reliably associate the payment (or portion of the payment) with documentation upon which it is permitted to rely to treat the payment as exempt from withholding under §1.1471-2(a)(4) or the payment is made under a grandfathered obligation described in §1.1471-2(b). See §1.1471-2(b)(2)(i)(A)(2) for the definition of grandfathered obligation with respect to an obligation giving rise to a dividend equivalent. QI is also required to withhold 30 per cent of any withholdable payment made after June 30, 2014, to an account holder that is an NFFE unless either QI can reliably associate the payment (or portion of the payment) with a certification described in §1.1472-1(b)(1)(ii) or an exception to withholding under §1.1472-1 otherwise applies.

If QI is a participating FFI or registered deemed-compliant FFI (other than a reporting Model 1 FFI), QI will satisfy its requirement to withhold under Sects. 1471(a) and 1472(a) with respect to direct account holders that are entities by withholding on withholdable payments made to nonparticipating FFIs and recalcitrant account holders to the extent required under its FATCA requirements as a participating FFI or registered deemed-compliant FFI. See the FFI Agreement, §1.1471-5(f)(1), or the applicable Model 2 IGA for the withholding requirements that apply to withholdable payments made to account holders of the FFI that are individuals treated as recalcitrant account holders or non-consenting US accounts. If QI is a reporting Model 1 FFI or a registered deemed-compliant Model 1 IGA FFI, QI will satisfy its requirement to withhold under Sect. 1471(a) with respect to direct account holders by withholding on withholdable payments made to nonparticipating FFIs to the extent required under its FATCA requirements as a registered deemed-compliant FFI or registered deemed- compliant Model 1 IGA FFI. QI must, however, withhold in the manner described in Sections 3.02 and 3.03 of this Agreement for when QI assumes or does not assume primary withholding responsibility for purposes of chapters 3 and 4 regardless of its chapter 4 status.

**(B) Chapter 3 Withholding.**

To the extent that QI makes a payment of an amount subject to chapter 3 withholding, QI is required to withhold 30 per cent of the gross amount of any such payment made to an account holder that is (or is presumed) a foreign person unless QI can reliably associate the payment with documentation upon which it can rely to treat the payment as made to a payee that is a US person or as made to a beneficial owner that is a foreign person entitled to a reduced rate of withholding. See Sect. 5 of this Agreement regarding documentation requirements. With respect an amount subject to chapter 4 withholding that is also an amount subject to chapter 3 withholding, QI may credit any tax withheld under chapter 4 against its liability for any tax due under chapter 3 with respect to the payment so that no additional withholding is required on the payment for purposes of chapter 3. Nothing in chapter 4 or the regulations thereunder (including the FFI Agreement) or any applicable IGA relieves QI of its requirements to withhold under chapter 3 to the extent required in this Agreement.

**(C) Withholding on Amounts Realised and PTP Distributions.**

**(1) Withholding on an Amount Realised.**

If QI acts as a broker with respect to a payment of an amount realised from a transfer of a PTP interest, QI is required to withhold under Sect. 1446(f) 10-per cent of the amount realised paid to an account holder of QI that is the transferor and is (or is presumed to be) a foreign partner when QI assumes primary withholding responsibility for the payment under Sect. 3.03(C)(1) of this Agreement. QI is further required to withhold on a payment of an amount realised made to a foreign broker to the extent provided in §1.1446(f)-4(a)(2). QI is not required to withhold on a payment of an amount realised when an exception to withholding under §1.1446(f)-4(b) applies. Thus, for example, QI is not required to withhold under Sect. 1446(f) when it may rely on a qualified notice that states the applicability of the exception under §1.1446(f)-4(b)(3). See Sect. 5 of this Agreement regarding documentation requirements for other exceptions to withhold under §1.1446(f)-4(b).

**(2) Withholding on a PTP Distribution.**

If QI acts as a nominee for a PTP distribution under Sect. 3.03(C)(2) of this Agreement, QI is a withholding agent for purposes of the distribution and is required to withhold as described in this Sect. 3.01(C)(2). For an amount subject to withholding under Sect. 1446(a) identified on a qualified notice for a PTP distribution, QI is required to withhold on the amount paid to an account holder that is (or is presumed to be) a foreign partner except when an exception to withholding applies to an account holder that is a foreign entity described in Sect. 501(c)(3) or that claims an exemption from withholding under an income tax treaty. See Sects. 5.03 and 5.06(A) of this Agreement for documentation requirements for these exceptions and Sect. 1446(b) for the rate of withholding that applies under Sect. 1446(a). See also §1.1446-5(c) and (d) for how QI determines its withholding under Sect. 1446(a) on a PTP distribution paid to an account holder that is a foreign partnership. For an amount subject to withholding under chapter 3 and 4 on a PTP distribution, QI is required to withhold under Sects. 3.01(A) and (B) of this Agreement to the extent such amounts are identified on a qualified notice for the distribution. For an amount realised on a PTP distribution, QI's requirement to withhold under section 1446(f) is limited to the amount identified on a qualified notice as in excess of the PTP's cumulative net income, subject to the withholding exceptions referenced in Sect. 3.01(C)(1) of this Agreement. If QI does not receive a qualified notice for a distribution or to the extent the qualified notice for the distribution does not specify an amount attributable to the distribution, QI is required to withhold only to the extent provided in §1.1446-4(d)(1).

**Sec. 3.02. Primary Withholding Responsibility Not Assumed under Chapters 3 and 4 or with respect to PTP interests.**

Notwithstanding anything in Sects. 1.01 and 3.01 of this Agreement to the contrary, QI is not required to withhold to the extent provided in this Sect. 3.02.

**(A) Withholding under Chapters 3 and 4.**

QI is not required to withhold with respect to a payment of US source FDAP income if it: (a) does not assume primary withholding responsibility under Sect. 3.03(A) of this Agreement by electing to be withheld upon under §1.1471-2(a)(2)(iii) for purposes of chapter 4, (b) provides the withholding agent from which QI receives the payment with a valid withholding certificate described in Sect. 6 of this Agreement that indicates that QI does not assume primary withholding responsibility for chapters 3 and 4 purposes, and (c) provides correct withholding statements (including information regarding any account holders or interest holders of an intermediary or flow-through entity that holds an account with QI, other than a QI that assumes primary withholding responsibility, or a WP or WT) as described in Sect. 6.02 of this Agreement.

**(B) Withholding with respect to PTP interest.** QI is not required to withhold on a payment of a PTP distribution or an amount realised from the sale of a PTP interest except when QI assumes primary withholding responsibility for either of those payments under Sect. 3.03(C)(1) or (2) of this Agreement. QI does not assume primary withholding responsibility for a payment of a PTP distribution or amount realised from the sale of a PTP interest by providing to its withholding agent or broker a valid withholding certificate described in Sect. 6 of this Agreement indicating that it is a QI that does not assume primary withholding responsibility for the payment and provides correct withholding statements as described in Sect. 6.02 of this Agreement. See Sect. 3.05(C) of this Agreement for when QI is not responsible for primary Form 1099 reporting and backup withholding for broker proceeds that are an amount realised.

**(C) Residual Withholding Requirement.**

Notwithstanding its election not to assume primary withholding responsibility for a payment as described in Sect. 3.02(A) or (B) of this Agreement, QI shall, however, withhold the difference between the amount of withholding required and the amount actually withheld by another withholding agent if QI—

**(1)** Actually knows that the appropriate amount has not been withheld by another withholding agent; or

**(2)** Made an error which results in the withholding agent's failure to withhold the correct amount due (*e.g.*, QI fails to provide an accurate withholding statement with respect to the payment, including a failure to provide information regarding any account holders or any interest holders of an intermediary or flow-through entity that holds an account with QI to the extent required in Sect. 6 of this Agreement), and QI has not corrected the underwithholding under Sect. 9.05 of this Agreement.

**Sec. 3.03. Assumption of Primary Withholding Responsibilities under Chapters 3 and 4 (including by QDDs) or with respect to PTP interests.**

**(A) Withholding Assumed under Chapters 3 and 4.** QI may assume primary withholding responsibility for purposes of chapters 3 and 4 by providing a valid withholding certificate described in Sect. 6 of this Agreement to a withholding agent that makes a payment of US source FDAP income to QI and by designating on the withholding statement associated with such certificate the account(s) for which QI assumes primary withholding responsibility (if required). QI is not required to assume primary withholding responsibility for all accounts it holds with a withholding agent. If QI assumes primary withholding responsibility for any account, it must assume that responsibility under chapters 3 and 4 for all withholdable payments and amounts subject to chapter 3 withholding made by the withholding agent to that account. Notwithstanding the preceding sentence, QI assumes primary withholding responsibility on a PTP distribution (which includes an amount subject to withholding under chapter 3 or 4 on the distribution) only as provided in Sect. 3.03(C)(2) of this Agreement.

If QI is acting as a QSL for a substitute dividend payment, QI must assume primary withholding responsibility for any such payment made to any account holder receiving a US source substitute dividend payment, subject to the restrictions related to QDDs described in Sect. 1.01 of this Agreement. A QI not acting as a QSL and acting as an intermediary under this Agreement for a US source substitute dividend payment must also assume primary withholding responsibility for all US source substitute dividends received and paid by QI as an intermediary. QI may assume primary withholding responsibility for US source FDAP payments of substitute interest as described in §1.861-2(a)(7). If QI assumes primary withholding responsibility for payments of substitute interest (as described in this paragraph), it must assume primary withholding responsibility with respect to all such payments. QI assumes primary withholding responsibility for payments of substitute interest for purposes of this Agreement when it assumes such responsibility for payments of interest and substitute interest it receives in connection with a sale-repurchase or similar agreement, a securities lending transaction, or collateral that it holds in connection with its activities as a dealer in securities. As a result, QI may represent its status as a QI on the withholding certificate described in Sect. 6.01 of this Agreement with respect to payments it receives of interest and substitute interest described in the preceding sentence regardless of whether it acts as an intermediary or as a principal with respect to these payments. To the extent that QI assumes primary withholding responsibility under this Sect. 3.03(A), QI must withhold as described in Sect. 3.01(A) and (B) of this Agreement. QI is not required to withhold on amounts it pays to another QI that has assumed primary withholding responsibility with respect to the payment under chapters 3 and 4 or to a WP or a WT. A QI is not required to withhold on only the following payments to a QI acting as a QDD—

**(1)** a payment with respect to a potential Sect. 871(m) transaction that is not an underlying security,

**(2)** a payment of a dividend equivalent, and

**(3)** a payment of a dividend received in calendar year 2023 or 2024 by that QDD in its equity derivatives dealer capacity.

**(B) Assumption of Withholding Responsibility by a QDD.** If QI is acting as a QDD, it must assume primary chapters 3 and 4 withholding responsibility for any dividend equivalent payment that it makes and must withhold with respect to a dividend equivalent payment on the dividend payment date for the applicable dividend (as determined in §1.1441-2(e)(4)). A QDD must treat any dividend equivalent (including any Sect. 871(m) amount) as a dividend from sources within the United States for purposes of Sects. 871(a) and 881 and chapter 3 and chapter 4 consistent with Sect. 871(m) and the regulations thereunder. A QDD may reduce the rate of withholding under chapter 3 on dividends and dividend equivalents only based on a beneficial owner's claim of treaty-reduced withholding for portfolio dividends under the dividends article of an applicable income tax treaty. A QDD must also assume primary chapter 3 and chapter 4 withholding responsibility for payments made with respect to a potential Sect. 871(m) transaction even if the payment is not a dividend equivalent if the amount paid is an amount subject to chapter 3 or 4 withholding. See Sect. 3.03(A) of this Agreement for when a QDD makes a payment subject to withholding under chapter 3 or 4 to another QI (including a QDD). If the QDD is a partnership or a branch of a partnership, it must also assume primary chapters 3 and 4 withholding responsibility for its partners on the Sect. 3.09 amounts as modified for a QDD that is a partnership (or branch of a partnership), treating the dividend equivalent payment as made on the dividend payment date for the applicable dividend (as determined in §1.1441-2(e)(4)). In addition, the QDD must notify each payee in writing that it will withhold on the dividend payment date before the time for determining the payee's first dividend equivalent payment (as determined under §1.871-15(j)(2)).

**(C) Withholding Assumed with respect to PTP Interests.**

**(1) Withholding Assumed on Amount Realised.** QI may assume primary withholding responsibility for a payment of an amount realised from the sale of a PTP interest only when the QI provides to the broker making the payment to QI a valid withholding certificate described in Sect. 6 of this Agreement stating that it assumes primary responsibility for the payment. In such a case, QI is required to withhold on the payment as described in Sect. 3.01(C)(1) of this Agreement, excluding an amount realised paid to another QI that has assumed primary withholding responsibility with respect to the amount realised.

**(2) Withholding Assumed on PTP Distribution.** QI may assume primary withholding responsibility for a payment of a PTP distribution only when the QI provides to the PTP or nominee paying the distribution to QI a valid withholding certificate described in Sect. 6 of this Agreement stating that QI assumes primary responsibility by acting as a nominee for the distribution under §1.1446-4(b)(3). QI may act as a nominee for a PTP distribution only when QI assumes primary withholding responsibility for all of the amounts subject to withholding on the PTP distribution under Sects. 1446(a) and (f) and chapters 3 and 4. When acting as a nominee, QI is required to withhold on a PTP distribution as required under Sect. 3.01(C)(2) of this Agreement, excluding a PTP distribution paid to another QI that has assumed primary withholding responsibility as a nominee with respect to the distribution or paid to a WP or WT with respect to an amount subject to withholding under chapter 3 or 4 on the distribution.

**Sec. 3.04. Backup Withholding Under Sect. 3406 and Form 1099 Reporting Responsibility.**

**(A) Backup Withholding.** QI is a payor under Sect. 3406 with respect to reportable payments. Under Sect. 3406, unless an exception to backup withholding applies, a payor is required to deduct and withhold 241 per cent from a reportable payment to an account holder that is a US non-exempt recipient if the US non-exempt recipient has not provided its US TIN in the manner required under that section; the IRS notifies the payor that the US TIN furnished by the payee is incorrect; there has been a notified payee underreporting described in Sect. 3406(c); or there has been a payee certification failure described in Sect. 3406(d).

**(B) Coordination of Chapter 4 Withholding and Backup Withholding.** With respect to a withholdable payment that is also a reportable payment subject to backup withholding under Sect. 3406, QI is not required to withhold under Sect. 3406 if QI withheld on such payment under chapter 4. See §31.3406(g)-1(e). Alternatively, if QI is a participating FFI or a registered deemed-compliant FFI (other than a reporting Model 1 FFI), it may elect to satisfy its obligation to withhold under chapter 4 (or the FFI Agreement) on a withholdable payment made to a recalcitrant account holder that is a US non-exempt recipient by satisfying its backup withholding obligation under Sect. 3406 provided that the payment is also a reportable payment. See Sect. 4 of the FFI Agreement. Nothing in chapter 4 (including the FFI Agreement) or any applicable IGA relieves QI of its requirements to backup withhold under Sect. 3406 to the extent required by this Agreement.

**(C) Form 1099 Reporting.** If QI applies backup withholding (as described in Sect. 3.04(B) of this Agreement), it must report the amount subject to backup withholding on Form 1099 and not on Form 1042-S.

**Sec. 3.05. Primary Form 1099 Reporting and Backup Withholding Responsibility for Reportable Payments Other Than Reportable Amounts.** QI is responsible for Form 1099 reporting and backup withholding on reportable payments other than reportable amounts to the extent required under this Sect. 3.05 and Sect. 8.06 of this Agreement, whether or not QI assumes primary Form 1099 reporting and backup withholding responsibility with respect to reportable amounts under Sect. 3.07 of this Agreement. Further, no provision of this Agreement which requires QI to provide another withholding agent with information regarding reportable amounts shall be construed as relieving QI of its Form 1099 reporting and backup withholding obligations with respect to reportable payments that are not reportable amounts. For when withholding under Sect. 1446(a) or (f) is applied on a payment to an account holder that is a US person, however, see Sect. 8.02 of this Agreement. Also see, §31.3406(g)-1(e), providing that a payor (irrespective of whether the payor is a US or non-US payor) is not required to backup withhold under Sect. 3406 on a reportable payment that is paid and received outside the United States with respect to an offshore obligation or on gross proceeds from a sale effected outside the United States, unless the payor has actual knowledge that the payee is a US person.

**(A) US Payor.** Except as provided in Sect. 3.05(C) of this Agreement, if QI is a US payor, QI has primary Form 1099 reporting and backup withholding responsibility for reportable payments other than reportable amounts. For example, if QI is a US payor, it has primary Form 1099 reporting and backup withholding responsibility for payments of foreign source income as well as all broker proceeds paid to account holders that are, or are presumed to be, US non-exempt recipients.

**(B) Non-US Payor.** If QI is a non-US payor, QI has primary Form 1099 reporting and backup withholding responsibility for broker proceeds described in Sect. 2.69(B)(2) of this Agreement and foreign source fixed and determinable income other than income paid and received outside United States as described in Sect. 2.69(B)(3) of this Agreement if such payments are made (or presumed made) to US non-exempt recipients.

**(C) Special Procedure for Broker Proceeds.** If QI is a US payor, QI may request another payor that is either a US financial institution or another QI to report on Form 1099 and, if required, backup withhold with respect to broker proceeds from a sale that is effected at an office outside the United States (as defined in §1.6045-1(g)(3)(iii)) that QI is otherwise required to report under Sect. 3.05(A) and Sect. 8.05 of this Agreement, provided the other payor actually receives the broker proceeds. In such a case, QI will not be responsible for primary Form 1099 reporting and backup withholding with respect to broker proceeds, provided that the other payor agrees to do the reporting and backup withholding and QI provides all of the information necessary for the other payor to properly report and backup withhold. QI, however, remains responsible for primary Form 1099 reporting and backup withholding if the other payor does not agree to report and backup withhold, or if QI knows that the other payor failed to do so. If, however, QI is a participating FFI or registered deemed-compliant FFI (other than a reporting Model 1 FFI) that reports an account on Form 1099 in order to satisfy its US account reporting requirement under chapter 4, as described in Sect. 8.04 of this Agreement, QI is responsible for reporting on Form 1099 with respect to reportable payments made to such US account and must report in the manner described in the FFI Agreement. Notwithstanding the preceding provisions of this Sect. 3.05, for a payment of broker proceeds that is an amount realised from the sale of a PTP interest, QI will not be excepted from responsibility for primary Form 1099 reporting and backup withholding if QI provides a valid withholding certificate described in Sect. 6 of this Agreement to the broker paying the proceeds to QI that indicates that QI assumes primary withholding responsibility for the amount realised.

**Sec. 3.06. Primary Form 1099 Reporting and Backup Withholding Responsibility for Reportable Amounts Not Assumed.** Notwithstanding Sects. 1.01 and 3.04 of this Agreement, QI shall not be required to report on Form 1099 and backup withhold with respect to a reportable amount if QI does not assume primary Form 1099 reporting and backup withholding responsibility and it provides a payor from which it receives a reportable amount the Forms W-9 of its US non-exempt recipient account holders (or, if a US non-exempt recipient fails to provide a Form W-9 or information regarding the account holder's name, address, and US TIN, if a US TIN is available) together with the withholding rate pools attributable to US non-exempt recipient account holders so that such payor may report on Form 1099 and, if required, backup withhold. If QI elects to backup withhold on withholdable payments that are also reportable amounts made to recalcitrant account holders that are also US non-exempt recipients, QI shall not be required to report on Form 1099 and backup withhold with respect to a reportable amount if it provides a payor from which it receives a reportable amount information regarding such recalcitrant account holders. See Sect. 6.03 of this Agreement and Sect. 4 of the FFI Agreement. If QI reports its US accounts on Forms 1099 under its FATCA requirements as a participating FFI or registered deemed-compliant FFI, see Sect. 8.04(A) of this Agreement providing that QI cannot delegate to a withholding agent its requirement to report its US accounts. If QI elects not to assume primary Form 1099 reporting and backup withholding responsibility, QI must provide the withholding agent with such information regarding any account holders or interest holders of an intermediary or flow-through entity that holds an account with QI. Notwithstanding its election not to assume primary Form 1099 reporting and backup withholding responsibility, QI shall backup withhold and report a reportable amount to the extent required under Sects. 3.04 and 8.06 of this Agreement if—

**(A)** QI actually knows that a reportable amount is subject to backup withholding and that another payor failed to apply backup withholding, or

**(B)** Another payor has not applied backup withholding to a reportable amount because of an error made by QI (*e.g.*, QI failed to provide the other payor with information regarding the name, address, US TIN (if available), and withholding rate pool for a US non-exempt recipient account holder subject to backup withholding, including a failure to provide information regarding any account holders or interest holders of an intermediary or flow-through entity that holds an account with QI to the extent required in Sect. 6 of this Agreement).

**Sec. 3.07. Primary Form 1099 Reporting and Backup Withholding Responsibility Assumed.** QI may assume primary Form 1099 reporting backup withholding responsibility with respect to reportable amounts without obtaining approval from the IRS. QI that assumes such responsibility is subject to all of the obligations imposed by chapter 61 and Sect. 3406, as modified by this Agreement, and QI shall be subject to any applicable penalties for failure to meet those obligations. QI shall inform a payor from which it receives a reportable amount that it has assumed primary Form 1099 reporting and backup withholding responsibility by providing the payor with a valid withholding certificate described in Sect. 6 of this Agreement and by identifying on the withholding statement associated with such certificate the account(s) for which QI assumes primary Form 1099 reporting and backup withholding responsibility (if required). QI is not required to assume primary Form 1099 reporting and backup withholding responsibility for all accounts it holds with a payor. However, if QI assumes primary Form 1099 reporting and backup withholding responsibility for any account, it must assume that responsibility for all reportable amounts made by a payor to that account. If QI is acting as a QDD, it must assume primary Form 1099 reporting and backup withholding responsibility for any reportable payments that are made with respect to a potential Sect. 871(m) transaction. Thus, for example, if QI acts as a QDD with respect to an NPC that is a potential Sect. 871(m) transaction and makes a payment pursuant to the NPC to a US person that is a US non-exempt recipient, QI must backup withhold and report any amount paid to the US person to the extent required under Sect. 3406 and §1.6041-1(d)(5). In addition, if QI is assuming primary withholding responsibility for payments of substitute interest (as described in Sect. 3.03(A) of this Agreement), it must assume primary Form 1099 reporting and backup withholding responsibility with respect to all such payments (with a similar requirement for Form 1099 reporting if QI assumes primary withholding responsibility for any payments of substitute dividends or acts as a QSL under Sect. 3.02(A) of this Agreement).

QI is not required to backup withhold on a reportable amount it makes to a WP, WT, or another QI that has assumed primary Form 1099 reporting and backup withholding responsibility with respect to the reportable amount. QI is also not required to backup withhold on a reportable amount that QI makes to an intermediary or flow-through entity that is a participating FFI, registered deemed-compliant FFI, or another QI that does not assume primary Form 1099 reporting and backup withholding responsibility with respect to the payment provided that such intermediary or flow-through entity allocates the payment on its withholding statement to a chapter 4 withholding rate pool of US payees and the withholding statement is associated with a valid Form W-8IMY that provides the applicable certification(s) for allocating the payment to this pool or allocates the payment on its withholding statement to a chapter 4 withholding rate pool of recalcitrant account holders.

**Sec. 3.08. Deposit Requirements.** If QI assumes primary withholding responsibility for a payment under Sect. 3.03 of this Agreement, it must deposit amounts withheld at the time and in the manner provided under Sect. 6302 (see §1.6302-2) by electronic funds transfer as provided under §31.6302-1(h). If QI is a non-US payor that does not assume primary withholding responsibility under Sect. 3.03 of this Agreement but withholds under Sect. 3.02(C) of this Agreement, QI must deposit amounts withheld by the 15th day following the month in which the withholding occurred.

**Sec. 3.09. QDD Tax Liability.** In addition to satisfying its withholding tax liability as described in this Agreement, a QDD must satisfy its QDD tax liability. The QDD's QDD tax liability is the sum of:

**(A)** its tax liability under Sect. 881 for its Sect. 871(m) amount (as defined in Sect. 2.73 of this Agreement) for each dividend on each underlying security reduced (but not below zero) by the amount of tax paid by the QDD under Sect. 881(a)(1) on dividends received with respect to that underlying security on that same dividend in its capacity as an equity derivatives dealer;

**(B)** its tax liability under Sect. 881 for dividend equivalent payments received as a QDD in its non-equity derivatives dealer capacity; and

**(C)** its tax liability under Sect. 881 for any payments, such as dividends or interest, received as a QDD with respect to potential Sect. 871(m) transactions or underlying securities that are not dividend equivalent payments, to the extent the full liability was not satisfied by withholding.

A QDD that is a foreign branch of a US financial institution does not have a QDD tax liability. Instead, such a QDD must determine and report its tax liability in accordance with chapter 1 and the appropriate US tax return for the US corporation. In the case of a QDD that is a partnership or a branch of a partnership, the QDD tax liability for each QDD will be the gross income components of this Sect. 3.09 instead of the tax liability under Sect. 881 amounts. More specifically, the amount under Sect. 3.09(B) is the dividend equivalent payments received as a QDD in its non-equity derivatives dealer capacity, and the amount under Sect. 3.09(C) is any payments, such as dividends or interest, received as a QDD with respect to potential Sect. 871(m) transactions or underlying securities that are not dividend equivalent payments. The Sect. 3.09(C) amount is not reduced by withholding, although QDD will take any prior withholding into account when reporting the amounts covered by Sect. 3.09(C) to the QI's partners and determining the appropriate withholding to those partners.

Further, the QDD tax liability includes any withholding required of the partnership with respect to its partners on the Sect. 3.09 amounts as modified for a QDD that is a partnership (or branch of a partnership).

For calendar years 2023 and 2024, the QDD (and its partners when the QDD is a partnership or a branch of a partnership) will not be liable for tax under Sect. 871(a) or 881 on actual dividends on physical shares or deemed dividends or dividend equivalents that the QDD receives in its equity derivatives dealer capacity. The QDD is (and in the case of a QDD that is a partnership or a branch of a partnership, the QDD's direct and indirect partners are) liable for tax on actual dividends on physical shares or deemed dividends or dividend equivalents received in its non-equity derivatives dealer capacity and on any other US source FDAP payments received by the QDD.

**(D) Timing for Determining QDD Tax Liability.** A QDD must determine its QDD tax liability due under Sects. 3.09(A) and (B) on the date provided in §1.871-15(j)(2) for the applicable dividend. A QDD must determine its QDD tax liability due under Sect. 3.09(C) when the payments are treated as received under the Code and the regulations promulgated thereunder. A QDD that is a partnership or a branch of a partnership must determine its QDD tax liability under Sects. 3.09(A) and (B), including the dividend equivalent payments received as a QDD in its non-equity derivatives dealer capacity, on the date provided in §1.871-15(j)(2) for the applicable dividend for withholding and reporting purposes. See Sect. 7.01(C) of this Agreement regarding a QI that is acting as a QDD's responsibility to report QDD tax liability on the appropriate US tax return and to maintain a reconciliation schedule for its Sect. 871(m) amount and other amounts related to its QDD tax liability. See also Sect. 7.01(C) of this Agreement for additional information regarding the reporting and other responsibilities of a QDD that is a partnership or branch of a partnership.

## Section 4. Private Arrangement Intermediaries and Certain Partnerships and Trusts

**Sec. 4.01. Private Arrangement Intermediaries–In General.** If QI is an FFI, QI may enter into a private arrangement with another intermediary under which the other intermediary agrees to perform all of the obligations of QI under this Agreement, except as modified in Sect. 4.02 of this Agreement. QI, however, may not enter into a private arrangement under this Sect. 4.01 with any account holder for which it acts as a QDD.

The agreement between QI and the other intermediary shall be between QI and all the offices of the other intermediary located in a particular jurisdiction, which must be one for which the IRS has approved the know-your-customer rules. Such an intermediary is referred to in this Agreement as a private arrangement intermediary (PAI). By entering into a PAI agreement, QI is not assigning its liability for the performance of any of its obligations under this Agreement. Therefore, QI shall remain liable for any tax, penalties, interest, and any other sanctions that may result from the failure of the PAI to meet any of the obligations imposed by its agreement with QI. QI agrees not to assert any defences against the IRS for the failures of the PAI or any defences that the PAI may assert against QI. For purposes of this Agreement, the PAI's actual knowledge or reason to know of facts relevant to withholding or reporting shall be imputed to QI. QI's liability for the failures of the PAI shall apply even though the PAI is itself a withholding agent and a payor under chapter 61 and Sect. 3406 and is itself separately liable for its failure to meet its obligations under the Code. Notwithstanding the foregoing, QI shall not be liable for tax, interest, or penalties for failure to withhold and report under chapters 3, 4, and 61 and Sects. 1446(a), 1446(f), and 3406 unless the underwithholding or the failure to report amounts correctly on Forms 945, 1042, 1042-S, 1099, or 8966 is due to QI's or its PAI's failure to properly perform its obligations under this Agreement. The PAI is not required to enter into an agreement with the IRS but must respond (either directly or through QI) to IRS inquiries related to its compliance, as described in Sect. 10.08 of this Agreement. The IRS may, however, in its sole discretion, refuse to permit an intermediary to operate as a PAI by providing notice to QI. QI may, however, appeal the IRS's determination by following the notice and cure provisions in Sect. 11.06 of this Agreement. For purposes of this Agreement, an intermediary shall be considered a PAI only if the following conditions are met:

**(A)** The PAI is a certified deemed-compliant FFI (other than a registered deemed-compliant Model 1 IGA FFI) that acts as an intermediary with respect to reportable amounts and has provided QI with a certification that it has maintained such certified deemed-compliant FFI status during each certification period;

**(B)** The PAI does not act as an intermediary for a direct account holder that is a QI, WP, WT, participating FFI, registered deemed-compliant FFI, or a registered deemed-compliant Model 1 IGA FFI;87

**(C)** The PAI is, pursuant to a written agreement between QI and the PAI (PAI agreement), subject to all the obligations of QI under this Agreement, except to the extent modified by Sects. 4.02 and 4.03 of this Agreement;

**(D)** For purposes of chapter 4, the PAI agrees to comply with the FATCA requirements applicable to its chapter 4 status as a certified deemed-compliant FFI, as modified by Sects. 4.02 and 4.03 of this Agreement, and is not required to fulfil QI's FATCA requirements as a participating FFI, registered deemed-compliant FFI, or registered deemed-compliant Model 1 IGA FFI;

**(E)** QI identifies the PAI on QAAMS before the first payment for which the PAI is operating under the PAI agreement;

**(F)** The PAI agrees, to the extent necessary for QI to satisfy its compliance obligations (*i.e.*, if QI does not receive a waiver described in Sect. 10.07 of this Agreement), either to provide its documentation and other information to QI for inclusion in QI's periodic review described in Sect. 10.04 of this Agreement or to conduct an independent periodic review in accordance with the procedures described in Sect. 10.05 of this Agreement and provide QI with the same certification as is required for QI's responsible officer under Sect. 10.03 of this Agreement for each certification period in order to allow the responsible officer of QI to make a certification to the IRS regarding PAI's compliance. The PAI agrees to respond (either directly or through QI) to IRS inquiries regarding its periodic review and agrees to provide QI (and the IRS, upon request) with a periodic review report (as described in Sect. 10.06 of this Agreement);

**(G)** The PAI furnishes QI with a Form W-8IMY and withholding statement described in Sect. 6 of this Agreement as modified by this Sect. 4.01(G). The PAI is required to provide QI with Forms W-9 (or, in absence of the form, the name, address, and US TIN (if available)) of the PAI's US non-exempt recipient account holders and the withholding rate pool information for those account holders as required by section 6.03(D) of this Agreement so that the QI (or the payor) may report on Form 1099 and, if required, backup withhold. In addition, the PAI is required to disclose to QI any account holder of PAI that is a passive NFFE with one or more substantial US owners (or one or more controlling persons that is a specified US person) as defined in §§1.1471-1(b)(74) and 1.1473-1(b), respectively (or in the applicable IGA), and the account holders or interest holders of any nonqualified intermediary or flow-through entity, respectively, which has an account with the PAI, and provide all of the documentation and other information relating to those account holders and interest holders that is required for the QI, or another withholding agent, to report the payments made to those account holders and interest holders to the extent required by Sects. 8.02(B) and 8.05 of this Agreement. Except to the extent the PAI provides its information to QI for purposes of performing the periodic review, the PAI is not required to disclose to QI, or another withholding agent, its direct account holders that are foreign persons other than a passive NFFE with one or more substantial US owners (or one or more controlling persons that is a specified US person). The limitations on a PAI's disclosure of its direct account holders do not, however, apply with respect to the PAI's direct account holders' receipt of payments of PTP distributions or amounts realised from sales of PTP interests. For either such payment, a PAI is required to disclose to QI its direct account holders and provide any information requested by QI for QI to meet its withholding and reporting requirements specified in Sect. 4.02(D) of this Agreement; and

**(H)** The PAI agrees to notify QI if the PAI no longer meets the requirements for certified deemed-compliant status, and upon such notification, the agreement between the PAI and QI will terminate.

**Sec. 4.02. Modification of Obligations for PAI Agreements.**

**(A) Payments Reportable under Chapters 3 and 4.** The agreement between QI and a PAI must provide that QI shall report all payments of amounts subject to chapter 3 or 4 withholding made by the PAI on QI's Forms 1042 and 1042-S as if QI had made the payments directly to the PAI's account holders. Therefore, QI shall report payments made to each of the following types of a PAI's account holders as follows:

**(1)** A direct account holder of the PAI that is a nonparticipating FFI, QI shall report an amount subject to chapter 4 withholding using the chapter 4 reporting pool described in Sect. 8.03 of this Agreement with the PAI reported as the recipient with respect to the pool.

**(2)** A direct foreign account holder of the PAI for which no withholding is required under chapter 4 (other than an intermediary, custodian, nominee, agent, or flow-through entity described below), QI shall, except as otherwise provided in Sect. 4.02(D) of this Agreement, report an amount subject to chapter 3 withholding (excluding an amount subject to chapter 3 withholding on a PTP distribution) using the chapter 3 reporting pools as described in Sect. 8.03 of this Agreement, with the PAI reported as the recipient.

**(3)** A direct foreign account holder of the PAI that is a nonqualified intermediary or flow- through entity, QI shall report payments of amounts subject to chapter 4 withholding with respect to any indirect account holders of the PAI that the nonqualified intermediary or flow-through entity includes in a chapter 4 withholding rate pool of nonparticipating FFIs using the chapter 4 reporting pool for such account holders described in section 8.03 of this Agreement with the nonqualified intermediary or flow-through entity reported as the recipient and shall report payments of amounts subject to chapter 3 withholding made with respect to indirect foreign account holders of the PAI that are not subject to chapter 4 withholding by reporting the payments as made to specific recipients under the rules of Sect. 8.02 of this Agreement.

**(B) Form 1099 Reporting and Backup Withholding.** The agreement between QI and a PAI must also provide that QI shall report all reportable payments made by the PAI on QI's Forms 945 and 1099 to the extent required under this Sect. 4.02(B). QI shall file Forms 1099 and backup withhold, if required, on reportable payments made by QI (including by a PAI) to US non-exempt recipients that are direct or indirect account holders of a PAI in accordance with the terms of this Agreement.

**(C) Form 8966 Reporting.** The agreement between QI and a PAI must also provide that QI shall report all withholdable payments made by the PAI on Form 8966 to the extent required under this Sect. 4.02(C). QI shall file Forms 8966 to report withholdable payments made by QI (including by a PAI) to passive NFFEs with one or more substantial US owners (or one or more controlling persons that is a specified US person) that are direct or indirect account holders of a PAI in accordance with Sect. 8.05 of this Agreement.

**(D) Payments of Amounts Realised or PTP Distributions.** The agreement between QI and a PAI must provide that QI will satisfy the requirements set forth in Sect. 8.07 of this Agreement with respect to each account holder of PAI that is a partner receiving from QI a PTP distribution or amount realised from the sale of a PTP interest for which a statement under Sect. 6031(b) is required for the taxable year (and for which the PAI will provide QI the necessary partner information). The agreement between QI and a PAI must further provide that QI shall treat the PAI as if the PAI were a disclosing QI with respect to both of the following—

**(1)** QI's reporting on Forms 1042 and 1042-S of an amount realised from the sale of a PTP interest or an amount subject to withholding on a PTP distribution paid to a direct account holder of the PAI (as further described in Sect. 8 of this Agreement); and

**(2)** QI's determination of the withholding required on any such amount.

**Sec. 4.03. Other Requirements of PAI Agreements.** QI shall require a PAI to provide QI with all the information necessary for QI to meet its obligations under this Agreement. No provisions shall be contained in the agreement between QI and a PAI that preclude, and no provisions of this Agreement shall be construed to preclude, the PAI's joint and several liability for tax, penalties, and interest under chapters 3,4, and 61 and Sect. 3406 to the extent that underwithholding, penalties, and interest have not been collected from QI and the underwithholding or failure to report amounts correctly on Forms 945, 1042, 1042-S, 1099, or Form 8966 are due to a PAI's failure to properly perform its obligations under its agreement with QI. Nothing in the agreement between QI and a PAI shall be construed to limit the PAI's requirements under chapter 4 or an applicable IGA. Further, nothing in the agreement between QI and a PAI shall permit the PAI to assume primary chapters 3 and 4 withholding responsibility, primary Form

1099 reporting and backup withholding responsibility, or primary withholding responsibility for a PTP distribution or an amount realised from the sale of a PTP interest.

**Sec. 4.04. Termination of Arrangement.** Except as otherwise provided in Sect. 4.01(H) of this Agreement, QI shall cease to treat an intermediary as a PAI within 90 days from the day QI knows that the PAI is in default of its agreement with QI unless the PAI has cured the event of default before the expiration of such 90-day period. QI must provide the IRS with notice of any PAI agreement that has been terminated within 30 days of the termination by removing the intermediary as a PAI on QAAMS.

**Sec. 4.05. Joint Account Treatment for Certain Partnerships and Trusts.**

**(A) In General.** If QI is an FFI, QI may enter an agreement with a non-withholding foreign partnership or non-withholding foreign trust that is either a simple or grantor trust described in this Sect. 4.05(A) to apply the simplified joint account documentation, reporting, and withholding procedures provided in Sect. 4.05(B) of this Agreement. QI and a partnership or trust that apply this Sect. 4.05 to any calendar year must apply these rules to the calendar year in its entirety. QI and the partnership or trust may not apply this Sect. 4.05 to any calendar year in which the partnership or trust has failed to make available to QI or QI's reviewer the records described in this Sect. 4.05(A) within 90 days after these records are requested, and the partnership or trust must waive any legal prohibitions against providing such records to QI. If the partnership or trust has failed to make these records available within the 90-day period, or if QI and the partnership or trust fail to comply with any other requirements of this Sect. 4.05, QI must apply the provisions of §§1.1441-1(c) and 1.1441-5(e) to the partnership or trust as a non-withholding foreign partnership or non-withholding foreign trust, must correct its withholding for the period during which the failure occurred in accordance with Sect. 9.05 of this Agreement, and cannot apply this Sect. 4.05 to subsequent calendar years. QI and a partnership or trust that apply this Sect. 4.05 to any calendar year are not required to apply this Sect. 4.05 to subsequent calendar years. A partnership or trust is described in this Sect. 4.05(A) of this Agreement if the following conditions are met:

**(1)** The partnership or trust has a chapter 4 status as a certified deemed-compliant FFI (other than a registered deemed-compliant Model 1 IGA FFI), an owner-documented FFI with respect to QI, an exempt beneficial owner, or an NFFE or is covered as an account that is excluded from the definition of financial account under Annex II of an applicable IGA or under §1.1471-5(a);

**(2)** The partnership or trust is a direct account holder of QI;

**(3)** None of the partnership's or trust's partners, beneficiaries, or owners is a flow- through entity or is acting as intermediary for a payment made by QI to the partnership or trust;

**(4)** None of the partnership's or trust's partners, beneficiaries, or owners is a US person and none of its foreign partners, beneficiaries, or owners is subject to withholding or reporting under chapter 4 (*e.g.*, a nonparticipating FFI and certain passive NFFEs); and

**(5)** The partnership or trust agrees to make available upon request to QI or QI's reviewer for purposes of QI's periodic review under Sect. 10 of this Agreement (including to respond to IRS inquiries regarding its compliance review) records that establish that the partnership or trust has provided QI with documentation for purposes of chapters 3 and 4 for all of its partners, beneficiaries, or owners.

**(B) Modification of Obligations for QI.**

**(1)** QI may rely on a valid Form W-8IMY provided by the partnership or trust and may rely on a withholding statement that meets the requirements of §1.1441-5(c)(3)(iv) or (e)(5)(iv), and §1.1471-3(c)(3)(iii)(B) (if the payment is a withholdable payment) and that provides information for all partners, beneficiaries, or owners together with valid Forms W-8 or, in the case of a partnership or trust that is a certified deemed-compliant FFI, documentary evidence permitted under the applicable know-your-customer rules from each partner, beneficiary, or owner, and, for a withholdable payment, documentation that meets the requirements of §1.1471-3(d) to establish the partner's, beneficiary's, or owner's chapter 4 status. The withholding statement need not provide any allocation information. QI may not, however, rely on a Form W-8IMY that is associated with a PTP distribution or amount realised from the sale of a PTP interest for purposes of this Sect. 4.05.

**(2)** QI must treat payments to the partnership or trust as allocated solely to a partner, beneficiary, or owner that is subject to the highest rate of withholding under chapter 3 and must withhold at that rate.

**(3)** QI may pool report amounts distributed to, or included in the distributive share of, the partnership's or trust's direct partners, beneficiaries, or owners in chapter 3 reporting pools on Form 1042-S as described in Sect. 8.03(B) of this Agreement.

**(4)** After QI has withheld in accordance with Sect. 4.05(B)(2) of this Agreement, it may file a separate Form 1042-S for any partner, beneficiary, or owner who requests that it do so. If QI issues a separate Form 1042-S for any partner, beneficiary, or owner, it cannot include such partner, beneficiary, or owner in its chapter 3 reporting pool. If QI has already filed a Form 1042-S and included the partner, beneficiary, or owner in a chapter 3 reporting pool, it must file an amended return to reduce the amount of the payment reported to reflect the amount allocated to the recipient on the recipient's specific Form 1042-S. QI may file a separate Form 1042-S for a partner, beneficiary, or owner only if the partnership or trust provides a withholding statement that includes allocation information for the requesting partner, beneficiary, or owner and only if the partnership or trust has agreed in writing to make available to QI or QI's reviewer the records that substantiate the allocation information included in its withholding statement.

**(5)** QI may not include any payments made to a partnership or trust to which QI is applying the rules of this Sect. 4.05 in any collective refund claim made under Sect. 9.04 of this Agreement.

**Sec. 4.06. Agency Option for Certain Partnerships and Trusts.**

**(A) In General.** QI may enter an agreement with a non-withholding foreign partnership or non-withholding foreign trust that is either a simple or grantor trust described in Sect. 4.06(A) of this Agreement under which the partnership or trust agrees to act as an agent of QI with respect to its partners, beneficiaries, or owners, and, as QI's agent, to apply the provisions of the QI agreement to the partners, beneficiaries, or owners. QI, however, may not enter an agreement under this Sect. 4.06 with any account holder for which it acts as a QDD. By entering into an agreement with a partnership or trust as described in this Sect. 4.06, QI is not assigning its liability for the performance of any of its obligations under this Agreement. QI and the partnership or trust to which QI applies the rules of this Sect. 4.06 are jointly and severally liable for any tax, penalties, and interest that may result from the failure of the partnership or trust to meet any of the obligations imposed by its agreement with QI. QI and a partnership or trust that applies the agency option to any calendar year must apply these rules to the calendar year in its entirety. Generally, QI and a partnership or trust that applies the agency option to any calendar year are not required to apply the agency option to subsequent calendar years. If, however, QI withholds and reports any adjustments required by corrected information in a subsequent calendar year under Sect. 4.06(B)(2) of this Agreement, QI must apply the agency option to that calendar year in its entirety. QI and a partnership or trust may not apply the agency option to any calendar year when the partnership or trust has failed to make available to QI or QI's reviewer the records described in Sect. 4.06 of this Agreement within 90 days after these records are requested, and the partnership or trust must waive any legal prohibitions against providing such records to QI. If, for any calendar year, the partnership or trust has failed to make these records available within the 90-day period, or if QI and the partnership or trust fail to comply with any other requirement of this Sect. 4.06, QI must apply §§1.1441-1(c) and 1.1441-5(e) to the partnership or trust as a non-withholding foreign partnership or non-withholding foreign trust, must correct its withholding for the period in which the failure occurred in accordance with Sect. 9.05 of this Agreement, and cannot apply the agency option to subsequent calendar years. A partnership or trust is described in this Sect. 4.06(A) of this Agreement if the following conditions are met:

**(1)** The partnership or trust is either a direct account holder of QI or an indirect account holder of QI that is a direct partner, beneficiary, or owner of a partnership or trust to which QI also applies the agency option.

**(2)** The partnership or trust has a chapter 4 status as a certified deemed-compliant FFI (other than a registered deemed-compliant Model 1 IGA FFI), an owner-documented FFI, an NFFE, an exempt beneficial owner, or is covered as an account that is excluded from the definition of financial account under Annex II of an applicable IGA or under §1.1471-5(a) and has provided QI with a certification that it has maintained such chapter 4 status during each certification period;

**(3)** None of the partnership's or trust's partners, beneficiaries, or owners is a WP, WT, participating FFI, registered deemed-compliant FFI, registered deemed-compliant Model 1 IGA FFI, or another QI acting as an intermediary for a payment made by QI to the partnership or trust.

**(4)** The partnership or trust agrees to permit QI to treat its direct partners, beneficiaries, or owners as direct account holders of QI under this Agreement and to treat its indirect partners, beneficiaries, or owners as indirect account holders of QI under this Agreement.

**(5)** The partnership or trust agrees, to the extent necessary for QI to satisfy its compliance obligations (*e.g.*, if the QI does not receive a waiver described in Sect. 10.07 of this Agreement), either to provide its documentation and other information to QI for inclusion in QI's periodic review described in Sect. 10.04 of this Agreement or to conduct an independent periodic review in accordance with the procedures described in Section 10.05 of this Agreement, provide QI with the certification required under Sect. 10.03 of this Agreement for each certification period in order to allow the responsible officer of QI to make a certification to the IRS regarding the partnership's or trust's compliance with this Sect. 4.06, and respond (either directly or through QI) to IRS inquiries regarding its compliance review, as described in Sect. 10.08 of this Agreement, including providing the QI and the IRS with the results of the reviewer's testing of transactions and accounts described in Sect. 10.06 of this Agreement.

**(6)** For a partnership or trust to which QI pays an amount subject to withholding under Sect. 1446(a) on a PTP distribution, the partnership is not a PTP, and the trust is a grantor trust (with the partnership or trust providing its US TIN to QI). For a partnership or trust to which QI pays an amount realised, the partnership is a partnership providing a certification for a modified amount realised, and the trust is a grantor trust (with the partnership or trust providing its US TIN to QI).

**(B) Modification of Obligations for QI.**

**(1) In General.** QI may rely on a valid Form W-8IMY provided by the partnership or trust, together with a withholding statement described in §1.1441-5(c)(3)(iv) or (e)(5)(iv) and §1.1471-3(c)(3)(iii)(B) (if the payment is a withholdable payment) that includes all information necessary for QI to fulfil its withholding, reporting, and filing obligations under this Agreement. The withholding statement may include chapter 3 withholding rate pools for partners, beneficiaries, or owners that are not intermediaries, flow-through entities (or persons holding interests in the partnership or trust through such entities), US persons, or passive NFFEs with one or more substantial US owners (or one or more controlling persons that is a specified US person), and the partnership or trust need not provide to QI documentation for these partners, beneficiaries, or owners. The withholding statement may also include a chapter 4 withholding rate pool of nonparticipating FFIs described in Sect. 6.03 of this Agreement for payments of amounts subject to chapter 4 withholding. Notwithstanding the preceding sentences of this Sect. 4.06(B)(1), the partnership or trust is required to disclose to QI any interest holder that is a passive NFFE with substantial US owners (or controlling persons that are specified US persons) or that is a US non-exempt recipient, as well as the account holders or interest holders of any nonqualified intermediary or flow-through entity, respectively, which has an interest in the partnership or trust, and to provide all of the documentation and other information relating to those account holders and interest holders that is required for the QI, or another withholding agent, to report the payments made to those account holders and interest holders to the extent required by Sects. 8.02(B) and 8.05 of this Agreement.

**(2) Timing of Withholding.** QI must withhold on the date it makes a payment to the partnership or trust based on a withholding statement provided by the partnership or trust on which QI is permitted to rely. The amount allocated to each partner, beneficiary, or owner in the withholding statement may be based on a reasonable estimate of the partner's, beneficiary's, or owner's distributive share of income subject to withholding for the year. The partnership or trust must correct the estimated allocations to reflect the partner's, beneficiary's, or owner's actual distributive share and must provide this corrected information to QI on the earlier of the date that the statement required under Sect. 6031(b) (*i.e.*, Schedule K-1) or the Beneficiary Statement or Owner Statement is mailed or otherwise provided to the partner, beneficiary, or owner, or the due date for furnishing the statement (whether or not the partnership or trust is required to prepare and furnish the statement). If that date is after the due date (without regard to extensions) for QI's Forms 1042 and 1042-S for the calendar year, QI may withhold and report any adjustments required by the corrected information in the following calendar year.

**(3) Payments Reportable Under Chapters 3 and 4.** QI shall report on Form 1042-S all amounts subject to chapters 3 and 4 withholding distributed to, or included in the distributive share of, the partnership or trust as follows:

**(i)** For a direct partner, beneficiary, or owner of the partnership or trust that is a nonparticipating FFI, QI shall report an amount subject to withholding using the chapter 4 reporting pool described in Sect. 8.03(A) of this Agreement with the partnership or trust reported as a recipient.

**(ii)** For a direct partner, beneficiary, or owner of the partnership or trust that is a foreign person for which no withholding is required under chapter 4 (other than an intermediary, agent, or flow-through entity described below), QI shall report an amount subject to chapter 3 withholding using the chapter 3 reporting pools described in Sect. 8.03(B) of this Agreement with the partnership or trust reported as a recipient.

**(iii)** For a direct or indirect partner, beneficiary, or owner of the partnership or trust that is a nonqualified intermediary or foreign flow-through entity, QI shall report payments of amounts subject to chapter 4 withholding in a chapter 4 withholding rate pool of nonparticipating FFIs using the chapter 4 reporting pool for such partner, beneficiary, or owner with the nonqualified intermediary or foreign flow-through entity95 reported as the recipient, and QI shall report payments of amounts subject to chapter 3 withholding for which no chapter 4 withholding is required by reporting the payments as made to specific recipients as described in Sect. 8.02 of this Agreement.

**(4) Payments Reportable under Sect. 1446(a) or (f).** QI shall report on Form 1042- S payments of amounts realised or amounts subject to withholding under Sect. 1446(a) in accordance with Sect. 4.06(B)(3) of this Agreement, taking into account the reporting required on these payments under Sect. 8.02 of this Agreement with respect to a flow-through entity or nonqualified intermediary.

**(5) Form 1099 Reporting and Backup Withholding.** The agreement between QI and the partnership or trust must also provide that QI shall include all reportable payments made by the partnership or trust in QI's Forms 945 and 1099 to the extent required under this Sect. 4.06(B)(4). QI shall file Forms 1099 and backup withhold, if required, on reportable payments made by QI to US non-exempt recipient that are direct or indirect partners, beneficiaries, or owners of the partnership or trust in accordance with the terms of this Agreement.

**(6) Form 8966 Reporting Requirements.** The agreement between QI and the partnership or trust must also provide that QI shall report all withholdable payments made by the partnership or trust on Form 8966 to the extent required under this Sect. 4.06(B)(5). If the partnership or trust is itself a passive NFFE and if any of its partners, beneficiaries, or owners is a passive NFFE with one or more substantial US owners (or one or more controlling persons that is a specified US person), QI shall file Forms 8966 to report all withholdable payments made by QI to any such passive NFFE in accordance with Sects. 8.04 and 8.05 of this Agreement.

**(C) Other Requirements of Agency Agreement.** QI shall require the partnership or trust to provide QI with all the information necessary for QI to meet its obligations under this Agreement. No provisions shall be contained in the agreement between QI and the partnership or trust that preclude, and no provisions of this Agreement shall be construed to preclude, the partnership or trust's joint and several liability for tax, penalties, and interest under chapters 3, 4, and 61 and Sect. 3406, to the extent that the underwithholding, penalties, and interest have not been collected from QI and the underwithholding or failure to report amounts correctly on Forms 945, 1042, 1042-S, 1099, or 8966 is due to the partnership's or trust's failure to properly perform its obligations under its agreement with QI. Nothing in the agreement between QI and the partnership or trust shall be construed to limit the partnership or trust's requirements under chapter 4 as a certified deemed-compliant FFI, owner-documented FFI, NFFE, or exempt beneficial owner. Further, nothing in the agreement between QI and the partnership or trust shall permit the partnership or trust to assume primary chapters 3 and 4 withholding responsibility or primary Form 1099 reporting and backup withholding responsibility.

## Section 5. Documentation Requirements

### Sec. 5.01. Documentation Requirements.

**(A) General Documentation Requirements.** QI agrees to use its best efforts to obtain documentation from account holders that receive a reportable payment to determine whether withholding applies or whether a payment is reportable under this Agreement. Under Sect. 11.06 of this Agreement, failure to obtain documentation from a significant number of direct account holders constitutes an event of default. If QI is an FFI obtaining documentary evidence, QI also agrees to adhere to the know-your-customer rules that apply to QI with respect to the account holder from whom the documentary evidence is obtained. If QI cannot reliably associate a reportable payment with valid documentation from the account holder, it must apply the applicable presumption rules to determine if withholding is required under chapter 3 or 4 or if backup withholding is required under Sect. 3406. QI agrees to review and maintain documentation in accordance with this Sect. 5 and, in the case of documentary evidence obtained from direct account holders, in accordance with the applicable know-your-customer rules. QI also agrees, if the performance of an external review is requested by the IRS (as described in Sect. 10.08(C) of this Agreement), to make documentation (together with any associated withholding statements and other documents or information) available upon request for inspection by QI's external reviewer. QI represents that none of the laws to which it is subject prohibit disclosure of the identity of any account holder or account information to QI's reviewer.

If QI is acting as a QDD, QI is required to apply the rules of this Sect. 5 to each account holder of an account for which it is acting as a QDD and to which it makes a reportable payment in accordance with the applicable requirements in Sect. 5.01(A) and (B) of this Agreement. In addition, if QI is a partnership and is or has a branch that is a QDD, QI is required to apply the rules of this Sect. 5 to each of its partners (looking through partners that are flow-through entities) in determining its withholding under Sect. 3.03(A) of this Agreement.

If QI makes a payment of an amount realised on a sale of a PTP interest or a payment of a PTP distribution, QI also agrees to use its best efforts to obtain the documentation that is described in Sect. 5.02 of this Agreement. For purposes of obtaining a US TIN from an account holder that is a partner with respect to documentation required under Sect. 5.02(B) or (C) of this Agreement, QI is treated as using its best efforts when QI makes a written solicitation (initial solicitation) for the account holder's US TIN in 2023 or the calendar year in which an account holder acquires a PTP interest through QI (if later). If an account holder's US TIN is not provided based on the initial solicitation, QI is required to make an additional written solicitation for the account holder's US TIN in the calendar year following the calendar year of the initial solicitation, and, if necessary, a further written solicitation in the calendar year following the year of the additional solicitation. Nothing in the preceding sentence shall, however, be construed to allow QI to apply a reduced rate of withholding under Sect. 1446(a) or (f) with respect to a payment made to a foreign account holder that fails to provide a US TIN to QI for any calendar year. QI further agrees to treat a partner as a foreign partner and a broker as a foreign broker when required under Sect. 5.13(C)(5) of this Agreement for a payment of an amount realised or the amount of a PTP distribution subject to withholding under Sect. 1446(a).

**(B) Coordination of Chapter 3 and Chapter 4 Documentation Requirements.**

**(1) QI that is an FFI.** If QI is an FFI, for each account holder for whom QI is acting under this Agreement, QI is required to perform the due diligence procedures under its FATCA requirements as a participating FFI, registered deemed-compliant FFI, or registered deemed-compliant Model 1 IGA FFI to determine if the account is a US account (or US reportable account) and to determine each account holder that is a nonparticipating FFI and, if applicable, recalcitrant account holder (or non-consenting US account). If an account holder receiving the payment is not the payee, QI is also required to establish the chapter 4 status of the payee or payees to determine whether withholding applies under chapter 4. For purposes of this Sect. 5, with respect to documenting an account holder for chapter 4 purposes, documentary evidence also includes any documentary evidence allowed under an applicable IGA. To the extent an account holder receives a payment with respect to which QI has determined that withholding is not required under chapter 4, QI shall obtain, unless already collected, documentation that meets the requirements of this Sect. 5 to determine whether the account holder is a foreign person for which QI is required to withhold under chapter 3 or a US payee for which QI is required to backup withhold under Sect. 3406 or report on Form 1099 under chapter 61. See, however, Sect. 8.06 of this Agreement providing the circumstances in which reporting of US accounts (or US reportable accounts) under its FATCA requirements as a participating FFI, registered deemed-compliant FFI, or registered deemed-compliant Model 1 IGA FFI satisfies QI's Form 1099 reporting responsibilities.

**(2) QI that is an NFFE.** If QI is an NFFE, QI is required to document the chapter 4 status of each account holder for whom QI is acting to determine if withholding and reporting apply under Sect. 1471 or 1472 on withholdable payments made to the account holder. QI is required to obtain, unless already collected, a valid Form W-8 or Form W-9 from each account holder to determine whether QI is required to withhold under chapter 3 or 4 or report on

Form 1099 under chapter 61 and backup withhold under Sect. 3406. The allowance in this Sect. 5 for QI to obtain documentary evidence does not apply if QI is an NFFE. QI may, however, obtain appropriate documentary evidence as additional documentation to establish the foreign status of an account holder.

**Sec. 5.02. Documentation for Foreign Account Holders.**

**(A) Documentation for Chapters 3 and 4.** QI may treat an account holder as a foreign beneficial owner of an amount for purposes of chapter 3 or 4 if the account holder provides a valid Form W-8 (other than Form W-8IMY unless provided by a QI that is acting as a QDD that is a corporation (or a branch of a corporation) and meets the requirements of Sect. 5.07(E) of this Agreement or a QI that is assuming primary withholding responsibility for a substitute interest payment) or valid documentary evidence that supports the account holder's status as a foreign person. QI may not treat an account holder that provides documentation indicating that it is a bank, broker, intermediary, or agent (such as an attorney) as a beneficial owner unless QI receives a statement, in writing and signed by a person with authority to sign such a statement, stating that such account holder is the beneficial owner of the income. Further, QI may not reduce the rate of withholding with respect to an indirect account holder that is a foreign beneficial owner unless the certification provided by the direct account holder is a valid Form W-8IMY, and then only to the extent that QI can reliably associate the payment with valid documentation that establishes that withholding does not apply under chapter 4 in the case of a withholdable payment made to the account holder and establishes that the indirect account holder is entitled to a reduced rate of withholding under chapter 3.

**(B) Documentation for Sect. 1446(a).** QI must treat an account holder that is a partner receiving a payment of a PTP distribution subject to withholding under Sect. 1446(a) as a foreign partner if the account holder provides a valid Form W-8 other than a Form W-8IMY provided by an intermediary, grantor trust, or partnership (excluding a PTP) that includes the account holder's US TIN. Alternatively, QI must treat an account holder described in the preceding sentence as a foreign partner when QI has both valid documentary evidence that supports the account holder's status as a foreign person and the account holder's US TIN. See, however, §1.1446-4(e)(4) for QI's requirement to provide Forms W-8 for the amount of a PTP distribution subject to withholding under Sect. 1446(a) when acting as a disclosing QI and Sect. 5.01(A) of this Agreement for the extent of QI's requirement to collect US TINs from its account holders for purposes of Sect. 1446(a).

**(C) Documentation for Sect. 1446(f).** QI must treat an account holder receiving a payment of an amount realised as a foreign partner if the account holder provides a valid Form W-8 (other than a Form W-8IMY provided by a broker or grantor trust) that includes the account holder's US TIN. Alternatively, QI must treat an account holder described in the preceding sentence as a foreign partner when QI has both valid documentary evidence that supports the account holder's status as a foreign person and the account holder's US TIN. See, however, §1.1446(f)-4(a)(7)(iii) for QI's requirement to provide Forms W-8 when acting as a disclosing QI for an amount realised and Sect. 5.01(A) of this Agreement for the extent of QI's requirement to collect US TINs from its account holders for purposes of Sect. 1446(f). With respect to an amount realised QI pays to a broker, QI may rely on documentation that is permitted under §1.1446(f)-4(a)(5) for treating the broker as a foreign person.

**Sec. 5.03. Beneficial Owner's Claim of Treaty Benefits.** To the extent an account holder receives a payment that is not subject to withholding under chapter 4, QI may not reduce the rate of withholding under chapter 3 based on a beneficial owner's claim of treaty benefits unless QI obtains the documentation required by Sect. 5.03(A) of this Agreement. In addition, QI agrees to establish procedures to inform account holders of the terms of limitation on benefits provisions of a treaty (whether or not those provisions are contained in a separate article entitled Limitation on Benefits) under which the account holder is claiming benefits. QI is required to obtain a Form W-8BEN-E with the appropriate limitation on benefits certification or, if QI is allowed to and obtains documentary evidence, the written certification included in the treaty statement as described in Sect. 5.03(B) of this Agreement. For a direct account holder documented by QI on or after January 1, 2018, using documentary evidence, QI must have a permanent residence address for the account holder in the jurisdiction associated with the documentary evidence to reduce the rate of withholding under this Section 5.03.

If an account holder that is a foreign partner receives an amount subject to withholding under Sect. 1446(a) on a PTP distribution or an amount realised, the documentation described in Sect. 5.03(A)(1) of this Agreement shall be permitted for the partner's claim of treaty benefits (except that a US TIN for the foreign partner is required), and Sects. 5.03(A)(2) and (3) of this Agreement shall not apply. See, however, Sect. 5.07 of this Agreement in the case of an amount realised paid to a nonqualified intermediary.

**(A) Treaty Documentation.** The documentation required by this Sect. 5.03(A) is as follows:

**(1)** The account holder has provided a properly completed Form W-8BEN or Form W- 8BEN-E on which a claim of treaty benefits is made, including, for an entity, the appropriate limitation on benefits and Sect. 894 certifications, as provided in §1.1441- 6(b)(1). A US TIN or foreign TIN shall not be required, however, if the beneficial owner is a direct account holder. An indirect account holder is required to have a either a US TIN or foreign TIN to claim treaty benefits unless it is claiming treaty benefits on income from marketable securities;

**(2)** The account holder has provided documentary evidence that has been obtained pursuant to the know-your-customer rules that apply to the account holder, and the account holder, if it is an entity, has made the treaty statement (if applicable) required by Sect. 5.03(B) of this Agreement; or

**(3)** The account holder provides the type of documentary evidence required under §1.1441-6 to establish entitlement to a reduced rate of withholding under a treaty, and the account holder, if it is an entity, has made the treaty statement (if applicable) required by Sect. 5.03(B) of this Agreement.

**(B) Treaty Statement.** The treaty statement required by an entity account holder under this Sect. 5.03(B) is as follows: [Name of entity account holder] meets all provisions of the applicable treaty that are necessary to claim a reduced rate of withholding, including any limitation on benefits provisions, and derives the income within the meaning of Sect. 894, and the regulations thereunder, as the beneficial owner. QI is only required to obtain the treaty statement required by this Sect. 5.03(B) from an account holder that is an entity. QI shall not be required to obtain a treaty statement required by this Sect. 5.03(B) from an individual who is a resident of an applicable treaty country or from the government, or its political subdivisions, of a treaty country. QI is also required to collect and to report, on a Form 1042-S issued under Sect. 8.02(P) of this Agreement, the specific category of limitation on benefits provision claimed from all of its entity account holders (i.e., the specific article of the treaty or that no article applies), including a government (or its political subdivisions).

**Sec. 5.04. Documentation for International Organisations.** To the extent an account holder receives a payment that is not subject to withholding under chapter 4, QI may not treat the account holder as an international organisation entitled to an exemption from withholding under Sect. 892 unless the name provided on the documentation (including a Form W-8EXP) is the name of an entity designated as an international organisation by executive order pursuant to 22 United States Code 288 through 288(f) and the documentation is valid under Sect. 5.10 of this Agreement. An international organisation may not, however, claim benefits under this Sect. 5.04 with respect to QI's requirement to withhold under Sect. 1446(a) or (f). If an international organisation is not claiming benefits under Sect. 892 but under another Code exception, the provisions of Sect. 5.02 of this Agreement shall apply rather than the provisions of this Sect. 5.04.

**Sec. 5.05. Documentation for Foreign Governments and Foreign Central Banks of Issue.**

**(A) Documentation From a Foreign Government or Foreign Central Bank of Issue Claiming an Exemption from Withholding Under Sect. 892 or Sect. 895.** To the extent an account holder receives a payment subject to withholding under chapter 3 that is not subject to withholding under chapter 4, QI may not treat an account holder as a foreign government or foreign central bank of issue exempt from withholding under Section 892 or 895 unless—

**(1)** QI receives from the account holder a Form W-8EXP or documentary evidence establishing that the account holder is a foreign government or foreign central bank of issue;

**(2)** The income paid to the account holder is the type of income that qualifies for an exemption from withholding under Sect. 892 or 895; and

**(3)** QI does not know, or have reason to know, that the account holder is a controlled commercial entity as described in Sect. 892, that the income owned by the foreign government or foreign central bank of issue is being received from a controlled commercial entity, or that the income is from the disposition of an interest in a controlled commercial entity.

**(B) Treaty Exemption.** To the extent an account holder receives a payment that is not subject to withholding under chapter 4, QI may treat an account holder as a foreign government or foreign central bank of issue entitled to a reduced rate of withholding under an income tax treaty for purposes of chapter 3 if it has valid documentation that is sufficient to obtain a reduced rate of withholding under a treaty as described in section 5.03 of this Agreement.

**(C) Other Code Exception.** If a foreign government or foreign central bank of issue is not claiming benefits under Sect. 892 or under an income tax treaty but under another Code exception (*e.g.*, the portfolio interest exception under Sect. 871(h) or 881(c)), the provisions of Sect. 5.02 of this Agreement apply rather than the provisions of this Sect. 5.05. A foreign government or foreign central bank of issue may not claim benefits under Sect. 892 with respect to QI's requirement to withhold under Sect. 1446(a) or (f).

**Sec. 5.06. Documentation for Foreign Tax-Exempt Organisations.** To the extent an account holder receives a payment that is subject to withholding under chapter 3 or Sect. 1446(a) on a PTP distribution but not under chapter 4, QI may not treat an account holder as a foreign tax-exempt organisation and reduce the rate of or exempt the account holder from withholding unless it satisfies the requirements provided in Section 5.06(A), (B), or (C) of this Agreement.

**(A) Reduced Rate of Withholding Under Sect. 501.** QI may not treat an account holder as a foreign organisation described under Sect. 501(c), and therefore exempt from withholding under chapter 3 (or, if the account holder is a foreign private foundation, subject to withholding at a 4-per cent rate under Sect. 1443(b)) unless QI obtains a valid Form W-8EXP on which Part IV of the form is completed.

**(B) Reduced Rate of Withholding Under Treaty.** QI may not treat an account holder as a foreign organisation that is tax-exempt on an item of income pursuant to an income tax treaty unless QI obtains valid documentation as described under Sect. 5.03 of this Agreement that is sufficient for obtaining a reduced rate of withholding under the treaty and the documentation establishes that the account holder is an organisation exempt from tax under the treaty on that item of income.

**(C) Other Exceptions.** If a tax-exempt entity is not claiming a reduced rate of withholding because it is a foreign organisation described under Sect. 501(c) or under a treaty article that applies to exempt certain foreign organisations from tax but is claiming a reduced rate of withholding under another Code or income tax treaty exception, the provisions of Sect. 5.02 or 5.03 (as applicable) of this Agreement shall apply rather than the provisions of this Sect. 5.06. A tax-exempt entity may not claim a reduced rate of withholding under Sect. 501 for purposes of QI's withholding under Sect. 1446(f).

**Sec. 5.07. Documentation from Intermediaries or Flow-Through Entities and QDDs.** QI must apply the presumption rules to a payment made to a nonqualified intermediary or flow-through entity that is a direct account holder of QI to the extent QI fails to obtain the documentation set forth below. If QI receives documentation for the account holders or interest holders of an intermediary or flow-through entity, QI must apply the rules of this Sect. 5 to determine the validity of such documentation. Notwithstanding the previous provisions of this Sect. 5.07, for an amount realised paid to a nonqualified intermediary, QI is required to apply the presumption rule provided in Sect. 5.13(C)(5) of this Agreement regardless of whether the nonqualified intermediary provides a valid Form W-8IMY and documentation with respect to the account holders receiving the amount realised.

**(A) Withholdable Payments Made to Nonqualified Intermediaries and Flow- Through Entities.** With respect to a withholdable payment made to a nonqualified intermediary or flow-through entity—

**(1)** QI receives a valid Form W-8IMY provided by the nonqualified intermediary or the flow-through entity receiving the payment that establishes the chapter 4 status of the intermediary or flow-through entity; and

**(2)** If the payment is not subject to withholding under chapter 4 based on such entity's chapter 4 status (or to the extent the payment is received on behalf of exempt beneficial owners), QI can reliably associate the payment with a withholding statement that meets the requirements of §1.1471-3(c)(iii)(B) that includes the account holders or interest holders of the intermediary or flow-through entity in chapter 4 withholding rate pools to the extent permitted or with valid documentation described in this Sect. 5 provided by account holders or interest holders of the intermediary or flow-through entity that are not themselves nonqualified intermediaries or flow-through entities and that QI can treat as not subject to withholding under chapter 4.

**(B) Reportable Payments Other than Withholdable Payments or Payments with respect to PTP interests Made to Nonqualified Intermediaries and Flow-Through Entities.** With respect to a reportable payment that is not a withholdable payment or an amount realised made to a nonqualified intermediary or flow-through entity—

**(1)** QI receives a valid Form W-8IMY and a withholding statement with the information specified in §1.1441-1(e)(3)(iv)(C) (which includes an alternative withholding statement) provided by the nonqualified intermediary or the flow-through entity regardless of whether the form includes a chapter 4 status of the nonqualified intermediary or flow-through entity unless such entity provides a withholding statement allocating a payment to a chapter 4 withholding rate pool of US payees; and

**(2)** QI can reliably associate the payment with a chapter 4 withholding rate pool of US payees or valid documentation described in this Sect. 5 provided by account holders or interest holders of the nonqualified intermediary or flow-through entity that are not themselves nonqualified intermediaries or flow-through entities.

**(C) Payments with respect to PTP Interests Made to Nonqualified Intermediaries and Flow-Through Entities.**

**(1) Amount Realised.** With respect to a payment by QI of an amount realised from the sale of a PTP interest made to a flow-through entity or nonqualified intermediary, the documentation that QI receives is a valid Form W-8IMY from the entity except for a foreign simple trust (for which a Form W-8BEN-E may instead be received) and a US grantor trust (for which a document similar to Form W-8IMY may be received). In the case of a foreign partnership providing the certification on a valid Form W-8IMY for a modified amount realised (which requires a US TIN for the partnership) QI is required to obtain from the partnership the documentation described in this Sect. 5 with respect to the partners that QI can reliably associate with the payment. For a grantor trust to which QI pays an amount realised, QI is further required to obtain valid documentation described in this Sect. 5 that QI can reliably associate with each grantor or owner of the trust and must obtain a US TIN for the trust.

**(2) PTP Distribution.** With respect to a payment by QI of a PTP distribution to a nonqualified intermediary, the documentation that QI receives from the intermediary is a valid Form W-8IMY (including its chapter 4 status for an amount of a distribution attributable to a withholdable payment) and documentation for each of the account holders of the nonqualified intermediary that are partners in the PTP that QI can reliably associate with each amount subject to withholding on the distribution (including by applying Sect. 5.13(B)(1) of this Agreement for any amount realised on the distribution). With respect to a payment by QI of a PTP distribution to a flow-through entity, the documentation that QI receives from the flow-through entity is as follows—

**(i)** For the amount of the distribution subject to withholding under Sect. 1446(a) made to a foreign partnership, QI receives a valid Form W-8IMY from the partnership and, for a foreign partnership other than a PTP, valid documentation described in this Sect. 5 on each of the partners in the partnership that QI can reliably associate with the distribution (including a US TIN for the partnership in both cases). See §§1.1446-4 and 1.1446-5(c). For the portion of the distribution subject to withholding under Sect. 1446(a) made to a trust, QI receives a valid Form W-8BEN-E or W-8IMY from a simple trust or, in the case of a foreign grantor trust, a valid Form W-8IMY from the trust (or similar document from a US grantor trust) and valid documentation on each grantor or owner of the trust permitted under this Sect. 5 for a payment subject to Sect. 1446(a) withholding that QI can reliably associate with the distribution (including a US TIN for the grantor trust).

**(ii)** For the amount of the distribution subject to withholding under chapter 3 or 4, QI receives a valid Form W-8IMY from the flow-through entity (which includes the entity's chapter 4 status with respect to any amount of a distribution attributable to a withholdable payment) and valid documentation on the interest holders in the entity (other than nonqualified intermediaries or flow-through entities) permitted under this Sect. 5 for a payment subject to chapter 3 or 4 withholding that QI can reliably associate with the distribution.

**(iii)** For the amount realised on the distribution, QI receives from the flow-through entity valid documentation specified in Sect. 5.07(C)(1) of this Agreement applicable to a flow-through entity that QI can reliably associate with the distribution.

**(D) Reportable Payments and Payments with respect to PTP Interests Made to QIs, WPs, and WTs.** With respect to a reportable payment made to a QI, WP, or WT, QI receives a valid Form W-8IMY provided by the QI, WP, or WT that includes the entity's chapter 4 status for a payment that is a withholdable payment and, for those payments for which a QI has not assumed primary chapters 3 and 4 withholding responsibility or primary Form 1099 reporting and backup withholding responsibility, QI can reliably associate the payment with withholding rate pools, as described in Sect. 6.03 of this Agreement, or a valid Form W-9 for a US non-exempt recipient account holder not included in a withholding rate pool.

With respect to a payment of an amount realised on the sale of a PTP interest made by QI to a QI, QI receives a valid Form W-8IMY provided by the other QI that includes the QI's chapter 4 status if the QI provides a withholding statement allocating a payment to a chapter 4 withholding rate pool of US payees. Additionally, for an amount realised for which the other QI does not assume primary withholding responsibility nor act as a disclosing QI, QI can reliably associate the payment with withholding rate pools, as described in Sect. 6.03 of this Agreement, or a valid Form W-9 for a US partner not includible in a chapter 4 withholding rate pool of US payees under chapter 4. See §1.1446(f)-4(a)(7)(iv). For an amount realised described in the preceding sentence that QI pays to a QI acting as a disclosing QI, QI receives valid documentation permitted under Sect. 5.02(C) of this Agreement with respect to the account holders of the other QI, including a valid Form W-9 for a US partner not includible in a chapter 4 withholding rate pool of US payees permitted under chapter 4.

With respect to a PTP distribution paid by QI to a QI, QI receives a valid Form W-8IMY provided by the other QI that includes the QI's chapter 4 status for any portion of the PTP distribution attributable to a withholdable payment. Additionally, for a PTP distribution for which the other QI does not assume primary withholding responsibility nor act as a disclosing QI, QI can reliably associate the payment with withholding rate pools, as described in Sect. 6.03 of this Agreement, or a valid Form W-9 for each partner that is a US person. For a PTP distribution that QI pays to a QI acting as a disclosing QI, QI receives with respect to the account holders of the other QI valid documentation required of a disclosing QI under Sect. 5.02(B) of this Agreement for an amount subject to withholding under Sect. 1446(a) on the distribution, valid documentation permitted under the preceding paragraph of this Sect. 5.07(D) for an amount realised on the distribution, and, for an amount subject to withholding under chapter 3 or 4 on the distribution, valid documentation described in Sect. 5.07(A) or (B) of this Agreement.

With respect to a PTP distribution paid to a WP or WT, QI receives a valid Form W-8IMY provided by the WP or WT that QI can reliably associate with an amount subject to withholding under chapter 3 or 4 on the distribution.

**(E) Payments Made to QIs Acting as QDDs.** For payments with respect to potential Sect. 871(m) transactions or underlying securities made to a QI acting as a QDD, if QI receives a valid Form W-8IMY provided by the QI acting as a QDD that includes the QI's chapter 4 status and the required certification that the QI is acting as a QDD and assumes primary withholding responsibility for payments it makes when the QI is acting as a QDD and QDD withholding statement, then QI can reliably associate the payments as made to the QI acting as a QDD. Additionally, in the case of a QDD identified on a valid Form W-8IMY as a partnership (or a branch of a partnership), the QI can reliably associate a payment described in Sect. 3.09 of this Agreement, as modified for a QDD that is a partnership or branch of a partnership, with withholding rate pools to the extent permitted in Sect. 6.03 of this Agreement for an account holder, or specific partner information, with respect to the QDD partners (looking through partners that are foreign flow-through entities). The requirement for the partner information specified in the preceding sentence does not apply to a payment described in Sects. 3.03(A)(1)-(3) of this Agreement.

**(F) Private Arrangement Intermediaries.** If QI has an agreement with a PAI, QI obtains from the PAI a Form W-8IMY completed as if the PAI were a QI that is an FFI (with the exception that the PAI must not provide a QI-EIN on the Form W-8IMY) and QI can reliably associate the payment with a withholding statement, as described in Sect. 4.01(G) of this Agreement, and the information described in this Sect. 5.07 for any account holders of the PAI that are intermediaries or flow-through entities and the documentation for any passive NFFE with one or more substantial US owners (or one or more controlling persons that is a specified US person if QI is a reporting Model 1 or reporting Model 2 FFI). For a payment of an amount realised from the sale of a PTP interest or PTP distribution, however, QI must reliably associate the payment with a withholding statement and the information described in this Sect. 5 with respect to both the direct account holders of the PAI and account holders of an intermediary or flow-through entity that is an account holder of the PAI.

**(G) Partnerships or Trusts to which QI Applies the Agency Option.** If QI has an agreement with a partnership or trust under which the partnership or trust agrees to act as an agent of QI, QI obtains from the partnership or trust a Form W-8IMY completed as if the partnership or trust were a QI (with the exception that the partnership or trust must not provide a QI-EIN on the Form W-8IMY) and QI can reliably associate the payment with a withholding statement, as described in Sect. 4.06(B)(1) of this Agreement, and the information described in this Sect. 5.07 for any account holders that are intermediaries or flow-through entities and the documentation for any passive NFFE with one or more substantial US owners (or one or more controlling persons that is a specified US person if QI is a reporting Model 1 or reporting Model 2 FFI).106

**Sec. 5.08. Documentation for US Exempt Recipients.** QI shall not treat an account holder as a US exempt recipient unless QI obtains from the account holder—

**(A)** A valid Form W-9 on which the account holder includes an exempt payee code to certify that the account holder is a US exempt recipient for purposes of chapter 4 reporting;

**(B)** Documentary evidence that is sufficient to establish that the account holder is a US exempt recipient; or

**(C)** Documentary evidence that is sufficient to establish the account holder's status as a US person and QI can treat the person as an exempt recipient under the rules of §§1.6045-2(b)(2)(i) or 1.6049-4(c)(1)(ii), as appropriate, without obtaining documentation.

**Sec. 5.09. Documentation for US Non-Exempt Recipients.** QI shall not treat an account holder as a US non-exempt recipient unless QI obtains a valid Form W-9 or other similar agreed form under its FATCA requirements as a participating FFI, registered deemed-compliant FFI, or registered deemed-compliant Model 1 IGA FFI from the account holder, QI knows an account holder is a US non-exempt recipient, or QI must presume a person is a US non-exempt recipient to the extent required under Sect. 5.13(C)(3) or (4) of this Agreement.

**Sec. 5.10. Documentation Validity.**

**(A) In General.** QI may not rely on documentation if QI has actual knowledge or, for a payment other than an amount realised, reason to know that the information or certifications contained in the documentation or account information are unreliable or incorrect, or if there is a change in circumstances with respect to the information or statements contained in the documentation or account information that affects the reliability of the account holder's claim. See §§1.1441-1(e)(4)(viii), 1.1441-6(b)(1)(ii), and 1.1441-7(b)(2) for general rules for reliance on documentation for purposes of chapter 3, Sect. 1446(a) (including for a claim of treaty benefits), and §1.1446(f)-4(b) for reliance on documentation for purposes of Sect. 1446(f). For purposes of chapter 3, also see §1.1441-7(b)(4) for general rules applicable to withholding certificates, §1.1441-7(b)(7) for general rules applicable to documentary evidence, and §1.1441- 7(b)(8)(i) for rules regarding documentary evidence received before January 1, 2001. See Sect. 5.10(B) of this Agreement for limitations that apply to certain QIs for when they are considered to have reason to know that documentation is unreliable or incorrect for chapter 3 purposes and Sect. 5.10(C) of this Agreement for when QI may rely on documentation notwithstanding the preceding requirements of this Sect. 5.10(A). See §31.3406(h)-3(e) for rules regarding when QI may rely on a Form W-9. A change in circumstances affecting withholding information, including allocation information or withholding rate pools contained in a withholding statement, will also cause the documentation provided with respect to that information to no longer be reliable. See §1.1441-1(e)(4)(ii)(D) for the definition of change in circumstances and a withholding agent's obligation with respect to a change in circumstances for purposes of chapter 3. In addition to the above requirements for reliance on documentation, QI may not rely on a permanent residence address provided by an account holder that is subject to a hold mail instruction except as provided in Sect. 5.10(D) of this Agreement. See §1.1441- 1(c)(38)(i) for the definition of permanent residence address and §1.1441-1(c)(38)(ii) for the definition of a hold mail instruction. See §1.1441-7(b)(8)(ii) for the requirement that documentary evidence received after December 31, 2001, may not be treated as valid if a withholding agent does not have a permanent residence address for the account holder.

If QI becomes aware of information resulting in the documentation no longer being reliable or correct and QI has not assumed primary withholding responsibility under chapters 3 and 4 or primary Form 1099 reporting and backup withholding responsibility, QI agrees that it will promptly provide a withholding agent with corrected information (*e.g.*, corrected withholding rate pools, corrected Forms W-9, or corrected US TINs) within 30 days after QI knows or has reason to know that the documentation upon which it has relied is unreliable or incorrect. If QI receives notification from the IRS that documentation provided by an account holder is unreliable or incorrect (*e.g.*, that the US TIN provided by an account holder is incorrect), QI shall follow the procedures set forth in §31.3406(d)-5. See also QI's FATCA requirements as a participating FFI, registered deemed-compliant FFI, or registered deemed-compliant Model 1 IGA FFI or an NFFE's requirements as a withholding agent under Sects. 1471 and 1472 following a change in circumstances

**(B) Limits on Reason to Know.**

**(1) Direct Account Holders.** If QI is a financial institution as defined in §1.1471-5(e), an insurance company (without regard to whether such company is a specified insurance company), or a broker or dealer in securities, QI shall be considered to have reason to know that documentation provided by a direct account holder is unreliable or incorrect with respect to the account holder's claim of foreign status for purposes of chapter 3 or 4 only as prescribed in §1.1441-7(b)(5) or (8), without regard, however, to §1.1441- 7(b)(5)(i) and §1.1441-7(b)(8)(ii), with respect to the conditions for when documentation is considered to be unreliable or incorrect based on QI having a US mailing address or US residence address in its account information. In place of those conditions in §1.1441-7(b)(5)(i) and §1.1441-7(b)(8)(ii), QI is required to treat documentation as unreliable or incorrect only if QI has a US mailing address or US residence address for the account holder.

A QI that is an entity described in the first sentence of this Sect. 5.10(B)(1) shall be considered to have reason to know that documentation provided by a direct account holder is unreliable or incorrect with respect to the account holder's residence for purposes of a claim of treaty benefits for chapter 3 and 4 only as prescribed in §1.1441- 7(b)(6) and (9) (including when QI does not have a permanent residence address for an account holder in the jurisdiction for which treaty benefits are claimed). For a direct account holder that QI documented before January 1, 2018, however, a QI is not required to treat an account holder's claim of treaty benefits as unreliable or incorrect solely because QI does not have an address for the account holder in the jurisdiction for which the treaty benefits are claimed provided that QI does not have an address for the account holder outside of the jurisdiction for which the treaty benefits are claimed (or QI otherwise satisfies the validity requirements for relying on the documentation for such a case).

**(2) Indirect Account Holders.** QI shall be considered to have reason to know that relevant information or statements contained in documentation provided by an indirect account holder are unreliable or incorrect if a reasonably prudent person in the position of a QI would question the claims made. QI shall have reason to know that documentation provided by a nonqualified intermediary or a flow-through entity is unreliable or incorrect if the nonqualified intermediary or flow-through entity does not provide QI with, to the extent required, the names of the indirect account holders, their addresses, allocation information allocating payments to each indirect account holder, and sufficient information for QI to report payments on Forms 1042-S and 1099. In addition, QI shall have reason to know that an indirect account holder is not entitled to a reduced rate of withholding under an income tax treaty if the nonqualified intermediary or flow-through entity has not provided sufficient information so that QI can verify that the indirect account holder has provided a US TIN or foreign TIN, if required, and made the necessary statements regarding limitations on benefits provisions and deriving the income under Sect. 894 and the regulations thereunder. See §1.1441- 7(b)(10) and Sect. 5.03 of this Agreement.

**(3) Limitation on Benefits Provisions (Entity Account Holders).** With respect to a specific limitation on benefits provision cited by an entity for purposes of a claim of treaty benefits (including when identified on a treaty statement under Sect. 5.03(B) of this Agreement), QI may rely on the provision cited absent actual knowledge that it is unreliable or incorrect.

**(C) Curative Rules for Reliance on Documentation.** If under Sect. 5.10(A) of this Agreement QI knows, or has reason to know, that documentation provided by an account holder is unreliable or incorrect to establish the account holder's foreign status for purposes of chapter 3 (including on account of a change in circumstances), QI may rely (or continue to rely) on the documentation when it obtains the additional documentation described in §1.1441-7(b)(5) or (b)(8) (as applicable depending on whether a Form W-8 or documentary evidence was collected from the account holder). If under Sect. 5.10(A) of this Agreement QI knows, or has reason to know, that documentation provided by an account holder is unreliable or incorrect to establish the account holder's residence for purposes of claiming benefits under an applicable income tax treaty for purposes of chapter 3 (including on account of a change in circumstances), QI may rely (or continue to rely) on the documentation when it obtains the additional documentation described in §1.1441-7(b)(6) or (b)(9) (as applicable depending on whether a Form W-8 or documentary evidence was collected from the account holder). For a payment subject to withholding under Sect. 1446(a), QI must obtain a valid Form W-8 for the account holder once it knows or has reason to know that the documentation provided is unreliable or incorrect (including on account of a change in circumstances).

**(D) Curative Documentation for Hold Mail Instruction.** QI may rely on a permanent residence address subject to a hold mail instruction as an account holder's permanent residence address when the account holder provides the documentary evidence described in §1.1471-3(c)(5)(i) (without regard to the requirement in §1.1471-3(c)(5)(i) that the documentary evidence contain a permanent residence address). The documentary evidence must support the account holder's claim of foreign status, or in the case of an account holder claiming treaty benefits, the account holder's residence in the country where the account holder is claiming a reduced rate of withholding under an income tax treaty. If, after documentation is provided, an account holder's permanent residence address is subsequently subject to a hold mail instruction, the addition of the hold mail instruction is a change in circumstances under Sect. 5.10(A) of this Agreement requiring an account holder to provide the documentary evidence described in this Sect. 5.10(D) in order for QI to continue to rely on the permanent residence address.

**Sec. 5.11. Documentation Validity Period.**

**(A) Documentation Other than Form W-9.** QI may rely on valid documentary evidence obtained from account holders in accordance with applicable know-your- customer rules as long as the documentary evidence remains valid under those rules or until QI knows, or has reason to know, that the information contained in the documentary evidence is incorrect. However, for purposes of a claim of treaty benefits, QI may only rely on documentary evidence provided pursuant to §1.1441-6(c)(3) or (4) (i.e., not provided under applicable know-your-customer rules), and statements regarding entitlement to treaty benefits described in §1.1441-6(c)(5)(i) or Sect. 5.03(B) of this Agreement until their validity expires under §1.1441-1(e)(4)(ii)(A)(2). For establishing an account holder's chapter 3 status (as defined in §1.1441-1(c)(45)) or foreign status for chapter 61 purposes, QI may rely on a Form W-8 until its validity expires under §1.1441-1(e)(4)(ii) and may rely on documentary evidence (other than documentary evidence obtained pursuant to applicable know-your-customer rules) until its validity expires under §1.6049-5(c). The validity periods referenced in the preceding sentence also apply for purposes of Sects. 1446(a) and (f).

**(B) Form W-9.** QI may rely on a valid Form W-9 as long as it has not been informed by the IRS or another withholding agent that the form is unreliable or incorrect. If QI has primary Form 1099 reporting and backup withholding responsibility, it may rely on a Form W-9 unless one of the conditions of §31.3406(h)-3(e)(2)(i) through (v) applies.

**Sec. 5.12. Maintenance and Retention of Documentation.**

**(A) Maintaining Documentation.** QI shall maintain documentation by retaining the original documentation, a certified copy, a photocopy, a scanned copy, a microfiche, or other means that allow reproduction (provided that the QI has recorded receipt of the documentation and is able to produce a hard copy). For a direct account, if QI is not required to retain copies of documentary evidence under its know-your-customer rules, QI may instead retain a notation of the type of documentation reviewed, the date the documentation was reviewed, the document's identification number (if any, *e.g.*, a passport number), and whether such documentation contained any US indicia. For direct accounts opened before January 1, 2001, if QI was not required under its know- your-customer rules to maintain originals or copies of documentation, QI may rely on its account information if it has complied with all other aspects of its know-your-customer rules regarding establishment of an account holder's identity, it has a record that the documentation required under the know-your-customer rules was actually examined by an employee of QI in accordance with the know-your-customer rules, and it has no information in its possession that would require QI to treat the documentation as invalid.

**(B) Retention Period.** QI shall retain a record of the account holder's documentation obtained under this Sect. 5 for as long as the documentation is relevant to the determination of QI's tax liability or reporting responsibilities under Sects. 871, 881, 1461, 1474(a), and 3406.

**Sec. 5.13. Application of Presumption Rules.**

**(A) In General.** QI shall apply the presumption rules of Sect. 5.13(C) of this Agreement if QI cannot reliably associate a payment with valid documentation from an account holder. The presumption rules cannot be used to grant a reduced rate of withholding. For example, the portfolio interest exception of Sects. 871(h) and 881(c) shall not apply to a person that is presumed to be foreign. Further, QI must apply the presumption rules when required and may not rely on its actual knowledge regarding an account holder's chapter 4 status or status as a US or foreign person to apply a reduced rate of withholding. Failure to follow the presumption rules may result in liability for underwithholding, penalties, and interest. Notwithstanding the preceding sentences, QI must rely on its actual knowledge regarding an account holder rather than what is presumed if, based on such knowledge, it should withhold an amount greater than the withholding rate under the presumption rules or it should report on Form 1042-S or Form 1099 an amount that would otherwise not be reported.

**(B) Reliably Associating a Payment with Documentation.** Generally, QI can reliably associate a payment with documentation if, for that payment, it holds valid documentation from the account holder; it can reliably determine how much of the payment relates to the valid documentation provided by such account holder; and it has no actual knowledge or reason to know that any of the information, certifications, or statements in or associated with the documentation are incorrect. See §1.1441-1(b)(2)(vii) or, for a withholdable payment, §1.1471-3(c) for rules regarding when a payment can be reliably associated with documentation. See also §1.1471-3(e)(4)(vi)(B) for when a QI that is an FFI may rely on documentation and information permitted in an applicable IGA to document an account holder's chapter 4 status. For documentation reliance rules for purposes of Sects. 1446(a) and (f), see §§1.1446-1(c)(2)(iii) and 1.1446(f)-4(b). Sections 5.13(B)(1) through (7) of this Agreement describe when a payment is reliably associated with documentation if the payment is made to an account holder that is an intermediary or flow-through entity (other than a nonparticipating FFI that is not acting on behalf of exempt beneficial owners or that is paid an amount realised).

(1) **Reliably Associating a Payment with Documentation Provided by a Nonqualified Intermediary or Flow-Through Entity.** Generally, QI can reliably associate a payment with documentation provided by a nonqualified intermediary or flow-through entity if it can reliably associate the payment with a valid Form W-8IMY provided by the nonqualified intermediary or flow-through entity, and it can determine the portion of the payment that relates to valid documentation associated with the Form W-8IMY for an account holder or interest holder of the nonqualified intermediary or flow- through entity that is not itself a nonqualified intermediary or flow-through entity; and the nonqualified intermediary or flow-through entity provides sufficient information for QI to report the payments on Form 1042-S, Form 1099, or Form 8966 if reporting is required.

If the payment is a withholdable payment, the Form W-8IMY must provide the nonqualified intermediary's or flow-through entity's chapter 4 status to the extent required for chapter 4 purposes. In lieu of the nonqualified intermediary or flow-through entity providing documentation for an account holder that is subject to chapter 4 withholding, QI can reliably associate a withholdable payment with valid documentation associated with the Form W-8IMY from the nonqualified intermediary or flow-through entity if it can determine the portion of the payment allocable to a chapter 4 withholding rate pool (to the extent permissible under §1.1471-3(c)(3)(iii)(B)).

If the payment is a reportable amount, QI can reliably associate such payment with documentation provided by a nonqualified intermediary or a flow-through entity that is a participating FFI or registered deemed-compliant FFI if, in lieu of providing documentation for its account holders that are US persons, such nonqualified intermediary or flow-through entity allocates the payment to a chapter 4 withholding rate pool of US payees and also certifies on a valid Form W-8IMY that it meets the requirements of §1.6049-4(c)(4)(iii) with respect to any account holder of an account it maintains within the meaning of §1.1471-5(d)(5) (*i.e.*, a direct account holder) that receives a payment included in this pool or allocates a payment that is a withholdable payment to a chapter 4 withholding rate pool of recalcitrant account holders.

Notwithstanding the preceding sentences in this Sect. 5.13(B)(1), to the extent a payment is not subject to reporting on Form 1042-S, Form 1099, or Form 8966, QI can reliably associate the payment with documentation if it can determine the portion of the payment that is allocable to a group of account holders for whom QI holds valid documentation (other than nonqualified intermediaries or flow-through entities) for112 whom withholding and reporting is not required. For example, QI can treat a payment of short term OID allocable to a group of documented foreign account holders as reliably associated with valid documentation. Further, if the documentation attached to a nonqualified intermediary's or flow-through entity's Form W-8IMY is documentation from another nonqualified intermediary or flow-through entity, then QI must apply the rules of this paragraph to that other nonqualified intermediary or flow-through entity.

With respect to a payment of an amount realised from the sale of a PTP interest, QI can reliably associate the payment with documentation when QI can reliably associate the payment with a valid Form W-8IMY provided by a flow-through entity except for a trust that is a simple trust (for which a valid Form W-8BEN-E may instead be provided). Additionally, QI can reliably associate the payment with documentation to permit a modified amount realised paid to a foreign partnership to the extent that QI can reliably associate the payment with a valid Form W-8IMY provided by the partnership that includes the certification for a modified amount realised and the partnership provides valid documentation for each partner allocated an amount of gain (if any) arising from the sale. For a payment of an amount realised made to a grantor trust, QI can reliably associate the payment with documentation when it can reliably associate the payment with a valid Form W-8IMY from the trust indicating its status as a foreign grantor trust (or similar document from a US trust) and can determine the percentage of the amount realised that is associated with valid documentation provided by each grantor or owner of the trust.

With respect to QI's payment of an amount realised from the sale of a PTP interest made to a nonqualified intermediary, QI cannot reliably associate the payment with documentation regardless of whether a valid Form W-8IMY is provided by the nonqualified intermediary together with valid documentation for its account holders that QI can associate with the payment. See Sect. 8.02(N) of this Agreement, however, for when a QI may rely on account holder documentation provided by a nonqualified intermediary for purposes of reporting under Sect. 8 of this Agreement.

With respect to a PTP distribution QI pays to a nonqualified intermediary, QI can reliably associate the distribution with documentation when QI can reliably associate the payment with a valid Form W-8IMY provided by the nonqualified intermediary (including its chapter 4 status for an amount of a distribution attributable to a withholdable payment) and can determine the portion of each amount subject to withholding on the distribution (as determined under Sect. 3.01(C)(2) of this Agreement) that is associated with valid documentation for each partner or beneficial owner with respect to the distribution that is an account holder of the nonqualified intermediary (as applicable, depending on the amount subject to withholding on the distribution and taking into account the preceding paragraph of this Sect. 5.13(B)(1) for an amount realised on the distribution).

With respect to a PTP distribution QI pays to a flow-through entity, QI can reliably associate the distribution with documentation to the extent it reliably associates with documentation each amount subject to withholding on the distribution as follows—

**(i)** For an amount subject to withholding under Sect. 1446(a), QI can determine the portion of the amount associated with—

**(a)** A valid Form W-8IMY from a partnership and, for a partnership other than a PTP, when QI can determine the amount associated with valid documentation provided by each of the partners of the partnership;

**(b)** A valid Form W-8BEN-E or Form W-8IMY from a simple trust; or

**(c)** A valid Form W-8IMY from a trust that identifies itself as a foreign grantor trust (or similar document from a US grantor trust), when QI can associate the portion of the amount with valid documentation provided by each grantor or owner of the trust.

**(ii)** For an amount subject to withholding under chapter 3 or 4 that QI can determine is reliably associated with a valid Form W-8IMY provided by the flow-through entity (which includes the entity's chapter 4 status with respect to an amount of a distribution attributable to a withholdable payment) and the portion of the amount

associated with valid documentation provided by each interest holder in the flow-through entity other than an intermediary or flow-through entity.

**(iii)** For an amount realised that QI can determine is reliably associated with valid documentation provided by the flow-through entity and the portion of the amount associated with an interest holder in the entity to the extent specified in this Sect. 5.13(B)(1) for an amount realised paid to a flow-through entity.

**(2) Reliably Associating a Payment with a Withholding Certificate Provided by Another QI that Does not Assume Primary Chapters 3 and 4 Withholding or Primary Form 1099 Reporting and Backup Withholding Responsibility.** Generally, QI can reliably associate a payment with documentation provided by another QI that does not assume either primary chapters 3 and 4 withholding responsibility or primary Form 1099 reporting and backup withholding responsibility if it can reliably associate the payment with a valid Form W-8IMY and, if the form is associated with a withholdable payment, it includes the QI's chapter 4 status to the extent required for chapter 4 purposes. Additionally, the Form W-8IMY must be associated with a withholding statement that allocates the withholdable payment among the chapter 4 withholding rate pools (to the extent permissible under §1.1471-3(c)(3)(iii)(B)), and with respect to a payment of an amount subject to chapter 3 withholding that is either not a withholdable payment or a withholdable payment for which no chapter 4 withholding is required, that allocates such payment among chapter 3 withholding rate pools for foreign account holders as described in Sect. 6.03(C) of this Agreement.

If the payment is a reportable amount, QI can reliably associate the payment with documentation provided by another QI if the withholding statement allocates the payment to withholding rate pools attributable to US non-exempt recipients and the documentation includes a valid Form W-9 for each US non-exempt recipient account holder for which the other QI is required to report on Form 1099 and, if required, backup withhold. QI can also reliably associate a reportable amount with valid documentation provided by another QI that is a participating FFI or registered deemed-compliant FFI if, in lieu of providing documentation for each US non-exempt recipient account holder, the QI allocates the payment to a chapter 4 withholding rate pool of US payees and provides the applicable certification(s) on a valid Form W-8IMY for allocating the payment to this pool or allocates a payment that is a withholdable payment to a chapter 4 withholding rate pool of recalcitrant account holders. Notwithstanding the preceding sentences in this Sect. 5.13(B)(2), the presumption rules shall not apply if a payment cannot be allocated to each US non-exempt recipient account holder or to a chapter 4 withholding rate pool of US payees to the extent the alternative procedures of section 6.03(D) of this Agreement apply.

**(3) Reliably Associating a Payment with Documentation Provided by a QI that Assumes Primary Chapters 3 and 4 Withholding Responsibility and Does not Assume Primary Form 1099 Reporting and Backup Withholding Responsibility.** Generally, QI can reliably associate a payment with valid documentation provided by another QI that assumes primary chapters 3 and 4 withholding responsibility, but not primary Form 1099 reporting and backup withholding responsibility, if it can associate the payment with a valid Form W-8IMY from the QI and, if the form is associated with a withholdable payment, it includes the QI's chapter 4 status to the extent required for chapter 4 purposes. Additionally, the Form W-8IMY must be associated with a withholding statement that allocates a payment that is a withholdable payment or an amount subject to chapter 3 withholding that is not a withholdable payment among a single withholding rate pool for all account holders with respect to which the QI assumes primary chapters 3 and 4 withholding responsibility.

If the payment is a reportable amount, QI can reliably associate the payment with documentation provided by another QI if the withholding statement allocates the payment to withholding rate pools attributable to each US non-exempt recipient, as described in Sect. 6.03(D), and the documentation includes a valid Form W-9 for each US non-exempt recipient account holder for which the other QI is required to report on Form 1099 and, if required, backup withhold. QI can also reliably associate such payment with valid documentation provided by another QI that is a participating FFI or registered deemed-compliant FFI if, in lieu of providing documentation for each US non-exempt recipient account holder, the QI allocates the payment made to the US non-exempt recipient to a chapter 4 withholding rate pool of US payees and provides the applicable certifications on a valid Form W-8IMY for allocating the payment to this pool or allocates a payment that is a withholdable payment to a chapter 4 withholding rate pool of recalcitrant account holders. Notwithstanding the preceding sentences in this Sect. 5.13(B)(3), the presumption rules shall not apply if a payment cannot be allocated to each US non-exempt recipient account holder or to a chapter 4 withholding rate pool of US payees to the extent the alternative procedures of Sect. 6.03(D) of this Agreement apply.115

**(4) Reliably Associating a Payment with Documentation Provided by a QI that Assumes Primary Form 1099 Reporting and Backup Withholding Responsibility.** Generally, QI can reliably associate a payment with valid documentation provided by another QI that assumes primary Form 1099 reporting and backup withholding responsibility, but not primary chapters 3 and 4 withholding responsibility, to the extent it can associate the payment with a valid Form W-8IMY from the QI that, if the payment is a withholdable payment, includes the QI's chapter 4 status to the extent required for chapter 4 purposes. Additionally, the Form W-8IMY must be associated with a withholding statement that allocates a payment that is a withholdable payment among chapter 4 withholding rate pools (other than a pool of US payees and to the extent permissible under §1.1471-3(c)(3)(iii)(B)) and, with respect to a payment that is an amount subject to chapter 3 withholding but is either not a withholdable payment or a withholdable payment for which no chapter 4 withholding is required, allocates the payment among chapter 3 withholding rate pools for foreign account holders as described in Sect. 6.03(C) of this Agreement, and identifies the portion of the payment for which QI assumes primary Form 1099 reporting and backup withholding responsibility.

**(5) Reliably Associating a Payment with Documentation Provided by a QI that Assumes Both Primary Chapters 3 and 4 Withholding Responsibility and Primary Form 1099 Reporting and Backup Withholding Responsibility.** Generally, QI can reliably associate a payment with valid documentation provided by another QI that assumes both primary chapters 3 and 4 withholding responsibility and primary Form 1099 reporting and backup withholding responsibility if QI can associate the payment with a valid Form W-8IMY from the QI that, if the payment is a withholdable payment, includes the QI's chapter 4 status. Additionally, the Form W-8IMY must also designate the accounts for which the other QI is acting as a QI and is assuming primary chapters 3 and 4 withholding and primary Form 1099 reporting and backup withholding responsibility. If the other QI is acting as a QDD, the Form W-8IMY (or withholding statement) must also designate those accounts (1) for which the QDD is receiving payments with respect to potential Sect. 871(m) transactions or underlying securities as a QDD, (2) for which the QDD is receiving payments with respect to potential Sect. 871(m) transactions (and that are not also underlying securities) for which withholding is not required, and (3) for which the QDD is receiving payments with respect to underlying securities for which withholding is required. The QDD's Form W-8IMY must also (1) for calendar years 2023 and 2024, identify the dividends that are received by the QDD that year in its equity derivatives dealer capacity (which may be done by designating one or more accounts, if the only dividends that can be received by those accounts are in the QDD's equity derivatives dealer capacity) and (2) if the QDD is a partnership or branch of a partnership, provide valid documentation or withholding rate pool information with respect to the QDD's partners to the extent required under Sect. 5.07(E) of this Agreement. If the other QI is acting as a QDD, the Form W-8IMY (or withholding statement) must also identify the home office or branch acting as a QDD that is receiving the payment. If the QI receiving a payment assumes both primary chapters 3 and 4 withholding responsibility and primary Form 1099 reporting and backup withholding responsibility for substitute interest payments as described in Sect. 3.03(A), the Form W-8IMY must indicate that the QI is assuming primary withholding responsibility for all such payments.

**(6) Reliably Associating a Payment with Documentation Provided by a QI that Assumes Primary Withholding Responsibility for a PTP Distribution or Amount Realised from the Sale of a PTP Interest.** QI can reliably associate with documentation a payment of a PTP distribution or amount realised from the sale of a PTP interest made to another QI that assumes withholding responsibility for the payment when QI can reliably associate the payment with a valid Form W-8IMY provided by the QI that indicates that the QI assumes primary responsibility for the amount realised or PTP distribution.

**(7) Reliably Associating a Payment with Documentation Provided by a QI that Does not Assume Primary Withholding Responsibility for a PTP Distribution or Amount Realised from the Sale of a PTP Interest.** QI can reliably associate with documentation a payment of an amount realised from the sale of a PTP interest made to a QI that does not assume primary withholding responsibility for the payment when QI reliably associates the payment with a valid Form W-8IMY provided by the other QI and can determine the portion of the payment associated with a valid Form W-9 for a US partner (or a chapter 4 withholding rate pool of US payees when permitted under chapter 4) and, with respect to other partners, either withholding rate pools, as described in Sect. 6.03(C) of this Agreement or, for a disclosing QI, when QI can determine the portion of the payment that is associated with valid documentation for each of the account holders of the disclosing QI not includible in a chapter 4 withholding rate pool of US payees under chapter 4. QI can reliably associate with documentation a payment of a PTP distribution made to another QI that does not assume primary withholding responsibility for the payment when QI can reliably associate the payment with a valid Form W-8IMY provided by the QI and can determine the portion of the distribution associated with withholding rate pools, as described in Sect. 6.03(C) of this Agreement, or a valid Form W-9 for a US partner, or, for a disclosing QI, when QI can determine the portion of each amount subject to withholding on the distribution that is associated with valid documentation for each of the account holders of the disclosing QI as described in Sect. 5.07(D) of this Agreement.

**(C) Presumption Rules.** With respect to a withholdable payment made to a foreign entity, if QI is an NFFE, it must follow the presumption rules of §1.1471-3(f) when it cannot reliably associate a withholdable payment with valid documentation. With respect to a payment that is an amount subject to chapter 3 withholding that is either not a withholdable payment or a withholdable payment for which no chapter 4 withholding is required, the presumption rules are the rules under §1.1441-1(b)(3) that a withholding agent must follow to determine the status of a beneficial owner (*i.e.*, as a US person or foreign person and as an individual or entity (and the entity's classification)) when it cannot reliably associate a payment with valid documentation. With respect to a reportable payment (including a withholdable payment made to an entity) that is not an amount subject to chapter 3 withholding, the presumption rules are the rules of §1.6049-5(d) that a payor must follow to determine the status of a payee (*e.g.*, as a non-exempt recipient) when it cannot reliably associate a payment with valid documentation. The presumption rules are as follows:

**(1) Certain Withholdable Payments Made with Respect to an Offshore Obligation.** A withholdable payment paid outside of the United States as defined under §1.6049-5(e) with respect to an offshore obligation (as defined in §1.1471-1(b)(88)) that is made to an entity is presumed made to a nonparticipating FFI for purposes of chapter 4. A withholdable payment that is not an amount subject to chapter 3 withholding, that is paid outside the US with respect to an offshore obligation, and that is treated as made to a payee that is an individual is presumed made to a US person when the payee has any of the indicia of US status that are described in §1.1441-7(b)(5). If QI is a participating FFI or registered deemed-compliant FFI (other than a reporting Model 1 FFI), see the rules under its FATCA requirements as a participating FFI or registered deemed-compliant FFI for classifying account holders as recalcitrant account holders. If QI is an FFI, see also Sect. 8.06 of this Agreement for whether QI is required to report such payments on Form 1099.

**(2) Amounts Subject to Withholding under Chapter 3 that are Paid with Respect to an Offshore Obligation.** An amount that is subject to chapter 3 withholding that is not a withholdable payment is presumed made to an undocumented foreign account holder if the payment is made outside of the United States with respect to an offshore obligation. If QI is an NFFE or an FFI that is not required to withhold on recalcitrant account holders pursuant to the terms of an applicable Model 1 or Model 2 IGA, an amount subject to chapter 3 withholding that is a withholdable payment and that is treated as made to a payee that is an individual is also presumed made to an undocumented foreign account holder if the payment is made outside of the United States with respect to an offshore obligation. QI must treat an amount described in this Sect. 5.13(C)(2) as subject to withholding under chapter 3 at a rate of 30 per cent on the gross amount of the payment and must report the payment as made to an unknown recipient on Form 1042-S.

**(3) Payments on Certain Short-Term Obligations and Bank Deposit Interest.** An amount of US source original issue discount on the redemption of a short-term obligation or US source bank deposit interest not subject to chapter 4 withholding is presumed made to an undocumented US non-exempt recipient account holder regardless of whether paid to an individual or entity. QI must report an amount described in this Sect. 5.13(C)(3) on Form 1099. QI must backup withhold and report such amounts on Form 1099 unless it provides sufficient information to another payor from which it receives such amounts to backup withhold and report the payments and QI does not know that the other payor has failed to backup withhold or report.118

**(4) Foreign Source Income, Broker Proceeds, and Certain Other Amounts Made with Respect to an Offshore Obligation.** A payment of an amount that is not a withholdable payment and is not an amount subject to chapter 3 withholding (other than payments of short-term OID and bank deposit interest described in Sect. 5.13(C) of this Agreement) that is paid outside the United States with respect to an offshore obligation and that is made to a payee that is an individual is presumed made to a US non-exempt recipient when the payee has any of the indicia of US status that are described in Sect. 5.10(B) of this Agreement. If the payment is made to a payee that is an entity, QI must apply the principles of §1.1441-1(b)(3)(ii), §1.1441-5(d)(2), or §1.1441-5(e)(6) (as applicable) without regard to §1.1441-1(b)(3)(ii)(D) for purposes of this paragraph 5.13(C)(4). For a payment of gross proceeds for which QI is a broker under §1.6045-1, similar rules apply to a payment made with respect to a sale that is effected at an office outside the United States under §1.6045-1(g)(1)(ii). QI must report an amount described in this Sect. 5.13(C)(3) as paid to a presumed US non-exempt recipient on Form 1099 to the extent required under Sect. 8.06 of this Agreement.

Backup withholding shall not be required, however, if the exception provided in §31.3406(g)-1(e) applies.

**(5) Other Payments.** For any payment not covered in Sects. 5.13(C)(1), (2), (3), or (4) of this Agreement, see the presumption rules provided in §1.1441-1(b)(3) or §1.6049-5(d)(2) (as applicable). In the case of a payment of an amount realised, an account holder that is the partner or a broker receiving the payment shall be presumed a foreign person for which a reduced rate of withholding under Sect. 1446(f) shall not apply. See, however, §1.1446(f)-4(b)(4) in the case of an amount realised for which withholding under Sect. 3406 is required. In the case of an amount subject to withholding under Sect. 1446(a) on a PTP distribution, an account holder that is a partner in the PTP receiving the distribution shall be presumed a foreign person, with the rate of withholding based on the status of the partner (as an individual or corporation) as determined under §1.1446-1(c)(3), or as otherwise determined under §1.1446-4(d)(1)(iii) (when applicable).

**Section 6. Qualified Intermediary Withholding Certificate and Disclosure of Account Holders to Withholding Agent**

**Sec. 6.01. Qualified Intermediary Withholding Certificate.** QI agrees to furnish a qualified intermediary withholding certificate to each withholding agent from which it receives a reportable amount as a QI or to each withholding agent or broker from which QI receives a PTP distribution or amount realised from the sale of a PTP interest (including when QI acts as a disclosing QI for the distribution or amount realised). The qualified intermediary withholding certificate is a Form W-8IMY (or acceptable substitute form) that certifies that QI is acting as a QI, contains QI's QI-EIN, and provides all other information required by the form. If QI receives a withholdable payment (including on a PTP distribution), QI must certify to its chapter 4 status and provide its GIIN (if applicable). QI must also certify its chapter 4 status as a participating FFI or registered deemed-compliant FFI when QI provides a Form W-8IMY that certifies that it meets the requirements of §1.6049-4(c)(4)(iii) with respect to any account holder of an account it maintains that is included in a chapter 4 withholding rate pool of US payees on QI's withholding statement for a payment subject to withholding under chapter 3 or 4 or an amount realised from the sale of a PTP interest.

If QI is acting as a QSL for a substitute dividend payment, QI must also certify that it is acting as a qualified securities lender and provide all other information required by Form W-8IMY.

If QI is acting as a QDD for payments with respect to potential Sect. 871(m) transactions or underlying securities, it must certify that it is acting as a QDD for those payments and assumes primary chapters 3 and 4 withholding responsibility and primary Form 1099 reporting and backup withholding responsibility for any payments with respect to potential Sect. 871(m) transactions that it makes as required by this Agreement, and it must provide all other information required by Form W-8IMY with respect to the certification.

If QI is acting with respect to payments of substitute interest as described in Sect. 3.03(A) of this Agreement, it must certify that it is assuming primary chapters 3 and 4 withholding responsibility and primary Form 1099 reporting and backup withholding responsibility for all such payments, in addition to the other certifications it makes and information it provides as a QI as required by this Agreement. Except as otherwise provided in Sect. 6.02 of this Agreement, QI also agrees to furnish each withholding agent to whom it provides a Form W-8IMY with the withholding statement described in Sect. 6.02 of this Agreement. QI is not required to disclose, as part of its Form W-8IMY or its withholding statement, any information regarding the identity of a direct or indirect account holder that is a foreign person or a US exempt recipient or a holder of a US account except when acting as a disclosing QI. To the extent QI does not assume primary Form 1099 reporting and backup withholding responsibility under Sect. 3.04 of this Agreement or is not excepted from reporting under Sect. 8.06 of this Agreement, for each US non-exempt recipient account holder on whose behalf QI receives a reportable amount, QI must provide to a withholding agent the Form W-9, or if any such account holder has not provided a Form W-9, the name, address, and US TIN (if available).

**Sec. 6.02. Withholding Statement.**

**(A) In General.** QI agrees to provide to each withholding agent from which QI receives reportable amounts as a QI a withholding statement described in this Sect. 6.02 and §1.1441-1(e)(3)(iv). A withholding statement shall not be provided to a withholding agent if QI assumes both primary chapters 3 and 4 withholding responsibility and primary Form 1099 reporting and backup withholding responsibility for all of its accounts for which QI receives reportable amounts as a QI, unless QI is acting as a QDD. The withholding statement forms an integral part of the Form W-8IMY. The withholding statement shall be updated as often as necessary for the withholding agent to meet its reporting and withholding obligations under chapters 3,4, and 61 and Sect. 3406. For120 a payment received by QI of a PTP distribution or an amount realised from the sale of a PTP interest, QI agrees to provide a withholding statement described in this Sect. 6.02 unless QI assumes primary withholding responsibility for the payment.

**(B) Content of Withholding Statement.** The withholding statement must contain sufficient information for a withholding agent to apply the correct rate of withholding on payments allocable to the accounts identified on the statement and to properly report such payments on Forms 1042-S and Forms 1099, as applicable. The withholding statement must—

**(1)** Designate those accounts for which QI acts as a QI;

**(2)** Designate those accounts for which QI assumes primary chapters 3 and 4 withholding responsibility or primary Form 1099 reporting and backup withholding responsibility (including accounts for which QI is acting with respect to payments of US source substitute interest (as described in Sect. 3.03(A) of this Agreement));

**(3)** If QI is acting as a QDD, designate the accounts (1) for which the QDD is receiving payments with respect to potential Sect. 871(m) transactions or underlying securities as a QDD, (2) for which the QDD is receiving payments with respect to potential Sect. 871(m) transactions (and that are not underlying securities) for which withholding is not required, and (3) for which QDD is receiving payments with respect to underlying securities for which withholding is required, and, if applicable, identifying the home office or branch that is treated as the owner for US income tax purposes. In addition, for calendar years 2023 and 2024, the withholding statement must identify the dividends that it receives in its equity derivatives dealer capacity (which may be done by designating one or more accounts, if the only dividends that can be received by those accounts are in the QDD's equity derivatives dealer capacity). Also, for a QDD that is a partnership or a branch of a partnership, the withholding statement must, for a payment of an amount under Sect. 3.09 of this Agreement (as modified for a QDD that is a partnership or branch of a partnership), include withholding rate pool information to the extent permitted in Sect. 6.03 of this Agreement for an account holder, or specific partner information, with respect to its partners receiving the amount (looking through partners that are foreign flow-through entities). The requirement to include the partner information specified in the preceding sentence does not apply to a payment described in Sects. 3.03(A)(1)-(3) of this Agreement.

**(4)** If applicable, designate the accounts for which QI is acting as a QSL with respect to any US source substitute dividend payments received from the withholding agent;

**(5)** Designate those accounts for which QI assumes primary withholding responsibility for a payment of a PTP distribution or an amount realised from the sale of a PTP interest; and

**(6)** Provide information regarding withholding rate pools, as described in Sect. 6.03 of this Agreement, when necessary, except that Sect. 6.03(C) of this Agreement shall not apply when QI acts as a disclosing QI for a payment (including for an amount subject to chapter 3 or 4 withholding on a PTP distribution), and references to a chapter 4 withholding rate pool of US payees in Sect. 6.03(B) of this Agreement shall not apply to an amount subject to withholding under Sect. 1446(a) on a PTP distribution. See also Sect. 2.91(E) of this Agreement for a disclosing QI's requirement to provide specific payee information on a withholding statement for a PTP distribution or amount realised from the sale of a PTP interest.

**Sec. 6.03. Chapters 3 and 4 Withholding Rate Pools.**

**(A) In General.** QI shall provide as part of its withholding statement withholding rate pool information in a manner sufficient for the withholding agent to meet its chapters 3 and 4 and backup withholding responsibilities and its Form 1042-S and Form 1099 reporting responsibilities. QI's requirement for its withholding statement described in the preceding sentence also applies to a withholding statement QI provides to the withholding agent or broker for a payment of a PTP distribution or amount realised from the sale of a PTP interest. Additionally, for a PTP distribution, the withholding rate pool information provided by QI on its withholding statement must take into account each amount subject to withholding on the distribution as determined by the withholding agent that pays the distribution to QI.

**(B) Chapter 4 Withholding Rate Pools.** If QI receives a withholdable payment on behalf of its account holders, QI may allocate the payment to a chapter 4 withholding rate pool. A chapter 4 withholding rate pool is a payment of a single type of income (*e.g.*, interest or dividends) that is allocated to payees that are nonparticipating FFIs. If QI is a participating FFI or registered deemed-compliant FFI (other than reporting Model 1 FFI), it may also allocate a withholdable payment to a chapter 4 withholding rate pool of recalcitrant account holders (if applicable). If QI is a participating FFI or registered deemed-compliant FFI receiving a reportable amount that is excepted from reporting under Sect. 8.06(A) of this Agreement (excluding Sects. 8.06(A)(2) and (A)(3) of this Agreement when the payment is subject to chapter 4 withholding and Sect. 8.06(A)(4) of this Agreement), QI may allocate the payment to a chapter 4 withholding rate pool of US payees. See Sect. 6.03(D) of this Agreement for the alternative procedures that may be used in this case. Except as otherwise provided in this Sect. 6.03(B), if QI receives a withholdable payment, QI must provide the information required under §1.1471-3(c)(3)(iii)(B)(2). Further, if QI elects under its FATCA requirements as a participating FFI or registered deemed-compliant FFI to backup withhold instead of withholding under chapter 4 with respect to certain recalcitrant account holders, QI's withholding statement must indicate the portion of such payment subject to backup withholding under Sect. 3406 that is allocated to such account holders and must provide all other information relating to such account holders that is required under chapter 61 for the withholding agent to report with respect to the payment.

If QI has an account holder that is another intermediary (whether a QI, NQI, or PAI) or a flow-through entity, QI may combine the account holder information provided by the intermediary or flow-through entity with QI's direct account holder information to determine the amounts allocable to each of QI's chapter 4 withholding rate pools described in this Sect. 6.03(B). If QI is an NFFE that has an account holder that is another intermediary or flow-through entity that is a participating FFI or registered deemed-compliant FFI, QI may provide the account holder's chapter 4 withholding rate pools of recalcitrant account holders and US payees to the extent applicable.

**(C) Chapter 3 Withholding Rate Pools.** With respect to any portion of the payment that is attributable to payees for which no chapter 4 withholding is required, a chapter 3 withholding rate pool is a payment of a single type of income, determined in accordance with the categories of income reported on Form 1042-S, that is subject to a single rate of withholding (*e.g.*, 0%, 10%, 15%, 30%, or 37%) and a single chapter 4 exemption code. QI shall determine chapter 3 withholding rate pools based on valid documentation obtained under Sect. 5 of this Agreement or, if a payment cannot be reliably associated with valid documentation, on the presumption rules of Sect. 5.13(C) of this Agreement. If QI has an account holder that is another intermediary (whether a QI, NQI, or PAI) or a flow-through entity (other than a nonparticipating FFI that is not acting on behalf of any exempt beneficial owners), QI may combine the account holder information provided by the intermediary or flow-through entity with QI's direct account holder information to determine the amounts allocable to each of QI's chapter 3 withholding rate pools with respect to the portion of the payment allocable to an account holder to which chapter 4 withholding does not apply. For a payment of an amount realised, however, QI may combine its account holder information with the account holder information provided by an intermediary only if the intermediary is a QI other than a disclosing QI.

**(D) US Non-Exempt Recipients Subject to Backup Withholding or Form 1099 Reporting and Alternative Procedures for Allocating**

**Payments on Withholding Statements.** To the extent QI does not assume primary Form 1099 reporting and backup withholding responsibility and is not excepted from reporting on Form 1099 under Sect. 8.04 of this Agreement, QI's withholding statement must establish a separate withholding rate pool for each US non-exempt recipient account holder that QI is required to report on Form 1099 and has disclosed to the withholding agent. QI may, by mutual agreement with the withholding agent, establish a single withholding rate pool (not subject to backup withholding) for all US non-exempt recipient account holders for whom QI is required to report on Form 1099 and has provided Forms W-9 before the withholding agent paying any reportable amounts or, if applicable, designated broker proceeds to which backup withholding does not apply. QI must establish a separate withholding rate pool for all US non-exempt recipient account holders subject to backup withholding before the withholding agent paying any reportable amounts or, if applicable, designated broker proceeds. Alternatively, QI may include US non-exempt recipients in a zero-rate withholding pool that includes US exempt recipients and foreign persons for which no withholding is required under chapters 3 and 4 and Sect. 3406 and may include payments allocated to a chapter 4 withholding rate pool of US payees in this pool to the extent permitted to be provided by QI under Sect. 6.03(B) of this Agreement. If QI chooses the alternative procedure of this paragraph, QI must provide sufficient information to the withholding agent no later than January 15 of the year following the year in which the reportable amounts and designated broker proceeds, if applicable, are paid in order to allocate to each US non-exempt recipient account holder or to a chapter 4 withholding rate pool of US payees (when applicable). Failure to provide such information will result in the application of penalties to QI under Sects. 6721 and 6722 and shall constitute an event of default under Sect. 11.06 of this Agreement.

**Section 7. Tax Return Obligations**
**Sec. 7.01. Form 1042 (or Other Tax Return) Filing Requirement.**

**(A) In General.** QI shall file a return on Form 1042, whether or not QI withheld any amounts under chapter 3 or 4, on or before March 15 of the year following any calendar year in which QI acts as a QI and makes a payment of an amount subject to chapter 3 or 4 withholding. A separate Form 1042 must be filed by each legal entity that is a QI covered by this Agreement in accordance with the instructions to Form 1042 (including to the extent of any requirement to reconcile amounts reported on Form 1042 with amounts reported on Forms 1042-S). Form 1042 shall be filed at the address indicated on the form, at the address at which the IRS notifies QI to file the return, or in accordance with the instructions to file Form 1042 electronically. In addition to the information specifically requested on Form 1042 and the accompanying instructions, if QI made any overwithholding or underwithholding adjustments under §§1.1461-2 and 1.1474-2 and Sects. 9.02 and 9.05 of this Agreement, QI must attach a statement setting forth the amounts of any overwithholding or underwithholding adjustments and an explanation of the circumstances that resulted in the overwithholding or underwithholding.

**(B) Extensions for Filing Returns.** QI may request an extension of the time for filing Form 1042, or any of the information required to be attached to the form, by submitting Form 7004, *Application for Automatic Extension of Time to File Certain Business Income Tax, Information, and Other Returns*, on or before the due date of the return.

**(C) QDD Tax Liability Requirements for QDDs.** In addition to its requirements under Sect. 7.01(A) of this Agreement, a QI that is acting as a QDD also must report its QDD tax liability on the appropriate US tax return (in the manner prescribed by the IRS), including separately identifying each part of the QDD tax liability described in Sect. 3.09(A) through (C) of this Agreement separately for the home office and each branch that is acting as a QDD (if applicable), and in the case of a QDD that is a partnership or branch of a partnership, taking into account the modifications in Sect. 3.09 and separately stating the withholding associated with any of the QDD tax liability amounts). For QDDs that are foreign corporations or branches of foreign corporations, the appropriate US tax return is a Form 1120-F, including all required Schedules Q. For QDDs that are partnerships or branches of partnerships, the appropriate US tax return is a Form 1065, including all required attachments and schedules, and to the extent any amount is subject to withholding with respect to a foreign partner of the QDD, Forms 1042 and 1042-S. In addition, if the QDD is a partnership or a branch of a partnership, the partnership must attach a statement to its Form 1065 for each QDD and, if the QDD has a fiscal year rather than a calendar year, a separate statement for each QDD for each portion of the fiscal year that falls within the calendar year that includes the information that would have been included on the Form 1120-F Schedule Q, in the manner specified in the instructions to the Form 1065. A QDD must also report any other information required by the appropriate return with respect to its QDD tax liability (including any part thereof). In each case, the form will be filed by the QI on behalf of its QDD(s) and the Form 1120-F or Form 1065, as applicable, must be filed whether or not the QI would be required to file the form if it were not a QDD. U.S financial institutions with a foreign branch that acts as a QDD must file the appropriate US income tax return (e.g.,

Form 1120, US Corporation Income Tax Return) for the tax year covered by this Agreement to report and pay its tax liability under chapter 1 and will not have a separate QDD tax liability. Similarly, any United States person that is an individual or a corporation and a direct or indirect partner of a QI partnership that is or has a QDD must report and pay its tax liability under chapter 1 and would not have a separate QDD tax liability for the amounts from the QDD. A QDD must also maintain, and make available to the IRS upon request, a reconciliation schedule that tracks across calendar years the Sect. 871(m) amount for each dividend with respect to each underlying security referenced by a potential Sect. 871(m) transaction separately for the home office and each branch that is a QDD (if applicable). The reconciliation schedule must separately state total amounts received as a QDD, as well as the dividends received in its equity derivatives dealer capacity and the Sect. 881 tax paid on those amounts (or in the case of a QI that is a partnership, the withholding by the partnership on its partners for those amounts and the reporting of the amounts to its partners), the amount of dividends that were effectively connected with the conduct of a trade or business in the United States, the amount of stock owned in its equity derivatives dealer capacity that was not effectively connected with the conduct of a trade or business in the United States, the amount of dividend equivalent payments it received in its equity derivatives dealer capacity, its long positions, its short positions, its net delta for business purposes (if any), its adjustments to the net delta used for business purposes (if any, such as adjustments to exclude transactions that, for federal income tax purposes, are not treated as transactions of a QDD, do not exist, or that are effectively connected with the conduct of a trade or business in the United States), the dividend amount per share, its tax liability under Sect. 881 (or if QI is a partnership, the withholding by the partnership on its partners and the reporting of the amounts to its partners) for its Sect. 871(m) amount, its net delta exposure, and the Sect. 871(m) amount for each dividend with respect to each underlying security referenced by a potential Sect. 871(m) transaction it received as a QDD, and any adjustments thereto, for transactions in its equity derivatives dealer capacity. The reconciliation schedule may be maintained in any manner or format that permits the IRS to reconcile the amount reported by the QDD for the calendar year.125

**Sec. 7.02. Form 945 Filing Requirement.** QI shall file a return on Form 945 on or before January 31 following the calendar year in which QI backup withheld an amount under Sect. 3406. Separate Forms 945 must be filed by each legal entity that is a QI covered by this Agreement. The form must be filed at the address specified in the instructions for Form 945, at the address at which the IRS notifies QI to file the return under the provisions of Sect. 12.06 of this Agreement, or in accordance with the instructions to file Form 945 electronically.

**Sec. 7.03. Retention of Returns.** QI shall retain Forms 945 and 1042 (including, with respect to a QI acting as a QDD, its reconciliation schedule) for the applicable statute of limitations on assessment under Sect. 6501.

## Section 8. Information Reporting Obligations

**Sec. 8.01. Form 1042-S Reporting.** Except as otherwise provided in Sect. 8.02 of this Agreement, QI is not required to file Forms 1042-S for amounts paid to each separate account holder for whom such reporting would otherwise be required. Instead, QI shall file a Form 1042-S reporting the pools of income (reporting pools) as determined in Sect. 8.03 of this Agreement. QI must file its Forms 1042-S in the manner required by the regulations under chapters 3 and 4 (or in the case of a participating FFI, in the manner required under the FFI Agreement) and the instructions to the form, including any requirement to file the forms magnetically or electronically. Separate Forms 1042-S must be filed by each legal entity that is a QI covered by this Agreement. A QI acting as a QDD that also has QI activities must file separate Forms 1042-S in its QDD capacity and its QI capacity (*i.e.*, other than when acting as a QDD). Each QI covered by this Agreement may also allow its individual branches not acting as QDDs to file Forms 1042-S provided that all Forms 1042-S contain the QI-EIN of the legal entity of which the branch forms a part and, to the extent required for chapter 4 purposes, the GIIN of the branch. If QI is acting as a QDD, the home office and each branch acting as a QDD must file separate Forms 1042-S for payments made as a QDD. Any Form 1042-S required by this Sect. 8 shall be filed on or before March 15 following the calendar year in which the payment reported on the form was made. QI may request an extension of time to file Forms 1042-S by submitting Form 8809, *Application for Extension of Time to File Information Returns*, by the due date of Forms 1042-S in the manner required by (and to the extent permitted on) Form 8809. For when a payment is subject to reporting on Form 1042-S, see generally §1.1461-1(c)(2). For when an amount realised from a transfer of a PTP interest under Sect. 1446(f) or an amount subject to withholding under Sect. 1446(a) on a PTP distribution is subject to reporting on Form 1042-S, see Sect. 2.91(B) of this Agreement and §1.1461-1(c)(2)(i)(P).

**Sec. 8.02. Recipient Specific Reporting.** QI (whether or not it assumes primary withholding responsibility under Sect. 3.03 of this Agreement) is required to file separate Forms 1042-S for amounts paid to each separate account holder as described in this Sect. 8.02. QI must file separate Forms

1042-S by income code, exemption code, recipient code, chapter 3 or 4 withholding rate pool, and withholding rate. In the case of a payment to a QDD, separate Forms 1042-S must be filed for each QDD, even if a single legal entity. For when a Form 1042-S is issued to an account holder that is a US person to report withholding under Sect. 1446(a) or (f), see the instructions for Form 1042-S. In addition, in the case of a QDD that is a partnership or a branch of a partnership, separate Forms 1042-S must be filed for each of the QDD's foreign partners with respect to each partner's share of the QDD's QDD tax liability subject to withholding under Sect. 3.09 of this Agreement, as modified for a QDD that is a partnership or branch of a partnership.

**(A)** QI must file a separate Form 1042-S for each account holder that is a QI (to the extent such payment is required to be reported under §1.1461-1) WP, WT, or QSL that. receives from QI an amount subject to withholding under chapter 3 or 4 (or, in the case of a QSL, that receives a US source substitute dividend payment), regardless of whether such account holder is a direct or indirect account holder of QI.

**(B)** QI must file a separate Form 1042-S for each account holder that is a nonqualified intermediary or flow-through entity that is a participating FFI, registered deemed-compliant FFI, or registered deemed-compliant Model 1 IGA FFI and that receives an amount subject to chapter 4 withholding from QI that is allocable to each of such FFI's chapter 4 withholding rate pools of recalcitrant account holders, nonparticipating FFIs, and pool of US payees, if applicable, regardless of whether such FFI is a direct or indirect account holder of QI.

**(C)** QI must file a separate Form 1042-S for each account holder that is a nonqualified intermediary or flow-through entity that is not described in Sect. 8.02(B) of this Agreement (other than a nonparticipating FFI) that receives from QI an amount subject to chapter 4 withholding allocable to such entity's chapter 4 withholding rate pool of payees that are nonparticipating FFIs, regardless of whether such intermediary or flow-through entity is a direct or indirect account holder of QI.

**(D)** QI must file a separate Form 1042-S for each account holder of QI that is a PAI or a partnership or trust to which QI applies the agency option that receives from QI an amount subject to chapter 4 withholding allocable to such entity's chapter 4 withholding rate pool of payees that are nonparticipating FFIs or an amount subject to chapter 3 withholding that is either not a withholdable payment or a withholdable payment for which no chapter 4 withholding is required and that is allocable to such entity's chapter 3 withholding rate pools.

**(E)** QI must file a separate Form 1042-S for each unknown recipient with respect to an account holder that is a nonqualified intermediary, flow-through entity, or QI that does not assume primary chapters 3 and 4 withholding responsibility and that receives an amount subject to chapter 4 withholding from QI that QI must presume is allocable to such entity's chapter 4 withholding rate pool of payees that are nonparticipating FFIs under the presumption rule of §1.1471-3(f)(5).

**(F)** QI must file a separate Form 1042-S for each foreign account holder (or interest holder) of a nonqualified intermediary or flow-through entity that is a nonparticipating FFI that is receiving a withholdable payment on behalf of an exempt beneficial owner (regardless of whether the nonqualified intermediary or flow-through entity is a direct or indirect account holder of QI) to the extent QI can reliably associate such amounts with valid documentation from such nonqualified intermediary or flow-through entity as to the payment allocable to one or more exempt beneficial owners. In addition, QI must file separate Forms 1042-S in the same manner for each foreign account holder (or interest holder) of a nonqualified intermediary or flow-through entity that is described in the preceding sentence and that is a direct or indirect account holder (or interest holder) of a PAI of QI or a partnership or trust to which QI applies the agency option.

**(G)** QI must file separate Forms 1042-S for each foreign account holder (or interest holder) of a nonqualified intermediary or flow-through entity that is receiving an amount subject to chapter 3 withholding that is either not a withholdable payment or a withholdable payment for which no chapter 4 withholding is required to the extent QI can reliably associate such amounts with valid documentation from an account holder that is not itself a nonqualified intermediary or flow-through entity. In addition, QI must file separate Forms 1042-S in the same manner for each foreign account holder (or interest holder) of a nonqualified intermediary or flow-through entity that is described in the preceding sentence and that is a direct or indirect account holder (or interest holder) of a PAI of QI or a partnership or trust to which QI applies the agency option.

**(H)** QI must file a separate Form 1042-S for each direct account holder that is receiving a withholdable payment and that establishes its status as a passive NFFE but fails to provide the information regarding its owners as required under §1.1471-3(d)(12)(iii) (unless such information was reported by the withholding agent).

**(I)** If QI is acting as a QDD, QI must file a separate Form 1042-S for any amount subject to chapter 3 withholding with respect to a potential Sect. 871(m) transaction made to another QDD.

**(J)** If QI acts as a disclosing QI with respect to a payment of a PTP distribution or an amount subject to reporting under Sect. 1446(f) made to an account holder that is a foreign partner, QI must file a Form 1042-S to report the payment when QI knows or has reason to know that the Form 1042-S has not been filed with respect to the partner or the rate of withholding shown on the Form 1042-S is incorrect. In the case of a PTP distribution that QI must report in accordance with the preceding sentence, QI must file a separate Form 1042-S for each amount associated with the distribution by the PTP to the extent required in the instructions for Form 1042-S. Notwithstanding the preceding provisions of this Sect. 8.02(J), see Sect. 8.02(M) of this Agreement for an amount subject to reporting under Sect. 1446(f) paid to a nonqualified intermediary.

**(K)** If a QI makes a payment of a PTP distribution or an amount subject to reporting under Sect. 1446(f) to an account holder that is a QI not acting as a disclosing QI for the payment, QI must file a Form 1042-S for the other QI. If QI instead receives information on a foreign partner from a QI that is an account holder and that acts as a disclosing QI for a payment referenced in the preceding sentence, QI must file a separate Form 1042-S to report the payment when QI assumes primary withholding responsibility for the payment or knows or has reason to know that the Form 1042-Shas not been issued with respect to the foreign partner. In such a case, QI must file the Form 1042-S reporting the disclosing QI as an intermediary, with the foreign partner reported as the recipient. In the case of a payment of a PTP distribution made to a QI that acts as a disclosing QI for the distribution and that QI is required to report in accordance with this Sect. 8.02(K), QI must file a separate Form 1042-S to the extent required in the instructions to Form 1042-S. For any Form 1042-S QI files with respect to a payment made to an account holder of a disclosing QI, QI must also furnish to the disclosing QI a recipient copy of the Form 1042-S.

**(L)** If QI receives specific information on a foreign partner that is a direct account holder of a PAI that receives from QI a payment of an amount subject to withholding on a PTP distribution or an amount subject to reporting under Sect. 1446(f), QI must file a separate Form 1042-S to report each amount paid to the partner to the extent required in accordance with Sect. 8.02(K) of this Agreement for a QI that is a disclosing QI (but as applied to a PAI instead of a disclosing QI).

**(M)** If QI makes a payment of a PTP distribution to a nonqualified intermediary, QI must file a separate Form 1042-S for each foreign partner or beneficial owner of the distribution that is an account holder of the nonqualified intermediary. If QI makes a payment of an amount subject to reporting under Sect. 1446(f) to a nonqualified intermediary, QI shall file the Form 1042-S for an unknown recipient of the nonqualified intermediary, except that QI may instead file the Form 1042-S for an account holder of the nonqualified intermediary receiving the payment when—

**(1)** QI has in place an agreement with the nonqualified intermediary that QI will report (or ensures that another QI or broker will report) under Sect. 1461 with respect to the amount allocated to each of the transferors of the PTP interest (and, if required, under Sect. 6045) and that QI will provide the nonqualified intermediary a recipient copy of each Form 1042-S issued as a result of QI's reporting;

**(2)** QI can reliably associate the payment with documentation for each transferor under Sect. 5.13 of this Agreement;

**(3)** QI receives from the nonqualified intermediary the statement described in §1.6031(c)-1 T(a)(1) with respect to each partner that is an account holder of the nonqualified intermediary for which a statement under Sect. 6031(b) is required to be issued (which meets the requirements in Sect. 8.07 of this Agreement) with respect to the partner's PTP interest for the year in which the payment was made; and

**(4)** The nonqualified intermediary appoints the QI as its agent for providing the statement to the PTP (or PTP's agent). See §1.6031(c)-1 T(f).

**(N)** QI must file a separate Form 1042-S for a grantor or owner of a grantor trust for purposes of Sect. 1446(a) or (f), except when QI applies the provisions of Sect. 4.06 of this Agreement with respect to the trust.

**(O)** QI must file a separate Form 1042-S for a foreign partnership holding a PTP interest directly with QI to the extent that QI determines a modified amount realised with respect to the partnership for purposes of Sect. 1446(f), or to the extent the partnership receives a payment subject to withholding under Sect. 1446(a), when the foreign partnership is not a PTP, but excluding either case when QI applies the provisions of Sect. 4.06 of this Agreement with respect to the partnership.

**(P)** QI must file a separate Form 1042-S with respect to an account holder that requests a Form 1042-S from QI by a written request made within two full calendar years following the year in which QI made the payment for which the Form 1042-S is requested. If, however, QI filed a Form 1042-S to report a payment of an amount subject to withholding under Sect. 1446(a) on a PTP distribution or an amount subject to reporting under Sect. 1446(f) with respect to an account holder for the same calendar year for which the account holder requests a separate Form 1042-S for any payment, QI must file a separate Form 1042-S for each amount reportable on Form 1042-S that was paid to the account holder for the calendar year. A request made in a case described in the preceding sentence must be made in writing within three full calendar years following the year in which QI made the payment for which the Form 1042-S is requested. Any request by an account holder for a separate Form 1042-S referenced in this Sect. 8.02(P) requires that the account holder provide its US TIN to QI.

**Sec. 8.03. Reporting Pools for Form 1042-S Reporting.**

**(A) Chapter 4 Reporting Pools.** Except for amounts required to be reported under Sect. 8.02 of this Agreement, if QI is an FFI, QI shall report all amounts subject to chapter 4 withholding by reporting pools on a Form 1042-S if those amounts are paid to direct account holders of QI. A separate Form 1042-S shall be filed for each type of reporting pool. A chapter 4 reporting pool is a payment of a single type of income, determined in accordance with the categories of income reported on Form 1042-S, that is allocable to a chapter 4 withholding rate pool consisting of either recalcitrant account holders or payees that are nonparticipating FFIs. QI must report recalcitrant account holders in pools based upon a recalcitrant account holder's particular status described in §1.1471-4(d)(6), with a separate Form 1042-S issued for each such pool. If QI is an FFI, it may report in a chapter 4 withholding rate pool of US payees an account holder that is (or is presumed) a US person and that QI reports as a US account under its applicable FATCA requirements as a participating FFI or registered deemed-compliant FFI provided that QI is excepted from Form 1099 reporting with respect to the payment under Sect. 8.06(A)(1) of this Agreement or Sect. 8.06(A)(2) and (A)(3) of this Agreement if the payment is excepted from Form 1099 reporting, is not subject to withholding under chapter 4, and is not a PTP distribution. If QI is an NFFE, QI shall report all amounts subject to chapter 4 withholding by reporting pools on a Form 1042-S if those amounts are paid to direct account holders that are nonparticipating FFIs in a chapter 4 reporting pool of nonparticipating FFIs.

**(B) Chapter 3 Reporting Pools.** Except for amounts required to be reported under Sect. 8.02 of this Agreement or when QI acts as a disclosing QI for a payment, QI shall report an amount subject to chapter 3 withholding or withholding under Sect. 1446(a) or (f) for which no chapter 4 withholding is required and that is paid to a foreign account holder by reporting pools on a Form 1042-S if paid to a direct account holder of QI, or to a direct account holder of a PAI of QI or a partnership or trust, to the extent permitted undersection 4 of this Agreement. A separate Form 1042-S shall be filed for each type of reporting pool. A chapter 3 reporting pool is a payment of a single type of income that falls within a particular withholding rate, chapter 3 exemption code, and, if the payment is a withholdable payment, chapter 4 exemption code as determined on Form 1042-S. QI may use a single chapter 3 pool reporting code (*e.g.*, QI- withholding rate pool- general) for all reporting pools except for amounts paid to foreign tax-exempt recipients, for which a separate chapter 3 pool reporting code (*e.g.*, QI- withholding rate pool- exempt organisation) must be used. For this purpose, a foreign tax-exempt recipient includes any organisation that is not subject to chapter 3 withholding and is not liable to tax in its jurisdiction of residence because it is a charitable organisation, a pension fund, or a foreign government.

**Sec. 8.04. FATCA US Account Reporting.**

**(A) QI that is an FFI.** If QI is an FFI, QI is required to report each US account (or, in the case of an FFI that is a reporting Model 1 FFI or a registered deemed-compliant Model 1 IGA FFI, each US reportable account) that it maintains and for whom QI is acting consistent with its FATCA requirements as a participating FFI, registered deemed-compliant FFI, or registered deemed-compliant Model 1 IGA FFI. If QI is a participating FFI or registered deemed-compliant FFI (other than a reporting Model 1 FFI or registered deemed-compliant Model 1 IGA FFI), QI must report its US accounts on Form 8966 in the time and manner required under its FATCA requirements as a participating FFI or registered deemed-compliant FFI except to the extent QI is reporting under §1.1471-4(d)(5) on Form 1099 with respect to its US accounts. If QI is a reporting Model 1 FFI or registered deemed-compliant Model 1 IGA FFI, QI must report each US reportable account on Form 8966 as required under the applicable Model 1 IGA. QI cannot delegate to its withholding agent its requirements to report US accounts (or US reportable accounts) regardless of whether QI does or does not assume primary Form 1099 reporting and backup withholding responsibility under Sect. 3 of this Agreement. See Sect. 8.06 of this Agreement for when the reporting described in this Sect. 8.04 satisfies QI's Form 1099 reporting responsibilities with respect to reportable payments under chapter 61.

**(B) QI that is an NFFE.** If QI is an NFFE acting as a QI on behalf of persons other than its shareholders, QI shall file Form 8966 to report withholdable payments made to an account holder that is an NFFE (other than an excepted NFFE) with one or more substantial US owners if the NFFE is the beneficial owner of the withholdable payment received by QI. See §1.1471-1(b)(8) for the definition of beneficial owner. QI must report on Form 8966 in accordance with the form and its accompanying instructions. Such report must include the name of the NFFE that is owned by a substantial US owner; the name, address, and US TIN of each substantial US owner; the total of all withholdable payments made to the NFFE during the calendar year; and any other information as required by the form and its accompanying instructions. If QI is acting as a sponsoring entity on behalf of an NFFE for chapter 4 purposes, QI is not required to report as described in this paragraph if QI reports the NFFE as part of QI's requirements as a sponsoring entity. See §1.1472-1(c)(5)(ii) for the reporting requirements of a sponsoring entity.

**Sec. 8.05. Form 8966 Reporting for Payees that are NFFEs.** QI shall file Form 8966 to report withholdable payments made to an intermediary or flow-through entity that provides information regarding an account holder (or interest holder) that is an NFFE other than an excepted NFFE with one or more substantial US owners (or one or more controlling persons that is a specified US person under an applicable IGA). QI must report on Form 8966 in the time and manner provided in §1.1474-1(i)(2). Such report must include the name of the NFFE that is owned by a substantial US owner (or controlling person); the name, address, and US TIN of each substantial US owner; the total of all withholdable payments made to the NFFE during the calendar year (or reportable period under the applicable IGA); and any other information as required by the form and its accompanying instructions. QI is not required to report, however, to the extent permitted under §1.1474-1(i)(2) on a payment made to a participating FFI or registered deemed-compliant FFI if such information is reported pursuant to Sect. 8.04 of this Agreement or if the intermediary or flow-through entity certifies on its withholding statement that it is reporting the account holder (or interest holder) as a US account pursuant to its FATCA requirements as a participating FFI, registered deemed-compliant FFI, or registered deemed-compliant Model 1 IGA FFI.

**Sec. 8.06. Form 1099 Reporting Responsibility.** QI shall file Forms 1099 and, unless filing magnetically, Form 1096, *Annual Summary and Transmittal of US Information Returns*, for reportable payments made to persons described in this Sect. 8.06. Forms 1099 shall be filed on or before the date prescribed for the particular Form 1099 under chapter 61 and in the manner required by regulations under chapter 61 and the instructions to the forms (including the requirements for filing the forms magnetically or electronically). Extensions of the time to file Forms 1099 may be requested by submitting Form 8809 in the manner required by the form. If QI is required to file Forms 1099, it must file the appropriate form for the type of income paid (*e.g.*, Form 1099-DIV for dividends, Form 1099-INT for interest, Form 1099-B for broker proceeds). QI must file Forms 1099 to report a reportable payment other than in the situations listed in Sects. 8.06(A) and (B) of this Agreement.

**(A) Reportable Amount.** QI must file a Form 1099 in accordance with the instructions to the form for the aggregate amount of a particular type of reportable amount paid to an account holder that is (or is presumed) a US non-exempt recipient (whether a direct or indirect account holder). However, QI is not required to file a Form 1099 on a reportable amount if—

**(1)** QI is a non-US payor reporting the account holder of a US account under its FATCA requirements as a participating FFI or registered deemed-compliant FFI (including a reporting Model 1 FFI) and the other conditions of §1.6049-4(c)(4)(i) are satisfied;

**(2)** QI reports the account holder's account as held by a recalcitrant account holder or, in the case of a QI that is a reporting Model 2 FFI or nonreporting Model 2 FFI treated as registered deemed-compliant, as a non-consenting US account under its FATCA requirements as a participating FFI or registered deemed-compliant FFI and the other conditions of §1.6049-4(c)(4)(ii) are satisfied;

**(3)** QI is a non-US payor that is a reporting Model 1 FFI or registered deemed-compliant Model 1 IGA FFI and determines that the account has US indicia for which appropriate documentation sufficient to treat the account as held by a specified US person has not been provided and reports the account as a US reportable account and the other conditions of §1.6049-4(c)(4)(ii) are satisfied;

**(4)** QI has not assumed primary Form 1099 reporting and backup withholding responsibility with respect to the account holder's account and has provided a Form W-9 to a withholding agent or has provided withholding rate pool information with respect to such account holder to a withholding agent to apply backup withholding and QI does not know that the withholding agent has failed to report or backup withhold as required;

**(5)** With respect to an account holder of an intermediary or flow-through entity (other than a QI) that is a direct or indirect account holder of QI, the intermediary or flow-through entity allocates the payment to a chapter 4 withholding rate pool of US payees and provides a Form W-8IMY containing a certification that the entity meets the requirements of §1.6049-4(c)(4)(iii); or

**(6)** With respect to an account holder of another QI that is a direct or indirect account holder of QI, the QI allocates the payment to a chapter 4 withholding rate pool of US payees and provides the applicable certification on a valid Form W-8IMY for allocating the payment to this pool.

**(B) Reportable Payments other than Reportable Amounts.** QI must file a Form 1099 for a reportable payment (other than a reportable amount) paid to each US non- exempt recipient (whether a direct or indirect account holder), or to any account holder that is presumed to be a US non-exempt recipient under Sect. 5.13(C) of this Agreement. Notwithstanding the previous sentence, QI is not required to file a Form 1099 for a reportable payment (other than a reportable amount) paid to a direct account holder that is (or is presumed) a US non-exempt recipient if—

**(1)** QI is a non-US payor reporting the account holder of a US account under its FATCA requirements as a participating FFI or registered deemed-compliant FFI (including a reporting Model 1 FFI) and the other conditions of §1.6049-4(c)(4)(i) are satisfied;

**(2)** QI reports the account holder's account as held by a recalcitrant account holder or, in the case of a QI that is a reporting Model 2 FFI or nonreporting Model 2 FFI treated as registered deemed-compliant, as a non-consenting US account under its FATCA requirements as a participating FFI or registered deemed-compliant FFI and the other conditions of §1.6049-4(c)(4)(ii) are satisfied;

**(3)** QI is a non-US payor that is a reporting Model 1 FFI or registered deemed- compliant Model 1 IGA FFI and determines that the account has US indicia for which appropriate documentation sufficient to treat the account as held by a specified US person has not been provided and reports the account as a US reportable account and the other conditions of §1.6049-4(c)(4)(ii) are satisfied; or

**(4)** With respect to a reportable payment that is broker proceeds paid to a US non-exempt recipient, QI has applied the procedures of Sect. 3.05(C) of this Agreement and QI does not know that the other payor has failed to report or backup withhold on the payment as required.

**Sec. 8.07. Section 6031 Reporting Responsibility with respect to Partner Holding PTP Interest.**

**(A) In General.** A QI must comply with the requirements of this Sect. 8.07 for each calendar year for purposes of QI's requirement to report under §1.6031(c)-1 T with respect to its account holders. A nominee for purposes of this Sect. 8.07 is an entity (including a broker) that holds a PTP interest directly or indirectly on behalf of another person. An account holder for purposes of this Sect. 8.07 is a partner or intermediary that during a calendar year receives from QI a PTP distribution or sells a PTP interest for which QI pays to it an amount realised and is—

**(1)** A direct account holder of QI excluding an account holder that is a QI or nonqualified intermediary referenced in Sect. 8.07(A)(2) or (3) of this Agreement;

**(2)** An account holder of another QI acting as a disclosing QI for a PTP distribution or amount realised (including an account holder of the other QI that is itself a QI but not acting as a disclosing QI); or

**(3)** An account holder of a nonqualified intermediary when QI either receives the information required for reporting under this Sect. 8.07 with respect to an account holder receiving the distribution or, for the amount realised paid to the account holder, satisfies the conditions of Sect. 8.02(M) of this Agreement (or is otherwise a PAI).

**(B) QI not Acting as Disclosing QI.** A QI that does not act as a disclosing QI for a PTP distribution or amount realised paid to an account holder for a calendar year with respect to the account holder's PTP interest may provide the statement with respect to the account holder specified in §1.6031(c)-1 T(a) to the PTP in which the interest is held (or PTP's agent), in the time specified in §1.6031(c)-1 T(b). For purposes of this Sect. 8.07(B), the statement specified in §1.6031(c)-1 T(a) must include a US TIN for a foreign account holder only when provided by the account holder to QI. If QI does not provide the statement described in the two preceding sentences, QI must issue to each account holder receiving the distribution or amount realised the statement that is described in §1.6031(c)-1 T(h) for the calendar year with respect to the PTP interest for which the distribution or amount realised was paid, in the time specified in §1.6031(c)-1 T(h). For purposes of this Sect. 8.07(B), the statement described in §1.6031(c)- 1 T(h) may be a copy of the statement issued under Sect. 6031(b) to QI for the year when QI includes with the statement an accurate designation of the percentage of each amount shown on the statement attributable to the account holder's PTP interest held with QI. In a case in which QI provides to an account holder the statement described in §1.6031(c)-1 T(h) or the preceding sentence, QI is also required to request from the PTP the PTP's deemed sale information for purposes of §1.864(c)(8)-2(b)(2) with respect to an account holder requesting (directly or through another intermediary) this information from QI (which, in turn, QI must provide to the account holder).

**(C) QI Acting as Disclosing QI.** A QI that acts as a disclosing QI for a PTP distribution or amount realised paid to an account holder for a calendar year with respect to the account holder's PTP interest is required to provide the statement with respect to the account holder specified in §1.6031(c)-1 T(a) (including with a US TIN only when required under Sect. 8.07(B) of this Agreement) to the PTP in which the interest is held (or PTP's agent), or QI's nominee for the payment, in the time specified in §1.6031(c)-1 T(b). A QI need not provide the statement described in the preceding sentence to the extent that QI's nominee maintains a fully segregated and disclosed account for which QI has already provided the information required for the statement (including a US TIN only when required under Sect. 8.07(B) of this Agreement). Additionally, in a case in which QI provides the statement to QI's nominee or the information referenced in the preceding sentence to its nominee, QI must obtain from the nominee a written representation that the nominee is acting as an agent of the PTP for purposes of §1.6031(c)-1 T(a) unless QI otherwise appoints the nominee as its agent for purposes of §1.6031(c)-1 T(a). See §1.6031(c)-1 T(f).

**Section 9. Adjustments for Over and Underwithholding; Refunds**

**Sec. 9.01. Adjustments for Overwithholding by Withholding Agent When QI Does not Assume Primary Withholding Responsibility.** QI may request that a withholding agent make an adjustment for amounts paid to QI when the withholding agent has overwithheld under chapter 3 or 4 by applying either the reimbursement procedure described in Sect. 9.01(A) of this Agreement or the set-off procedure described in Sect. 9.01(B) of this Agreement within the time period prescribed for those procedures. Nothing in this section shall be interpreted to require a withholding agent to apply the reimbursement or set off procedures under Sects. 9.01 (A) or (B) of this Agreement. See §1.1474-2(a)(2) for the definition of overwithholding that applies for purposes of this Sect. 9 with respect to an amount withheld under chapter 4. The reimbursement and set-off procedures that apply to an amount overwithheld by QI's withholding agent under chapter 3 and 4 also apply to an amount overwithheld on an amount realised or an amount subject to withholding under Sect. 1446(a) on a PTP distribution by QI's broker (for an amount realised), or a nominee or PTP (for a PTP distribution).

**(A) Reimbursement Procedure.** QI may request that a withholding agent repay QI for any amount overwithheld and for the withholding agent to reimburse itself under the reimbursement procedures described in §§1.1461-2(a)(2)(i) and 1.1474-2(a)(3) by making the request in the time permitted to apply those procedures with respect to a beneficial owner or payee.

**(B) Set-off Procedure.** QI may request that a withholding agent repay QI by applying the amount overwithheld against any amount which otherwise would be required to be withheld under chapter 3 or 4 from income paid by the withholding agent to QI under the set-off procedures of §§1.1461-2(a)(3) and 1.1474-2(a)(4). QI must make the request in the time permitted to apply those procedures with respect to a beneficial owner or payee.

**Sec. 9.02. Adjustments for Overwithholding by QI Assuming Primary Withholding Responsibility.** QI may make an adjustment for amounts paid to its account holders when QI has overwithheld by applying either the reimbursement or set-off procedures described in this Sect. 9.02 within the time period prescribed for those procedures. The reimbursement and set-off procedures that apply to an amount QI overwithheld under chapter 3 and 4 also apply to an amount QI overwithheld on an amount realised or an amount subject to withholding under Sect. 1446(a) on a PTP distribution.

**(A) Reimbursement Procedure.** QI may repay its account holders for an amount overwithheld under chapter 3 or 4 and reimburse itself by reducing, by the amount of tax actually repaid to the account holders, the amount of any subsequent deposit of tax required to be made by QI under Sect. 3.08 of this Agreement. For purposes of this Sect. 9.02(A), an amount that is overwithheld shall be applied in order of time (*i.e.*, sequentially) to each of the QI's subsequent deposit periods in the same calendar year to the extent that the withholding taxes required to be deposited for a subsequent deposit period exceed the amount actually deposited. An amount overwithheld in a calendar year may be applied to deposit periods in the calendar year following the calendar year of overwithholding only if:

**(1)** The repayment occurs in the time specified in §§1.1461-2(a)(2) and 1.1474-2(a)(3);

**(2)** QI states on a Form 1042-S (issued, if applicable, to the account holder or otherwise to a chapter 3 or 4 reporting pool), filed in the time specified in §§1.1461-2(a)(2) and 1.1474-2(a)(3), the amount of tax withheld and the amount of any actual repayments; and

**(3)** QI states on a Form 1042, filed in the time specified in §§1.1461-2(a)(2) and 1.1474-2(a)(3), that the filing of the Form 1042 constitutes a claim for credit in accordance with §1.6414-1.

**(B) Set-Off Procedure.** QI may repay its account holders by applying the amount overwithheld against any amount which otherwise would be required under chapter 3 or 4 to be withheld from a payment made by QI to the account holders when the requirements of §1.1461-2(a)(3) (for chapter 3 withholding) or §1.1474-2(a)(4) (for chapter 4 withholding) are satisfied. For purposes of making a return on Form 1042 or 1042-S for the calendar year of overwithholding, and for purposes of making a deposit of the amount withheld, the reduced amount shall be considered the amount required to be withheld from such income under chapter 3 or 4.

**Sec. 9.03. Repayment of Backup Withholding.** If QI erroneously withholds, as defined under §31.6413(a)-3, an amount under Sect. 3406 from an account holder, QI may refund the amount erroneously withheld as provided in §31.6413(a)-3.

**Sec. 9.04. Collective Credit or Refund Procedures for Overwithholding.** If there has been overwithholding on amounts subject to chapter 3 or 4 withholding paid to QI's account holders during a calendar year and the amount has not been recovered under the reimbursement or set-off procedures as described in Sect. 9.01 or 9.02 of this Agreement, QI may request a credit or refund of the total amount overwithheld by following the procedures of this Sect. 9.04. QI shall follow the procedures set forth under Sects. 6402 and 6414, and the regulations thereunder, to claim the credit or refund. No credit or refund will be allowed after the expiration of the statutory period of limitation for refunds under Sect. 6511.

**(A) Payments for which a Collective Refund is Permitted.** Except as otherwise provided in this Sect. 9.04, QI may use the collective refund procedures with respect to all amounts subject to chapters 3 and 4 withholding. With respect to amounts withheld under chapter 3 or 4, QI shall not include in its collective refund claim tax withheld on payments made to an indirect account holder or a direct account holder of QI that is a nonqualified intermediary or flow-through entity, and with respect to amounts withheld under chapter 4, if QI is a participating FFI or registered deemed-compliant FFI, QI shall not include in its collective refund claim tax withheld on payments made to any account holder described in the FFI agreement or in §1.1471-4(h)(2). QI also shall not include in its collective refund claim any overwithholding of tax on an amount realised on a sale of a PTP interest or any amount of tax withheld on a PTP distribution.

**(B) Requirements for Collective Refund.** QI may use the collective refund procedures under this Sect. 9.04 only if the following conditions are met:

**(1)** QI must not have issued (and will not issue) Forms 1042-S to the account holders that received the payment that was subject to overwithholding;

**(2)** QI must submit together with its amended Form 1042 on which it provides a reconciliation of amounts withheld and claims a credit or refund, a copy of the Form 1042-S furnished to QI by its withholding agent reporting the taxes withheld to which the claim relates (if applicable) and a statement that includes the following information and representations—

**(i)** The reason(s) for the overwithholding;

**(ii)** QI deposited the tax for which a refund is being sought under Sect. 6302 or received a Form 1042-S from its withholding agent showing the amount of tax withheld, and neither QI nor its withholding agent has applied the reimbursement or set-off procedure of §§1.1461-2 and 1.1474-2 to adjust the tax withheld to which the claim relates;

**(iii)** QI has repaid or will repay the amount for which refund is sought to the appropriate account holders;

**(iv)** QI retains a record showing the total amount of tax withheld, credits from other withholding agents, tax assumed by QI, adjustments for underwithholding, and reimbursements for overwithholding as it relates to each account holder and also showing the repayment (if applicable) to such account holders for the amount of tax for which a refund is being sought;

**(v)** QI retains valid documentation that meets the requirements of chapter 3 or 4 (as applicable) to substantiate the amount of overwithholding with respect to each account holder for which the refund is being sought; and

**(vi)** QI has not issued and will not issue a Form 1042-S (or such other form as the IRS may prescribe) to any account holder with respect to the payments for which the refund is being sought.

**Sec. 9.05. Adjustments for Underwithholding.** If QI knows that an amount should have been withheld under chapter 3 or 4 from a previous payment made to an account holder but was not withheld, QI may either withhold from future payments made pursuant to chapter 3 or chapter 4 to the same account holder or payee or satisfy the tax from property that it holds in custody for such person or property over which it has control. QI may also withhold from future payments as described in the preceding sentence with respect underwithholding on an amount realised or PTP distribution. The additional withholding or satisfaction of the tax owed described in the previous sentence must be made before the due date (not including extensions) of the Form 1042 for the calendar year in which the underwithholding occurred. QI's responsibilities under this Sect. 9.05 will be met if it informs a withholding agent from which it received the payment of the underwithholding and the withholding agent satisfies the underwithholding.

**Sec. 9.06. Underwithholding After Form 1042 Filed.** If, after a Form 1042 has been filed for a calendar year, QI, QI's reviewer, or the IRS determines that QI has underwithheld tax for such year, QI shall file an amended Form 1042 to report and pay the underwithheld tax. QI shall pay the underwithheld tax, the interest due on the underwithheld tax, and any applicable penalties at the time of filing the amended Form 1042. If QI fails to file an amended return, the IRS shall make such return under Sect. 6020 and assess such tax under the procedures set forth in the Code.

## Section 10. Compliance Procedures

### Sec. 10.01. Compliance Program

**(A) In General.** QI is required to adopt a compliance program under the authority of a responsible officer or, if QI adopts a consolidated compliance program, under the authority of a responsible officer of a Compliance QI (as described in Sect. 10.02(B) of this Agreement). QI's compliance program must include policies, procedures, and processes sufficient for QI to satisfy the documentation, reporting, and withholding requirements of this Agreement and sufficient for a responsible officer of QI (or a Compliance QI) to make the certifications required under Sect. 10.03 of this Agreement. If QI is acting as a QDD, QI's compliance program must also include policies, procedures, and processes sufficient for it to satisfy and report its QDD tax liability and other reporting required as a condition of its status as a QDD. QI must also perform or arrange for the performance of a periodic review described in Sect. 10.04 of this Agreement to the extent required by that section. As part of the responsible officer's certification, QI must provide to the IRS the factual information as required by and referenced in Sects. 10.04 and 10.05 and in Appendix I to this Agreement. QI must also satisfy the requirements of Sect. 10.06 of this Agreement with respect to the report covering the periodic review and must comply with the IRS review described in Sect. 10.08 of this Agreement.

**(B) Coordination with FATCA Requirements as a Participating FFI, Registered Deemed-Compliant FFI, or Registered Deemed-Compliant Model 1 IGA FFI and, for a Direct Reporting NFFE, the Requirements of §1.1472-1(c)(3).** As a condition for maintaining QI status, QI must maintain its chapter 4 status with respect to each branch of QI operating under this Agreement. Therefore, QI must, as part of the compliance procedures described in this Sect. 10 determine whether it is compliant with its FATCA requirements as a participating FFI, registered deemed-compliant FFI, or registered deemed-compliant Model 1 IGA FFI.

**(C) Phase-in Years for 871(m).** In enforcing the regulations issued with respect to dividend equivalents under Sects. 871(m), 1441, 1461, and 1473 (the "Sect. 871(m) regulations"), the IRS will take into account the extent to which the QI (including QIs that are not QDDs) made a good faith effort to comply with the Sect. 871(m) regulations for any delta-one Sect. 871(m) transaction in calendar years 2023 and 2024 and any139 non-delta-one Sect. 871(m) transaction in calendar year 2025. Similarly, for purposes of the IRS's enforcement and administration of the QDD rules in the Sect. 871(m) regulations and the relevant provisions of this Agreement, the IRS will take into account the extent to which the QDD made a good faith effort to comply with the Sect. 871(m) regulations and the relevant provisions of this Agreement for calendar years 2023 and 2024. For calendar years 2023 and 2024, a QDD is not required to perform a periodic review with respect to its QDD activities (as otherwise required by Sect. 10.04 of this Agreement) or provide factual information in Appendix I with respect to its QDD activities. In addition, for the QI certification on material failures in calendar years 2023 and 2024, the only certification that a QDD is required to make with respect to its QDD activities for this period is that it has made a good faith effort to comply with the Sect. 871(m) regulations and the relevant provisions of this Agreement for those activities. A revised certification of internal controls (and factual information and other certifications) applicable to a QI's QDD activities will be added to this Agreement for purposes of certification periods ending after December 31, 2024. For calendar years 2023 and 2024, a material failure relevant to a QDD has not occurred unless the QDD failed to make a good faith effort to comply with the Sect. 871(m) regulations and the relevant provisions of this Agreement. Similarly, for calendar years 2023 and 2024, a QI will not be considered to have a material failure with respect to a delta-one Sect. 871(m) transaction unless the QI failed to make a good faith effort to comply with the Sect. 871(m) regulations for any of those transactions in those years. For calendar year 2025, a QI will not be considered to have a material failure with respect to a non-delta-one Sect. 871(m) transaction unless the QI failed to make a good faith effort to comply with the Sect. 871(m) regulations for any of those transactions in that year. For any reliance on the good faith standard, the QI must disclose any Sect. 871(m) transactions included in the review that the QI believes should be subject to the good faith standard for purposes of reporting the factual information with its periodic certification and include a brief description of the reason QI relied on the good faith standard, how the QI will address it, and why the good faith standard should apply. A QI will be considered to satisfy its obligations for purposes of this Sect. 10 that apply specifically to Sect. 871(m) transactions for calendar years 2023 and 2024 provided that the QI made a good faith effort to comply with the relevant terms of this Agreement. Any QI that has not made a good faith effort to comply with its section 871(m) requirements or QDD obligations under this Agreement will not be given any relief from IRS administration or enforcement for calendar years 2023 and 2024, including penalties.

**10.02. Responsible Officer.** QI must appoint an individual as a responsible officer as defined in Sect. 2.72 of this Agreement. The responsible officer must be identified on QAAMS as QI's responsible party, and such person may, but is not required to, be the same responsible officer for purposes of compliance with QI's FATCA requirements as a participating FFI, registered deemed-compliant FFI, or registered deemed-compliant Model 1 IGA FFI. The responsible officer must establish a compliance program that meets the requirements of this Sect. 10.02 and must make the periodic certifications to the IRS described in Sect. 10.03 of this Agreement. The responsible officer of QI must be an officer of QI with sufficient authority to fulfil the duties of a responsible officer described in this Sect. 10. The responsible officer (or a delegate appointed by the responsible officer) must also serve as the point of contact for the IRS for all issues related to this Agreement and for complying with IRS requests for information or additional review procedures under Sect. 10.07 of this Agreement. References in this Sect. 10.02 to the responsible officer include a responsible officer's designee, where appropriate.

**(A) Compliance Program.** The responsible officer must establish a program for QI to comply with the requirements of this Agreement that includes the following—

**(1) Written Policies and Procedures.** The responsible officer must ensure the drafting and updating, as necessary, of written policies and procedures sufficient for QI to satisfy the documentation, withholding, reporting, and other obligations of this Agreement, including, with respect to QI that is acting as a QDD, satisfying its QDD tax liability. Such written policies and procedures must include a process for employees of QI to raise issues to the responsible officer (or the responsible officer's designee) that concern QI's compliance with this Agreement.

**(2) Training.** The responsible officer must communicate such policies and procedures to any line of business of QI that is responsible for obtaining, reviewing, and retaining a record of documentation under the requirements of Sect. 5 of this Agreement; making payments subject to withholding under Sect. 3 of this Agreement; reporting payments and accounts as required under Sects. 7 and 8 of this Agreement; or entering into potential Sect. 871(m) transactions, in the case of QI that is acting as a QDD.

**(3) Systems.** The responsible officer must ensure that systems and processes are in place that will allow QI to fulfil its obligations under this Agreement. For example, in order to fulfil QI's obligations to report on Forms 1042-S, 1099, and 8966 under Sect. 8 of this Agreement, QI must establish systems for documenting account holders and for recording the information with respect to each such account that QI is required to report under that section.

**(4) Monitoring of Business Changes.** The responsible officer must monitor business practices and arrangements that affect QI's compliance with this Agreement, including, for example, QI's acquisition of lines of businesses or accounts that give rise to documentation, withholding, or reporting obligations under this Agreement.

**(5) QDD Tax Liability Determinations.** If QI is (or has a branch that is) acting as a QDD, the responsible officer must ensure that each QDD has appropriate systems in place to make the necessary determinations and calculations to identify Sect. 871(m) transactions, potential Sect. 871(m) transactions, the amount of dividends received in its QDD equity derivatives dealer capacity and the Sect. 881 taxes paid thereon, its net delta exposure, the dividend amount per share, the stock owned by the QDD included in its net delta exposure long position, its long position, its short position, its Sect. 871(m) amount and the Sect. 881 taxes paid thereon, its QDD tax liability amount, and the amount of dividend equivalent payments made by the QDD, as well as any other necessary information. In the case of a QDD that is a partnership or a branch of a partnership, instead of determining the Sect. 881 taxes, the partnership must have appropriate systems to determine the Sect. 3.09 amounts on a gross basis and the chapter 3 and 4 withholding required with respect to any of its partners with respect to those amounts (as well as any other amounts required to be determined under Section 7.01(C) of this Agreement). In addition, the responsible officer must ensure that the QDD has appropriate systems in place to determine whether a transaction is as a principal or non-principal, whether a transaction is in an equity derivatives dealer or non-equity derivatives dealer capacity, whether the transaction exists for federal income tax purposes, whether the transaction is owned by the QDD, and whether the transaction is effectively connected with the conduct of a trade or business in the United States. This includes appropriate systems to, where required, calculate the delta for a potential Sect. 871(m) transaction, perform the substantial equivalence test described in §1.871-15(h), calculate the amount of a dividend equivalent, determine any QDD tax liability amount (and each part thereof) and its timing, and determine what payments are received or made with respect to potential Sect. 871(m) transactions and underlying securities as a principal and whether in its equity derivatives dealer capacity or non- equity derivatives dealer capacity and by which home office or branch that is acting as a QDD. The systems must also take into account information received pursuant to §1.871-15(p).

**(6) Periodic Review.** Unless QI receives a waiver (the requirements of which are described in Sect. 10.07(B) of this Agreement), the responsible officer must designate a reviewer that meets the qualifications described in Sect. 10.04(A) of this Agreement to perform the periodic review as described in Sect. 10.05 of this Agreement, to the extent required.

**(7) Certification of Internal Controls.** The responsible officer must make the periodic certification as described in Sect. 10.03 of this Agreement, including ensuring that corrective actions are taken in response to any material failures (as defined in Sect. 10.03(B) of this Agreement).

**(B) Consolidated Compliance Program.** The IRS, in its discretion, may permit a consolidated compliance program that includes two or more QIs that are members of a group of entities under common ownership when the QIs: (i) operate under a uniform compliance program for purposes of this

Agreement; (ii) share practices, procedures, and systems subject to uniform monitoring and control; and (iii) are subject to a consolidated periodic review that includes a review of internal controls and testing of transactions relevant to this Agreement with respect to each QI in the consolidated compliance program. Each QI that is a member of a consolidated compliance program (CCG member) must designate a Compliance QI to act on its behalf, and the responsible officer of the Compliance QI must identify itself as such when making its periodic certification and must comply with the identification, certification of internal controls, and periodic review requirements for the QI consolidated compliance program as the IRS may prescribe. Each CCG member must further designate the Compliance QI as its agent for executing a Form 872, *Consent to Extend the Time to Assess Tax,* with respect to any assessment of tax relevant to this Agreement for the period covered by the consolidated compliance program. The Compliance QI must agree to execute any Form 872 on behalf of all of its CCG members and be jointly and severally liable for the obligations and liabilities of any CCG member relating to this Agreement for the period covered by the consolidated compliance program. For purposes of this Sect. 10.02(B), a Compliance QI is required to provide this agreement and the designations from its CCG members in connection with a request by the IRS Foreign Intermediaries Program for an executed Form 872 from the Compliance QI. QIs that want to operate a consolidated compliance program must contact the IRS Foreign Intermediaries Program for approval.

**10.03. Certification of Internal Controls by Responsible Officer.** A QI's responsible officer must make the certification described in either Part II.A (Certification of Effective Internal Controls) or Part II.B (Qualified Certification) of Appendix I to this Agreement and must disclose any material failures that occurred during the certification period or during any prior period if the material failure was not disclosed as part of a prior certification or written disclosure made by QI to the IRS. If the responsible officer has identified a material failure that QI has not corrected as of the date of the certification or an event of default applicable to the certification period, the responsible officer cannot make the certification in Part II.A of Appendix I (Certification of Effective Internal Controls) and must make the certification in Part II.B of Appendix I (Qualified Certification) and attach the remediation plan described in Part II.B.3 of Appendix I. Regardless of which certification is made, QI must provide with its certification a copy of the periodic review report that is described in Sect. 10.05 of this Agreement unless QI applies for a waiver of its review requirement under Sect. 10.07(B) of this Agreement. For a QI that uses the third year of the certification period for its periodic review, the certification is due on or before December 31 of the year following the certification period. For a QI that uses the first or second year of the certification period for its periodic review or a QI that obtains a waiver of the periodic review requirement, the certification is due on or before July 1 of the year following the certification period. The initial certification period is the period ending on the third full calendar year that this Agreement is in effect (including renewals of this Agreement). Subsequent certification periods are every three calendar years following the initial certification period (including renewals of this Agreement). The certification of internal controls required by this Sect. 10.03 applies only to the internal controls related to QI's compliance with this Agreement and its FATCA requirements as a participating FFI, registered deemed-compliant FFI, or registered deemed-compliant Model 1 IGA FFI and, in the case of a direct reporting NFFE, its requirements under §1.1472-1(c)(3), with respect to accounts for which it acts as a QI, and does not relate to any other obligations or requirements. The responsible officer may rely on any reasonable procedure, process, review, or certification that enables the responsible officer to make the certification described in this Sect. 10.03. If the responsible officer relies on an internal or external review for this purpose (*i.e.*, for purposes of determining whether QI has effective internal controls), the internal or external reviewer must be independent, as described in Sect. 10.04 of this Agreement. The responsible officer must document the procedures, processes, reviews, or certifications relied upon in making the certification. QI's responsible officer (or the responsible officer of its Compliance QI) must make the certifications of compliance in such manner as the IRS may prescribe.

**(A) PAIs and Partnership or Trust to which QI Applies the Agency Option.** Unless QI has received a waiver of the periodic review requirement, any PAI with which QI has an agreement and any partnership or trust to which QI applies the agency option must provide its documentation and other information to QI for inclusion in QI's periodic review or conduct an independent periodic review and provide a written certification to QI regarding its compliance with the requirements of the PAI or agency agreement. Such certification must be available to the IRS upon a request made as part of the review described in Sect. 10.08 of this Agreement (with a certified translation into English if the certification is not in English).

**(B) Material Failures.**

**(1) Material Failures Defined.** A material failure is generally a failure of QI to fulfil the requirements of this Agreement or its FATCA requirements as a participating FFI, registered deemed-compliant FFI, or registered deemed-compliant Model 1 IGA FFI. For purposes of the certifications described in

Parts II.A and B of Appendix I to this Agreement, a material failure is limited to the following:

**(i)** QI's establishing of, for financial statement purposes, a tax reserve or provision for a potential future tax liability related to QI's failure to comply with this Agreement, including its FATCA requirements as a participating FFI, registered deemed-compliant FFI, or registered deemed-compliant Model 1 IGA FFI, and with respect to QI that is acting as a QDD, failure to satisfy its QDD tax liability and its obligations pursuant to Sect. 871(m) and the regulations under that section.

**(ii)** QI's failure to establish written policies, procedures, or systems sufficient for the relevant personnel of QI to take actions consistent with QI's obligations under this Agreement, or if QI is acting as a QDD, its obligations as a QDD under this Agreement or pursuant to Sect. 871(m) and the regulations under that section.

**(iii)** A criminal or civil penalty or sanction imposed on QI (or any branch or office thereof) by a regulator or other governmental authority or agency with oversight over QI's compliance with AML/KYC procedures to which QI (or any branch or office thereof) is subject and that is imposed due to QI's failure to properly identify account holders under the requirements of those procedures.

**(iv)** A finding (including a finding noted in the periodic review report described in Sect. 10.06 of this Agreement) for one or more years covered by this Agreement that QI failed to—

**(a)** Withhold an amount that QI was required to withhold under chapter 3 or 4 or under Sect. 3406 as required under Sect. 3 of this Agreement or, if QI is acting as a QDD, failing to timely pay its QDD tax liability;

**(b)** Provide information sufficient for another withholding agent to perform withholding and reporting to the extent required when QI does not assume primary chapters 3 and 4 withholding responsibility or primary Form 1099 reporting and backup withholding responsibility;

**(c)** Provide allocation information as described in Sect. 6.03(D) of this Agreement (regarding US non-exempt recipient account holders) by January 15 as required by that section when QI applies the alternative withholding rate pool procedures;

**(d)** Make deposits in the time and manner required by Sect. 3.08 of this Agreement or make adequate deposits to satisfy its withholding obligations, or, if QI is acting as a QDD, timely satisfy its QDD tax liability, taking into account the procedures under Sect. 9 of this Agreement;

**(e)** Report or report accurately on Forms 1099 as required under Sect. 8.06 of this Agreement or provide information to the payor to the extent QI does not assume primary Form 1099 reporting and backup withholding responsibilities;

**(f)** Report or report accurately on Forms 1042 and 1042-S under Sects. 7 and 8 of this Agreement;

**(g)** Report or report accurately on Form 8966 under Sects. 8.04 and 8.05 of this Agreement;

**(h)** Withhold an amount required to be withheld or report accurately with respect to US source substitute dividend payments or make timely and adequate deposits of tax due with respect to such payments for which QI is a QSL and acts as a dealer or intermediary;

**(i)** Withhold an amount that QI was required to withhold on a payment of an amount realised from the sale of a PTP interest or on a PTP distribution as required under Sect. 3 of this Agreement or provide correct information to a withholding agent or broker when QI does not assume primary withholding responsibility for either payment under Sect. 3.02 of this Agreement; or

**(j)** Comply with the requirements of Sects. 5.01(A) and 8.07 of this Agreement with respect to one or more account holders that are partners holding PTP interests (including, for purposes of Sect. 8.07 of this Agreement, account holders of another intermediary when QI acts as an agent for meeting these requirements).

**(2) Limitations on Material Failures.** A failure described in Sect. 10.03(B)(1)(iv) of this Agreement is a material failure only if the failure was the result of a deliberate action on the part of one or more employees of QI to avoid the requirements of this Agreement with respect to one or more account holders of QI or was an error attributable to a failure of QI to establish or implement internal controls necessary for QI to meet the requirements of this Agreement. Regardless of these limitations for certification purposes, QI is required to correct a failure to withhold or deposit tax under Sect. 3 of this Agreement, or to report under Sect. 7 or 8 of this Agreement, or, for a QI that is acting as a QDD, to timely pay its QDD tax liability and timely file the appropriate return (or amended return).

**Sec. 10.04. Periodic Review Absent Waiver.** Unless the QI receives a waiver (the requirements of which are described in Sect. 10.07(B) of this Agreement), when QI provides the certification described in Sect. 10.03 of this Agreement, QI must also provide certain factual information regarding its accounts, withholdable payments, amounts subject to chapter 3 withholding and withholding under Sects. 1446(a) and (f), and, if QI is acting as a QDD, Sect. 871(m) transactions, potential Sect. 871(m) transactions, and its QDD tax liability based on the results of a periodic review. The factual information requested is included in Appendix I to this Agreement.

**(A) Independent Reviewer.** The periodic review may be performed by an internal reviewer (such as an internal auditor) that is an employee of QI or an employee of an affiliate of QI (including an employee of a Compliance QI in the case of a consolidated compliance program) ("internal reviewer"), or a certified public accountant, attorney, or third-party consultant ("external reviewer"), or any combination thereof.

**(1) Internal Reviewer.** QI may designate an internal reviewer to perform the periodic review (or a portion of the periodic review) only when the internal reviewer is competent with respect to the requirements of this Agreement. The internal reviewer must also be able to report findings that reflect the independent judgement of the reviewer. The internal reviewer must not be reviewing its own work, procedures, or results (*e.g.*, the internal reviewer, in reviewing QI's documentation cannot be part of the team primarily responsible for collecting and validating documentation). The results of the periodic review and the internal reviewer's reporting of such results to the responsible officer cannot influence or affect the compensation, bonus, employment status, or employee review of the internal reviewer. The IRS has the right to request the performance of the periodic review by an alternative reviewer if the IRS, in its sole discretion, reasonably believes that the reviewer selected by QI was not independent, as described in this Agreement, or did not perform an effective periodic review under this Agreement. In the case of a consolidated compliance program, the Compliance QI may designate an internal reviewer to perform the consolidated periodic review (or a portion of the consolidated periodic review). See Sect. 10.02(B) of this Agreement. The internal reviewer of the Compliance QI must meet the requirements of this section with respect to both the Compliance QI and each QI that is a member of the consolidated compliance program. If QI designates an internal reviewer that is an employee of an affiliate of QI but is not part of a consolidated compliance program, QI must ensure that the internal reviewer has access to all necessary information in order to complete the review. In addition, QI must permit the IRS to communicate directly with such internal reviewer.

**(2) External Reviewer.** QI may engage an external reviewer that is a certified public accountant, attorney, or third-party consultant that is regularly engaged in the practice of performing reviews of clients' policies, procedures, and processes for complying with accounting, tax, or regulatory requirements (including assisting clients in determining such compliance) and that is sufficiently independent of the QI to conduct the review objectively. For this purpose, an external reviewer must (as a minimum) apply the standards of independence that would otherwise apply to its engagement to conduct the periodic review (such as the standards for an agreed-upon procedures engagement by a certified public accountant). The external reviewer must be in good standing with and comply with any applicable professional standards for maintaining its license as an accountant or attorney (or other third-party consultant that has similar professional standards or requirements). The external reviewer is not required to make an attestation or render an opinion regarding QI's compliance with this Agreement or QI's compliance with its FATCA requirements as a participating FFI, registered deemed-compliant FFI, or registered deemed-compliant Model 1 IGA FFI, but the reviewer must be able to perform the periodic review as specified in Sect. 10.05 of this Agreement. QI must permit the external reviewer to have access to all relevant records of QI for purposes of performing the review, including information regarding specific account holders. Additionally, the engagement between the external reviewer and QI must impose no restrictions on QI's ability to provide the results of the review to the IRS. However, the external reviewer is not required to divulge the identity of QI's account holders to the IRS, except as otherwise provided under QI's FATCA requirements as a participating FFI, registered deemed-compliant FFI, or registered deemed-compliant Model 1 IGA FFI. QI must permit the IRS to communicate directly with the external reviewer, and any legal prohibitions that prevent the IRS from communicating directly with the reviewer must be waived.

**Sec. 10.05. Scope and Timing of Review.** The responsible officer of QI (or of the Compliance QI) must require the reviewer to test accounts related to QI's documentation, withholding, reporting, and other obligations under this Agreement, including its requirements related to withholding and reporting under Sects. 1446(a) and (f), its QDD tax liability if QI is acting as a QDD, and its FATCA requirements as a participating FFI, registered deemed-compliant FFI, or registered deemed-compliant Model 1 IGA FFI for accounts for which it is acting as a QI, and to identify deficiencies in meeting these obligations. Any PAI with which QI has an agreement and any partnership or trust to which QI applies the agency option must provide the information necessary for QI to test accounts and transactions of such entity as part of QI's periodic review unless such entity conducts its own periodic review and provides QI with the report documenting the results of such review as described in Sect. 10.06 of this Agreement. Unless otherwise approved by the IRS, the review must include the steps described in Sect. 10.05(A) through (E) of this Agreement. QI is required to arrange for the performance of one review for the certification period to evaluate QI's documentation, withholding, and reporting practices. If QI is acting as a QDD, this review should also include a review of its determination as to whether transactions are Sect. 871(m) transactions, its computations and determinations of dividend equivalent amounts, dividends and taxes paid thereon, whether transactions are in its equity derivatives dealer capacity, net delta exposure, its Sect. 871(m) amount, and its calculation of its QDD tax liability, as well as any other amounts required to be included on the reconciliation schedule. The review may be conducted for any calendar year covered by the certification period. However, all results of the review must relate to one calendar year. QI may conduct a review for a particular calendar year if, on the due date for reporting the factual information relating to the periodic review (provided in Sect. 10.04 of this Agreement), there are 15 or more months available on the period for assessment under Sect. 6501(a) of the calendar year for which the review is to be conducted or the QI submits, upon request, a Form 872, *Consent to Extend the Time to Assess Tax*, that will satisfy the 15-month requirement. The Form 872 must be mailed to the IRS at the address provided in Sect. 12.06 of this Agreement. QI may use a sample to test accounts if there are more than 60 accounts to review. If QI has fewer than 60 accounts, it must review all accounts and cannot use a sample to test accounts. To the extent applicable, the reviewer must separately review its QI activities (when not acting in its QDD capacity) and QDD activities. The reviewer is required to record its sampling procedures and to maintain the ability to reconstruct the sample. Further, the review is not required to include statistical sampling procedures for testing transactions, but the reviewer must document its methodology for sampling determinations. A safe harbour methodology and additional information on the use of statistical sampling is provided in Appendix II to this Agreement. If the reviewer determines that underwithholding has occurred, QI shall report and pay any amount due. QI must also notify the IRS Foreign Intermediaries Program in accordance with Sect. 12.06 of this Agreement if the underwithholding is discovered in the review. See Appendix II to this Agreement for information required to be provided when reporting underwithholding and information regarding any projection of underwithholding determined when using a sampling method.

**(A) Documentation.** The reviewer must—

**(1)** Review QI's accounts, to ensure that QI obtained documentation that meets the requirements described in Sects. 5.01 through 5.09 of this Agreement with respect to payments subject to withholding under chapter 3 (including when attributable to PTP distributions);

**(2)** Review QI's accounts for which treaty benefits are claimed to ensure that QI obtained the treaty statements and limitation on benefits information required by Sect. 5.03(B) of this Agreement for entity account holders;

**(3)** Review information contained in account holder files to determine if the documentation validity standards of Sect. 5.10 of this Agreement have been met for a QI to rely on documentation. For example, the reviewer must verify that changes in account holder information (*e.g.*, a change of an account holder's foreign address to a US address, a change of account holder status from foreign to US, or a change in an entity's chapter 4 status from participating FFI to non-participating FFI) are being conveyed by QI to QI's withholding agents and are otherwise being taken into account by the QI for determining its reliance on documentation;

**(4)** Review the accounts for which QI is acting as a QI to ensure that QI is obtaining, reviewing, and maintaining documentation in accordance with its FATCA requirements as a participating FFI, registered deemed-compliant FFI, or registered deemed-compliant Model 1 IGA FFI and determining the status of account holders for purposes of chapter 4 or an applicable IGA;

**(5)** Review accounts held by US non-exempt recipient account holders, to determine if QI obtained Forms W-9, and, if QI does not assume primary Form 1099 reporting and backup withholding responsibility, that QI transmitted those forms to a withholding agent when required under this Agreement;

**(6)** Review accounts to which QI makes payments of PTP distributions subject to withholding under Sect. 1446(a) to determine whether QI has documented the status of the account holders under the requirements described in Sects. 5.01 through 5.09 of this Agreement applicable to those payments (including documenting partners of account holders that are foreign partnerships (other than PTPs), documenting grantors and owners of grantor trusts, and requesting the US TINs of account holders receiving these payments under Sect. 5.01(A) of this Agreement);

**(7)** Review accounts to which QI makes payments of amounts realised to determine whether QI has documented the status of account holders under the requirements described in Sects. 5.01 through 5.09 of this Agreement applicable to those payments (including documenting partners of account holders that are foreign partnerships certifying to modified amounts realised, documenting grantors and owners of grantor trusts, and requesting the US TINs of account holders receiving these payments under Sect. 5.01(A) of this Agreement);

**(8)** For a QI that is a QDD, review accounts that received a reportable payment for which QI is acting as a QDD to determine whether QI has documented the status of account holders under the requirements described in Sects. 5.01 through 5.09 of this Agreement;

**(9)** For a QI that assumes primary chapters 3 and 4 withholding responsibility for payments of US source substitute interest, review accounts of persons to which QI pays the interest to determine whether QI has documented the status of such persons under the requirements described in Sects. 5.01 through 5.09 of this Agreement; and

**(10)** For QI that is a QSL or that otherwise assumes primary withholding responsibility as an intermediary for US source substitute dividend payments, review accounts to which QI pays US source substitute dividends to determine whether QI has documented the status of the account holders under the requirements described in Sections 5.01 through 5.09 of this Agreement.

**(B) Withholding Rate Pools.** The reviewer must—

**(1)** Perform checks using account holders assigned to each withholding rate pool, and cross check that assignment against the documentation provided by the account holder (or the presumption rule applied under Sect. 5.13 of this Agreement), the type of income earned, and the withholding rate applied to the pool, taking into account the results of the documentation review under Sect. 10.05(A) of this Agreement and the appropriate withholding rate to be applied to a treaty claim (or withholding rate otherwise applicable to the income paid), to determine any underwithholding. For purposes of these checks, at a minimum the last payment of each income type paid to the account for the year (by reference to the income classifications on Form 1042-S as compared (for accuracy) to the income reported in QI's account statements for the account holder) may be used.

**(2)** Determine that appropriate withholding rate pools are established for US non-exempt recipients that received reportable amounts, and if QI is using the procedure for US non-exempt recipients described in Sect. 6.03(D) of this Agreement, verify that QI is providing sufficient and timely information to withholding agents to allocate reportable amounts to US non-exempt recipients; and

**(3)** With respect to a partnership or trust described in Sect. 4.05 of this Agreement, determine whether the partnership or trust has a chapter 4 status permitted under Sect. 4.05(A) of this Agreement and perform test checks using account holder documentation for the selected partners, beneficiaries, or owners and records of each type of reportable amount paid by QI to the entity to determine whether the highest rate of withholding applicable to each type of reportable amount is reflected in QI's withholding rate pools. Determine any underwithholding resulting from either of these review steps.

**(C) Withholding Responsibilities.** Taking into account the results of the documentation review under Sects. 5.10(A) of this Agreement, the appropriate withholding rate applied to a treaty claim (or otherwise applicable to the income paid), and the presumption rules (when applicable) under 5.13 of this Agreement, the reviewer must determine any underwithholding by applying the review steps below—

**(1)** To the extent QI has assumed primary chapters 3 and 4 withholding responsibilities, perform test checks, using recalcitrant account holders (when applicable) and nonparticipating FFIs, to verify that QI withheld the proper amounts under chapter 4;

**(2)** To the extent QI has assumed primary chapters 3 and 4 withholding responsibility, perform test checks, using foreign account holders for which no withholding is required under chapter 4 based on the payee's chapter 4 status, to verify that QI withheld the proper amounts under chapter 3 and properly applied the exemptions from chapter 4 withholding;

**(3)** To the extent QI has not assumed primary chapters 3 and 4 withholding responsibility, perform test checks to verify that QI has fulfilled its withholding responsibilities under Sect. 3.02 of this Agreement (including any required withholding by QI if QI provided to its withholding agent any incorrect withholding rate pools by comparison to the correct withholding rates for payments associated with a withholding rate pool);

**(4)** To the extent QI has assumed primary Form 1099 reporting and backup withholding responsibility for account holders receiving reportable payments from QI, perform test checks using US non-exempt recipient account holders to verify that QI backup withheld when required;

**(5)** To the extent QI has not assumed primary Form 1099 reporting and backup withholding responsibility for account holders receiving reportable payments, perform test checks using US non-exempt recipient account holders to verify that QI fulfilled its backup withholding responsibilities under Sects. 3.04 through 3.06 of this Agreement;

**(6)** To the extent QI has assumed primary withholding responsibility on payments of PTP distributions, perform test checks of payments to accounts to which QI pays PTP distributions, to verify QI withheld the proper amounts under chapters 3 and 4, and Sects. 1446(a) and (f) on the distributions, including by determining the amounts subject to withholding by reference to the qualified notice issued for a distribution or applying the default rule of §1.1446-4(d)(1);

**(7)** To the extent QI has assumed primary withholding responsibility on amounts realised from sales of PTP interests, perform test checks of payments to accounts to which QI pays amounts realised, to verify QI withheld the proper amounts for purposes of Sect. 1446(f), including that QI applied the "10-percent exception" of §1.1446(f)- 4(b)(3) to exempt any amounts from withholding only as permitted under that section;

**(8)** To the extent QI has not assumed primary withholding responsibility on payments of PTP distributions or amounts realised from sales of PTP interests and provides withholding rate pools to a withholding agent, perform test checks to determine whether QI has satisfied any withholding required under Sect. 3.02 of151 this Agreement by comparison to the correct withholding rates for payments associated with a withholding rate pool;

**(9)** To the extent that QI acts as a disclosing QI, perform test checks to compare the withholding reported on Forms 1042-S issued to QI and QI's direct account holders (other than QIs or NQIs) to the correct withholding to verify that QI withheld to the extent required under Sect. 3.02 of this Agreement;

**(10)** To the extent that QI is acting as a QDD, perform test checks to determine that QI withheld when required on payments that it made with respect to potential Sect. 871(m) transactions;

**(11)** To the extent that QI acts as a QSL or otherwise assumes primary chapter 3 and 4 withholding responsibility as an intermediary on payments of US source substitute dividends, perform test checks to determine that QI withheld when required on such payments and determine whether QI has a policy in effect to assume primary withholding responsibilities on all such payments;

**(12)** To the extent that QI assumes chapter 3 and 4 withholding responsibility on payments of US source substitute interest, perform test checks to determine that QI withheld when required on such payments and determine whether QI has a policy in effect to assume primary withholding responsibilities on all such payments;

**(13)** To the extent that QI assumes primary withholding responsibility for payments to a partnership or trust described in Sect. 4.05 of this Agreement, perform the review steps described in Sect. 10.05(b)(3) of this Agreement (as applied to QI's own withholding rather than QI's withholding rate pools); and

**(14)** Perform test checks to verify that amounts withheld by QI were timely deposited in accordance with Sect. 3.08 of this Agreement.

**(D) Return Filing and Information Reporting.** The reviewer must—

**(1)** Obtain copies of original and amended Forms 1042 and 945, and any schedules, statements, or attachments required to be filed with those forms, verify that the forms have been filed, and determine whether the amounts of income, taxes, and other information reported on those forms are accurate by—

**(i)** Reviewing copies of Forms 1042-S that withholding agents have provided QI to determine whether QI properly reported the amount of taxes withheld by other withholding agents on Form 1042;

**(ii)** Reviewing account statements and correspondence from withholding agents;

**(iii)** Determining that adjustments to the amount of tax shown on Form 1042 (and any claim by QI for refund or credit) properly reflect the adjustments to withholding made by QI using the reimbursement or set off procedures under Sect. 9.02 of this Agreement and are supported by sufficient documentation;

**(iv)** Reconciling amounts shown on Forms 1042 with amounts shown on Form 1042-S (including the amount of taxes reported as withheld);

**(v)** If QI is acting as a QDD, reviewing the reconciliation schedule described in Sect. 7.01(C) of this Agreement and any information used to prepare such schedule or compute its QDD tax liability, including information received pursuant to §1.871-15(p), reviewing the amounts required to determine its Sect. 871(m) amounts and its QDD tax liability over the applicable period, and reviewing such information to determine whether the Sect. 871(m) amounts and QDD tax liability have been properly calculated;

**(vi)** If QI is acting as a QDD, reviewing amounts shown on Forms 1042 (including all required Schedules Q) and Forms 1042-S, as well as any information received pursuant to §1.871-15(p), to determine whether the QDD properly took the information into account (*e.g.*, to calculate its QDD tax liability);

**(vii)** To the extent QI acts as a QSL, determine that QI properly reported the gross amount of the US source payments of substitute dividends to which the recipient would have otherwise been entitled before consideration of any withholding tax obligations; the amount of tax withheld by the withholding agent; and the amount of tax withheld by other withholding agents in the series of securities lending or sale-repurchase transaction;

**(viii)** In the case of collective credits or refunds, reviewing the statements attached to amended Forms 1042 filed to claim a collective refund, determine whether those forms are accurate, and—

**(a)** Determine the causes of any overwithholding reported and ensure QI did not issue Forms 1042-S to persons whom it included as part of its collective credit or refund;

**(b)** Determine that QI repaid the appropriate account holders and that the amount of the claim is accurate and supported by adequate documentation; and

**(c)** Determine that QI did not include payments made to a partnership or trust described in Sect. 4.05 of this Agreement or a payment of an amount subject to withholding under Sect. 1446(f) or on a PTP distribution.

**(2)** Obtain copies of original and corrected Forms 1042-S and Forms 1099 filed by QI, together with the work papers used to prepare those forms, and determine whether the amounts reported on those forms are accurate by—

**(i)** Reconciling payments and tax reported on Forms 1042-S received from withholding agents with amounts (including characterisation of income) and taxes reported by QI as withheld on Forms 1042-S and determining the reason(s) for any variance;

**(ii)** Reviewing the Forms W-8IMY and the associated withholding statements that QI has provided withholding agents;

**(iii)** Reviewing account statements issued by QI to account holders;

**(iv)** Determining, in the case in which QI utilised the reimbursement or set-off procedure that QI satisfied the requirements of Sect. 9.02 of this Agreement and that the adjusted amounts of tax withheld are properly reflected on Forms 1042-S.

**(3)** Obtain copies of original and amended Forms 8966 (or, for QI that is a reporting Model 1 FFI, any analogous forms used for reporting account information pursuant to the applicable Model 1 IGA) of accounts for which QI is acting as a QI, and determine whether the amounts of income and other information reported on Forms 8966 are accurate by—

**(i)** Reviewing US accounts (or US reportable accounts for which QI acts as a QI) to determine that such accounts were reported in accordance with QI's FATCA requirements as a participating FFI, registered deemed-compliant FFI, or registered deemed-compliant Model 1 IGA FFI;

**(ii)** If QI is an NFFE acting as a QI on behalf of persons other than its shareholders, confirming that if QI is acting on behalf of a passive NFFE with substantial US owners, withholdable payments made to the passive NFFE and the information regarding its substantial US owners were reported;

**(iii)** Confirming with respect to any nonqualified intermediary or flow-through entity that provides information regarding an account holder (or interest holder) that is an NFFE (other than an excepted NFFE) with one or more substantial US owners that such substantial US owners were reported to the extent required under Sect. 8.04(B) of this Agreement;

**(iv)** Reviewing the documentation provided by a PAI or a partnership or trust to which QI applied the agency option to determine that QI reported on Form 8966 to the extent required under Sect. 4 of this Agreement; and

**(v)** Reviewing work papers used to prepare these forms.

**(4)** Obtain records of any reportable payments paid by QI to its US account holders to identify any US account holders for which QI failed to file an applicable Form 1099 (to the extent required) or report on a Form 8966 (or analogous reporting under an applicable Model 1 IGA).

**(5)** If QI is acting as a QDD, review accounts designated as accounts for which QI acted as a QDD to determine whether QI is acting as a QDD with respect to all potential Sect. 871(m) transactions and underlying securities for which it is required to act as a QDD and not any other transactions and whether the Sect. 871(m) amount includes the amounts in its equity derivatives dealer capacity and not amounts in its non-equity derivatives dealer capacity.

**(6)** Obtain records of account holders to which QI paid a PTP distribution or an amount realised from a sale of a PTP interest to verify that QI properly provided the statements or other information required under Sect. 8.07 of this Agreement with respect to the account holders.

**(7)** Determine whether QI has any agreements in place under Sect. 8.02(M) of this Agreement to report on Form 1042-S amounts realised paid to an NQI's account holders and, if so, verify that QI reported on Form 1042-S as agreed or otherwise has a written agreement in place with another withholding agent to report these amounts.

**(E) Significant Change in Circumstances.** The reviewer must verify that in the course of the review it has not discovered any significant change in circumstances, as described in Sect. 11.04(A), (D), or (E) of this Agreement.

**Sec. 10.06 Periodic Review Report.**

**(A) In General.** The results of the periodic review must be documented in a written report addressed to the responsible officer of QI and submitted to the IRS with the certification described in Sect. 10.03 of this Agreement (with a certified translation into English if the report is not in English). The report must describe the scope of the review and the actions performed to satisfy each requirement of Sect. 10.05(A) through (E), including the methodology for sampling determinations. The report may include explanatory footnotes to clarify the results of the report. Recommendations may be included but are not required to be provided in the report. The periodic review report should form the basis for the factual information provided by QI that is set forth in Appendix I. In addition to the findings of Sect. 10.05 of this Agreement, the periodic review report should also include details regarding the documentation and tax deposit and payment failures identified by the reviewer but then cured before the periodic review report is finalised. While the curing of inadequate documentation is permissible, the factual information reported (as set forth in Appendix I) should report the results of the review as it was performed and should not reflect the results after curing (unless stated otherwise). Any curing process should not delay certification of internal controls or factual information required in Appendix I to this Agreement. To the extent necessary, the periodic review report should include the dates on (or time period during) which curative documentation was received for accounts with respect to which the reviewer determined that underwithholding had occurred, the number of accounts for which curative documentation was obtained and a revised calculation of the underwithholding or additional backup withholding.

**(B) Periodic Review Report for QDDs.** If QI is acting as a QDD, the periodic review report should also include the number of accounts that were not correctly treated as (i) principal accounts (except accounts that are effectively connected with the conduct or a trade or business within the United States within the meaning of Sect. 864), (ii) non-principal accounts, (iii) principal accounts that are effectively connected with the conduct or a trade or business within the United States within the meaning of Sect. 864, (iv) equity derivatives dealer accounts, and (v) non-equity derivatives dealer accounts. The report should also include any other issues related to the QDD tax liability (*e.g.*, incorrect determination of whether an account is a potential Sect. 871(m) transaction or a Sect. 871(m) transaction, the dividends received in the QDD's equity derivatives dealer capacity and the taxes paid on those dividends, the net delta exposure, the Sect. 871(m) amount and the taxes on the Sect. 871(m) amount, the amount of dividend equivalent payments made, or any other amounts subject to tax (or required to compute the tax liability) under Sect. 871(a) and 881 (including the QDD tax liability)) for each QDD.

**(C) PAI Certification and Partnership or Trust to which QI Applies the Agency Option**. Any PAI with which QI has an agreement and any partnership or trust to which QI applies the agency option that does not provide its documentation and other information to QI for inclusion in QI's periodic review described in Sect. 10.04 of this Agreement, must conduct an independent periodic review in accordance with the compliance procedures described in Sect. 10.05 of this Agreement. The performance results of the periodic review must be documented in a written report addressed to the responsible officer of QI and must be available to the IRS upon request (with a certified translation into English if the report is not in English).

**(D) Retention of Report and Certifications.** The report and certifications described in this Sect. 10.06 must be retained by QI (or the Compliance QI) for as long as this Agreement is in effect.

**Sec. 10.07. Waiver of Periodic Review Requirement.**

**(A) In General.** A QI that is not acting as a QDD and that is an FFI that meets the requirements of Sect. 10.07(B) may apply for a waiver of the periodic review requirement. Notwithstanding the prior sentence, a QI that is acting as a QDD and otherwise qualifies to apply for a waiver of the periodic review requirement, may do so for calendar year 2023 or 2024. QI must request a waiver of the periodic review requirement under this Sect. 10.07 when the responsible officer makes the certification described in Sect. 10.03 of this Agreement. QI's application for such a waiver must be approved by the IRS, and waiver applications are not approved automatically. QI must apply for a waiver for each certification period for which a waiver is requested. If QI's request for a waiver of the periodic review requirement is granted, such approval is only to waive QI's obligations under Sects. 10.04 and 10.05 of this Agreement, and QI is still required to make the certification described in Sect. 10.03 of this Agreement. The waiver also does not preclude the IRS from requesting information or conducting a correspondence review as described in Sect. 10.07 of this Agreement. QI must include the information of any PAI with which QI has an agreement and any partnership or trust to which QI applies the agency option in its waiver application which is set forth in Part III of Appendix I to this Agreement. QI must also provide the information set forth on Appendix III to this Agreement for each year of the certification period.

**(B) Eligibility.** QI is eligible to apply for a waiver of the periodic review requirement if it meets the following requirements—

**(1)** QI must be an FFI and, for calendar years after 2024, that is not also acting as a QDD;

**(2)** QI is not part of a consolidated compliance program;

**(3)** For each calendar year covered by the certification period, the reportable amounts received by QI do not exceed $5 million (including the amount of PTP distributions subject to withholding under chapter 3 or 4);

**(4)** QI timely filed its Forms 1042, 1042-S, 945, 1099, and 8966 (or the reporting otherwise required under an applicable IGA), as applicable, for all calendar years covered by the certification period;

**(5)** QI made all periodic certifications and reviews required by Sects. 10.02 and 10.03 of this Agreement as well as all certifications required pursuant to QI's FATCA requirements as a participating FFI, registered deemed-compliant FFI, or registered deemed-compliant Model 1 IGA FFI; and

**(C) Documentation Required with Waiver Application.** When applying for a waiver under this Sect. 10.07, QI must include the information described in Appendix I to this Agreement using the most recent calendar year covered by the certification period and reporting such results without any curing or remediation.

**(D) Approval.** If QI's request for a waiver of the periodic review requirement is approved, the IRS will notify QI. If QI requests a waiver but such request is not approved, QI will be granted a six-month extension from the date of denial of the waiver to complete the periodic review. Such extension will not be granted if QI has made the request for waiver in bad faith.

**Sec. 10.08. Periodic Review.**

**(A) In General.** Based upon the certifications made by the responsible officer and the disclosure of material failures, the information reported on Forms 945, 1042, 1042-S, 1099, and 8966 filed with the IRS during the certification period, or otherwise at the IRS's discretion for compliance purposes, the IRS may initiate requests of QI under this Sect. 10.08. The IRS may pre-emptively request remediation or the conduct of a limited periodic review earlier than the time period provided in this Sect. 10 if, based on the information described above, the IRS identifies, in its discretion, a presence of factors indicating systemic or significant compliance failures by QI. The IRS may also request that QI designate a replacement responsible officer if QI's responsible officer has not complied with its responsibilities (including responding to requests by the IRS for additional information) or the IRS has information that indicates the responsible officer may not be relied upon to comply with its responsibilities.

**(B) Correspondence Review.** The IRS may, in its discretion, conduct additional fact finding through a correspondence review. In such a review, the IRS will contact the responsible officer of QI (or the Compliance QI) in writing and request information about QI's compliance with this Agreement or the compliance of a PAI or a partnership or trust to which QI applied the agency option, including, for example, information about documentation, withholding, or reporting processes, its periodic review, and information about any material failures that were disclosed to the IRS (including remediation plans). The IRS may request phone or video interviews with employees of QI (and the Compliance QI), a PAI, or a partnership or trust to which QI applied the agency option as part of the IRS's correspondence review. QI is required to respond in a reasonable time to any such requests.

**(C) Additional Review Procedures.** In limited circumstances, the IRS may direct QI (or the Compliance FFI) or any PAI or partnership or trust to which QI applies the agency option to perform additional, specified review procedures. The IRS reserves the right to require QI (or the Compliance QI) or a PAI, or a partnership or trust to which QI applied the agency option to engage an external reviewer to perform the additional review procedures regardless of whether such reviewer performed the periodic review. The IRS will provide the responsible officer of QI with a written plan describing the additional review procedures and will provide a due date of not more than 120 days for the QI to provide to the IRS a report covering the reviewer's findings.

**Section 11. Expiration, Termination, Merger and Default**

**Sec. 11.01. Term of Agreement.** This Agreement begins on the effective date referenced in Sect. 2.22 of this Agreement and expires on December 31, 2028, unless terminated before that time under Sect. 11.02 of this Agreement. This Agreement may be renewed for a further term as provided in Sect. 11.08 of this Agreement.

**Sec. 11.02. Termination of Agreement.**

**(A) In General.** This Agreement may be terminated by either the IRS or QI before the end of its term by delivery of a notice of termination to the other party, in accordance with Sect. 12.06 of this Agreement. The IRS, however, shall not terminate this Agreement unless there has been a significant change in circumstances, as defined in Sect. 11.04 of this Agreement, or an event of default has occurred, as defined in Sect. 11.06 of this Agreement, and the IRS determines, in its sole discretion, that the significant change in circumstances or the event of default warrants termination of this Agreement. In addition, the IRS may also terminate this Agreement before the end of its term if as a result of an amendment in accordance with Sect. 12.02 of this Agreement, the QDD is no longer entitled to act as a QDD. The IRS shall not terminate this Agreement for an event of default if QI can establish to the satisfaction of the IRS that all events of default for which it has received notice have been cured within the time period agreed upon. The IRS shall notify QI that an event of default has occurred and that the IRS intends to terminate the Agreement unless QI cures the default or establishes that no event of default occurred. A notice of termination sent by either party shall take effect on the date specified in the notice, and QI is required to notify its withholding agent of the date that its status as a QI is terminated. The termination of the Agreement shall not affect any of QI's reporting, tax filing, withholding, depositing, or payment responsibilities arising in the calendar years for which this Agreement was in effect and portion of the calendar year in which termination is requested. The IRS shall revoke QI's QI-EIN within a reasonable time after the reporting, tax filing, and depositing requirements for such years are satisfied. The termination of this Agreement is not intended to affect any other federal income tax consequences.

**(B) Periodic Review and Final Certification after Termination of Agreement.** Upon termination of this Agreement, QI must provide to the

IRS, within six months of the date of termination, the certification described in Sect. 10.03 of this Agreement covering the period from the end of the most recent certification period (or, if the first certification period has not ended, the effective date of this Agreement) to the date of termination.

Additionally, QI must submit a periodic review report that meets the requirements of Sect. 10.06 of this Agreement with its final certification if this Agreement is terminated in the final year of QI's certification period. QI may request a waiver of the periodic review requirement for this purpose if it is otherwise eligible for a waiver under Sect. 10.07 of this Agreement. If a waiver is not granted, QI must use one of the two prior years of the certification period for its periodic review. Regardless of whether QI is required to submit a periodic review report under this Sect. 11.02(B), the IRS may request that QI perform specified review procedures in accordance with Sect. 10.08(C) of this Agreement with respect to QI's final certification period. See Sect. 11.05(B) of this Agreement for a case in which a QI terminating this Agreement merges into or is acquired by another QI.

**Sec. 11.03. Loss of QDD Status.** If QI is acting as a QDD and the home office or branch, as applicable, fails to qualify as an eligible entity during the term of this Agreement, the home office or branch shall lose its QDD status immediately upon the QDD failing to qualify as an eligible entity and as of that date can no longer act as a QDD. QI is required to notify its withholding agent of the date that the QDD failed to qualify as an eligible entity and no longer was permitted to act as a QDD. The QDD's loss of QDD status shall not affect any of QI's QDD reporting, tax filing, withholding, depositing, or payment responsibilities for the period QI was acting as a QDD as provided in this Agreement, including paying its QDD tax liability.

**Sec. 11.04. Significant Change in Circumstances.** For purposes of this Agreement, a significant change in circumstances includes, but is not limited to—

**(A)** An acquisition of all, or substantially all, of QI's assets in any transaction in which QI is not the surviving legal entity;

**(B)** A change in US federal law, or applicable foreign law, that affects the validity of any provision of this Agreement, materially affects the procedures contained in this Agreement, or affects QI's ability to perform its obligations under this Agreement;

**(C)** A ruling of any court that affects the validity of any material provision of this Agreement;

**(D)** A material change in the applicable know-your-customer rules and procedures;

**(E)** A significant change in QI's business practices that affects QI's ability to meet its obligations under this Agreement;

**(F)** If QI is an FFI, QI's failure to maintain its status as a participating FFI, registered deemed-compliant FFI, or registered deemed-compliant Model 1 IGA FFI;

**(G)** If QI is acting as a sponsoring entity on behalf of a sponsored FFI or sponsored direct reporting NFFE, if it fails to comply with the due diligence, withholding, reporting, and compliance requirements of a sponsoring entity; or

**(H)** If QI is acting as a QDD, the home office or branch, as applicable, ceases to qualify as an eligible entity, including as a result of a change in its business or regulatory status (see Sect. 11.03).

**Sec. 11.05. Merger.**

**(A) In General.** If a QI (predecessor QI) merges with or is acquired by another QI (successor QI), and the successor QI assumes all the rights, debts, and obligations of the predecessor QI as it relates to the predecessor QI's QI agreement, the predecessor QI must notify the IRS that it intends to terminate this Agreement before the end of its term by delivery of a notice of termination and merger in accordance with Sect. 12.06 of this Agreement. A notice of termination and merger shall take effect on the date specified in the notice, and QI is required to notify its withholding agent of the date that its status as a QI is terminated and designate the successor QI to receive payments in its capacity as a QI for any accounts previously covered by the predecessor QI's QI agreement. The successor QI must ensure that all reporting and tax filing obligations are fulfilled and any withholding is deposited in accordance with the procedures outlined in Rev. Proc. 99-50, 1999-2 C.B. 757, when applicable, that arose in the calendar years and portion of the calendar year in which termination is requested and for which this Agreement was in effect (including for Form 1042-S filed to report withholding under chapter 4). To the extent QI is acting as a QDD, it must use the standard procedure outlined in Rev. Proc. 99-50 and cannot use the alternative procedures. See QI's FATCA Requirements as a participating FFI, registered deemed-compliant FFI, or registered deemed-compliant Model 1 IGA FFI for the procedures, if any, for reporting on Form 8966 in the case of a merger or acquisition. The IRS shall revoke the predecessor QI's QI-EIN within a reasonable time after the reporting, tax filing, and depositing requirements for such years are satisfied. The termination of this Agreement is not intended to affect any other federal income tax consequences.

**(B) Periodic Review and Certification after Merger.** A predecessor QI that is terminating its QI agreement and that is required to submit a periodic review report under Sect. 11.02(B) of this Agreement may satisfy this requirement through a combined periodic review. A combined periodic review for purposes of this section 11.05(B) is a periodic review that covers a calendar year that the predecessor QI is permitted to use under Sect. 11.02(B) of this Agreement and that includes accounts of both the predecessor QI and successor QI in the population of accounts for purposes of the review steps of Sect. 10.05 of this Agreement covering documentation and withholding requirements. See Appendix II of this Agreement for information on designing a statistical sample for a combined periodic review. The certifications required for both the predecessor QI and successor QI for the period covered by the combined review must include the factual information specific to each QI that is required under Appendix I of this Agreement. A predecessor QI may obtain a six-month extension of the time to submit a final certification under Sect. 11.02(B) of this Agreement for purposes of this Sect. 11.05(B). The request for an extension must indicate that it is being made due to the combined periodic review and be delivered to the IRS in accordance with Sect. 12.06 of this Agreement before the time otherwise required for the final certification.

**Sec. 11.06. Event of Default.** For purposes of this Agreement, an event of default occurs if QI fails to perform any material duty or obligation required under this Agreement and the responsible officer had actual knowledge or should have known of the facts relevant to the failure to perform any material duty. An event of default includes, but is not limited to, the occurrence of any of the following:

**(A)** QI fails to implement adequate procedures, accounting systems, and internal controls to ensure compliance with this Agreement;

**(B)** QI underwithholds a material amount of tax that QI is required to withhold under chapter 3, Sect. 1446(a), Sect. 1446(f), or chapter 4, or backup withhold under Sect. 3406 and fails to correct the underwithholding by filing an amended Form 1042 or 945 reporting, and paying, the appropriate tax;

**(C)** QI makes excessive refund claims;

**(D)** Documentation described in Sect. 5 of this Agreement is lacking, incorrect, or unreliable for a significant number of direct account holders under the requirements of Sect. 5.01(A) of this Agreement;

**(E)** QI files Forms 945, 1042, 1042-S, 1099, or 8966 that are materially incorrect or fraudulent, or fails to comply materially with the requirements of Sect. 8.07 of this Agreement with respect to account holders that are partners holding PTP interests (including account holders of another intermediary when QI acts as an agent for meeting these requirements);

**(F)** If QI is an FFI, QI fails to materially comply with its FATCA requirements as a participating FFI, registered deemed-compliant FFI, or registered deemed-compliant Model 1 IGA FFI;

**(G)** If QI is a sponsoring entity, QI fails to materially comply with the due diligence, withholding, reporting, and compliance requirements of a sponsoring entity;

**(H)** QI fails to materially comply with the requirements of a nonqualified intermediary under chapters 3 and 61, and Sects. 1446 and 3406 with respect to any account for which QI does not act as a QI.

**(I)** QI fails to perform a periodic review when required or document the findings of such review in a written report;

**(J)** QI fails to cooperate with the IRS on its compliance review described in Sect. 10.08 of this Agreement;

**(K)** QI fails to inform the IRS of any change in the applicable know-your-customer rules within 90 days of the change becoming effective;

**(L)** QI fails to inform the IRS within 90 days of any significant change in its business practices to the extent that change affects QI's obligations under this Agreement;

**(M)** QI fails to inform the IRS of any PAI of QI, as described in Sect. 4 of this Agreement;

**(N)** QI fails to cure a material failure identified in the qualified certification described in Part II.B of Appendix I to this Agreement or identified by the IRS;

**(O)** QI makes any fraudulent statement or a misrepresentation of material fact with regard to this Agreement to the IRS, a withholding agent, or QI's reviewer;

**(P)** The IRS determines that QI's reviewer is not sufficiently independent, as described in this Agreement, to adequately perform its review function, and QI fails to arrange for a periodic review conducted by a reviewer approved by the IRS;

**(Q)** An intermediary with which QI has a PAI agreement is in default with that agreement and QI fails to terminate that agreement within the time period specified in Sect. 4.04 of this Agreement;

**(R)** A partnership or trust to which QI applies the agency option is in default with that agreement and QI fails to terminate that agreement within the time period specified in Sect. 4.06 of this Agreement; and

**(S)** If QI is acting as a QDD, QI fails to timely pay a material amount of its QDD tax liability and fails to correct the underpayment and pay the appropriate tax amount.

**Sec. 11.07. Notice and Cure.** Upon the occurrence of an event of default, the IRS will deliver to QI a notice of default specifying each event of default. QI must respond to the notice of default within 60 days (60-day response) from the date of the notice of default. The 60-day response shall contain an offer to cure the event of default and the time period in which to cure or shall state why QI believes that no event of default occurred. If QI does not provide a 60-day response, the IRS will deliver a notice of termination as provided in Sect. 11.02 of this Agreement. If QI provides a 60-day response, the IRS shall either accept or reject QI's statement that no default has occurred or QI's proposal to cure the event of default. If the IRS rejects QI's contention that no default has occurred or rejects QI's proposal to cure the event of default, the IRS may offer a counter proposal to cure the event of default with which QI will be required to comply within 30 days. If QI fails to provide a 30-day response, the IRS will send a notice of termination in accordance with Sect. 11.02 of this Agreement to QI, which QI may appeal within 30 days of the date of the notice by sending a written appeal to the address specified in Sect. 12.06 of this Agreement. If QI appeals the notice of termination, this Agreement shall not terminate until the appeal has been decided. If an event of default is discovered in the course of a review, the QI may cure the default, without following the procedures of this Sect. 11.07, if the external reviewer's report describes the default and the actions that QI took to cure the default and the IRS determines that the cure procedures followed by QI were sufficient. If the IRS determines that QI's actions to cure the default were not sufficient, the IRS shall issue a notice of default and the procedures described in this Sect. 11.07 shall be followed.

**Sec. 11.08. Renewal.** If QI intends to renew this Agreement, it must submit an application for renewal to the IRS on QAAMS. This Agreement will be renewed only upon the agreement of both QI and the IRS. A QI that seeks to renew its QI agreement and also seeks to become a QDD (that was not previously acting as a QDD) must supplement the renewal request by providing a statement containing all information required by Form 14345 relating to a QDD.

**Section 12. Miscellaneous Provisions**

**Sec. 12.01.** QI's application to become a QI, all Appendices to this Agreement and know-your-customer rules included in a country attachment on IRS.gov relevant to QI (or a branch of QI), and, if QI is an FFI, its FATCA requirements as a participating FFI, registered deemed-compliant FFI, or registered deemed-compliant Model 1 IGA FFI, are hereby incorporated into and made an integral part of this Agreement. This Agreement constitutes the complete agreement between the parties. A QI may only represent its status as a QI for payments described in this Agreement and may not act as a QI for any payments without having the Agreement in effect for the applicable year.

**Sec. 12.02.** This Agreement may be amended by the IRS if the IRS determines that such amendment is needed for the sound administration of the internal revenue laws or internal revenue regulations. This Agreement will only be modified through published guidance issued by the IRS and US Treasury Department. Any such modification imposing additional requirements will in no event become effective until the later of 90 days after the IRS provides notice of such modification or the beginning of the next calendar year following the publication of such guidance.

**Sec. 12.03.** Any waiver of a provision of this Agreement is a waiver solely of that provision. The waiver does not obligate the IRS to waive other provisions of this Agreement or the same provision at a later date.

**Sec. 12.04.** This Agreement shall be governed by the laws of the United States. Any legal action brought under this Agreement shall be brought only in a United States court with jurisdiction to hear and resolve matters under the internal revenue laws of the United States. For this purpose, QI agrees to submit to the jurisdiction of such United States court.

**Sec. 12.05.** QI's rights and responsibilities under this Agreement cannot be assigned to another person.

**Sec. 12.06.** Except as otherwise provided on QAAMS, all written notices sent to the IRS by QI must be sent by either e-mail to lbi.fi.qiwpissues@IRS.gov or by registered, first class airmail (with each such notice to include the QI's name, QI-EIN, GIIN (if applicable), and the name of its responsible officer), addressed as follows:

Internal Revenue Service
Foreign Payments Practice
Foreign Intermediaries Program
290 Broadway, 12th Floor NW
New York, New York 10007-1867

Written notices provided to QI under this Agreement shall be sent by IRS by secure e- mail to the responsible officer of the QI and all contact persons identified by QI.

**Sec. 12.07.** QI, acting in its capacity as a QI or in any other capacity, does not act as an agent of the IRS, nor does it have the authority to hold itself out as an agent of the IRS.

# Appendix 3: DAC6

**Council Directive (EU) 2018/822 of 25 May 2018 amending Directive 2011/16/EU as regards mandatory automatic exchange of information in the field of taxation in relation to reportable cross-border arrangements**

THE COUNCIL OF THE EUROPEAN UNION,

Having regard to the Treaty on the Functioning of the European Union, and in particular Article 113 and 115 thereof,

Having regard to the proposal from the European Commission,

After transmission of the draft legislative act to the national parliaments,

Having regard to the opinion of the European Parliament,

Having regard to the opinion of the European Economic and Social Committee,

Acting in accordance with a special legislative procedure,

Whereas:

(1) In order to accommodate new initiatives in the field of tax transparency at the level of the Union, Council Directive 2011/16/EU has been the subject of a series of amendments over the last few years. In this context, Council Directive 2014/107/EU introduced the Common Reporting Standard ('CRS') developed by the Organisation for Economic Cooperation and Development (OECD) for financial account information within the Union. The CRS provides for the automatic exchange of information on financial accounts held by non-tax residents and establishes a framework for that exchange worldwide. Directive 2011/16/EU


R. K. McGill and K. V. Pitkin, *Qualified Intermediary*,
https://doi.org/10.1007/978-3-031-81410-5

was amended by Council Directive (EU) 2015/2376, which provided for the automatic exchange of information on advance cross-border tax rulings, and by Council Directive (EU) 2016/881, which provided for the mandatory automatic exchange of information on country-by-country reporting of multinational enterprises between tax authorities. In light of the use that anti-money-laundering information can have for tax authorities, Council Directive (EU) 2016/2258 placed an obligation on Member States to give tax authorities access to customer due diligence procedures applied by financial institutions under Directive (EU) 2015/849 of the European Parliament and of the Council. Although Directive 2011/16/EU has been amended several times in order to enhance the means tax authorities can use to react to aggressive tax planning, there is still a need to reinforce certain specific transparency aspects of the existing taxation framework.

(2) Member States find it increasingly difficult to protect their national tax bases from erosion as tax-planning structures have evolved to be particularly sophisticated and often take advantage of the increased mobility of both capital and persons within the internal market. Such structures commonly consist of arrangements which are developed across various jurisdictions and move taxable profits towards more beneficial tax regimes or have the effect of reducing the taxpayer's overall tax bill. As a result, Member States often experience considerable reductions in their tax revenues, which hinder them from applying growth-friendly tax policies. It is therefore critical that Member States' tax authorities obtain comprehensive and relevant information about potentially aggressive tax arrangements. Such information would enable those authorities to react promptly against harmful tax practices and to close loopholes by enacting legislation or by undertaking adequate risk assessments and carrying out tax audits. However, the fact that tax authorities do not react to a reported arrangement should not imply acceptance of the validity or tax treatment of that arrangement.

(3) Considering that most of the potentially aggressive tax-planning arrangements span across more than one jurisdiction, the disclosure of information about those arrangements would bring additional positive results where that information was also exchanged among Member States. In particular, the automatic exchange of information between tax authorities is crucial in order to provide those authorities with the necessary information to enable them to take action where they observe aggressive tax practices.

(4) Recognising how a transparent framework for developing business activity could contribute to clamping down on tax avoidance and evasion in the internal market, the Commission has been called on to embark on initiatives on the mandatory disclosure of information on potentially aggressive tax-planning arrangements along the lines of Action 12 of the OECD Base Erosion and Profit Shifting (BEPS) Project. In this context, the European Parliament has called for tougher measures against intermediaries who assist in arrangements that may lead to tax avoidance and evasion. It is also important to note that in the G7 Bari Declaration of 13 May 2017 on fighting tax crimes and other illicit financial flows, the OECD was asked to start discussing possible ways to address arrangements designed to circumvent reporting under the CRS or aimed at providing beneficial owners with the shelter of non-transparent structures, considering also model mandatory disclosure rules inspired by the approach taken for avoidance arrangements outlined within the BEPS Action 12 Report.

(5) It is necessary to recall how certain financial intermediaries and other providers of tax advice seem to have actively assisted their clients in concealing money offshore. Furthermore, although the CRS introduced by Directive 2014/107/EU is a significant step forward in establishing a framework of tax transparency within the Union, at least in terms of financial account information, it can still be improved.

(6) The reporting of potentially aggressive cross-border tax-planning arrangements can contribute effectively to the efforts for creating an environment of fair taxation in the internal market. In this light, an obligation for intermediaries to inform tax authorities of certain cross-border arrangements that could potentially be used for aggressive tax planning would constitute a step in the right direction. In order to develop a more comprehensive policy, it would also be necessary that as a second step, following the reporting, the tax authorities share information with their peers in other Member States. Such arrangements should also enhance the effectiveness of the CRS. In addition, it would be crucial to grant the Commission access to a sufficient amount of information so that it can monitor the proper functioning of this Directive. Such access to information by the Commission does not discharge a Member State from its obligations to notify any State aid to the Commission.

(7) It is acknowledged that the reporting of potentially aggressive cross-border tax-planning arrangements would stand a better chance of achieving its envisaged deterrent effect where the relevant information

reached the tax authorities at an early stage, in other words before such arrangements are actually implemented. To facilitate the work of Member States' administrations, the subsequent automatic exchange of information on such arrangements could take place every quarter.

(8) To ensure the proper functioning of the internal market and to prevent loopholes in the proposed framework of rules, the reporting obligation should be placed upon all actors that are usually involved in designing, marketing, organising or managing the implementation of a reportable cross-border transaction or a series of such transactions, as well as those who provide assistance or advice. It should not be ignored either that, in certain cases, the reporting obligation would not be enforceable upon an intermediary due to a legal professional privilege or where there is no intermediary because, for instance, the taxpayer designs and implements a scheme in-house. It would thus be crucial that, in such circumstances, tax authorities do not lose the opportunity to receive information about tax-related arrangements that are potentially linked to aggressive tax planning. It would therefore be necessary to shift the reporting obligation to the taxpayer who benefits from the arrangement in such cases.

(9) Aggressive tax-planning arrangements have evolved over the years to become increasingly more complex and are always subject to constant modifications and adjustments as a reaction to defensive countermeasures by the tax authorities. Taking this into consideration, it would be more effective to endeavour to capture potentially aggressive tax-planning arrangements through the compiling of a list of the features and elements of transactions that present a strong indication of tax avoidance or abuse rather than to define the concept of aggressive tax planning. Those indications are referred to as "hallmarks".

(10) Given that the primary objective of this Directive concerning the reporting of potentially aggressive cross-border tax-planning arrangements should focus on ensuring the proper functioning of the internal market, it is critical not to regulate at the level of the Union beyond what is necessary to achieve the envisaged aims. This is why it would be necessary to limit any common rules on reporting to cross-border situations, namely those involving either more than one Member State or a Member State and a third country. In such circumstances, due to the potential impact on the functioning of the internal market, one can justify the need for enacting a common set of rules, rather than leaving the matter to be dealt with at the national level. A Member State could take further national reporting measures of a similar nature, but any

information collected in addition to what is reportable in accordance with this Directive should not be communicated automatically to the competent authorities of the other Member States. That information could be exchanged on request or spontaneously according to applicable rules.

(11) Considering that the reportable arrangements should have a cross-border dimension, it would be important to share the relevant information with the tax authorities in other Member States in order to ensure the maximum effectiveness of this Directive in deterring aggressive tax-planning practices. The mechanism for the exchange of information in the context of advance cross-border rulings and advance pricing arrangements should also be used to accommodate the mandatory and automatic exchange of reportable information on potentially aggressive cross-border tax-planning arrangements among tax authorities in the Union.

(12) In order to facilitate the automatic exchange of information and enhance the efficient use of resources, exchanges should be carried out through the common communication network ('CCN') developed by the Union. In this context, information would be recorded in a secure central directory on administrative cooperation in the field of taxation. Member States should have to implement a series of practical arrangements, including measures to standardise the communication of all requisite information through the creation of a standard form. This should also involve specifying the linguistic requirements for the envisaged exchange of information and upgrading the CCN accordingly.

(13) In order to minimise costs and administrative burdens both for tax administrations and intermediaries and to ensure the effectiveness of this Directive in deterring aggressive tax-planning practices, the scope of automatic exchange of information in relation to reportable cross-border arrangements within the Union should be consistent with international developments. A specific hallmark should be introduced to address arrangements designed to circumvent reporting obligations involving automatic exchanges of information. For the purposes of that hallmark, agreements on the automatic exchange of financial account information under the CRS should be treated as equivalent to the reporting obligations laid down in Article 8(3a) of Directive 2014/107/EU and in Annex I thereto. In implementing the parts of this Directive addressing CRS avoidance arrangements and arrangements involving legal persons or legal arrangements or any other similar structures,

Member States could use the work of the OECD, and more specifically its Model Mandatory Disclosure Rules for Addressing CRS Avoidance Arrangements and Opaque Offshore Structures and its Commentary, as a source of illustration or interpretation, in order to ensure consistency of application across Member States, insofar those texts are aligned with the provisions of Union law.

(14) While direct taxation remains within the competence of Member States, it is appropriate to refer to a corporate tax rate of zero or almost zero, solely for the purpose of clearly defining the scope of the hallmark that covers arrangements involving cross-border transactions, which should be reportable under Directive 2011/16/EU by intermediaries or, as appropriate, taxpayers, and about which the competent authorities should exchange information automatically. Moreover, it is appropriate to recall that aggressive cross-border tax-planning arrangements, the main purpose or one of the main purposes of which is to obtain a tax advantage that defeats the object or purpose of the applicable tax law, are subject to the general anti-abuse rule as set out in Article 6 of Council Directive (EU) 2016/1164[1] .

(15) In order to improve the prospects for the effectiveness of this Directive, Member States should lay down penalties against the violation of national rules that implement this Directive. Such penalties should be effective, proportionate and dissuasive.

(16) In order to ensure uniform conditions for the implementation of this Directive and in particular for the automatic exchange of information between tax authorities, implementing powers should be conferred on the Commission to adopt a standard form with a limited number of components, including the linguistic arrangements. For the same reason, implementing powers should also be conferred on the Commission to adopt the necessary practical arrangements for upgrading the central directory on administrative cooperation in the field of taxation. Those powers should be exercised in accordance with Regulation (EU) No 182/2011 of the European Parliament and of the Council.[2]

(17) The European Data Protection Supervisor was consulted in accordance with Article 28(2) of Regulation (EC) No 45/2001 of the European Parliament and of the Council.[3] Any processing of personal data carried

---

[1] https://eur-lex.europa.eu/legal-content/EN/TXT/HTML/?uri=CELEX:32018L0822#ntr9-L_2018139EN.01000101-E0009

[2] https://eur-lex.europa.eu/legal-content/EN/TXT/HTML/?uri=CELEX:32018L0822#ntr10-L_2018139EN.01000101-E0010.

[3] https://eur-lex.europa.eu/legal-content/EN/TXT/HTML/?uri=CELEX:32018L0822#ntr11-L_2018139EN.01000101-E0011.

out within the framework of this Directive must comply with Directive 95/46/EC of the European Parliament and of the Council[4] and Regulation (EC) No 45/2001.

(18) This Directive respects the fundamental rights and observes the principles recognised in particular by the Charter of Fundamental Rights of the European Union.

(19) Since the objective of this Directive, namely to improve the functioning of the internal market by discouraging the use of aggressive cross-border tax-planning arrangements, cannot sufficiently be achieved by the Member States but can rather, by reason of the fact that it targets schemes which are developed to potentially take advantage of market inefficiencies that originate in the interaction among disparate national tax rules, be better achieved at Union level, the Union may adopt measures, in accordance with the principle of subsidiarity as set out in Article 5 of the Treaty on European Union. In accordance with the principle of proportionality as set out in that Article, this Directive does not go beyond what is necessary in order to achieve that objective, especially considering that it is limited to cross-border arrangements concerning either more than one Member State or a Member State and a third country.

(20) Directive 2011/16/EU should therefore be amended accordingly.

## HAS ADOPTED THIS DIRECTIVE:

*Article 1*

Directive 2011/16/EU is amended as follows:

(1) Article 3 is amended as follows:
(a) point 9 is amended as follows:
(i) in the first subparagraph, point (a) is replaced by the following:
'(a) for the purposes of Article 8(1) and Articles 8a, 8aa and 8ab, the systematic communication of predefined information to another Member State, without prior request, at pre-established regular intervals. For the purposes of Article 8(1), reference to available information relates to information in the tax files of the Member State communicating the information, which is retrievable in accordance with the procedures for gathering and processing information in that Member State;';

(continued)

[4] https://eur-lex.europa.eu/legal-content/EN/TXT/HTML/?uri=CELEX:32018L0822#ntr12-L_2018139EN.01000101-E0012.

(continued)

(ii) in the first subparagraph, point (c) is replaced by the following:

'(c) for the purposes of provisions of this Directive other than Article 8(1) and (3a) and Articles 8a, 8aa and 8ab, the systematic communication of predefined information provided in points (a) and (b) of this point';

(iii) in the second subparagraph, the first sentence is replaced by the following:

'In the context of Articles 8(3a), 8(7a) and 21(2), Article 25(2) and (3) and Annex IV, any capitalised term shall have the meaning that it has under the corresponding definitions set out in Annex I';

(b) the following points are added:

'18"cross-border arrangement" means an arrangement concerning either more than one Member State or a Member State and a third country where at least one of the following conditions is met:

(a) not all of the participants in the arrangement are resident for tax purposes in the same jurisdiction;
(b) one or more of the participants in the arrangement is simultaneously resident for tax purposes in more than one jurisdiction;
(c) one or more of the participants in the arrangement carries on a business in another jurisdiction through a permanent establishment situated in that jurisdiction and the arrangement forms part or the whole of the business of that permanent establishment;
(d) one or more of the participants in the arrangement carries on an activity in another jurisdiction without being resident for tax purposes or creating a permanent establishment situated in that jurisdiction;
(e) such arrangement has a possible impact on the automatic exchange of information or the identification of beneficial ownership

(continued)

(continued)

For the purposes of points 18 to 25 of this Article, Article 8ab and Annex IV, an arrangement shall also include a series of arrangements. An arrangement may comprise more than one step or part

19 "reportable cross-border arrangement" means any cross-border arrangement that contains at least one of the hallmarks set out in Annex IV

20 "hallmark" means a characteristic or feature of a cross-border arrangement that presents an indication of a potential risk of tax avoidance, as listed in Annex IV

21 "intermediary" means any person that designs, markets, organises or makes available for implementation or manages the implementation of a reportable cross-border arrangement

It also means any person that, having regard to the relevant facts and circumstances and based on available information and the relevant expertise and understanding required to provide such services, knows or could be reasonably expected to know that they have undertaken to provide, directly or by means of other persons, aid, assistance or advice with respect to designing, marketing, organising, making available for implementation or managing the implementation of a reportable cross-border arrangement. Any person shall have the right to provide evidence that such person did not know and could not reasonably be expected to know that that person was involved in a reportable cross-border arrangement. For this purpose, that person may refer to all relevant facts and circumstances as well as available information and their relevant expertise and understanding

In order to be an intermediary, a person shall meet at least one of the following additional conditions:

(a) be resident for tax purposes in a Member State;
(b) have a permanent establishment in a Member State through which the services with respect to the arrangement are provided;
(c) be incorporated in, or governed by the laws of, a Member State;
(d) be registered with a professional association related to legal, taxation or consultancy services in a Member State

22 "relevant taxpayer" means any person to whom a reportable cross-border arrangement is made available for implementation, or who is ready to implement a reportable cross-border arrangement or has implemented the first step of such an arrangement

23 for the purposes of Article 8ab, "associated enterprise" means a person who is related to another person in at least one of the following ways:

(a) a person participates in the management of another person by being in a position to exercise a significant influence over the other person;
(b) a person participates in the control of another person through a holding that exceeds 25% of the voting rights;
(c) a person participates in the capital of another person through a right of ownership that, directly or indirectly, exceeds 25% of the capital;
(d) a person is entitled to 25% or more of the profits of another person

If more than one person participates, as referred to in points (a) to (d), in the management, control, capital or profits of the same person, all persons concerned shall be regarded as associated enterprises

(continued)

(continued)

If the same persons participate, as referred to in points (a) to (d), in the management, control, capital or profits of more than one person, all persons concerned shall be regarded as associated enterprises

For the purposes of this point, a person who acts together with another person in respect of the voting rights or capital ownership of an entity shall be treated as holding a participation in all of the voting rights or capital ownership of that entity that are held by the other person

In indirect participations, the fulfilment of requirements under point (c) shall be determined by multiplying the rates of holding through the successive tiers. A person holding more than 50% of the voting rights shall be deemed to hold 100%

An individual, his or her spouse and his or her lineal ascendants or descendants shall be treated as a single person

24 "marketable arrangement" means a cross-border arrangement that is designed, marketed, ready for implementation or made available for implementation without a need to be substantially customised

25 "bespoke arrangement" means any cross-border arrangement that is not a marketable arrangement';

(2) the following Article is inserted:

'Article 8ab

**Scope and conditions of mandatory automatic exchange of information on reportable cross-border arrangements**

1. Each Member State shall take the necessary measures to require intermediaries to file information that is within their knowledge, possession or control on reportable cross-border arrangements with the competent authorities within 30 days beginning:

(a) on the day after the reportable cross-border arrangement is made available for implementation; or

(b) on the day after the reportable cross-border arrangement is ready for implementation; or

(c) when the first step in the implementation of the reportable cross-border arrangement has been made,

whichever occurs first

Notwithstanding the first subparagraph, intermediaries referred to in the second paragraph of point 21 of Article 3 shall also be required to file information within 30 days beginning on the day after they provided, directly or by means of other persons, aid, assistance or advice

2. In the case of marketable arrangements, Member States shall take the necessary measures to require that a periodic report be made by the intermediary every 3 months providing an update which contains new reportable information as referred to in points (a), (d), (g) and (h) of paragraph 14 that has become available since the last report was filed

3. Where the intermediary is liable to file information on reportable cross-border arrangements with the competent authorities of more than one Member State, such information shall be filed only in the Member State that features first in the list below:

(continued)

(continued)

(a) the Member State where the intermediary is resident for tax purposes;
(b) the Member State where the intermediary has a permanent establishment through which the services with respect to the arrangement are provided;
(c) the Member State which the intermediary is incorporated in or governed by the laws of;
(d) the Member State where the intermediary is registered with a professional association related to legal, taxation or consultancy services

4. Where, pursuant to paragraph 3, there is a multiple reporting obligation, the intermediary shall be exempt from filing the information if it has proof, in accordance with national law, that the same information has been filed in another Member State
5. Each Member State may take the necessary measures to give intermediaries the right to a waiver from filing information on a reportable cross-border arrangement where the reporting obligation would breach the legal professional privilege under the national law of that Member State. In such circumstances, each Member State shall take the necessary measures to require intermediaries to notify, without delay, any other intermediary or, if there is no such intermediary, the relevant taxpayer of their reporting obligations under paragraph 6

Intermediaries may only be entitled to a waiver under the first subparagraph to the extent that they operate within the limits of the relevant national laws that define their professions

6. Each Member State shall take the necessary measures to require that, where there is no intermediary or the intermediary notifies the relevant taxpayer or another intermediary of the application of a waiver under paragraph 5, the obligation to file information on a reportable cross-border arrangement lie with the other notified intermediary, or, if there is no such intermediary, with the relevant taxpayer
7. The relevant taxpayer with whom the reporting obligation lies shall file the information within 30 days, beginning on the day after the reportable cross-border arrangement is made available for implementation to that relevant taxpayer, or is ready for implementation by the relevant taxpayer, or when the first step in its implementation has been made in relation to the relevant taxpayer, whichever occurs first

Where the relevant taxpayer has an obligation to file information on the reportable cross-border arrangement with the competent authorities of more than one Member State, such information shall be filed only with the competent authorities of the Member State that features first in the list below:

(a) the Member State where the relevant taxpayer is resident for tax purposes;
(b) the Member State where the relevant taxpayer has a permanent establishment benefitting from the arrangement;
(c) the Member State where the relevant taxpayer receives income or generates profits, although the relevant taxpayer is not resident for tax purposes and has no permanent establishment in any Member State;
(d) the Member State where the relevant taxpayer carries on an activity, although the relevant taxpayer is not resident for tax purposes and has no permanent establishment in any Member State

(continued)

(continued)

8. Where, pursuant to paragraph 7, there is a multiple reporting obligation, the relevant taxpayer shall be exempt from filing the information if it has proof, in accordance with national law, that the same information has been filed in another Member State
9. Each Member State shall take the necessary measures to require that, where there is more than one intermediary, the obligation to file information on the reportable cross-border arrangement lie with all intermediaries involved in the same reportable cross-border arrangement

An intermediary shall be exempt from filing the information only to the extent that it has proof, in accordance with national law, that the same information referred to in paragraph 14 has already been filed by another intermediary

10. Each Member State shall take the necessary measures to require that, where the reporting obligation lies with the relevant taxpayer and where there is more than one relevant taxpayer, the relevant taxpayer that is to file information in accordance with paragraph 6 be the one that features first in the list below:

(a) the relevant taxpayer that agreed the reportable cross-border arrangement with the intermediary;

(b) the relevant taxpayer that manages the implementation of the arrangement

Any relevant taxpayer shall only be exempt from filing the information to the extent that it has proof, in accordance with national law, that the same information referred to in paragraph 14 has already been filed by another relevant taxpayer

11. Each Member State may take the necessary measures to require that each relevant taxpayer file information about their use of the arrangement to the tax administration in each of the years for which they use it
12. Each Member State shall take the necessary measures to require intermediaries and relevant taxpayers to file information on reportable cross-border arrangements the first step of which was implemented between the date of entry into force and the date of application of this Directive. Intermediaries and relevant taxpayers, as appropriate, shall file information on those reportable cross-border arrangements by 31 August 2020
13. The competent authority of a Member State where the information was filed pursuant to paragraphs 1 to 12 of this Article shall, by means of an automatic exchange, communicate the information specified in paragraph 14 of this Article to the competent authorities of all other Member States, in accordance with the practical arrangements adopted pursuant to Article 21
14. The information to be communicated by the competent authority of a Member State under paragraph 13 shall contain the following, as applicable:

(a) the identification of intermediaries and relevant taxpayers, including their name, date and place of birth (in the case of an individual), residence for tax purposes, TIN and, where appropriate, the persons that are associated enterprises to the relevant taxpayer;

(b) details of the hallmarks set out in Annex IV that make the cross-border arrangement reportable;

(continued)

(continued)

(c) a summary of the content of the reportable cross-border arrangement, including a reference to the name by which it is commonly known, if any, and a description in abstract terms of the relevant business activities or arrangements, without leading to the disclosure of a commercial, industrial or professional secret or of a commercial process, or of information the disclosure of which would be contrary to public policy;
(d) the date on which the first step in implementing the reportable cross-border arrangement has been made or will be made;
(e) details of the national provisions that form the basis of the reportable cross-border arrangement;
(f) the value of the reportable cross-border arrangement;
(g) the identification of the Member State of the relevant taxpayer(s) and any other Member States which are likely to be concerned by the reportable cross-border arrangement;
(h) the identification of any other person in a Member State likely to be affected by the reportable cross-border arrangement, indicating to which Member States such person is linked

15. The fact that a tax administration does not react to a reportable cross-border arrangement shall not imply any acceptance of the validity or tax treatment of that arrangement
16. To facilitate the exchange of information referred to in paragraph 13 of this Article, the Commission shall adopt the practical arrangements necessary for the implementation of this Article, including measures to standardise the communication of the information set out in paragraph 14 of this Article, as part of the procedure for establishing the standard form provided for in Article 20(5)
17. The Commission shall not have access to information referred to in points (a), (c) and (h) of paragraph 14
18. The automatic exchange of information shall take place within one month of the end of the quarter in which the information was filed. The first information shall be communicated by 31 October 2020';

(3) in Article 20, paragraph 5 is replaced by the following:

'5. The Commission shall adopt standard forms, including the linguistic arrangements, in accordance with the procedure referred to in Article 26(2), in the following cases:

(a) for the automatic exchange of information on advance cross-border rulings and advance pricing arrangements pursuant to Article 8a before 1 January 2017;
(b) for the automatic exchange of information on reportable cross-border arrangements pursuant to Article 8ab before 30 June 2019

Those standard forms shall not exceed the components for the exchange of information listed in Articles 8a(6) and 8ab(14), and such other related fields which are linked to these components which are necessary to achieve the objectives of Articles 8a and 8ab, respectively

(continued)

(continued)

| |
|---|
| 'The linguistic arrangements referred to in the first subparagraph shall not preclude Member States from communicating the information referred to in Articles 8a and 8ab in any of the official languages of the Union. However, those linguistic arrangements may provide that the key elements of such information shall also be sent in another official language of the Union'; |

| | |
|---|---|
| (4) | in Article 21, paragraph 5 is replaced by the following:<br>'5. The Commission shall by 31 December 2017 develop and provide with technical and logistical support a secure Member State central directory on administrative cooperation in the field of taxation where information to be communicated in the framework of Article 8a(1) and (2) shall be recorded in order to satisfy the automatic exchange provided for in those paragraphs<br>The Commission shall by 31 December 2019 develop and provide with technical and logistical support a secure Member State central directory on administrative cooperation in the field of taxation where information to be communicated in the framework of Article 8ab(13), (14) and (16) shall be recorded in order to satisfy the automatic exchange provided for in those paragraphs<br>The competent authorities of all Member States shall have access to the information recorded in that directory. The Commission shall also have access to the information recorded in that directory, however within the limitations set out in Articles 8a(8) and 8ab(17). The necessary practical arrangements shall be adopted by the Commission in accordance with the procedure referred to in Article 26(2)<br>Until that secure central directory is operational, the automatic exchange provided for in Article 8a(1) and (2) and Article 8ab(13), (14) and (16) shall be carried out in accordance with paragraph 1 of this Article and the applicable practical arrangements'; |

| | |
|---|---|
| (5) | in Article 23, paragraph 3 is replaced by the following:<br>'3. Member States shall communicate to the Commission a yearly assessment of the effectiveness of the automatic exchange of information referred to in Articles 8, 8a, 8aa and 8ab as well as the practical results achieved. The Commission shall, by means of implementing acts, adopt the form and the conditions of communication for that yearly assessment. Those implementing acts shall be adopted in accordance with the procedure referred to in Article 26(2)'; |

(6) Article 25a is replaced by the following:
*'Article 25a*
**Penalties**
Member States shall lay down the rules on penalties applicable to infringements of national provisions adopted pursuant to this Directive and concerning Articles 8aa and 8ab, and shall take all measures necessary to ensure that they are implemented. The penalties provided for shall be effective, proportionate and dissuasive';

(7) Article 27 is replaced by the following:
*'Article 27*
**Reporting**
1. Every five years after 1 January 2013, the Commission shall submit a report on the application of this Directive to the European Parliament and to the Council
2. Every two years after 1 July 2020, the Member States and the Commission shall evaluate the relevance of Annex IV and the Commission shall present a report to the Council. That report shall, where appropriate, be accompanied by a legislative proposal';

(8) Annex IV, the text of which is set out in the Annex to this Directive, is added

*Article 2*

1. Member States shall adopt and publish, by 31 December 2019 at the latest, the laws, regulations and administrative provisions necessary to comply with this Directive. They shall immediately inform the Commission thereof.They shall apply those provisions from 1 July 2020.
2. When Member States adopt those provisions, they shall contain a reference to this Directive or be accompanied by such a reference on the occasion of their official publication. Member States shall determine how such reference is to be made.Member States shall communicate to the Commission the text of the main provisions of national law which they adopt in the field covered by this Directive.

*Article 3*

This Directive shall enter into force on the twentieth day following that of its publication in the *Official Journal of the European Union*.

*Article 4*

This Directive is addressed to the Member States.

Done at Brussels, 25 May 2018.

*For the Council*
*The President*
V. GORANOV

# Annex

## Annex IV

### Hallmarks

### Part I. Main Benefit Test

Generic hallmarks under category A and specific hallmarks under category B and under points (b)(i), (c) and (d) of paragraph 1 of category C may only be taken into account where they fulfil the "main benefit test".

That test will be satisfied if it can be established that the main benefit or one of the main benefits which, having regard to all relevant facts and circumstances, a person may reasonably expect to derive from an arrangement is the obtaining of a tax advantage.

In the context of hallmark under paragraph 1 of category C, the presence of conditions set out in points (b)(i), (c) or (d) of paragraph 1 of category C can not alone be a reason for concluding that an arrangement satisfies the main benefit test.

### Part II. Categories of Hallmarks

#### A. Generic Hallmarks Linked to the Main Benefit Test

| | |
|---|---|
| 1 | .An arrangement where the relevant taxpayer or a participant in the arrangement undertakes to comply with a condition of confidentiality which may require them not to disclose how the arrangement could secure a tax advantage vis-à-vis other intermediaries or the tax authorities |

| | |
|---|---|
| 2 | An arrangement where the intermediary is entitled to receive a fee (or interest, remuneration for finance costs and other charges) for the arrangement and that fee is fixed by reference to:<br>(a) the amount of the tax advantage derived from the arrangement; or<br>(b) whether or not a tax advantage is actually derived from the arrangement. This would include an obligation on the intermediary to partially or fully refund the fees where the intended tax advantage derived from the arrangement was not partially or fully achieved |

| | |
|---|---|
| 3 | An arrangement that has substantially standardised documentation and/or structure and is available to more than one relevant taxpayer without a need to be substantially customised for implementation |

## B. Specific Hallmarks Linked to the Main Benefit Test

| | |
|---|---|
| 1 | An arrangement whereby a participant in the arrangement takes contrived steps which consist in acquiring a loss-making company, discontinuing the main activity of such company and using its losses in order to reduce its tax liability, including through a transfer of those losses to another jurisdiction or by the acceleration of the use of those losses |

| | |
|---|---|
| 2 | An arrangement that has the effect of converting income into capital, gifts or other categories of revenue which are taxed at a lower level or exempt from tax |

| | |
|---|---|
| 3 | An arrangement which includes circular transactions resulting in the round-tripping of funds, namely through involving interposed entities without other primary commercial function or transactions that offset or cancel each other or that have other similar features |

## C. Specific Hallmarks Related to Cross-border Transactions

| | |
|---|---|
| 1 | An arrangement that involves deductible cross-border payments made between two or more associated enterprises where at least one of the following conditions occurs:<br>(a) the recipient is not resident for tax purposes in any tax jurisdiction;<br>(b) although the recipient is resident for tax purposes in a jurisdiction, that jurisdiction either:<br>(i) does not impose any corporate tax or imposes corporate tax at the rate of zero or almost zero; or<br>(ii) is included in a list of third-country jurisdictions which have been assessed by Member States collectively or within the framework of the OECD as being non-cooperative;<br>(c) the payment benefits from a full exemption from tax in the jurisdiction where the recipient is resident for tax purposes;<br>(d) the payment benefits from a preferential tax regime in the jurisdiction where the recipient is resident for tax purposes; |

| | |
|---|---|
| 2 | Deductions for the same depreciation on the asset are claimed in more than one jurisdiction |

3 Relief from double taxation in respect of the same item of income or capital is claimed in more than one jurisdiction

4 There is an arrangement that includes transfers of assets and where there is a material difference in the amount being treated as payable in consideration for the assets in those jurisdictions involved

## D. Specific Hallmarks Concerning Automatic Exchange of Information and Beneficial Ownership

1 An arrangement which may have the effect of undermining the reporting obligation under the laws implementing Union legislation or any equivalent agreements on the automatic exchange of Financial Account information, including agreements with third countries, or which takes advantage of the absence of such legislation or agreements. Such arrangements include at least the following:

(a) the use of an account, product or investment that is not, or purports not to be, a Financial Account, but has features that are substantially similar to those of a Financial Account;

(b) the transfer of Financial Accounts or assets to, or the use of jurisdictions that are not bound by the automatic exchange of Financial Account information with the State of residence of the relevant taxpayer;

(c) the reclassification of income and capital into products or payments that are not subject to the automatic exchange of Financial Account information;

(d) the transfer or conversion of a Financial Institution or a Financial Account or the assets therein into a Financial Institution or a Financial Account or assets not subject to reporting under the automatic exchange of Financial Account information;

(e) the use of legal entities, arrangements or structures that eliminate or purport to eliminate reporting of one or more Account Holders or Controlling Persons under the automatic exchange of Financial Account information;

(f) arrangements that undermine, or exploit weaknesses in, the due diligence procedures used by Financial Institutions to comply with their obligations to report Financial Account information, including the use of jurisdictions with inadequate or weak regimes of enforcement of anti-money-laundering legislation or with weak transparency requirements for legal persons or legal arrangements

| | |
|---|---|
| 2 | An arrangement involving a non-transparent legal or beneficial ownership chain with the use of persons, legal arrangements or structures:<br>(a) that do not carry on a substantive economic activity supported by adequate staff, equipment, assets and premises; and<br>(b) (b) that are incorporated, managed, resident, controlled or established in any jurisdiction other than the jurisdiction of residence of one or more of the beneficial owners of the assets held by such persons, legal arrangements or structures; and<br>(c) (c) where the beneficial owners of such persons, legal arrangements or structures, as defined in Directive (EU) 2015/849, are made unidentifiable |

## E. Specific Hallmarks Concerning Transfer Pricing

| | |
|---|---|
| 1 | An arrangement which involves the use of unilateral safe harbour rules |

| | |
|---|---|
| 2 | An arrangement involving the transfer of hard-to-value intangibles. The term "hard-to-value intangibles" covers intangibles or rights in intangibles for which, at the time of their transfer between associated enterprises:<br>(a) no reliable comparables exist; and<br>(b) at the time the transaction was entered into, the projections of future cash flows or income expected to be derived from the transferred intangible, or the assumptions used in valuing the intangible are highly uncertain, making it difficult to predict the level of ultimate success of the intangible at the time of the transfer |

| | |
|---|---|
| 3 | An arrangement involving an intragroup cross-border transfer of functions and/or risks and/or assets, if the projected annual earnings before interest and taxes (EBIT), during the three-year period after the transfer, of the transferor or transferors, are less than 50% of the projected annual EBIT of such transferor or transferors if the transfer had not been made |

# Appendix 4: Trace AI Agreement

**Agreement Authorising Financial Intermediary to Act as an Authorised Intermediary with Respect to Income Arising in [Country]**

**WHEREAS**, [Financial Intermediary] (the —Applicant||) has submitted an application to become an Authorised Intermediary with respect to certain types of income arising in [Country] (the —Source Country||);

**WHEREAS**, the Applicant and the Affiliates of the Applicant designated in Appendix A to this Agreement that are signatories to this Agreement (individually and collectively referred to as —the AI||), and [the competent authority of the Source Country] (the —Competent Authority||) desire to enter into an agreement (this —Agreement||) to establish the AI's rights and obligations regarding documentation, information reporting,

and compliance with respect to certain types of income arising in the Source Country;

**WHEREAS,** the AI and the Competent Authority (the —Parties||) have accepted the procedures designated in Appendix B to this Agreement (the —Procedures||), as such Procedures may be modified by this Agreement;

**NOW, THEREFORE**, in consideration of the following terms, representations, and conditions, the Parties agree as follows:

1. The AI agrees to undertake the responsibilities and assume the liabilities of an Authorised Intermediary as set out in the Procedures, as they may be modified by this Agreement, and the Competent Authority agrees to allow the AI to act as an Authorised Intermediary in accordance with, and subject to, those Procedures.


R. K. McGill and K. V. Pitkin, *Qualified Intermediary*,
https://doi.org/10.1007/978-3-031-81410-5

2. The Parties agree that the definition of Covered Payment set forth in the Procedures shall be modified to include the following types of income:

[];

and to exclude:

[].

3. The Parties agree that the definition of Reportable Payment set forth in the Procedures shall be modified to include the following types of income:

[];

and to exclude:

[].

4. The Parties agree that the term —Eligible Countries|| shall mean: [list of countries and jurisdictions identified by the Source Country, taking into account factors including whether the Source Country has with that country or jurisdiction an effective exchange of information relationship, whether that country or jurisdiction has in effect adequate Know Your Customer Rules, and whether the IMPLEMENTATION PACKAGE country or jurisdiction is a member of a multilateral organisation or community or grouping of countries that adopt common standards and approaches to issues of tax compliance, including mutual assistance (such as the Member States of the European Union or Organisation for Economic Co-Operation and Development)];

5. [The Parties agree that the AI will/will not undertake [primary] withholding responsibilities unless specified otherwise in Appendix A. [In undertaking such [primary] withholding responsibilities, the AI agrees to comply with the additional procedures set out in Appendix C to this Agreement.]]

6. For purposes of providing Tax Rate Information to a Payor in accordance with Paragraph IV.A of the Procedures, the rate of withholding that will apply to:

(a) a Covered Payment in respect of a resident of the Source Country with respect to which the AI has received a valid Investor Self-Declaration, either directly from the AI's own Direct Account Holder that is an Investor, or indirectly through a Contractual Intermediary, is/are [the applicable rate(s) provided in the Source Country's domestic law at the time this Agreement is entered into for the relevant category or categories of residents of the Source Country with respect to each relevant income type], as such rate may be modified by [reference to relevant provision(s) of domestic law];

(b) a Covered Payment in respect of a resident of the Source Country with respect to which the AI has not received a valid Investor Self-Declaration either directly from the AI's own Direct Account Holder that is an Investor, or indirectly through a Contractual Intermediary is/are [the back-up rate(s) provided in the Source Country's domestic law at the time this Agreement is entered into for the relevant category or categories of residents of the Source Country with respect to each relevant income type, if applicable], as such rate may be modified by [reference to relevant provision(s) of domestic law];

(c) a Covered Payment in respect of a non-resident of the Source Country with respect to which the AI has received a valid Investor Self-Declaration, either directly from the AI's own Direct Account Holder that is an Investor, or indirectly through a Contractual Intermediary, is/are the [lower of the] applicable rate(s) provided in the relevant tax treaty with respect to income of that type, but excluding lower rates applicable to companies receiving dividends from companies in which they own a specified percentage of the capital or voting rights

(or some combination thereof)[, or in [cross-reference to relevant provisions of domestic law providing a reduction or an exemption from withholding tax]];

[(d) a Covered Payment with respect to which the AI has assumed [primary] withholding responsibilities [or with respect to which the AI has received a valid Intermediary Declaration from a Withholding agent] is zero;]

(e) a Covered Payment with respect to which the AI has received from an Authorised Intermediary a valid Intermediary Declaration and Tax Rate Information is/are the rates specified in that Tax Rate Information; and

(f) all other Covered Payments, is/are [standard rate(s) for the relevant income types provided under Source Country law at the time this Agreement is entered into for undocumented investors], as such rate(s) may be modified by [reference to relevant provision(s) of domestic law]. AGREEMENT ATHORISAING FINANCIAL INTERMEDIARY TO ACT AS AN ATHORISED INTERMEDIARY WITH RESPECT TO INCOME ARISING IN [COUNTRY]

Implementation Package

7. The Parties agree that the period for retention of Tax Rate Information for purposes of Paragraph IV.C of the Procedures shall be [description of applicable document retention period in the Source Country, including starting date] and for retention of documentation for purposes of Paragraph V.E of the Procedures shall be [description of applicable document retention period in the Source Country, including starting date].

8. The Parties agree that claims made under paragraph VI.A.3 of the Procedures will be processed only if they are filed by [description of applicable statute of limitations in the Source Country, including starting date].

9. The Parties agree that the applicable period for purposes of Paragraph II.B (regarding claims against the AI for underwithholding) shall be

[description of applicable statute of limitations in the Source Country for an assessment by the Competent Authority with respect to underwithholding on an Investor, including starting date].

10. The Parties agree that, unless changed in accordance with Paragraph VIII.B.6 of the Procedures, the Independent Reviewer shall be: [] If different from the above, the Independent Reviewer of each Affiliate is set out in Appendix A.

11. Notices shall be directed as follows:

To the Competent Authority:

Contact:

____________________________________________

Address:

____________________________________________

City: ______________ Province, State or Locality: ____________
Country: _______________Postal Code: __________________
Telephone: ______________Fax: __________________
e-mail: ____________________

To the AI:

Contact: ____________________________________________

Address:

____________________________________________

City: ______________ Province, State or Locality: ____________
Country: ____________ Postal Code: ______________________
Telephone: _________________Fax: ___________________
e-mail: ______________________

To the Independent Reviewer:

Contact: ____________________________________________

Address:

____________________________________________

City: _____________ Province, State or Locality: ________________
Country: ____________ Postal Code: ________________________
Telephone: _______________Fax: ________________
e-mail: __________________________

If different from the above, the address of the Affiliates' Independent Reviewers is set out in Appendix A.

12. The Agreement shall be governed by the laws of the Source Country. Any legal action brought under this Agreement shall be brought only in [appropriate court of the Source Country]. For this purpose, the AI agrees to submit to the jurisdiction of such court.

13. This Agreement shall enter into effect on [] and shall remain in effect indefinitely unless terminated by either Party in accordance with Section IX of the Procedures.

14. The AI's application to become an Authorised Intermediary and all the Appendices to this Agreement and Annexes to the Procedures are hereby incorporated into and made an integral part of this Agreement, which shall constitute the entire agreement between the Parties.

15. Terms used in this Agreement shall have the meaning given to them in the Procedures, except as explicitly modified by this Agreement.

16. The Applicant's Authorised Intermediary Identification Number shall be [] and those of its Affiliates designated in Appendix A to this Agreement shall be as set out therein.

17. The AI hereby gives permission to the Competent Authority to disclose its status as an Authorised Intermediary or to make such information publicly available and, if the Competent Authority designates the Applicant or any Affiliate designated in Appendix A as an Excluded Intermediary, to disclose such Excluded Intermediary's status as such to any person or to make such information publicly available.

THIS AGREEMENT is made in duplicate by and between the Applicant, any Affiliates of the Applicant designated in Appendix A to this Agreement, and the Competent Authority by:

On behalf of the Competent Authority:

______________________________

Signature
Date

______________________________

Name of Signatory in block capitals or type

______________________________

Title of Signatory

On behalf of the Applicant: AGREEMENT ATHORISING FINANCIAL INTERMEDIARY TO ACT AS AN ATHORISED INTERMEDIARY WITH RESPECT TO INCOME ARISING IN
[COUNTRY]

______________________________

Signature
Date

______________________________

Name of Signatory in block capitals or type

______________________________

Title of Signatory

[Additional signature blocks, if necessary, for affiliates]– APPENDIX A: AFFILIATES OF THE APPLICANT AUTHORISED TO ACT AS AUTHORISED INTERMEDIARIES

**Appendix A:**
**Affiliates of the Applicant Authorised to Act as Authorised Intermediaries**

The following Affiliates of the Applicant are authorised to act as Authorised Intermediaries with respect to Covered Payments arising in the Source Country, and their AIINs are as indicated:

**Name of Affiliate**

**Address of Affiliate**

**AIIN of Affiliate**

[[**Primary**] **Withholding Responsibility:** Yes/No]

**Independent Reviewer (if different from Applicant's Independent Reviewer)**

**Address of Independent Reviewer**

[to be repeated for each Affiliate]APPENDIX B: PROCEDURES REGARDING THE OPERATION OF A FINANCIAL INTERMEDIARY AS AN AUTHORISED INTERMEDIARY

**Appendix B:**
**Procedures Regarding the Operation of a Financial Intermediary as an Authorised Intermediary**

**I. Purpose**

This document provides guidance regarding the procedures (the —Procedures||) to be followed by a financial intermediary in fulfilling its obligations under an agreement (the —Agreement||), to which these Procedures are appended as Appendix B, with the taxing authority of [Country] (the —Source Country||) to be an Authorised Intermediary with respect to certain payments arising in the Source Country. These Procedures form part of the Agreement and are subject to the specific undertakings contained therein.

**II. Obligations of the Authorised Intermediary**

**(A) In General.** The AI shall:

1. determine the correct withholding rate to be applied to its Account Holders on the basis of the documentation requirements of Section V;

2. make claims for reduced withholding rates on behalf of its Account Holders by providing Tax Rate Information, as described in Section IV, to Payors of Covered Payments;

3. collect Tax Rate Information provided by other Authorised Intermediaries in accordance with paragraph IV.D.1;

4. report to the Competent Authority on an annual basis information regarding Reportable Payments paid by the AI to Account Holders, in the manner described in Section VII;

5. retain records of such Tax Rate Information and other relevant declarations and notifications, including Investor Self-Declarations, in the manner described in Paragraphs IV.C and V.E and, upon request, make all such records available for inspection by the Competent Authority or Independent Reviewer as provided for in

Section VIII; and

6. use its best efforts to operate these Procedures in accordance with their terms.

**(B) Liability of the AI.** The AI acknowledges that it is liable for the payment of any underwithholding of tax that occurs with respect to a Covered Payment received on behalf of an Investor, whether a Direct Account Holder or an Indirect Account Holder, unless that Investor is also an Account Holder with respect to another Authorised Intermediary that has received the Covered Payment, directly or indirectly, through the AI. For these purposes, —underwithholding|| does not include the failure to deposit (by any person other than the AI) amounts that have been withheld. This paragraph shall apply notwithstanding that the AI may have complied with these Procedures with respect to the Covered Payments to which such underwithholding relates. Claims by the Competent Authority under this paragraph shall be barred, however, if they are made after the period set out in Paragraph 9 of the Agreement has run.

**(C) Scope of the Agreement.** The Agreement shall apply to each Office of the AI located in the Eligible Countries, but only to the extent that such an Office receives a Covered Payment with respect to an account that the AI has designated as an account for which it is acting in its capacity as an Authorised Intermediary, in accordance with Paragraph IV.A of these Procedures.

**III. Definitions.**

For purposes of these Procedures, the terms set out below shall have the meaning provided by this Section III.

**(A) "Account Holder"** means any person that is a Direct Account Holder or an Indirect Account Holder and with respect to which the AI acts as an Authorised Intermediary. A Direct Account Holder is any person (including another Intermediary) who has an account directly with an Authorised Intermediary. An Indirect Account Holder is any person who receives amounts that have been paid through an Authorised Intermediary but who does not have a direct account relationship with the Authorised Intermediary. For example, a person that has an account with a foreign Intermediary which, in turn, is a Direct Account Holder of the AI is an Indirect Account Holder. A person is an Indirect Account Holder even if there are multiple tiers of Intermediaries (each of which would also be a Direct or Indirect Account Holder of the Authorised Intermediary) between the person and the Authorised Intermediary. If a Fiscally Transparent Entity acts as an Intermediary under these Procedures by making claims on behalf of its partners, beneficiaries, or similar persons, each such partner, beneficiary or similar person shall be treated as an Account Holder.

**(B) "Affiliate"** means any person that controls the Applicant, that is controlled by the Applicant, or that is under common control with the Applicant.

**(C) "the AI"** means the Applicant and its Affiliates designated as Authorised Intermediaries in the Agreement of which these Procedures form a part;

**(D) "the Applicant"** means the Intermediary that submitted the application to enter into the Agreement of which these Procedures form a part;

**(E) "Authorised Intermediary"** means any Intermediary, including the AI, that has entered into an agreement with the Competent Authority to be treated as an Authorised Intermediary and acts in its capacity as an Authorised Intermediary;

**(F) "Authorised Intermediary Identification Number" or "AIIN"** means a unique combination of numbers assigned by the Source Country to an Intermediary upon the Source Country's conclusion of an agreement to treat the Intermediary as an Authorised Intermediary;

**(G) "Competent Authority"** means the tax authority of the Source Country designated in the Agreement of which these Procedures form a part;

**(H) "Contractual Intermediary"** means any Intermediary that is neither an Excluded Intermediary with respect to the Source Country nor acting as an Authorised Intermediary and with respect to which the AI has received a valid Intermediary Declaration (original or copy) in the form set out in Annex 1 for Contractual Intermediaries certifying that the Intermediary is subject to Know Your Customer Rules (except to the extent that it is an Intermediary only by reason of being a Fiscally Transparent Entity) with respect to the Account Holders for which claims are made through the AI, authorising the disclosure of the declaration to relevant tax authorities in accordance with its terms and agreeing to specified procedures for the recovery of under-withheld tax;

**(I) "Covered Payment"** means, except to the extent modified by the Agreement, any payment of dividends or interest arising in the Source

Country received by the AI with respect to an account that has been designated by the AI in accordance with Paragraph IV.A as one for which it is acting in its capacity as an Authorised Intermediary;

**(J) "Eligible Countries"** means the countries and jurisdictions designated as such in the Agreement of which these Procedures form a part;

**(K) "Excluded Intermediary"** means an Intermediary that has been designated as such by the Competent Authority in accordance with Paragraph V.D or IX.C;

**(L) "Fiscally Transparent Entity"** means an entity or arrangement that has not provided an Investor Self-Declaration on its own behalf because, with respect to Covered Payments its partners, beneficiaries or similar persons are treated as deriving the payments directly;

**(M) "Independent Reviewer"** means the third party designated in the Agreement to perform a review of the AI's compliance with its obligations under these Procedures;

**(N) "Independent Reviewer's Report"** means a report of the Independent Reviewer described in Section VIII and in Annex 2;

**(O) "Intermediary"** means any person that acts on behalf of another person such as a custodian, broker, nominee or other agent, including a Fiscally Transparent Entity, with respect to a Covered Payment;

**(P) "Intermediary Declaration"** means the certification, in one of the forms set out in Annex 1, provided by an Intermediary to another Intermediary, authorising the disclosure of the declaration to relevant tax authorities in accordance with its terms and agreeing to specified procedures for the recovery of under-withheld tax;

**(Q) "Investor"** means any person that receives a Covered Payment and that is not acting as an Intermediary with respect to that Covered Payment;

**(R) "Investor Self-Declaration"** means the certification, in one of the forms set out in Annex 1, provided by an Account Holder to an Intermediary, certifying that the Account Holder is the beneficial owner of the income to be paid or credited to the account(s) to which the certification relates, providing certain additional information

relevant to determining the appropriate rate of withholding to be applied to the income to be received, authorising the disclosure of the declaration to relevant tax authorities in accordance with its terms and agreeing to specified procedures for the recovery of under-withheld tax;

**(S) "Know Your Customer Rules"** means customer due diligence and record- keeping requirements relating to the opening and maintenance of accounts with financial services firms that are based on the relevant principles established by the Financial Action Task Force, including in particular

Recommendations 4-11 of the 40 Recommendations relating to measures to prevent money laundering and terrorist financing and the 9 Special Recommendations relating to terrorist financing as they relate to financial institutions found at www.fatf-gafi.org;

**(T) "Office"** means any branch, agency, representative office or other establishment through which any of the Intermediaries designated in the Agreement as the AI conducts its business.

**(U) "Payor"** means any person that makes a Covered Payment, directly or indirectly, to an Authorised Intermediary;

**(V) "Reportable Payment"** means, except to the extent modified by the Agreement, any Covered Payment, but only to the extent that the Covered Payment (1) is paid directly, or indirectly through one or more Contractual Intermediaries, to another Authorised Intermediary acting in its capacity as an Authorised Intermediary, or (2) if not so paid, is a payment that qualifies for a reduction or exemption from withholding tax in accordance with Paragraph 6 of the Agreement;

**(W) "Tax Rate Information"** means pooled information provided by an Authorised Intermediary to a Payor regarding the withholding rate to be applied to a payment;

**(X) "Taxpayer Identification Number"** means a unique combination of letters or numbers, however described, assigned by a country or other taxing authority to its residents and used to identify the residents in the course of collecting taxes; and

**(Y) "Withholding Agent"** means the person who is required, under the laws of the Source Country, to withhold tax on a Covered Payment and remit it to the Competent Authority (or other body responsible for accepting tax payments). The term includes an Authorised Intermediary that has assumed [primary] withholding responsibility under an agreement with the Source Country.

**IV. Provision of Tax Rate Information.**

**(A) In General.** The AI agrees to provide to each Payor from which the AI receives a Covered Payment in its capacity as an Authorised Intermediary Tax Rate Information that meets the requirements of this Section IV. The Tax Rate Information must contain sufficient information for a Payor to apply the correct rate of withholding on Covered Payments with respect to which the AI is acting in its capacity as an Authorised

Intermediary and, to the extent so required, to properly report such payments on the form in Annex 1 for reporting of Reportable Payments to Authorised Intermediaries. For purposes of this paragraph, the AI shall be treated as acting in its capacity as an Authorised Intermediary only with respect to those accounts with the Payor which have been so designated by the AI by providing the appropriate Intermediary Declaration.

**(B) Determination of Appropriate Tax Rate.** For purposes of providing Tax Rate Information to the Payor, the AI will determine the appropriate rate of tax based on the rate(s) of tax set out in Paragraph 6 of the Agreement. For purposes of that paragraph, the AI shall treat an Investor Self-Declaration as valid only if the AI has satisfied the requirements of Section V with respect to that Investor Self-Declaration.

**(C) Form and Retention of Tax Rate Information.** The Tax Rate Information may be provided in any manner, and in any form, to which the AI and the Payor mutually agree, so long as it allows the Payor to determine the number of shares or other securities that are subject to each applicable withholding rate (rather than a —blended rate applied to all the shares or securities in the account). For example, the AI may agree to establish a procedure to furnish Tax Rate Information with respect to each payment of income accruing on securities held in a single —omnibus account. Alternatively, the AI may establish with the Payor separate accounts for securities that are subject to different withholding rates. The AI would then shift securities from one account to another as necessary to take account of any transfers between investors. By establishing the accounts and communicating to the Payor the rate that should apply to each account, the AI will have provided Tax Rate Information within the meaning of this paragraph. The AI must retain records of all Tax Rate Information received by the AI from other Authorised Intermediaries and all Tax Rate Information provided by the AI to Payors (including Tax Rate Information provided in electronic form) for the period set out in Paragraph 7 of the Agreement.

**(D) Information from Intermediaries.** If the AI has an Account Holder that is an Authorised Intermediary or a Contractual Intermediary, the AI may combine the account holder information described in this paragraph and provided by the Intermediary with information held by the AI with respect to its Direct Account Holders that are Investors in order to provide aggregate Tax Rate Information to a Payor. The AI may not combine the information received from such other Intermediary with its own information if the AI knows or should have known that the information provided by the Intermediary is incorrect or incomplete.

**(1) Information from other Authorised Intermediaries.** If the Direct Account Holder with the AI is another Authorised Intermediary that has designated the relevant account as one for which it is acting in its capacity as an Authorised Intermediary, then the AI may combine the Tax Rate Information provided by the Authorised Intermediary with the AI's own account information.

**(2) Information from Contractual Intermediaries.** If the Direct Account Holder with the AI is a Contractual Intermediary, the AI may combine the information received from the Contractual Intermediary with the AI's own account information in order to provide aggregate Tax Rate Information to a Payor only if the AI receives from the Contractual Intermediary, in addition to a valid Intermediary Declaration from the Contractual Intermediary, the following information:

(a) with respect to each Indirect Account Holder of the AI that is an Investor and for which a reduced rate of withholding tax has been claimed, a copy of the Investor Self-Declaration provided by that Account Holder that supports the claim for the reduced withholding tax, unless that Investor is also an Account Holder with respect to another Authorised Intermediary that provides Tax Rate Information in accordance with clause (b) and that Investor receives amounts paid through the Contractual Intermediary through that other Authorised Intermediary;

(b) with respect to each Indirect Account Holder of the AI that is an Intermediary with an Account Holder for whom documentation is required to be provided under clause (a) and that holds through the Contractual Intermediary, a copy of the Intermediary Declaration provided by that Intermediary and, if the Intermediary is an Authorised Intermediary, Tax Rate Information originating with that Authorised Intermediary (unless that Authorised Intermediary is also an Account Holder with respect to another Authorised Intermediary that provides Tax Rate Information in accordance with this clause (b) and that Intermediary receives amounts paid through the Contractual Intermediary through that other Authorised Intermediary); and

(c) allocation information enabling the AI to match income payments to each underlying Account Holder for whom documentation is required under clause (a) or (b).

**(3) Information from Other Intermediaries.** The AI may not combine with its own account information Tax Rate Information or Investor Self-Declarations provided by an Intermediary that is neither an Authorised Intermediary nor a Contractual Intermediary. Accordingly, the appropriate rate of tax to be applied to any Covered Payment to be paid, directly or indirectly, to or through such an Intermediary shall be the rate provided in subparagraph 6.f of the Agreement.

**V. Documentation Requirements.**

**(A) Direct Account Holders.** The AI may make a claim for a reduced rate of withholding with respect to a Covered Payment paid to a Direct Account Holder that is an Investor only if the AI has received from such Direct Account Holder a properly completed and duly executed Investor Self-Declaration that supports the claim to be made and the AI does not know or have reason to know that the Investor Self-Declaration is unreliable or incorrect. The AI shall base the Tax Rate Information it provides to a Payor under Section IV of these Procedures, as well as the information to be reported to the Competent Authority in accordance with Section VII, on the documentation rules of this Section V.

**(1) Account-Opening Procedures.** In connection with the opening of an account, the AI shall use reasonable efforts to obtain an Investor Self-Declaration from each of its Direct Account Holders that is an Investor. The AI shall review the Investor Self-Declaration and other information that is in its possession, including the Investor's account information and other information that the AI may have as a result of complying with applicable Know Your Customer Rules in order to determine whether the Investor Self-Declaration is unreliable or incorrect.

**(2) Continuing Validity of an Investor Self-Declaration.**

(a) **In General.** Except as provided in this paragraph, a properly completed and duly executed Investor Self-Declaration shall expire on the last day of the fifth calendar year following the year in which the Investor Self-Declaration is signed. The Investor Self-Declaration shall remain valid indefinitely, however, if it is provided with respect to a government (including a central bank of issue, agency or instrumentality) or an international organisation. If the Source Country develops procedures that provide for electronic confirmation of the information contained in the Investor Self-Declaration, then the validity of the Investor Self-Declaration may be extended in accordance with terms of such procedures.

(b) **Updating Investor Self-Declarations.** The AI shall institute appropriate measures to ensure that changes in an Account Holder's account information that could affect the Investor's Investor Self-Declaration (such as a change of address) will result in a review and, if necessary, an updating of the Investor Self-Declaration. The AI shall inform the Investor at the time the Account is opened and at regular intervals thereafter of the Investor's obligation to update an Investor Self-Declaration if the information contained therein becomes incorrect.

**(B) Unreliable or Incorrect Investor Self-Declarations.**

(1) In General. The AI may not make claims on the basis of an Investor Self- Declaration if the AI knows, or should have known, that the information or statements contained in the Investor Self-Declaration are unreliable or incorrect. The determination of whether the AI knows, or should have known, that the Investor Self-Declaration is unreliable or incorrect will be made by taking into account all of the information that the AI has in its possession, including the Investor's account information and other information that the AI may have in its possession as a result of complying with applicable Know Your Customer Rules. Once the AI knows, or has reason to know, that the Investor Self-Declaration provided by an Investor is unreliable or incorrect, it can no longer make claims for a reduced withholding rate on the basis of that Investor Self-Declaration. Without prejudice to Paragraph VI(A)(2), if the AI discovers that information contained in an Investor Self-Declaration is unreliable or incorrect, or if the AI receives notification from the Competent Authority that the Investor Self-Declaration provided by the Investor is unreliable or incorrect (e.g., that a Taxpayer Identification Number provided by an Investor is incorrect), the AI agrees that it will correct its records in relation to the Investor within 30 days after the AI discovers or is notified that the Investor Self-Declaration is unreliable or incorrect.

(2) Specific Examples. This section provides a non-exhaustive list of circumstances in which the AI shall be considered to have reason to know that an Investor Self-Declaration provided by a Direct Account Holder is unreliable or incorrect. If a Direct Account Holder has provided an Investor Self-Declaration that is not reliable under the rules of this Paragraph V.B., the AI shall require new documentation to the extent necessary to comply with the requirements set out below.

(a) If the Investor is a natural person, and the AI has examined, in order to comply with applicable Know Your Customer Rules, the passport of the Investor, an Investor Self-Declaration provided by the Investor will be deemed unreliable if the photograph in the passport does not match the appearance of the person presenting the passport.

(b) The AI may not rely on an Investor Self-Declaration to reduce the withholding rate that would otherwise apply if the Investor Self-Declaration is incomplete, contains information that is inconsistent with the Investor's claim, or the AI has other information that is inconsistent with the Investor's claim.

(c) The AI shall not treat an Investor as a resident of a country other than the Source Country if the permanent residence address on the Investor Self-Declaration is outside the Source Country but the AI has a mailing or residence address for the Investor inside the Source Country. The AI nevertheless may treat the Investor as a resident of a country other than the Source Country if the AI has in its possession or obtains additional corroborative documentation that supports the Investor's claim not to be a resident of the Source Country.

(d) The AI shall not treat an Investor as a resident of a country under an income tax treaty if the permanent residence address on the Investor Self-Declaration is not in the applicable treaty country. The AI nevertheless may treat the Investor as a resident of the applicable treaty country if the AI has in its possession or obtains additional corroborative documentation that supports the Investor's claim that it is a resident of the applicable treaty country.

(e) The AI shall not treat an Investor as a resident of a country under an income tax treaty if the permanent residence address on the Investor Self-Declaration is in the applicable treaty country but the AI has a mailing or residence address for the Investor outside the applicable treaty country. If the AI has a mailing or residence address for the Investor outside the applicable treaty country, the AI may nevertheless treat the Investor as a resident of the applicable treaty country if the AI has in its possession or obtains additional corroborative documentation that supports the Investor's claim that it is a resident of the applicable treaty country.

(f) The AI may not rely on an Investor Self-Declaration to reduce the withholding rate on an income payment if: a) the AI has been involved in arranging or structuring a transaction pursuant to which the person that provided the Investor Self-Declaration obtained from the AI the security which generates the income payment; and b) under the law of the Source Country that person is not entitled to a reduced rate with respect to income on securities received pursuant to such transaction.

(g) The AI shall not treat an investor as a resident of a country under an income tax treaty if the only residence or mailing address it has for an investor in that country is an in-care-of address or a P.O. Box. The AI may nevertheless treat the Investor as a resident of the applicable treaty country if the AI has in its possession or obtains additional corroborative documentation that supports the Investor's claim that it is a resident of the applicable treaty country.

(h) The AI will be considered to know that the information contained in the Investor Self-Declaration is incorrect if it has been informed by the Investor, the Competent Authority or a Payor or another Intermediary that the information contained in the Investor Self-Declaration is unreliable.

**(C) Unreliable or Incorrect Information relating to Indirect Account Holders.**

The AI shall be considered to know that relevant information or statements contained in documentation, including Tax Rate Information, relating to an Indirect Account Holder are unreliable or incorrect if a reasonably prudent person in the position of an Authorised Intermediary would question the claims made. The AI shall be considered to have reason to know that a claim for a reduced withholding rate provided by a Contractual Intermediary is unreliable or incorrect if the Contractual Intermediary does not provide the AI with the information set out in Paragraph IV.D.2. A Payor, including an Authorised Intermediary, may not in any case rely on, or make a claim on the basis of, information originating with an Excluded Intermediary even if such information is provided to the Payor or Authorised Intermediary by a Contractual Intermediary.

**(D) Designation as an Excluded Intermediary.** The Competent Authority may, in its discretion, determine that information provided by a specific Intermediary is by definition unreliable. Such determination should be based on (1) objective evidence that information provided by the Intermediary in connection with these Procedures (whether with respect to the Source Country or another country) has repeatedly been unreliable or incorrect and that such information has resulted in material underwithholding of tax that has not been promptly corrected in accordance with Section VI, or paid by the Intermediary or (2) in the case of a Contractual Intermediary, the Intermediary's failure to fulfil significant procedural obligations, including a failure to make documents described in Paragraph V.F available for inspection in accordance with that paragraph. Upon making such determination, the Competent Authority shall designate the Intermediary an Excluded Intermediary and shall add such Intermediary to the list maintained by the Competent Authority in accordance with Paragraph X.B. With respect to the Intermediary so designated, such designation shall take effect immediately, subject to Paragraph IX.C and the Intermediary so designated immediately shall cease to make any claims for reductions in the rate of withholding tax to be applied to Covered Payments. With respect to Covered Payments to be paid by the AI, directly or indirectly, to the Intermediary so designated, the designation will take effect for payments with respect to which entitlement to the payment is determined 15 days or more after the earliest of: (1) the date the Excluded Intermediary notifies the AI that a previously-provided Intermediary Declaration is no longer correct; (2) the date the AI has been notified by the Competent Authority that the Intermediary is an Excluded Intermediary (which, for this purpose, may be satisfied by an email to the appropriate person at the AI identified in Paragraph 11 of the Agreement); or (3) the date the AI otherwise discovers that the Intermediary has been designated an Excluded Intermediary. The Intermediary shall remain on such list unless it becomes an Authorised Intermediary, subject to these Procedures, with respect to the Source Country, or the Competent Authority determines that the Intermediary may be treated as a Contractual Intermediary.

**(E) Maintenance and Retention of Documentation.** The AI shall retain the original Investor Self-Declaration, a certified copy thereof, or a secure electronic scan thereof with respect to each Account Holder that is an Investor, and the Intermediary Declaration, a certified copy thereof, or a secure electronic scan thereof, with respect to each Account Holder that is an Intermediary. The AI shall also retain any other relevant information from the Account Holder's file. All such documentation shall be saved for the period specified in Paragraph 7 of the Agreement. However, if the Competent Authority has notified the AI that there is an open audit or investigation for which documentation in the Account Holder's file and/or an Intermediary Declaration is relevant, such documentation may not be destroyed but must be retained until the Competent Authority has notified the AI that the audit or investigation has been completed.

**(F) Access to Documentation.** The AI shall make the Investor Self-Declarations and any Intermediary Declarations received in accordance with Paragraph IV.D.2, associated Tax Rate Information provided to Payors and any other information referred to in this Section V (including information received as a result of complying with Know Your Customer Rules) available upon request for inspection by the Independent Reviewer and the Competent Authority in accordance with Section VIII. The AI shall also use its best efforts to make available to the Independent Reviewer and the Competent Authority any information described in the preceding sentence that is held by any Contractual Intermediary that is an Affiliate of the AI. The AI shall, upon request, transmit the documents and information described in this paragraph to the Competent Authority in the Source Country or, to the extent possible, make such documents and other information available to the Competent Authority for inspection at the Offices of the AI.

**VI. Adjustments for Over- and Under-Withholding.**

**(A) Adjustments by AI before Annual Report is Filed.** If, at any time prior to the filing of the Annual Report required by Section VII, the AI discovers that the Tax Rate Information provided to a Payor, and/or the withholding tax collected by the Payor, was incorrect, the procedures provided in this Paragraph A shall apply. Any adjustments that have been made in accordance with this Paragraph shall be reflected in the annual information reports required by Section VII.

**(1) Overwithholding.** The AI may request that a Payor make an adjustment for amounts paid to the AI with respect to which too much tax has been withheld. Such adjustment may be made by way of the reimbursement procedure described in clause(a) or the set-off procedure described in clause (b). Such adjustment must be requested and made within the time period prescribed in such clauses. An Account Holder that has received a Covered Payment with respect to which too much tax has been withheld may request that the AI make the request described in this paragraph. The AI shall use its best efforts to ensure that any request for adjustment is made in a timely manner and shall co-operate with the Payor to facilitate a prompt adjustment. If an adjustment has not been made before the end of the period prescribed in clause (a) or (b) below, the AI shall withdraw its request and shall file a claim for refund in accordance with Paragraph B below. The AI may also withdraw its request and file a claim for refund in accordance with Paragraph B below if the time period in clause (a) or (b) has not expired but 2 months have elapsed since the date of the request and no adjustment has been made.

(a) **Reimbursement Procedure**. The AI may request that a Payor repay the AI for any amount over-withheld, in which case the Payor may make a similar request of any other Payor from which it has received a Covered Payment. The AI must make such request to the Payor prior to the due date for filing the report required by Paragraph VII.B.

(b) **Set-Off Procedure.** The AI may request that a Payor repay the AI by applying the amount over-withheld against any amount that otherwise would be required to be withheld from Covered Payments made by the Payor to the AI. The AI must make such request to the Payor prior to the due date for filing the report required by Paragraph VII.B.

**(2) Underwithholding.** If the AI knows that an amount should have been withheld from a previous Covered Payment made to an Account Holder but it has not been withheld (or the amount withheld was too low), the AI shall notify the Payor and shall agree with the Payor as to the appropriate course to remedy the shortfall. For example, the Payor, if it is a Withholding Agent with respect to the Covered Payments, may withhold from future payments made to the AI with respect to the relevant Account Holder. Alternatively, the AI may arrange covering payment from the Account Holder or, if necessary, satisfy the obligation out of property of the Account Holder over which it has control, by making payment to, or to the order of, the Payor.

**(B) Adjustments by AI with Year-End Summary.** In connection with filing the information report required by Section VII, the AI shall also file the Year-End Summary of Covered Payments in the form set out in Annex 1. Any adjustments for over- or underwithholding of tax that have not been made in accordance with Paragraph A shall be reflected in the Year-End Summary. The AI shall pay any additional tax reflected on the Summary at the time the Summary is filed with the Competent Authority.

**(C) Adjustments by AI after Annual Report is filed.** If, at any time after the filing of the Annual Report required by Section VII, the AI is aware that the Tax Rate Information provided to a Payor, and/or the withholding tax collected by the Payor, was incorrect, the procedures provided in this Paragraph C shall apply.

**(1) Overwithholding.** If an AI has provided Tax Rate Information to a Payor that results in too much tax being withheld from a Covered Payment, or the Payor collected too much withholding tax, and the AI was not able to make a request for an adjustment, or has withdrawn such a request, in accordance with Paragraph A.1 of this Section, the AI may make a claim for refund of the over-withheld tax by filing a claim on behalf of Account Holders that are Investors directly with the Competent Authority at the address provided in the Agreement or electronically using [description of transmission format]. If the overwithholding is attributable to Tax Rate Information originating with an underlying Authorised Intermediary in accordance with Paragraph IV.D.1, the claim for refund shall be made by the Authorised Intermediary that originated the Tax Rate Information, not by the AI. All claims under this Paragraph VI(C)(1) must be filed by the date specified in Paragraph 8 of the Agreement, using the form in Annex 1.

**(2) Underwithholding.** If within the period set out in Paragraph 9 of the Agreement, the AI discovers that tax has been under-withheld for which it is liable, in accordance with Section II.B, the AI shall file an amended Year-End Summary and pay any additional tax due as soon as possible but no later than 30 days after the under- withholding was discovered.

**(D) Adjustments Originating with the Competent Authority.** If the Competent Authority determines that tax has been under-withheld and that, in accordance with Section II.B, the AI is liable for the under-withheld tax, the Competent Authority shall so notify the AI before proceeding against any other Intermediary and/or a Withholding Agent. The AI shall have 30 days to demonstrate to the satisfaction of the Competent Authority that the tax in fact was not under-withheld, or to pay the under-withheld tax. If the AI has not paid the under-withheld tax by the expiration of such period and the Competent Authority still considers that tax was under-withheld, nothing in this paragraph shall prevent the Competent Authority from proceeding against any party with liability.

**VII. Information Reporting.**

**(A) In General.** The AI shall be required to report to the Source Country detailed information regarding Reportable Payments paid, directly or through one or more Contractual Intermediaries, to its Account Holders that are Investors as well as those that are Authorised Intermediaries, during the calendar year. In connection with filing such information reports, the AI shall also file the Year-End Summary of Covered Payments in the form set out in Annex 1.

**(B) Contents of Information Report.** The information report shall include:

(1) the name, address, and AIIN of the AI;

(2) the name, address and Taxpayer Identification Number of the Account Holder (or other form of information or combination of information (e.g., address and birth date) used by a country or other taxing authority to identify its residents for purposes of collecting taxes) and country of residence in the case of an Account Holder that is not an Authorised Intermediary (unless the Account Holder has no fiscal residency); and

(3) information regarding the amount of a Reportable Payment (in the currency of the securities in respect of which the payment was made), the date on which it was paid or credited to the Account Holder, details of the securities in respect of which the payment was made and amount of tax withheld from the Reportable Payment.

In the case of a Reportable Payment paid to another Authorised Intermediary, the relevant Taxpayer Identification Number shall be the Authorised Intermediary Identification Number.

**(C) Format and Filing.** Reporting with respect to Account Holders that are not Authorised Intermediaries shall be made on the relevant form required by Annex 1. Reporting with respect to Authorised Intermediaries shall be made on the relevant form required by Annex 1. Such forms shall be filed annually, on or before 30 April of theyear following any calendar year in which the AI receives Reportable Payments in its capacity as an Authorised Intermediary. The AI may file such reports electronically using the format developed for these purposes by the Organisation for Economic Co-Operation and Development.

**(D) Amended Year-End Summary or Information Reports.** If within the period set out in Paragraph 9 of the Agreement, the AI discovers an error in the Year-End Summary or in the Information Reports it has filed, it shall file an amended Year-End Summary or Information Reports as soon as possible and no later than 30 days after the error was discovered.

**VIII. Compliance.**

**(A) In General.** In order to assess compliance by the AI with its obligations under the Agreement and these Procedures, the Competent Authority may require the delivery of an Independent Reviewer's Report in accordance with Paragraph B of this Section. The Competent Authority shall, in addition, maintain the right to review directly the AI's compliance with these Procedures and the Agreement.

**(B) Report of the Independent Reviewer.** The Independent Reviewer's Report shall focus on the AI's compliance with its obligations under the Agreement and these Procedures. In this regard, the Independent Reviewer's Report will review the AI's processing of Covered Payments, including the application of tax withholding in accordance with Paragraph 6 of the Agreement and the documentation secured under Section V, and its reporting to the Source Country in accordance with Section VII. The Independent Reviewer's Report shall be prepared in accordance with Annex 2.

**(1) Access to Information.** The AI shall permit the Independent Reviewer to have access to all relevant records of the AI for purposes of completing the Independent Reviewer's Report, including information regarding specific Account Holders receiving Covered Payments. The AI shall permit the Competent Authority to examine the Independent Reviewer's work papers and reports.

**(2) Timing and Filing of Independent Reviewer's Report.**

(a) In General. The AI shall have the Independent Reviewer prepare an Independent Reviewer's Report for the first full calendar year that the AI has in effect an agreement with any country pursuant to which it acts as an Authorised Intermediary in accordance with these Procedures. Thereafter, the Independent Reviewer will prepare an Independent Reviewer's Report only upon request by any tax authority that is a Competent Authority under any such agreement, which shall be no more often than every third year unless a Competent Authority has good cause for requesting a more frequent Independent Review, including that a prior review of the AI has indicated a significant failure by the AI to meet its obligations under the Agreement and these Procedures and/or the risk of default. Notwithstanding the preceding sentences, if the Independent Reviewer's Report identifies material or systemic failures by the AI to meet its obligations under the Agreement and these Procedures, the years between the last reviewed year and the year subject to the Independent Reviewer's Report shall also be subject to review, but only if the AI would be liable under Paragraph II.B with respect to any claim by the Competent Authority with respect to such year.

(b) First Year of the Agreement. Upon the entry into effect of the Agreement, the AI shall provide the Competent Authority with a copy of the most recent (if any) Independent Reviewer's Report prepared in accordance with subparagraph (a). If the first full calendar year that the Agreement is in effect is not a year for which an Independent Review otherwise would be performed in accordance with subparagraph (a), the Competent Authority nevertheless may elect to have an Independent Review performed for that year. However, such Independent Review shall be limited to a review, in accordance with Sections III to V of Annex 2, of the processing of two Covered Payments arising in the Source Country unless, after receiving the results of that review, the Competent Authority has reasonable concerns regarding the AI's compliance with the Agreement. In that case, the Competent Authority may request a supplementary review as described in Section VI of Annex 2. Thereafter, Independent Reviews with respect to the Source Country will be performed on the same schedule as set out in subparagraph (a).

(c) Notice and Filing. A Competent Authority requesting an Independent Review in accordance with subparagraph (a) or (b) must notify the AI that a report will be required no later than 31 December of the year to which the report is to relate. The Independent Reviewer shall provide a copy of any Independent Reviewer's Report prepared pursuant to subparagraph (a) to each country with which the AI has in effect an agreement pursuant to which it acts as an Authorised Intermediary in accordance with these Procedures no later than 30 September of the year following the year to which the report relates. A Competent Authority may, however, upon request by the Independent Reviewer, extend the due date for the Independent Reviewer's Report upon a showing of good cause.

**(3) Scope of the Independent Reviewer's Report.** In connection with the Independent Reviewer's Report prepared with respect to the first full calendar year that an Agreement is in effect, the Independent Reviewer must review the AI's compliance with the Agreement and these Procedures in accordance with the agreed procedures for review set forth in Annex 3. At a minimum, the Independent Reviewer must review the AI's processing of Covered Payments, including the application of tax withholding in accordance with paragraph 6 of the Agreement and the documentation secured under Section V, and its reporting to the Source Country in accordance with Section VII. With respect to later years, if the Competent Authority requests further review by the Independent Reviewer, such review may encompass any reasonable combination of the elements in Annex 3. The Independent

Reviewer's Report must fully describe the scope of the review, the methodologies (including sampling techniques) used to determine whether the AI is in compliance with the provisions of the Agreement and these Procedures and address each of the items in the preceding sentences.

**(4) Use of Statistical Sampling.** If a procedure in Annex 2 requires an Independent Reviewer to make a determination based on a valid sample of accounts, it shall use a statistical sampling whenever an examination of all accounts within a particular class of accounts would be unreasonable in terms of time and expense. If it is reasonable to examine all accounts in connection with a particular issue, statistical sampling techniques shall not be used.

**(5) Consolidated Review of the AI.** The Independent Reviewer may conduct a consolidated review of the AI, so long as (1) the members of the group making up the AI operate with uniform practices and procedures and shared systems for performing the functions being reviewed, and (2) those practices and procedures and shared systems are subject to uniform monitoring and control.

**(6) Designation of Independent Reviewer.** The AI shall propose to the Competent Authority an initial Independent Reviewer that is subject to laws, regulations or rules that impose sanctions for failure to exercise its independence and to perform the review competently. The AI's initial Independent Reviewer is designated in Paragraph 10 of the Agreement. The Competent Authority may, however, revoke its acceptance of the Independent Reviewer if it reasonably believes that the reviewer designated is not independent or cannot perform an effective review under these Procedures. In such case, the Competent Authority shall notify the AI by June 30 of the year preceding the year for which an Independent Review is to be conducted. Within 90 days of such notification, the AI shall propose a substitute for the Independent Reviewer that the AI reasonably believes to be subject to laws, regulations or rules that impose sanctions for failure to exercise its independence and to perform the review competently. The Competent Authority shall approve or reject the substitute Independent Reviewer within 30 days of receiving the proposal from the AI.

**(C) Review by the Competent Authority.** The Competent Authority may also review the AI's compliance with the Agreement. Such a review may take the form of spot checks, pursuant to which the Competent Authority would request from the AI information regarding a certain percentage or number of Account Holders receiving a specific Covered Payment, in order to determine whether the amount of withholding tax collected, and any information required to be reported, was correct. In connection with such a spot check, the Competent Authority might also examine other information held by the AI with respect to the relevant Account Holders, such as information collected in the course of complying with Know Your Customer Rules, or information on the underlying transaction on the basis of which the Account Holder has acquired the relevant securities. The Competent Authority may also decide to confirm the claims for benefits, with respect to specific Account Holders or a random sample of Account Holders, by requesting that the country listed on the Investor Self-Declaration as the Account Holder's country of residence confirm that the Account Holder is in fact a resident of that country. In addition to such spot checks, the Competent Authority may also pursue a more expansive examination of the AI's operations and procedures. Such an examination might occur, for example, when the Independent Reviewer's Report and/or the spot checks described in this paragraph suggest a persistent and pervasive failure by the AI to meet its obligations under the Agreement and these Procedures or when the Competent Authority becomes aware of problems that might not be discovered as a result of the information reporting required by Section VII. In those cases, the Competent Authority will meet with the AI in order to clarify and resolve those problems, with a view to avoiding a default that would necessitate termination of the Agreement. The AI agrees that, upon request of the Competent Authority, the review by the Competent Authority may take place at the offices of the AI, subject to any required consents obtained by the Competent Authority from the competent authority of the country in which the AI is established and in accordance with applicable laws, including any bilateral or other agreements between the two countries.

**IX. Termination of Agreement**

**(A) In General.** Subject to Paragraph B of this Section, the Agreement may be terminated by either the Competent Authority or the AI by delivery of a notice of termination to the other party in accordance with Paragraph X.E. A notice of termination sent by either party shall take effect on the date specified in the notice, which in the case of a notice sent by the Competent Authority shall be at least 30 days after the date on which the notice is received by the AI.

**(B) Termination for Cause.** During the period beginning with the effective date provided in Paragraph 13 of the Agreement (without regard to any later effective date applicable with respect to any modification of the Agreement) and ending seven years thereafter, the Competent Authority shall not terminate the Agreement unless there has been a significant change in circumstances, as defined in Subparagraph 1, or an event of default has occurred, as defined in Subparagraph 2. Before delivering notice of termination for cause, the Competent Authority shall follow the resolution procedures in Subparagraph 3.

**(1) Significant Change in Circumstances.** For purposes of these Procedures, a significant change in circumstances includes, but is not limited to –

(a) An acquisition of all, or substantially all, of the AI's assets in any transaction unless, in the case of a merger, the AI is the surviving legal entity;

(b) A change in any applicable law or policy that affects the validity of any representation made by the AI in its application to become an Authorised Intermediary, affects the validity of any provision of the Agreement, materially affects the procedures contained in these Procedures or affects the AI's ability to perform its obligations under the Agreement and these Procedures;

(c) A final ruling of any court that affects the validity of any provision of the Agreement or these Procedures; or

(d) Any other significant change in the AI's circumstances that affects the AI's ability to meet its obligations under the Agreement and these Procedures.

**(2) Events of Default.** For purposes of these Procedures, an event of default occurs if the AI fails to perform any material duty or obligation required under the Agreement and these Procedures, and includes, but is not limited to, the occurrence of any of the following:

(a) The AI fails to reasonably implement adequate procedures, accounting systems, and internal controls to ensure compliance with the Agreement and these Procedures;

(b) The AI makes a misrepresentation with respect to Tax Rate Information that results in substantial underwithholding by a Withholding Agent;

(c) The AI fails to notify a Payor that an amount that should have been withheld from a previous Covered Payment made to the AI has not been withheld (or the amount withheld was too low), and/or fails to take the actions specified in Section VI to remedy the underwithholding;

(d) The AI makes refund claims in excess of the amount to which its Account Holders are entitled;

(e) The AI fails to timely file the forms required by Section VII, or files forms that are materially incorrect or fraudulent;

(f) The AI fails to have the Independent Reviewer prepare an Independent Reviewer's Report required by Section VIII.B, the AI fails to cooperate with the Independent Reviewer, or the AI or its Independent Reviewer fails to provide reasonable cooperation with the Competent Authority;

(g) The AI fails to inform the Competent Authority within 45 days of any significant change in its circumstances to the extent that change affects the AI's obligations under the Agreement and these Procedures;

(h) The AI fails to cure a material error, omission or deficiency identified by the Competent Authority or by an Independent Reviewer within a reasonable time;

(i) The AI makes any fraudulent statement or a misrepresentation of material fact with regard to the Agreement to the Competent Authority, a Payor or Withholding Agent, or the AI's Independent Reviewer;

(j) The AI fails to provide the Competent Authority with an Independent Reviewer's Report that complies with Section VIII; or

(k) The AI is prohibited for any reason (including by law or contract) from disclosing the identity of an Account Holder or account information to the AI's Independent Reviewer or any relevant tax authorities for the purposes of monitoring the AI's performance under the Agreement.

**(3) Resolution Process.** Upon the occurrence of an event of default, the Competent Authority may deliver to the AI a notice of default specifying the event of default that has occurred and proposing a date for a meeting between the Competent Authority, the AI and, if necessary, the Independent Reviewer, which date shall be within 45 days of the date of the notice. The purpose of such meeting shall be to clarify and resolve any underlying problems that have led to the event of default. In advance of that meeting, the AI may provide an offer to cure the event of default, including the time period in which the cure will be accomplished, or a statement giving any reasons why the AI does not agree that an event of default has occurred. The Competent Authority may provide its own counter-proposal regarding the method of cure and the applicable timetable and/or a response to any statement by the AI regarding the existence of an event of default. If the Competent

Authority and the AI reach a satisfactory resolution regarding whether an event of default exists and a method and timetable for the cure of any such default, or a timetable for further discussions that might lead to such a satisfactory resolution, the Competent Authority shall not terminate the Agreement so long as the AI complies with the terms of any such resolution or discussions that might lead to such a resolution are on-going. If the Competent Authority and the AI cannot reach a satisfactory resolution at the meeting, and cannot agree to a timetable for further discussions that might lead to such a resolution, the Competent Authority may deliver a notice of termination in accordance with this Paragraph B. The Competent Authority may also deliver a notice of termination for cause if the AI does not agree to hold a meeting within 45 days of the delivery of the notice of default or fails to attend the scheduled meeting, unless the AI can show good cause for such a delay or failure and agrees to hold such a meeting as soon as practicable and within a time frame acceptable to the Competent Authority. If an event of default is discovered in the course of an Independent Review, the AI may cure the default, without following the procedures of this paragraph, if the Independent Reviewer's report describes the default and the actions that the AI took to cure the default and the Competent Authority determines that the cure procedures followed by the AI were sufficient. If the Competent Authority determines that the AI's actions to cure the default described in the preceding sentence were not sufficient, the Competent Authority shall issue a notice of default and the procedures described in this paragraph shall be followed.

**(C) Co-Ordination with Designation as an Excluded Intermediary.** If the Competent Authority designates the AI as an Excluded Intermediary in accordance with Paragraph V.D, such designation shall, at the request of the AI, be treated as an event of default to which the resolution process provided in Paragraph B will apply. However, in such case the initial meeting generally will take place within 15 days of such designation. If a satisfactory resolution is reached, the Competent Authority may suspend the designation so long as the AI complies with the terms of such resolution. If a satisfactory solution is not reached or the AI fails to comply with such resolution, the designation of the AI as an Excluded Intermediary shall become effective in accordance with the terms of Paragraph V.D. In addition, if the Competent Authority terminates the Agreement for cause in accordance with Paragraph B, the AI shall thereafter be treated as an Excluded Intermediary for a period of five years, unless the Competent Authority agrees before the expiry of such period (1) that the Intermediary may be treated as a Contractual Intermediary or (2) that the Intermediary may act as an Authorised Intermediary. After the expiry of the five year period, the Intermediary may re-apply for authorisation to act as Authorised Intermediary.

**X. Miscellaneous Provisions.**

**(A) List of Authorised Intermediaries.** The Competent Authority shall maintain a list of Intermediaries that have been authorised by the Competent Authority to act as Authorised Intermediaries with respect to income arising in the Source Country and whose authorisations have not been revoked. The Competent Authority will make available to any person the name and address of any such Intermediaries which have been so authorised and may if they so choose publish such information.

**(B) List of Excluded Intermediaries.** The Competent Authority shall maintain a list of Intermediaries that have been identified as Excluded Intermediaries. Such list shall include those Intermediaries whose authorisation to act as Authorised Intermediaries has been terminated by the Competent Authority in accordance with Section IX and any other Intermediaries designated by the Competent Authority in accordance with Paragraph V.D.

The Competent Authority will make available to any person the name and address of any such Intermediaries which have been so designated and may if they so choose publish such information.

**(C) Waiver.** Any waiver of a provision of the Agreement or these Procedures by the Competent Authority is a waiver solely of that provision. The waiver does not obligate the Competent Authority to waive other provisions of the Agreement or these Procedures or the same provision with respect to a later period.

**(D) No Assignment.** The AI's rights and responsibilities under the Agreement and these Procedures cannot be assigned to another person.

**(E) Notices.** Notices provided under the Agreement shall be mailed registered, first class mail with, if permissible, a copy sent by e-mail. Such notices shall be directed as provided in the Agreement. All notices sent to the Competent Authority must include the AI's AIIN.

**(F) No Agency.** The AI, acting in its capacity as an Authorised Intermediary, or in any other capacity, does not act as an agent of the Competent Authority, nor does it have the authority to hold itself out as an agent of the Competent Authority.

# Index




R. K. McGill and K. V. Pitkin, *Qualified Intermediary*,
https://doi.org/10.1007/978-3-031-81410-5

GPSR Compliance
The European Union's (EU) General Product Safety Regulation (GPSR) is a set of rules that requires consumer products to be safe and our obligations to ensure this.

If you have any concerns about our products, you can contact us on

ProductSafety@springernature.com

In case Publisher is established outside the EU, the EU authorized representative is:

Springer Nature Customer Service Center GmbH
Europaplatz 3
69115 Heidelberg, Germany

www.ingramcontent.com/pod-product-compliance
Lightning Source LLC
Chambersburg PA
CBHW072132160625
28292CB00004B/271
* 9 7 8 3 0 3 1 8 1 4 0 9 9 *